THE AFRICANA BIBLE

THE AFRICANA BIBLE

READING ISRAEL'S SCRIPTURES
FROM AFRICA AND THE AFRICAN DIASPORA

Hugh R. Page Jr., *General Editor*

Randall C. Bailey, Valerie Bridgeman, Stacy Davis,

Cheryl Kirk-Duggan, Madipoane Masenya (ngwan'a Mphahlele),

Nathaniel Samuel Murrell, Rodney S. Sadler Jr., *Associate Editors*

FORTRESS PRESS

Minneapolis

THE AFRICANA BIBLE
Reading Israel's Scriptures from Africa and the African Diaspora

Cover image: *Jacob and the Angel*, Anthony Armstrong, copyright © Anthony Armstrong (www.armstrongart.net).
      Used by permission.
Cover design: Laurie Ingram
Book design: Zan Ceeley, Trio Bookworks

Library of Congress Cataloging-in-Publication Data

The Africana Bible : reading Israel's Scriptures from Africa and the African diaspora / Hugh R. Page, Jr., general editor ; Randall C. Bailey . . . [et al.], associate editors.
    p. cm.
  Includes bibliographical references and index.
  ISBN 978-0-8006-2125-4 (alk. paper)
  1. Bible. O.T.—Criticism, interpretation, etc.—Africa. 2. Apocryphal books (Old Testament)—Criticism, interpretation, etc.—Africa. 3. Black theology. 4. Theology—Africa. I. Page, Hugh R. II. Bailey, Randall C., 1947–
  BS1171.3.A37 2009
  221.7—dc22
                              2009011353

The paper used in this publication meets the minimum requirements of American National Standard for Information Sciences—Permanence of Paper for Printed Library Materials, ANSI Z329.48-1984.

Manufactured in the U.S.A.

14   13   12   11   10   1   2   3   4   5   6   7   8   9   10

To our forefathers and foremothers for their steadfast faith, tenacity,
and struggles to claim life at all costs

To those ancestors who rest in the belly of the Atlantic,
cast into the deep during the *Maafa*

To *Africana* scholars, preachers, teachers, and believers
who have made the Bible live

To African and African Diasporan scholars who blazed a trail that we might be,
and that this volume might come to fruition

To our families, who have supported our journeys of faith, life, and learning

And to God, who makes all things possible

❧ CONTENTS ❧

READING THE HEBREW BIBLE

THE HEBREW BIBLE: Torah

THE HEBREW BIBLE: Prophets

THE HEBREW BIBLE: Writings

THE DEUTEROCANONICAL
AND PSEUDEPIGRAPHIC WRITINGS

IMAGES

Gallery following page 214

1. Map of the African Diaspora. Map by Mapping Specialists, LLC.
2. The Africana World today. Map by Mapping Specialists, LLC.
3. Stone relief of a man tending a small plant. Mari, Syria, 3000–2685 B.C.E. National Museum, Damascus. Photo: Erich Lessing/Art Resource, N.Y.
4. Figurine of a man's head, found in a sanctuary at Ashdod, Israel. Israel Museum (IDAM), Jerusalem. Photo credit: Erich Lessing / Art Resource, N.Y.
5. Figurine of a woman's head with diadem of pearls. Reuben and Edith Hecht Collection, Haifa University, Haifa, Israel. Photo credit: Erich Lessing / Art Resource, N.Y.
6. Figurine of a woman's head with Egyptian hairdo. Reuben and Edith Hecht Collection, Haifa University, Haifa, Israel. Photo credit: Erich Lessing / Art Resource, N.Y.
7. A woman's face carved in ivory. Phoenician, ninth–eighth century B.C.E. 11 x 8.85 cm; British Museum, London. Photo: Trustees of the British Museum/ArtResource, N.Y.
8. Comb (wood, 336 mm), from a village of the Djuka maroons on the Tapanahoni River, Surinam, collected in the 1920s. Photo: Denis Finnin; American Museum of Natural History Library.
9. A small domestic shrine, the model of a temple with two pillars with voluted capitals, probably dating from the beginning of the Israelite monarchy; from Megiddo. Clay; Israel Museum (IDAM), Jerusalem. Photo: Erich Lessing/Art Resource, N.Y.
10. Small domestic shrine. Clay; around 800 B.C.E. Israel Museum (IDAM), Jerusalem. Photo: Erich Lessing/Art Resource, N.Y.

Images

CONTRIBUTORS

EDITORS

Hugh R. Page Jr. is Associate Professor of Theology and African Studies and Dean of the First Year of Studies at the University of Notre Dame. He is, by academic training, a philologist, theologian, and historian; via on-the-job experience, an ethnologist and academic administrator; by spiritual formation, a left-leaning, decidedly liberal Anglican priest; by disposition, an aspiring *homo universalis*, martial artist, contemplative, Bluesman, and poet. His research centers on ancient Near Eastern myth; early Hebrew poetry; the comparative study of Afroasiatic cultures; *Africana* esoteric traditions; and the reclamation of the *lexicon*, *materia medica*, and worldview of *Africana conjure* traditions in the North American Diaspora as raw materials for fashioning modern spiritualities of resistance, sustainability, and hope. As scholar, his work blends close reading with *sociopoetics* and *autoethnography*; it seeks evocatively to blur the traditional boundaries between scholarship and art. He is author of *The Myth of Cosmic Rebellion: A Study of Its Reflexes in Ugaritic and Biblical Literature* (Brill, 1996) and *Exodus* (Bible Reading Fellowship—People's Bible Commentary Series, 2006), as well as editor of *Exploring New Paradigms in Biblical and Cognate Studies* (Mellen Biblical Press, 1996).

⏩ Contributors

Randall C. Bailey is the Andrew W. Mellon Professor of Hebrew Bible at the Interdenominational Theological Center in Atlanta. He is an ideological critic concentrating on the intersections of race/ethnicity, class, gender, sexuality, and power in the biblical text. He is co-editor with Jacquelyn Grant of *The Recovery of Black Presence: An Interdisciplinary Exploration* (Abingdon, 1995); co-editor, with Tina Pippin, of *Race, Class, and the Politics of Bible Translation* (*Semeia* 76, 1996); editor of *Yet with a Steady Beat: Contemporary U.S. Afrocentric Biblical Interpretation* (SBL, 2003); co-editor, with Tat-siong Benny Liew and Fernando Segovia, of *They Were All Together in One Place: Toward Minority Biblical Criticism* (SBL, 2009); and author of *David in Love and War: The Pursuit of Power in 2 Samuel 10–12* (JSOT, 1990); and *Open with Caution: The Bible and Sexuality* (Westminster John Knox, 2009).

Valerie Bridgeman, Associate Professor of Hebrew Bible and Homiletics and Scholar of Theology and the Arts at Lancaster Theological Seminary in Lancaster, Pennsylvania, is a biblical studies scholar and a poet. She concentrated in Hebrew Bible (Old Testament) for her Ph.D. from Baylor University with a minor in ethics. Her interest in the Bible was fomented and nurtured in Sunday School classes at Pine Grove Baptist Church in rural central Alabama. Later, when she joined the holiness movement into which her father was converted, the interest was sealed. Called to ministry at the age of eighteen, she has had the Bible in her hand for a long time. Her interests also are artistic: As a poet, she is always looking for a turn of phrase to provoke the next poem and finds the Hebrew Bible is replete with them.

Stacy Davis is Assistant Professor of Religious Studies at St. Mary's College in Notre Dame, Indiana. Raised Pentecostal but currently in voluntary exile from her church, she finds her tradition's recent interpretation of the good news and its willingness to align with Christian fundamentalism a sore spot. Nonetheless, the Pentecostal belief in reading Scripture for oneself and being open to the Holy Spirit shapes her scholarly life. She studies the history of biblical interpretation, or how specific religious communities read and sometimes misread sacred texts.

Cheryl A. Kirk-Duggan, Professor of Theology and Women's Studies at Shaw University Divinity School in Raleigh, North Carolina, is former editor of *Semeia*, an experimental biblical journal, and author and editor of over twenty books and numerous articles. She is an ordained elder in the Christian Methodist Episcopal Church. She declares that she is known for her "6 Ps" as professor, preacher, priest, prophet, poet, and performer. Dr. Kirk-Duggan is an avid athlete and musician, loves to tinker with her roses, and embraces laughter as her best medicine with the quest for a healthy, holistic, spiritual life as foundation. She resides in Raleigh with her beloved husband, Mike.

Madipoane Masenya (ngwan'a Mphahlele) is chair of the department of Old Testament and Ancient Near Eastern Studies at the University of South Africa in Pretoria. She describes herself as being birthed by a rural context, politically not-so-conscious yet culturally conscious, in rural South Africa. A child born in the heydays of apartheid, she saw, smelled, and felt racial segregation from early childhood. The Eurocentric, Africana-unconscious Bible and theology that she received early in life, she states, were not helpful in the rediscovery and redefinition of her identity as an African-South African *mosadi* (woman) with unique experiences. Although she continues to be clergy in a Pentecostal church, the mainline and Pentecostal ecclesiastical settings that nurtured her failed, she says, to sharpen her conscience regarding the social injustices perpetrated by a racist, classist, and sexist South African system. She employs a *bosadi* hermeneutic to deliberately foreground African-South African women's experiences, grappling with issues such as post-apartheid racism, xenophobia, Xhosaism, HIV/AIDS, and sexism. These are also critiqued if and when she encounters them in the biblical text or biblical interpretation as she continues her quest for a justice-seeking, life-affirming hermeneutic for African-South African peoples.

Nathaniel Samuel Murrell is Associate Professor of Philosophy and Religion at the University of North Carolina, Wilmington. He is an Afro Caribbean-born scholar and clergyman trained in religious studies and Bible and received his college education in Jamaica and Trinidad and graduate degrees from Wheaton College (Illinois), Drew University Graduate School (New Jersey), and the Graduate School of Education, Rutgers University. He is one of the cofounders of the Caribbean Graduate School of Theology in Jamaica, where he still holds a visiting lectureship in biblical studies. He co-authored *Religion, Culture and Tradition in the Caribbean* (2000) and the popular *Chanting Down Babylon: The Rastafari Reader* (1998). His most recent book is *Afro-Caribbean Religions* (fall 2009). He has been an active participant or consultant in several projects related to Blacks/Africans/African Americans and the Bible including Vincent Wimbush's *African Americans and the Bible* (2000) and R. S. Sugirtharajah's *Voices from the Margin: Interpreting the Bible in the Third World* (2006). He says he generates as much passion teaching African religions, African American religions, Caribbean religions, Gandhi, King, and civil rights, and sacred texts of world religions as he does preaching in southeastern North Carolina. He states that he finds in scriptures many voices, places for many levels of conversation, competing interests, and people power.

Rodney S. Sadler Jr. is Associate Professor of Bible at the Union Theological Seminary and Presbyterian School of Christian Education at Charlotte, North Carolina. Sadler is a native of Philadelphia and was raised between that city, Bermuda, and Camden, New Jersey. He is a graduate of Howard University (B.A., M.Div.) and Duke University (Ph.D. in Hebrew Bible and Biblical Archaeology). He is the author of *Can A Cushite Change His Skin? An Examination of Race, Ethnicity, and Othering in the Hebrew Bible* (T. & T. Clark, 2005) and the managing editor of *The African American Devotional Bible* (Zondervan, 1997). He served as Director of Black Church Studies at Duke University Divinity School (2000-2002). An ordained Baptist minister, Rodney is married to Madeline McClenney-Sadler and father of Ariyah Sadler.

CONTRIBUTORS

David Tuesday Adamo is Dean of the Faculty of Arts and Sciences and Professor of Biblical Studies at Kogi State University in Anyigba, Nigeria. He has published several books, among which are *Africa and Africans in the Old Testament* (Wipf & Stock, 2001), *Africa and Africans in the New Testament* (University Press of America, 2006), *Reading and Interpreting the Bible in African Indigenous Churches* (Wipf & Stock, 2001), *Biblical Interpretation in African Perspective* (University Press of America, 2006), and *Black-American Heritage?* (D. T. Adamo, 1985).

Dorothy B. E. A. Akoto (*née* Abutiate) is at the Trinity Theological Seminary in Legon, Ghana. She hails from Avatime-Biakpa and Asadame/Anyako, among the Ewe peoples of the Volta Region, and was born in Akuse, Eastern Region, S.E. Ghana, West Africa. Growing up there furnished her with her earliest self-awareness of the similarities between the Hebrew Bible and the African cultural context and allowed her to see the former as distinctly African. She construes biblical interpretation and practice as a form of "grafting" of the Hebrew (Western) scriptures on to the African/Ghanaian/Ewe religiocultural "tree." This and her interest in Wisdom literature and feminist studies have greatly influenced her interpretation of the book of Esther.

Wilma Ann Bailey is Professor of Hebrew and Aramaic Scripture at the Christian Theological Seminary in Indianapolis, Indiana. She is an African American woman who is descended from enslaved and free people and currently lives in a mid-American city that has a 25 percent African American population. In the past, the city was racially segregated. Informal and illegal practices of segregation in schools, housing, hospitals, restaurants, and recreational facilities were maintained well into the twentieth century. Those patterns are still visible in certain areas, particularly housing and schools. The institution where she works, though predominantly European American, has increased significantly in its diversity (racial/ethnic, male/female, American/international, denominational) during the tenure of the current president, who is African American.

Harold V. Bennett is President and Dean at the Charles H. Mason Theological Seminary, Interdenominational Theological Center in Atlanta, Georgia. He is the third president and dean of the Seminary (affiliated with the Church of God in Christ, COGIC). He also teaches religious studies at Morehouse College in Atlanta, Georgia. His most recent book is *Injustice Made Legal* (Eerdmans, 2002) and his most recent published articles include "Justice" in *The New Interpreters' Dictionary of the Bible* (Abingdon, 2006-9), "Deuteronomy" in *The Cambridge Dictionary of Christianity* (Cambridge University Press, 2008), and "Triennial Tithes and the Underdog: A Revisionist Reading of Deut 14:22-29 and 26:12-15" in *Yet With A Steady Beat: Contemporary U.S. Afrocentric Biblical Interpretation*, ed. R. C. Bailey (SBL, 2003).

Theodore W. Burgh is Associate Professor of Philosophy and Religion at the University of North Carolina in Wilmington, North Carolina. In addition to researching and teaching courses in Hebrew Bible/Old Testament, anthropology, and music of the ancient world, he works as an archaeologist in Jordan where he is an Associate Field Supervisor of the Tell Jalul Project. He earned a B.A. in music from Hampton University and advanced degrees in religious studies and archaeology from Howard University and the University of Arizona, respectively. His academic interests are in the areas of archaeology, the Hebrew Bible/Old Testament, and music and musical instruments of the ancient Near East.

Dexter E. Callender Jr. is Associate Professor of Religious Studies at the University of Miami in Miami, Florida. He was born in Boston, Massachusetts, to parents whose families had emigrated to the U.S. and Canada from Barbados and Jamaica, and he grew up with Caribbean-American sensibilities during the stormy days of court-ordered desegregation. He attended predominantly white schools but spent his afternoons and evenings at the Elma Lewis School of Fine Arts (National Center for Afro American Artists) in the heart of Boston's black community. Although raised in the United Church of Christ, he later joined Twelfth Baptist Church, a direct descendant of the historic First African Meeting House. An early interest in the Bible, particularly with respect to questions of origins, led ultimately to his pursuit of graduate work in Near Eastern Languages and Civilizations.

Steed Vernyl Davidson is Assistant Professor of Old Testament at Pacific Lutheran Theological Seminary in Berkeley, California. Professor Davidson received his education in the Caribbean and the United States. A graduate of the University of the West Indies, Boston University, and Union Theological Seminary in the City of New York, his research and writings center on postcolonial theory and the reading of the Bible. Having to navigate the complex world of identities created by colonialism and neo-colonialism through his education and upbringing, Davidson writes with sensitivity to the multiple locations where persons of African descent live and read texts.

Elelwani B. Farisani is with the Department of Old Testament and Ancient Near Eastern Studies at the University of South Africa in Pretoria, South Africa. He was born in apartheid South Africa. His father had three wives, and although his father could read and write, his three mothers had no formal education. Just like many other black South African families, his family was subjected to the cruelly discriminatory apartheid system. In line with the apartheid policy of classifying and separating black people according to their ethnic backgrounds, his family was forcefully removed and had to relocate against their will at least three times. His research concentrates on how African indigenous languages can be used in the teaching and learning of biblical Hebrew and on showing how, with the use of sociological analysis, biblical texts can best be used to address some of the current challenges facing the African continent. He is the former principal of the Lutheran Theological Institute, which is attached to the School of Religion and Theology at the University of Kwazulu-Natal, South Africa.

Judy Fentress-Williams is Associate Professor of Hebrew Bible at the Virginia Theological Seminary in Alexandria, Virginia. According to her, she was reading the Bible (in the King James Version) at age four. The language, images and stories of the Bible have shaped her worldview and her research at a denominational seminary. She is fascinated with the oral dimensions of the text, and her experiences have taught her there is always a story behind or beyond the one being told. She states that when we remember, recount, and preach biblical narrative, we are shaping the narrative and informing a tradition. She is intrigued with God's command to remember the exodus and with the way African captives remembered the story, making it their own.

Naomi Franklin is Chair of the Religious Studies Department at Virginia Union University in Richmond, Virginia. She is also adjunct faculty in biblical studies at the School of Theology at Virginia Union University and co-founder and former Dean of the St. Jerome Biblical Studies Institute, St. Kitts, W.I., where she also served as Professor of Biblical Studies and Languages. She is the author of "Naomi the Other Job," presented at the SBL Annual Meeting in 2006, and of "Hidden in Plain Sight," presented at the conference on Women, Power, and Spirituality in Biblical Times in 2001. She earned her Ph.D. in Old Testament at Duke University in 1990.

Wil Gafney is Associate Professor of Hebrew and Old Testament at Lutheran Theological Seminary at Philadelphia in Pennsylvania. She is an African American woman whose engagement with the Hebrew Scriptures takes place in Jewish and Christian communities. She is ordained in the Episcopal Church, U.S.A., a predominantly white church in a global Anglican Communion that is predominantly black and brown. She began her clergy and academic vocations in the predominantly black African Methodist Episcopal Zion Church. She is also a member of a Reconstructionist *minyan* and is particularly interested in how Jews and Christians interpret the texts they hold in common. While she has lived most of her life in the United States, she has spent some months traveling in Africa and Asia, three months in Kenya and Tanzania in the 1980s, six weeks in Israel and Jordan in the 1990s, and two trips to India in 2007.

Contributors

Wallace Hartsfield II is Pastor of the Metropolitan Missionary Baptist Church in Kansas City, Missouri. The Rev. Dr. Hartsfield studied music at the Conservatory of Music and psychology at the University of Missouri, Kansas City and also holds an MDiv from the Interdenominational Theological Center and a PhD in Hebrew Bible from Emory University. He has taught at Morehouse College and the Interdenominational Theological Center.

John W. D. Holder is Bishop of the Diocese of Barbados (Anglican). The Rt. Rev. John W. D. Holder is a graduate of Codrington College (DipTh), the University of the West Indies (B.A.), and the University of the South (STM). He earned the Ph.D. degree in Old Testament from King's College, University of London (1985). Ordained to the diaconate in 1974 and to the priesthood in 1975, he was elected Bishop of the Anglican Church in Barbados in 2000. He has held academic positions in the U.S. and Barbados. His recent published works include *Reflections on Priesthood* (Diocese of Barbados, 2001); *The Bible in the Anglican Tradition—The Bible and Human Sexuality* (2004); and "Sexuality in the Old Testament," in *The Anglican Communion and Homosexuality*, ed. Philip Groves (SPCK, 2008).

Jamal-Dominique Hopkins is Assistant Professor of New Testament at the Interdenominational Theological Center in Atlanta, Georgia. He earned his PhD at the University of Manchester (U.K.) where his research focused on intertestamental literature of the late Second Temple period, primarily in the area of the Dead Sea Scrolls and Qumran studies. His dissertation was titled "Sacrifice in the Dead Sea Scrolls: Khirbet Qumran, the Essenes and Cultic Spiritualization." Hopkins is a product of the Black church and a Black undergraduate college education. An ordained elder of the Church of God in Christ, he earned his BA from Howard University in Washington, D.C., where he began to develop a critical consciousness with regard to the intertextual and intercultural aspects of literary hermeneutics. He is the author of "Dead Sea Scrolls: Jerusalem Priesthood in the Scrolls," *Encyclopedia of the Historical Jesus* (Routledge, 2008), and "The Authoritative Status of *Jubilees* at Qumran," *Henoch: Journal of Studies in Judaism and Christianity from Second Temple to Late Antiquity* 30 (2009/10).

Leslie R. James is Associate Professor in Religious Studies and Director of the Black Studies Program at DePauw University in Greencastle, Indiana. He is Convenor of the Committee for Institutional Commitment to Educational Equity (CICEE) of the Great Lakes Colleges Association (GLCA). He holds membership in several professional organizations and is a research associate in The Institute for Signifying Scriptures (ISS). One of his major areas of scholarship is African diasporic history and religion.

Vivian L. Johnson is Associate Professor of Hebrew Bible at United Theological Seminary in Dayton, Ohio. Two key parts of her life that bear on her work in academia are growing up in the Pentecostal church that her grandmother founded and pastored and having primarily Jewish teachers through her K–12 educational experience. She states that she is indebted to both her Pentecostal church leaders and her Jewish instructors for emphasizing the importance of learning. Her Pentecostal upbringing with its focus on studying the Word bears on her scholarly and religious life. While she is exploring religious traditions that best suits her theological sensibilities, she appreciates her Pentecostal roots for inculcating the significance of each word in the Bible. This attentiveness to scripture forms her academic quests to translate texts for herself and proffer fresh interpretations. Her research centers on linguistic, literary, and narrative analyses of the First Testament.

Willa Mathis Johnson is Assistant Professor of Religion at the University of Mississippi in Oxford, Mississippi. She describes herself as a middle-aged African American woman, privileged by opportunities and education. The mother of an intelligent nine-year-old and the twenty-year spouse of a sociologist, she identifies most readily with her race, gender, and disabled status. She states that, clearly, not everyone understands or desires to acknowledge racism's history or its inequities. As an assistant professor at the University of Mississippi, she is made cognizant continuously of race-related matters. Additionally, with her physical disability and history of breast cancer, the constant threat of serious illness and the possibility of one day not having health insurance are daunting. These daily issues constitute the quality of her life and inform her view of the world.

Temba L. J. Mafico is Associate Vice President for Academic Services, Associate Provost, and Professor of Hebrew Bible Interdenominational Theological Center in Atlanta, Georgia. He also directs the ITC Holy Land Pilgrimage for Pastoral Renewal. His publications include "Yahweh's Emergence as 'Judge' among the Gods: A Study of the Hebrew Root *špt*"; *Judges* (International Bible Commentary); "Judge/Judging," "Just/Justice," and "Ethics of the Old Testament," *Anchor Bible Dictionary*; "The Divine Name Yahweh Elohim and Israel's Polytheistic Monotheism," *Journal of Northwest Semitic Language* 22:1 (1996), 155-83; and "Patriarchs," *New Interpreters' Dictionary of the Bible* (forthcoming). He is is also Pastor of the Village of Hope Missionary Baptist Church in Stone Mountain, Georgia.

Herbert Marbury is Assistant Professor of Hebrew Bible at Vanderbilt University in Nashville, Tennessee. He describes himself, reluctantly, as a *post-* "Black Nationalist," acknowledging that this moniker evokes images of an era long gone, filled with "Black Power" signs, paramilitary attire, dark glasses, dashikis, and fiery rhetoric, all public expressions of deep disaffection with the economic and political inequities shaping the American body politic. The phrase also conveys the temporal tension he feels with which he struggles as he negotiates his identity in a post–civil rights, postmodern, post-Katrina world where race, once an unambiguous signifier, no longer easily signifies right and wrong or distinguishes between oppressed and oppressor. In a world where white crowds, energized by Barack Obama's ideas, clamored to make him the United States' first African American president and thousands of African Americans simultaneously struggle against the degradation of post-Katrina neglect and where young white men wearing T-shirts emblazoned with the words "I want to be like Mike [Michael Jordan]" could savagely beat a young black man who happened to be strolling through "the wrong neighborhood," the insidious permanence and yet the complex ambiguity of race constitute his identity.

Andrew M. Mbuvi is Assistant Professor of Biblical Studies at Shaw University Divinity School in Raleigh, North Carolina. A native of Kenya, he completed his pre-doctoral studies there before embarking on a Ph.D. in hermeneutics and biblical interpretation at Westminster Seminary in Philadelphia. Upon completion, he was offered a year of postdoctoral studies at Duke University in Durham, N.C., in 2004, following which he commenced a full-time teaching career in biblical studies at Shaw University Divinity School (High Point Campus). In 2007 Professor Mbuvi's first book, *Temple, Exile and Identity in 1 Peter* (T. & T. Clark), was published and he is currently working on a commentary for *Jude and 2 Peter* for Cascade Publishers.

Contributors

Dora Rudo Mbuwayesango is Associate Professor of Old Testament at Hood Theological Seminary in Salisbury, North Carolina. Originally from Zimbabwe, she reads the Bible from feminist and postcolonial perspectives. Although she is based in the U.S.A., she is concerned about developments on the African continent and especially in southern Africa, where the devastating impact of the legacy of past and present imperialism is highly visible.

Madeline McClenney-Sadler is President of the Exodus Foundation in Charlotte, North Carolina. She describes that she first received Christ at age five. She holds a business and divinity degree from Howard University and a Ph.D. in religion with a specialization in Hebrew Bible from Duke University. She is a born-again, moderate ordained minister from a middle-class black enclave in Virginia and says she has been "affectionately" addressed as "honkey" by a youthful peer, as "you black people" by a racist Ph.D. instructor, and with the question "why aren't you home making your husband's dinner?" by a pastor in the library where she studied for a doctoral language exam. She states: "pressed down on every side, but not destroyed: Ain't I black and female in Africana?"

C. L. Nash is a doctoral student in systematic theology at the University of Edinburgh, Scotland. She anticipates graduation during 2009. Her work is grounded in nineteenth-century history, where she uses postmodern theory to help deconstruct standards of genderized and racialized normativity. Her published works include "More Than Race, More Than Gender" (in *The International Journal of Diversity in Organisations, Communities and Nations,* Paul James and Mary Kalantzis, eds.; Common Ground Publishing, 2009). Nash's book reviews have appeared in such journals as *The Black Theology Journal, Studies in World Christianity,* and *Literature and Theology.* Nash is an ordained minister in the American Baptist Church and has also served with the United Reformed Church in Edinburgh, Scotland.

Kenneth Ngwa is Assistant Professor of Hebrew Bible at Drew University Theological School in Madison, New Jersey. He researches and teaches courses on Israelite Wisdom literature, African proverbs, and the Exodus story. His publications include *The Hermeneutics of the 'Happy' Ending in Job 42:7-17* and an article, "Did Job Suffer for Nothing? The Ethics of Piety, Presumption and the Reception of Disaster in the Prologue of Job" (*JSOT,* March 2009). Born in Cameroon, Dr. Ngwa is an ordained minister with the Presbyterian Church in Cameroon and a board member of the African Renaissance Ambassador, a non-governmental organization working for the continuous development of African society.

Makhosazana K. Nzimande is a Senior Lecturer of Theology at University of Zululand in South Africa. She is a South African from Umlazi Township, Durban, and holds a Ph.D. in biblical interpretation from Brite Divinity School, Texas Christian University. Her doctoral dissertation, *Postcolonial Biblical Interpretation in Post-Apartheid South Africa: The Gebirah in the Hebrew Bible in the Light of Queen Jezebel and the Queen Mother of Lemuel,* explores the utilization of a postcolonial hermeneutical framework in interpreting some Old Testament texts. Nzimande is currently the Acting Head of Department, Department of Theology and Religion Studies, University of Zululand, KwaDlangezwa, South Africa. Nzimande is a member of the Anglican Church of Southern Africa (ACSA).

Emerson B. Powery is Professor of Biblical Studies at Messiah College in Grantham, Pennsylvania. He is a part of the first generation of his family born in the United States, and his two older siblings were born in the Caribbean (in the Cayman Islands), while his two younger siblings were born in the U.S. His parents moved to New York City in the early 1960s for economic and missionary purposes. This West Indian American family comfortably receives other ethnic labels—Afro-Caribbean, African American—by which many identify them in the so-called multiethnic environment of the U.S. He describes that this mixed racial identity enhances his sensitivity towards ethnic hybridity, differences, and tensions within the ancient biblical stories, including the literature of the Maccabees.

Stephen B. Reid is Professor of Christian Scriptures at Truett Theological Seminary, Baylor University in Waco, Texas. He says that contingency shapes his reading. He grew up in a Black working class family with middle-class values. Both of his parents were orphans, and they raised their children with preparation that they may be orphans themselves some day. Even though he was an academic dean for five years—an academic dean is the shop steward of a seminary faculty—he says he "read the world," including the Bible, from the perspective of the worker, not the boss. These factors mean that he asks questions about the power relationships in a text and views even the text with a certain skepticism.

Cleotha Robertson is Assistant Professor at Alliance Theological Seminary in New York City, New York. He received his Ph.D. from New York University and has taught at New York Theological Seminary and Hartford Seminary as well as Alliance Theological Seminary. Since 1994, he has served as the Senior Pastor of Sound View Presbyterian Church (PCUSA), which is a diverse, vibrant and community-involved African American congregation of the Presbytery of New York City.

Jerome Ross is Assistant Professor of Old Testament at the Samuel DeWitt Proctor School of Theology at Virginia Union University in Richmond, Virginia. He has published works including "The Cultural Affinity between the Ancient Yahwists and the African Americans: A Hermeneutic for Homiletics" in *Born to Preach*, ed. Samuel K. Roberts (Judson Press, 2000) and "Jubilee in Lev. 17–26" in the *Holy Bible: The African American Jubilee Edition* (American Bible Society, 1999).

Kimberly N. Ruffin is Assistant Professor of English at Roosevelt University in Chicago, Illinois. She credits the Black church, particularly Sunday School, in fostering her love for critical thinking, the Bible, and the arts. She is a member of New Faith Baptist Church International (Matteson, Illinois) who considers activists such as evangelist Charlotte Keys (founder, Jesus People Against Pollution) and Wangari Maathai (founder, Green Belt Movement) as models of how Black Christians can be leaders in creating a sustainable common life on Earth.

David T. Shannon was from Atlanta, Georgia. An internationally recognized pastor, scholar, and educator, the late Rev. Dr. David T. Shannon (1934–2008) shared his far-reaching gifts with the church, the academy, and the global community. He served as dean of Pittsburgh Theological Seminary and president of three institutions: Andover Newton Theological School (Newton Centre, Mass.); Virginia Union University (Richmond, Va.); and Allen University (Columbia, S.C.). He was well known for his ecumenical and interfaith endeavors; his involvement in organizations promoting cooperation among ecclesial bodies (for example, the National Council of Churches and World Council of Churches); and his ministry within his own denomination (American Baptist Churches, U.S.A.). His published works include *The Old Testament Experience of Faith* (Judson, 1977) and (as co-editor with Gayraud Wilmore) *Black Witness to the Apostolic Faith* (Eerdmans, 1988).

Adam Stokes is currently a Ph.D. student in Hebrew Bible/Old Testament at Princeton Theological Seminary in Princeton, New Jersey, and a licensed Baptist minister in the Progressive National Baptist Church. His interests include the book of Job and the depiction of the sea monster in ancient Near Eastern mythology. He is also interested in the appropriation of biblical motifs and themes found in traditional African American folklore.

Michelle Ellis Taylor is a Ph.D. candidate at Brandeis University in Waltham, Massachusetts, and is an instructor in the Religion Department at Huntingdon College in Montgomery, Alabama. She is currently completing her dissertation, entitled "'In this Way You will Purge the Evil From Your Midst': A Comparison of Dt 21:1-9 and Num 19." She is a native of Montgomery, Alabama, and holds a B.S. in business administration from the University of Alabama, as well as an M.A. in theological studies from United Theological Seminary in Dayton, Ohio.

Justin S. Ukpong is Professor of New Testament and Vice-Chancellor (President) at Veritas University, the Catholic university in Abuja, Nigeria. A Catholic priest from Nigeria, he holds a doctorate degree in Biblical Theology from the Pontifical Urban University, Rome, and has taught in Nigeria, Switzerland, South Africa, and the U.S.A. In 2000, he received an honorary doctorate degree in theology from the University of Bern, Switzerland. Dr. Ukpong is a member of the Society of Biblical Literature, the Studiorum Novum Testamentum Societas, and the Catholic Biblical Association. His publications include monographs and articles in series and journals such as *Concilium*, *Semeia*, *Journal of Theology for Southern Africa*, *Mission Studies*, and *International Review of Mission*.

Robert Wafawanaka is Assistant Professor of Biblical Studies at Virginia Union University in Richmond, Virginia. He describes his social location as emerging from a dual African and North American context. Having lived in both continents for almost the same length of time, he hase been influenced by the cultural values of both locations. While he grew up in a traditional environment defined by colonialism, oppression, and liberation, he has also lived in a modern and academic American setting in his adult life. He states that his reading of Baruch is informed by these contexts.

Renita J. Weems is an Independent Scholar from Nashville, Tennessee. A former member of the faculty of Vanderbilt Divinity School and former Visiting Professor at Spelman College, she is now a writer, an ordained minister, and a full-time blogger. She has numerous books, commentaries, and articles on the Bible and prophetic religion to her credit. Her book *Listening for God: A Minister's Journey through Silence and Doubt* (Simon & Schuster, 2000) won the Religious Communicators' Council's prestigious 1999 Wilbur Award for excellence in communicating spiritual values to the secular media. She is a columnist at Beliefnet.com for their "Progressive Revival" page, which is dedicated to the revival of religious progressivism and its influence in American politics.

Gosnell L. Yorke is Professor of Religion and Dean of the School of Graduate Studies at Northern Caribbean University in Mandeville, Jamaica. He describes that he was born in a relatively poor family in St. Kitts, the first British colony in the Caribbean, and was educated there and in Trinidad and Tobago, as well as in the U.S., Canada, and South Africa where he has lived and worked for many years. From time to time, he visits not only Britain, where his father has lived for over forty years, but his mother as well, who is now a retiree in the Dutch-speaking Caribbean country of Curacao. In addition to English as his mother tongue, he also speaks French, Spanish, Portuguese, and some Kiswahili, since he has also lived and worked in Kenya for a number of years.

PREFACE

CULTURE AND LIFE CIRCUMSTANCES affect the way people read sacred literature. Folkways influence popular attitudes about those texts that people typically classify as "Scripture." These attitudes, in turn, help to determine the methods by which readers apply their "Scriptures" in making sense of the highs and lows of daily existence.

That sacred texts shape values is hardly disputed. That they contain ideas about the divine, nature, society, and self that are considered foundational in various parts of the globe is generally accepted. That certain holy books have transcended their communities of origin and have been adopted, in whole or in part, by others is well known. That several have given rise to vibrant interpretive traditions, some of which have spawned new bodies of lore, is well documented. That some have been used to justify war, the building of empire, human bondage, and various forms of social exclusion is a sad but true fact.

To declare that the aforementioned truisms apply in large measure to the Christian Bible may surprise some. The Bible's place in the modern Western imagination affords it such privileged status that many consider it to be in a class by itself. Some find it difficult to accept that it contains ideas objectionable to anyone or that it could be used to harm others. Nonetheless, history bears witness to the many ways in which the Old and New Testaments have influenced our world. With regard to peoples of African descent, the Christian Bible, in its various canonical versions, is a pivotal text with which many on the continent of Africa and in the African Diaspora have a complex relationship.

On the one hand, it has been an invaluable resource in struggles for freedom, as we see in the rhetoric of Frederick Douglass and Maria Stewart. Its ideals have been used as touchstones for shaping common life, influencing discourse on everything from the traditional Sabbath laws to debates over homosexuality, abortion, and racial reconciliation. Many Fundamentalist, Evangelical, and other Africana (that is African and African Diasporan) Christian bodies feel that it is the inerrant word of God. For such persons, the Bible is the textbook for determining proper behavior and morals, both public and private. In North America and elsewhere, biblical passages, imagery, and rhetoric are integral parts of civic discourse. Politicians from Jesse Jackson Sr. to Barack Obama draw on them. Motivational speakers, such as Les Brown and Iyanla Vanzant, deploy them. Biblical metaphors and tropes saturate Africana religious parlance and popular speech. Preachers, athletes, actors, musicians, and other public figures utilize them.

On the other hand, the Christian Bible has been a source of disruption and instability in the lives of Africana peoples. It has been used as a tool of oppression. Certain passages have been used to justify policies inimical to independence and self-governance in Africa and elsewhere. At times, the freedom to read and preach from it have been tightly regulated.

For some time, scholars have been working diligently to understand the extraordinary relationship between Africana peoples and the Christian Bible. Part of the process has included exploring and acknowledging the various ways in which the Bible has been read and interpreted in Africa and the Black Diaspora globally. It has also included an effort to create new models for interpretation that draw heavily on the traditions and lore of Africana peoples worldwide. Within the past two decades, African and African Diasporan scholars have made significant contributions to this rapidly growing body of work. The results have been widely circulated in assorted monographs, articles, and edited collections. They attest to the emergence of a new academic subfield: Africana biblical studies.

This field will take its place alongside current disciplines dedicated to the study of biblical interpretation in the American Diaspora (African American biblical hermeneutics), the Caribbean Diaspora, and Africa. Its focus will be analytical and comparative. Among its aims are to: (1) identify interpretive strategies that transcend local and regional boundaries in the Africana world; (2) discover patterns of biblical appropriation common to multiple life settings on the African continent and within the Black Diaspora; and (3) promote the development of reading strategies that place the particularities of Africana life at the center, rather than on the periphery, of the interpretive process. These strategies have already begun to change the face of biblical scholarship.

The Africana Bible is a significant step in further developing this new subfield. It is an interdisciplinary and multicultural encounter with that portion of the Christian Bible known variously as the Old Testament, the First Testament, or the Hebrew Bible. It also includes chapters on apocryphal and selected pseudepigraphic books that many within the Africana community classify as scripture (that is, as a sacred and authoritative book). It examines some of the critical issues, theological perspectives, and interpretive challenges found within these texts; sheds light on the lives, cultures, and faith traditions of persons of African descent globally; and seeks to call attention to the points of intersection and divergence that exist between the Old/First Testament, read as scripture, and contemporary readers. It opens a window onto the Africana world and the strategies used by peoples of African descent on the African continent, in the Caribbean, in the Americas, in Europe, and elsewhere in deriving meaning from it. It features the work of scholars familiar with, and willing to read, the biblical text through the lenses of Africana history, literature, and culture. It asks how such issues as globalization, immigration, discrimination, and identity construction influence, and are influenced by, the First Testament and other ancient Jewish texts.

It also takes on the difficult task of critically evaluating the role the First Testament has played in African and African Diasporan history and contemporary life. In addition to entries on specific canonical and extracanonical books, it also contains prefatory articles that offer a rationale for reading the First Testament through an Africana lens; examine the impact that living in Diaspora has had on biblical interpretation; sample various African and African Diasporan reading strategies; give an overview of how the Bible is viewed in twenty-first-century Africa; offer a perspective on how Africana women encounter the Bible; look at some of the problematic dimensions of the Bible and its relationship to those living in Africa and the African Diaspora; offer guidelines on how one might engage in a more responsible reading of the First Testament; and survey how the First Testament has been used in Africana art, music, and popular culture.

Insofar as it offers African, African American, and Afro-Caribbean readings of books constituting the First Testament and the Apocrypha, *The Africana Bible* is a fitting complement to the recently released *True to Our Native Land: An African American New Testament Commentary* (Blount et al. 2007). However, it differs from the latter in several regards. First, the current volume seeks to be something more than a standard commentary on scripture. In fact, one of its goals is to call into question whether any secondary exposition, Africana or otherwise, can do more than simply converse with a primary text such as the First Testament. We hope that it also serves as a stimulus for all who read the First Testament, in academic or religious settings, to both hear and heed the challenge issued by Vincent Wimbush:

> We must collect ourselves as a larger, more complexly constituted group and orient ourselves so as to begin (in some cases, perhaps begin *again*) to fathom how "scriptures" developed, what work we make them do within and across the societies and cultures, and with what historical and perduring political consequences. Such fathoming should be carried out across the scholarly guilds, across the academic departments and programs, across school types, across social situations and settings. (2008: 3)

Second, we have made the primary point of reference for this volume the worldwide Africana community, rather than the African American community exclusively. Clearly, every perspective and locale within that vast landscape is not presented. Nonetheless, our hope has been to "sample," perhaps like the contemporary "D.J." or "MC," contributors *and* perspectives that represent the richness and diversity of the whole. Our goal in so doing is to encourage readers to see themselves as part of an ongoing global dialogue about the Bible and even about Africana life itself. We recognize, as do many scholars today, that identity, whether one is speaking of individuals or groups, is fluid and contingent. Cultural boundaries are porous and permeable, rather than fixed. Texts, whether literary or oral, classic or popular, are often points of reference in negotiating concepts of self and society. They are also used in creating and maintaining social boundary markers. At times, they determine who is "in" and who is "out." They also help determine who is allowed to stand at the "center" and who is to be relegated to the "margin" in matters familial, political, or religious. Reading of the First Testament and cognate sources requires an awareness of how such dynamics are realized within these sources as well as in those places where the texts are read.

Third, the current volume uses various methodologies, some more traditional and others decidedly experimental. Contributors to *The Africana Bible* have been encouraged to "step outside" of established disciplinary and genre boundaries and to employ African and African Diasporan stories, poetry, art, and music as actual dialogue partners in the interpretive process. They have been encouraged to be responsibly "playful" in their interpretive work and to demonstrate how Africana traditions, lore, and lived experience can be creatively deployed in reading, probing, conversing with, challenging, (at times) ignoring, extending, and creating meaning from and in partnership with the First Testament, the Apocrypha, and the Pseudepigrapha. Given that one can see examples of all of these strategies in the history of Africana biblical interpretation to date, it is appropriate that such strategies be featured in this volume. Readers should leave this volume with an appreciation of the remarkable diversity, scope, and tone that characterize modern

» Preface

Africana encounters with the First Testament. They will also see that there is indeed considerable latitude in the ways that canons of "scripture" are determined, the ways the boundaries of Africana culture are drawn, and the way Africana interpretation of the First Testament is conducted.

Our hope is that *The Africana Bible* will be a tool that helps to increase both awareness of Africana life throughout the world and greater interest in the history, current challenges, and future prospects of the peoples of Africa and the Black Diaspora worldwide. The North American context is but one of many in which peoples of African descent have read, and continue to read, the First Testament. Our understanding of the African cultural landscape has grown exponentially in recent years. Our awareness of the geographical extent, diversity, and breadth of African Diasporan communities around the globe has also increased. Our knowledge of the role that the Bible and other sacred literatures have played in Africa and the African Diaspora is constantly evolving as well.

The agenda of *The Africana Bible* is both discursive and constructive. On the one hand, we want its constituent entries to be informative. On the other, we want the perspectives and readings found herein to invite all who use it to join the conversation about the First Testament and the Black experience today—however one understands it—and to see the voices represented herein as a model of the heterogeneous Africana community that we are and seek more fully to become.

We trust that Bible scholars, seminary faculty, students, clergy, laity, Christian educators, those with an interest in the study of the Bible as literature, and other readers intent on exploring the cultural dimensions of faith will find it a useful tool. We trust that it will be successful in honoring the legacy of our predecessors, within and outside of the academy, whose creative use of scripture—the First Testament, the Apocrypha, and the Pseudepigrapha in particular—is the foundation on which our work is built.

As an editorial group, we wish to thank all of those who, over the years, have contributed to the completion of this project. This includes the many women and men in Africa, the Americas, the Caribbean, Europe, and elsewhere for whom the First Testament has been a touchstone in navigating the difficult terrain of human existence; those countless *Africana* scholars who have shared, and continue to air, their work on the Bible in print (see, for example, Felder 1991; West and Dube 2000; and Holter 2006) and through presentations at the meetings of professional organizations such as the Society of Biblical Literature and the American Academy of Religion; and the clergy and laity within Africana churches worldwide, for many of whom the First Testament is an essential part of the scriptural whole from which light and life proceed. We would also like to express our gratitude to the University of Notre Dame, in Indiana, for the hospitality extended to us at various points during the completion of this work by the staff of the Center for Continuing Education/McKenna Hall and the faculty, staff, and students of the Departments of Theology and Africana Studies (through the Initiative for the Study of Religion and Culture in Africa and the African Diaspora). We acknowledge, in particular, funding for our editorial work made available through the aegis of the Walter Chair in Theology. Finally, to Neil Elliott and our publishing partners at Fortress Press, we wish to extend our profound thanks for their belief in this project, their counsel, and their substantial material support, without which the completion of *The Africana Bible* would not have been possible.

—Hugh R. Page Jr., GENERAL EDITOR;
Randall C. Bailey, Valerie Bridgeman, Cheryl Kirk-Duggan,
Stacy Davis, Rodney S. Sadler Jr., Nathaniel Samuel Murrell,
Madipoane Masenya (ngwan'a Mphahlele), ASSOCIATE EDITORS

References

Blount, Brian K., Cain Hope Felder, Clarice J. Martin, and Emerson B. Powery, eds. 2007. *True to Our Native Land: An African American New Testament Commentary*. Minneapolis: Fortress Press.

Felder, Cain, ed. 1991. *Stony the Road We Trod: African American Biblical Interpretation*. Minneapolis: Fortress Press.

Holter, Knut, ed. 2006. *Let My People Stay!: Researching the Old Testament in Africa*. Nairobi, Kenya: Acton.

West, G. O., and Musa W. Dube, eds. 2000. *The Bible in Africa: Transactions, Trajectories, and Trends*. Leiden: Brill.

Wimbush, Vincent. 2008. "TEXTures, Gestures, Power: Orientation to Radical Excavation." In *Theorizing Scriptures: New Critical Orientations to a Cultural Phenomenon*, ed. V. Wimbush. New Brunswick, N.J.: Rutgers University Press.

MAPS

1. The Ancient Near East

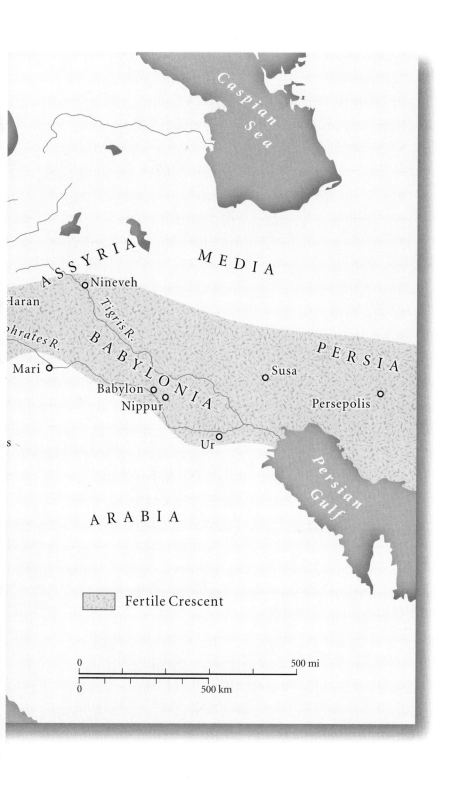

Fertile Crescent

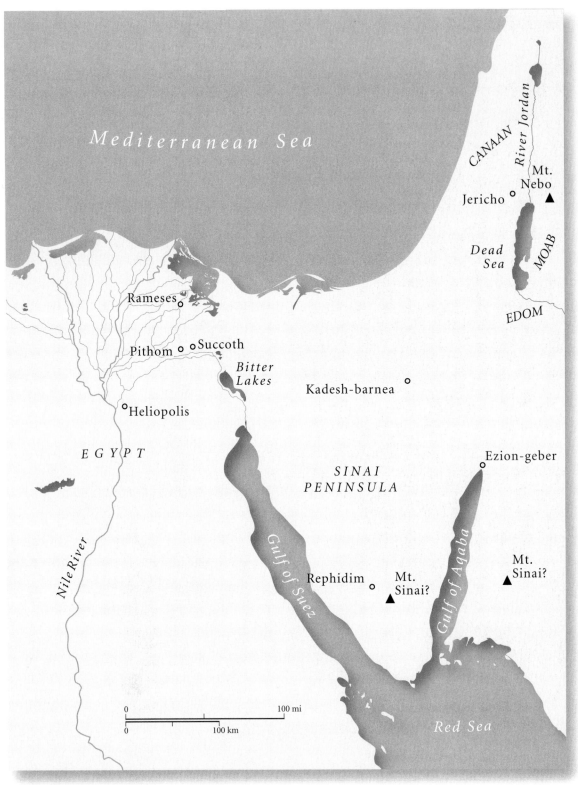

Mediterranean Sea

CANAAN

River Jordan

Mt.
Nebo ▲

Jericho ○

Dead
Sea

MOAB

EDOM

Rameses ○

Pithom ○ ○ Succoth

Bitter
Lakes

Kadesh-barnea ○

Heliopolis ○

EGYPT

SINAI
PENINSULA

Ezion-geber ○

Gulf of Suez

Nile River

Rephidim ○   Mt.
Sinai? ▲

Gulf of Aqaba

Mt.
Sinai? ▲

0   100 mi

0   100 km

Red Sea

2. The Geography of Exodus

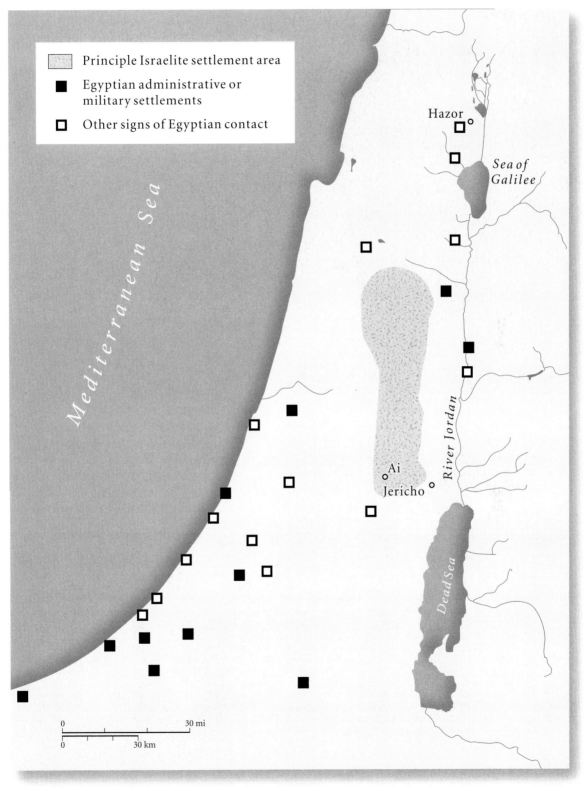

3. The Emergence of Israel in Canaan

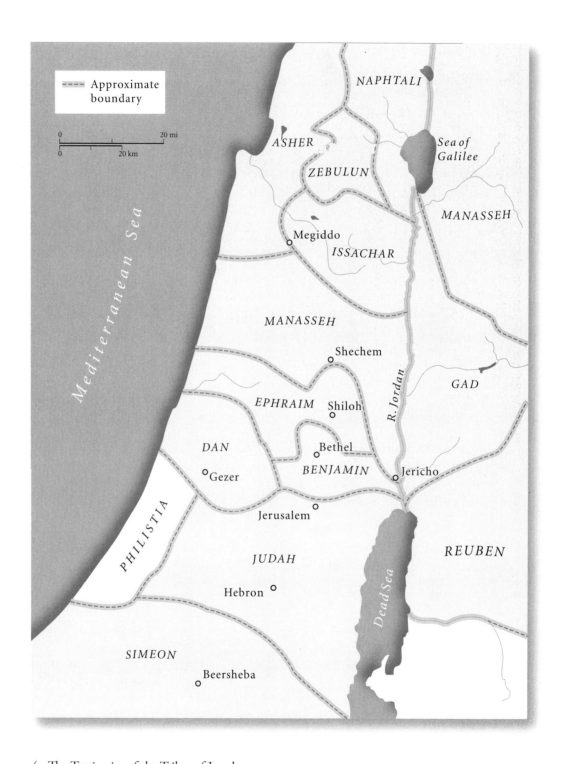

Legend: Approximate boundary

0   20 mi
0   20 km

Mediterranean Sea

NAPHTALI

ASHER

ZEBULUN

Sea of Galilee

MANASSEH

Megiddo

ISSACHAR

MANASSEH

Shechem

R. Jordan

GAD

EPHRAIM

Shiloh

DAN

Bethel

Gezer

BENJAMIN

Jericho

Jerusalem

JUDAH

REUBEN

Hebron

Dead Sea

PHILISTIA

SIMEON

Beersheba

4. The Territories of the Tribes of Israel

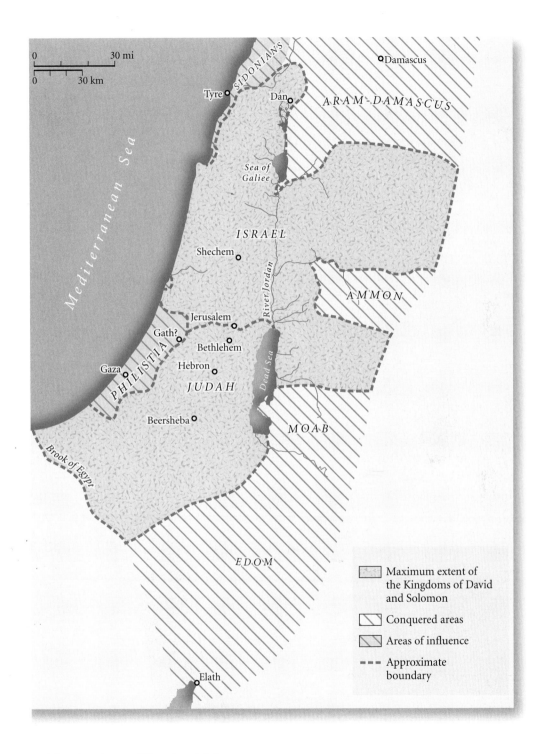

5. The Kingdoms of David and Solomon

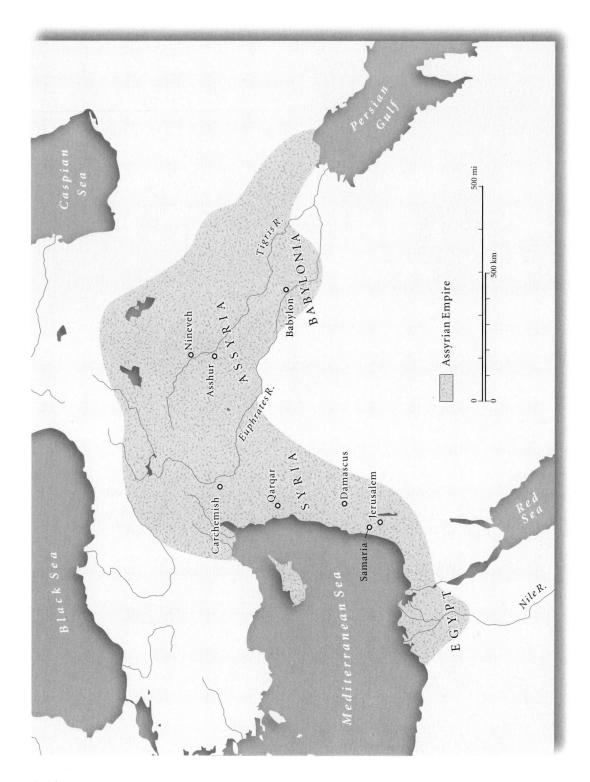

Caspian Sea

Persian Gulf

500 mi

500 km

Assyrian Empire

Tigris R.

Nineveh

Asshur

A S S Y R I A

Babylon

B A B Y L O N I A

Euphrates R.

Qarqar

S Y R I A

Damascus

Jerusalem

Carchemish

Samaria

Black Sea

Mediterranean Sea

Red Sea

E G Y P T

Nile R.

6. The Assyrian Empire

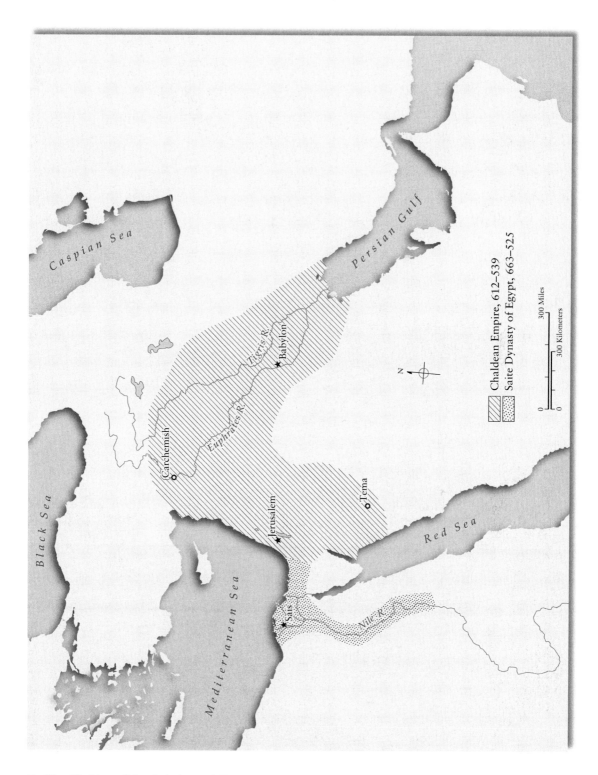

Caspian Sea

Persian Gulf

Tigris R.

Babylon

Euphrates R.

Carchemish

Black Sea

Tema

Jerusalem

Red Sea

Mediterranean Sea

Sais

Nile R.

N

Chaldean Empire, 612–539
Saite Dynasty of Egypt, 663–525

300 Miles

300 Kilometers

0

0

7. The Chaldean (Neo-Babylonian) Empire

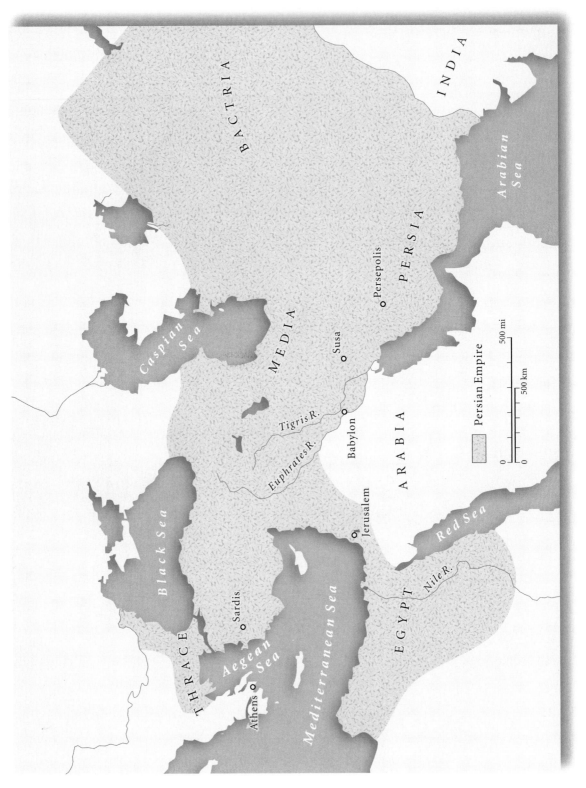

8. The Persian Empire

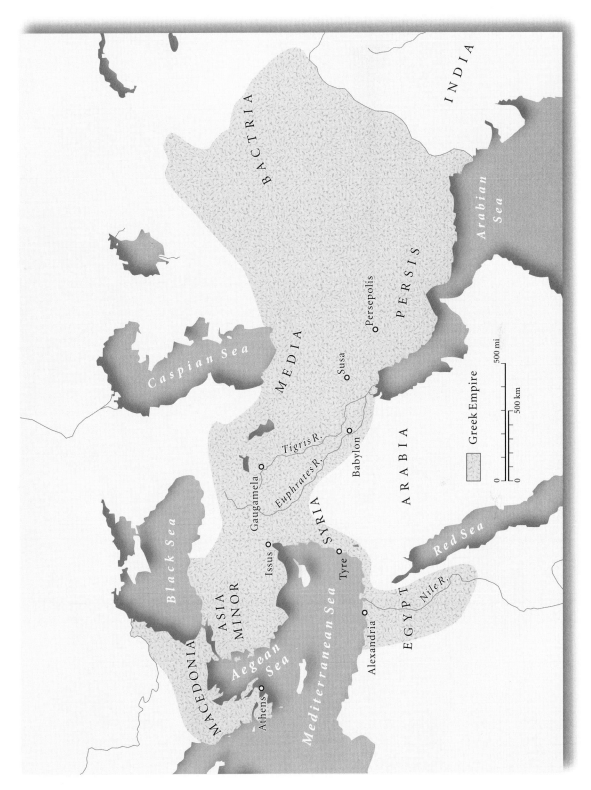

INDIA

BACTRIA

Arabian Sea

PERSIS

Persepolis

MEDIA

Caspian Sea

Susa

ARABIA

Babylon

Tigris R.

Euphrates R.

Gaugamela

Greek Empire

500 mi

500 km

Black Sea

SYRIA

Issus

Tyre

Red Sea

Nile R.

ASIA
MINOR

Mediterranean Sea

Alexandria

EGYPT

MACEDONIA

*Aegean
Sea*

Athens

9. The Hellenistic Empire

READING THE
HEBREW BIBLE

The AFRICANA BIBLE

A RATIONALE

Hugh R. Page Jr.

THE STORY IN THE NAME

It would be misleading to speak of *The Africana Bible* as a scriptural commentary, particularly given what we have come to know of works that traditionally fall within that genre.[1] It is, by contrast, an interlocutor with scripture. Its articles present critical and impressionistic reflections on books that have been accorded sacred status by Jewish and Christian audiences. Collectively, its articles do not seek to be the "last word" on how the primary sources with which they "converse" are to be understood. The secondary literature cited is intentionally selective. The bibliographies at the end of each article are neither exhaustive nor strictly inclusive of those monographs and articles typically construed as central to the field of biblical studies. The context and questions that animate this volume emerge from the heart and soul of the Africana experience, an ethos that itself defies essentialization. The constitutive elements of Black life on the African continent and within its myriad diasporas—forced, voluntary, historical, current, created, and imagined—are as varied as the voices of the authors heard within this volume. *The Africana Bible* mirrors this diversity.

In some ways, the title *The Africana Bible* seems an odd designation for a work that seeks, in its conversation with the Bible, to bring to bear the intellectual riches of the peoples and cultures of Africa and the African Diaspora. Why the Latin terminology (that is, *Africana*) instead of a name derived from Akan, Kiswahili, or some other African language? Why not a simpler, perhaps catchier title? Would not a straightforward designation such as *The African and African American Commentary on the Hebrew Bible/Old Testament* be preferable? In some circles, an appeal to nomenclature is made to resolve, once and for all, the fraught issues of classification and ownership. In others, it is one stage, albeit an important one, in an analytical process. For example, in categorizing emotions, physical maladies, cultures, academic pursuits, or literature, typological assignation is a pivotal preliminary task. For those working with biblical and cognate literatures, *Gattungsforschung* (that is, the identification of literary genres) is foundational for exegesis. For those occupying the role of expositor, especially with regard to the Bible, naming can be seen as a strategy for arranging, cataloging, controlling, and laying claim to that text. Moreover, to categorize a work as Bible commentary is to give it representational power and authoritative *gravitas* among readers. All too often, an appeal to what a Bible commentary "says" seems to be the point at which probative reading ends. Books so categorized come to be seen as providing *the* key to understanding a sacred and pluriform anthology whose mysteries are deep and, at times, inscrutable. In this regard, the term *commentary*, when used in relation to modern works that claim to interpret the Bible, can be understood as a cultural cipher for that which, more often than not, limits discourse.

However, naming can also indicate problems that exist in defining genres, roles, and relationships. It can call attention to the inchoate nature of realities that appear to be fixed. It can raise questions about artifacts, cultures, or ideas. It can allude to processes intended to promote reflection or foster contemplation. Such is the case with the title *The Africana Bible*. It suggests a mode of discourse that does not easily fit into the genre of commentary, insofar as that classification is popularly construed. Its articles represent an assortment of textual interventions. The approaches used span the gamut of creative engagements and critical methodologies. Throughout, it attempts to use an array of experiential, literary, artistic, and material resources hailing from African and African Diasporan peoples the world over as touchstones for reading, reacting to,

querying, embracing, and—on occasion—looking both through and beyond the Bible at Africana life.

This volume's authors are steeped in one or more of these traditions. Our contributions create, in effect, a literary and ideational cosmos akin to the community we collectively represent—diverse, heterogeneous, dynamic, contingent, evolving, and constantly under negotiation. They represent the continuation, rather than the conclusion, of an ongoing conversation about the Bible and Africana life. Thus, the title encourages readers to consider the place that the Bible occupies in the lives of peoples of African descent. At the same time, it challenges them to think further about the meaning of such basic terms as *Bible*, *Africa*, *Diaspora*, and *Africana*.

If anything, this volume could well be spoken of as *An Africana Bible* rather than *The Africana Bible* insofar as it is one of many possible contemporary exegetical encounters with the scriptures of Israel. One could well speak of it as a twenty-first-century midrash on selected Jewish and early Christian writings. One might also think of it as one recension of a dynamic and pluriform Africana "interpreted Bible," to borrow James Kugel's terminology (1997: xv). Whereas Kugel uses the former designation in speaking of a diverse body of scriptural texts and interpretive traditions acknowledged as normative by Jews and Christians, I use it here to refer to the Bible and those secondary "texts" to which it has given rise in an assortment of Africana cultural domains. Following the recent lead of Vincent Wimbush (2008: 4), one might go further and classify *The Africana Bible* as an anthology of scholarly "riffs" that probe, challenge, and problematize biblical, apocryphal, and pseudepigraphic writings considered by various communities (in antiquity and today) as scripture.

Insofar as the articles contained herein embody a poetics both critical and creative, at once intellectual and artistic, it is equally fitting to apply Barbara Holmes's designation *griosh* to the present volume. Holmes's reflections on this term are instructive:

I have coined a different word to refer to hermeneutical skills that are particular to black biblical interpretation. The word is *griosh*, which is derived from the word *griot*, referring to African storytellers, who were also historians and keepers of cultural memory. The sound *sh* is a symbolic marker of the hush arbors where Christian diasporan faith perspectives were honed. (Holmes 2004: 120)

I see *The Africana Bible* as a work produced by those who function as poets and "storytellers" in academic, church, and other settings. One of its major functions is to empower readers to ask questions and to consider further the meaning and implications of the First Testament and cognate writings for communities that revere them, that have been shaped by them, and that—in some instances—have been destabilized by interpretations of them.[2] As is the case with many scholars working in the discipline of Africana studies, this book should encourage readers to *trouble* terms like *Africana* (that is, pertaining to things African and African Diasporan), *Bible, commentary*, and *community*. It should promote consideration of important questions such as these: Once texts are generated, are they no longer "owned" by their authors? How do texts and their potential meanings change once they are gathered into an anthology like the Hebrew Bible? Is there truly an overarching Africana culture? Can we speak any longer of the existence of *a* (that is, a single) Bible acknowledged as authoritative in the Africana world? What are the distinguishing markers of a community—Africana or other? To what extent is identity, within a community or on an individual basis, an absolute and noncontingent construction? At a time when scholarship on Africa and the larger Black Diasporan world is engaging these and related questions, this book should have wide appeal within and beyond the confines of the Black church. In fact, it is hoped that it will help recent scholarly efforts, such as those of Stacey Floyd-Thomas and others (2007: xxiii–xxiv), to

develop a more expansive notion of that important institution.

Thus, *The Africana Bible* is an invitation to critical reflection on Africana life and the role that the First Testament has played in it. It is also a guide for a more discerning exploration of a body of literature and a theological tradition whose canonical shape and content have been, and continue to be, variously configured and whose impact on Africa, the Black Diaspora, and the Atlantic world has been, and remains, profound.

AN OVERVIEW OF CONTENT

Contributors to *The Africana Bible* have been encouraged to use the entire spectrum of intellectual, artistic, and religious resources found within the Africana *milieu* in their hermeneutical engagement of Israel's scriptures. Consistent with this aim, contributors have been asked to employ a wide range of critical biblical scholarship—as well as an array of African and African Diasporan expressive genres, including narrative, poetry, dance, photography, and music—as dialogue partners and interpretive lenses. They have been given license to stress the role of the First Testament as a sacred text embedded within a larger ecology of sacred texts and traditions within both African and Black Diasporan settings. The goal has been to ensure that *The Africana Bible* can be a tool that: (1) increases awareness of Black lived experience throughout the world; (2) promotes conversation about the history, current challenges, and future prospects of peoples of African descent internationally; (3) enables Black experience today to be viewed from a global perspective; and (4) can be used as a literary medium that promotes convergence and community building.

The members of our editorial board have tried to ensure that each entry has sufficient breadth and depth to serve the needs of specialist and nonspecialist readers in academic and other settings. To enable access to such a diverse audience, contributors have been asked to be sensitive to several issues in the preparation of their essays: theological perspectives and cultural challenges found within the Bible; the lives, cultures, and faith traditions of persons of African descent living around the world; and points of intersection and divergence that exist between the Bible (understood as scripture) and contemporary readers. They have also been asked to demonstrate awareness of sociocultural and religious realities in the multiplicity of interlocking Africana cultural settings as well as of the complex network of African Diasporas historically and in the present by: (1) foregrounding the work of African and African Diasporan scholars; (2) reading the biblical text in light of maxims and methodologies derived from Africana history, literature, and culture; (3) focusing on issues of concern (such as globalization, immigration, discrimination, and identity construction) within the Black community worldwide; and (4) highlighting and questioning the role that the Bible has played in African and African Diasporan intellectual history.

Contributors have also been asked to provide brief autobiographical statements that disclose their social location to reveal to readers the perspective(s) from which their articles have been written. Each article in the commentary is accompanied by a short bibliography so that readers can continue the conversation about the Bible and Africana life initiated therein.

BECOMING THE AUDIENCE WE SEEK TO ENGAGE

The academic training received by most authors contributing to *The Africana Bible* privileges post-Enlightenment critical approaches. At the same time, many of the authors have been, and continue to be, formed by individuals and institutions in Africa and the Black Diaspora that represent various ideas about the nature of life, ways of knowing, and salvation. Our challenge has been to find ways to articulate and employ these ideas about being, knowing, and discovering meaning in life through our textual readings. We recognize that this anthology must be a viable resource for a worldwide Africana community continuing to wrestle with issues of identity, economic disenfranchisement, marginalization, heterogeneity, interconnectedness, and interdependence.

Given the importance of commentaries to those who read the Bible, it is surprising that biblical scholars receive little formal training in how to write them. Even more alarming is that—given our knowledge of the impact the Bible has had on the formation of Western society—more energy has not been devoted to examining the genre in a critical manner. For example, anyone writing a commentary on the First or Second Testaments should have some awareness of the ways that commentaries: (1) shape readers' encounters with these texts; (2) promote, directly and indirectly, political and religious ideologies; (3) commodify the Bible and ideas about how it should be interpreted; (4) generate reading communities; (5) reify cosmologies and myths of origin; (6) privilege particular interpretive strategies; (7) construct and dissolve social boundaries; and (8) sustain and deconstruct social groups. In this regard, they have the capacity to take on a status and authority comparable to the Bible itself.[3]

Commentaries are, therefore, examples of persuasive discourse. They use meta-narration to inform and guide readings of the text. Approaches to this task often range from heavy-handed to minimally intrusive. Writers can assume various roles in producing these secondary treatments. Some adopt the posture of expert, while others prefer that of intellectual fellow traveler or spiritual guide. In certain instances, an author's perspective appears to be opaque by intention. In others, it may be aligned closely with that of either a consensus opinion or the Deity itself as conceived by a given commentator. Such strategies tend to deprive readers of agency and minimize their responsibility in negotiating meaning.

The Africana Bible seeks to be an empowering text that is unambiguous about its intentions. As contributors, we have challenged ourselves to be clear about the major presuppositions informing our work and, to the extent possible, straightforward in revealing the implications of our findings for the global Africana community. We have an acute appreciation for the dynamism and diversity of Africana life. We are familiar with, and writing from within, the Africana ethos as we understand it.

Several principles have informed our efforts. The first is general recognition of our need for immersion in Africana intellectual and cultural traditions. In most instances, this has involved creative rereading of Israel's scriptures as well as archival and experiential research. In some cases, it has entailed becoming reacquainted with sources long forgotten and rarely referenced in traditional biblical scholarship. In others, it has necessitated continuing education—that is, (re)familiarization with Africana literature, music, art, and ideas heretofore outside of our personal or professional scope.

The second principle is a commitment to identify clearly for readers the places within the Africana tradition from which we are doing our hermeneutical work as well as those major factors that have helped to shape our agenda as readers. The third is a consensus that Africana touchstones—that is, persons and resources representing a broad cross section of life experiences and cultural domains—should be given primacy of place in our interpretive interventions. The fourth is a willingness to present our findings in a manner conducive to conversation and the building of inclusive and liberating communities of independent First (and Second) Testament readers. The fifth principle is that the marketing and distribution of *The Africana Bible* should embody the animating values of the global Africana community that we *are* and seek more fully to *become*.

The authors of the following articles are not attempting to articulate a single authoritative perspective, what in contemporary academic circles would be called totalizing hegemonic meta-narration. Instead, they seek to explore the potential meanings that emerge when biblical texts are viewed in light of African and African Diasporan lived experience. These interpretive forays are experiential "readings" or "explorations" that seek to formulate a common idiom from what Vincent Wimbush has termed the "dark script" (Wimbush 2000: 28) of the First Testament and the *koine* of Africana daily life. By beginning with, or referencing, images or tropes from Black life, authors have allowed the realities of day-to-day existence on the African continent and throughout the African Diaspora to have a prominent place in the process by which meaning is derived from the First Testament and other ancient texts deemed authoritative by Africana readers today.

AN EDITORIAL SELF-DISCLOSURE

As general editor, I view *The Africana Bible* as an investment in the full realization of a compassionate, unified, and diverse global community. This community consists of the peoples of Africa, the global African Diaspora, and the entirety of the human family. As priest (the Episcopal Church), Bible scholar, philologist, poet, and child of the African Diaspora, I recognize the pivotal roles that those in the academy, faith communities, the arts, and the Africana world must play if we are to realize this teleological objective. I also recognize that we must be more attentive to, and appreciative of, the processes by which texts are created, collected, read, edited, interpreted, canonized, appropriated, and applied.

My commitment to this goal comes from a profound appreciation of the theological complexity, breadth, and depth of the Hebrew Bible; an embrace of the Christian Bible's elegant truths;[4] the theological latitude characteristic of the Anglican worldview; and those core values enshrined in both African American spirituals and the soul-blues musical continuum (particularly those expressed in the music of Junior Wells; Marvin Gaye; Roberta Flack; Stevie Wonder; Parliament; Earth, Wind, and Fire, and others). My thinking has been influenced by many sources: contemporary artists who have shaped, reappropriated, and extended that soul-blues tradition, including Ben Harper, Cree Summer, Prince, and John Legend; (re)discovery of the blues (Hoodoo Blues in particular) through actual performance and the work of James Cone (2001), Francis Davis (2003), LeRoi Jones (1963), Albert Murray (2000), Robert Palmer (1982), Jon Michael Spencer (1994), and Gayle Dean Wardlow (1998); blues art; the Black contemplative and esoteric traditions, mediated by the visual art of Pamela Coleman Smith, the photographs and poetry of Gordon Parks (1971), the extant eighteenth-century sermons of Prince Hall, the autobiography and other writings of Howard Thurman (1979), and the work of Barbara Holmes (2004); and African American *conjure*, via participant observation, the fiction of Zora Neale Hurston (1991), the modern *conjure* tales collected by Nalo Hopkinson (2003), and the work of Theophus Smith (1994), Catherine Yronwode (2002, 2004), Yvonne Chireau (2003), Stephanie Mitchem (2007), and others.[5] I see the aforementioned as *matrices* within which Africana identities, Bible-reading strategies, and spiritualities have taken shape and continue to develop.

For those who might wonder about the legitimacy and theological value of the above endeavors, and of *The Africana Bible* overall, I would posit that both are nuanced responses to the late Robert Hood's haunting question, "Must God remain Greek?" (1990: xi). They are answers that create, in his words, "an opportunity for Christian life and thought to be enriched and enhanced by appropriating the treasury of non-Western insights into the human condition and the divine life," rejoinders that confirm that the Africana experience is indeed a "theological trove" (Hood 1990: xii) that can be mined productively by those in theology's central and ancillary subfields.

In the end, *The Africana Bible* is, in my mind, a product of Africana "expressive culture" (Ember and Ember 1999: 505). It is part of our lore. In the traditional sense, it is an explanatory work. Viewed from a slightly different perspective, it can be categorized as what Norman Denzin terms a "messy text" that brokers "multiple interpretive experiences," alternates "between description, interpretation, and voice," and charts, from various reflexive points of view, "the multiple discourses that occur in a given social space" (1997: 225). Throughout, its entries converse—at times directly, at other times obliquely—with selected writings that were either included in or excluded from the Jewish *Tanak* and the Christian First Testament. They do likewise for Africana life itself. In some respects, *The Africana Bible* is a (re)inscription of the Black experience. It blurs the boundaries between literary prose, critical scholarship, and (at points) poetry. It is a discursive performance that embodies resistance to oppression; hope for the creation of inclusive and welcoming Africana communities of conscience; and a promise to use the First Testament and other sacred texts creatively and responsibly in the realization of Martin Luther King Jr.'s "beloved community."[6]

Notes

1. I wish to express my sincere thanks to the members of the editorial board for *The Africana Bible*—Randall Bailey (Interdenominational Theological Center), Cheryl Kirk-Duggan (Shaw University Divinity School), Stacy Davis (Saint Mary's College), Rodney Sadler (Union Seminary–PSCE at Charlotte), Valerie Bridgeman (Lancaster Theological Seminary), Nathaniel Samuel Murrell (University of North Carolina, Wilmington), and Madipoane Masenya (ngwan'a Mphahlele) (University of South Africa)—for their feedback on the ideas expressed in this essay as well as their suggestions for its expansion and improvement.

2. Scholars today are divided as to the appropriate use of such terms as *Hebrew Bible, Old Testament, Tanak, First Testament,* and *scriptures of Israel.* Thus, usage by authors contributing to *The Africana Bible* varies. My interchangeable use of *First Testament* and *Israel's scriptures* is a way of honoring the cultural settings within which these texts were born as well as the full sweep—historical and modern—of the Jewish and Christian continuums within which they have been read. The arrangement of articles in this volume follows the threefold textual subdivision of the Jewish canon. It also includes entries on a number of so-called apocryphal (or deuterocanonical) and pseudepigraphic works. Our goal, as an editorial board, has been to represent a broad cross section of works considered authoritative within the Africana world.

3. Elsewhere (Page 2007: 56–57), I provide a more fully developed list of tropes accompanying the process by which texts are accorded authoritative (that is, scriptural) status.

4. By "elegant truths," I refer to the timeless and universal maxims about the divine, nature, society, and life's meaning that can be derived from its various books and canonical configurations.

5. I have found particularly insightful the modern reappropriations of the *conjure* tradition by such researcher-practitioners as Luisah Teish (1985), Tayannah Lee McQuillar (2003), Stephanie Rose Bird (2004), and Catherine Yronwode (2002).

6. For King's definition of this concept, see his 1957 Christian Century article in the anthology by James Washington (1990: 8).

References

Bird, Stephanie Rose. 2004. *Sticks, Stones, Roots and Bones: Hoodoo, Mojo and Conjuring with Herbs.* St. Paul, Minn.: Llewellyn.

Chireau, Yvonne P. 2003. *Black Magic: Religion and the African American Conjuring Tradition.* Berkeley: University of California Press.

Cone, James. 2001. *The Spirituals and the Blues: An Interpretation.* Reprint of 1972 original ed. New York: Orbis.

Davis, Francis. 2003. *The History of the Blues: The Roots, The Music, The People.* Reprint of 1995 ed. Cambridge, Mass.: Da Capo.

Denzin, Norman. 1997. *Interpretive Ethnography: Ethnographic Practices for the 21st Century.* Thousand Oaks, Calif.: Sage.

Ember, Carol R., and Melvin Ember. 1999. *Anthropology.* 9th ed. Upper Saddle River, N.J.: Prentice-Hall.

Floyd-Thomas, Stacey, Juan Floyd-Thomas, Carole B. Duncan Jr., Stephen G. Ray, and Nancy Lynne Westfield, eds. 2007. *Black Church Studies: An Introduction.* Nashville: Abingdon.

Holmes, Barbara A. 2004. *Joy Unspeakable: Contemplative Practices of the Black Church.* Minneapolis: Fortress Press.

Hood, Robert. 1990. *Must God Remain Greek: Afro Cultures and God-Talk.* Minneapolis: Fortress Press.

Hopkinson, Nalo, ed. 2003. *Mojo: Conjure Stories.* New York: Warner.

Hurston, Zora Neale. 1991. *Moses, Man of the Mountain.* Reprint of 1939 ed. New York: HarperPerennial.

Jones, LeRoi. 1963. *Blues People: The Negro Experience in America and the Music That Developed from It.* New York: Morrow.

Kugel, James. 1997. *The Bible as It Was.* Cambridge, Mass.: Belknap.

McQuillar, Tayannah Lee. 2003. *Rootwork: Using the Folk Magick of Black America for Love, Money, and Success.* New York: Fireside.

Mitchem, Stephanie. 2007. *African American Folk Healing.* New York: New York University Press.

Murray, Albert. 2000. *Stomping the Blues.* 25th anniversary ed. New York: Da Capo.

Page, Hugh R., Jr. 2007. "The Dynamics of Scripturalization." In *Theorizing Scriptures: New Critical Orientations to a Cultural Phenomenon.* New Brunswick, N.J.: Rutgers University Press.

Palmer, Robert. 1982. *Deep Blues.* New York: Penguin.

Parks, Gordon. 1971. *In Love.* Philadelphia: Lippincott.

Smith, Theophus. 1994. *Conjuring Culture: Biblical Formations of Black America.* New York: Oxford University Press.

Spencer, Jon Michael. 1994. *Blues and Evil*. Knoxville: University of Tennessee Press.

Teish, Luisah. 1985. *Jambalaya: The Natural Woman's Book of Personal Charms and Practical Rituals*. San Francisco: HarperSanFrancisco.

Thurman, Howard. 1979. *With Head and Heart: The Autobiography of Howard Thurman*. San Diego: Harcourt Brace Jovanovich.

Wardlow, Gayle Dean. 1998. *Chasin' That Devil Music: Searching for the Blues*. San Francisco: Miller Freeman.

Washington, James M., ed. 1990. *A Testament of Hope: The Essential Writings and Speeches of Dr. Martin Luther King, Jr.* New York: HarperOne.

Wimbush, Vincent. 2008. "TEXTures, Gestures, Power: Orientation to Radical Excavation." In *Theorizing Scriptures: New Critical Orientations to a Cultural Phenomenon*, ed. Vincent L. Wimbush. New Brunswick, N.J.: Rutgers University Press.

———, ed. 2000. *African Americans and the Bible: Sacred Texts and Social Textures*. New York: Continuum.

Yronwode, Catherine. 2002. *Hoodoo Herb and Root Magic: A Materia Magica of African-American Conjure*. Forestville, Calif.: Lucky Mojo Curio.

Yronwode, Cathering. 2004. Hoodoo Rootwork Correspondence Course. Forestville, Calif.: Lucky Mojo Curio.

The AFRICAN DIASPORA *as* CONSTRUCT *and* LIVED EXPERIENCE

Leslie R. James

WHAT IS THE RELATIONSHIP between the African Diaspora and the Bible? The potential answers to such a question vary widely. My answer is that the forced migration, or dispersion, of millions of Africans into the crucible of the modern Atlantic plantation economy as cheap labor is pivotal for understanding Africana biblical interpretation. African New World slavery was central to this economic system; it affected the African continent as well as the Americas. Those forcibly transported to the New World, and elsewhere, engaged in a process of resistance and culture creation designed to transcend the limits of slavery. The Bible, the central text of Western civilization, played a central, though contested, role in structuring the unequal relations between master and slave in the Americas. In the face of the dehumanizing and humiliating condition of slavery, African-descended peoples

in the New World searched the Bible when they encountered it for vestiges of freedom, hope, justice, and an alternative future. This means that Afro-Diasporic peoples played a major role in the construction of freedom in the Americas (North and South America and the Caribbean) and the modern world. The Bible was an important, though not the only, resource in this emancipatory project of self-representation.

In other words, Africana biblical hermeneutics, particularly in the Americas, has always been in a dialectical relationship with the Black struggle to transcend slavery. In light of this thesis, *The Africana Bible* is an Afro-Diasporic midrash on the Bible. The major sections of the Hebrew Bible (Tanak), the Torah/Law, the Prophets, the Writings, and extracanonical literature therefore have a distinctive type of discourse in relationship to the

African Diasporic experience. The various authors of *The Africana Bible* enunciate these discourses. According to Stuart Hall: "It is because this New World is constituted for us as a place, a narrative of displacement, that it gives rise so profoundly to a certain imaginary plenitude, recreating the endless desire to return to 'lost origins,' to be one again with the mother, to go back to the beginning. . . . Who has not known, at this moment, the surge of an overwhelming nostalgia for lost origins, for 'times past'?" (Hall 1990: 236).

To remember that the word *diaspora* can refer simply to "migration" forced debates over the term, and the ethnic and other types of hostage to which it is subsumed, into insignificance. Feelings of exile, slavery, disjunction, loss, alienation, social death, resistance, remembrance, and return accompanied the forced dispersion of Africans from their native homeland. Since these are also major themes in the Bible, subaltern Africans in the Americas or in Africa could read and identify with the biblical texts, especially the Hebrew Bible narratives. These texts gave them a new imagination that became a major resource to resist slavery and re-create themselves as historical subjects.

The religious, philosophical, cultural, and political reflections that emerged from this diasporic condition, despite its historical continuum, are massive. Much of it still remains to be unearthed, not just for academic purposes but, above all, to serve humankind in its journey into the future. My focus is, therefore, on African Diasporic culture. Its diasporic mirror leads to the interpretation of the Bible as a diasporic canon. This horizon of diaspora, or exile, is multifaceted and complex, synchronic and diachronic. This study, while recognizing different diaspora styles and experiences, seeks to bring those different styles together under one "canopy" without hegemonic intention. Dialectically, diaspora is a major metaphor for liberation and transcendence. If anything, a major goal of this project is to name the present moment in time, globally speaking, so that Africana peoples, at home and abroad, might be empowered

to name themselves as subjects in the face of new challenges to define them otherwise. The biblical text became a major tool, a mirror, in this historical and existential project of representing the Black presence, the *Présence Africaine*, in the New World.

THREE MOMENTS IN HISTORY

In Africa and its Diaspora, the biblical canon was embedded in the historical process of transcending slavery and its legacy. In a somewhat Hegelian fashion, three major moments in diasporic history may be highlighted to illustrate the point. These moments reflect the history of the diasporic pilgrimage. They are, in effect, major shifts in European history and intellectual thought. These shifts affected dominant Western biblical scholarship. I argue that these major shifts in European biblical scholarship were related to the Black struggle for freedom in the Americas.

The first moment—slavery and the creation of the African Diaspora—began around the seventeenth century and matured around the eighteenth with the development of slavery and the Atlantic plantation economic system. It is coterminous with the rise of critical biblical scholarship in Europe. In the wake of Renaissance humanism, the breakdown of feudalism, the Reformation, and the modern era, the metaphorical fence was removed from around the biblical text. The Catholic Church's hold on the Bible during the Middle Ages was now removed. The printing press made the biblical text popular and secular. This development in Europe took place while the Caribbean and the Americas were discovered, conquered, and colonized. The biblical text that played a major role in the birth of European humanism and nationalism did not play a similar role in the Americas. On the contrary, the Bible was used primarily to legitimate conquests, colonization, slavery, and empire. Since the biblical canon was now open, other peoples, not only Europeans, were free to explore its deep wells of emotion. They could also utilize it to fashion new identities. This applied particularly to African Diasporic people.

Against the background of slavery and the development of plantation society that led to the formation of African Diasporic communities, the slave narrative became a significant genre of literature up to the eighteenth century. The classic piece of literature in this regard is generally considered to be *The Interesting Narrative of Olaudah Equiano or Gustavus Vassa, the African*. Published in 1789, the year of the French Revolution, Equiano's constant reference to himself as African and "oppressed Ethiopian" echoed his diasporic consciousness, the centrality of African slavery in the formation of the modern African Diaspora and Atlantic civilization, and his commitment to abolition and freedom for all Africans. Slavery, to Equiano, could not be vindicated "by the law of Moses and by that of Christ in the Gospel" (Equiano 1789/1995: 335). In essence, he saw freedom from slavery as central to the First and Second Testaments of the Bible. Thus the *Présence Africaine* in the New World claimed the Bible as a constitution to represent themselves in the crucible of slavery and beyond. The Bible, especially the First Covenant, was on their lips as they declared through the centuries, right up to the 1960s Civil Rights era, "I have a dream!"

The dream, so eloquently articulated in its United States version, is the reversal in the condition of the *Présence Africaine*. Stuart Hall defines this condition as the site of the repressed. Apparently silenced beyond memory by the power of the experience of slavery, Africa was in fact present everywhere, in the everyday life and customs of the slave quarters. This was the case in the languages and *patois* of the plantations, as well as in names and words. Often disconnected from their native taxonomies, the *Présence Africaine* was manifest in the secret syntactical structures through which other languages were spoken, in the stories and tales told to children, in religious practices and beliefs, in spiritual life, the arts, crafts, musical forms and rhythms of both slave and postemancipation societ-

ies. Africa, the signified that could not be represented directly in slavery, remained and remains the unspoken, unspeakable "presence" in Caribbean culture and, arguably, elsewhere in the Americas. It is "hiding" behind every verbal inflection, every narrative twist of Caribbean cultural life. It is the secret code with which every Western text was "reread." It is the ground-bass of every rhythm and bodily movement. This was—is—the "Africa" that "is alive and well in the diaspora" (Hall 1990: 230). Pedagogically, the *Présence Africaine* revised or signified or "reread" every Western text, including the Bible, the central text of Western civilization. The heuristic goal, if not the reconstruction of Western civilization, was and remains the representation of the African Diasporic presence.

The second moment, which is still ongoing, was in response to the first. While the first moment marked the destructuring of traditional African social existence, the second marked the restructuring of that social existence. It led to African Diasporic cultural reconfigurations in the African New World Diaspora. This process began in the Middle Passage, in the holds of the slave ships, as different African tribal groups bonded together in the womb of slavery and forged new corporate and collective identities in various New World societies. Resistance was a marked aspect of this process.

This in-between, liminal period is important from a diasporic perspective. It led to the creation of a variety of African Diasporic cultures in which religion is a central feature. This moment, from the development of the African New World plantation economy in the eighteenth century to abolition and emancipation in the nineteenth, was marked by a history of slave rebellions throughout the Caribbean and the Americas. The classic event in this phase, one that sent the shock waves of revolution throughout the New World plantation system, was the Haitian Revolution (1791–1801). This was the Age of Revolution, and the rebellion in Haiti was classic. It struck a lethal blow to the heart of the French empire and European hegemony and led to the birth of the first independent Black nation in the modern world. It also contributed, paradoxically, to the emergence of the United States as an American empire.

In spring 1803, Napoleon abandoned his plan to create a French empire in the Americas and sold the huge Louisiana territory to the United States of America, a sale that ultimately led to the significant expansion of the United States. The slave rebellion in Haiti (or, as the French called it, Saint Domingue) deserves major recognition for its impact on Napoleon's decision, for it subverted Napoleon's plan to construct a western empire, with Louisiana as its center. Napoleon lost, and never recovered.

Under the leadership of Toussaint L'Ouverture, the Haitian slaves' defeat of Napoleon's forces, led by General Leclerc, made redeployment of those forces to Louisiana strategically impossible, and sabotaged Napoleon's efforts. The strain of providing resources for Leclerc's expedition and the subsequent drain of resources from Saint Domingue disrupted operations in Louisiana as well (Paquette 1997: 209).

Leclerc's death on January 11, 1803, put the final nail in the coffin of Napoleon's western design. Napoleon was forced to sell Louisiana to U.S. president Thomas Jefferson. The Louisiana Purchase brought a vast amount of territory into the American domain; it simultaneously assimilated Napoleon's western design into the American sphere of influence and the young nation's political self-understanding. The successful Haitian Revolution virtually destabilized the French empire and the United States as well.

Looking at the broader sweep of history during this second "moment," one development is worthy of note: that is, that critical biblical scholarship underwent significant changes and could be said to have reached a high point toward the end of the nineteenth and beginning of the twentieth century. Two events related to this should be noted: the First Vatican Council, with its new norms for biblical interpretation, and Albert Schweitzer's publication of *The Quest of the Historical Jesus*. As is

well known, Schweitzer's work, which interpreted Jesus as a misguided apocalyptic prophet, set the tone for much of biblical scholarship in the ensuing decades of the twentieth century. But seen in retrospect, it might well have signified also the decline of European Christianity and civilization, the decline of European man—an occurrence that had a decided impact on Africana life globally. Schweitzer wrote, in the famous conclusion to this magisterial work, that Jesus "comes to us as One unknown, without a name, as of old, by the lakeside, He came to those men who knew Him not, He speaks to us the same word: 'Follow thou me!' and sets us the tasks which He has to fulfill for our time" (Schweitzer 1906/1968: 403). This European relinquishment of the figure of Jesus contrasts with the concluding statement of another, later classic, the Algerian Frantz Fanon's *The Wretched of the Earth*, in which Fanon writes that "for Europe, for ourselves and for humanity, comrades, we must make a new start, develop a new way of thinking, and endeavor to create a new man" (Fanon 1963/2004: 239). The juxtaposition of Schweitzer, representing the European imperial colonizer, and Fanon, representing the Pan-African de-colonizer, allow us to recognize a shift away from messianic visions based upon the European construction of Jesus to alternative messianic definitions, available beyond and outside Europe, that breached the continuity between the First and Second Testaments.

Fanon opened the door for a different approach, especially an African Diasporic one, to emerge in response to the Hebrew Bible. One goal of *The Africana Bible* is to develop this approach, to enunciate and develop various methods of biblical interpretation that reflect the complex African Diasporic reality. Among other things, it must enunciate the African Diasporic voice that was silenced in the New World because the voice of the *Présence Européenne*, heavily articulated through theologies that tap into biblical hopes and promises, excluded the *Présence Africaine* from its vision of paradise.

The third moment in the history of the African Diaspora, from the end of the nineteenth century to the middle of the twentieth, was the era of diasporic reconnection with Africa. The biblical mantra of this period is the famous text "Ethiopia shall stretch forth her hand to God" (Psalm 68:31). The greater the impact of their encounter with biblically oriented Protestant Christianity, the more African and African-descended peoples creolized the Bible to promote their freedom in resistance to slavery and its legacy of racism. Historical, cultural, political, and economic conditions caused some African Diasporic religious traditions to emphasize certain portions of the Bible more than others. The relationship between the biblical text and identity is nevertheless constant in African Diasporic biblical interpretation. The Jamaican Rastafari, for example, emphasized notions of repatriation or return to Africa from exile in Babylon. The diasporic experience mutated in dialectic with history, as did biblical interpretation. In this third moment, the dominant mode of biblical hermeneutics has been the historical-critical method. This method was by no means foreign to the African Diasporic mind, which had always interpreted the Bible in relationship to historical realities and contexts. A major goal of this interpretive process among African-descended scholars has been the restoration and reclamation of African identity. We have seen a paradigm shift in biblical interpretation, the product of a different set of cultural interactions that have come to term, especially in the second part of the twentieth century, with the emancipation of a number of African and Caribbean countries from colonial tutelage as well as the Civil Rights movement of the 1960s. This emancipatory process reached a high point with the demise of South African apartheid in 1994. This shift prepares for the task of African Diasporic social life in the new millennium, a reality marked by globalization.

TASKS FOR AFRICAN DIASPORA INTERPRETATION

The implications of these insights for African and African Diasporic biblical interpretation are far-reaching. Among other things, it means that the biblical text will have to be deconstructed. It also means that a number of important issues must be foregrounded.

First, the issue of definition has to be addressed. The need for lucidity is as important as the need to name the African Diaspora in relation to this present moment in time. The underlying reason, as we have shown, is the fluidity of biblical interpretation in relationship to historical changes and contradictions. According to Harris:

> The African diaspora concept subsumes the following: the global dispersion (voluntary and involuntary) of Africans throughout history; the emergence of a cultural identity abroad based on origin and social condition; and the psychological or physical return to the homeland, Africa. Thus viewed, the African diaspora assumes the character of a dynamic, continuous, and complex phenomenon across time, geography, class, and gender. (Harris 1993: 3–4)

Harris provides a very useful working definition. Critical consideration must be given to the appropriateness of the term in relation to the dispersal of African peoples across time and space. The intention of *The Africana Bible* is to reflect the "dynamic, continuous, and complex phenomenon [of Diaspora] across time, geography, class, and gender." Undoubtedly, the privileging of modern Atlantic slavery is clear through the work. It discloses the role of the Bible in the cause of Black freedom, humanization, identity reconstruction, agency, culture, economic and political self-determination and sovereignty, nation building, and integration.

As an African Diasporic person, my context has always forced me to investigate the role of the Bible, especially the First Testament, in the development of newly independent nations. Stuart Hall's attempt to define the term *diaspora* in relation to American (New World) history is instructive in this regard. According to Hall, the "New World" presence (America, Terra Incognita) is the beginning of diaspora, diversity, hybridity, and difference. His argument applies to African American and other peoples of African descent in the contemporary global world. Hall's use of the term *diaspora* is metaphorical, not literal. By *diaspora*, Hall does not refer to those scattered tribes whose identity can be secured only in relation to some sacred homeland to which they must at all costs return, even if it means pushing other people into the sea. Writes Hall: "This is the old, the imperializing, hegemonising form of 'ethnicity.'" Rather, the diasporic experience as he understands it is characterized "not by essence or purity, but by the recognition of a necessary heterogeneity and diversity; by a conception of 'identity' which lives with and through, not despite, difference; by hybridity." By *diaspora,* Hall refers to those identities that are "constantly producing and reproducing themselves anew, through transformation and difference" (Hall 1990: 235). The significance of this point should not be missed. Among other things, it explains the use of such hyphenated terms as *African-American, Afro-Caribbean*, and *Afro-Brazilian*. It also demonstrates the importance of such constructs as the African Diaspora.

Attention must be paid to the issue of complexity, agency, creativity, sensitivity, and the overlapping of diasporic identities or worldviews in the African Diaspora. This includes the often ignored, but very important, aspect of contested notions of diasporic identities. Contestation is an important aspect of identity construction. *The Africana Bible* is conceived as a text that simultaneously reflects not only diasporic complexity but also unity and clear dialogical intent. The notion of diaspora has to be related to the larger world, to patterns of imperialism and globalization. This consideration defines

the African Diaspora as a subversive trope involving a pedagogy of resistance. It is heuristic. The notion of pedagogies of resistance, to hegemony and global homogenization, has a direct bearing on biblical interpretation. The ways in which this is fleshed out vary with respect to the First and Second Testaments. They depend on different conjunctions in time, as reflected in the texts. The political conjunctures tend to shift from North Africa (Egypt) to the Ancient Middle East to the Greco-Roman Mediterranean Basin. Though the zones of conjuncture have changed, they have remained rather focused around the crossroads between North Africa, Europe, and the Middle East. That might well be a matter of remembrance. The diasporic orientation of *The Africana Bible* represents a shift in consciousness and the locus of biblical interpretation to the Atlantic Basin.

Diaspora has to be perceived as ontological, epistemological, ecumenical, political, and practical. The ecumenical dimension is salient. It signifies that notions of chosenness have to be critically examined in dialectic with pluralism and hybridity. Introduction of the question of diaspora, in its complex diversity, in biblical studies—particularly African Diasporic biblical studies—combats notions of chosenness and ethnic purity that have caused so much grief in the twentieth and twenty-first centuries. W. E. B. DuBois's notion of the "color-line" counsels caution. African Diasporic biblical hermeneutics bears in mind that the problem of the twentieth century will also be the problem of the twenty-first century. It has not disappeared because Joseph, who was sold by his brothers into slavery, has done well in Egypt. Consequently, *The Africana Bible* reflects critically on its situatedness and stances of reflection.

Finally, the concept of diaspora, as it applies to the First Testament, must radically engage the canonical texts and the process of canonization. The Black Diasporic perspective must, historically speaking, reflect on the actual cultural condition of enslaved Africans in their enforced migration across the Atlantic. African-descended peoples did not lose all vestiges of their ancestral cultures and worldviews in their cross-Atlantic migration, despite assertions to the contrary. Migration, rather than erasing their ancestral roots, led to a process of transmission and fusion of different ancestral traditions in the interest of maintaining self and constructing alternative communities at the dawn of the modern era of globalization. An African Diasporic consciousness and approach to biblical interpretation endows us with what Nettleford calls "a unique knowledge of the crafting of a new sensibility, not out of some void as in the Book of Genesis, but out of the lived reality of different cultures" (Hall/Nettleford, 2006: 302). Nettleford echoes the sentiments of the Genesis tradition that declared "and God saw that it was good" when he wrote that "this unique knowledge" is "cause for celebration rather than self-negation, self-contempt or self-doubt" (Hall/Nettleford, 2006: 302).

Diasporic knowledge, or consciousness, is the African Diasporic power to revise the First Testament; to remap, to re-narrate the environment and the world-as-we-know-it. It is the power to enter into a genuine dialogue or conversation with the text(s), with slavery, exile, terror, tempests, hurricanes and storms (Ivan and Katrina), identity, contestation, plurality, complexity, diversity, and globalization; to recast those texts, or discover within those texts, some more than others, the power to confront reality in the process of self-representation. *The Africana Bible* is a work of self-discovery and purpose in which African Diasporic peoples name themselves and their historical purpose in collaboration with the God of their ancestors, the "God of our weary years."

Black Christianity in America has notably mined the resources of the First Testament for signs of social freedom and hope. Indeed, this search is grounded in the First Testament to a large extent. African Diasporic peoples are conscious, on the one hand, that they have departed from slavery. On the other hand, they know they have not reached the Land of Promise. Their search for the Land

of Promise has often pointed them in different, and at times conflicting, directions. Nevertheless, Africa, real or imagined, remains a vital source in their pilgrimage from the past into the future. This journey is often filled with deep feelings of disjunction. It is out of this feeling of disjunction that *The Africana Bible* emerges as an expression of the strivings of African Diasporic people for new moments of conjunction as they journey into the future. *The Africana Bible* is therefore more than a supplement or "mining" of the First Covenant for inspiration. It is a highly sophisticated work that represents a paradigm shift in reading the texts.

The Africana Bible is a work of art that shows that the Bible should be conceived not just as literature but also as ritual in which the First Testament is a point of departure to experience new ways of communal self-representation and re-narration. It is a historical, communal, and eschatological appropriation of the text. *The Africana Bible* is an African Diasporic gaze into the Bible, which sees the eyes of God looking at threats to reverse the gains made by African Diasporic peoples in their journey toward a future of promise yet making that timeless invocation "Go down Moses, say to Pharaoh, let my people go."

References

Burton, Richard D. E. 1997. *Afro-Creole: Power, Opposition, and Play in the Caribbean*. Ithaca, N.Y.: Cornell University Press.

Cone, James H. 2005. *God of the Oppressed*. Rev. ed. Maryknoll, N.Y.: Orbis.

DuBois, W. E. B. 1990. *Black Folk, Then and Now*. New introduction by Herbert Aptheker. Millwood, N.Y.: Kraus-Thomson.

———. 1996. *The World and Africa: An Inquiry into the Part Which Africa Has Played in World History*. New York: International.

———. 2003. *The Souls of Black Folk*. Centennial edition. Introduction by David Levering Lewis. New York: Modern Library.

Equiano, Olaudah. 1789/1995. *The Interesting Narrative and Other Writings*. New York: Penguin.

Fanon, Frantz. 1963/2004. *The Wretched of the Earth*. Translated by Richard Philcox. New York: Grove.

Genovese, Eugene D. 1976. *Roll, Jordon, Roll: The World the Slaves Made*. New York: Vintage.

Gilroy, Paul. 1993. *The Black Atlantic: Modernity and Double Consciousness*. Cambridge, Mass.: Harvard University Press.

Hall, Kenneth O., ed. 2006. *Rex N: Rex Nettleford Selected Speeches*. Kingston, Jamaica: Ian Randle.

Hall, Stuart. 1990. "Cultural Identity and Diaspora." In *Identity: Community, Culture, Difference*, ed. Jonathan Rutherford. London: Lawrence & Wishart, 223–37.

Harris, Joseph E., ed. 1993. *Global Dimensions of the African Diaspora*. 2nd ed. Washington, D.C.: Howard University Press.

Hine, Clark Darlene, and Jacqueline McLeod, eds. 1999. *Crossing Boundaries: Comparative History of Black People in Diaspora*. Bloomington: Indiana University Press.

Levine, Lawrence W. 1977. *Black Culture and Black Consciousness: Afro-American Folk Thought from Slavery to Freedom*. Oxford: Oxford University Press.

Lovejoy, Paul E. 1977. "The African Diaspora: Revisionist Interpretations of Ethnicity, Culture and Religion under Slavery." *Studies in the World History of Slavery, Abolition, and Emancipation*, 2, no. 1 (1977). Available at http://www.h-net.msu .edu/~slavery/essays/esy9701love.html.

Mintz, Sidney W., and Richard Price. 1992. *The Birth of African-American Culture: An Anthropological Perspective*. Boston: Beacon.

Okpewho, Isidore, Carole Boyce Davies, and Ali A. Mazrui, eds. 1999. *The African Diaspora: African Origins and New World Identities*. Bloomington: Indiana University Press.

Paquette, Robert L. 1997. "Saint Dominque in the Making of Territorial Louisiana." In *A Turbulent Time: The French Revolution and the Greater Caribbean*, ed. David Barry Gaspar and David Patrick Geggus, 204–25. Bloomington: Indiana University Press.

Raboteau, Albert J. 1995. *A Fire in the Bones: Reflections on African-American Religious History*. Boston: Beacon.

———. 2004. *Slave Religion: The "Invisible Institution" in the Antebellum South*. Updated ed. Oxford: Oxford University Press.

Schweitzer, Albert. 1906/1968. *The Quest of the Historical Jesus: A Critical Study of Its Progress from Reimarus to Wrede*. Introduction by James M. Robinson. New York: Macmillan.

Shepperson, George. 1966. "The African Abroad or the African Diaspora." *African Quarterly* 2, no. 1:76–93.

Stuckey, Sterling. 1987. *Slave Culture: Nationalist Theory and The Foundations of Black America*. New York: Oxford University Press.

Thornton, John. 1998. *Africa and Africans in the Making of the Atlantic World, 1400–1800*. 2nd ed. Cambridge: Cambridge University Press.

AFRICAN *and* AFRICAN DIASPORAN HERMENEUTICS

READING *the* HEBREW BIBLE *as* JOURNEY, EXILE, *and* LIFE *through* MY/OUR PLACE

Randall C. Bailey, Cheryl Kirk-Duggan, Madipoane Masenya (ngwan'a Mphahlele), and Rodney S. Sadler Jr.

THE ADAGE "the grass is always greener on the other side" draws attention to the fact that how one perceives text, places, people, or things depends on the lens one uses. The grass may or may not be greener; it may not even be green. One's lens or hermeneutical matrix has a great deal to do with what one hears or sees and one's perceptions of what one has heard or seen.

Africana biblical hermeneutics are contextual, particular, and powerful. This introductory essay provides a thumbnail sketch of the ways in which African and African Diasporan experiences affect how people read, hear, interpret, and engage the Hebrew Bible, cognizant of the impact of cultural context, gender, race, and class. This composite essay reflects brief, candid perspectives from four Hebrew Bible scholars as they share their sociocultural, historical, and theological contexts and hermeneutical strategies that reflect their passion about who they are and what they do. We hear voices committed to integrity and transformation reflecting (1) an Afrocentric journey; (2) a South African in exile; (3) life reading scripture and scripture reading life; and (4) an African Diasporan/Bermudian place of discourse. These readings are invitational, not normative; creative, not elitist; passionate, liberative, and pedagogical.

MY JOURNEY INTO AFROCENTRIC BIBLICAL INTERPRETATION

Randall C. Bailey

My commitments to Afrocentric biblical interpretation grow out of my experiences in the Civil Rights struggles in the northern United States during the 1960s and 1970s. The role of the church in the movement and the preaching of Black clergy interpreting the gospel in liberation perspectives were integral to my conversion experience. Commitments to justice and bringing about the "Beloved Community" were central to my theological understandings of who God is and what God requires of us. My return to the church as an adult was concurrent with the rise of the Black Theology Movement (BTM) in the United States. My focus as a biblical scholar was to do the exegesis that would further the goals of the BTM and bring about Black liberation.

Since there was little Black biblical scholarship published in my graduate school years, I relied on feminist biblical scholarship to help me develop liberatory methods of interpretation. In this process, I became convinced of the interrelationships of liberation movements and the need for intersectionality in biblical interpretation. My early publications in Afrocentric biblical interpretation built on the works of Copher and Felder, which established Black presence in the text. Thus, I followed the feminist model of exploring the narratives and speeches in which "Africans" appeared in the text. From this, I developed a modality of interpreting the African presence as being from the south, militarily strong, politically mighty, wealthy, wise, and the standard of valuation for ancient Israel and the Early Church. Ancient people "showed themselves approved" by rising to the status of Africans. My research also pointed to biblical writers holding anti-African and antiliberationist messages.

The rise of ideological criticism greatly influenced my Afrocentric hermeneutic. Weems's work on the use of sexual violence against women as a metaphor for divine punishment, Warrior's challenge to the BTM around embracing the conquest materials, and Mosala's work on how the notion of the "Bible as Word of God" leads to the acceptance of oppressive ideas all pushed me to acknowledge that not all of the Bible speaks to promoting justice or liberation of the oppressed. This also made me see parallels between the struggles of Palestinians and same-gender-loving people and our struggles for freedom and liberation.

Identifying African Diasporan life with that of the Canaanites, Moabites, Ammonites, Samaritans, and first-century Jews led to new issues for Afrocentric "readings from the underside." For instance, how do our experiences of having been sexualized by white supremacist myths coincide with calling the Philistines the "uncircumcised ones," where they are identified by their genitals? How do our experiences of being used as tools of the political left and right help us to resist the New Testament's portrayal of Jesus as primarily a miracle worker and not a revolutionary fighting Rome? How do we reclaim the hermeneutic of suspicion shown in the Negro spirituals, where they changed biblical stories to fit their needs and used religious language to focus on liberation and freedom? These are the issues central to my understanding of Afrocentric biblical interpretation.

EXILED IN MY OWN HOME: AN AFRICAN–SOUTH AFRICAN PERSPECTIVE ON THE BIBLE

Madipoane Masenya (ngwan'a Mphahlele)

I write from Africa, my home continent. Africa is, however, a stranger in the global village, as it cannot participate as an equal partner. Hence, even within academia, resources developed in Africa are not always taken seriously, if at all, by the powerful. More specifically, I write from South Africa, my home country, yet as a stranger. I therefore do biblical scholarship as one "exiled" at home (compare the introduction to Jeremiah in the present volume).

In the following paragraphs, I give a brief overview of the context that contributes to my identity as a stranger. Foreignness among others characterizes one's exilic state. Having been born wearing a darker skin color in apartheid South Africa meant becoming a foreigner from the moment of birth, ironically a stranger in the land of one's ancestors.

Such foreignness was compounded in baby girls' lives given the underlying African cultural perception that a girl child "naturally" belonged to her future husband's home, a situation that also privileged boy children over girl children in terms of education (Masenya 2002: 99).

My gender continues to determine my place in a patriarchal context. Life in the latter context is typified by constant fear on account of the pervasive acts of violence perpetuated against female bodies. One's sex still has a say in the place where and the extent to which one can exercise one's God-gifting in ministry. Whether one is at home or in the public sphere of work, church, and the broader society, one remains an exile—despite fourteen years of "independence" in South Africa!

Growing up within a marginalized culture, I was intimidated into choosing to be called by my foreign name rather than my African name. The circumstances, then, dictated that I despise my culture in favor of the hegemonic Eurocentric culture, a situation that continues even to this day. An attempt to foreground one's African context within Eurocentric epistemologies (which continue to shape the South African higher education curriculum) is still viewed with suspicion. One's state of captivity is thus felt even in the academy. Elsewhere I have argued:

Ours is a theological education characterized by one assuming the role of an insider in one

context and that of an outsider in another context. One becomes an insider as one is being trained as a student, an insider to the theologies which are foreign to oneself, an insider as one trains African students in Western-oriented studies of the Bible, an insider as one does research. If the research conducted is not played according to the rules inside the game, it will not earn this "insider/outsider" accreditation to the Western academic status quo, which itself remains basically an outsider to the African status quo. (Masenya 2004: 460)

My skin color also determined the socioeconomic exile that had to be my lot since the colonial era up to today. In my continued search for justice, I am shaped by such a context as I interact with the Bible in an attempt to do justice to my struggles and those of fellow African peoples.

LIFE READING SCRIPTURE, SCRIPTURE READING LIFE: AN AFRICAN AMERICAN BIBLICAL HERMENEUTIC
Cheryl A. Kirk-Duggan

A trinitarian God-presence and an awareness of the Bible emerged through my daily experiences of family, church, and culture. My womanist, interdisciplinary response, an African Diasporan biblical hermeneutic reflecting how life can read scripture, allows for fluidity embracing improvisation, voice, spiritual health, emotional growth, and moral accountability. Womanist hermeneutics exposes oppression toward nurturing humanity holistically and requires human integrity and responsibility. Such an epistemology involves tempered cynicism, creativity, courage, commitment, candor, curiosity, and the comedic or gift of humor amid faith. This way of thinking and knowing helps me to challenge what people value, to wrestle with the paradoxical, and to accept that which I do not understand; to have a worldview that is contrary to accepted reality; and to expose the various oppressions in the text, seeking for justice. In so doing, the resulting reading works to be inclusive, to honor justice and love, moving toward communal and individual healing and transformation.

People engage the Bible in multiple texts—spoken word, song, story, art, and dance—in multiple places and spaces. For me, these places and spaces integrated family life and rituals: Sunday School, Bible study, and religious pageants, including church community as nurturing place and musical performance space, rooted in biblical texts.

Advanced studies exposed scripture in music, literature, and culture. Doctoral studies provided new awareness of complex issues emerging from biblical interpretation—revealing how tradition often skews meanings of texts and uses scripture to perpetrate harm. My interdisciplinary sensibilities, faith, and consciousness of the biblical impact within Western culture pressed me to contrast a popular familiarity with a more sophisticated biblical awareness.

Within many African American experiences, biblical texts have bolstered courage and empowered communities to face oppression without complete acquiescence or dying. Black folks' struggle framed by a religious life reshapes oppression toward an ideology of personal reformulation, amid celebration and caution toward interpretative integrity. Exegetical hermeneutics provide a lens where scripture witnesses to culture, content, and consciousness, helping to heighten Black folks' awareness of our African reality from the Middle Passage through recent Gulf wars, seeking liberation in the United States. Problematically, contradictions between biblical themes of justice and those that distort and devalue Black humanity, along with narrow evangelical, oppressive interpretations adapted as good news, produce spiritual death. Our interpretations often reflect more about our reality than biblical texts. My readings of texts problematize issues of injustice.

The Pentateuch or Torah presents creation, sin, liberation, celebration, regulations, injustice, the mystery of God, and the import of faith. Royal histories warn us about messianism, flawed leaders, and seductive failures of empires. Unfortunately, prophets for justice often demonize women to show Israel/Judah their errors. Wisdom literature, especially the Psalms, provides a liturgical corpus for confession, petition, and thanksgiving. The Gospels examine Jesus' life, times, and teachings. Epistles orient us toward early church history, revealing complications around leadership, community, and human nature.

As an African Diasporan biblical scholar, I work to expose white supremacist interpretation, debunk oppressive ideologies, and avoid romanticizing the text and its problems. Aware that biblical texts witness to particular human realities, doing exegesis, preaching, and teaching cognizant of generating new questions and newer paradigms is critical.

As life reads scripture and scripture reads life, we must wrestle with texts from our own contexts, questioning usage and interpretation in town and gown. Careful to avoid bibliolatry, a wealth of imaginative discourse emerges when we engage ancient texts for contemporary use.

READING AFRICANA: READING FROM "MY" PLACE
Rodney S. Sadler Jr.

For me, the word *Africana* references ideological, artistic products of native or diasporan peoples from Africa. Africana biblical interpretation involves holistic encounters, comprising complex compositions of Africana identity with scripture. Trained through Eurocentric lenses, an Africana reading occurs when we retrain ourselves to *read text(s) from our own contexts*. Our broad Africana contexts include common, competing notions of reading, living, and being, as well as people from African, European, Caribbean, Asian, and North and South American nations, coming from distinct, homogenetic material as well as mixed, diverse genetic material. A unifying theme in Africana reading is historical Western oppression, from domestic colonialism to enslavement, to devaluation and dehumanization. My reading reflects our heritage, amid our right to read particular to *our* experiences, eschewing absolute definitions.

Reading from "my" place has an African American, Bermudian flavor: African American teen parents in West Philly, late 1960's; a fragmented home, relocation with my mother and new dad to Bermuda, later as a teen back to the States with my father and new mom; feeling alien in both contexts; a purgatory between affluent privilege of private schooling *and* economically depressed barrio subsistence—two geographic and three sociocontextual worlds framed by morally conservative, socially progressive Christianity, with roots-rock-reggae theologies, amid "racial" justice ideologies.

My Africana reading engages rich biographies of early black visionaries: slave narratives; our first literati; our interpretations since Scripture collided with us; our quest for universal freedom and justice. I reclaim inclusivity and universal justice over against fragmenting prosperity messages, while many remain enslaved to pain and oppression.

My reading engages aesthetics of African Diasporan communities responding to our sacred scripts. By engaging a seminal Africana text—the Bible, a living North African artifact—we have reclaimed, reimagined, and restored our faith. This reading decenters normative "whiteness," where Western Christianity recast everyone, including God's self, as "white" and *wrote us out of it*, and celebrates the "mixed multitude" (Exod. 12:38) roots of biblical Israel, used to bring God's word to humanity.

Historically descriptive, ministerially significant, and socially prescriptive of hope, my reading speaks of where we have been, notes where we are, and suggests where we "ought" to be. A Christian minister's reading from 1960s justice activities, my reading is Yahwistic amid *tsedek*-justice-righteousness traditions; Jesuistic, from the enfleshed Jesus; and Rastafarian, "I and I" theology. I engage historical criticism to access the formulative conceptual world of the Hebrew Bible, yet without privileging these methodologies, and employ ancestral subversive reading strategies toward a "playful," *purposeful* reading. I recognize these texts had a "particular" history that excluded foreign "goys" and acknowledge scripture as God's word with human fingerprints, never to be confused with God God's self.

My writing engages my call: commitments to my God, my people, and my race (the human race). I write as a Progressive National/American Baptist, raised by Episcopalian and Methodist parents, mentored by a UCC preacher uncle, trained in Brethren, Southern Baptist, National Baptist, Pentecostal, Holiness, and A.M.E. congregations, educated at Baptist, Congregational, Methodist, and Quaker schools, and teaching in a Presbyterian seminary. I am ethically conservative, socially progressive, theologically Pente-Baptist or Baptecostal, writing as faithful witness to God.

EPILOGUE:
HAVING READ, READ SOME MORE

From South Africa to the United States and Bermuda, from music and poetry through feminist and womanist strategies, these four scholars have evoked passionate scenarios of how their lived lifelong contexts inform their reading. Similarly, your context shapes your reading. How do you read? What can you learn from an Africana reading?

References

Bailey, Randall C. 1991. "Beyond Identification: The Use of Africans in Old Testament Poetry and Narratives." In *Stony the Road We Trod: African-American Biblical Interpretation*, ed. Cain H. Felder, 165–84. Minneapolis: Fortress Press.

———. 1994. "They're Nothing but Incestuous Bastards: The Polemical Use of Sex and Sexuality in Hebrew Canon Narrative." In *Reading from This Place*, vol. 1, *Social Context and Biblical Interpretation in the United States*, ed. Fernando Segovia and Mary Ann Tolbert, 121–38. Minneapolis: Fortress Press.

———. 1998. "The Danger of Ignoring One's Own Cultural Bias in Interpreting the Text." In *The Postcolonial Bible*, ed. R. S. Sugirtharajah, 66–90. Sheffield, Eng.: Sheffield University.

Cannon, Katie G. 1995. *Katie's Canon: Womanism and the Soul of the Black Community*. New York: Continuum.

Copher, Charles B. 1993. *Black Biblical Studies: An Anthology of Charles B. Copher*. Chicago: Black Light Fellowship.

Felder, Cain Hope. 1989. "Biblical Meaning and the Black Religious Experience." In *Troubling Biblical Waters: Race, Class and Family*, ed. Cain Hope Felder, 5–21. Maryknoll, N.Y.: Orbis.

Love, Velma. 2000. "The Bible and Contemporary African American Culture 1." In *African Americans and The Bible*, ed. Vincent Wimbush, 49–65. New York: Continuum.

Masenya (ngwan'a Mphahlele), Madipoane. 2002. "'… But You Shall Let Every Girl Live': Reading Exodus 1:1-2:10 the Bosadi (Womanhood) Way." *Old Testament Essays* 15, no. 1:99–112.

———. 2004. "Teaching Western-Oriented Old Testament Studies to African Students: An Exercise in Wisdom or in Folly?" *Old Testament Essays* 17, no. 3:455–69.

Mosala, Itumeleng J. 1989. *Biblical Hermeneutics and Black Theology in South Africa*. Grand Rapids, Mich.: Eerdmans.

Shopshire, James. 2000. "The Bible as Informant and Reflector in Social-Structural Relationships of African Americans." In *African Americans and the Bible*, ed. Vincent Wimbush, 123–37. New York: Continuum.

Warrior, Robert Allen. 1995. "A Native American Perspective: Canaanites, Cowboys and Indians." In *Voices from the Margin: Interpreting the Bible in the Third World*, ed. R. S. Sugirtharajah, 235–41. Maryknoll, N.Y.: Orbis.

Weems, Renita J. 1995. *Battered Love: Marriage, Sex, and Violence in the Hebrew Prophets*. Minneapolis: Fortress Press.

The BIBLE *in* TWENTY-FIRST-CENTURY AFRICA

David Tuesday Adamo

WHAT IS THE BIBLE? The word *Bible* comes from the name Byblos, a port city on the coast of Syria that grew the papyrus leaves that were originally used for writing materials in antiquity. The word eventually came to refer to the sacred text that contains the Old and the New Testament books. Among most African Christians and scholars, the Old and New Testaments contain the word of God.[1] The Bible is held to contain the ancient revelation that God gave to Israel and other nations. God is felt to have spoken directly to the prophets, priests, and sages. Those words of God were preserved and written down. They were then passed on to us through the medium of the Bible.

In Africa, this inspired word of God is the rule of faith followed by Christians and non-Christians. God's self-disclosure to the human family is recorded in the Bible. Mary Getui puts it this way:

"[The] Christian believes that the Bible is the written Word of God. It is inspired by God, meaning that the thoughts of God were breathed into the holy men of God who spoke or wrote God's word. The Bible is the marvelous drama of God revealing himself to his people, and of the inspired prophets of God expressing that revelation in human thought forms" (Getui 1997: 87).

Among Africans, Christians and non-Christians, the Bible is a liberative document. This has been especially true in recent years during the apartheid regime in South Africa. Bible passages were used extensively to combat apartheid. Scholars like Alan Boesak and Desmond Tutu not only found liberating themes in the Bible but also saw the Bible itself as the liberative word of God (West and Dube 2000: 82). The pervasive suffering on the continent demanded the use of materials present in the Bible as means for liberating people on the continent from oppression, sickness, and other difficulties. Unlike in the West, many African Christians consider the Bible to be a manual for life. It is regularly consulted for advice.

THE SIGNIFICANCE OF THE BIBLE IN AFRICAN CHRISTIANITY IN THE TWENTY-FIRST CENTURY

In twenty-first-century Africa, the Bible is the basis of African Christianity. Without the Bible, there could be no Christianity in Africa. John Mbiti has rightly observed that the Bible's potential and actual influence in shaping African theology and Christianity is tremendous (Mbiti 1979: 84, 87). Similarly, Henri Daniel-Rops views the Bible as the unique and inexhaustible book in which all there is to say about God and humanity has been said (Daniel-Rops 1958).

Within African Christianity, people see themselves in the Bible. The Bible becomes a mirror in which human beings can see their inadequacies, successes, and nature. The consequences of original sin can be seen in the Bible. The stories in the Bible are stories of everyone's life journey. Thus, Getui suggests that "there is no position in life, no phase of human experience, for which the Bible does not contain valuable instruction. Ruler, and subject, master and servant, buyer and seller, borrower and lenders, parent and child, teacher and student—all may here find lessons of priceless worth" (Getui 1997: 88). The Bible contains a unique perspective on ethics, law, sociology, economics, and politics that is difficult to comprehend without first understanding the message of the Bible.

The Bible is a unifying factor in twenty-first-century African Christianity. Its role in the life of the Christian Church in Africa is not unlike that which it holds in the church universal. Of this role, Wright and Fuller say:

Christianity has always held that the Bible is a very special book unlike any other book in the world. It is the most important of all books because in it and in it alone, the true God has made himself known to man with clarity. The world is full of sacred literature and it is full of gods. But in the vast confusion the one source which can be relied upon for the truth is the Bible. There we are told about the events which brought the church into being and the purpose for its being. There we encounter the answer to the meaning of our own lives and of the history in which we live, there the frightening gulf between our weak, ignorant and mortal lives and the infinity of power and peace in our universe is really bridged. There we discover our duty defined and our God revealed. The many segments of the Christian Church have said all this in a great variety of ways with a great emphasis; but all have agreed that the Bible has been the fountain from which have come the Church and its faith. It is the common starting point to which we must continually return for guidance and stimulation. (quoted in Mugambi 1997: 89)

The Bible aids the coming together of churches in Africa. African scholars have also begun to use the Bible to interpret Africa. The Old Testament, in particular, is used as a point of comparison with African traditions and religions. Several scholars, such as Madipoane Masenya (ngwan'a Mphahlele), have compared the Old Testament with Northern Sotho proverbs (Masenya 2001: 133–46). Constance Shisanya used the Hagar narrative to illumine the perspective of African women (Shisanya 2001: 147–52). Adamo and Ewhubare compare the African wife of Abraham, Hagar, with marriage practices in the Urhobo tradition (Adamo and Ewhubare 2005). Pauline Otieno provides a perspective on the use of the Old Testament within the Coptic Church in Kenya (Otieno 2001: 159–64).

THE BIBLE IN THE EARLIER CENTURIES IN AFRICA

The story of the Bible in Africa is long and complex. From the standpoint of the Christian Church, it was the basis of doctrine. Therefore, those within the church were compelled not simply to read the Bible but to interpret it as well. The truth is that "the interpretation of Scripture is the principal bond between the ongoing life and thought" of Christians (Grant 1984). In interpreting that Bible, various methods of interpretation were employed. One could rightly say that the story of the Bible in Africa is tied to the history of biblical interpretation on the continent (Grant 1984).

During the first and second centuries, the only authoritative written document was the Old Testament (Adamo 2006). Paul, Jesus, and the authors of the New Testament assert its authority. Acts 8:26-40, the account of the so-called Ethiopian Eunuch, makes clear the status of the book of Isaiah. The New Testament indicates that there were African prophets and teachers (Acts 13:1) who were probably missionaries in Antioch (Adamo 2006). Apollos of Alexandria was an African missionary, and there were teachers who served as interpreters of scripture in Ephesus and Corinth (Acts 18:24-28; 19:1). Rufus, the son of Simon of Cyrene, was an African pastor in Rome (Rom. 16:13).

Africa can rightly be considered the cradle of biblical interpretation (Ukpong 2000: 11–28). Among early interpreters can be numbered Gnostic proponents Basilides and Valentinus. The establishment of a major catechetical center at Alexandria in Egypt was a pivotal event in the history of African biblical interpretation. It served as home to such eminent African scholars as Panteanus (its first head), Clement of Alexandria (Grant 1984: 114), Origen, Didymus the Blind, Tertullian, Cyprian of Carthage, Athanasius, Cyril of Alexandria, and Augustine of Hippo. Alexandrian scholars became major proponents of allegorical interpretation.

Historically, Africans who were exploited made use of the Bible because they found in it revolutionary potential. They used the Bible to fight against oppression. Among the Bantu churches, the Hebrew scriptures were foundational. In the nineteenth century, the Bible came to sub-Saharan Africa through missionary colonial expansionism (West 2002: 65–94). The one million European settlers had more land than the five million native Africans who were resettled and restricted to the barren area known as Bantu Land. This led the native community to say accusingly, "At first we had this land, and you had the Bible. Now we have the Bible and you have the land" (Sundkler 1948: 33).

John Colenso, Anglican bishop of Natal, who translated the Bible into the Zulu language, is illustrative of colonial missionary efforts to translate the Bible into indigenous tongues and to provide interpretive works that made it accessible to African audiences.

AFRICAN EMANCIPATORY MOVEMENTS AND THEIR BIBLE IN THE TWENTIETH CENTURY

Of course, Bible transmission and interpretation on the continent of Africa have not been one-sided affairs. Africans were not "mute" and passive receivers of the Bible (Sugirtharajah 2001: 105). Their response was often complex and varied. It involved both resistance and assimilation in response to colonial efforts to encourage acceptance of the Bible. While resistance was employed by native emancipatory movements, assimilation was the tactic employed by local integrative movements (Sugirtharajah 2001: 105). Both approaches made use of creative reading strategies. In some, attention was called to liberating figures such as Moses. In others, biblical stories of miracles, exorcism, healing, spiritual power, and spirit possession were stressed (Sugirtharajah 2001: 107–8).

BIBLICAL INTERPRETATION
IN TWENTY-FIRST-CENTURY AFRICA

Any discussion of the Bible in Africa must take into account African biblical interpretation. This is absolutely necessary because such interpretation allows one to see how the Bible was received and read by African audiences, both academic and nonacademic. During the twentieth century, a distinctive African tradition of interpretation began to emerge. A serious departure from the Western methodological approaches to the Bible began to take place, as noted by Justin Ukpong:

> African ways of reading the Bible are being taught along side classical methods in academic institutions; the Bible is being studied against the background of African context; and African contextual issues form the agenda for reading the Bible; . . . African conceptual frame of reference is competing with that of the West as (hitherto considered universal and normal) a methodological tool of exegetical practices; the ordinary people's approach to the Bible is informing scholarly reading practices; critical reading masses are being nurtured at the grassroots, and the hitherto muted voices of the ordinary people are coming alive in academic biblical discourse. (Ukpong 2002: 9–10)

In the first decade of the twenty-first century, African scholars have assumed greater prominence. In Africa, access to the Bible has become democratized in the academy. African biblical scholars, though mostly trained in the West, have the freedom to question the relevance of Western methods of reading the Bible in which they have been trained.[2] They are free to express hermeneutical suspicion about the universality of such methods. This process amounts to a reclaiming of the Bible as the word of God. I term this method of interpreting the Bible "African Cultural Hermeneutics."[3] It must be stated that the use of this African method does

not require a total rejection of dominant Western approaches. Occasionally, these methods are used alongside each other. Below I describe several ways of reading the Bible that fall under or are closely allied with the African cultural approach.

AFRICA AND AFRICANS IN THE BIBLE

This method, which focuses on the identification of Africa and Africans in the Bible, has been fully accepted in Africa and has become one of the favorite ways of interpreting the Bible. It began, of course, among African Americans in the United States in the early twentieth century and spread to Africa. It calls attention to the fact that Africa and Africans are mentioned more than any other nation, except Israel, in the Bible. There are some 867 references to Africa and Africans in both the Old and New Testaments (Adamo 2001a, 2006). According to this method, the best way to interpret and fully understand the Bible is to pay close attention to the presence of Africa and Africans and their contributions to the military, economic, social, religious, and cultural life of ancient Israel as found in the Bible.

Africa has a very close connection with biblical Christianity and thus with the Bible itself. This connection is celebrated in great African personalities present in the Bible. Today, greater awareness exists of the significant role these personalities have played in both the Old and New Testaments. Such individuals include the African wife of Moses (Kushit) in Numbers 12:1; the Queen of Sheba in 1 Kings, who provided the wood and precious stones for the beautification of the Temple of Solomon; Ebed-Melech, who rescued one of the most important prophets of the Old Testament; the so-called Ethiopian Eunuch in Acts 8; Simon of Cyrene, who assisted Jesus in carrying the cross; Apollos of Alexandria (Acts 18:24-28; 19:1); and Rufus the Evangelist (Rom. 16:13), who helped in evangelizing Asia and Africa during the period of the New Testament.[4]

Using Africa to Interpret the Bible

This interpretive approach uses African culture and tradition to interpret the Bible in order to shed light on the understanding of the Bible and Africans. While historical-critical methodology is used to analyze the text, the anthropological/sociological method is used to analyze African cultures and situations for the purpose of understanding fully both the biblical text and African tradition (Ukpong 2000: 11–28). The purpose of this method is also for the interpreter to arrive at an understanding of authentic African Christianity that is both biblical and African (Ukpong 2000: 11–28). Sometimes, biblical scholars also interpret the Bible to evaluate African culture (Adamo 2003: 9–33).

African Comparative Approach

It is during the current century that the African comparative approach has reached its zenith. It centers on the critical examination and comparison of elements within African cultures (especially in sub-Saharan Africa) found in the Bible. This is a change from the dominant Western method in which comparative evidence is drawn primarily from the ancient Near East. Furthermore, in such comparative work, Egypt is regarded as part of Africa.

African Bibliographical Studies Approach

In nineteenth- and twentieth-century Africa, there were few interpretive resources produced by Africans that facilitated the study of the Bible. Most of the work available was produced by missionaries and conservative Bible expositors. Scarcely any of the notes and explanatory references written by Africans, and geared to an African context, were compiled or published. While these sources were not taken seriously by missionaries and colonial masters, among Africa readers today great importance is attached to materials on the Bible written by both Africans and non-Africans in African contexts. Africans no longer depend on foreign presses

for publication of their research materials. Articles, journals, and other heretofore unpublished materials are being sought and put in distributable form for easy reference and access by African biblical scholars. These are also becoming readily available in African seminaries, universities, and Bible study centers. In fact, some are now made available in electronic form for free access.

The Bible as Power Approach

This is an existential and reflective approach to the study of the Bible developed by African Indigenous Churches. To African Christians and even non-Christians, the Bible is relevant to everyday life. When African Indigenous Churches were dissatisfied with the approach of mainline missionary churches, they searched the Bible and discovered that it contained power to solve many everyday life problems. They felt that the missionaries and colonial powers were hiding from them the power inherent in the word of God as stated in Hebrews 4:12—that is, that the word of God is "quick, and powerful and sharper than any two-edged sword piercing even to the dividing asunder of soul and spirit." As they read the Bible with African eyes, they discovered that the word is used for miracles by prophets, as well as by Jesus in the New Testament. They claimed those words for healing, protection, and success in life. Specific passages, especially in the book of Psalms, are used for this purpose, mostly within African Indigenous Churches. It must be said that this also reflects the use of the word of God for healing, protection, and success in life in African indigenous traditions (Adamo 2001b). For example, Psalms 5, 6, 28, 35, 37, 54, 55, 83, and 109 are classified as protective Psalms. Psalms 1, 2, 3, 16, 27, 28, 51, 100, 102, and 109 are considered therapeutic Psalms. Psalms 4, 8, 9, 23, 24, 27, 46, 51, 134 and others are seen as success Psalms. One important fact is that this method of reading the Bible not only is practiced by African Indigenous Churches throughout Africa, but is also practiced by members of mainline missionary churches in Africa.

One also sees comparable usage among Christians in various parts of the African Diaspora.

READING THE BIBLE WITH ORDINARY READERS

Two African biblical scholars, Justin Ukpong and Gerald West, are the pioneers for this methodology. They recognized that the majority of people who read the Bible are ordinary readers. The people we call "ordinary readers" are typically poor, oppressed, underprivileged, and untrained biblical scholars. This approach to the Bible is most common in Africa. Unlike in the West, where the majority of people who do biblical studies are trained biblical scholars, in Africa the majority of people who do biblical interpretation are common people—that is, those who are not formally trained in the art of biblical interpretation.

This approach involves having trained biblical scholars sit down with ordinary readers to do Bible study. Such reading takes place not only in the church but also outside the church for the purpose of education and liberation (Ukpong 2000: 11–28). Trained biblical scholars do not direct the reading. Instead, they facilitate reading. The reading agenda is that of the community (Yorke 1997: 145–46). This helps to create a reading group that has the liberty of using its socioreligious and cultural institutions, as well as its thought systems and practices, in interpretation (Ukpong 2002: 17–32). This approach to interpretation also empowers people to read the Bible critically. This is one of the most recent approaches to interpreting the Bible in Africa, one that helps to create an interface between ordinary readers and academic Bible readers (Ukpong 2002: 17–32). I believe very strongly that this type of African reading should be classified alongside other academic approaches to the Bible (Ukpong 2000: 11–28).

The methods above demonstrate the importance of the Bible and the seriousness with which African Christians and non-Christians treat it in Africa today.

CONCLUSION

In conclusion, let me offer some personal observations on what the Bible means to Africans, whether they are academic or ordinary readers. In so doing, I will reference some of the ideas already expressed by scholars and nonscholars in Africa (Getui 2001: 181–88).

- First, the Bible is regarded as the source of authority for African Christians. It is highly respected because it is held to have come directly from God. Therefore, without the Bible, there can be no faith and no Christianity.
- Second, the Bible is a unifying factor among denominations in Africa. The source of ecumenism among churches is the Bible. Despite doctrinal differences among numerous denominations, the Bible remains a uniting force.
- Third, the Bible is the word of God and possesses power. According to African belief, there is power in the word. There is protection, healing, and a means to success in life found within the Bible. For this reason, in most parts of Africa, Bible quotations are written on vehicles, houses, and even motorcycles. Some write them on pieces of papers and then wrap them and place them in pockets or under pillows for protection against enemies.
- Fourth, most Africans, whether Christians or non-Christians, believe that the Bible is the most familiar book in Africa because it is the most widely translated and the most read book in Africa.
- Fifth, popular opinion in Africa indicates that the Bible is highly esteemed and central in the experiences of Christians and non-Christians.
- Sixth, despite the fact that the Bible is a uniting force in Africa, it is also a dividing force and has been used as a document

for oppression. Thus, J. S. Mbiti has correctly argued that the Bible's influence and potential in shaping African theology and Christianity is tremendous (Mbiti 1979: 83–94). The development of a distinctive African hermeneutic ensures that the Bible will remain an important part of African life. In fact, my prediction is that the Bible is going to be more influential in shaping people's lives in future generations, particularly given the exponential growth of Christianity in Africa.

- Finally, the Bible is regarded no longer as a European book in Africa but indeed as an African book. I believe this will be the case for years to come.

Notes

1. The meaning of the word of God differs considerably from person to person. Unfortunately, space does not permit a detailed examination of these various definitions.

2. See Justin Ukpong, "Reading the Bible in a Global Village: Issues and Challenges from African Readings" (Ukpong et al. 2002). He maintains that the difference between African exegesis and Western exegesis is that African exegesis links the biblical text with African realities.

3. See Ukpong, "Reading the Bible in the Global Village" (Ukpong et al. 2002, 10). Ukpong calls this method "inculturation hermeneutics."

4. For further discussion of these personalities, see D. T. Adamo, *Africa and Africans in the Old Testament* and *Africa and Africans in the New Testament* (Adamo 2001a, 2006).

References

Adamo, D. T. 2001a. *Africa and Africans in the Old Testament.* Eugene, Ore.: Wipf and Stock.

———. 2001b. *Reading and Interpreting the Bible in African Indigenous Churches.* Eugene, Ore.: Wipf and Stock.

———. 2003. "The Historical Development of Old Testament Interpretation in Africa." *Old Testament Essays* 16, no. 1:9–33.

———. 2006. *Africa and Africans in the New Testament.* Lanham, Md.: University Press of America.

Adamo, David, and E. F. Ewhubare. 2005. "The African Wife of Abraham (Gn 16:1-16; 21: 8-21)." *Old Testament Essays* 18: 455–71.

Bent, Ans J. van, ed. 1982. *Handbook of WCC Member Churches.* Geneva: World Council of Churches. P. 257.

Daniel-Rops, Henri. 1958. *What Is the Bible?* New York: Hawthorn.

Getui, Mary. 1997. "The Bible as a Tool for Ecumenism." In *The Bible in African Christianity: Essays in Biblical Theology*, ed. Hannah W. Kinoti and John M. Waliggo. Nairobi: Acton.

———. 2001. "The Bible in African Theology." In *Interpreting the Old Testament in Africa*, ed. Mary Getui, Knut Holter, and Victor Zinkurature, 181–88. New York: Peter Lang.

Grant, Robert M. 1984. *A Short History of the Interpretation of the Bible.* London: SCM.

Lemarquuand, Grant. 2000. "New Testament Exegesis in (Modern) Africa." In *The Bible in Africa Transactions, Trajectories and Trends*, ed. Gerald O. West and Musa Dube. Leiden: Brill.

Masenya, Madipoane (ngwan'a Mphahlele). 2001. "Wisdom and Wisdom Converge: Selected Old Testament and Northern Sotho Proverbs." In *Interpreting the Old Testament in Africa*, ed. Mary Getui, Knut Holter, and Victor Zinkurature. New York: Peter Lang.

Mbiti, J. S. 1979. "The Biblical Basis for Present Trends in African Theology." In *African Theology en Route*, ed. Kofi Appiah-Kubi and Sergio Torres. Maryknoll, N.Y.: Orbis.

Mugambi, J. N. K. 1997. "The Bible and Ecumenism in African Christianity." In *The Bible in African Christianity: Essays in Biblical Theology*, ed. H. W. Kinoti and J. M. Waliggo. Nairobi, Kenya: Acton.

Otieno, Pauline. 2001. "Interpreting the Book of Psalms in the Coptic Orthodox Church in Kenya." In *Interpreting the Old Testament in Africa*, ed. Mary Getui, Knut Holter, and Victor Zinkurature, 159–64. New York: Peter Lang.

Shisanya, Constance. 2001. "A Reflection on the Hagar Narratives in Genesis through the Eyes of a Kenyan Woman." In *Interpreting the Old Testament in Africa*, ed. Mary Getui, Knut Holter, and Victor Zinkurature, 147–52. New York: Peter Lang.

Sugirtharajah, R. S. 2001. *The Bible and the Third World.* Cambridge: Cambridge University Press.

Sundkler, Bengt G. M. 1948. *Bantu Prophets in South Africa.* London: Lutherworth.

Ukpong, Justin. 2000. "Developments in Biblical Interpretation in Africa: Historical and Hermeneutical Directions." In *The Bible in Africa: Transactions, Trajectories, and Trends,* ed. Gerald O. West, and Musa W. Dube. Leiden: Brill. 2000: 11–28.

———. 2002. "Inculturation Hermeneutics: An African Approach to Biblical Interpretation." In *The Bible in the World Context: An Experiment in Contextual Hermeneutics*, ed. Walter Dietrich and Luz Urich, 17–32. Grand Rapids, Mich.: Eerdmans.

Ukpong, Justin, Musa Dube, Gerald West et al., eds. 2002. *Reading the Bible in the Global Village.* Atlanta: Society of Biblical Literature.

West, Gerald. 2002. "Unpacking the Package That Is the Bible in African Biblical Scholarship." In *Reading the Bible in the Global Village*, ed. Justin Ukpong, Musa Dube, Gerald West, et al., 65–94. Atlanta: Society of Biblical Literature.

West, Gerald O., and Musa Dube, eds. 2000. *The Bible in Africa Transactions, Trajectories and Trends.* Leiden: Brill.

Yorke, G. L. O. 1997. "The Bible and the Black Diaspora." In *The Bible in African Christianity: Essays in Biblical Theology*, ed. Hannah W. Kinoti and John M. Waliggo, 145–64. Nairobi: Acton.

WOMEN, AFRICANA REALITY,

and the BIBLE

Madipoane Masenya (ngwan'a Mphahlele)

Senzeni na   (What have we done?)   [repeated eight times]

Isono sethu ubumnyama   (Our sin is our blackness)   [repeated eight times]

Amabhunu ayizinja   (Whites are dogs)   [repeated eight times]

IN THE HEYDAY OF APARTHEID in South Africa, the above Zulu song used to be sung by protesting Black masses. The latter could have been Soweto pupils protesting against Afrikaans as the medium of instruction, women marching to the Union buildings to protest against passbooks, and so forth. It was sung in anger and frustration. The question was directed not only to the oppressor but also to God. What is it that Blacks have done wrong to deserve the harsh treatment they received then? We speculated that our "sin" was our Black skin color. *Isono sethu ubumnyama*! Let me add one more line in order to connect my African–South African reality with that of my fellow Africana sisters: *Isono sethu ubulili bethu besifazane*—"Our sin is our female sex." Our "sin" is not only our skin color but also our female sex: we are Black women, daughters of Africa.

What immediately comes to mind when I further ponder my connectedness with my sisters and the Bible is my encounter with the latter at the Elminah Castle in Ghana in 2000. I stood in one of the rooms, angered by a poster with a quotation from Psalm 132:14. The core of the poster's message was that God was in the place of slavery! There, at the western corner of the African continent, I remembered how this book, which has come to be valued and shunned by many Africana peoples, functioned to sanction all forms of oppression that were to become their painful legacies. Some were hurled from that same location to the Americas, while some remained to be subjugated and colonized. I remembered how the Bible was systematically used to sanction racial segregation in South Africa. As sons and daughters of Africa bore, and still bear, the brunt of their Blackness, the daughters have been, and still are, at the receiving end. The latter are connected in their struggles against a variety of life-denying forces in their local contexts and globally. To this connectedness, we will later return. These are women whose realities, as they interact with the Bible, I will attempt to describe.

In differing Africana grassroots contexts, the concept of "Bible" does not need any further qualification. When it is mentioned, listeners usually assume that it refers to the Christian Bible. That, however, does not imply that Christianity is the only religion in their contexts. Given the fact that *The Africana Bible* is targeted toward such contexts, and the significant role that the Christian Bible continues to play in varying Africana settings, the concept "Bible" will hereafter be used to refer to the Christian scriptures.

My goal is to investigate the kind of interaction, if any, that exists between Africana women's realities and the Bible. It will be impossible, if not presumptuous, to assume that one could speak on behalf of all Africana women's experiences as they do or do not relate to the Bible. Therefore, my goal will be to use the story of Bathepa Maja as the main narrative through which broad linkages can be forged. Her story therefore serves as a hermeneutical lens through which one can get a small glimpse of Africana women's realities in relation to the Bible.

Let me begin with a brief personal disclosure.

NGWAN'A MPHAHLELE'S ENCOUNTER WITH THE BIBLE

I first encountered the Bible in early childhood at home (ga-Mphahlele), in the church, and later at school. My family formed part of a group designated *majakane*, a church-going African people who supposedly (that is, mainly in public) shunned African traditional customs. The *majakane* stood in contrast to the so-called heathens (*bahedene*) who

openly rejected Christianity. They freely engaged in African traditional life. In that setting, the Bible was successfully used to divide kindred peoples! I later came to embrace it in my teen years when I got attracted to Pentecostal theology. Later, I encountered it as a university student in biblical studies classes, as a graduate student of Hebrew Bible, and now as a *bosadi* (womanhood) Hebrew Bible scholar.

Earlier on, I noted the connectedness of Africana women. How connected are they?

OUR CONNECTEDNESS

African women are connected as theologians, biblical scholars, and members of the Christian laity challenging patriarchy in religion, society (local and global), African culture, the academy, and so forth. The origins of the Circle of Concerned African Women Theologians in 1989 bears witness to African women's determination to take their experiences seriously, in view of the Ecumenical Association of Third World Theologians' perceived failure in that regard (see Oduyoye and Kanyoro 1992).

The introduction of womanist and Black feminist biblical and theological discourses was motivated by the determination of African American women to ensure that their realities are also taken into account. As Demetrius Williams notes:

> In their use of the Bible, African Americans rejected biblical passages that sanctioned slavery, oppression and race prejudice. This makes it puzzling, then, that the African American interpretive traditions, which found within the Bible models and paradigms of liberation from race and class oppression, were unwilling to explore the Bible to find equally liberating models to challenge the traditional roles and status of women, especially Black women who suffered under the same harsh system of race and class oppression. (Williams 2003: 40)

In the South African context, I continue to be amazed by how many Black men, who equally still bear the scars of marginalization on account of their race, find it difficult to listen to the concerns of those who are marginalized on account of their gender (Masenya 2004, 2005).

Althea Spencer Miller acknowledges the historical significance of women in Caribbean families (see also Leo-Rhyne 2003). She notes that both Caribbean women and men are colonial subjects. Nevertheless, she argues regarding patriarchy as follows: "Subject though the Caribbean man is to *kyriarchy*, he is not an innocent victim in the situation. He is fully capable of exerting the values of patriarchy even as he rails against the impact of colonialism upon himself. His perceptions of traditional gender roles also need critical analysis" (Spencer Miller 2005: 224). As Africana women, we experience patriarchy from those of our own kind even as we, together with them, at times on account of the abuse of the Bible, remain subjected to American and European imperialism through globalization and neocolonialism.

We therefore challenge sexism from those of our own kind, in the church and its scriptures, even as we continue to fill the church pews on Sundays. In one instance at a church in Kingston, Jamaica, in 2003, I marveled as I found myself in an almost all female church!

We are connected in challenging such life-denying forces as racism (in, for example, the United States and South Africa in particular), sexism (in the broader society and within African cultures for those located on the continent), classism, xenophobia, HIV/AIDS, neocolonialism, and globalization. Though connected, ours are different realities.

A RICH VARIETY OF AFRICANA WOMEN'S REALITIES

What comes to mind when one ponders Africana women's varied realities and their interaction with

the Bible is that in aural African cultures, and in light of the traditional tendency to give priority to boy children in terms of education, not all women can read from the Bible themselves. This is not unlike the situation encountered by early African slaves in the Americas. The painful story of Howard Thurman's grandmother comes to mind here. She was not keen to hear any text from the Pauline letters. When asked why, she responded:

> Always the white minister used as his text something from Paul. At least three or four times a year he used as his text: 'Slaves, be obedient to them that are your master, . . . as unto Christ.' Then he would go on to show how it was God's will that we were slaves and how, if we were good and happy slaves, God would bless us. *I promised my Maker that if I ever learned to read and if freedom ever came, I would not read that part of the Bible.*" (Weems 1993: 34, emphasis mine)

These women and many others who can read, but who lack the privileges of academic Bible readers, are able to select texts that they find resonate with their experiences while leaving out those that do not (for example, Thurman's grandmother's distaste for "slave" texts). They go further and interpret the Bible in a way that affirms their individual circumstances. Bible interpretation cannot be a preserve for the elite in these settings. Another example in this regard is noteworthy, a refreshing rereading of Psalm 37:25 by Lucy Bailey. Spencer Miller describes Bailey's hermeneutic as follows: "Her experience was that the main theme of this psalm, that God would vindicate the righteous, rang true in her own life. Biologically childless, there were, nonetheless children of many ages who nestled in the warmth of her lap and of her dress folds. She knew that God was with her. Her seed, she knew, would not suffer" (Spencer Miller 2005: 210).

Some church women may read the Bible in their private closets, while not being allowed to read in the church! The Zionist Christian Church in South Africa, probably among the largest African Independent Churches (AICs) on the continent, is one such example. Women can never be allowed to serve as ministers in this church. This is an interesting power dynamic demonstrating how even after the struggle against early colonial imperialism (see the origins of AICs), patriarchy continues to reign supreme. Not only is such a problematic dynamic the lot of African women in some of these churches, but it remains the fate of African women in a democratic South Africa (Masenya 2004, 2005), in post-independence African states on the continent (Oduyoye and Kanyoro 1992; Oduyoye 1995; Phiri), in the Black church in North America (Kirk-Duggan 2003; Weems 1993), and even in women-centered families within the Caribbean (Spencer Miller 2005; Lewis 2003).

Although I have pointed to a sense of connectedness regarding the concerns shared by Africana women theologians and biblical scholars, it is fair also to acknowledge that various ideologies, local concerns, and themes inform their works. Having considered the unity and diversity typical of our experiences as Africana women, let us now focus on an exemplary narrative: Bathepa Maja's story.

ENCOUNTERING BATHEPA MAJA

"How Worthy Is the Woman of Worth" is the topic I was invited to address at an occasion celebrating the achievement of seventy-year-old Bathepa Maja. The invitation came from the Women's Ecumenical Fellowship of the South African Council of Churches, Limpopo Province (hereafter referred to as WEFSACCLP). In 2006, Bathepa Maja obtained the Shoprite-Checkers Woman of the Year award for her tireless efforts toward establishing the Sentahle Community Home-Based Care in her rural village of ga-Maja (located in Limpopo Province). How did the old retired nurse come to be motivated to engage in that great project in this

poor province? As a church woman, Maja, together with other women, visited an ailing older woman to offer prayers for her. They prayed and left the patient's house. On their next visit, the patient was dehydrated, even as she struggled to interact with them. After a few weeks, she died. Says Maja:

I felt very guilty. What did I do as a nurse? Prayer women did spiritual healing, but what about nursing interventions—nothing. During her memorial service these women (prayer women) were singing and dancing . . . praising this woman when preaching. This remained indelible in my mind. This was my starting point of Sentahle, as I thought of those who are far from us. My profession is not for me, but for the community. (2006:3)

From then on, Bathepa Maja determined to relentlessly search out needy families at ga-Maja to provide the necessary interventions. Through that demanding exercise, she managed to identify needy families—such as those with members who were sick, hungry, or had children in need. After identifying them, she *walked* from house to house, at times traversing difficult terrain, to address these various needs. She bathed patients, provided medication, and fed the hungry. Earlier on in her "missionary" endeavors, Maja enlisted the help of volunteers for care-giving responsibilities. With the steady support of donors Maja has been able to secure full-time workers. She continues, as well, to seek external support. It was through the relentless efforts of this prayerful, Bible-oriented church woman that a Community Care Center was built! The Center now caters to the various needs of the ga-Maja community (Mailula 2007).

What I find intriguing and empowering about Bathepa Maja is her ability to integrate her African–South African realities with what she has gleaned from the Bible. Her understanding that her faith needs to be accompanied by outreach to the needy is refreshing. Her commitment to the Bible-based teachings of the WEFSACCLP, whose focus has always been on holistic salvation, should challenge those of us who have adopted a narrow, self-centered view of God's salvation to reassess such a problematic view. She reminds Africana women to be wary of "prosperity gospel teachings," mostly from the U.S. televangelists, which promise material blessings by prayer, giving (to rich preachers), and faith only! Her African communal caring mentality is certainly worth noting. It is no wonder that WEFSACCLP felt it necessary to recognize her achievement. I felt honored to be part of those who celebrated this Woman of Worth! I am intrigued by her hermeneutic. It does not require a background in Bible studies or biblical language proficiency. It is functional and oriented toward helping the needy. Hers is a transformational African woman's hermeneutic. This is a refreshing break from those approaches to hermeneutics and theology that most of us have been trained to employ, particularly during the apartheid era: individualistic, detached, spiritual, and futuristic.

Bathepa Maja's story reveals what has been noted previously about the accessibility of the Bible not only to scholars but to many Africana grassroots women. Does it not make sense for such readers, who are closer to Africana realities than many scholars, to make use of this book, which has been used for better and for worse, to effect positive change in our communities? All of us might benefit not only by listening to their stories but also by allowing ourselves to learn from their experiences. As we do so, we will enable those who choose the Bible as a resource to let it serve Africana realities in a positive way:

> In the service of humanity,
> For better, for worse,
> Through calm and storms,
> In sorrows, in joy,
> For division and unity,
> Servicing humanity.
>
> For enslavement and freedom,
> Conquering and repossessing,

> Oppressing and liberating,
> For death, for life,
> Serving Africana woman humanity,
> The Christian Bible.

References

Byron, Gay L. 2005. "The Challenge of 'Blackness' for Rearticulating the Meaning of Global Feminist New Testament Interpretation." In *Feminist New Testament Studies: Global and Future Perspectives*, ed. Kathleen O'Brien Wicker, 85–101. New York: Palgrave Macmillan.

Dube, Musa W., ed. 2001. *Other Ways of Reading: African Women and the Bible*. Atlanta: Society of Biblical Literature; Geneva: World Council of Churches.

Kanyoro, Musimbi R. A. 2002. *Introducing Feminist Cultural Hermeneutics: An African Perspective*. New York: Sheffield Academic.

Kirk-Duggan, Cheryl A. 2003. "Let My People Go: Threads of Exodus in African American Narratives." In *Yet with a Steady Beat: Contemporary U.S. Afrocentric Biblical Interpretation*, ed. Randall Bailey, 123–43. Atlanta: Society of Biblical Literature.

Leo-Rhyne, E. 2003. "Poverty and the Caribbean Family." Unpublished Paper read at the Pan-African Seminar on Religion and Poverty, Kingston, Jamaica.

Maja, Bathepa. 2006. Sentahle Community Home-Based Care Organisation. Organisational Profile and Report, Polokwane.

Mailula (nee Mabapa), Malehu E. 2007. Telephone conversation, 30 April 2007

Masenya (ngwan'a Mphahlele), Madipoane. 2004. *How Worthy Is the Woman of Worth? Rereading Proverbs 31:10-31 in African–South Africa*. New York: Peter Lang. 2005.

———."Their Hermeneutics Was Strange! Ours Is a Necessity! Rereading Vashti as African-South African Women." In *Her Master's Tools? Feminist Challenges to Historical-Critical Interpretations: Global Perspectives on Biblical Scholarship*, ed. Caroline Van der Stichele & Todd Penner, eds, 179–94. Atlanta: SBL.

Madipoane Masenya (ngwan'a Mphahlele)

Oduyoye, Mercy A. 1995. "The Bible and African Women." In *Reading from this Place*, vol. 2, *Social Location and Bible Interpretation in Global Perspective*, ed. Fernando F. Segovia and Mary A. Tolbert, 33–51. Minneapolis: Fortress Press.

Oduyoye, Mercy A., and Musimbi R. A. Kanyoro. 1992. *The Will to Arise: Women, Tradition and the Church in Africa*. Maryknoll, N.Y.: Orbis.

Okure, Teresa. 1995. "Reading from this Place: Some Problems and Prospects." In *Reading from This Place*, vol. 2, *Social Location and Bible Interpretation in Global Perspective*, ed. Fernando F. Segovia and Mary A. Tolbert, 52–66. Minneapolis: Fortress Press.

Phiri, Isabel A. 2000. *Women, Presbyterianism and Patriarchy: Religious Experience of Chewa Women in Central Malawi*. Blantyre: CLAIM (Christian Literature Association in Malawi).

Sentahle Community Home-Based Care Organisation. Organisational Profile and Report, 2006. Polokwane, South Africa.

Spencer Miller, Althea. 2005. "Lucy Bailey Meets the Feminists." In *Feminist New Testament Studies: Global and Future Perspectives*, ed. Kathleen O'Brien Wicker, 209–38. New York: Palgrave Macmillan.

Weems, 1993. "Reading Her Way through the Struggle: African American Women and the Bible." In *The Bible and Political Liberation: Political and Social Hermeneutics*, eds. Norman K. Gottwald, and Richard A. Horseley, 31–50. Maryknoll, N.Y.: Orbis.

Weems, Renita J. 2002. "Rereading for Liberation: African-American Women and the Bible." In *Feminist Interpretation of the Bible and the Hermeneutics of Liberation*, ed. Sylvia Schroer and S. Bietenhard, 19–32. London: Sheffield Academic, 2002.

Williams, Demetrius K. 2003. "The Bible and Models of Liberation in the African American Experience." In *Yet with a Steady Beat: Contemporary U.S. Afrocentric Biblical Interpretation*, ed. Randall C. Bailey, 33–59. Atlanta: Society of Biblical Literature.

The BIBLE *and* AFRICANA LIFE

A PROBLEMATIC RELATIONSHIP

Steed Vernyl Davidson, Justin Ukpong, and Gosnell Yorke

You gave I King James Version; King James was a white man; . . .
Bring back Macabee [sic] Version; that God gave to black man.
— Max Romeo, Jamaican songwriter

Africans embrace the Bible with a stubborn belief in its liberatory power and capacity (Yorke 2001: 137). Yet, as Romeo's lyrics above suggest, there exist at best two Bibles: one of oppression and one of freedom. In the encounter with Europeans and Christianity, Africans have experienced the Bible in these ambiguous ways. Though there are few instances of rejection of the Bible, in general Africans in various locations have read the Bible on their own terms and against the dominant oppressive culture. While this may mean omitting offensive texts, it also means subverting texts from their normative positions or even "blackening" texts to foreground African heroes. Consequently, Africans produce a different Bible through these varied reading practices.

THE BIBLE IN AFRICA

Christians in West Africa view the Bible as a popular text. Phrases such as "The Lord is my Shepherd" or "The Lord is my light and my salvation" written on commercial vehicles suggest the place of the Bible in the lives of Africans. Many Christians sleep with the Bible under their pillows, believing in its power to ward off evil spirits. They read the Bible to derive comfort and consolation in moments of trouble. They see it as a rule of life and a source of morality. This scenario, however, belies the historical problematic relationship that has existed between the Bible and Africans.

Two popular African stories exemplify the relationship. One story relates that when white missionaries first came to Africa, they presented Africans with the Bible and asked them to close their eyes for prayer. On opening their eyes, Africans discovered that the whites had taken away their land and left them with the Bible. The story is meant to show that the coming of the Bible to Africa is implicated in the colonial oppression of Africans.

The other story tells of an African woman who carried the Bible with her wherever she went. When asked why she did that, she responded that it was because the Bible was the only book that could read her. This story, unlike the previous one, takes a positive stance toward the Bible. It affirms the Bible as a source of empowerment—hence the woman's attachment to it.

Why are Africans so attached to the Bible introduced by Europeans who turned out to be oppressors? What are the issues in the dialectical relationship between the Bible and Africans? The responses to these questions lie in the historical process of the arrival of the Bible in Africa.

The Bible came to Africa, south of the Sahara, through white missionaries at the time Africa was being colonized. The missionaries used the Bible to condemn aspects of African culture and religion. Africans had to sing hymns they did not understand and that held no meaning for them. John Pobee speaks of Africans who had no idea of snow singing, "See amidst the winter snow" (Pobee 1979: 41). The missionaries referred to African cultures and religions as pagan, needing to be exterminated in order to implant European culture through Christianity. They used the Bible to justify the subjugation of Africans. White Christians who came to South Africa saw themselves as God's chosen people on a divine mission like the Israelites (Grundlingh and Sapire 1989: 19–38).

African reaction to the Bible and the colonial project has gone in two directions. One is a total rejection of the Bible by a few. The "Goddian" religion in Nigeria (Onuwa 1989: 116–25; see also *Goddian Religion Handbook*) and "Africania" religion in Ghana (Bediako 1995: 17–20) represent a clear dismissal of the Bible and Christianity. These religions, modern expressions of African traditional religion, practice animal sacrifice, offer libations to ancestors, and worship African deities. Founded by former Christians and led by (formerly Christian) theologians, these religions offer an indigenous African religious experience untouched by Western Christianity and the Bible.

The other response by Africans to the Christian Bible lies in accepting and reading the Bible but in an African way. Part of the process of colonization was teaching Africans how to read and write so that they could occupy subservient roles in the colonial government. Missionaries translated the Bible into local languages. As Africans became more literate, they discovered that there is more in the Bible than the missionaries let them know. They saw in the New Testament a Jesus who heals the sick, liberates the downtrodden, and drives away demons. In a situation where people are afflicted by evil spirits, hunger, and oppression, Africans discovered a "Bible" that makes an impression on them. They developed strategies to circumvent the oppressive use of the Bible and came to read it differently.

Philip Turner's analysis of African acceptance of Christianity illustrates African acceptance of the Bible. Turner identifies three ways Africans accept Christianity (Turner 1971: 46). The first way of acceptance results in "immediate adaptation." In terms of the Bible, this refers to a situation where elements in the Bible are taken as "another version of something already familiar." Thus, Africans can accept the concept of God and the Ten Commandments because these are similar to their own culture.[1]

Turner calls the second way of acceptance the way of "compartmentalization." In this way, new elements deemed strange or incompatible with indigenous culture are "locked up in tight compartments and become operative only in certain situations." In missiological terms, this appears as "syncretism." For example, for Africans, religion is meant to solve practical problems. Accepting the Bible therefore guarantees answers to problems. In instances where the guaranteed result does not occur, African Christians seek recourse in traditional religions.

The third way deals with elements too strange to be compatible with the indigenous culture.

These elements either radically modify or destroy some elements of the indigenous culture. An example of this is the practice in some parts of Africa of killing twins at birth because they are believed to be a curse from God. Another example is human sacrifice that was practiced in some parts of Africa. Today, with the influence of the Bible, these practices are no longer in vogue.

Though the historical process of the entry of the Bible was accompanied with oppression, most Africans accept it but circumvent its oppressive use through inventive means to read it profitably. African scholars have developed new approaches, including comparative reading, evaluative reading, and inculturation reading (Ukpong 2000: 3–19), bypassing Western reading strategies and arriving at biblical readings for Africans.

THE BIBLE AND AFRICANS IN THE CARIBBEAN

A great number of slaves in the New World knew too well already the teachings and stories of the Old Testament. . . . Many slaves who learned to read and write did so by using the King James Version as a basic textbook.
—Peebles 1983: 8

This section focuses on the "older African Diaspora"[2] as well as limiting its gaze principally to the Anglophone component. Consequently, not much will be said about the African Diaspora in French-, Spanish-, Portuguese-, or Dutch-speaking countries of the Caribbean.[3] In the Caribbean, defining the Bible remains a challenge. In a region populated by a mix of Protestants and Catholics in noticeable numbers, different forms of the Old Testament, for example, exist. The canonical confusion becomes sharper when considering the ideological attachment of Jamaican Rastafarians to Ethiopia. The Bible of the Ethiopian Orthodox Church, originally published in Ge'ez back in the sixth century C.E., has fifty-four books in the Old Testament section

alone—eight more than in the Roman Catholic canon (Noss 2004: 11). This marked difference informs the notion in Romeo's lyrics that the European Bible is not the same as the African Bible.

Regardless of the canonical complexities surrounding the biblical canon, when it comes to the Bible in the Caribbean, relating to it is both programmatic and problematic. It is programmatic because there is a conviction that God speaks meaningfully to the "afro-existential situation" through figures such as Moses. The text comes as a sustaining and liberating word of life and one that serves to keep hope alive in the most pathological of contexts.

In the Caribbean, creative blends of motifs from the Bible are used in various ways. At times, the Bible functions like a talisman. At other times, the Bible is a means to engage in the religio-magical practices of divining, proving, or curing. The hermeneutical ritual of illumination—in which the Bible is opened at random and texts chosen at random (especially from Daniel, Psalms, and Ezekiel), followed by a "call upon the Holy Ghost for assistance in interpreting the text" (Glazier 1983: 46–48)—reflects a belief in the numinous power of the Bible. This belief also demonstrates itself in the vibrant blend of themes from the Bible and African religio-cultural traditions based on deities such as Ogun and Shango and the Akan worship of obosom (Bisnauth 1989: 87–88).

At the height of missionary activity among slaves in the Caribbean, it was not uncommon to use the King James Version to teach and preach a self-submissive piety and passivity meant to keep the slaves accepting of their lot in life. This version of the Bible derived further authority since it spoke in the language of the slave master and reflected the cultural tendencies of colonial society. The predisposition to use the Bible as a "text of terror" was countered by the stubborn commitment of the enslaved in the Caribbean to be free. This commitment spawned an interpretive tradition that persists. Such interpretations were never an uncritical, fundamentalistic, anti-intellectual consumption of the Bible as taught and preached, as it seems in some contemporary "afro-diasporic circles" (Washington 1986: 493). Essentially, an uncritical and self-injurious embrace of the entire Bible itself did not take place.

The nonacceptance of the entire Bible resulted in the unconscious adoption of an inevitable "canon within the canon." Africans in the Caribbean engaged in creative rhetorical rereading of biblical traditions. For example, the story of Cain slaying his brother Abel "with a great big club" (Segal 1995: 64) proves the contention that whites have their roots in Cain, who was bleached or turned white as a result of divine punishment. This reading counteracts the myth of the "curse of Ham" and his becoming black because of it (Yorke 2004: 159). Similarly, Rastafarians offer a mythological reconstruction of Ethiopian history by appealing to the divinization of Haile Selasie, foregrounding Africans in the biblical narrative (Chevannes 1994, 1998, 2006; Erskine 2007).

The Bible serves the slaves' mulish commitment to be free in the here and now. Its usage in Caribbean life reflects the notion that a liberating version supposedly meant for "the black man" was replaced by the oppressive version and tool of King James. The active use of the Bible in diverse areas of Caribbean life demonstrates the commitment to replace this liberating version of the Bible.

THE BIBLE AMONG AFRICANS IN NORTH AMERICA

It must be admitted that there [was] a strong temptation on the part of the masters to use the Scriptures as an auxiliary to the overseer
—Drew 1968: 9

The Africans who encountered Christianity in North America in the seventeenth century faced a hostile environment that welcomed them only for their labor. This environment, shaped by the Bible, prescribed the place of Africans in the society. Slaveholding plantations justified the forced labor

of Africans with appeal to the so-called curse of Ham (Gen. 9:24-27). This mistaken exegesis served to uphold what was regarded by the largely Protestant North American slave society as faithful adherence to scripture. These Christians saw the Bible as a repository for morals and piety and understood slavery as both justified and requiring the dutiful submission of the slave as a means of replicating a divinely ordered hierarchy. Consequently, Africans encountered the Bible as an intimidating text that denied their freedom. This oppressive text they rejected and embraced instead a different canon, a different theology, and a story world produced by the same Bible (Drew 1968: 32).

The initial encounter between Africans transported to North America and the Bible is best described as preliterary but critical. Hindered in their access to the text, Africans in North America encountered the stories of the Bible and discovered a world of mystery, miracle, and justice. The stories of deliverance from Egypt, of redemption of persons in dire circumstances, and of Jesus who suffers for the sake of others echoed their own experiences of suffering, injustice, and oppression. Through the cycle of telling and hearing, African slaves developed a canon of liberation that theologizes a God of freedom and justice (Wimbush 1989: 141).

This canon differed markedly from that which slaveholders possessed or even textualized. The canon came alive in the songs and preaching of slave gatherings initially held mostly in secret. In this underground world, a hermeneutic of resistance recognized the contradictions between the God of Egyptian deliverance (Felder 1989: 157) and that communicated through the household codes (Eph. 6:5-9, Col. 3:22-25, 1 Pet. 2:18-25) (Drew 1968: 89). Consequently, texts used to justify slavery and to encourage pious acceptance of suffering and oppression do not appear with the same level of authority in the discourse of Africans in North America. Even though unaccustomed to textual traditions, Africans constructed a Bible out of the stories of freedom highlighting persons like Moses, Joshua, Daniel, and Elijah. This Bible has Jesus as savior but little of Paul since he appears to support slavery (Weems 1991: 61). The Bible in the hands of Africans differs from that held by Euro-Americans.

Toward the end of the colonial era in the United States and Canada, as slaves acquired more skills to function in a Europeanized society, the critical relationship with the Bible turned to the actual texts. Biblical scholars dismantle the myth supported by the Hamite curse (Copher 1989: 121). They expose the exclusion of the African presence from the Bible by arguing that geographically Egypt belongs to Africa, acknowledge the contributions of Cush and its citizens in the Bible, and connect displaced Jews with Africans (Copher 1991: 148). While most of these efforts have received mixed reactions from users of the Bible, the work of scholars like Charles Copher have resulted in Africans in North America taking a greater pride in the Bible as a book about Africa and Africans.

Africans in North America, like other users of the Bible in the nineteenth and twentieth centuries, develop affinities for European methods of biblical study and reading strategies. These methods tend to focus on producing a universally applicable interpretation of what the text meant in its original context. Under the guise of faithful Bible reading, North American Africans have unlearned the "this-world-liness" of the Bible that their forebears discovered. Consequently, incidents such as slavery, segregation, and economic deprivation, which mark the African experience in North America, remain unvalued and unmentioned in reading strategies (Bailey 1998: 76).

In the midst of African cultures in North America, the Bible looms large in music, art, drama, and hip-hop. This suggests an active engagement with the Bible in contemporary popular culture that points to the historical relationship between people of African descent and the Bible in their struggles. Vincent Wimbush advocates a reading strategy that values the African experience as the starting text for any engagement with the Bible (Wimbush 2000: 22). Arguably, this Bible and its reading are not like any other. This reading of the Bible starts with the African experience and ends with the African experience.

CONCLUSION

The Bible exists as a strange book for those who would embrace an Afrocentric worldview. Africans have always understood the power of the Bible since they can be numbered among its victims. Despite this and the few instances of rejection, a wholesale dismissal of the Bible is hard to find among Africans around the world. However, the European Bible—the slave Bible, with its unjust God and distorted history of interpretations—has been rejected. Africans continue to write another Bible out of their lived history of oppression and freedom, of struggle and perseverance.

Notes

1. Bennett argues that one reason African slaves embraced Christianity is the similarities between Christian theology and African theology (Bennett 1989: 131).
2. A distinction can be made between the "older African Diaspora" produced by the transatlantic slave trade and a "newer African Diaspora" resulting from liberalization of immigration policies in the United States and Europe.
3. Additionally, comments on how the King James Version equivalents such as the Louis Segond Version, the Reina Valera Version, the Almeida Version, or the Statevertaling Version impacted these non-English diasporas will be left to a larger work.

References

Bailey, Randall C. 1998. "The Danger of Ignoring One's Own Cultural Bias in Interpreting the Text." In *The Postcolonial Bible*, ed. R. S. Sugirtharajah. Sheffield: Sheffield Academic.

Bediako, Kwame. 1995. *Christianity in Africa: The Renewal of a Non-Western Religion*. Maryknoll, N.Y.: Orbis.

Bennett, Robert A. 1989. "Black Experience and the Bible." In *African American Religious Studies: An*

Interdisciplinary Anthology, ed. Gayraud S. Wilmore. Durham, N.C.: Duke University Press.

Bisnauth, Dale. 1989. *History of Religions in the Caribbean.* Kingston, Jamaica: Kingston.

Chevannes, B. 1994. *Rastafari: Roots and Ideology.* New York: Syracuse University Press.

———. 1998. *Rastafari and Other African-Caribbean Worldviews.* New Brunswick, N.J.: Rutgers University Press.

———. 2006. *Betwixt and Between: Explorations in an African-Caribbean Mindscape.* Kingston, Jamaica: Ian Randle.

Copher, Charles B. 1989. "Three Thousand Years of Biblical Interpretation with Reference to Black People." In *African American Religious Studies: An Interdisciplinary Anthology*, ed. Gayraud S. Wilmore. Durham, N.C.: Duke University Press.

———. 1991. "The Black Presence in the Old Testament." In *Stony the Road We Trod: African American Biblical Interpretation*, ed. Cain Hope Felder. Minneapolis: Fortress Press.

Drew, Benjamin. 1968. *The Refugee: Or the Narratives of Fugitive Slaves in Canada.* New York: Negro University Press.

Erskine, N. L. 2007. *From Garvey to Marley: Rastafari Theology.* Gainesville, Fla.: University Press of Florida.

Felder, Cain Hope. 1989. "The Bible, Recontextualization and the Black Religious Experience." In *African American Religious Studies: An Interdisciplinary Anthology*, ed. Gayraud S. Wilmore. Durham, N.C.: Duke University Press.

Glazier, Stephen. 1983. *Marchin' the Pilgrims Home: Leadership and Decision Making in an Afro-Caribbean Faith.* Westport, Conn: Greenwood.

Goddian Religion Handbook. 1977. Nigeria, Lagos: n.p.

Grundlingh, Albert, and Hilary Sapire. 1989. "From Feverish Festival to Repetitive Ritual: The Changing Fortunes of Great Trek Mythology in an Industrializing South Africa, 1938–1988." *South African Historical Journal* 21:19–37.

Noss, P. "Traditions of Scripture Translation: A Pan-African Overview." 2004. In *Bible Translation and African Languages*, ed. Gosnell Yorke and P. Renju. Nairobi, Kenya: Acton: 7–24.

Onunwa, Udobata R. 1989. "Goddianism: A Resurgence of an Old Cult in Christian Garb." *Africa Theological Journal* 18 (2): 116–25.

Peebles, J. W. 1983. "Preface." In *The Original African Heritage Study Bible (King James Version)*, ed. Cain H. Felder. Nashville: James C. Winston.

Pobee, John S. 1979. *Toward an African Theology.* Nashville: Abingdon.

Segal, R. 1995. *The Black Diaspora.* London: Faber & Faber.

Turner, Philip. 1971. "The Wisdom of Our Fathers and the Gospel of Christ: Some Notes on Christian Adaptation in Africa." *Journal of Religion in Africa* 4 (1): 45–68.

Ukpong, Justin S. 2000. "Developments in Biblical Interpretation in Africa: Historical and Hermeneutical Directions." *Journal of Theology for Southern Africa* 108 (N): 3–18.

Washington, James, ed. 1986. *A Testament of Hope: The Essential Writings and Speeches of Martin Luther King, Jr.* San Francisco: Harper SanFrancisco.

Weems, Renita J. 1991. "African American Women and the Bible." In *Stony the Road We Trod: African American Biblical Interpretation*, ed. Cain Hope Felder. Minneapolis: Fortress Press.

Wimbush, Vincent. 1989. "Biblical Historical Study as Liberation: Toward an Afro-Christian Hermeneutic." In *African American Religious Studies: An Interdisciplinary Anthology*, ed. Gayraud S. Wilmore. Durham, N.C.: Duke University Press.

———, ed. 2000. *African Americans and the Bible: Sacred Texts and Social Textures.* New York: Continuum.

Yorke, Gosnell. 2001. "The Bible and the Black Diaspora: Links with African Christianity." In *The Bible in Africa: Transactions, Trajectories and Trends*, ed. Gerald West and Musa Dube. Boston: Brill Academic.

———. 2004. "Bible Translation in Anglophone Africa and Her Diaspora: A Postcolonialist Agenda." *Black Theology: An International Journal* (formerly Black Theology in Britain: A Journal in Contextual Praxis) 2 (2): 153–66.

READING *the* HEBREW BIBLE RESPONSIBLY

Wil Gafney

THE ISSUE OF READING the Hebrew Bible responsibly is on one level an issue for all readers; however, this article will address responsible Christian readings of the scriptures of Israel. Using the categories of race/ethnicity, gender, and religious identity as examples, it will briefly examine historic Western Christian exegeses justifying slavery, subordination of women, anti-Judaism, and anti-Semitism. The article will also suggest appropriate readings of relevant texts in those categories.

While many Christians encounter the scriptures of Israel as the "Old Testament," these texts are more than a prologue to the Christian New Testament. They are an independent body of literature, a collection of individual works with their own macronarratives and micronarratives, completely independent of the Christian New Testament. A responsible engagement with the scriptures of Israel begins by recognizing and respecting their independence and cohesiveness.

WHAT'S IN A NAME?

There is power in naming. Naming is the invocation of language to define. There is power in language. Language is regularly a colonizing agent, a tool of subjugation. In the African Diaspora, dominant culture names historically were imposed on subjugated peoples, cultures, and texts. These colonizing naming practices continue throughout the Diaspora, accompanied by regular acts of resistance. The names we construct for religious literature, characters, and the divine are frequently definitive, however inadequate. Responsible reading means pausing before we write or speak on what we have read to reflect on the implications of the language we will use before we use it.

THE SCRIPTURES OF ISRAEL

What do we call this literature and why? I use the term *scriptures of Israel*. Scriptures are written sacred texts in any religious tradition—for example, the Qur'an, Bible, Upanishads, Bhagavad-Gita, I Ching, and Sutras. *Scriptures of Israel* is a term that is independent of the Jewish and Christian traditions, which are subsequent to the text itself. It includes each canonical configuration validated in ancient Israel, whether in Hebrew or Greek, therefore including the Deuterocanon (or Apocrypha). It also includes the Aramaic Targumim and Peshitta. *Bible* is a broad term that refers to the written sacred texts (scriptures) of Jewish or Christian traditions in a number of canonical formulations in both tradition streams. For example, the Samaritan Jewish "Bible" would consist only of the Torah; nothing else is canonical in that tradition of Judaism.

The title "Old Testament" presupposes not only a Christian framework but regularly a supercessionist one in which the "old" is inferior to or at least replaced by the "new." This nomenclature also presupposes the canonicity of the Old and New Testaments together, with or without the Deuterocanon. The linguistic designation "Hebrew Bible" presupposes a framework in which the text is independent of subsequent texts and can reflect either a cultural/literary context or a Jewish religious context. This term also presupposes a normative Hebrew canon, generally based on the Masoretic Text (MT), excluding not only the New Testament but also the Greek Jewish writings that form the majority of the Deuterocanon and, regularly, the Greek version of the Hebrew scriptures, the Septuagint (LXX). The acronym "Tanakh" (TaNaKh = Torah, Nevi'im, Kethuvim) is synonymous with "Hebrew Bible."

The "Christian Scriptures" cover all of the literature that Christians deem canonical. Great variety, of course, exists among the Christian canons. The sixty-six-book canon, accepted by most Protestant communions, is the most narrow collection of Christian scripture. The majority of Christians (represented by the Roman Catholic and Anglican communions) recognize a seventy-three-book canon that includes expanded versions of Daniel and Esther and lectionary readings from Ecclesiasticus (also known as the Wisdom of Jesus Ben Sirach). The canon of the Greek Orthodox Church is larger, and the canon of the Slavonic Orthodox Church is larger yet. The most expansive is that of the Ethiopian Orthodox Church, which has never published a canon list or even a Bible but whose liturgies include readings from Enoch and Jubilees.

There are also Aramaic scriptures, canonical to Christians and Jews. The Targumim—translations of the Hebrew Bible into Aramaic, with commentary—dates from the time of Ezra. The Peshitta, the Aramaic Bible containing Old and New Testaments, is the canon of the Syrian Orthodox Church. In this tradition, authoritative manuscripts for the New Testament are in the Syriac dialect of Aramaic, not Greek, which are believed to be corrupt translations. The Greek scriptures are largely Christian scriptures. Historically, Jewish readers abandoned the Septuagint to Christian readers after the third century C.E., with a few contemporary scholarly exceptions. The Greek New Testament, with or without the Septuagint, is a Christian text.

The scriptures of Israel then are all of the texts deemed canonical at any time in ancient Israel, including those preserved in the MT, the LXX, the Samaritan Pentateuch (SP), biblical scrolls from Qumran (Q), the Aramaic Targumim (T), and the Syriac Peshitta (P). Responsible exegesis of the scriptures of Israel requires recognizing their plurality, particularly in the African Diaspora, where there is no one, singular canon of scripture.

THE DIVINE NAME

Let me begin by telling you a story: Once upon a time, a man encountered a burning bush ablaze with fire that did not consume the bush. Hearing his own name called not once but twice, the man entered into conversation with the Voice coming from the bush. When asked for a name, the Voice-in-the-Bush said, "I AM/WILL BE WHO I AM/WILL BE." When he came down from the mountain, naming the Voice-in-the-Bush, the man said, "He said his name is the LORD."

The man, wrestling with the infinite mystery hidden and revealed in a name that was a statement of ontological being, and with his own cultural and social limitations, did not repeat the name given by the Voice-in-the-Bush, "I AM." In "I AM," there is neither specification of gender nor sexuality, orientation, color, nationality, ethnicity, ability, disability, age, or youth. The man shifted the divine name from first to third person, introducing gender, which was not present in the original declaration. The man substituted the human male elite title "lord" for "I AM" and added hierarchy to the divine name. The man is, of course, Moshe, Moses; the story is that of the burning bush and God's disclosure of the most holy name in Exodus 3.

The Hebrew equivalent of the letters YHWH, the Tetragrammaton, represents the most holy name of God in the Hebrew scriptures. The divine name is never spelled out in the text and has no certain pronunciation or exact translation. (It is most probably related to the Hebrew and Aramaic verbs for being—that is, the underpinning of the burning bush naming, "I AM"—but is not an exact match for either language.) Due to its holiness, the divine name was traditionally replaced with a plural possessive common title for male human dignitaries, "adonai," "lord." In the Hebrew text, the letters YHWH are pointed with the vowel-signs that indicate the appropriate substitution. Attempts to forcibly combine the consonantal letters and vowels have produced a number of bastardizations of the divine name.

Another, more recent tradition is the capitalization of "Lord" (using large and small capital letters) when translating God's most holy name to distinguish it from other "lords" in the Scriptures. Moshe, Moses, is credited with initiating the tradition of referring to the I AM as "the LORD." And now, the signifier, "the LORD," has become the signified, "YHWH": "God-Whose-Name-Is-Too-Holy-To-Be-Pronounced," "God-Who-Simply-Is," "God-Without-Gender-or-Hierarchy."

If the divine name is never spelled out in the Hebrew scriptures, why are there scholarly texts with a name fully spelled out? First, it should be noted that the name is never spelled out in Jewish texts or pronounced in Jewish community. In fact, the practice of spelling out and pronouncing a name is entirely gentilic and Christian, traceable to the historical-critical movement in biblical studies in nineteenth-century Western Europe and perpetuated by their ideological descendants. Second, it should be noted that the full spelling and articulation are entirely speculative, drawn from informed scholarly speculation but speculative nonetheless.

The reception of the scriptures of Israel into the Christian canon was and is marked by usurpation, colonization, anti-Judaism, and anti-Semitism. Specifically, in the West and in cultures colonized by the West, the scriptures of Israel have regularly been mediated through gentile culture and languages, particularly German, which is especially onerous in a post-Holocaust world. Let me conclude this section with a popular American (U.S.) aphorism: "What would Jesus do?" What did Yeshua, Jesus, say with reference to the divine name? The Gospel of John relates a number of "I am" sayings, but did he say the divine "I AM"? Most likely he spoke originally in Aramaic as preserved in the Peshitta; his words have also been preserved in Greek. In neither Greek nor Aramaic—nor in biblical Hebrew, for that matter—is "I am" directly equivalent to the divine name. For example, in the Peshitta, "I am the bread of life" in John 3:28 is literally "I, I, the bread of life," lacking the verb. In the Greek New Testament, "I am the bread of life" uses only part of the divine self-disclosure of Exod. 3:14 in the LXX, "I am the one who is"; there is no Greek equivalent for the Tetragrammaton.

Readers of the scriptures of Israel who identify Yeshua, Jesus of Nazareth, as the Son of God and/or as God Godself may want to frame their naming of God as *imitatio Christi*. Yeshua, Jesus, never pronounced the divine name. Responsible exegesis of the scriptures of Israel requires respecting the text itself, the traditions preserved in the text, and the God of the text.

BIBLICAL NAMES

Many students of the biblical languages are shocked to find that the names of biblical characters with which they are most familiar are not the characters' names at all. English readers of the Bible, in particular, are surprised to find that names they have cherished and after which they have named their children have been translated through a number of languages, including Latin, German, and occasionally Arabic, sometimes randomly, and are frequently only slightly recognizable.

Here are a few examples. The prophet Isaiah is originally "Yeshayahu" in Hebrew, "Isaiae" in Latin, and "Jesaja" in German. The prophet Jeremiah is originally "Yirmeyahu" in Hebrew, "Hieremiae" in Latin, and "Jeremias" in German. Note that the English "Isaiah" is derived from Latin, while the English "Jeremiah" is derived from German, yet both begin with a "Y" in Hebrew. The English "Solomon" is more closely related to the Arabic "Suleiman" than to the Hebrew "Shlomo." When biblical translators translate the names of biblical characters into their own languages, they are subjugating and colonizing the scriptures, their language, and their culture. The translator substitutes his language and culture and re-creates the identity of the biblical characters in his own image. In the African Diaspora, the work of biblical translation has largely been done by white men who not only translate the text in their own image but also then impose their Anglo-Germanic name-calling on subject African peoples.

The original Hebrew idiom of the text is regularly suppressed in gentilic translations of the scriptures of Israel and in their Christian trajectory. It has long been the anti-Semitic and anti-Judaistic practice of translators to Europeanize the names of New Testament characters, eradicating the Semitic forms preserved in the Greek and Aramaic texts of the New Testament. This is particularly striking when the names of those characters are preserved in Semitic form in the Hebrew scriptures. For example, the Hebrew "Yaakov" and the Greek "Iakob" are translated "Jacob" in the Torah and "James" in the Epistles, in the same way "Miryam" becomes "Mary." Nor are place names immune to anti-Semitic and anti-Judaistic linguistic colonization. For example, "K'far Nachum," the "Town of Nahum," is nearly unrecognizable as "Capernaum." What's in a name? Liberation or oppression. Responsible exegesis of the scriptures of Israel requires respect for and fidelity toward the Semitic languages, peoples, and cultures of the scriptures of Israel. This means putting an end to the mediation of the scriptures through gentilic languages, especially German, in this post-Holocaust world.

MULTICULTURAL ISRAEL

Responsible reading of the scriptures of Israel also calls for revisiting the ways in which racial constructs are imposed on the text. Israelite identity is, like all identities, a constructed identity; in its earliest formulation, it is a cultural rather than a biological identity. Yaakov the Heel-Grabbing-Sneak, who becomes Israel the God-Wrestler, is the grandson of Abraham the Chaldean in Gen. 11:28. His Chaldean kinfolk would eventually evolve into the Babylonian Empire that decimated his descendants—so the Israelites and Babylonians shared biology but not culture. The tribes of Ephraim and Manasseh shared African maternity because of Joseph's marriage to Asenat, the Egyptian in Gen. 41:45. Even Moshe, Moses, the Torah-Vessel, married non-Israelite women—Zipporah the Midianite in Exod. 2:21 and an unnamed Nubian woman in Num. 12:1—meaning that some of the priestly community had multicultural heritage. A non-Israelite, mixed multitude accompanied Israel when they departed Egypt in Exod. 12:38 and became absorbed into the community. In 2 Sam. 22:51, David—called "meshiach," or "messiah" in Hebrew, and "christos," or "christ" in Greek (although generally translated "anointed" in English)—was the grandson of a Moabite woman (Ruth 4:22).

The multicultural nature of Israel is especially important to read over and against racialized constructions of Israel as ethnically and racially monolithic, and their construction as "white" in the nineteenth and twentieth centuries. The supposed whiteness of biblical Israel has been used to sanctify colonization of black, brown, and beige peoples around the globe, invoking the ahistorical "Conquest of Canaan" as paradigmatic.

SLAVERY AND COLONIZATION

It is impossible to overstate the power of Noah's cursing narrative in Gen. 9:29ff—misnamed "the Curse of Ham" in post-Enlightenment exegesis—in the African Diaspora. The tortuous "reasoning" was that since Ham was the ancestor of African peoples including Egypt and Nubia, the cursing of his son, Canaan, meant that the enslavement of Africans was the will of God illustrated by this biblical narrative. Providing specious support, Ham's name was interpreted as "hot," representing the African continent, thereby including all African peoples in the misnamed "Curse of Ham" and failing to take into account that Ham also means "father-in-law" in Gen. 38:13 and 35.

The Israelite system of debt-slavery is distorted and exploited to justify slavery of African peoples

and their forced dispersion as a "biblical" construction. However, there the North Atlantic slave trade and ensuing slavocracy were anything but Torah observant. For example:

1. Contrary to Exod. 20:10, African slaves regularly worked on the Sabbath.
2. Contrary to Exod. 21:2, African slaves did not have the option of being freed every seven years.
3. Contrary to Exod. 21:16, slave traffickers were not put to death for kidnapping persons in order to sell those persons.
4. Contrary to Exod. 21:20, slave owners who killed their slaves were not punished.
5. Contrary to Exod. 21:26, African slaves who were maimed by their owners were not set free.
6. Contrary to Deut. 15:13, freed African slaves did not receive liberally from their previous owner's livestock and other income that they helped produce prior to being freed (when and if they were freed at all).
7. Contrary to Deut. 21:13, captured African women were not treated as wives and were sold as slaves after having sexual relations with their abductors.

Responsible exegesis of the scriptures of Israel requires abandoning racialized constructions of the ancient Israelites and naming those contexts in which contemporary racial constructions have been imposed on the text.

DIVINE AND HUMAN GENDER

Biblical Hebrew is a gendered language, inviting reflection on understandings of human and divine gender. Virtually all biblical names for God are grammatically masculine, yet the spirit of God is grammatically feminine, recalling that human

Wil Gafney

beings, created in the divine image, are male and female. In Gen. 1:1-2, two verbs are used for God: in verse 1, "he, God created," and in verse 2, "the Spirit of God, She was brooding." The language of human gender in Gen. 1:27 is less egalitarian. The word for female, *neqevah*, is derived from a term meaning "pierced" or "penetrated"; the word for male, *zakar*, is derived from a term for memory. By etymology, women are "fill-able" while men are "memorable." This is particularly ironic since God does not in the scriptures of Israel possess the organ of memory, the penis, through which men's memory is perpetuated through descendants.

The only reproductive organ that God possesses in the text is a womb (Job 38:29). God's womb is also present in the text through the tender love and nurture that emanates from the divine womb. The verb *r-ch-m*, unfortunately regularly translated "compassion," is the emotion that emanates from the *recham*, or womb. This is the love that God has for God's people throughout the scriptures of Israel:

> Hos. 1:6-7: Gomer conceived again and gave birth to a daughter. Then YHWH said to Hosea, "Name her No Mother-Love, for I will no longer have mother-love for the house of Israel or forgive them. But I will mother-love the house of Judah, and I will save them by YHWH their God; I will not save them by bow, or by sword, or by war, or by horses, or by horsemen."

It is certainly the case that the scriptures of Israel are androcentric, contain patriarchal jurisprudence (e.g., Deut. 22:13-30) and discourse (e.g., Genesis 16 and 21), and narratives detailing violence against women (e.g., Judg. 20:20ff), sanctioned by God (e.g., Num. 311:15ff), instructed by God (e.g., Deut. 21:10ff), and occasionally carried out by God (e.g., Ezekiel 16 and 23). It is also the case that women's voices are heard in the scriptures of Israel; that there are narratives in which women have power (e.g., 2 Kings 11), agency (e.g., Genesis 24), and authority (e.g., Judges 4 and 5); and that there is a recognition in the text that ancient Israelite society is dependent on the labor and contribution of women and men (e.g., Lev. 27:1-7).

As it pertains to the analysis of gender constructions and gender roles in the scriptures of Israel, responsible exegesis requires intentionality in text selection, translation, and interpretation. Those interpretive communities and individuals who use biblical portrayals of gender roles to construct contemporary gender roles must and do choose among liberative, egalitarian, and oppressive paradigms.

References

Abbey, Tetteki Rose. 2001. "Rediscovering Ataa Naa Nyonmo—The Father Mother God." In *Talitha Cum! Theologies of African Women*, ed. Nyamnbura Njoroge and Musa W. Dube. Pietermaritzburg, South Africa: Cluster.

Anderson, Cheryl. 2004. *Women, Ideology, and Violence: Critical Theory and the Construction of Gender in the Book of the Covenant and the Deuteronomic Law*. New York: T. & T. Clark.

Bailey, Randall, and Tina Pippin. 1996. *Race, Class and Politics of Biblical Translation. Semeia* 76. Atlanta: Society of Biblical Literature.

Castelli, Elizabeth. 1993. "*Les Belles Infideles*: Fidelity or Feminism? The Meaning of Feminist Biblical Translation." In *Searching the Scriptures: A Feminist Introduction*, vol. 1, ed. Elizabeth Schüssler Fiorenza. New York: Crossroad.

Dube, Musa W. 2000. *Postcolonial Feminist Interpretation of the Bible*. St. Louis: Chalice.

———. 2006. *Toward Postcolonial Feminist Translations of the Bible*. Unpublished Paper.

Gafney, Wilda C. M. (forthcoming) "Hearing the Word—Translation Matters: A Fem/Womanist Exploration of Translation Theory and Practice for Proclamation in Worship." In *Angles of Vision, Biblical Studies and the Life of the Mind, Culture, and*

Spirit: Essays in Honor of Bruce M. Metzger, ed. J. Harold Ellers.

———. (forthcoming) "Mother Knows Best: Messianic Surrogacy and Sexploitation in Ruth." In *Mother Goose, Mother Jones, Mommy Dearest: Mother/Daughter, Mother/Son Relationships in the Bible*, ed. Cheryl A. Kirk-Duggan and Tina Pippin. *Semeia Studies*.

———. 2006. "Study in Genesis." In *Pastor's Bible Study Volume III*. Nashville: Abingdon.

Patte, Daniel et al., eds. 2004. *Global Bible Commentary*. Nashville: Abingdon.

Pippin, Tina. 1999. "Translation Happens: A Feminist Perspective on Translation Theories." In *Escaping Eden: New Feminist Perspective on the Bible*. New York: New York University Press.

Plaskow, Judith. 1993. "Anti-Judaism in Feminist Christian Interpretation." In *Searching the Scriptures: A Feminist Introduction*, vol. 1, ed. Elizabeth Schüssler Fiorenza. New York: Crossroad.

Pui-Lan, Kwok. 1993. "Racism and Ethnocentrism in Feminist Biblical Interpretation." In *Searching the Scriptures: A Feminist Introduction*, vol. 1, ed. Elizabeth Schüssler Fiorenza. New York: Crossroad.

Scholz, Susanne. 2003. *Biblical Studies Alternatively: An Introductory Reader*. Upper Saddle River, N.J.: Prentice Hall.

Segovia, Fernando F., and Mary Ann Tolbert. 1995. *Reading from this Place: Social Location and Biblical Interpretation in the United States*. Minneapolis: Fortress Press.

Stein, David et al., eds. 2006. *The Contemporary Torah: A Gender-Sensitive Adaptation of the JPS Translation*. Philadelphia: Jewish Publication Society.

Trible, Phyllis. 1984. *Texts of Terror: Literary-Feminist Readings of Biblical Narratives*. Philadelphia: Fortress Press.

Van Wijk-Bos, Johanna W. H. 2005. *Making Wise the Simple: The Torah in Christian Faith and Practice*. Grand Rapids, Mich.: Eerdmans.

———. 2000. "Writing on the Water: The Ineffable Name of God." In *Jews, Christians and the Theology of the Hebrew Scriptures*, ed. Alice Bellis. Atlanta: Society of Biblical Literature.

Weems, Renita. 1995. *Battered Love: Marriage, Sex, and Violence in the Hebrew Prophets*. Minneapolis: Fortress Press.

Yorke, Gosnell L.O.R. 2004. *Bible Translation and African Languages*. Nairobi: Acton.

———. "Bible Translation in Anglophone Africa and Her Diaspora: A Postcolonialist Agenda." In *Black Theology: An International Journal* 2, no. 2 (July 2004): 153–66.

The HEBREW BIBLE *in* AFRICANA ART, MUSIC, *and* POPULAR CULTURE

Kimberly N. Ruffin

THE WORLD'S BEST-SELLING BOOK has a distinct presence in artistic traditions spanning the centuries and geographies of the Africana world. High rates of biblical literacy in Africa and its Diaspora make the Bible a common popular culture reference that affirms the artistic abilities of both everyday people and professional artists. Accompanying people ranging from the "Lost Boys of Sudan" during their long search for safety to Kenya's Nobel Prize winner Wangari Maathai as she advocates for environmentalism, the Bible has been a dynamic source of religious, social, and political comfort and controversy. The Bible permeates life in the Africana world so deeply that even nonreligious artists engage its contents. The Hebrew Bible, in particular, has been a source of inspiration and elucidation for people across faiths both before and after European colonization and the transatlantic slave

trade. Interpretive stances from the fundamentalist to the iconoclastic illustrate that the Bible saturates the religious, political, spiritual, and cultural lives of people of African descent. As part of the grand march of history, these biblical readings have never been static, but Africana art, music, and popular culture provide a window into distinct patterns in this interpretive panoply.

During and after the period of the transatlantic slave trade, passages of Hebrew scriptures were used as rhetorical support for racialized slavery. Biblical interpretations that supported racialized slavery fueled the arts and mass media of world cultures that demonized "blackness" and promulgated negative images of Africanity. These long-standing global traditions of disparaging Africans and African cultures are a backdrop for understanding aspects of Africana Hebrew Bible interpretation in the verbal and visual arts. Artists who seek to counter this discourse respond with force to racist hermeneutics by using the Hebrew Bible to celebrate Africans as important contributors to not only contemporary life but also biblical antiquity. In centuries past, art in this vein could be found in live speech (whether conveyed in song, sermon, or oratorical events) and the printed word, the predominant vehicles for popular culture.

Both of these methods were crucial in the circulation of the pamphlet *Appeal, in Four Articles; Together with a Preamble, to the Colored Citizens of the World, but in Particular, and Very Expressly, to Those of the United States of America*, written by David Walker in 1829. The destitute conditions of the enslaved moved David Walker (son of a free Black woman and an enslaved man) to circulate the *Appeal* with the help of Black and White mariners. Understanding that many of the enslaved suffered from imposed illiteracy, Walker encouraged literate Blacks to share its contents orally with those who could not read. He addresses the psychological damage of racialized slavery by interpreting the Hebrew Bible in ways that highlight the presence of Africa in biblical antiquity. The explicit statement of geographic locales within Africa in the Hebrew Bible, such as Ps. 68:31, bolstered the cause of Africana abolitionists, who knew that pinpointing Africa as a positive part of biblical antiquity eroded the power of racialized slavery.

Walker raises awareness about the severity of racialized slavery by contrasting American and Egyptian enslavement. First, to historicize the powerlessness people of African descent faced in America, he stresses that Egyptians were African and that they had the power to enslave Israelites. Although this is an abolitionist text, it makes the argument that African people were in positions of power in the Hebrew Bible to empower enslaved Africans in Walker's day to imagine themselves beyond bondage. In addition, it distinguishes the type of enslavement in Egypt as being less harsh than American slavery because it did not rely on the dehumanization of Israelites. His prime example is

that Moses was raised by Pharaoh's daughter and could have "been seated on the throne of Egypt." He later debunks arguments supporting American slavery by addressing passages of the Hebrew Bible pertaining to Cain and Ham. He champions the "sons of Ham" as incredible contributors to the "arts and sciences," in contrast to interpretations that read Ham's offspring as condemned to slavery. He refutes boldly the assertion that people of African descent are the "seed of Cain" suffering from the curse of "a dark stain." Later, he warns against those who doubt slavery will come to an end through references to Noah, Lot, and Moses as instances in which God works on behalf of the righteous. This address to the "Colored Citizens of the World" represents the strain of Hebrew biblical interpretation that unites verbal artistry with political purposes to dismantle racist discourse and to uplift a racialized human group.

The same oral and written transmission of Hebrew Bible interpretation that David Walker relied on has been a cornerstone of Africana religious ceremony as well. Although sanctions against acquiring scribal literacy during enslavement contributed to the frequency of the spoken transmission of the biblical text, they do not account fully for the vibrant oral/aural traditions within Africana communities. After the transatlantic slave trade, African rhetorical and musical traditions were transformed into the languages of "New World" cultures. These artistic styles, along with those that persisted on the African continent, have informed the transmission of the Hebrew Bible in religious contexts. An award-winning and best-selling CD recording of both Hebrew and Christian scriptures, *The Bible Experience*, capitalizes on the appreciation of oral expertise and preferences to connect to the Bible's word aurally. Music is combined with the dramatic reading of the Hebrew Bible by African American clergy, actors, singers, and rappers, including Forest Whitaker, Angela Basset, LL Cool J, and Cicely Tyson. The creative presentation of biblical scripture through African American artists connects audiences to the material in a manner that is culture affirming and scripturally/religiously posi-tive. Ancient illustrated Ethiopian Bibles combine biblical scripture with visual imagery and accom-plish this aim as well. These are artistic traditions in which the actual presentation of the biblical text is to be artful and reflective of Africana people and imagery.

One artistic preference that informs the use of the Hebrew Bible in many Africana liturgical contexts is the combination of the exposition of predetermined scripture with the seemingly spon-taneous, "spirit-inspired" inclusion of scripture from anywhere in the Hebrew or Christian texts. This often results in multiple references to Hebrew and Christian texts within a single artistic product (such as a sermon or a song). It also points to the fact that part of the worldwide acclaim for Africana sermonic traditions has been built on a textual mastery demonstrated through cross-references to multiple texts. The role of the artist, usually a cler-gyperson, in this case is to identify biblical passages that are especially relevant to unique circumstances of the gathering of worshipers. Weekly church services highlight this dynamic tradition; the inter-national circulation of the work of "mega-church" ministers with this skill (such as Bishop T. D. Jakes) gives Africana biblical interpretation a presence in all forms of popular culture media (television, print, Internet, podcast, CD, DVD, audiocassette tape, and film).

Characterizations of Africana churches as places of "syncretic" worship mean that both Afri-can and non-African (usually European) worship styles influence the use of texts from the Hebrew Bible, often resulting in worship styles that encour-age spontaneous, participatory, and kinesthetically and orally expressive worship. These traditions can be experienced throughout the Diaspora and on the African continent, especially in African Pentecostal-ist "spirit churches." Dr. Martin Luther King Jr.'s "I've Been to the Mountaintop" speech, in which he heralds the inevitable triumph of the Civil Rights Movement through the story of the Exodus narrative, demonstrates the lasting impact these

sermonic traditions have had in the world at large.

James Weldon Johnson's 1927 tribute to the "old-time Negro preacher" in *God's Trombones*, a collection of sermon-inspired poems, sought to transform his childhood memories of the oral performance of sermonic skill into print. Inter-pretations of Hebrew biblical passages in the text reveal the extent to which sermons were aimed at addressing both religious and cultural concerns specific to Africana people. Johnson dramatizes the opening books of Genesis in "The Creation," giving a highly personified image of God that concludes with a simile comparing God's love to that of a Black mother for her child. Harlem Renaissance visual artist Aaron Douglass's illustrations for the book have been noted for their affirmation of Black people and culture. Johnson's re-creation of the Moses narrative in "Let My People Go" is typical of Africana depictions that emphasize Moses as a liberator as opposed to traditions that define his central importance as a law-giver.

Throughout the poems, Johnson is mindful of linguistic elements that give the sermonic traditions of the Africana church great accessibility. While he is insistent that he wants to avoid a demeaning depiction of dialect, he incorporates a vernacular style that can be read in "Noah Built the Ark": "Sinners came a-running down to the ark / Sinners came a-swimming all round the ark . . . But Noah'd done barred the door" (36). *The Bible Experience*, sermonic traditions, and *God's Trombones* represent an Africana tradition of Hebrew biblical interpreta-tion that stresses verbal and sonic artfulness, acces-sibility, and cultural and temporal relevancy.

Contemporary Africana authors extend the scope of religious interpretation by using the Hebrew Bible as a springboard to address the psychological and spiritual needs of Africana people. Religious self-help literature, such as P. K. McCary's *Black Bible Chronicles from Genesis to the Promised Land: A Survival Manual for the Streets* (1993), modernizes persons and principles from the Hebrew Bible to address the circumstances of contemporary, urbanized Africana people. This self-help genre oftentimes targets specific groups, as can be read in *Be Restored! God's Power for African American Women* (2006), by Debra Berry, which uses the book of Nehemiah as the focus for spiritual maturation, or in the edited collections *From One Brother to Another: Voices of African-American Men* (volumes 1 and 2, 1996, 2008), which represent several interpretations of the Hebrew Bible as part of advice giving. This genre has a scholarly punctuation in *Grant Me Justice! HIV/AIDS and Gender Readings of the Bible*, edited by Musa W. Dube and Musimbi Kanyoro; here, readings of Job, Ezekiel, Genesis, and the Prophets by Africana scholars are brought to bear on a public health emergency. In both the scholarly and mainstream publications, written art serves a utilitarian purpose.

The Hebrew Bible references in African American spirituals incorporate advice giving through typology about heroic people, such as Job, Abraham, Jacob, Joshua, and David. The interpretative premise here is that these biblical heroes had qualities that were instructive for postbiblical people; stories of biblical triumph signified that God rewarded steadfastness and righteousness. For example, the spiritual "Didn't My Lord Deliver Daniel?" makes the following argument: "He delivered Daniel from de lion's den, Jonah f'om the belly of de whale, An' de Hebrew chillum from de fiery furnace, An' why not every man." Initially created and transmitted orally in enslaved communities, spirituals were eventually put into print by the founders of the Fisk University Jubilee Singers, George White and Ella Shephard. The Jubilee Singers raised funds for Fisk University with tours in the United States and Europe. Their reception as "Black Victorians" made great strides in counteracting negative images of African Americans, as the derogatory art form of minstrelsy emerged around the same time as spirituals. Both art forms signaled the growth of "popular culture" in America, which would surpass local and regional art forms in prominence and would unite Americans with the opportunity to experience common artistic products. Contemporary Gospel songs, such as "3 Hebrew Boys," continue this tradition of celebrating the heroes of Hebrew scripture begun in the music of enslaved people.

Spirituals also included "signal-songs" that identified opportunities for escape from bondage via the help of people collaborating in networks such as the Underground Railroad. One such signal-song, "Go Down Moses," makes reference to who is perhaps the Hebrew Bible figure with the most eminence in Africana culture. The large-scale experience of enslavement and the continued need for libratory discourse contribute to this widespread reference in religious, political, and extra-religious domains. Harriet Tubman was renowned as the "Moses of her people" because of her work as a "conductor" on the Underground Railroad. Reggae music legend Bob Marley's musical songbook is filled with intertwined references to both Hebrew and Christian texts, characteristic of Rastafarian hermeneutics. However, his song "Exodus" stresses the epic themes of collective struggle and emancipation by calling for another "Brother Moses" to help complete the aim of crossing the "Red Sea." R&B songster Isaac Hayes's album *Black Moses* includes a typological narrative written by Chester Higgins, who declares Hayes as a "soulful prophet" among the "Chosen People" who must fight the forces of "racial hatred and bigotry." Novelist Zora Neale Hurston's *Moses, Man of the Mountain* emphasizes the miraculous/mystic elements of the Exodus narrative as Hurston also identifies Moses as a figure in several world cultures. Infusing such biblical people as Joshua, Miriam, Aaron, and Zipporah with African American dialect, the novel addresses topics such as racial purity, leadership, war, and magic. The long-standing presence of Moses as a revered figure in Africana life created the context for then–U.S. senator (D-Illinois) Barack Obama's metaphorical proclamation of his peer group to be the "Joshua Generation," who needed to build on the gains made by the preceding "Moses Generation."

In the realm of visual art, Moses is just one of the many biblical personages who has served as inspiration. Cheick Oumar Sissoko sets his epic film *La Genèse* (1999) in Sissoko's birth country of Mali to tell the story of Jacob, Esau, and Joseph. Films such as this have been crucial in providing images of the people of biblical antiquity as people of African descent. Harriet Powers's "Bible Quilt," part of the Smithsonian's collections, is an early example of fabric art by African American women. Among the images in the quilt are Adam and Eve, Cain and Abel, and Jacob (who is also honored in the spiritual "We Are Climbing Jacob's Ladder"). In the twenty-first century, the museum exhibit "Threads of Faith: Recent Works from the Women of Color Quilters Network" cataloged contemporary examples of artists who choose to capture biblical images in fabric. Michael Davis is the creator of faith-based comic books that feature Black characters, such as members of the group "Genesis 5," "a band of teenage angels who battle dark forces while attending high school." Davis's work is published by Urban Ministries, Inc., a company that has been crucial in providing church literature, such as vacation Bible school materials, specifically targeted to people of African descent, featuring images of and addressing issues important to people of African descent. Yet these modern examples are not the only evidence of visual biblical interpretation. The rock-hewn churches of Lalibela, Ethiopia, are perhaps the earliest example. These religious castles have been recognized by UNESCO (the United Nations Educational, Scientific, and Cultural Organization) as a "World Culture" site. Elaborately carved, mammoth structures, the castles take inspiration from such biblical settings as the River of Jordan and the Mount of Olives.

Although artistic Africana biblical interpretation can be accurately characterized as largely celebratory of organized religion, there are notable contributions from artists who question the Bible's authority or who apply its contents outside religious contexts. One such example is John Edgar Wideman's novel *Two Cities*. In this work, the biblical book of Lamentations becomes the inspiration for the central female character, Kassima, to turn

her individual mourning into a communal dirge that helps cope with a devastated African American neighborhood. A childhood victim of classist discrimination in a Black church, Kassima boldly declares that the Bible is for everyone, even those outside organized religion. Musical artists such as Prince expand this application in songs that are undoubtedly secular and highly sensual but nevertheless inspired by imagery from biblical books such as Genesis ("And God Created Woman") and Song of Solomon ("When Doves Cry"). Bone Thugs in Harmony is just one example of hip-hop artists who make references to Hebrew scripture but who do not fall into the category of religious music. In fact, many such artists record music that would not be welcome in a church setting, yet their application of the texts reveals that the Bible's resonance in the Africana world goes beyond religious communities.

While she is appreciative of the sociopolitical power of the Black church, writer Alice Walker has forwarded an iconoclastic reading of Moses that focuses on actions she interprets as imperialistic and oppressive to women. Novels such as *The Color Purple* reflect pagan theological notions that counter traditions supported by the Hebrew Bible. Another iconoclastic look comes from the music of Me'Shell N'dege Ocello, whose songs (such as "Leviticus: Faggot" and "Deuteronomy: Niggerman") address how Hebrew Scripture has been interpreted in ways that oppress human groups. Honoreé Fanonne Jeffers offers a look into the lives of biblical women, including Sarai, Hagar, Lot's wife, and Lot's daughters, in the poetry of *Outlandish Blues*. Her sympathetic reflection on these women's perspectives is accentuated by African American vernacular speech patterns.

Africana people's relationship to the Hebrew Bible is multitextured and complex. They have been drawn to it for numerous reasons, and their artistic products reflect that their hermeneutical traditions have been infused with an in-depth knowledge of scripture and the desire for cultural syncretism. Although elements of these scriptures were used to oppress them, Africana people around the world have used the text's liberatory aspects to fuel their liberation. Anywhere in a range from iconoclastic to celebratory, the artistic interpretations of the Hebrew Bible in the Africana world strive to balance the contents of the ancient book with the demands and debates of the current day.

References

Berry, Debra. 2006. *Be Restored! God's Power for African American Women*. Birmingham, Ala.: New Hope.

The Bible Experience: Old Testament. 2007. Grand Rapids, Mich.: Zondervan ChurchSource.

Dube, Musa W., and Musimbi Kanyoro, eds. 2004. *Grant Me Justice! HIV/AIDS and Gender Readings of the Bible*. Maryknoll, N.Y.: Orbis.

Hayes, Isaac. 1971. *Black Moses*. Stax Records. (B000000ZMS).

Hurston, Zora Neale. 1991. *Moses, Man of the Mountain*. New York: Harper Perennial.

Jeffers, Honorée. 2003. *Outlandish Blues*. Middletown, Ct.: Wesleyan University Press.

Johnson, James Weldon. 1969. *The Books of American Negro Spirituals*. New York: Da Capo.

———. 1990. *God's Trombones: Seven Negro Sermons in Verse*. New York: Penguin.

Key, William, and Robert Johnson-Smith II, eds. 1996, 2008. *From One Brother to Another: Voices of African-American Men*. Vols. 1 and 2. Valley Forge, Pa.: Judson.

McCary, P. K. 1993. *Black Bible Chronicles, Book One: From Genesis to the Promised Land*. New York: African American Family.

NdegeOcello, Me'Shell. 1996. *Peace beyond Passion*. Mavrick. (B000002N2B)

Prince. *Purple Rain*. 1984. Warner Bros . (B000002L68).

Prince and the New Power Generation. 1992. *The Love Symbol Album*. Warner Bros. (B000008JLP).

Sissoko, Cheick Oumar. 1999. *La Genèse*. San Francisco: California Newsreel.

Walker, Alice. 1982. *The Color Purple*. New York: Pocket.

Walker, David. 1965. *Appeal, in Four Articles; Together with a Preamble, to the Colored Citizens of the World, but in Particular, and Very Expressly, to Those of the United States of America*. New York: Hill and Wang.

Wideman, John Edgar. 1998. *Two Cities*. Boston: Houghton Mifflin.

THE AFRICANA BIBLE

READING ISRAEL'S SCRIPTURES

FROM AFRICA AND THE AFRICAN DIASPORA

THE
HEBREW BIBLE
Torah

EARLY HEBREW POETRY *and* ANCIENT PRE-BIBLICAL SOURCES

Hugh R. Page Jr.

EVERYTHING HAS MEANING

As a child, I often wondered why my parents and grandparents were so attentive to the placement of photographs and knickknacks throughout the house. Wandering through the homes of my African American friends elsewhere in Baltimore, I noticed that their families were equally attentive to such things. Each picture and item seemed to have a history. The location of a framed portrait, a letter opener, or a bronzed shoe was anything but haphazard. Whether in the living room, dining room, or bedroom, on the fireplace mantle or a kitchen shelf, it became clear to me that certain apparently mundane places and items within a home were "special."

As a child, the word *axé*—a term used in the Afro-Brazilian tradition of Cadomblé for the power coursing through life—was not part of my everyday lexicon.[1] I knew nothing of Rudolf Otto's concept of the *numinous* (1958: 7) and nothing of the sacral nature of Black diasporan landscapes.[2] That visual representations and material possessions could be and in fact were imbued with power was not part of my basic understanding of how the world worked. In my youthful *naiveté*, I simply assumed a picture was a picture; bric-a-brac was bric-a-brac; pots and pans were pots and pans; diplomas were diplomas; and tables were tables. I had no idea that a table could be an altar; that a diploma could serve as a talisman; that pots and pans could be sacred vessels; that knickknacks could represent pieces of a fragmented and reconstituted identity; or that pictures could be icons through which communion with ancestors could be established. I knew nothing of the concept of Diaspora—either Jewish or African—or of the role that assemblages of artifacts might play in community formation and the constitution of the self among peoples dispersed from a homeland.

It wasn't until I began to learn more about ritual practices and the nature of the sacred within and outside of the Africana world that I gained a visceral understanding of what I had seen. The process of realization was gradual, informed by reading, talking with family members, and—of all things—poetic musing. The poem "Family Altar" represented my first theological exploration of this theme in print. Its opening quatrain conveys my thinking, at the time of its writing and now, that Africana assemblages have a transcendent character (Page 1997: 7).

> Black and white photos in bright silver frames
> Mantles and living room table displays
> Ancestral spirits from celluloid film
> Speak of your journey that we may be whole

Over the years, my awareness of the relationship between diaspora, identity, and collecting has been greatly enhanced through academic research[3] and exposure to explorations of these themes in cinema.[4]

PICKING UP AND ASSEMBLING THE PIECES

Opposing social forces have shaped the Africana ethos from the fifteenth century C.E. of the Common Era to the present. On the one hand, the Atlantic slave trade and European hegemony in Africa caused social disorientation and psychological fragmentation. On the other, the attempts by Africana peoples, on the continent and elsewhere, to fight against dehumanization, dismantle power structures built on racist ideologies, and ensure political independence have produced life ways that have served to counter the worldview and values dominant in the industrialized West. Moreover, they have promoted creative reconceptualizations

of basic ideas about community and personhood. It is through the radical act of "picking up pieces" and building assemblages—for example, "pieces" of ideas, memories, traditions, texts, peoples, and so on—that Africana worldviews are continually formed, occasionally modified, and at times refashioned. The requirements of survival before the abolition of the slave trade and after the collapse of Apartheid have forced the peoples of Africa and the African Diaspora to become collectors, curators, and interpreters of artifacts. This is the case whether such *realia* are indigenous or borrowed from the cultures in which Africana peoples live as sojourners.

The First Testament is one such entity. Some might argue that it is, strictly speaking, an Africana artifact—one that has been composed in two languages (Hebrew and Aramaic) that are part of the Afroasiatic language phylum. Others might suggest that it is perhaps better seen as a source "appropriated" by African and African Diasporan readers. Both perspectives have merit. The First Testament belongs to a vast body of Afroasiatic texts. Insofar as this is the case, it fits within a much larger domain of Africana literature. On the other hand, the First Testament is in fact an anthology of ancient Jewish texts with which Africana readers have long interacted, on the continent of Africa and in various locales where African peoples live in Diaspora. The Old Greek (or Septuagint), Coptic, Ethiopic, Nubian, and (quite possibly) some of the Old Latin translations are examples of such biblical interactions that took place in an African setting.[5] The Africana literature, art, music, and religious discourse that consciously interpret, respond to, and appropriate the First Testament are further examples.

Burton Visotzky offers a slightly different way of thinking about the issue of ownership, based in part on Vincent Wimbush's extension of Henry Lewis Gates's concept of "signifying." Visotzky makes a pivotal distinction between Jewish *midrash* and the concept of "signifying" as conceived by both Wimbush and Gates. He contends that Jewish *midrash* was done with a text over which the Jewish community claimed ownership, the Tanak (in other words, the Jewish canon consisting of Torah, Prophets, and Writings). By contrast, "signifying" has been done with a text that has been externally imposed on a community (2008: 252). Nonetheless, Visotzky suggests that Africana readers might construe Hebrew scriptures "through the lens of ownership, and not just through the hermeneutic of identification with the slave narratives while capitulating the canon to white hegemony" (2008: 253). He offers two Jewish approaches whereby Africana readers might reclaim the Tanak:

> The first . . . is to view the Tanakh as an African Document (African-Israelite/African-American). It is most certainly not a WASP (white) document. The second paradigm is that of Midrash and "signifying scriptures." (2008: 253)

Visotzky's approach has much to commend it. However, it is important to remember that opinion among Africana readers about the "ownership" of the First Testament is far from uniform. In fact, questions of spiritual, cultural, and human "property" in general have been sources of considerable debate and trauma within the Africana community. This is true whether the point of reference is the territorial boundaries of modern nation states, natural resources, religious traditions, ideas, or human bodies. Such concerns are intimately linked to larger issues such as empire building, colonial expansion, and political authority.

I choose to hold in abeyance the rather contentious issue of who ultimately "owns" the disparate elements with which Africana peoples have traditionally constituted themselves. The ancient and modern anthologies and translations of Israel's scriptures used in this endeavor have been and remain quite varied. Nonetheless, one could suggest that all are treated as part of that assemblage from which Africana ideas about the self, community, and the unseen world have been and continue to be

fashioned. These traditions are, without question, some of the more important *tesserae* in the Africana cultural mosaic. They are pieces about which vigorous debates as to ownership, usage, and value continue today. In this regard, they are not unlike the various poems, songs, sayings, and narratives brought together to form the Tanak and its first five books, the Torah/Pentateuch.

THE TORAH/PENTATEUCH AS DIASPORAN ASSEMBLAGE

The history of biblical criticism in the era after the European Enlightenment is replete with scholarly attempts to make sense of the disparate sources that were brought together to make the first five books of the Bible a united whole and to make sense of that unit's major themes. Within this massive body of work, the contributions of Benedict Spinoza (1632–1677), Jean Astruc (1684–1766), Alexander Geddes (1737–1802), W. M. L. de Wette (1780–1849), Julius Wellhausen (1844–1918), Hermann Gunkel (1862–1932), Albrecht Alt (1883–1956), Paul Haupt (1858–1926), Gerhard von Rad (1901–1971), Martin Noth (1902–1968), and William F. Albright (1891–1971) are often noted as foundational.[6] These scholars used names (divine, personal, and place names); distinctive themes; evidence of literary redaction; and comparative data from other ancient Near Eastern cultures to isolate sources used in the composition of the Pentateuch and to generate hypotheses as to its historical evolution.

As groundbreaking and enduring as many of their efforts have been, they were not value-neutral. They reflected, as does scholarship produced in any era, the personal interests of each author, as well as the social ethos in which they lived.[7] Thus, in some respects, to read their descriptions of Israel's early history and the Pentateuch's origins is to view, through their eyes, the historical and intellectual landscape of Europe and the Americas from the late seventeenth through the late twentieth centuries. It is a landscape upon which the saga of European colonial expansion as well as the trans-Atlantic slave trade and its aftermath unfolded. However, few resonances of these historical realities—or of the influence of the Bible on Africana peoples—are to be found in their work on the Pentateuch. Needless to say, the touchstones of their research do not primarily reflect the concerns of members of the Society of Friends in Pennsylvania articulating an agenda for the abolition of slavery (1688); of maroons fighting for freedom in Jamaica during the 1730s and 1790s; of the delegates to the first Pan-African Congress (1900);[8] or even of Martin Luther King Jr. as he penned his famous apologia while incarcerated in a Birmingham, Alabama, prison.[9] Their quest to understand the mystery of the Pentateuch's unity and diversity placed Genesis, Exodus, Leviticus, Numbers, and Deuteronomy into conversation with those interpretive paradigms and events of the day deemed pivotal for the creation and spread of an academic discipline—biblical studies. However, it did not *center* on the crises confronting Africana peoples, particularly during the period extending from the 1600s to the early 1970s. Many of the Africana notables in North America for whom such interests were pivotal made their contributions to our understanding of the Pentateuch largely outside of the biblical studies guild.[10] Among such interpreters can be numbered the creators of African American spirituals like "Go Down Moses," "Walk Together Children," and "We are Climbing Jacob's Ladder" (see Herder and Herder 2001: 22, 89, and 90); authors such as Phillis Wheatley,[11] Paul Lawrence Dunbar,[12] Zora Neale Hurston (1991), and Ishmael Reed;[13] and countless other poets, preachers, artists, and public intellectuals.[14]

From looking at the historical sweep of Pentateuchal criticism from the Enlightenment to the present, two assertions can be made. The first is that the fragmentary nature of the Pentateuch has taken precedence in most studies over the fragmenting impact the ideologies embedded in its books have had on the lives of Africana and other formerly colonized peoples. The second is that the analysis of editorial strategies used by biblical compilers to gather sources and form a unified body of sacred tradition have been placed in the foreground of such research, while those methods employed by people on the social margins to reconstitute their lives and rebuild their communities through the reading of these texts have been relegated to the background. As crucial as prior work on the origins of the Bible's first five books has been, it represents a lost opportunity to look more probingly at the impact of trauma on identity (individual and communal), memory, and cultural rebirth as such are reflected in those books and in the lives of those peoples subjugated in part by ideas found in them.

Although quibbling continues about several of the fine points of these and other efforts aimed at uncovering the secrets of the Torah's origins, many scholars have little difficulty with the assertion that the Torah is a composite work reflecting many centuries of compilation and redaction. This opinion is not universally held. Some hold that we should continue to regard as plausible that Moses played a role in the process by which these books assumed their current form.[15] For a few, the impact of special collections, such as early Hebrew poems (among these, Genesis 49; Exodus 15; Judges 5; Numbers 23–24; Deuteronomy 32–33) in shaping the Pentateuch and the entirety of the canon is pivotal.[16] There are, nonetheless, telltale signs throughout the Pentateuch of its composite nature. Sayings and poetry, perhaps considered "classic"[17] and, hence, worthy of preservation, are "embedded" into narratives (see, for example Gen. 2:23; 3:14-19; Exod. 20:1-17; Lev. 10:3; Num. 6:24-26; 10:35-36; and Deut. 26:5-10). We find evidence of the use of external sources (Num. 21:14). Parallel traditions are preserved (compare, for example, Gen. 1:26-27 with Gen. 2:7-24 and Exod. 20:1-17 with Deut. 5:6-21). Different historiographic perspectives are juxtaposed (compare Exod. 14:21-29 with Exod. 15:1-18). Thus there are very strong indications that the Tanak is an "assemblage," that is a collection of materials brought together with a specific set of theological aims in mind.

One could go on to add that the Torah's constituent parts bear some of the distinguishing marks of authors and editors experiencing diaspora. By this I mean signs of forced or voluntary separation from an actual or imagined homeland. Such separation engenders, one could argue, an ontological crisis of unpredictable duration, traces of which can be found in literature and other products of culture.[18] How one defines oneself, how one understands the concept of family, and even one's relationship to places of origin and residence are radically altered. It is an experience in which social disintegration and coalescence exist in dynamic tension.

Various strategies are deployed within the Pentateuch to address the challenges presented by this social and religious crisis—efforts aimed at promoting cohesion through the picking up and re-assembling of pieces. For example, one encounters in the Torah an assortment of literary genres. These include

creation accounts (Gen. 1:1—2:4a; 2:4b-25)
stories of remarkable births
(Gen. 18:10-15; 21:1-7; Exod. 2:1-10)
genealogies (Gen. 5:1-32; 11:10-30)
myths of cultural origin (Gen. 10; 19:30-38)
theophanies
(Gen. 12:1-3; 15:12-21; 16:7-12; 18:1-32; Exod. 3; 19:1-6)
etiologies (Gen. 19:18-22; 28:16-19; 32:30; Exod. 15:22-24)
lists (Gen. 36:31-40; Exod. 6:14-25; Num. 1:5-43; 13:4-15; 33:3-48)
vision/dream narratives
(Gen. 28:10-15; 32:22-29; 41:17-24)
curses (Gen. 3:14-19; 9:25; Deut. 27:15-26)
blessings
(Gen. 14:19-20; 48:15-16; Num. 6:24-26; Deut. 28:3-13)
laws (Exod. 20:1-17; 21:1—23:19)

speeches
(Gen. 2:23; 8:21-22; 27:39-40; Deut. 30:11-20)
epics
(Gen. 12:1-25:11; Exod. 2:1—Num. 36:13; Deut. 31–34)
illustrative prudential stories
(Gen. 37; 39–48; 49:29—50:26; Exod. 4:24-26; 18:1-27; Lev. 10:1-3; Num. 22:21-34)
oracles (Num. 23:6-10, 18-24)
sacerdotal regulations
(Exod. 25:1-31:11; 35:4—40:33; Lev. 1:1—8:36; Num. 9:1-14)
and ancient poems
(Gen. 49:1-27; Exod. 15:1-18, 21; Lev. 10:3; Num. 21:27-30; Deut. 26:5-10; 32:1-43; 33:1-29).

The inclusion of such a wide variety of materials was perhaps aimed at giving voice to the full range of life settings and forms of communication typical within ancient Israelite society.

One also finds materials reflective of several theological perspectives. In Gen. 1:1—2:4a we have a creation hymn echoing the values of those who served as priests. In the story of Moses's revelatory experience at Horeb (Exod. 3:1-17), we see a weaving together of disparate ancestral traditions about the name(s) and identifying character traits of the deity through whom the Israelites are to be rescued. We even encounter a version of the Decalogue (Deut. 5:1-22) that has been reformulated so as to reflect the philosophy of a group that idealized Moses as lawgiver and mediator of the divine will. This may have been a strategy employed to honor the diversity of the "multi-cultural assemblage" (Exod. 12:38, my translation) within which these books would be read and applied.

In certain instances, attention is paid in stories to the creation and dissolution of boundaries, physical or spiritual. The narratives of the Tower of Babel (Gen. 11:1-9) and of the construction of the Tabernacle (Exod. 35:4—40:33) are good examples of this. The former deals with the attempt to transgress the boundary separating the divine dwelling place from the locus where humans reside. The latter concerns the proper demarcation of the earthly domain where the deity's cloud "encamps" and which its glory "fills" (Exod. 40:35). One can see from these stories a concern with marking space. Here I have in mind territory, whether real or imagined, and the ways in which one obtains, controls, and hallows it. For those experiencing diaspora, a sense of both belonging and wholeness are often tied to particular sites: communities, homes, sanctuaries for worship, and the like.

The themes of displacement, relocation, transition, resettlement, assimilation, and remembering are predominant from the beginning of Genesis through the final chapter of Deuteronomy. Journeys—whether from Eden (Gen. 3:22-24), Ur (Gen. 12:1), Egypt (Exod. 12:31-33), or Sinai (Num. 10:11-13); via Ark (Num. 7:6-16) or "the wings of eagles" (Exod. 19:4)—are tropes that propel Pentateuchal narratives from the first day of creation (Gen. 1:5) to that of Moses's death and mysterious interment (Deut. 34:5-6). These journeys mark the matriarchs, patriarchs, sojourners, and pilgrims in search of the land of promise as children of various diasporas: some voluntary, others necessitated by circumstance.

BRIC-A-BRAC, DIASPORA, AND PENTATEUCH—THEIR BEARING ON AFRICANA LIFE

Once again, in my experience, bric-a-brac has extended meanings in many Africana homes within North America. One might call it part of the "sacred miscellany" through which sense is made of the incongruities of Black life. Such collections remind one that there is more to the world than meets the eye; that (re)assembled pieces can—according to an Africana poetics of collecting[19]—

make ancestors breathe and, sometimes, open windows to the future. The art of placing those pieces is a skill transferable to other aspects of existence. Africana life requires that one find, repair, and assemble such pieces—families, identities, and dreams. It will be for most a constant struggle.

Likewise, the Pentateuch is a literary miscellany whose various parts speak of its authors' struggle for unity against forces that seek to fragment the communities of which they are a part. It is an anthology deftly "pieced together" so as to overcome the social fragmentation that is the fruit of forcible diaspora, and to foster unity through liturgical and other re-enactments of its texts. Like the collections of items strategically and lovingly placed on the shelves and tables of many Africana homes in North America, it is an assemblage. For some, it contains *axé* with which the gifted can conjure freedom. For others, it is a sword, whose passages represent "edges" with the capacity to heal or harm. Within the larger Africana community there are those who believe it is to be read; "prayed"; regarded with suspicion; or simply ignored.[20] For many Jews and Christians it contains part of a sacred story continuing to unfold. As a whole, it is suggestive of life's joys, sorrows, and incongruities. It speaks of realities with which Africana peoples throughout the world are familiar.

To think of Genesis, Exodus, Leviticus, Numbers, and Deuteronomy as the result of careful selection and arrangement of things tangible (objects) and intangible (ideas) is to call to mind that such processes tend to be, in Africana settings, liberating and healing arts. A statement by the late Erskine Peters is illustrative of how this occurs.

> Although I understand that I am a biological and cultural fragment of Africans, Europeans, and Native Americans, I have no problems with wholeness due to being made of fragments. That's because I perceive the axis of my being to be the human essence, not the ethnic or racial essence. (Peters 1992: 9)

Peters speaks of perceiving his ontological "axis" as "human." Such self-perception deconstructs external forces that seek to render the Black experience as "other," and affirms the integrity of Africana peoples as part of the larger human family. To make a conscious choice about which memories, knowledge systems, languages, and rituals—past and present—are to be embraced and to put them together in ways that promote wholeness, social solidarity, and a transcendent encounter with the ineffable, however one conceives it, accomplish the same aims. Such actions were central to the agenda of Pentateuchal compilers and editors. They have been, and are today, mainstays of Africana existence.

Thus, engaging the Torah from an Africana perspective calls attention to how an assemblage of disparate pieces can reflect, influence, and be in dialogue with those for whom diaspora is a haunting memory; a mixed blessing;[21] a reality enacted daily; an imagined *milieu*; or an eschatological hope.[22]

Notes

1. On the use of this term, see Harding (2000: 77–79, 163) and Dow (1997: 21–22, 226).

2. About this, see the collection edited by Gundaker (1998), and the essay by Thompson, who argues cogently for a continuation of Kongo tradition in African American aesthetics, and notes the importance of elevated places and shelving therein (1998: 37–38, 60, 64).

3. I owe my current understanding of the taxonomy and poetics of collecting to the work of Pearce (1995: xiii), who argues convincingly that collections of artifacts play an important role in identity construction.

4. My appreciation of the fragmentary and contingent nature of identity was heightened after seeing Mweze Ngangura's *Pieces D'Identités* (1998) many years ago.

5. On these and other translations, see the work of Metzger (2001: 13, 30, 35–37, 44–46, 50-51).

6. Dates for these scholars have been taken from the two-volume dictionary of Hayes (1999a, 1999b). Others could certainly be added to this list. I consider those cited particularly worthy of note, because their research has set the parameters within which much subsequent discussion about the Pentateuch has taken place.

7. For critical assessments of Albright's work, see Long (1997) and the essays collected in the edited volume of Van Beck (1989).

8. The aforementioned dates and events are taken from the timeline in the Schomburg Center's African American Desk Reference (Koslow 1999: 3, 4).

9. See his 1964 "Letter from Birmingham Jail" (Gates and McKay 1997: 1854–66).

10. Here I refer specifically to several categories of persons: those holding academic degrees in biblical studies; those holding academic positions with teaching responsibilities and/or research profiles focusing on the Bible and its interpretation; those generally recognized persons in the aforementioned groupings as contributors to discourse in the field; and those accounted by historians of the discipline of Biblical Studies as having contributed in some substantial way to its development. Among the twentieth-century's more important Africana trailblazers working within the North American guild were Charles Copher (1989) and Robert Bennett (1970, 1976). Africana scholars have long been under-represented in First Testament Studies. For example, the total number of African American Hebrew Bible scholars in 2000 numbered only twenty-one (see Bailey 2000: 707).

11. See, in particular, her letter "To Samson Occom" (in Gates and McKay 1997: 176).

12. See his "An Ante-Bellum Sermon" (in Gates and McKay 1997: 891).

13. See his "Neo-HooDoo Manifesto" (in Gates and McKay 1997: 2297–2301).

14. The typical synopsis of modern Pentateuchal criticism does not make reference to these figures. See, for example, those of Duff (on the Pentateuch and Hebrew Bible as a whole, 1910: 129–87), Houtman (1999), and Arnold (Arnold 2003).

15. See, for example, the measured statement of Alexander (2003: 70).

16. This can be inferred from the work of Cross and Freedman (1997).

17. On the possible preservation of "classic" texts in Egyptian literature and the Bible's corpus of Wisdom traditions, see Weeks (1994: 159–60).

18. See Gomez's treatment of issues animating the study of the African Diaspora and features suggestive of a common Black Diasporan experience (Gomez 2005: 2).

19. Here, I commend a melding of the research of Susan Pearce with that of Theophus Smith (Smith 1994) in suggesting that just as there is a "European poetic" (Pearce 1995: 32) for collecting, there exist, as well, Africana poetic(s) for creating assemblages that are—in and of themselves—"conjurational performances" (Smith 1994: 3) intended to heal, instruct, and liberate.

20. This latter strategy deserves further exploration. To "ignore" something, one must—it seems—initially acknowledge (if only tacitly) its presence before looking around, beyond, or through it. The ways in which certain Africana artifacts ignore the Bible deserves greater attention. One artifact, Blues, displays a complex evolution in which biblical themes are at times mirrored, critiqued, expanded, and selectively ignored (see Spencer 1994: 1–6, 72–77, 84–89, 99–100, 137). This continuum of engagement also needs further exploration.

21. Here, I echo Gilroy, who cites Martin Delany's 1859 travelogue as evidence of a longstanding "ambivalence over exile and homecoming" (1993: 24) among Africana peoples in Western society.

22. On the creative dimensions of diaspora—including its imaginary and eschatological dimensions—see Holt (2001: 36–37).

References

Alexander, T. Desmond. 2003. Authorship of the Pentateuch. In *Dictionary of the Old Testament: Pentateuch*, ed. T. D. Alexander and D. W. Baker. Downers Grove, Ill.: InterVarsity.

Arnold, Bill T. 2003. Pentateuchal Criticism, History of. In *Dictionary of the Old Testament: Pentateuch*, ed. T. D. Alexander and D. W. Baker. Downers Grove, Ill.: InterVarsity Press.

Bailey, Randall C. 2000. Academic Biblical Interpretation among African Americans in the United States. In *African Americans and the Bible: Sacred Texts and Social Textures*, ed. V. L. Wimbush. New York: Continuum.

Bennett, Robert A., Jr. 1970. Africa and the Biblical Period. *Harvard Theological Review* 64:483–500.

———. 1976. *God's Work of Liberation*. Wilton, Conn.: Morehouse-Barlow.

Copher, Charles. 1989. Three Thousand Years of Biblical Interpretation with Reference to Black Peoples. In *African American Religious Studies: An Interdisciplinary Anthology*. Durham, N.C.: Duke University Press.

Cross, Frank Moore, and David Noel Freedman. 1997. *Studies in Ancient Yahwistic Poetry*. 2nd ed., *The Biblical Resource Series*. Grand Rapids, Mich.: Eerdmans.

Dow, Carolyn L. 1997. *Saravá!: Afro-Brazilian Magic*. St. Paul, Minn.: Llewellyn.

Duff, Archibald. 1910. *History of Old Testament Criticism*. New York: Knickerbocker.

Gates, Henry Louis, Jr., and Nellie Y. McKay, eds. 1997. *The Norton Anthology of African American Literature*. New York: Norton.

Gilroy, Paul. 1993. *The Black Atlantic: Modernity and Double Consciousness*. Cambridge, Mass.: Harvard University Press.

Gomez, Michael. 2005. *Reversing Sail: A History of the African Diaspora*. Ed. M. Klein, *New Approaches to African History*. Cambridge, UK: Cambridge University Press.

Gundaker, Grey, ed. 1998. *Keep Your Head to the Sky: Interpreting African American Home Ground*. Charlottesville, Va.: University Press of Virginia.

Harding, Rachel E. 2000. *A Refuge in Thunder: Candomblé and Alternative Spaces of Blackness*. Bloomington, Ind.: Indiana University Press.

Hayes, John H., ed. 1999a. *Dictionary of Biblical Interpretation, A–J.* Nashville: Abingdon.

———, ed. 1999b. *Dictionary of Biblical Interpretation, K–Z.* Nashville: Abingdon.

Herder, Nicole Beaulieu, and Ronald Herder, eds. 2001. *Best-Loved Negro Spirituals: Complete Lyrics to 178 Songs of Faith.* Mineola, N.Y.: Dover.

Holt, Thomas C. 2001. Slavery and Freedom in the Atlantic World: Reflections on the Diasporan Framework. In *Crossing Boundaries: Comparative History of Black People in Diaspora*, ed. D. C. Hine and J. McLeod. Bloomington, Ind.: Indiana University Press.

Houtman, C. 1999. Pentateuchal Criticism. In *Dictionary of Biblical Interpretation, K-Z*, ed. J. H. Hayes. Nashville: Abingdon.

Hurston, Zora Neale. 1991. *Moses, Man of the Mountain.* Reprint of 1939 ed. New York: HarperPerennial.

Koslow, Philip, ed. 1999. *African American Desk Reference.* New York: Wiley.

Long, Burke O. 1997. *Planting and Reaping Albright: Politics, Ideology, and Interpreting the Bible.* University Park, Penn.: Pennsylvania State University Press.

Metzger, Bruce M. 2001. *The Bible in Translation: Ancient and English Versions.* Grand Rapids, Mich.: Baker Academic.

Ngangura, Mweze. 1998. Pieces D'Identites. Congo / Belgium.

Otto, Rudolf. 1958. *The Idea of the Holy: An Inquiry into the Non-Rational Factor in the Idea of the Divine and its Relation to the Rational.* New York: Oxford University Press.

Page, Hugh R., Jr. 1997. *Waves, Clouds, and Flames: Impressions from Journeys Past and Present.* South Bend, Ind.: Quiet Fire.

Pearce, Susan M. 1995. *On Collecting: An Investigation into Collecting in the European Tradition.* London: Routledge.

Peters, Erskine. 1992. *African Americans in the New Millennium: Blueprinting the Future.* Berkeley, Calif.: Regent.

Smith, Theophus. 1994. *Conjuring Culture: Biblical Formations of Black America.* New York: Oxford University Press.

Spencer, Jon Michael. 1994. *Blues and Evil.* Knoxville, Tenn.: University of Tennessee Press.

Thompson, Robert Farris. 1998. "Bighearted Power: Kongo Presence in the Landscape and Art of Black America." In *Keep Your Head to the Sky: Interpreting African American Home Ground*, ed. G. Gundaker. Charlottesville, Va.: University Press of Virginia.

Van Beck, Gus W., ed. 1989. *The Scholarship of William Foxwell Albright.* Ed. J. Frank Moore Cross. Vol. 33, *Harvard Semitic Studies.* Atlanta, Ga.: Scholars.

Visotzky, Burton. 2008. In "Hoc Signum Vincent: A Midrashist Replies." In *Theorizing Scriptures: New Critical Orientations to a Cultural Phenomenon*, ed. V. L. Wimbush. New Brunswick, N.J.: Rutgers University Press.

Weeks, Stuart. 1994. *Early Israelite Wisdom.* Oxford Theological Monographs. Oxford: Clarendon.

GENESIS

Rodney S. Sadler Jr.

FROM THE STORIES of the creation of the world to the interfamilial conflict of the early Hebrew clans, throughout our experience with the Judeo-Christian scriptures Genesis has captured the imagination of Africana authors. This attraction is due not only to the poignant narratives that ably speak to commonplace experiences in family life but also to the fact that Genesis introduces us to an awesome God who holds a good world in loving hands. Such a deity has been comforting, as we Africana peoples have needed a source of hope in a world dominated by those opposed to our very being. After enduring the governance of European domination, oppression, slavery, segregation, and genocide, scripture's emphasis of God's ultimate control over the horrors of this world was requisite. Genesis provides a context to understand God's control *in spite of*—in spite of all the horrors we

have faced, we have needed to know that there is yet a reason to keep on keeping on.

God's control in this book is presented in tension with human agency, thus providing theological grounding for how a loving God could overcome the evils that brothers and sisters work against one another in this world. Just as Abel's murder by his brother did not go unnoticed (4:1-16), our ancestors knew that their suffering would be vindicated. Even as Joseph, though sold by his brothers (37:23-28), prospered in the slave master's land (41:39-52), this narrative testified of the God who would prosper us in the land(s) of our sufferings.

This article explores the recurrent themes of familial function, dysfunction, and redemption, and the prevalence of divine providence, matters that are not only key to Genesis but also central concerns in the lives of Africana peoples. Genesis is placed in dialogue with other Africana fiction, biography, poetry, and song to see how the latter give us insight into the former. Alice Walker's seminal text, *The Color Purple* (*CP*), like Genesis, occupies itself with familial and theological issues and provides insight into characters often silenced in Genesis. *CP* also provides the woman's voice all but missing from Genesis and offers a woman's story that serves as a requisite balance to a generally patriarchal text. *CP* is a powerful counterpoint as it speaks to the fascinating arrangements that have been deemed family in our communities, where fictive family lines run deep and closest cousins and favorite aunts and uncles often share no blood but much love.

CREATION IN GENESIS 1–3: CREATED IN "GOD'S IMAGE"

Guess who they say the snake is? . . . Whitefolks sign for they parents. They was so mad to git throwed out and told they was naked they made up they minds to crush us wherever they find us, same as they would a snake. . . . [The Olinka] think, after the biggest of the white folks no longer on the earth, the only way to stop making somebody the serpent is for everybody to accept everybody else as a child of God, or one mother's children, no matter what else they look like or how they act. (Walker 1982: 274–75)

As Celie recounts in *CP* the Olinka understandings of Creation, a clear Africana tendency is present. She notes that the familial relationship between God and humanity provides the impetus to overcome the inevitable tendency of humans to demonize the Other.

For Africana peoples, one of the most significant messages from Genesis 1 is that as earthlings we are each created *betselem 'elohim*, or in the "image of God." The image of God is a strong grounding motif for the universal worth of all humanity, evidenced by its reuse in Judeo-Christian contexts such as Gen. 9:5-6 as a prohibition against violence. It is ironic that the Hebrew people who

eschew crafting images of their deity (Exod. 20:4-6; Deut. 5:8-10) find such meaning in bearing that image in their flesh. The charge to revere human life because of the *imago Dei* is also evidenced in other Africana sources.

The artist Prince, in his spiritual b-side cut "God," engages this passage lyrically. The ethereal song "God" celebrates God's creation of a good universe, reaching its zenith with a multipart harmonious chant: "God made U, God made me, He made us all, equally." Herein is the key to the Creation narrative for Prince, for the song celebrates in its climactic crescendo a notion of universal human worth.

God's creation of humanity figures prominently in one of the most familiar poems penned by Africana giant James Weldon Johnson. "The Creation," an artistic retelling of Genesis 1–2, finds its raison d'être in God's need for human companionship: "And God said: I'm lonely still. . . . He thought: I'll make me a man!" (Johnson, "The Creation"). Johnson's God is an interesting combination of male and female attributes. Though consistently referenced with masculine pronouns, Johnson appeals to imagery familiar to his people to describe God's loving nature as "a mammy bending over her baby." This poignant simile of God as an African American mother both intentionally violates the patriarchal Judeo-Christian assumptions of God's masculinity and playfully modifies this tradition by ascribing divinity to marginalized African American female flesh. It is *this* God that toils "over a lump of clay till He shaped it in His own image."

The prominence of the *imago Dei* has not been limited to fictional literature and song; it has also played a critical role in the sociopolitical rhetoric of Martin Luther King Jr.: "Man is a child of God made in His image, and therefore must be respected as such. Until men see this everywhere, until nations see this everywhere, we will be fighting wars" (King 1986: 255). Crafting his vision of the beloved community, King finds a prominent place for this ideology as the ground for his vision of universal human worth. As in Celie's letters, until human beings recognize this crucial fact, human conflict is inevitable.

As such, this hermeneutical appropriation plays a key role in the liberative thought of Africana peoples aesthetically and practically. Because we are a people who have known what it means to be deemed less than human, or made "*In His Image . . . But*" (Smith 1798), we have returned time and again to this affirmation of our collective worth. Our appropriations of these texts have been playful and creative, using elements that supported universal human worth and conflating elements from both Genesis 1 and 2, while avoiding details (like the oppressive concepts of subduing and dominating in 1:26-28) that may be seen as problematic. The *imago Dei* and our ability to playfully recraft these narratives are key reasons why the Creation accounts in Genesis 1–2 are key Africana resources.

CREATION OF HUMAN BEINGS: GENDER EQUALITY AND CO-REGENCY

Adam is . . . (t)he first man that was white.
Not the first man. They say nobody so crazy they think they can say who was the first man. But everybody notice the first white man cause he was white.
(Walker 1982: 272–73)

The narrative of the creation of the world finds its climactic moment in the creation of human beings. The term occasionally translated "human beings" in the NRSV and generally as "man" in most other English versions is *'adam* or *ha'adam*. Now this clearly is not a personal name (that is, Adam) as the KJV ill-advisedly begins to indicate at about Gen. 2:19. A better translation of this term, however, would be "the earthling" since the term is derived from the term *'adamah*, meaning "land" or "earth." Such a translation clarifies better than "man" or even "human being" that the origi-

nal intent of the author is to emphasize that God made "earthlings" as a whole, *not just males*, in God's image. As such, a better translation of verses 27-28 would be:

> And God created the earthling in God's image, in the image of God God created *it*, male and female God created *them*.
> And God blessed *them* and God said to *them*, "(y'all) be fruitful and multiply and fill the earth and subdue it, and exercise dominion over the fish of the sea and the foul of the heavens and over all the living beings that teem upon the earth."

Such a translation takes into consideration that the term *'adam* is meant to function as a collective term referring to both the male and female. Thus, we should note that *'adam* is here not a name or an ascription of gender but a collective term for "earthlings" in general; this is emphasized by the author's choice of the plural pronoun *'otham*, and the use of the plural verbs *veyirddu* and *urdu*, meaning in 1:26 and 1:28 "let *them* have dominion," further reiterates the inclusive nature of the term *'adam*. In the Creation account in Genesis 1:1—2:4a, both genders are vested with authority as stewards over the earth and all that is in it. It is in this way that the family begins, with this functional procreative unit: two beings reflecting God's glory in human form united in common cause.

This is an important theme because Africana families continue to struggle with the dysfunction of androcentrism and misogyny. If we are to overcome this tendency, we have to acknowledge that Creation offers no biblical precedent to the notion that we are created qualitatively differently as males and females; in Genesis 1 and 2, both genders were created with equal expressions of God's image, equal authority over the earth, and equal value as human beings. Herein is the basis of a functional union from which the human family arises in all of its forms.

NOAH'S OFFSPRING IN GENESIS 9–10: FROM CURSES TO "RACES"

There is a white woman missionary . . . who has lived in Africa for the past twenty years. She is said to be much loved by the natives even though she thinks they are an entirely different species from what she calls Europeans. . . . She says an African daisy and an English daisy are both flowers, but totally different kinds. (Walker 1982: 136)

GENESIS 9:18-27:
THE ORIGINS OF A "RACIAL" CURSE

Genesis 9:18-27, "Curse of Ham/Canaan," is a passage with one of the most notorious histories of interpretation in all of the Hebrew scriptures. In terms of its narrative content, it is a tale replete with familial dysfunction; it begins with a drunken father, offers hints of sexual abuse, features two favored sons, and ends with a third getting cursed. A close reading of the narrative reveals that it contains an enigmatic curse leveled against a now-extinct ethnic group, the Canaanites, that justified their loss of land and servitude to the Shemites (read "Israelites"). In this regard, the author's wholly problematic intent is often overlooked by contemporary readers since the oppression of an extinct ethnopolitical entity seems passé as a cause for concern amid the plethora of existing instances of subjugation. Yet this passage was revived and reinterpreted in the seventeenth and eighteenth centuries by Euro-Americans and leveled against a new target of oppression. In this latter instance, Africana peoples were deemed the "Sons of Ham" and this curse of perpetual servitude was leveled against our ancestors as a theological justification for their enslavement.[1]

The curse itself is the result of an act whereby Ham (or Canaan in an earlier version of this account) sexually abused or was sexually abused by his father, Noah (Bailey 1994). This is one of numerous Genesis texts that employ some form of sexual exploitation as a means to denigrate a foe (for example, Gen. 9:18-27—Canaanites;

16—Ishmaelites; 19:1-29—Sodomites; 19:30-38—Moabites and Ammonites) or further the plot of a larger narrative (Gen. 30:1-13, 38). There is a danger to these uses of sexuality for they tend to imply that problematic sexual acts are sources of denigration for entire ethnic groups (Bailey 1994).

We should note that because this text was composed to justify the disenfranchisement of one group of people by another, it is inherently precarious. It establishes a theological precedent for the abuse of an "Other" by a favored group and can easily be adopted as a proof text by subsequent groups seeking to legitimate theologically their superiority over or oppression of another "othered" group. Though the authors of this pericope did not intend to legitimate an oppressive paradigm based on "racial" criteria, its no less problematic ethnically oppressive *Tendenz* made the narrative ripe for abuse. Thus this text is both intrinsically and hermeneutically problematic. When married to a "racialized" understanding of Genesis 10, subsequent supremacists readily misappropriated the text, applied it to a "racial" Other, and thereby found the theological justification for the disenfranchisement of Africans.[2] The dangers of pericopes like Gen. 9:18-27 that justify a dominant group's oppression of an "Other" should lead contemporary interpreters to exercise due diligence when preaching or teaching from them. Uncritical appropriation of biblical material has led to a host of social ills, from "racism" to nationalism to sexism to heterosexism, and the list continues. As those who have been victimized by the deliberate misreading of scripture, Africana peoples must ensure that our biblical interpretations do not perpetuate the abuses of the past.

GENESIS 10:
THE ORIGINS OF THE CURSE OF "RACE"

In the aftermath of the flood in Genesis 6–9, the "Table of Nations" in Genesis 10 describes the repopulation of the earth by the descendants of the sons of Noah. For many reasons, one could argue that this passage is the lynchpin without which "race" cannot be connected to the Judeo-Christian scriptures. When the concept of "race" came into vogue during the so-called Enlightenment (circa seventeenth century), Scripture was employed in ways that supported the theories that emerged during that period (see Hannaford 1996, Haynes 2002, Smith 1972, and West 2002). Theories of race made popular in Europe during this period were subsequently correlated with this patronymic that postulated a definitive moment for the differentiation of distinct human lineages (Haynes 2002: 3–19 and Sadler 2006: 386–403).

Hence, the story of Noah's sons was reinterpreted as the passage demonstrating the origins of "race" in the Bible. This passage lends itself to a "racial" interpretation for it shows how all of humanity is descended from three known individuals who can be assumed to be geographically circumscribed to three distinct regions (in theory, Africa, Asia, and Europe). As such, the genealogical list in Genesis 10 describes almost all people in the then-known world as descendants of Noah through one of his three sons: Shem (assumed to be the ancestor of "Euro-Asians," though all of his descendants are on the African continent, 10:21-32), Ham (assumed to be the ancestor of "Africans," though some of his descendants are in Europe and Asia, 10:6-20), and Japheth (assumed to be the ancestor of "Europeans," though most of his descendants are unknown peoples, 10:2-5). As a result, this passage has traditionally come to be known as the "Table of Nations," biblical evidence of the divine origins of ontologically distinct human "races."

Carefully examining this passage, however, makes it evident that the biblical authors had no concept of color-based "races" in mind in forming this genealogy. This is evident inasmuch as the terms *Shem, Ham,* and *Japheth* do not recur in scripture as essentializing terms describing the whole of these descendant groups (that is, we do not hear of the Japhethites doing such and such—

even concepts such as the Shemites or Semites and the Hamites are later, postbiblical terms) and Shem, Ham, and Japheth are never associated with color terms in subsequent biblical literature (Copher 1991: 146–53).

The familial linkage of all humanity is the key to understanding this passage and indeed Genesis itself. The *griots* who compose and relay this patronymic go to considerable lengths to demonstrate the kinship of humankind. The concept of "race" itself should be vigorously resisted (Sadler 2006: 401–43.)

ANCESTRAL SAGAS IN GENESIS 12–36: FAMILIAL FUNCTION, DYSFUNCTION, AND SEXUAL EXPLOITATION

[Robert Newsom] set out to purchase a replacement for his wife, dead now for nearly a year. . . . [F]rom the moment he purchased Celia, Newsom regarded her as both his property and his concubine.

. . . Newsom raped Celia, and by that act at once established and defined the nature of the relationship between the master and his newly acquired slave. . . . [I]t is entirely possible that he felt that his ownership of the young Celia entitled him to use her for his sexual pleasure. (McLaurin 1991: 21–25)

The ancestral narratives that comprise the vast majority of the corpus of Genesis address a central concern: the ability of God to fulfill the promises made to Abraham of an abundant family that will bless the world. Far from being exemplars of moral behavior in model family units, a close reading of the ancestral sagas reveal numerous flawed characters and persistent familial dysfunction. Characters like Abram/Abraham, who twice profits from the sale of his wife (Gen. 12:16—13:2 and 20:14-16) and takes sexual advantage of his wife's enslaved Egyptian woman (Genesis 16), and Jacob/Israel, who steals his brother's birthright (Genesis 25) and blessing (Genesis 28) and swindles his crooked uncle (Genesis 30), epitomize the kinds of skeletons found in many of our familial closets.

We should not be surprised that in these narratives barrenness and childlessness are recurrent motifs. Barrenness threatens to derail YHWH's promises to Abram time and again in these accounts whether with Sarai/Sarah or later with Rachel (chap. 30), as does childlessness in the case of Tamar (chap. 38). Initially childless Abram desires to fulfill this promise by his own agency, seeking an heir of his own choosing to inherit the promise. At first, the choice is his nephew Lot (12:5), yet he is unable to remain with Abram due to interfamilial conflict (13:5-12). The second choice was Eliezer, a man enslaved to his house, yet YHWH promises the heir will be one who is from his own seed (15:4). Thus his third choice comes about by his wife Sarai's agency (16:1-3). As a woman who lives in a world where "a woman's womb was her destiny," Sarai was compelled to find a way to provide her husband with the child she personally could not offer (Weems 1998: 3).

In 16:1, Hagar is introduced portentously as an enslaved Egyptian woman of barren Sarai. This introduction foreshadows what will become of this proud young woman, enslaved to a whimsical mistress embittered because of her childless condition. She is objectified, presented only as a solution to a problem for which she is not responsible. Sarai, thus, tells her husband, Abram, in verse 2 to bo`-na` ("go into") Hagar. That sexual language is used for this nonconsensual contact should remind us of enslaved Africana foremothers and forefathers raped by masters and enslavers who used their bodies for sexual gratification and their offspring as slaves.

> But he was my master. I was compelled to live under the same roof with him—where I saw a man forty years my senior daily violating the most sacred commandments of nature. He told me I was his property; thus I must be subject to his will in all things. My soul revolted against the mean tyranny. But where could I turn for protection? . . . My master met me at every turn, reminding me that I belonged to him, and swearing by heaven and earth that he would compel me to submit to him. (Jacobs, 44–46)

As we consider the plight of women victimized under a misogynistic system, we should note that Genesis provides no insight into the fear, betrayal, and incredulity that Hagar must have felt. Perhaps Celie's letters to God can serve as a window into Hagar's soul.

> He never had a kine word to say to me. Just say You gonna do what your mammy wouldn't. First he put his thing up gainst my hip and sort of wiggle it around. . . . When that hurt, I cry. He start to choke me, saying You better shut up and git used to it. (Walker 1982: 1)

We can imagine that Hagar's own letters would reflect a similar incredulity and innocence as she was passed on as a sexual surrogate to bear children for a man she neither loved nor who loved her. She was a functioning object used to bear a seed and produce an heir. When she bore a child, she was cast aside like Celie was after her second child by her incestuous Pa. Celie's letters are also a window into the pain felt by the enslaved Bilhah and Zilpah, and perhaps even by the unloved Leah too (Genesis 30), who though deemed wives of Jacob function in the shadow of his favoritism toward Rachel, as Celie did in Shug's shadow.

Yet the problem of offspring was not for Abram, Sarai, Hagar, Rachel, Leah, or any other human agent to resolve. It was ultimately YHWH's concern. Patiently, almost parentally, YHWH watches these attempts to fulfill the promise fail, and when all hope seems lost, YHWH provides an heir unexpectedly. Thus, in Gen. 21:1-4, the promise is fulfilled by the birth of Isaac, and in 30:22-24 the promise of a child through Jacob's beloved wife Rachel is fulfilled by the birth of Joseph (then, later in 35:18, Benjamin). The jealousy, bitterness, division, and dysfunction caused by human attempts

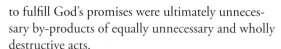

to fulfill God's promises were ultimately unnecessary by-products of equally unnecessary and wholly destructive acts.

And where is YHWH in these women's stories of rape, slavery, and sexual commodification? Because the *griots* who compose these texts are part of a patriarchal system that frequently devalues women, we should not be surprised that their portrayals of YHWH allow the Divinity silently to consent to the women's abuse. Yet there are glimpses of hope in the narrative that demonstrate God's concern for these matriarchs. Despite Sarai's claim in 16:2 that YHWH has made her barren, God in 17:16 and 18:10 promises to provide a son from her womb and fulfills the promise in 21:1-3. Despite the fact that YHWH initially returns Hagar to bondage (16:9; for an alternate interpretation, see Weems 1988: 13) and authorizes her abandonment (21:12), the Deity promises her a son (16:7-16) and then rescues her in the wilderness and promises "to make a great nation" from her son (21:17-21). Despite the misogynistic lens through which the *griots* view the Deity casting their God as an accomplice in their male characters' misdeeds, in contextually relevant ways they hint at YHWH's concern for the welfare of the progeny of the matriarchs but not for the women themselves.

So what do we as children of disenfranchised, enslaved, raped, and otherwise abused Africana peoples have to do with texts that assume the commonplace nature of such behavior? How can we sing "Father Abraham" without examining his exploitation of Hagar, or "We are Climbing Jacob's Ladder" without ever questioning his treatment of Bilhah, Zilpah, and Leah? How is it that we have traditionally identified with the protagonists of these narratives who have perpetrated the patterns of oppression, the legacy of which we continue to suffer? Increasingly, the answer has been to view such texts with a requisite hermeneutic of suspicion (for examples, see Weems 1988, Bailey 1998, and Harrison 2004); some scholars even question whether we should consider such content scripture to which we are beholden. But in the end, there is

a quandary for Africana peoples who have gleaned hope for liberation from a Bible replete with narratives that presume the legitimacy of oppression. Is our willingness to valorize these narratives a betrayal of our own interests and history? Whether our ability to read such texts with the protagonist is a manifestation of DuBoisian "double consciousness" or simply the result of a naively uncritical appropriation of a sacral tradition at odds with our life experiences, we owe it to ourselves to discern clearly what it is that these stories *really* say about the nature of God and family.

JOSEPH NOVELLA IN GENESIS 37–50: SELLING BROTHER JOSEPH

Today the people of Africa — having murdered or sold into slavery their strongest folks — are riddled with disease and sunk in spiritual and physical confusion. . . . Why did they sell us? And why do we still love them?
(Walker 1982: 139)

The story of Joseph begins in chapter 37 with a brief introduction in verse 2: "These are the generations of Jacob." This familiar Genesis refrain introduces the importance of Jacob's family in the following chapters. But the subsequent narratives focus less on the family and more on the account of the life of Joseph—hence the name for Genesis 37–50, the "Joseph Novella." The Joseph Novella is a generally coherent narrative that begins with an account of the relationship between Joseph and his brothers, which deteriorates rapidly from 37:2-11 as he tattles on them, tells them he is destined to rule over them, and even worse, tells them that his father favors him more than them. Jacob/Israel's favoritism here, as in the instance with his wives and the enslaved women (Genesis 30), undermines the integrity of his family. These details add tension to the story that culminates with Joseph's brothers—the children of Leah, the hated wife, and Bilhah and Zilpah, the raped enslaved women—capturing him, restraining him in a pit, and then selling him to Midianite traders in 37:27-28.

Joseph's story echoes the stories of many of our ancestors, for they found themselves similarly enslaved. It was their African brothers who sold them into slavery. Venture Smith chronicles his capture in his biography. Taken first by an invading tribe of fellow Africans, he was pinioned and dragged toward the coast with the remnants of his village who were not killed in the invasion. Later, his plunderers were plundered by yet another tribe.

> The very first salute I had from them was a violent blow to the head with the fore part of a gun, and at the same time a grasp round the neck. I then had a rope put about my neck (10). . . . I was then taken a second time. All of us were then put into the castle, and kept for market. On a certain time I and other prisoners were put on board a canoe, under our master, and rowed away to a vessel belonging to Rhode-Island, commanded by Capt. Collingwood, and the mate Thomas Mumford. . . . I was bought . . . for four gallons of rum, and a piece of calico. (Smith 1798: 13)

Because of its description of Joseph's plight, which paralleled many of their own ordeals, this story became typological for many enslaved people, including Phillis Wheatley, Jupiter Hammon, Albert Gronniosaw, Olaudah Equiano, and Venture Smith (Richards 2000: 221).

Nettie's words above to her sister about the Africana people among whom she was to minister provide a glimpse into the mind of Joseph. These are likely his own unasked questions as he would have pondered his own plight and struggled to make sense of his own brothers' disdain that led them to sell him into slavery. Why did they sell him? Why does he still love them?

These questions unasked in the text lurk beneath the surface only to recur at the end of the narrative. Once Joseph has overcome the manifold obstacles he faced—slavery, sexual harassment, imprisonment, and so forth—he rises to a position of penultimate authority in Pharaoh's administration in 41:39-44. It is then that he encounters his brothers who sold him into the hell of his early life in Egypt. His response to his brothers is guarded. Initially, he crafts tests to prove their hearts. But by 45:4 he reveals himself to them:

> Then Joseph said to his brothers, "Come closer to me." And they came closer. He said, "I am your brother, Joseph, whom you sold into Egypt. And now do not be distressed, or angry with yourselves, because you sold me here; for God sent me before you to preserve life.

Nettie's question is inescapable: "Why does [he] still love them?" Though this question is never addressed, the response to Nettie's initial question perhaps provides the answer to both queries: "Why did they sell [me]?" This question seems to demand the response of jealously or hatred or hard-heartedness; instead, Joseph offers a theologically potent response, "for God sent me before you to preserve life." This response seems wholly unsatisfying from a human perspective. Yet Joseph is not alone in finding a theological motivation for human suffering. Indeed, this is the same response Second Isaiah gives for the suffering of Judah during the Exile (Isa. 53:10). This is the same response Jesus offers as he prepares for his passion (Matt. 26:39). The suffering was accepted because it was seen as a means to further the will of the Lord.

Though wholly untenable to me in relation to the North Atlantic slave trade, this seemingly irrational response is not uncommon in Africana circles either. From the moment in the latter part of the eighteenth century when Phillis Wheatley penned

> TWAS mercy brought me from my pagan
> land,
> Taught my benighted soul to understand

African Americans have sought to reconcile their enslavement with a vision of a benevolent deity (Wheatley 1834: 42). When asked to reflect on the reason for the passion of Africans in the Americas, late-nineteenth-century Ethiopianists often mirrored Joseph's response that it was God's will:

> While it is true that we were brought here as captive heathens through the greed and avarice of the white man . . . I believe that an over-ruling Providence suffered it to be because there was a great and grand purpose to be sub-served, and that infinite wisdom intended to evolve ultimate good out of a temporary evil, and that in the ages to come, the glory of God will be made manifest and that millions will thank heaven for the limited toleration of American slavery.
> (Turner 1998: 777)

The conclusion from Genesis to the Ethiopianists is that through our collective sufferings, God had blessings in store for all humanity, including those very brothers who "sold us out" in the most literal of senses.

Notions of God's providence at work in hell-ish situations are dangerous inasmuch as they can serve to legitimate untold abuses in order to reconcile God's justice, love, and power with the worst instances of oppression. Yet they provide requisite hope that God still cares for people in pandemonium, letting them know that there is eschatological merit to their suffering. At the end of the day, their suffering will serve a higher purpose in a plan they are at a loss to explain. In this regard, the Joseph Novella provides the basis of a theology of hope for those desperately groping for God's hand in the midst of the overwhelming darkness of human inhumanity.

Notes

1. For a thorough discussion of the use of this passage in racialist discourse, see Copher 1991: 147–48; Felder 1991: 129–32; Haynes, 2002; and Peterson, 1978.

2. Haynes 2002 identifies Gen. 9:20-27 and its "cognate texts" as the most potent theological weapons in the arsenal of proslavery advocates in the American context used to undergird both slavery and subsequent racial discrimination in the United States. He notes particularly the mythic value of these texts for providing the "biblical sanctions for the inferiority of blacks, the evil of miscegenation, and the necessity—or at least permissibility—of racial segregation" (viii).

References

Bailey, Randall C. 1994. "They're Nothing but Incestuous Bastards: Polemical Use of Sex and Sexuality in Hebrew Canon Narrative." In *Reading from This Place*, vol. 1, *Social Context and Biblical Interpretation in the United States*, ed. Fernando Segovia and Mary Ann Tolbert, 121–25, 133–38. Minneapolis: Fortress Press.

———. 1998. "The Danger of Ignoring One's Own Cultural Bias in Interpreting the Text." In *The Postcolonial Bible*, ed. R. S. Sugirtharajah, 66–90. Sheffield: Sheffield University Press.

Bruce, John. E. 1998. "Reasons Why the Colored American Should Go to Africa." In *Lift Every Voice: African American Oratory 1787–1900*, ed. Philip S. Foner and Robert James Branham. Tuscaloosa: University of Alabama Press.

Campbell, Antony F., and Mark A. O'Brien. 1993. *Sources of the Pentateuch: Texts, Introductions, Annotations*. Minneapolis: Fortress Press.

Copher, Charles. 1991. "The Black Presence in the Old Testament." In *Stony the Road We Trod: African American Biblical Interpretation*, ed. Cain Hope Felder, 146–64. Minneapolis: Fortress Press.

Felder, Cain Hope. 1991. "Race, Racism, and the Biblical Narratives." In *Stony the Road We Trod:*

African American Biblical Interpretation, ed. Cain Hope Felder, 129–32. Minneapolis: Fortress Press.

Hannaford, Ivan. 1996. *Race: The History of an Idea in the West*. Washington, D.C.: Woodrow Wilson Center.

Harrison, Renee K. 2004. "Hagar Ain't Workin', Gimme Celie: A Hermeneutic of Rejection and a Risk of Re-appropriation." *Union Seminary Quarterly Review* 58 (3–4): 38–55.

Haynes, Stephen R. 2002. *Noah's Curse: The Biblical Justification of American Slavery*. New York: Oxford University Press.

Jacobs, Harriet A. 1861. *Incidents in the Life of a Slave Girl*. http://docsouth.unc.edu/fpn/jacobs/jacobs.html.

Japhet, Sara. 1993. *I & II Chronicles: A Commentary*. Louisville, Ky.: Westminster/John Knox, 58.

Johnson, James Weldon. 1920. "The Creation." In *The Norton Anthology of African American Literature*, gen. eds. Henry Louis Gates Jr. and Nellie Y. McKay, 775–77. New York: Norton, 1997.

King, Martin Luther, Jr. 1986. "A Christmas Sermon on Peace." In *A Testament of Hope: The Essential Writings and Speeches of Martin Luther King, Jr.*, ed. James M. Washington, 253–58. San Francisco: HarperSanFrancisco.

McLaurin, Melton A. 1991. *Celia, A Slave*. New York: Avon.

Peterson, Thomas. 1978. *Ham and Jepheth: The Mythic World of Whites in the Antebellum South*. Metuchen, N.J.: Scarecrow.

Rashkow, Ilona. 1998. "Daddy Dearest and the 'Invisible Spirit of Wine.'" In *Feminist Companion to Genesis*, 2nd series, ed. Athalya Brenner, 82–98. Sheffield: Sheffield Academic.

Richards, Phillip. 2000. "The 'Joseph Story' as Slave Narrative: On Genesis and Exodus as Prototypes for Early Black Anglophone Writing." In *African Americans and the Bible: Sacred Texts and Social Textures*, ed. Vincent L. Wimbush, 221–35. New York: Continuum.

Sadler, Rodney S., Jr. 2005. *Can a Cushite Change His Skin? An Examination of Race, Ethnicity, and Othering in the Hebrew Bible*. New York: T. & T. Clark.

———. 2006. "Can a Cushite Change His Skin?" In *Interpretation* 60 (4): 386–403.

Smith, H. Shelton. 1972. *In His Image, . . . But*. Durham, N.C.: Duke University Press.

Smith, Venture. 1798. *The Narrative Life and Adventures of Venture, a Native of Africa*. http://docsouth.unc.edu/neh/venture/venture.html.

Turner, Bishop Henry McNeal. 1998. "Justice or Emigration." In *Lift Every Voice: African American Oratory 1787–1900*, ed. Philip S. Foner and Robert James Branham, 775–90. Tuscaloosa: University of Alabama Press.

Walker, Alice. 1982. *The Color Purple*. Orlando, Fla.: Harcourt.

Weems, Renita. 1988. *Just a Sister Away: A Womanist Vision of Women's Relationships in the Bible*. San Diego: LuraMedia.

West, Cornel. 2002. "A Genealogy of Modern Racism." In *Race Critical Theories*, ed. Philomena Essed and David Theo Goldberg. Malden, Mass.: Blackwell.

Wheatley, Phillis. 1834. "On Being Brought from Africa to America." In *Memoir and Poems of Phillis Wheatley, a Native African and a Slave. Dedicated to the Friends of the Africans*. http://docsouth.unc.edu/neh/wheatley/wheatley.html.

EXODUS

Judy Fentress-Williams

It's the story everyone knows. It shows up in our movies, music, and literature. People who have never picked up the Bible know the story of the exodus—and just about everyone knows the name Moses. The exodus is pervasive in our popular culture. Its popularity belies its import in much the same way that James Brown's music is so widely used that many of those who enjoy his music don't know they are listening to the "Godfather of Soul" (Gordon 2006). This familiar story of the exodus is the formational and identifying event for Israel. It became the lens through which Israel interpreted her experiences and the foundation for her understanding of God. Thus the historical event developed into a transcendent moment—one that can occur again and again. And so it does, in the life of Israel and beyond.

PART ONE: THE EXODUS

REMEMBERING AS A REMIX

Before the exodus takes place, God commands the people to celebrate (Exod. 12:14), observe (12:24; 13:10), remember (13:3ff), and tell future generations: "You shall observe this day throughout your generations as a perpetual ordinance" (12:17). What the scripture makes clear is that remembering is as important as the event itself, if not more important. In an oral culture, repeating is the way that the events stay alive. If this event is central to Israel's identity, then the command to remember and retell is one oriented toward survival. Each time Israel repeats the story she reaffirms her identity.

Remembering the events of the exodus serves two purposes. It is an acknowledgment of who

God is, and it is a reminder of who the people are. Throughout the wilderness, God prefaces his commands to Israel with the words "I am the LORD your God who brought you out of the land of Egypt, out of the house of slavery" (Exod. 20:2). Service to God comes out of this relationship. It is not unlike the phrase some of us heard from our mothers, "I brought you into this world and I can take you out!" Both statements stake a claim that establishes a relationship and the listener's obligation that comes out of that relationship.

Israel remembers and retells her story as a means of affirming, preserving, and, at times, redefining her identity. No retelling of the story is the same. Each recounting of the event is shaped in part by the teller, the context, and the purpose of the story. In other words, when Israel obeys the command to remember, she is retelling. The events of the exodus were "remixed" as subsequent generations tried to find their way into the narrative. A remix is another version of a song, one distinct from the original in that different tracks are emphasized. It is achieved by adjusting the elements of the song, emphasizing or diminishing particular elements. For example, a remix might use a different baseline or highlight tracks that the original did not. A remix may be an extended version of the original, usually the version of the song that often is played in clubs for dancing. The remix often appears with the original on the same CD, allowing two versions of one song to coexist, reflecting back on each other.

The metaphorical language of the Bible is like music, allowing the story of the exodus to move from event to tradition and organizing motif. It can be retold with differing emphasis, resulting in a remix that seeks not to replace earlier accounts but to affirm and respond to the earlier accounts. For example, if the exodus is the point of orientation for Israel's identity and imagination, then the exile becomes the "anti-exodus" and the return to the land is a second exodus, all variations on a theme. In the prophetic tradition, the familiar language and images of the exodus are remixed to offer a new

understanding of who God is. Take the example of the prophet Amos:

> "Are you not like the Ethiopians to me, O people of Israel? says the LORD. Did I not bring Israel up from the land of Egypt and the Philistines from Caphtor and the Arameans from Kir?" (Amos 9:7).

In this passage, the prophet evokes language and images of God bringing Israel up, used heretofore to express the exclusive nature of Israel's relationship with God to suggest that God's work is not limited to a single people. Moreover, the work of God extends to those previously considered as enemies. Repeating/remixing allows for a tradition to expand and be inclusive.

The inclusivity of a remix stands in contrast to the practice of sampling. In sampling, a small segment of a recording is repeated, or looped, to form the foundation of another song. Sampling allows a song to cross genres and to fit into other settings. It is a way for music to live on in subsequent generations, as the example of James Brown makes clear. However, taken from its original arrangement, the small piece of music takes on a different character. The inherent danger of sampling is that the subsequent generations do not know the song in its entirety, the original artist, or the context.

A SAMPLE OF MEMORY

An example of sampling as a paradigm for remembering comes in the traditions surrounding the prophet Moses.

> All across the continent [Africa] there are the legends of the greatness of Moses. . . . He is revered because he had the power to go up to the mountain and bring them down. Many men could climb mountains. Anyone could bring down laws that had been handed to them. But who can talk with God face to face? . . . What other man has ever seen with his eyes even the back part of God's glory? (Hurston 1939: 337)

The figure of Moses looms large in the story of Israel, and it has shaped imaginations in the African Diaspora. African captives in America used the name Moses to refer to Harriet Tubman, along with many others who were deemed freedom fighters. Many African leaders after national independence were called Moses (Mugambi 2001: 14). Marcus Garvey was referred to as "black Moses," and Martin Luther King Jr. evoked the image of Moses atop Mt. Nebo, gazing over onto the Promised Land to conclude his last sermon, preached April 3, 1968, at Mason Temple in Memphis, Tennessee.

Separated from the roots of the narrative, these samples of the story depict Moses as a strong solitary figure. This image of Moses comes from a few elements or snapshots of the story that are sampled or repeated to the exclusion of the rest of the narrative. First, they forget that Moses was a reluctant, seemingly ill-suited leader who never made peace with his role as prophet. Second, they neglect the parts of the story that depict him as the recipient of liberation and not the liberator. Third, the practice of sampling overlooks the fact that the agents of redemption are women, sometimes foreign, and marginalized (Exod. 1:17—2:10). Unlike the tradition of Moses as a solitary prophet, the women in these stories work with others, using a variety of methods to redeem life. Thus the sampling paradigm for memory results in a theology that is limited to repeating the same old, tired elements again and again. In contrast, a remix maintains the themes of the music and the integrity of the narrative by engaging in dialogue with the original in a variety of contexts. What follows are examples of the exodus as remix.

Remix 1:
Pharaoh Don' Know Nothin' 'bout Birthin' Babies!

Exod. 1:1-14 provides the context and setting for the entire narrative. We begin with a genealogy that provides continuity with the Joseph narrative in Genesis, and then we are given the circumstances that lead to Israel's enslavement. Two groups of people once lived in community, but when the relationship dissolved, one group was perceived as a threat by the other and the response to that threat was oppression.

The story that begins in 1:15 is a preview to the exodus itself because it is a story about liberation. Pharaoh instructs the "midwives to the Hebrews" to kill the boys they deliver and to let the girls live. The phrase "midwives to the Hebrews" does not make the nationality of the midwives clear. They could be Hebrew or Egyptian. What matters in the narrative is their fear of God that enables them to defy Pharaoh. When summoned to explain why the Hebrew boys have not been killed, the midwives tell Pharaoh that the Hebrew women are "vigorous" or "lively" (*hayot*) and deliver before they arrive. Pharaoh, either because of his ignorance about women and childbirth or his belief that the Hebrews truly are "other" (in other words, less than human), believes their story. The midwives are in a position of very little power, yet they exploit Pharaoh's limited knowledge, which is due in part to his elevated position. The story foreshadows the exodus, in which Pharaoh's words will not stand. His orders will be subverted by unlikely, marginal characters. In this first deliverance story in Exodus, Pharaoh orders death for the Hebrew boys, but the midwives conspire to preserve that life.

Remix 2:
Moses Has Two Mommies

In chapter 2, the narrative shifts from the story of all the people to the story of one family, that of a Levite man and his wife. The woman bore a son and decided to hide him because he "was a fine baby" (*ki tov*). This phrase, "how good" (*ki tov*), appears in the Creation story as a description of God's work: "And God saw that it *was good*" (Gen. 1:18, 21, and 24). The use of the familiar phrase reminds the reader that the baby born under a death sentence is a part of God's created order. Moses is special not only in his mother's eyes but in the eyes of the Creator. His mother's inability to conceal him leads her to undertake a plan that is both desperate and hopeful: to place the baby on the river. She puts the baby in a waterproofed basket and in so doing fulfills Pharaoh's command that all the baby boys be tossed into the Nile River. This is the second story of deliverance in Exodus. Like the first story, the salvation of the child will require more than one person. Unlike the first story, this deliverance account has two components and two mothers.

Moses's basket is discovered by the daughter of Pharaoh, who not only rescues the baby but hires the child's mother to be his wet nurse. This story of deliverance stands out from what has gone before because the daughter of the Pharoah is "other" by virtue of her ethnicity, gender, and position. Like the previous stories we have examined, her rescue of the child involves the collaboration of others. What is most noteworthy in this account is the way that Pharaoh's daughter "prefigures" God's action in redeeming Israel. In 2:6, we read: "When she opened it, she saw the child. He was crying and she took pity on him. 'This must be one of the Hebrews' children,' she said."

Pharaoh's daughter *saw* the child, *heard* him (he was crying), and *took pity* on him. That action preceded her decision to keep him as her own. In Exod. 3:7, we hear YHWH say to Moses: "I have *observed* the misery of my people who are in Egypt; I have *heard* their cry on account of their taskmasters. Indeed *I know their sufferings*, and I have come down to deliver them from the Egyptians." Like Pharaoh's daughter, God *sees*, *hears*, and *has pity*.

Pharaoh's daughter rescues and names the child, making him her own. His name, Moses, works across language lines. His Egyptian mother named him Moses because "I drew him out of the water" (2:10). In Egyptian, the name Moses is likely derived from *Thutmose*, meaning "child of." In Hebrew, it means "the one who draws out," not "one drawn out" as Pharaoh's daughter claims. Here we can conclude that although Moses's adoptive mother had one thing in mind when she named him, there was another plan for his life embedded in that name.

Thus far, the would-be deliverer Moses is delivered again and again by women who model God's act of redemption. Each act of deliverance tells the reader something about how and why God will deliver Israel. In the story of the midwives, we learn that God will deliver Israel in defiance of Pharaoh and that God will dupe the Egyptian ruler. In the second story, we observe that Israel is God's child and that God's devotion to God's people is fierce like that of a mother to her baby. In the third story, we see that God's act of redemption will be made manifest through the collaboration of unlikely people. God's act of redemption is not limited by gender or race or by any of the lines of division created by humans.

Moses was nurtured by two women and most likely loved them both. As a result, he had two languages, two cultures, and two peoples. His upbringing demanded multiple consciousnesses. If he was connected to two peoples, how did he understand the prophetic words he uttered, "Let my people go"? Moses's multiple identities afforded him a perspective that revealed that the work of redemption was about more than any one people. God's work of redemption is relentless in its intentions to work across our designated boundaries so that all of God's people have the opportunity to be redeemed.

Remix 3:
Tell Ol' Pharaoh: African Americans and the Exodus

The exodus tradition shapes and is shaped by the people who tell the story. African captives in America found that the story of Israel's bondage and liberation spoke profoundly to their experiences of oppression and the struggle for liberation. Like Israel, their cultures were oral, and the story of the exodus readily fit into their cosmogony. They repeated it and made it their own. For Africans, this meant that they sang the story, because singing invokes the sacred. They took liberties with Old Testament narrative, "based on the tragedy of great need" (Thurman 1975: 14). As the enslaved Africans in the United

States recast the story, they laid claim to an identity as Israel, God's people. Pharaoh was the slave master, and Moses was the title given to anyone deemed a freedom fighter. The God of Moses and Israel bore a striking resemblance to the almighty creator God and judge of all who was already known to many of the captives (Raboteau 1978: 8). Having found their God in the story of the exodus, African captives were able to affirm their humanity and assert belief in a God who was on the side of the oppressed and downtrodden.

> When Israel was in Egypt's Land
> Let my people go
> Oppressed so hard, they could not stand
> Let my people go
>
> Go down Moses
> Way down in Egypt's land
> Tell ol' Pharaoh
> Let my people go

"Let My People Go," one of the better-known spirituals, is a fixture in American culture. When enslaved Africans in the United States used the exodus narrative to tell their own story, they employed "double voiced discourse," which is not limited to a single speaker and a single time. The double-voiced discourse moves between past, present, and future, using symbolic language and call-and-response. "When Israel was in Egypt's land" refers to a moment in history for Israel and the historical context of slavery in America. The time of oppression in this remix is tied to a particular location as the song identifies Egypt as the place of oppression for Israel. Line number three reminds the hearer that the people suffer not only because they are away from home but because of the oppression in this other place. The displacement speaks to a universal imbalance—one that only the creator God can repair.

In this particular remix of the exodus, the singer places herself alongside Moses by repeating the words of the prophet in lines two, four, and eight, "let my people go." If the song is sung as a call-and-

response, the voice of Moses is not a solitary one but a chorus, a community that calls for justice. The remix moves with ease from past to present, in and out of character, identifying with both the leader and those in need of one. Underlying these assertions is an assumed identity that the singers are "my people," namely "God's people." The identity as the people of God is the basis for humanity and a call to action that will end oppression.

Inherent in the liberation theology of these captives were the following assumptions:

- The God of Israel was the creator God, ruler of all the world.
- As God's children, they were fully human.
- As God's children (i.e., Israel), they had every right to expect deliverance.
- God's deliverance was not just a spiritual one but also political, socioeconomic, and physical.
- Deliverance would come because God was faithful and just.

This liberation theology of the African captives is the taproot of liberation theology in its varieties of expressions.

PART TWO: EXODUS AFTER THE EXODUS

Our traditions around the exodus tend to focus on the events in the first fifteen chapters. That emphasis overshadows the second, larger section of the book, which contains the wilderness and legal tradition. Free from the place of bondage, Israel is homeless. The God she follows does not appear to be anxious about this matter. To the contrary, God seems content to have Israel wander where she must depend on YHWH for everything. This is frustrating not only because of the realities of desert life, but because the exodus is tied from the very beginning to the land of promise. In Exod. 3:8a, God says: "I have come down to deliver them from the

Egyptians, and to bring them up out of that land to a good and broad land, a land flowing with milk and honey." The act of redemption has two parts. God goes down to deliver *and* to bring Israel up to a "good and broad land." That being said, the exodus is not complete until Israel reaches this promised land, and the remainder of the book is spent in a prolonged, agonizing anticipation as Israel exchanges the certainty of slavery for the unknown wilderness.

The wilderness section can be mapped out by location. Between Egypt and the elusive land of Canaan, the three locations that ground the narrative are the wilderness, Sinai, and the tabernacle. These locations will provide the interpretive lens for this section.

REMIX 4:
THE WILDERNESS—OH FREEDOM?

Freedom looks like the biggest thing that God ever made to me, and being a little hungry for the sake of it ought not to stop you. (Hurston 1939: 522–23)

The point of the exodus in Egypt was the creation of a people. Against the harsh backdrop of the desert, the Israelites learn that if they are to be the people of God, they must develop a faith born out of imagination.

Exodus 15:22-27 recounts Israel's first experience as a free people. In this brief account, the following key elements appear:

- The people follow Moses and God.
- They run out of water and are thirsty.
- They are led to water that they cannot drink.
- They cry out to Moses, who cries out to God.
- God instructs Moses on how to "cure" the water.
- God uses this opportunity to issue commands.

This first experience of freedom is a bitter one, as the Israelites learn what it means to be bought with a price. They were freed from Egypt but now belong to YHWH. They used to serve Pharaoh, but now they must serve YHWH and this God has the ability to inflict plagues as well as to heal. Moreover, their first experience of freedom reminds Israel that there is much to learn about this God. After all, what kind of God leads thirsty people to water they cannot drink?

The story of Exod. 15:22-27 is evocative for African Americans, whose first taste of freedom was a bitter one. The promise of forty acres and a mule was an empty one, and like the experience of Israel in the wilderness, newly freed slaves were arguably less safe than they were in slavery. The experiences of Reconstruction caused African Americans to ask, "Where is the land of promise?" The ongoing challenges to the African American community raise the question "Are we there yet?" and, more importantly, "Will we ever get there?" The provisional supply is satisfactory as a temporary plan, but many members of the African American community feel it has become a permanent way of life as African Americans, like Israel in the wilderness, move from one crisis to another.

This and other accounts of murmuring raise questions about the ability of God's people to trust God's provision. The word that is translated as "murmur," *rib*, has a legal context that speaks to the pursuit of what one is due legally. The very word *murmur* speaks to God's obligation of provision and presence to Israel. The murmuring accounts form a motif in scripture—one that is very much a part of many Africana religious traditions. The centrality of music to the people of the African continent makes for a tradition that embraces the practice of corporate murmuring. The community cries out, moans, and laments when there is a need, with the full expectation that God will answer. In fact, this act of crying out is a reflection of the strength of the bond between the people and God. The people cry to God because they understand that there is no greater power and no greater love. The *rib* comes from an intimate relationship. It is fraught with difficulty and frustration, but it is a bond like that between spouses or between parent and child. It is for that reason that Jeremiah describes the wilderness as a "honeymoon" for God: "I remember your devotion, your love as a bride, how you followed me in a land not sown" (Jer. 2:2).

The wilderness experience in Exodus picks up on a motif that is prevalent throughout scripture—namely, the desert being a place of encounter with God. In Genesis 12, Abram begins his sojourn in the wilderness, where he has multiple encounters with God. In Genesis 16 and 21, Hagar encounters God in the wilderness. Jacob, Abraham's grandson, also has multiple encounters with God in the wilderness (Genesis 28 and 32), and Moses meets God in the wilderness of Sinai. Now, the entire people of Israel are taken from bondage into the wilderness for an extended period of formation that is rooted in Israel's utter dependence on God.

The wilderness then is a place that is literal and metaphorical. It is the place of isolation and trial, but it is also the place of intimacy, where God places a mark on his bride. This mark is one born out of suffering. Belonging to God means sharing in the redemptive suffering of the world, and in the *ketubbah* there is no prenuptial agreement. Here the reality of being chosen by God comes into focus. God chooses people because we could not and would not willingly choose to share in redemptive suffering.

The experiences of African Americans and the Israelites make clear that the encounter and experience with God is the foundation for the covenantal relationship that enabled both communities to remain people of faith in the face of a harsh environment. One prominent example of the covenant is the Ten Commandments or Decalogue ("ten words").

Remix 5: Sinai and the Top Ten

The initial itinerary in the wilderness/legal tradition moves Israel to Sinai, the mountain of God. Sinai is the location of Moses's call, and it is from this location that God will give the law to Israel directly.

Exodus 20 begins as follows: "Then God spoke all these words." The Ten Commandments are unique as words spoken directly to the people from God. As such they hold a special place in Judaism and Christianity.

The first four commandments focus on Israel's relationship with her God, while commandments six through ten focus on people's relationships with their neighbors. Thus the Decalogue begins by establishing the centrality and scope of Israel's relationship with God. YHWH is God, first and foremost (first commandment). The commandments identify behavior that is evidence of this relationship. The prohibition of images in the second commandment prevents Israel from prescribing limits to how God works. The third commandment protects the sacred nature of God's name, binding Israel to honor any oath made invoking the divine name, and the fourth commandment directs Israel to "remember" or observe the Sabbath as sacred time. All four commandments prescribe behavior that reflects the nature of Israel's relationship with her God.

The remaining commandments understand that the nature of our relationship with God transforms our relationships with one another. Israel's behavior in community is a reflection of her relationship with God, and this begins in the family unit with parents (fifth commandment). Commandments six through ten regulate respect of our neighbor's life (prohibiting wrongful death), family, property, and integrity. The final prohibition against coveting is at the root of these other transgressions, so the final commandment speaks to regulating not just the outward behavior but our heart. In this way, it directs us back to the first command to have nothing and no one before God. God is the primary relationship, and God is the primary point of reference. The extent to which we uphold this will determine how we will live in community with one another.

The similarity between the Decalogue and the Hittite Suzerain treaty is significant, not only because of what that tells us about the extent to which Israel was a product of the ancient Near East. Its differences point to the ways in which Israel was an innovator as well. At the root of these commandments is the desire for relationship. YHWH does not simply want Israel's obedient behavior; the goal is Israel's heart.

Remix 6:
The Tabernacle: House Party

The isolation of the wilderness deprived Israel of an element essential to her identity. All the identifying markers of family, kinship group, and tribe are tied to land. In the establishment of the nation of Israel, God redefined all these elements. The people who come out of Egypt are a mixed group (Exod. 12:37-38). Although they maintain family and kinship groups, their primary marker of identity is that of belonging to God, to whom they are bound through covenant. Similarly, the elusiveness of the promised land provides an opportunity for God to redefine Israel's identity as it relates to homeland.

Few consider the wilderness home. The very geography demands a seminomadic life. Israel sojourns in the wilderness, in an effort to get to the land of Canaan. But this so-called sojourn takes a long time, forty years to be exact. So the exodus community finds itself in limbo, awaiting fulfillment of the promise made to Abraham and awaiting the completion of the act of the exodus. The expectation of "a good and broad land, a land flowing with milk and honey" must be balanced with God's announcement to Pharaoh, "Let my people go, so that they may celebrate a festival to me in the wilderness" (Exod. 5:1). God's declaration to Pharaoh gives a purpose of liberation that has nothing to do with the land of Canaan. Rather, it has to do with worship in the weary land of the wilderness. Is God sending mixed messages?

In the gap of anticipation of the promised land, the text devotes a significant amount of space to the tabernacle (chaps. 25–30 and 35–40). Before Canaan, there is a temporary home, a portable space that houses the ark of the Covenant. YHWH, like Israel, is in temporary housing. Yet, the amount of space the text devotes to the details of worship suggests this temporary space is not insignificant. To the contrary, it appears that the tent that is the tabernacle is the new definition of homeland. God marks the people at Sinai, and after that God is bound to the people by law/relationship, free to move wherever God's people move. Thus the people become YHWH's habitation. They are YHWH's homeland, and YHWH is their home.

To future generations, whether they are settled in Canaan or in exile, the tabernacle is a reminder that God's habitation is with Israel and that Israel's is with God. The tent of encounter is like a house party. Before teens can go to dance clubs, they bring the party into their own homes, usually the basement. A house party can take place wherever there is permission and space. It is not an official establishment, but when the people and music are there and the lights are turned down, there is a party—often one that will rival that at any club. It is, like the tabernacle, a movable celebration for people who do not have access to the official sites. During the times of segregation, when access to dance halls was limited, African Americans transformed existing spaces for dances. Africana history has a wealth of experiences around transforming and redeeming space.

Wilderness worship is the understanding that the sacred can occur anywhere. This concept was countercultural for the ancient Near East, where deities were tied to a place. This God wanted to be tied to a people. The God who moved with the people offered a word of hope to those in this wilderness of exodus, exile, and all subsequent wilderness experiences. This hope is what enabled African captives to find God in a foreign land. In the "hush arbors" under the cover of darkness, slaves experienced the transformation of any place into sacred space with the presence of God's spirit. They understood that the wilderness or the place of exile can be transformed into Canaan.

Judy Fentress-Williams

References

Fishbane, Michael. 1988. *Biblical Texts and Texture.* Oxford: Oneworld.

Gordon, Jason. 2006. "James Brown: Most Sampled Man in the Biz" in *Rolling Stone: Rock & Roll Daily.* December 26.

Hurston, Zora Neale. 1939. "Moses, Man of the Mountain." In *Zora Neale Hurston: Novels and Stories.* New York: Library of America.

Mugambi, Jesse. 2001. "Africa and the Old Testament." In *Interpreting the Old Testament in Africa.* Nairobi: Acton.

The Prince of Egypt. 1998. Dreamworks SKG. Film.

Raboteau, Albert J. 1978. *Slave Religion: The Invisible Institution in the Antebellum South.* New York: Oxford University Press.

Thurman, Howard. 1975. *Deep River* and *The Negro Spiritual Speaks of Life and Death.* Richmond, Ind.: Friends United.

Watkins, Ralph C. 2007. *The Gospel Remix: Reaching the Hip Hop Generation.* Valley Forge, Pa.: Judson.

Weems, Renita. 1988. *Just a Sister Away.* San Diego: Luramedia.

LEVITICUS

Madeline McClenney-Sadler

FROM THE WHITE HOUSE to Tiananmen Square, civil rights movements warn us that a lack of fairness in society leads to social upheaval. Around the world, marchers proclaim, "No justice! No peace!" In Leviticus, priestly exhortations make a similar proclamation. In a literarily complex arrangement of instructions, the prime directive is revealed at Leviticus's literary core in chapter 19: justice and peace come when you love your neighbor (Douglas 1999a: 343). Conversely, in Leviticus, a lack of love leads to a lack of justice and peace. Do the right thing in relationships and there will be right relationships in society. To see this attention to literary details in the arrangement of its chapters is key.

The following divisions in Leviticus illustrate a steady crescendo of theological notes that form a complete chord on justice and holiness in chapter 19: chapters 1–7, sacrifices; chapters 8–10, ordination of priests; chapters 11–15, the practice of purity; chapters 16–17, purity and atonement; chapter 18, purity and kinship; chapter 19, purity and justice; chapter 20, purity and punishment; chapters 21–26, purity and feasts; chapter 27, appendix. On either side of its core (chap. 19) stand chapters 18 and 20. Chapter 18 lists the incest prohibitions that make sex between family members off-limits (Lev. 18:1-18), and chapter 20 covers the punishments for idolatry and transgressing the incest prohibitions (20:1-27).

When reading Leviticus with chapter 19 as its compositional core, we find social justice is predicated upon sexual justice between individuals, within families, and between families. The demand of holiness is certain: a people who will be holy as God is holy (Lev. 19:2) recognize that Yahweh has a claim on the sexuality of those who acknowledge Yahweh as Lord.

Douglas argues that the compilers of Leviticus utilized a literary practice in Afro-Greco antiquity that arranges a composition according to an architectural structure. Specifically, the layout of Leviticus follows the layout of the desert tabernacle. Holiness is predicated upon just relationships between individuals. The closer we get to the core of Leviticus (chap. 19), the more we realize that all justice unravels when sexual justice within the family is abrogated by sex with close relatives and sex between people who are close to each other (such as a man having sex with sisters). Trauma within the family has a social cost, and sexual border crossing within the family is the pulled thread that initiates the tear.

> Pa never had a kine word to say to me.
> Just say "You gonna do what your mammy
> wouldn't." . . . when that hurt, I cry. He start
> to choke me, saying "You better shut up and
> git used to it." But I don't never get used to
> it. He act like he can't stand me no more. Say
> I'm evil an always up to no good. . . . I see him
> looking at my little sister. She scared. But I say,
> "I'll take care of you. With God help."
> (Walker 1982/2006: 1–3)

Purity and holiness are meaningless within the family if a father rapes a daughter (Lev. 18:17) or a mother rapes a son (Lev. 18:6). If a person can surrender to Yahweh his or her most prized possession, presumably control of his or her body, then he or she gains a spiritual discipline that increases the capacity to surrender possessions during the jubilee (Lev. 25:10), to utilize just weights in commerce (Lev. 19:36), to protect the assets of one's neighbor (Lev. 19:11), and to refuse to hate a brother (Lev. 19:17). To give Yahweh ritual service or a tithe but refuse to conduct oneself in a holy fashion is unclean (Isa. 1:10-17; Jeremiah 23). Holy persons of other groups who worship false gods sacrifice as little personally while placating the gods with the bodies of women and children (Lev. 18:21).

In an Africana Diaspora overcome by HIV/AIDS, mangled by coercive sex between girls and older boys and men, strangled by women pursuing young boys, twisted by older men seducing minor boys, dismembered by sexual tourism, and emotionally disordered by an underground sex slave industry and addiction to pornography, it is a matter of wisdom that we inspect more closely the commands for holy sexual conduct between kinfolk and friends in Leviticus 18.

There is no other verse in Leviticus that has been as instrumental to Africana communities as Lev. 19:18: "Love your neighbor as yourself, I am the Lord." To recognize this as the moral apex of Leviticus is to note its centrality to the sustaining theologies of two crucial figures in the Africana world: Jesus and Martin Luther King Jr.

> Agape means nothing sentimental or basically
> affectionate; it means understanding, redeem-
> ing good will for all men, an overflowing love
> which seeks nothing in return. It is the love
> of God working in the lives of men. When
> we love on the agape level we love men not
> because we like them, not because their atti-
> tudes and ways appeal to us, but because God
> loves them. (King 1957: 8–9)

For Jesus, love of neighbor is an essential aspect of his own theology. In his explanation of Jesus' conflation of Lev. 19:18 with Deut. 6:4-5 in the book of Mark, Powery notes: "The addition of 'love for neighbor' is not common and provides Jesus' theological understanding that love for the other elucidates most clearly one's love for God" (2003: 144).

Failure to engage in sexual acts that are loving and just undermines key relationship strengths, such as emotional intimacy, loyalty, and monogamy, all of which make healthy relationships of any kind between human souls possible. Grammy Award–winning singer Musiq Soulchild sings about the same human error that the Holiness Code of Leviticus seeks to correct. He sings: "Love . . . so many people use your name in vain." In the chorus, Soulchild conveys the importance of love in human relationships: "For better or worse, I still will choose you [love] first." Soulchild's song is representative of a commonplace in the Christian Africana Diaspora. Whether armed or unarmed in the fight against oppression, across many national borders, Christian Africans in the Diaspora have chosen to love their oppressors in the way King described above. If we fight against racists who hate, we know intuitively that we must not become like them.

In the United States, African American women's spirituality is often shaped in a crucible of heartache, assault, and neglect by those who use the name of love in vain. In her groundbreaking study of African American women's spirituality, Frederick addresses the intersection of faith and sexuality. She notes that it is fundamental for many African American women to connect sexuality and faith in a way that is empowering:

> Women hold certain ideas about sexual engagement, not only to protect their own sacred space, but also to protect the sacred space of others. Ideas about celibacy and marriage are presented as a means of protecting loved ones against high teenage pregnancy rates and sexually transmitted diseases. Within this discourse is a larger discussion about the need for biblical ideals of sexuality in order to facilitate the regeneration of society as a whole. (Frederick 2003: 197)

The regeneration of a functioning social structure is the aim of the hermeneutical key "love your neighbor" in Leviticus (19:18).

We could go shouting to Zion about the instructions in Leviticus and its divinely inspired moral apex were it not for the fact that the very same book that forbids abuses of power within the family (Lev. 18:6-18; 19:29), requires fairness (Lev. 19:36), and demands atonement for both unin-

tentional and intentional wrongdoing (Leviticus 16) also gives Israelites permission to enslave non-Israelites and use them as breeding machines (Lev. 25:44). As Roberta Flack and the Black Eyed Peas would ask, "Where is the love?" As Bailey (1995) cogently argues, Christians must be careful with the use and application of passages that appear to condone oppressive ideologies.

There is no twenty-first-century feel-good response that can make Lev. 25:44 spiritually comprehensible for a spiritual people seeking deliverance in the Africana Diaspora. Whether we treat servitude as a form of social welfare necessary to provide survival benefits to dislocated individuals and families in preindustrial societies, or whether we treat servitude in any circumstance as a heinous act against humanity, Leviticus allows it, as long as the person is non-Israelite. Given its accent on justice and its structural arrangement, which places love at its literary center, it is too simplistic to charge what I call its "literary personality" with hypocrisy. Leviticus is no more hypocritical than biblical readers who reject its authority because of this verse about slavery while receiving pensions and salaries built on slave and child labor profits.

Although it does not abolish slavery, the Levitical ethic of love attempts to weaken slavery by stopping it within its community of origin. To its credit, unlike many of our investment firms, it has fair labor standards. It does not permit the mistreatment of strangers and foreigners—that is, non-Israelites. It provides that "when a stranger resides with you in your land, you shall not wrong him. The stranger who resides with you shall be to you as one of your citizens; you shall love him as yourself, for you were strangers in the land of Egypt: I am the Lord your God" (19:33, 34). Levitical instructions are explicit in the expectation that all persons within the household be treated humanely—although whether this happened in practice is certainly questionable. All economic systems lend themselves to corruption. Most Bible readers eat the bread of a corrupted economic system with little thought of how the bread made it to the table. When we eat, we appear to condone the modern-day subsistence wages that make possible the consumption of fruit picked by enslaved Latino hands. We have not abolished low wages, though at the core many of us have that as our ultimate aim. Leviticus is no different with respect to slavery. At its core, chapter 19, slavery would have to be abolished. The egalitarian bent of Leviticus is also accented in the incest prohibitions of chapter 18.

It is exceedingly important to note that we have erred in identifying a patrilineal society in Lev. 18:6-18. Anthropologists have long known that patrilineality is universally associated with exogamy (McClenney-Sadler 2007: 73). That the status of women is elevated in ancient Israel is clear in a formal analysis and structural assessment of Leviticus 18. In cross-cultural comparative research, incest prohibitions are used to determine descent because incest rules identify family relationships. Utilizing anthropological methods in my analysis, a Normal Hawaiian social structure is revealed. It is characterized, in part, by bilateral descent and bilateral incest taboos. Bilateral descent means that family connections are traced through both the male and female lines. Comparative ethnographers have noted that where Hawaiian social structures exist, women are elevated in social status.

The presentation of the mother's rights before the father's in verse 7 reflects an increase in status that accrues to mothers as well as an increase in status for women in ambilocal societies like ancient Israel, where couples can live anywhere. The first rights recognized are the exclusive rights of a mother to a father (18:7); the final rights recognized are those of a wife to harmonious and nonthreatening relationships with her daughters, granddaughters, and sisters (18:17-18). The jural-literary movement from mother's rights to "wife's rights" forms an *inclusio* that makes the first last and the last first. The importance of wives and mothers in ancient Israelite culture is emphasized literarily, thus balancing gender asymmetry in these laws.

Although much neglected in Sunday Bible studies in the Africana Diaspora, Leviticus is a book of the Bible that should be used to guide us in maintaining just relationships. Even with its internal inconsistencies, it dares readers to see beyond its own literary extremes and focus on what lies at its center—a neighborly love (chap. 19) that cannot exist without holy sexual relations between humans on one side (chap. 18), and consequences for failure to maintain those relationships in a holy manner on the other (chap. 20). This is the trilogy of chapters, the climax of Leviticus, where God's justice is explained. As Douglas notes, for those who heed Levitical instructions, "holiness involves making their lives a transparent enactment of God's law" (1999a: 349).

References

Bailey, Randall C. 1995. "They're Nothing but Incestuous Bastards: The Polemical Use of Sex and Sexuality in Hebrew Canon Narrative." In *Reading from This Place: Social Location and Biblical Interpretation*, ed. Fernando F. Segovia and Mary Ann Tolbert, 121–38. Minneapolis: Fortress Press.

Black Eyed Peas. 2003. "Where Is the Love?" From the album *Elephunk*. A&M Records.

Douglas, Mary. 1999a. "Justice as the Cornerstone: An Interpretation of Leviticus 18–20." *Interpretation* 53:341–50.

———. 1999b. *Leviticus as Literature*. Oxford: Oxford University Press.

Flack, Roberta, and Donny Hathaway. 1972. "Where Is the Love?" From the album *Roberta Flack and Donny Hathaway*. Atlantic Records.

Frederick, Marla. 2003. *Between Sundays: Black Women and Everyday Struggles of Faith*. Berkeley: University of California Press.

King, Martin Luther, Jr. 1957. "Non-Violence and Racial Justice." *Christian Century*, 1–9.

McClenney-Sadler, Madeline. 2007. *Re-Covering the Daughter's Nakedness: A Formal Analysis of Israelite*

Kingship Terminology and the Internal Logic of Leviticus 18. New York: T. & T. Clark.

Music Soulchild. 2000. "Love." From the album *I Just Want to Sing.* Def Soul Records.

Powery, Emerson. 2003. *Jesus Reads Scripture: The Function of Jesus' Use of Scripture in the Synoptic Gospels.* Leiden: Brill.

Walker, Alice. 1982/2006. *The Color Purple.* New York: Harcourt Trade.

NUMBERS

Michelle Ellis Taylor

MUST THE OPPRESSED
BECOME THE OPPRESSOR?

"Why would God tell them to kill all those
    children?" I asked.
"'Cause that's the Lord's way child. They were
    sinful and would have led God's people to
    sin," the elderly lady answered.
"Weren't the Midianites God's children too?"
"No, they were a sinful nation."
"Why couldn't God change their hearts?"
"Because they were too hard-hearted."
"Weren't the Israelites sinful, too?"
"They were the children of the covenant."
"That doesn't seem fair," I responded.

Such were the answers I received as a child
when I questioned the stories of the Bible.

"Why does the Bible blame everything on
    women?" I asked.
"Because of Eve and the apple. The women of
    Baal Peor caused the men to sin because
    women are the weaker sex."
Not from what I can see, I thought. *God doesn't
    seem very fair at all.*

These are the thoughts that confront many who
attempt a critical reading of the book of Numbers
(so named for the census in chapters 1–4). The
Israelites, fresh out of slavery in Egypt, now on
their way to settle in the land of Canaan, are at
the point of birth as a nation and therefore have a
wonderful opportunity. With this new beginning,
they can become any kind of nation they choose.
They can treat each other fairly. They can respect
the nations they encounter on their trek to the

Land of Canaan and leave them unmolested. They can create laws that empower all their members. Once powerless, they now have power over others. How they use this power is up to them. But this is dreaming. The book of Numbers is known for its butchery of the nations Israel encounters along the way as well as its misogynistic laws. Nations that are treated with fellowship in the book of Exodus are butchered in Numbers. One of the few laws that gives parity to women in Numbers 27 is repealed in Numbers 31.

Many themes of Numbers are significant for people of African ancestry. Issues of slavery, oppression, racism, and abuse and subjugation of women resonate strongly with us. The slavery of the Bible was used to justify slavery of Africans and their descendents in much of the Western world in the nineteenth century, including the United States, the Caribbean, Mexico, and Brazil. Numbers is one of the very texts used to justify the sanctioned butchering of other nations in the name of expansion. The butchery found in the book of Numbers sets the pattern for the warfare and slaughter going on in much of the world today, whether a nation claims the Holy Bible or the Holy Qur'an as its model.

If Israelite men were threatened by foreigners, they were equally threatened by women—Israelite and foreign women alike. Thus the book of Numbers has several stories of women being put "in their place" when they dared step out.

MIRIAM AND MOSES'S CUSHITE WIFE

Miriam is both heroine and villain in this story in Numbers 12. She is too proud and free because she is a woman who has the audacity to lead. Miriam and Aaron both complain about Moses thinking too highly of himself because he is married to a Cushite woman. Because of later racial bias in religious texts, we often assume a negative interpretation of this text; however, Randall Bailey has

successfully argued that Cush (Ethiopia) and Egypt were the standards of beauty and success in ancient texts (Bailey 1991).

According to Bailey, they claim his marriage to a Cushite woman shouldn't make him more special since they themselves are Egyptians (Bailey 1995). Similarly, Aaron and Miriam argue that God has spoken not just through Moses but through them as well. In essence, both arguments are that Moses has nothing over them. Because of this complaint, God chastises Aaron and Miriam, telling them that God speaks to prophets in a vision or dream but that God speaks to Moses directly and Moses actually sees God. To further stress the point, God strikes Miriam with a skin disease we usually translate as "leprosy" or "scale disease" (not the disease known as leprosy today). Although Aaron also questioned Moses's authority and complained about Moses's Cushite wife, he is not struck with this disease, only Miriam. In contrast to the Black (Cushite) woman she complained about, she is struck with snow-white scales, "as one dead, who emerges from his mother's womb with half his flesh eaten away" (v. 12).

As to the issue of why Miriam was struck with the skin disease and not Aaron, perhaps to the biblical writer, Aaron, as a man, was within his right to question Moses and has the right to be a leader. Miriam, however, stepped out of the bounds dictated to her as a woman because, first, she had the audacity to be a leader and, second, to question the ultimate leader, Moses. God further shows Moses's authority because it is only after Moses prays for God to heal Miriam and asks that she instead be put outside the camp for seven days (see law in Leviticus 13–14) that she is healed. Aaron, however, apparently goes unpunished for questioning.

God doesn't seem very fair at all.

Although the biblical writer had problems with Miriam as a leader, the people still cannot leave until she is readmitted to the camp; thus, although chastised for daring to "act like a man," she continues as their leader and is respected as such.

THE DAUGHTERS OF ZELOPHEHAD

Numbers 27:1-11 and 36:1-12 tell of five audacious women—Mahlal, Noah, Hoglah, Milcah, and
Tirzah—whose father died before reaching the land
of Canaan and therefore could not receive his share
of the inheritance. His daughters did not want their
father's name to be left out, so they asked Moses
if they could inherit his portion of the land on his
behalf. Moses took the issue to God, and God told
Moses the daughters had a valid argument so he
should indeed issue Zelophehad's share of the land
to his daughters. God then gave Moses a new law:
if a man dies without sons but has a daughter, his
holdings are to be transferred to his daughter. These
audacious women got the entire law changed!

However, in 36:1-12, the patriarchs of the clan
could not stand for these women to step out of
their place and usurp what the men saw as theirs by
right and privilege, so they appealed to Moses on
the issue of women being land owners and pointed
out that if a woman married outside her clan, then
the land would go to that other clan and the clan of
her father would lose that land. With their bidding,
Moses then declared that any woman who inherits
land must marry within her father's clan, essentially
marrying her cousin and handing the land over
to him. Would it have been so difficult for Moses
to decree that the land would revert, upon the
woman's death, to the tribe of her father? No, the
issue is allowing women to inherit land in the first
place, a right reserved for the men of the clan. The
largesse of chapter 27 is taken away in chapter 36
so that a woman with no brothers is only allowed
to be a placeholder for the land until she finds a
husband to take it off her hands. As with the story
of Miriam and Moses's Cushite wife, here the biblical writer, under the guise of God, cannot tolerate a
woman being too proud or too free. The daughters
of Zelophehad are only allowed to break with tradition if and as long as they are keeping their father's
name alive; strength in a woman is allowed only in
service of patriarchy.

God doesn't seem very fair at all.

THE WOMEN OF BAAL PEOR: NUMBERS 25

She say, Miss Celie. You better hush. God might hear you.

*Let 'im hear me, I say. If he ever listened to poor colored women
the world would be a different place, I can tell you.*
(Walker 1982: 192)

The women of Baal Peor and an unnamed Midianite woman are blamed for the destruction of the
Midianites in this brutal story where the Moabites
and Midianites are interchangeable. They are called
whores because the Israelite men had sexual intercourse with them and made sacrifices to a Moabite
god, the god of Baal Peor, although the Moabites
also worshiped Yahweh, the God of Israel. For this
sin, God tells Moses to impale the chiefs of all the
people in the sun because of God's fierce anger at
this infraction. Moses orders the judges, "Each of
you shall kill any of your people who have yoked
themselves to Baal Peor," which leads to the Israelites killing their own family members (fratricide).
Although it is the women of Moab who are accused
of leading the Israelites astray, one foreign woman
is as good as another in justifying brutality against
an entire race of people, so in verse 6, when we are
told that an Israelite brought a Midianite woman
before the congregation of Israel, a plague from
God then strikes Israel, killing about twenty-four
thousand people. Then Phinehas, Aaron's zealous
son, kills the Midianite woman and the man who
brought her before the Israelites. Of course, God
then tells Moses to show hostility toward the Midianites, thus justifying the butchery of the Midianites. The foreignness, the otherness, of Midianite
and Moabite women is used in this story (chap. 25)
to justify the butchering of Midianite women, men,
and boys, and then the kidnapping and mass rape
of the Midianite girls too young to have had intercourse with a man (chap. 31).

*If [God] ever listened to poor colored women
the world would be a different place, I can tell you.*
(Walker 1982: 192)

ISRAEL AND THEIR KIN: THE MASSACRE OF THE MIDIANITES, NUMBERS 31

The most prominent theme in Numbers is the Israelites' butchering of their relatives to obtain their land in the name of the divine promise, God's promise that they would inherit the land of Canaan.

War
by Edwin Starr

War! Huh!
What is it good for?
Absolutely nothing!

War I despise
'cause it means destruction
of innocent lives

War means tears
To thousands of mothers' eyes
When their sons go to fight
And lose their lives

. . .

War, it ain't nothing
But a heartbreaker
War, friend only to the undertaker
War—It's an enemy to all mankind
The thought of war blows my mind
War has caused unrest
Within the younger generation
Induction then destruction
Who wants to die?

The names of the Moabites and the Midianites are often interchanged in the Bible. The Midianites were the direct descendants of Abraham, having descended from Midian, Abraham's son by Keturah, whom he married after the death of Sarah (Gen. 25:2). Moses's wife Zipporah and father-in-law Jethro were Midianites. Jethro was a Midianite priest (Exodus 18) who professed belief in Israel's God in verse 11: "Now I know that the Lord is greater than all the gods, because he delivered the people from the Egyptians." It was Jethro who advised Moses on appointing judges to help him rule the Israelite multitudes in Exod. 18:17-23. However, according to Numbers 31, Moses orders his father-in-law's people wiped out.

War!
It's nothing but a heartbreaker

The biblical text describes peaceful interaction between the Israelites and Moabites in Numbers 22–24 before God supposedly tells Israel to utterly destroy them. The prophet Balaam is a prophet of Yahweh, Israel's God. King Balak of Moab tells him to curse Israel. However, after listening to God, Balaam blesses Israel instead, explaining that he can only say what God tells him to say (22:38). However, in Numbers 31, this same Balaam is accused of causing the women of Baal Peor to lead the men of Israel astray. Thus, Balaam, friend to the Israelites, is killed (v. 8).

War!
Friend only to the undertaker

In chapter 31, the Israelites' annihilation of the Midianites is heartbreaking on so many levels if read with open eyes. They kill all the men and then take all the women and children as captives. But Moses is angry that they allow all the women to live, of course because they caused the men of Israel to worship Baal of Peor (recall, those were the Moabites, not Midianites). Moses then tells the Israelites to kill all the boy children and the women who are not virgins, but to keep the virgins for themselves, in the name of God. Then they take the girls as sex slaves. Thus we see that their foreignness was not the issue, but their suitability as sex slaves for the Israelite men, who apparently felt it was okay to have sexual intercourse with a foreigner, as long as she was not over age twelve.

> War is the enemy of all mankind
> The thought of war blows my mind

Frequently we see reports on the news of young boys being taken captive and forced to kill their own family members, forced to watch as their own mothers and sisters are raped, and told they will be killed themselves if they do not comply, if they do not join rebel forces. How can we continue to read such a text uncritically? Our easy explanation is that we can't understand God's ways. Would we want to know the ways of a God who was this brutal? Is it so impossible that these lines were written to justify war atrocities?

> Handed down from generation to generation
> Induction, destruction
> Who wants to die?

Such events as the butchering of their kin in God's name are as much war atrocities as those occurring in Iraq, Darfur, and Rwanda in our own time. Is God instructing such atrocities now? If God does not instruct such brutality now, why do we believe God instructed it in biblical times?

> Peace, love and understanding, tell me
> Is there no place for them today?
> They say we must fight to keep our own
>   freedom
> But Lord knows there's gotta be a better way
> Ahh, war, (Huh) Good God y'all
> What is it good for?

CONCLUSION

An Africana reading of this book would be to identify not with the Israelites but with the oppressed

and rejected, with those in whom the dominant power once trusted but then turned against—that is, with the Midianites and the Moabites (chaps. 25 and 31), with Miriam and Moses's Cushite wife (chap. 12), and with the daughters of Zelophehad (chaps. 27 and 31).

We accept difficult stories in the Bible because "God said it, so it must be okay," even when it is contrary to our image of a loving God, as in Num. 31:17-18: "Now therefore, kill every male among the little ones, and kill every woman who has known a man by sleeping with him. But all the young girls who have not known a man by sleeping with him, keep alive for yourselves." However, such acceptance without question, without examination, leads us to continue to persecute and oppress others, an even sadder fact because we ourselves are a people who have been persecuted and oppressed.

Or can we re-envision God as one who would not want us to be so brutal to one another? Perhaps God would want us to be the voice of reason that shouts, "This must stop! This slaughter of my children is not what I intended!"

> Darkness cannot drive out darkness; only light can do that. Hate cannot drive out hate; only love can do that. Hate multiplies hate, violence multiplies violence, and toughness multiplies toughness in a descending spiral of destruction. . . . The chain reaction of evil—hate begetting hate, wars producing more wars—must be broken, or we shall be plunged into the dark abyss of annihilation. (King 1981: 53)

References

Bailey, Randall C. 1991. "Beyond Identification: The Use of Africans in Old Testament Poetry and Narratives." In *Stony the Road We Trod: African American Biblical Interpretation*, ed. Cain Hope Felder, 156–84. Minneapolis: Fortress Press.

———. 1994. "They're Nothing but Incestuous Bastards: The Polemical Use of Sex and Sexuality in Hebrew Canon Narratives." In *Reading from This Place: Social Location and Biblical Interpretation*, vol. 1, ed. Fernando F. Segovia and Mary Ann Tolbert, 121–38. Minneapolis: Fortress Press.

———. 1995. "'Is That Any Name for a Nice Hebrew Boy?'—Exodus 2:1-10: The De-Africanization of an Israelite Hero." In *The Recovery of Black Presence: An Interdisciplinary Exploration*, ed. Randall C. Bailey and Jacquelyn Grant, 25–36. Nashville: Abingdon.

Dearman, Andrew. 1989. *Studies in the Mesha Inscription and Moab*. Atlanta: Scholars.

Felder, Cain Hope. 1991. "Race, Racism and the Biblical Narrative." In *Stony the Road We Trod: African American Biblical Interpretation*, ed. Cain Hope Felder, 127–45. Minneapolis: Fortress Press.

Gibb, H. A. R., and J. H. Kramers. 1995. *Concise Encyclopedia of Islam*. Leiden: Brill.

King, Martin Luther, Jr. 1981. *The Strength to Love*. Minneapolis: Fortress Press.

Lipka, Hillary. 2006. *Sexual Transgression in the Hebrew Bible*. Sheffield, Eng.: Sheffield Phoenix.

Starr, Edwin. 1970. *War*. Album. Motown Records.

Walker, Alice. 1982. *The Color Purple*. New York: Harcourt.

———. 1985. *The Color Purple*. Film. Amblin Entertainment.

DEUTERONOMY

Harold V. Bennett

"Mother to Son"

Well, son, I'll tell you:
Life for me ain't been no crystal stair.
It's had tacks in it,
And splinters,
And boards torn up,
And places with carpet on the floor —
Bare.
But all the time
I'se been a-climbin' on,
And reachin' landin's,
And turnin' corners,
And sometimes goin' in the dark
Where there ain't been no light.
So boy, don't you turn back.
Don't you set down on the steps
'Cause you finds it's kinder hard.
Don't you fall now —
For I'se still goin', honey,
I'se still climbin',
And life for me ain't been no crystal stair.

—Langston Hughes

THE POEM "Mother to Son" exemplifies the advice that a Black mother could give to her child. As the anonymous mother talks to her son, she shares what she has learned about life. She says:

> Well, son, I'll tell you:
> Life for me ain't been no crystal stair.
> It's had tacks in it,
> And splinters,
> And boards torn up,
> And places with carpet on the floor—
> Bare.

On the one hand, the unnamed woman in "Mother to Son" points out that life is replete with obstacles, hardships, and predicaments. On the other hand, Blacks in America, and especially in the American South, have a very similar story to tell. This experience surfaces in the backdrop against which to understand "The Negro National Anthem." The song says:

> Stony the road we trod,
> Bitter the chastening rod,
> Felt in the days when hope unborn had died

"The Negro National Anthem," then, implies that struggle, harsh conditions, adversity, abuse, and exploitation have been widespread in the plight of Blacks in the United States.

While one can view the guidance offered by the anonymous woman in "Mother to Son" and the experience of Blacks in American society through the lens of hardship, exploitation, alienation, discrimination, and abuse, the careful reader also notices that another storyline is present in both of these poems. The nameless woman in "Mother to Son" instructs her child on how to deal with existential impediments in life. She says:

> Don't you set down on the steps
> 'Cause you finds it's kinder hard.
> Don't you fall now—

She counsels him to reject an ethos that grounds itself in victimization, hopelessness, irresponsibility, and other moral ideals, which place a person on the defensive and lead to his or her dehumanization and constant frustration with the human condition. She instead counsels him to become proactive. The mother in "Mother to Son" directs her child to keep it moving: she urges him to take up an offensive position and to subscribe to an ethos that leads to empowerment and self-determination.

Words in "The Negro National Anthem" indicate also that triumph and accomplishment are features of the Black experience. The song points out:

> Yet with a steady beat,
> Have not our weary feet
> Come to the place for which our fathers
> sighed?

Although the counsel of the unnamed woman in "Mother to Son" and "The Negro National Anthem" are bases for claiming that a success narrative is present in the collective beingness of Black people in the world, these poems also invite the reader to raise questions about the institutional, systemic oppression and exploitation of Blacks in the United States.

This article draws from the collective experience of Blacks in the United States, sculpting a hermeneutic for viewing religious texts that elucidates institutional bases of oppression and introduces aspects of the success narrative into the hermeneutic. This hermeneutic, then, raises and seeks a response to the following questions: (1) What oppressed subgroups appear in the legislation in Deuteronomy? (2) What are the predicaments of these subgroups in the biblical communities? (3) Is there a systemic, institutional basis of oppression in the biblical community suggested by the book of Deuteronomy? (4) If so, how does this social convention contribute to the predicament of these oppressed groups in ancient Israelite society? And, finally, (5) if a success narrative is present in the responses of these groups to their circumstances, how can that success narrative be interpreted so that it can provide a philosophical framework for helping to ameliorate the circumstances of Blacks in the United States in general?

OVERVIEW OF DEUTERONOMY

Deuteronomy is the fifth book in the Old Testament. According to Jewish traditions, it is the fifth book of Moses. The title of this book in English grounds itself in the Greek translation of the Hebrew wording of Deut. 17:18. The Septuagint, the Greek version of the Hebrew Bible, uses the wording *to deuteronomiov touto* ("this second law") to reflect the Hebrew *mishnê hattorâ hazz'ôt* ("a copy of this law"). The English appellation, *Deuteronomy,* brings into play the notion that the fifth book of Moses is a second, distinct body of legal traditions.

Deuteronomy contains thirty-four chapters. What is more, distinct language appears in these texts. Characteristic of Deuteronomy are phrases such as the following: *with your whole heart and soul* (Deut. 11:13), *the place which the Lord thy God will choose* (Deut. 14:23-25), *to go after strange gods* (Deut. 13:3), and *the house of servitude* (Deut. 5:6). Moreover, diverse literary genres comprise this document. Chief among those types of literature present are narratives, hortatory addresses, laws, and poems. As Deuteronomy recounts the trek of the biblical community from Egypt to the plains of Moab, it also includes many of the literary traditions that recount the experience of biblical Israel in the wilderness.

The account about the reconnaissance of the land illustrates how Deuteronomy introduces new information or adapts extant traditions that appear elsewhere in the literary traditions of ancient Israel. One account about the report of the spies appears in Num. 13:1—14:45. In the story found in Numbers, the Deity commands Moses to send out scouts to obtain critical information about the promised land. Numbers 13:1—14:45 lists the individuals who comprised this group, and it specifies the length of the expedition. Moses, Aaron, and Caleb, not Joshua, play a major role in the account in Numbers. What is more, the account in Numbers indicates that the people suggested stoning the spies after they returned from surveying the promised land and offered their report about the prospect of the biblical community seizing the land from its inhabitants. Deuteronomy 1:19-46 is an alternative account of the report of the spies. In this account, the people ask Moses to organize a reconnaissance of the land. The names of the persons who comprised the group fail to appear in this account. No report about the desire of the people to stone the scouts is present. What is more, Deuteronomy introduces information that attempts to exculpate Moses of any wrongdoing in regard to taking possession of the land. Aaron appears nowhere in the account in Deuteronomy.

Deuteronomy also offers new information about the keeping of the Sabbath. Deuteronomy 5:12-15 indicates that one should keep the Sabbath because the Deity delivered the biblical community from slavery in Egypt. Exodus 20:8-11 indicates that one should keep the Sabbath because the Deity rested from work on the seventh day. The story about the spying out of the land of Canaan and the admonition to recognize the Sabbath day shows that collections of narratives and legal texts in Deuteronomy contain conspicuous innovations.

LITERARY-CRITICAL ANALYSIS OF DEUTERONOMY

Much debate exists about the composition and final form of Deuteronomy. Two main problems receive frequent consideration in this discussion: (1) how Deuteronomy arrived in its present state and (2) the relationship of Deuteronomy 12–26 to Exodus 21–23. Mainstream scholarship proffers two solutions to the first question. One alternative is that Deuteronomy, as we have it, is the result of a series of expansions or additions to an extant document. This extant document, or original Deuteronomy, played a part in the campaign of Josiah to centralize the cult within Jerusalem during the seventh century B.C.E. This book or document, which is believed to have received amplification, is also assumed to be a small collection of laws that contained neither a narrative introduction nor a narrative conclusion. Since the work of de Wette in 1805, it has become widely accepted that Deuteronomy 12–26 reflects or contains the contents of this original book.

The relationship of Deuteronomy 12–26 to Exodus 21–23 is another area of conversation in the literary-critical treatment of Deuteronomy. Deuteronomy 12–26, the Deuteronomic Code, follows the recapitulations of history in Deuteronomy 1–11 and immediately precedes the texts on blessings and curses in Deuteronomy 27–28. Many of the legislations that are in this corpus of law appear in the Covenant Code (found in Exodus 21–23). Some collections of law, which are present in Deuteronomy 12–26, are noticeably absent in Exodus 21–23, Leviticus 17–26 (the Holiness Code), Priestly Law (Exodus 25–31; 35–40; Numbers 1–10), and other collections of law in the Pentateuch. Prominent among these laws are injunctions that seek to centralize sites for worship of the Deity (Deut. 12:5-7, 11-12), regulations that govern the collection and distribution of triennial tithes (Deut. 14:28-29 and 26:12-15), prophecy (Deut. 13:1-18 and 18:15-22), monarchy (Deut. 17:14-20), divorce and remarriage (Deut. 24:1-4), levirate marriage (Deut. 25:5-10), and sexual intercourse with an engaged woman (Deut. 22:22-29). The literary relationship between the Covenant Code and the Deuteronomic Code, however, triggered the claim that the latter is perhaps a revision or adaptation of the laws that appear in the former.

The ideology, which appears in the legal traditions found within Deuteronomy 12–26, has far-reaching tentacles. It shapes the reconstructions of history in Joshua, Judges, 1–2 Samuel, and 1–2 Kings. In fact, it is probable that moral injunctions and ideology, which appear in Deuteronomy 12–26, played some role in the Josianic reformation (see 2 Kings 22–23 and 2 Chronicles 34–35). Moreover, Deuteronomy 12–26 and the book of Jeremiah share ideas about YHWH, social ethics, and the Israelite cultus. One way that scholars account for the fact that the fingerprints of Deuteronomy 12–26 are on documents elsewhere in the Hebrew Bible is to postulate the existence of a Deuteronomic movement at work in the biblical community.

HERMENEUTICAL CONCERNS AND DEUTERONOMY

Deuteronomy includes legal injunctions that position scholars to reconstruct and appreciate the shortcomings and ills of social life in ancient Israel. At the center of this claim is the belief that subgroups of law in the Deuteronomic Code that often get classified as humanitarian are not quite what they seem. These regulations suggest that laws in Deuteronomy 12–26 worked to the disadvantage of persons who were vulnerable socially, politically, or economically. Close examination of Deuteronomy 12–26 reveals that women, widows, strangers, orphans, and non-Israelite slaves fall especially within this category.

Subgroups of law in Deuteronomy make it difficult, if not totally improbable, that persons in the biblical community who existed in economic distress would obtain financial assistance from persons with the means to assist them. Deuteronomy 23:19-20 regulates the making of money on the lending of money, food, or anything that could earn interest. Noteworthy, however, is that this regulation governing the lending of money at a rate of interest stipulates that it is acceptable to lend money, at any rate conceivable, to a foreigner. The law prohibits the charging of interest on loans to fellow Israelites; it allows the lender to make as much money as he or she can if he or she lets somebody who is a non-Israelite borrow money. This law, then, promotes the making of a major return on investments by encouraging the lender to take the economic resources out of the community. Thus, the Israelite who is in economic distress and seeks a loan is in much trouble. Deuteronomy 15:1-6, thus makes a case for lending money to non-Israelites.

Subgroups of law in the book of Deuteronomy sanction slavery. Deuteronomy 15:12-18 and 23:15 justify a system based on using the enforced labor of people. The former passage allows for the release of a slave after he has been enslaved for seven years. What attracts attention is that this reprieve does not apply to slaves who are non-Israelite. Slaves who are not Israelite are slaves for life. What is more, Deut. 23:15 prohibits the return of a runaway slave to his master. Both legal injunctions endorse the institution of slavery. Neither regulation explicitly bans it. This is quite shocking, because texts that appear in Deuteronomy indicate that being delivered from slavery is that reality in which acceptable moral action should be grounded (Deut. 5:6; 6:12; 8:14; 13:5; 16:12; 24:18). This raises the question: Why would the biblical community force a circumstance on people that it did not want for itself? Israel could have easily banned slavery, all forms of it. Instead, she embraced it and wrote justification for it in her constitution. It therefore stands to reason that a significant population of non-Israelite slaves was present in the ancient biblical community. Legislations on slavery in Deuteronomy warrant this claim.

Subgroups of law in the book of Deuteronomy work to the socioeconomic disadvantage of marginal groups in ancient Israelite society. This claim brings into play the regulations on gleanings. This legal injunction conveys the idea that the crops and fruits that remained in the fields were for the sustenance of widows, strangers, and orphans. In short, these regulations posit that these vulnerable, socially weak individuals were to search the fields

for vegetables and fruits that might have been left by the reapers.

It is possible to argue that Deut. 24:19-22 breaks ground for the negative stereotyping of widows, strangers, and orphans in the biblical community. While this legislation implies that corporate generosity was a source for the material endowment of these people, it allows seeing this subgroup of persons as non-producers. These ordinances imply that these individuals were always recipients and consumers. These regulations convey the impression that widows, strangers, and orphans benefited from the labor of others but that these individuals gave nothing back to the community. This law therefore makes it possible for local peasant farmers and herders to argue that widows, strangers, and orphans were parasites and a scavenger class in ancient Israelite society. What is more, legislation that demands allocating leftovers for a social subgroup could contribute to the patronizing, demeaning, and capricious treatment of vulnerable persons. Legal injunctions on gleanings in Deuteronomy 12–26, then, could invite groups in the biblical community to discredit and to use negative terms to describe widows, strangers, and orphans in ancient Israel.

Law shaped social conventions and influenced private morality in ancient Israelite society. Since laws in Deuteronomy that seek to regulate morality toward some of the most distressed in the biblical community contain distinctive formulae, terminology, and pedagogies, it is possible to claim that subgroups of legal injunctions bolstered the improbability that economic inequality, marginalization, and exploitation were present, if not widespread, in ancient Israel. That being the case, it is important to part company with mainstream readings that use power and privilege as the lens through which to interpret laws relating to the poor and economically distressed in Deuteronomy and to unite with camps that proffer that an angle of vision on the text that grounds itself in the experience of this social subgroup should be brought into play. The voices of the poor and the disenfranchised need to be heard. Their situation needs to become visible and the starting point for approaching the biblical text, if we are going to understand power dynamics and appreciate fully the complexity of social life in ancient Israel.

Deuteronomy 24:19-22 conveys the idea that the crops and fruits that remained in the fields were for the sustenance of widows. In short, these regulations posit that these vulnerable, socially weak individuals were to search the fields for vegetables and fruits that might have been left by the reapers. This circumstance raises a serious question about the quantity of crops left or overlooked in fields or in the orchards, for it is probable that no produce remained in the fields after the harvest. Perhaps cultic officials sensed that local peasant farmers were lying about the yields of their crops; consequently, they developed strategies to influence local peasant farmers to gather everything from their fields. Widows had to embody *valiancy*. This subgroup of people had to act as a scavenger class.

What is more, Deut. 24:19-22 implies that corporate generosity was a source for the material endowment of the widow. The opinion that these individuals subsisted through welfare or public assistance, however, could contribute to the patronizing, demeaning, and capricious treatment of these persons by individuals or subgroups in biblical communities. It becomes possible that intrepidness was a characteristic of widows in ancient Israel. Legal injunctions on gleanings in the Deuteronomic code discourage widows from going into the fields and obtaining sustenance. These regulations allow seeing widows as non-producers, for these laws imply that such persons were always recipients and consumers. This code insinuates that these persons exploited the labor and industry of the masses. This law, therefore, makes it possible for widows to be anxious about local peasant farmers and herders. The story of widows in the biblical community brings courage into play.

Deuteronomy 14:28-29 and 26:12-15 seek to regulate morality toward widows, strangers, and orphans in the biblical community. This regulation implies that widows, in particular, often

demonstrated resourcefulness in their daily lives. Underpinning this claim is the belief that these laws prescribed sharing leftovers of corn, grain, wine, and other foodstuffs with these people and that Deut. 14:28-29 and 26:12-15 prescribed sharing foodstuffs with widows once every three years. This predicament positions the reader to surmise that these types of persons did something with virtually nothing and that they made ends meet in the meantime to take care of themselves.

Widows in ancient Israel, in particular, often embodied intrepidness and valiancy. Embodying these virtues positioned them to deal with their predicaments. Adherence to these moral ideals positions Blacks in America to adhere to the advice that the unnamed woman gives to her child in "Mother to Son":

> Don't you set down on the steps
> 'Cause you finds it's kinder hard.
> Don't you fall now—

References

Bennett, Harold V. 2002. *Injustice Made Legal: Deuteronomic Law and the Plight of Widows, Strangers, and Orphans in Ancient Israel*. Grand Rapids, Mich.: Eerdmans.

Brenner, Athalya, ed. 2000. *Exodus to Deuteronomy: A Feminist Companion to the Bible*. Sheffield: Sheffield Academic.

Brueggeman, Walter. 2001. *Deuteronomy*. Nashville: Abingdon.

Christensen, D. L., ed. 1993. *A Song of Power and the Power of Song: Essays on the Book of Deuteronomy*. Winona Lake, Ind.: Eisenbrauns.

Hughes, Langston. 1959. "Mother to Son." In *Selected Poems of Langston Hughes*, ed. Langston Hughes, 187. New York: Vintage.

Iseminger, Gary, ed. 1992. *Intention and Interpretation*. Philadelphia: Temple University Press.

Johnson, James Weldon. "Lift Every Voice and Sing" ("The Negro National Anthem"). http://historical textarchive.com/sections.php?op=viewarticle&artid=37.

Levinson, Bernard. 1997. *Deuteronomy and the Hermeneutics of Legal Innovation*. New York: Oxford University Press.

Nelson, Richard D. 2002. *Deuteronomy: A Commentary*. Old Testament Library. Louisville: Westminster John Knox.

Olson, Dennis. 1994. *Deuteronomy and the Death of Moses*. Overtures to Biblical Theology. Minneapolis: Fortress Press.

Person, Raymond F. 2002. *The Deuteronomic School: History, Social Setting, and Literature*. Atlanta: Society of Biblical Literature.

THE AFRICANA BIBLE

READING ISRAEL'S SCRIPTURES

FROM AFRICA AND THE AFRICAN DIASPORA

THE

HEBREW BIBLE

Prophets

INTRODUCTION

to the PROPHETS

Cheryl Kirk-Duggan and Valerie Bridgeman

THE WORD *PROPHET* conjures up a variety of meanings depending on one's context, scriptural awareness, and sociocultural location. In Africana settings, words from prophetic books, especially expressed in the King James Version, have some of the most profound, inspiring poetry in scripture: "Comfort ye my people"; "Ho, all who thirst"; and "They that wait on the Lord shall renew their strength." Simultaneously, some prophetic words can be incredibly scathing, cruel, abusive, xenophobic, and misogynistic. The prophet's propensity to use female metaphors and women as metaphors to describe ancient Israel's relationship with its God often demeans women, making them scapegoats. Both the beatific and the abusive ends of this spectrum inform how persons of African descent use these scriptures and how they understand God, community, relationships, suffering, life, and jus-

tice—from preachers and parishioners to artisans of word, music, dance, film, and canvas.

Who are these purveyors of such joy and sorrow? Twenty-first-century persons might think of prophets as fortune tellers, soothsayers, or psychics, like Miss Cleo. Biblical prophets, however, are a diverse cross section of men and women who believed they were called by God to serve in a sacred office as political advisors, interpreters, and visionaries. Some confronted rulers (2 Samuel 12; 2 Kings 1); others performed miraculous feats (2 Kings 6) or, like Huldah, interpreted sacred texts (2 Kings 22:13-20). We know most of the latter prophets by their words rather than their deeds, however. In either case, prophets attribute their divinely ordained relationship as the catalyst for their power and focus. The prophetic office often entails relaying revelation, religious reform, political advice, or faith and reasoning in the third person. With Mosaic theology as the prototype for Yahwistic prophetic tradition and theology, covenant and law come together. This theology makes apparent the prophet/king contrast. Biblical prophets often defend the Deity, hear and respond to individual and collective complaints, and note the distinction between faith and the state, the division between the prophetic and the political. Dissenting prophets and contradictory words are recorded in the text (for example, the controversy between Jeremiah and Hananiah in Jeremiah 28). Then there are times when the prophet seems to be at a loss as to particular meanings, where the prophet records a rhetorical question that the Divine leaves unanswered. In many religious settings—especially Africana settings—that take these words as sacred, these differences often are disregarded, dismissed, or explained away.

From a literary perspective, prophecy contains discourses between the prophet and the people; from the people to the prophet; and from the prophet to God on behalf of the people, and God's declarations and responses to those human events and inquires. Prophets and their disciples use literary devices that include (1) poetic oracles (brief rhythmic statements)—short, dateless pronouncements that rarely mention specific historic events, making references to wars or disasters applicable to a number of situations; (2) biography in prose form—that is, stories about prophets and oracles announced by a prophet; and (3) autobiography. One can divide prophecy thematically into judgment and salvation (cult prophecy) or into welfare and disaster, either addressing all of ancient Israel/Judah or their surrounding nation-state neighbors. National oracles are words of judgment spoken basically against foreign nations, usually with good news for ancient Israel.

Prophetic writings use a variety of schemes to convey a message, including reporting visions, dreams, and oracles; hearing and reporting their call experience; and extolling words of judgment and those of salvation as they sought to bring new understandings to people deemed wayward, rebellious, and sometimes incorrigible. Their often poetic renderings bemoan moral and spiritual corruption. Their foci vary, from almost nonexistent autobiography to more extensive information on the prophet's psychological, spiritual, and prophetic lived experiences.

Prophets spoke to a variety of audiences and were often consultants for military warfare. They often spoke to the community at large and probably engaged in cultic activity, including festivals. Prophets functioned in the cult (community of worshipers) and at the court (relating to the kings). From a historical perspective, prophets exist in an oral and written tradition, as pre-exilic, exilic, and postexilic operatives. Prophets ranked above kings on behalf of Yahweh. They must have enjoyed support from a large swath of the population, since they seemed to work unimpeded before power. Prophets could critique king or leaders, individually and collectively, and could critique merchants and other members of society they considered immoral. Prophets vigorously spoke against idolatry and oppression, for these egregious acts displayed misdirected trust. Prophets dealt with reality, often not with precise details but with personal words and religious power. As they addressed basic existing trends, they saw troubled humanity and a need for transformation. Classical prophecy can be said to have ended when Israel lost its political independence.

How one determines what is a prophetic book depends on the canon used. We have here included the books of 1–2 Samuel and 1–2 Kings under "prophets," following the Jewish canon rather than the Protestant/Catholic canons. Also included are the books listed as prophets in all these canons: Isaiah, Jeremiah, and Ezekiel, often called "Major Prophets" because they are contained in separate scrolls, and the Book of the Twelve, the Latter, or the Minor, Prophets, so named because they were contained in one scroll according to archeological findings. As such, they remain in one scroll for the Jewish canon. Some scholars believe that this rather substantial collection of books contains many themes that resonate with the theological perspective found in the book of Deuteronomy. It is for this reason that many classify Deuteronomy, Joshua, Judges, 1–2 Samuel, and 1–2 Kings as part of a single narrative that has been termed the *Deuteronomistic History* (in other words, a recounting of Israel's development told from the standpoint of the principles found in Deuteronomy). One can also see evidence of Deuteronomic themes in portions of the Major and Minor Prophets as well.

Classical prophecy begins in the eighth century B.C.E., with Amos and Hosea. Prior to their ministries, Samuel (judge/prophet), Nathan, Elijah, Elisha, and others were prophets to kings who did not fashion books.

The articles that follow present an overview of each prophetic book, providing some historical information and contextualized experiences of these prophetic texts as they have been transmitted and appropriated in Africa and the African Diaspora. We invite you to listen in new ways to thoughts about ancient words as you think through their implications for your life and those with whom you connect.

The DEUTERONOMISTIC HISTORY

Jerome Clayton Ross

BIBLICAL SCHOLARS LONG HAVE AGREED that editors shaped biblical texts to frame the way readers understood ancient Israel's/Judah's experiences with its neighbors and its deity. Scholars believe some redactors/editors produced the so-called Deuteronomistic History (DH). DH, the siglum (scribal abbreviation or symbol) for the Deuteronomistic History/Historian, consists of Deuteronomy, Joshua, Judges, 1–2 Samuel, and 1–2 Kings. CH, the siglum for the Chronistic History/Historian, is a postexilic redaction of DH (Gottwald 1985; Noth 1958; Coote and Ord 1989). DH and CH assumed that Jerusalem is the only authorized sanctuary. Every king—northern and southern—was judged according to his attitude toward the exclusive legitimacy of the temple in Jerusalem. DH and CH present the monarchy as the fundamental cause for Israel's defection from and unfaithfulness to YHWH.

Perhaps the most devastating event in these nations was the exile, colonizing the wealthiest, most productive citizens by removing them from the Fertile Crescent, dispersing them to far-flung areas of the Babylonian and later Persian empires. Written during this time, DH presented an apologetic theodicy defending YHWH's (in)justness/justice and explained that the exile happened because people violated Torah and covenant. These standards demanded faithfulness to YHWH. Abandoning idolatry and maintaining Jerusalem as the sole cult center gave evidence to such fidelity. The tone of DH was hopeful. According to it, judgment was not YHWH's last word and people were to understand history in light of YHWH's word accomplishing YHWH's will, as the prophets proclaimed.

DH argued that cultural diversity led to violating Yahwistic standards, coded as "statutes," "ordinances," "law," and "commandments." These violations resulted in national catastrophes. According to DH, repeated disobedience to "YHWH's word" caused the devastation. This cultural diversity was evidenced in allegiances to and arrangements with dominant or foreign nations/gods. DH reinforced the sense that YHWH was active in history by prolifically using the messenger formula, "thus said YHWH." Created by exiles from the South (ancient Judah), DH contributed significantly to Judaism's creation by endorsing Davidic-Zionistic Yahwism, minus a monarchy, to maintain communal continuity.

Next, DH appropriated several older customs. First, the custom of Shabbat rest became the symbol to sanctify time and presence with YHWH. In lieu of an operating (physical) sanctuary, DH promoted the pre-exilic custom of Shabbat rest as a means of regulating the Yahwistic colonists' community life. DH propagated the Shabbat to guarantee fellowship with YHWH. Thus the elimination of temple worship with the monarchical administration left a void filled by the revival of local cults and other customs. Second, Israelite paterfamilias cult observers scrupulously practiced circumcision to symbolize their covenant with YHWH—that is, male members' allegiance or loyalty to ancient Israelite ideology and lifestyle. They maintained Yahwistic traditions and solidarity by perpetuating and elevating circumcision as a prophylactic rite to secure identity as Yahwists (compare to circumcision and Passover). Third, DH proponents employed dietary laws to order daily life, for food items were categorized according to purity and distinction from the prevailing sacrifice and eating habits in foreign cultures (Coote and Ord 1991: 62–66; Douglas 1975: 249–75; Gammie 1989: 9–12). Thus, as vehicles for perpetuating Yahwistic identity, homes became auxiliary sanctuaries, parents acted like makeshift priests, and dinner tables served as makeshift altars (Milgrom 1991: 661 passim; Douglas 1999: 11 passim). Inevitably, a pronounced individualism emerged,

as Judahites democratized and universalized their traditions.

Closely related to the appropriating customs, the school responsible for the production of DH furthered the emergence of the Yahwistic canon. Heretofore, monarchical personnel created written, Yahwistic traditions and used them as political propaganda. Now, the editors and redactors of DH collected, revised, and used these traditions, minus a monarchy and temple, to reconstruct Yahwistic communities in contradistinction to extenuating circumstances and foreign influences. In regular assemblies, the traditions were read, discussed, and interpreted. Thus the origin of the synagogue emerges in this postexilic period, though no literature from this era concurs (Ross 1997: 148f; Levine 1996: 425–48). The synagogue marked an attempt to counter foreign influences, particularly cults that competed for Judahites' allegiance, offering obvious benefits to those who assimilated. DH edits the historical books toward a distinct view of the Deity and an apologetic that frames the exile.

References

Coote, Robert B., and David Robert Ord. 1989. *The Bible's First History: From Eden to the court of David with the Yahwist*. Minneapolis: Fortress Press.

———. 1991. *In the Beginning: Creation and the Priestly History*. Minneapolis: Fortress Press.

Douglas, Mary. 1975. "Deciphering a Meal." In *Implicit Meanings*, 249–75. London: Routledge and Kegan Paul.

———. 1999. *Leviticus as Literature*. Oxford: Oxford University Press.

Gammie, John G. 1989. *Holiness in Israel*. Overtures to Biblical Theology. Minneapolis: Fortress Press.

Gottwald, Norman K. 1985. *The Hebrew Bible: A Socio-Literary Introduction*. Philadelphia: Fortress Press.

Lemche, Niels Peter. 1995. *Ancient Israel: A New History of Israelite Society*. Sheffield, Eng.: Sheffield.

Levine, Lee I. 1996. "The Nature and Origin of the Palestinian Synagogue Reconsidered." *Journal of Biblical Literature* 115: 425–48.

Milgrom, Jacob. 1991. *Leviticus 1–16*. AB Commentary 3. New York: Doubleday.

Noth, Martin. 1958. *The History of Israel*. 3rd ed. Trans. Peter R. Ackroyd. New York: Harper and Row.

Ross, Jerome C. 1997. *The Composition of the Holiness Code (Lev. 17–26)*. Ph.D. diss., University of Pittsburgh; Ann Arbor: University of Michigan.

JOSHUA

Temba L. J. Mafico

ISRAEL'S FALLACY ABOUT THE HOLY WAR

In Josh. 8:18-26, we read that Yahweh said to Joshua: "Stretch out the sword that is in your hand toward Ai; for I will give it into your hand. . . . When the Israelites had finished slaughtering all the inhabitants of Ai. . . . [t]he total of those who fell that day, both men and women, was twelve thousand." Such statements as these make the book's readers wonder how God, the creator of the whole world, would select one race to slaughter people of another race so mercilessly. In this short discussion, I first deal with this problem of privileging one people group over another by providing a way of understanding the book of Joshua. I conclude with a comparative study of several themes of Joshua within an African tradition.

The book of Joshua is disturbing to those who interpret it literally. To enjoy and learn from this book, the reader must have some basic facts relating to the purpose of its authorship. Some of these basic facts are based on sheer common sense. First, readers must realize that the book of Joshua was written by ancient Israelites for ancient Israelites. A missionary for the global community of faith of all nations did not write this book. The ancient Israelites regarded Yahweh as the mighty god who fought for them against the gods of other nations. Although, ultimately, Yahweh became synonymous with Elohim (God), there is strong evidence that originally Yahweh was the action god of the divine council (Mafico 2007).

Second, Deuteronomistic historians wrote Joshua retrospectively. These writers reinterpreted the history of ancient Israel to conform it to an ideological perspective that affirmed that Yahweh blessed people and nations strictly according to their just deserts. Experiencing relentless political upheavals in the seventh century B.C.E. onward, ancient Israelites questioned the theology of Yahweh's past victories. They began to ask: "Was it not you who cut Rahab and pierced the dragon? Was it not you who dried up the sea, the waters of the great deep, who made the depths of the sea a way for the redeemed to cross over" (Isa. 51:9-10)?

Joshua, like the book of Jeremiah, says that it is not that Yahweh has become weak. Rather, Yahweh gave the ancient Israelites what they deserved, just like when Achan sinned by breaching the ban (Heb. *herem*). Yahweh abandoned them to be slaughtered by the dwellers of Ai. But if ancient Israel's leadership could be as obedient as Joshua was, then Yahweh would again fight for them. Thus Joshua is a hyperexaggerated book written to motivate ancient Israelites and their kings to be as faithful to Yahweh as in the days of Joshua.

THE INFORMED INTERPRETATION OF JOSHUA

Joshua should not be interpreted as a book relating the accurate historical events of ancient Israel's conquest of Canaan. Rather, it is a book that reflects its ideology of the conquest long after it had happened. Joshua portrays an ideal Israel under the leadership of an ideal leader, Joshua, a leader said to be so theocentric and obedient that his leadership was flawless—hence, Yahweh was with him. By idealizing ancient Israel in this way, the authors were criticizing the behavior of the contemporary kings who had deteriorated in their moral probity far beyond the folly of Solomon that led to the schism of the kingdom of Israel. The country of ancient Israel was languishing under great uncertainties, and there was a feeling that Yahweh was adverse to them. The book of Joshua was therefore written to inspire later generations to rally behind

Yahweh, who once rewarded ancient Israelites with the speedy conquest of the whole country simply because they were faithful to Yahweh alone. Additionally, the book highlights Joshua as a model king in contrast to the monarchs of Israel who ruled after the glorious reign of David. Furthermore, the reader must realize that the author's facts may be tainted by some propaganda that was prejudicial to other nations, particularly the Canaanites, whose land they had usurped. Did ancient Israel succeed in annihilating the Canaanites, as the first half of the book of Joshua claims?

THE CONTRADICTORY PROPAGANDA OF JOSHUA

A careful reading of the book of Joshua unveils some enigmatic inconsistencies that are imperceptible to biblicists or literal Bible interpreters. These inconsistencies are found in the structure and content of the book and also when in comparison with the other Deuteronomistic books (Judges, 1–2 Samuel, 1–2 Kings). To give two examples, Joshua 1–12 reports ancient Israel's speedy victory over the Canaanites, achieved with no single Israelite sustaining death or injury. But in Josh. 13:1 we are shocked to read: "Now Joshua was old and advanced in years and the Lord said to him, 'You are old and advanced in years, and very much of the land still remains to be possessed.'" The list of territories yet to be conquered comprises almost the entire land of Canaan. This statement entirely contradicts the statement found in the summary chapters (Josh. 11:16—12:24), which underscored that the whole land was liberated, leaving only slain bodies of all inhabitants and carcasses of their livestock. In Josh. 10:40-43, we have this strong summary:

> So Joshua defeated the whole land, the hill country and the Negeb and the lowland

and the slopes, and all their kings; he left no one remaining, but utterly destroyed all that breathed, as the Lord God of Israel commanded. And Joshua defeated from Kadesh-barnea to Gaza, and all the country of Goshen, as far as Gibeon. Joshua took all these and their land at one time, because the lord God of Israel fought for Israel. Then Joshua returned, and all Israel with him, to the camp at Gilgal.

To interpret the meaning of texts like these is only possible when the reader is familiar with the ideology of the Deuteronomist found in the books of Joshua to Kings. These books accentuate Yahweh's retributive justice—that is, do right and be blessed; sin and be cursed. Thus, beginning with Joshua 13, the redactor painted a more realistic picture of how ancient Israelites occupied the Canaanites' land. They won some battles and lost others (Judg. 2:11-15) and even served foreign rulers like Cushan-rishathaim for eight years (Judg. 3:8). The Israelites were even tempted to worship the baals of the Canaanites, a theme that recurs throughout the book of Judges and passim.

A final note regarding the misconception of the so-called holy war is this: the Canaanites were not subdued completely until the time of David. David conquered the Jebusites to build his capital on neutral land that belonged neither to the northern nor southern tribes (2 Sam. 5:6-10). One could surmise that ancient Israelites coexisted with Canaanites and in some cases even intermixed with them (Josh. 10:1-26). The polemic against syncretism is a good testimony to the threat that Baalism posed to Yahwism (compare to 1 Kings 18:20-24). The attempt to resolve the enigma of the holy war has left us little space to focus on the texts that reflect African traditional viewpoints. Contemporary commentaries adequately present the Western perspective on major themes of the book of Joshua. Hence it behooves us to hear the perspective of Black people on some of these themes.

PREPARATION FOR WAR AND CIRCUMCISION OF THE ANCIENT ISRAELITES

In Josh. 5:1-8, we read of God's injunction to Joshua to circumcise the children of Israel a second time. A careful reading, however, shows that this was not a second circumcision: it was the first time because this circumcision was for the children of the warriors who had left Egypt and then died in the wilderness. Their children, however, had not yet been circumcised (Josh. 5:7). Significantly, Joshua must use a flint stone that reminds us of what Zipporah used when she vicariously circumcised Moses. On his return to Egypt from Midian, Yahweh wanted to kill Moses (Exod. 4:24-26). Zipporah perceived that it was because he was uncircumcised, according to the text. She circumcised their son and touched Moses's feet with the son's foreskin to appease Yahweh.

Circumcision among the Gikuyu people of Kenya played a very pivotal role in their tribal cohesion. As with ancient Israelites, the circumcision rite was performed by an elder using the most traditional circumcision tool, a sharp stone knife. Circumcision played a critical role among Africans. Circumcision, a prerequisite for marriage, was also used as a rite of passage for boys ages thirteen to sixteen. By this rite, boys instantly transitioned from youth to adulthood. Significantly, the circumcised group stayed together for several months before and after circumcision. Elders disclosed to them the esoteric secrets of their tribe, the responsibilities for a man to his family and tribe. All elders present shouted together to ask the gods to bless them. At that moment, youth swore to keep tribal secrets, to cohere, and to defend their tribe against enemies. This covenant was sealed with the rite of circumcision. Each circumcision "boot camp" was given a distinct name and became a military troop that could be called to duty by its group name (Kenyatta 1965: 132).

Analogically, for ancient Israelites to remain resolutely united against the Canaanites, they needed their young warriors to be a covenanted military force. Their fathers had been united both by the Egyptian experience and by their sojourning together in the wilderness, where they witnessed Yahweh's glorious acts. Therefore it is reasonable to argue that the circumcision at Gilgal was a covenant ancient Israelites were making with one another and with Yahweh in preparation for the war against the Canaanites. It also was a requisite for marriage (compare to Gen. 34:13-17).

ACHAN'S SIN AND WHY IT CAUSED ANCIENT ISRAEL'S DEFEAT

The account of Achan intends to illustrate that it was not the ancient Israelites who were fighting the war against the Canaanites; it was Yahweh. This "holy war" fulfills promises Yahweh made to the patriarchs (Gen. 12:1; 16:17-20). Yahweh clears the land of Canaanites. To achieve victory, the children of Israel were to adhere to the *herem*, "the ban." Achan alone breached the ban, and the whole nation-state lost the battle against the Canaanites. To Westerners, this does not make sense. To Africans, this is easy to explain. War was won not by the prowess of the army but by the support of the Deity through the ancestral spirits. This was the African belief even during the wars of the liberation of Zimbabwe and other colonized African countries. The ban even included making love with one's wife (compare to 1 Sam. 11:8-13—Uriah refusing to go and sleep with a spouse while he was part of the troops fighting a war). Because of the bonding "covenant" that each young person made during circumcision, a breach by one was a breach by all. This solidarity concept is observed in all walks of African life. For example, the misbehavior of a child is a shame shared by the whole family and spreads to the extended family and the clan.

Analogically, the sanctification of ancient Israelites following Achan's sin was similar to the ancient African practice of extremely purging itself

of army misconduct in its midst. Interestingly, ancient Israel also was tainted by the presence of banned goods as long as those goods were among them. According to African and ancient Near Eastern concepts of *pars pro toto* (a part represents the whole), a banned object in the midst of ancient Israel contaminated Achan and his family, who, in turn, contaminated the whole of Israel. Thus an African person whose wound was bleeding while walking on a path would obliterate every drop of blood because any part of a person's body, hair, or clothing represented the whole person and thus could be used by an enemy for harm (Frankfort 1977: 12–14).

CHOOSE YOU THIS DAY

Ancient Israelite social structure is akin to African social stratification. In chapter 24, Joshua summoned the Israelites to appear before the gods (Heb. *'elohim*) at Shechem. First he summoned the elders—those whose age had accorded them the status of sages. These were followed by the heads of families. Today, elected African presidents work closely with elders, heads of families, mediums/ diviners (so-called biblical judges), and military officers because ordinary people will continue to follow their elders, heads of families, and mediums/ diviners (Mafico 1998).

To unite all ancient Israelites under Yahweh, Joshua followed Israelite social structure. He brought them before the *'elohim*, "the gods." While they were in front of their *'elohim*, he challenged them to make a choice between Yahweh and the *'elohim* of Canaan, the *'elohim* their ancestors brought from beyond the Euphrates and those they worshiped in Egypt. To help them make the right choice, he first listed the acts of Yahweh Elohim in verses 2-13. In this text, Yahweh explicitly says: "I did to Egypt . . ."; "I brought you out . . ."; "I gave you the land . . ."; and so forth. In these ten verses, Yahweh uses the "I" thirteen times to refer to his benevolent acts toward their ancestors. By the concept of *pars pro toto,* what Yahweh did for their ancestors he did for them. Yahweh's track record should help ancient Israelites choose who among the gods to follow with utmost fidelity. In one accord, the Israelites chose Yahweh as their plenipotentiary deity among the other gods (compare to Exod. 15:11). This text sounds like a requisite for the making or renewing of a covenant.

CONCLUSION

Many people are disturbed by the military tone of the book of Joshua and the callous killing of the Canaanites at the command of Yahweh. We have attempted to show that the book of Joshua should not be taken too literally. To get a balance of how Israel conquered the Canaanites, the book of Joshua should be read alongside the book of Judges, which shows that Yahweh was not a partial God. He was on the side of the Israelites only when they walked according to his statutes (Josh. 1:7-8). When they did not, the same deity used the Canaanites to massacre the Israelites (Judg. 2:11-16).

Joshua was written or finally edited by the Deuteronomistic historians several centuries after the breakup of the United Kingdom of Israel in order to make the kings of the eighth to the sixth century B.C.E emulate Joshua, whose total obedience to Yahweh won him many battles against the Canaanites; some of those victories were achieved without fighting—for example, the fall of Jericho (6:1-21). Since Joshua was written to motivate ancient Israelites during their political vicissitudes, the account of the battles is full of exaggerated accretions that are hideous to modern readers, especially those not acquainted with the critical methods of studying the Bible. But reading Joshua as the backdrop of the entire biblical account reveals that God was not impartial to Israel. God punished Israel harshly when they disobeyed, sometimes by calling Israel's enemies as his servants (Isa. 10:5-6; 45:1-3). God is consistent with his justice diachronically because God is the same from time immemorial hitherto (Isa. 41:4b; 43:10c).

References

Butler, Trent C. 1983. *Joshua: Word Biblical Commentary.* Waco, Tex.: Word.

Frankfort, H. 1977. *The Intellectual Adventure of Ancient Man.* Chicago: University of Chicago Press.

Kenyatta, J. 1965. *Facing Mount Kenya.* New York: Vintage.

Mafico, Temba. 1996. "The Divine Compound Name and Israel's Monotheistic Polytheism." *Journal of Northwest Semitic Languages*, 22 (1): 155–73.

———. 1998. "Judges." In *International Bible Commentary*, ed. W. Farmer. Collegeville, Minn.: Liturgical.

———. 2007. *The Emergence of Yahweh as "Judge" among the Gods.* New York: Mellen.

Mendenhall. G. E. 1955. *Law and Covenant in Israel and the Ancient Near East.* Pittsburgh: Biblical Colloquium.

JUDGES

Randall C. Bailey

TRADITIONALLY, the book of Judges gets its name from the charismatic leaders who rescue the "Israelites" from foreign oppression, the *šōpᵉtîm*, such as Jephthah, Abimelech, Gideon, and the like, who are called Major Judges.

With a surface reading of the book and an appreciation for the patriarchal nature of the biblical materials, one would think that the book is designed to lift up new heroes for the people. The problem is that all of the male *šōpᵉtîm* are flawed characters. Othniel cannot speak up to get a good land allotment (1:14). Barak will not go to war without Deborah (4:7). Gideon keeps testing YHWH (6:36-40). Ehud is left-handed (3:15). Manoah cannot get the angel to recognize his patriarchal authority (13:8-17). Samson never frees his people but keeps running women (14:1; 16:1, 4). On top of this, YHWH is portrayed as doing the

same thing over and over while expecting a different response (3:7-8, 12; 4:1-2; 6:1, and so forth).

Maybe we need another way of reading this book. As Mieke Bal has pointed out, the various stories in the book lead to the death and sacrifice of daughters. If so, an Africana tool for analysis of this book could be the song "Four Women" by Nina Simone, the famed Black jazz singer and composer who used aspects of Black life and political existence in the United States as the inspiration for her works. In "Four Women," Simone speaks to the experiences of Black women in the United States as exploited persons and as agents responding to their experiences of oppression. While the concentration on coloration as a tool of exploitation may not relate to what happens in the book of Judges, the aspects of social class and gender in this song relate to experiences of many of the women in the book. This article uses Simone's composition "Four Women" as a way of grouping the women in the book and of exploring their ways of being sacrificed by these "flawed men" with the hopes that we do not keep replicating such sacrifices in our own communities.

> My skin is black. My arms are long
> My hair is wooly. My back is strong
> Strong enough to take the pain
> It's been inflicted again and again
> What do they call me?
> My name is Aunt Sarah

The stories of several women in the book of Judges follow the claims of Aunt Sarah—that she is strong and retains her dignity in experiencing the oppression that comes upon her from an oppressive society. One problem with these women in the book of Judges who experience "Aunt Sarah's pain" is that they are all unnamed. Instead, they are identified by their relationship to a male character who gets them into trouble. In Judges 13, Manoah's wife gets the word from God that she is to have a male child. He is to be a Nazirite and save his people from the Philistines. She tells her husband, but he does not believe her and he asks for a divine visit. The angel comes back but appears only to her. She has to get her husband, who asks the angel what is to be done and is told, "I already told her!" This woman is in a marital relationship where her husband does not respect or trust her, but she carries forth the divine decree of bearing the child. Later readers have to identify her as the wife of the man who mistreats her.

In Judges 11, Jepthah promises God that if he wins the battle he will sacrifice the first one to come out of his house. In ancient times, women came out to sing and dance for returning armies. Jephthah's daughter learns she has to be sacrificed because of his vow. She responds by saying, "Do what you must, just let me bewail my virginity." She goes off for two months with her companions and then returns and is sacrificed. She models what

happens to women who accept crazy male leadership in the name of God.

In Judges 19, a woman flees her Levite husband and returns to her father's house for protection. He comes to get her and eventually is allowed to take her back. On the way back home, he is threatened by the Benjaminites. As a way of protecting himself, he throws her outside, where she is gang raped. In the morning, she is at the threshold of the house. He picks her up, takes her home, cuts her into twelve pieces, and calls for a war to avenge *his* honor.

As Aunt Sarah says, "It happens again and again."

> My skin is yellow. My hair is long
> Between two worlds I do belong
> My father was rich and white. He forced my
>   mother late one night
> What do they call me?
> My name is Siffronia

Siffronia bemoans situations in which daughters are caught in situations where adults and their actions beyond the daughters' control bring them harm. They live in the space between two warring cultures and nations and bear the pain of these situations. In Judges 20, the daughters of Shiloh go out to do their dance for the community festival. The Benjaminites' women have been killed in war after the Levite's concubine's death. To keep the vow not to give any other Israelite women to the Benjaminites, these men are allowed to kidnap, rape, and keep the daughters of Shiloh. In that way, the men of Shiloh will not have broken the vow not to give women to the Benjaminites.

Judges 11 tells us that Jepthah's mother was a prostitute and his father was Gilead. It is not clear if that is his father's name or whether his father was any of the men who had had sex with the prostitute. This woman evidently is not allowed to keep her child, since her son is banished from the community. Given the use of Gilead, it is not clear whether she was used by the men of the city as sport. She is not even given the title "mother"; rather, he is called "the son of a prostitute" (v. 1) / "another woman" (v. 2).

Samson married a Timnite woman in Judges 14. At a party he gives a riddle to stump the Philistines. They threaten her to get the answer to the riddle. She does and he calls her a heifer. Samson then burns the fields of the Philistines, who kill his wife. As Siffronia says, "Between two worlds I do belong."

> My skin is tan. My hair's alright, it's fine
> My hips invite you. And my lips are like wine
> Whose little girl am I?
> Well yours if you have some money to buy
> What do they call me?
> My name is Sweet Thing

Sweet Thing presents a narrative where women have to use their sexuality to survive the oppression in society. In Judges 1, Caleb puts his daughter Achsah up as a prize for whoever conquers Hebron. In fact, the name Achsah means "toy" or "trinket." She becomes Othniel's play thing. She is one of the few women in the book whose name is given.

Judges 16 gives us the story of Samson and Delilah. Like the Timnite wife, the Philistines force her to seduce Samson to discover the source of his strength. She and Samson play S&M sex games where she ties him up with bowstrings and ropes until he tells her that his strength is in his hair. She gets paid 1,100 pieces of silver by the Philistines. "Any one who has money to buy," says Sweet Thing.

> My skin is brown. And my manner is tough
> I'll kill the first mother I see. Cuz my life has
>   been too rough
> I'm awfully bitter these days. Because my par-
>   ents were slaves
> What do they call me?
> My
> Name
> Is
> Peaches

Peaches is the woman who openly fights the oppression that impacts her life. In Judges 4, 5, and 9, we get war stories that involve tough women. Deborah, in chapter 4, tells Barak to go to war. When he balks and says she must come, Deborah replies that she will *but* the glory will go to a woman. And so it does since Jael, not Barak, is the one who kills Sisera. In Judges 5, Deborah challenges the tribes who appear for battle and chides those who do not. In 9:53, Abimelech is trying to capture Thebez but an unnamed woman drops a millstone on his head and crushes his skull. Somehow, although the men get the titles and books named for them, it is often the sisters who get the job done. Could this be why you are bitter, Peaches? Or are you angry because the book does not show God intervening to help any of these women in dealing with the oppression they face or in saving their lives from the excesses and foolishness of the men in their lives?

References

Bal, Mieke. 1988. *Death and Dissymmetry: The Politics of Coherence in the Book of Judges.* Chicago: University of Chicago Press.

Boling, Robert. 1975. *Judges.* AB 6A. Garden City, N.Y.: Doubleday.

Fewell, Danna Nolan. 1998. "Judges." In *The Women's Bible Commentary*, exp. ed., ed. Carol A. Newsom and Sharon H. Ringe, 73–83. Louisville, Ky.: Westminster John Knox.

Simone, Nina. 1965. "Four Women." Produced by Hal Mooney. Lyrics and arranged by Nina Simone. On the album *Wild is the Wind.* Phillips.

Trible, Phyllis. 1984. *Texts of Terror: Literary-Feminist Readings of Biblical Narratives.* Overtures to Biblical Theology. Philadelphia: Fortress Press.

Weems, Renita J. 1989. *Just a Sister Away: A Womanist Vision of Women's Relationships in the Bible.* San Diego: LuraMedia.

1–2 SAMUEL

Theodore W. Burgh

THE FIRST BOOK OF SAMUEL treats Samuel, the transitional figure from the period of judges to kingship in Israel; Saul's problematic reign; and the transition of kingship from Saul to David. The second book of Samuel focuses primarily on the reign of David and David's family matters.

As an African American living in southeastern North Carolina at the beginning of the twenty-first century, I bring to the books of Samuel a plethora of sociocultural experiences—indelible nightmares as well as enjoyable memories—and ever-changing thoughts and perspectives, all of which shape how I perceive and navigate the world in which I live. I find in biblical figures characteristics that are reflected in many individuals from my own past and present, who have taught me: how to engage life's unforeseen trials; how, what, and when to celebrate; and to seek knowledge constantly. In these

ways they have given me more philosophical and theological questions than answers.

"Drama, drama, and more drama" would be a poignant way of describing this turbulent section of the Old Testament/Hebrew Bible. The book(s) of Samuel introduce us to new theological and political developments in Israelite culture. The saga begins with the biblical icon Samuel. The writings give us snapshots of a sort of "Renaissance man," living out different roles during the early Iron Age (ca. 1200–1000 B.C.E.), through the intricate literary portrayal of a complex, wise, and possibly troubled individual. Through the books of Samuel we witness the advent and embryonic evolution of Israelite kingship, the anointing of two of Israel's most prominent kings, and a host of remarkable events that help to define what we have come to know as Israelite culture. While the text describes episodes from thousands of years ago, many of the people, events, and activities presented there find parallels in daily life in African American culture today. Readers often connect with the trials and tribulations of Samuel, the perplexing decisions made by Saul, and the enigmatic popularity and convoluted relationships of David. Examining the actions taken by some of these figures may have an impact on our own daily life decisions.

THE FIRST BOOK OF SAMUEL

The Birth of Samuel and the Song of Hannah (1 Samuel 1–2)

The Deuteronomistic writers (on current views regarding authorship and composition of the Books of Samuel see the Introduction to the Deuteronomistic History) let the reader know even before his birth that Samuel will be special. His mother, Hannah, one of two wives of Elkanah, is barren. "YHWH had closed her womb," although we are not told why (1 Sam. 1:6). The theme is a common one in numerous biblical stories (Gen. 20:18; Gen. 25:21; Judg. 13:3). Feeling the pressure of the high value her society placed on bearing a child—particularly a male—in order to confirm her womanhood, she prays diligently to her god asking to become pregnant. Archaeological excavations have produced variously sized terra cotta statues, typically images of women, from Israelite and other Near Eastern cultures, which have been identified as fertility figurines. These artifacts demonstrate the need and importance attributed to bearing children. We also see Hannah's desire to be a mother and to give her love unconditionally to a child produced from her union with Elkanah. One should note that in instances of infertility in the Old Testament the onus is usually on the woman: concerns regarding conception are never attributed to the husband's physical problems. In this case, however, because Peninah, Elkanah's other wife, has given birth to "sons and daughters" fathered by him (1 Sam. 1:4),

Hannah clearly bears the brunt of the issue. Furthermore, Hannah's antagonistic rival torments her with vicious barbs and taunts. Hannah is caught in the midst of what could be understood in contemporary street vernacular as "baby mama drama."

Her diligence takes her to Shiloh, where she, with scheduled regularity, plants herself in the doorway of the temple and prays fervently to YHWH. She entreats silently with such passion and persistence that the priest Eli accuses her of being drunk. Yet Hannah's fervent prayer is not for herself: she requests that she become the mother of a male child via her husband Elkanah. Although she will give this child an undying mother's love, Hannah promises to dedicate him back to YHWH as a nazarite, with the faith and hope that he will make a major contribution to his people.

The latter aspiration continues to be the desire of many parents. No matter what the economic or societal circumstances of a child's birth, the hope is that the individual, through the assistance and blessing of God, will be a responsible citizen of the world and remain safe from harm. Hannah expresses this wish and gives thanks to YHWH in what some scholars have described as the song or prayer of Hannah (1 Sam. 2:1-10). Although Hannah's theme is more one of national thanksgiving, she still conveys personal gratitude for what has happened to her. In a similar fashion, contemporary hip-hop artist singer-songwriter Lauryn Hill expresses many of the same sentiments as she shares her own reflections of gratitude in a song titled "Zion," named after her newborn son (from the album entitled *The Miseducation of Lauryn Hill* 1998). Hill sings:

> But then an angel came to me one day
> Told me to kneel down and pray
> for unto me a manchild would be born
> Woe to this crazy circumstance, I knew his life
> deserved a chance
> Now let me pray to keep you from
> The perils that will surely come
> See life for you my prince has just begun

And I thank you for choosing me
To come through unto life to be
A beautiful reflection of his grace
Now the joy of my world is in Zion

Why does Hannah choose the nazarite lifestyle for her son? At that time in ancient Israel, a nazarite was a male or female who dedicated himself or herself, or who was dedicated to YHWH by others, through specific vows (Num. 6:1-21; Judg. 13:7). The term *nazarite*, which derives from the Hebrew word *nazar*, meaning "to consecrate," is typically understood to refer to one who adhered to pre-established vows that prohibited cutting one's hair or beard and partaking of wine or strong drink (including anything produced from grapes, such as vinegar), required a restricted diet, and generally involved declarations of purity of life and devotion. The nazarite existence could be for one's entire life or for a specified time period. The ancient nazarite life finds a parallel in the lifestyle of Rastafarianism today. Both have prescribed diets, the Rastafarian diet being closely aligned with commandments in the Hebrew Bible (for example, refraining from strong drink and "unclean" foods). Nazarites and Rastafarians alike let their hair take its natural course, which in the case of the latter are called dreadlocks. The comparison may be suggestive of Samuel's physical appearance. Although Samuel has no choice in the matter of becoming a nazarite initially, the text never gives any indication of his displeasure with the vows or desire to change from the lifestyle.

SAMUEL AS "RENAISSANCE MAN": JUDGE, PRIEST, PROPHET

Like Samuel, a number of women and men in African American communities also wear various hats. Many are janitors, entrepreneurs, teachers, preachers, church administrators, hair stylists, babysitters, and so on, while working simultaneously as judges, priests, prophets, and CEOs in their own homes. As a circuit judge, priest, and prophet, Samuel was a staunch pillar among his people. Yet, he still had the responsibilities of his own house, particularly in one role that is often overlooked by interpreters: that of parent. Often this crucial role is taken for granted and thought to be a job that anyone who can procreate can fulfill. Consider that some of the most noted civil rights activists of our time—for example, Martin Luther King, Fannie Lou Hamer, Coretta Scott King, Malcolm X, Ella Baker, and others—were constantly called upon to give service in several capacities to their people and communities, but they were at the same time husbands, wives, and parents who worked diligently to keep their families together. Although not on the same level as the figures just mentioned, I can speak from the experience of multitasking in a number of these roles and can say with authority that it is not an easy feat. In the case of Samuel, we learn that he appointed his two sons, Joel and Abijah (1 Sam. 8:1-3), as judges in Beersheba. They did not, however, follow in his ways in serving the people, even though Samuel and other members of the community set solid examples for them to emulate. Sadly, their service to the people was untrustworthy and underhanded (1 Sam. 2:34; 3:13; 4:11).

AGEISM AGAINST SAMUEL ON THE PART OF THE ELDERS

After all the competent leadership Samuel provided for the Israelite community and its people, the elders advise him that they want to go in another direction. Citing his sons' immoral activities, and more importantly, Samuel's age (1 Sam. 8:5), they request that he inquire of YHWH on their behalf to find them a king (1 Sam. 8:5-6). Samuel reluctantly obliges, and YHWH agrees to their request though with a strong expression of admonishment. Although their desire will be granted, YHWH gives Samuel a laundry list of events that will take place that will dramatically alter life in Israelite culture (1 Sam. 8:4-22). After all that the leader whom YHWH has appointed has done for the community, he has now been pushed aside, apparently without warning. In the larger scheme, the people have rejected the rule of YHWH. What is even more insulting to Samuel is that the leaders don't ask him to serve as king, even in an interim position. According to the biblical writers, Samuel essentially exercised the duties of a king and was selected by YHWH to lead and guide his people. From what we understand in the text, he did an excellent job. Although Moses, Noah, and others led people well into the twilight years of their lives, ageism appears to have been a major factor in Samuel's removal from his position. One has to consider that if Samuel had not been viewed as a member of the American Association of Retired Persons (AARP) crowd, the elders might have asked him to become king or to serve in some viable capacity during this transition to monarchy. Sadly, this is the way many senior citizens in the United States and in some African American communities are perceived today. A number of adults who have been blessed to live past certain ages are now perceived as useless, outdated, and irrelevant and essentially become invisible. The precious wisdom gained from years of skilled living and survival are often discarded and wasted in our communities because of perceptions of age. How much better off would we be if we worked to preserve and utilize these priceless resources!

Samuel the Judge vs. Saul the King?

We learn that although the elders request the change in leadership, YHWH determines who will be the first king of Israel in selecting Saul the Benjamite. Saul comes into a very difficult situation. He has never been king, nor has Israel ever had a king. There is no instruction manual available, no human resources department, or any previous king to serve as a mentor; further, Saul's reign begins during a period of transition. While he does have YHWH and a possibly disgruntled Samuel to guide him in his newly acquired job, it appears that Saul is essentially on his own. As expected in a high-pressure position such as this, Saul does not always make the best choices and angers Samuel

and YHWH. He is a successful military leader, but several of Saul's decisions actually lead to his demise and loss of the kingship.

The story raises some questions regarding the relationship between Samuel and Saul. Was there some animosity on Samuel's part toward Saul? Did he have Saul's best interest at heart? Remember, the people have rejected Samuel primarily due to his age, and Saul is his young, strong, willing, yet inexperienced replacement. Moreover, Samuel had to anoint and install the young man into the newly created leadership position, serve as his guide, and watch Saul make one mistake after another. Even though they are not royalty, consider the number of celebrities in our modern period who have publicly "fallen from grace" or from "the top" (one thinks of Mike Tyson, MC Hammer, or Whitney Houston). Some people may pose plausible arguments that one or another such figure lacked proper mentoring or blatantly ignored sound advice: as a consequence, they tumbled mightily. Was there a relationship comparable to that between Samuel and Saul somewhere in their lives? It is difficult to address these kinds of issues with any precision, of course, but the circumstances surrounding Samuel and Saul as presented in the biblical text invite comparison to certain types of attitude and behavior.

Nor is this sort of situation uncommon in African American daily life. For example, when one takes a new job in which one must be trained by the person one is replacing, or when one works with someone who applied for one's position and did not receive it, the circumstances can create a tense atmosphere. In situations such as these, one knows that any mistake one makes will be magnified. I've witnessed young or new ministers take a new pastoral post with a church and immediately find themselves in a Samuel-Saul relationship with angry associate ministers, self-centered deacons, and bitter church members.

As a consequence it appears in some ways that no matter what Saul did, he would have had limited success during his tenure as king. Although his fate is sealed when YHWH reveals that he regrets that he has made him king (1 Sam. 15:35), no one can deny that Saul was instrumental in establishing Israel as a respectable nation. As Saul's reign begins to unravel, David, the king-elect, has entrenched himself in Saul's court and family by serving as the king's personal musician, befriending Saul's son Jonathan, and marrying his daughter Michal. It is some time before David rules the entire country, but the writers present him as one who almost walks on water. He is a "man after God's own heart" (1 Sam. 13:14); the spirit of YHWH is with him even as YHWH has left Saul with an evil one (1 Sam. 16:14). We find that the handsome, ruddy young "bad boy" with beautiful eyes has an intoxicating charm. He is popular and adored by many. In a fashion similar to rap artist LL COOL J ("Ladies Love Cool James"), we could call the king-elect LL COOL D (the "Ladies Love Cool David")—and he loves them as well.

THE SECOND BOOK OF SAMUEL

The Fall of Saul and the Rise of David

In many ways, one could compare David's life to the lives portrayed by a number of rap and hip-hop artists at the beginning of the twenty-first century. At the pinnacle of his life, during what some consider his youth, David is considered successful, rich, and at the top of his game. He has an abundance of women at his beck and call and he is a recognized musical artist (lyre player, singer, and songwriter). David also made a mark for himself with his impromptu disrobing "praise dance" before YHWH and the people of Israel, much to his wife's displeasure (2 Sam. 6:14). Moreover, in hip hop/rap fashion, David and his camp have a long-running disagreement or "beef" with Saul and his camp. (One might compare similar contemporary feuds between hip-hop styles and artists, for example: East Coast vs. West Coast, Jay-Z vs. Naz, MC Lyte vs. Antoinette, or 2 Pac vs. Biggie). Like some of these artists, Saul is now paranoid, jealous, and afraid

of David and his rising celebrity. Of course, the obvious difference between the biblical figures and today's artists is that (at least early on) the battles between modern performers typically escalated no further than words and took place on "wax" or on stage behind a microphone; David and his foes, on the other hand, settled their conflicts on the battle-field with instruments of war. David and his adversaries also had much more at stake than reputations.

Continuing in this same line of comparison between hip-hop/rap and biblical figures, one could ask: Was David a "thug" or would he be considered a "gangsta?" The meanings of these urban terms are quite fluid, but in general, a thug is an individual who commits acts that are socially unacceptable. A gangsta (sometimes presented G.A.N.G.S.T.A.), depending upon context and use, can be perceived a bit more positively and has been defined as someone who is focused; serious about matters in their personal life; and willing to achieve their goals by any means necessary. Admittedly this way of framing the question may stand in distinct contrast to more traditional perceptions of David, and while he may not actually be either thug or gangsta, his actions display characteristics of both. There are times when he does or takes what he wants, without question (for example, 2 Sam. 5); he displays unmitigated devotion toward his friends; and there are instances in which people are harmed or killed based solely on his decision or his perspective on a particular situation (for example, the revenge in 2 Sam. 4). This inquiry and discussion are meant not as judgmental or to place David or any of the biblical figures in a negative light, but as another way to understand better and possibly to relate to the people and culture in which David and his contemporaries lived. Consider that some genres of contemporary media at times present hip-hop artists, athletes, rappers of color, and aspects of African American culture without complete understanding and rely on negative stereotypes, while at the same time employing and imitating aspects of African American culture in commercial advertising. Many of the sorts of acts on the part of African American celebrities that gain media attention today are not so far removed from the rest of the world, either past or present; the same can be said for some of the stories in the Bible. For instance, are David's revenge tactics and his taking of whatever he desires any different from the often-glorified actions of mafia-themed TV shows or movies (for example, *The Sopranos, Goodfellas,* or *New Jack City*) or the lifestyles displayed in numerous videos and video games (such as Jay Z's *99 Problems,* NWA's *F&#k tha Police,* or *Grand Theft Auto*)? When an Amalekite messenger comes to David and tells him that he has killed Saul (according to Saul's request), David, much like mafia captains or gang members presented in movies, has one of his "boys" kill the messenger (2 Sam. 1:16). Some would use the slang adjective "thug" or "gangsta" to describe this act. Whatever the name we use, we understand that when the biblical David spoke, things happened!

In another act that leaves an indelible mark upon David's record, we read that the king sleeps with the wife of Uriah the Hittite, a faithful soldier in his army, and then takes his life. Again, some may consider this move mafia-like, gangsta, or thuggish. However, one must also consider that Bathsheba may have committed a gangsta or thuggish move herself, as it is the son from their union, Solomon, who eventually takes the throne.

No matter what David does or causes to happen, it is evident that he truly loves his God. He is, the Bible tells us, a man after YHWH's own heart (1 Sam. 13:14). His compassion for his best friend's physically challenged son (2 Samuel 9), his repentant heart, and his love for his family and friends reveal the soul of a man whose true desire is to serve YHWH.

It's a Family Affair

While the scope of this essay does not permit thorough exploration of many subjects in the book(s) of Samuel, a few words about David's family are worth noting. While he had YHWH's favor and his reign is considered to have been successful, David's familial problems were abundant. Some of his family issues would generate top headlines and sales for today's papers such as the *Star* or *National Enquirer* and make engaging subjects for reality TV. David's family is clearly not the "traditional" husband, wife, and child. He has numerous wives, concubines, and children (2 Sam. 5:13-16). As we might expect, his family is beset by issues that are perplexing and disturbing and must have been hard on his mental state. We learn, for instance, that David's son Amnon rapes his stepsister Tamar, and her brother Absalom has Amnon killed for this. Absalom then rebels against his father, and Adonijah, another son, attempts to usurp the throne against Solomon. Yet through all of this, David loves them all unconditionally. A number of these familial events appear to parallel the decline of David's kingdom. Several of the disastrous events just mentioned followed the illicit affair with Bathsheba and the murder of her husband Uriah. Incest, the deaths of his children, family rebellion, plots of anarchy, and military conflicts required David's attention and energy. Although David was one after YHWH's own heart (1 Sam. 13:13-14), his actions affected his relationship with his God. As a result, his personal life and kingdom suffered. Nevertheless, David loved his family without question in much the same manner that YHWH loved him. Many practice this type of unconditional love today when it comes to relatives, as they are often able to look past insidious actions of individuals and see their hearts. There are instances, sadly, when a family member must endure difficult times alone before they come around. Yet unconditional love—as demonstrated in the relationship of YHWH and David—often comes from the family and remains constant no matter what.

The books of Samuel shed light on some overlooked struggles of leadership. Samuel, Saul, and David labored diligently to lead the people of Israel in the ways of YHWH. Saul and Samuel had to navigate uncharted waters in how to rule, as Israel had never had a king. David had to work to unite the country. In the midst of this, we see that each had to confront human emotions, desires, needs, and family issues.

It is important to remember that none of them asked to be king. YHWH chose each of them. While all of their decisions were not perfect, they played major roles in creating the culture and nation of Israel, YHWH's people.

References

Bailey, Randall C. 2002. *David in Love and War: The Pursuit of Power in 2 Samuel 10–12.* Sheffield: JSOT.

Dyson, Michael Eric. 2002. *Holla If You Hear Me.* Medford, N.J.: Plexus.

Franklin, Kirk. 2005. *Hero.* Gospelcentric.

Gilkes, Cheryl Townsend. 1993. "Womanist Ways of Seeing." In *Black Theology: A Documentary History Volume Two: 1980–1992,* ed. James H. Cone and Gayraud S. Wilmore. Maryknoll: Orbis, 321–24.

Hill, Lauryn. 1998. *The Miseducation of Lauryn Hill.* Sony Records.

Kirk-Duggan, Cheryl. 2000. "Hot Buttered Soulful Tunes and Cold Icy Passionate Truths: The Hermeneutics of Biblical Interpolation in R & B." In *African Americans and the Bible.* Ed. Vincent Wimbush. New York: Continuum.

Light, Alan. 1999. *The Vibe History of Hip Hop.* New York: Three Rivers.

Murrell, Samuel, William Spencer, and Adriane Anthony McFarland, eds. 1998. *Chanting Down Babylon: The Rastafarian Reader.* Philadelphia: Temple University Press.

Myers, William. 1991. "The Hermeneutical Dilemma of the African American Biblical Student." In *Stony the Road We Trod: African American Biblical Interpretation,* ed. Cain H. Felder. Minneapolis: Fortress Press, 40–56.

1–2 KINGS

Stephen Breck Reid

THE SOCIAL LOCATION OF THIS AUTHOR

My birth is a key element of my social location. Born in the mid-twentieth century, I grew up in Ohio. My father's family moved with the great migration from the South between the World Wars. My mother's family lived as farmers in Kentucky after moving from the Carolinas. Both of my parents were orphaned. My father grew up largely in a home in Xenia, Ohio. Conversely, my mother, whose parents divorced during her early teens, spent most of her childhood with her family. So she lived on the farm and in the city and experienced the slide into poverty that often accompanied African American women and their children after divorce. After my grandmother died, her daughters raised themselves with the help of the local community. My family of origin consistently rehearsed the fragility of life and the need for children to be ready for parental abandonment. I, too, have rehearsed this notion.

I grew up and have spent all my professional life working for a Eurocentric church. My family was one of the first African American families in our local church. Like many denominations, mine—the Church of the Brethren—reflects immigrant origins, which took race and identity for granted in its theological reflection. This context means that I continue to privilege a faith-based reading that educates the church. A more pernicious outgrowth is the unfortunate tendency to think of my work as the helpful voice of the "Other." Here my experience with the Institute for Black Catholic Studies continues to remind me of the importance of Afrocentric reading.

1–2 KINGS IN THE CANONICAL CONTEXT

The canonical location of 1–2 Kings is interesting. The book of Judges aspires to the mixed blessing of the monarchy. Material in 1–2 Samuel recounts ancient Israel's bittersweet political romance with the monarchy.

THE MYTHIC DAVIDIC DYNASTY (1 KINGS 1–4, 9, 12)

As a graduate student, I thought it odd that David's story bled onto Kings. As I get older, however, this canonical reality makes more sense. The dynasty leaned into exhaustion as David crept into death. The book begins with the statement that David "was old and advanced in years" (1:1). The story of Abishag the Shunammite figures into the court history and preoccupation with who will take the throne (1:1-4; 2:17; see Rost 1982). Adonijah aspired to the throne (1:5-10). Bathsheba comes to the fore as a force behind the throne (1:11-53). David's testament is an odd blend of moral exhortation, political accusations, and inferred vendetta (2:1-8). After a transition formula (2:9-11), the text returns to political intrigue and Solomon's legitimation tale. Remember that Adonijah was the elder brother, which created a stir. For this reason, Brueggemann argued that the writers of Genesis drew from the legitimacy crisis in the Davidic dynasty for the template for Jacob and Joseph, younger brothers who moved contrary to traditions (see Brueggemann 1968). The chapter ends a political thriller, with everyone who supported the losers like Adonijah and Joab fallen (2:46).

Henry Louis Gates Jr. used the African Eshu tradition to describe the double voiced nature of African orature (see Gates 1989). W. E. B. DuBois in *The Souls of Black Folk* (1961) makes the case for the double consciousness of African American people. The move from political thriller in chapter 2 to wisdom-piety petition and wisdom tale in

chapter 3 is jolting. In order to understand chapter 3, we must understand the juxtaposition of piety and power. I use a postcolonial, African reading, attending to its canonical context, to do so. Simultaneously, wisdom-piety elements in the petition and the tale (3:5-28) should bracket earlier material.

WOMANISH WOMEN OF THE BOOKS OF KINGS

Depictions of women in the books of Kings vacillate from metaphors of vulnerability (widow) to piety (the Queen of Sheba, Huldah the prophet) and finally to evil and apostasy (Jezebel and Athaliah). The Queen of Sheba, Jezebel, and Athaliah dominate the narrative and popular imagination that grows out of the Kings material.

- Scholars think the Queen of Sheba (1 Kings 10:1-13 and 2 Chronicles) is from Ethiopia, Eritrea, or Yemen. Some view her as the speaker in Song of Songs (1:5) who says she is black and beautiful. According to Josephus, the text depicts her as a lover of learning (see the Qur'an, chap. 27:23-44). Halle Berry starred in the 1995 movie *Solomon and Sheba*.
- Jezebel captured biblical and Western imagination as the most maligned female other than Eve. Daughter of Ithobaal I of Tyre, she remained true to her faith amid culture wars among Israelite prophets. As a Tyrian princess, she remained a prime example of the exogamy the editor of Kings and the Deuteronomistic History generally loathe. The usurper Jehu incites Jezebel's servants to defenestration (2 Kings 9:33). The New Testament depicts Jezebel as a cultural miscreant (Rev. 2:20). Sade's song "Jezebel" provides a counter reading. Boyz II Men take a different strategy.

- Athaliah shows more potential for womanist interpretation than yet actualized. She is a quintessential outsider. The pro-Davidic southern redactor marginalizes her (2 Kings 11:1-21). She is from Israel, living and reigning in Judah, a widow of an assassinated king.

TEMPLE (1 KINGS 5–8)

Readers today must understand that ancient Israel authorized a temple as a clue of sacred space, namely divine reality. We consider space, even that designated "sacred," as having symbolic power, but we stop short of any cosmological significance. When one reads from the perspective of classical African traditions, one can recapture cosmological significance. The cosmogram of ancient Bakongo culture stands closer to the biblical stories of Kings than the modernist and postmodernist readings of Western scholars.

The African Diasporan situation parallels the tabernacle's wandering traditions. From seventeenth-century colonial times to the present, the church functions more like the synagogue than the temple; it emphasizes gathering around the word and community rather than sacrifice.

The temple material in Kings connects with the stories of Samuel (especially 2 Samuel 7) that outline the divine affirmation of the temple building program. The "narrative spirituality" (Endres 1988) described here is presently embedded in Kings but arises earlier than the nationalist Deuteronomist movement (623–500 B.C.E.).

One element continues the royal romance of Solomon and picks up on the Davidic romance franchise. The temple, like the monarchy, remains an ambivalent symbol. The history of the temple and that of the monarchy remain as linked as they are ambivalent. The monarchy's rise saw the transformation from tabernacle to temple. The monarch's political adventures took a toll on the temple because it was a symbol and a repository of national wealth. When the northern kingdom, Israel, split off, it developed its own temple (922 B.C.E.). When the Babylonians took Jerusalem, they ransacked the temple (586 B.C.E.). When the colonial Persian Judean regime wanted to consolidate their power, they refurbished the temple (515 B.C.E.). Through poor intelligence, the Seleucids believed they could transform the temple into a Greek/Hellenistic temple without any political consequences (168 B.C.E.). Herod the Great again consolidated his power with the people through an extensive expansion of the temple (20 C.E.). The Roman general Titus had his army sack the temple (70 C.E.). At least three times, attempts to refurbish the temple were unsuccessful: during the second Jewish revolt (132–135 C.E.), during the reign of Julian the Apostate (362–363 C.E.), and again in the seventh century C.E. The temple symbolizes one element of the royal romance with power.

The use of a superscription alerts readers that building a temple is a part of the salvation history and includes the exodus from Egypt (1 Kings 6:1). The building had three parts, each twenty cubits wide: first, a ten-cubit vestibule; second, a forty-cubit nave; and third, a twenty-cubit inner sanctuary (1 Kings 6:2). The temple's description ends as it began—with a superscription (1 Kings 6:37-38). As if to accent the ambivalence of monarchy and temple, chapter 7 outlines the palace's opulence over against the temple's simplicity (1 Kings 7:1-12): Solomon's palace took twice as long to complete and was substantially larger than the temple, a royal sanctuary.

Hiram of Tyre (1 Kings 7:13-14) was the Benjamin Banneker of antiquity, the outsider who shapes a capital city matches quite well.

THE PROPHETIC BACKBONE OF KINGS

- Assorted prophets: 1 Kings 11, 12:21-33; 13
- Elijah cycle: 1 Kings 17—2 Kings 2
- Elisha cycle: 2 Kings 3–9, 13

From an Africana perspective, the world of the books of Kings is populated with prophets and kings, conjurers and chiefs. The Göttingen interpretive school posits that this is due to the influence of a prophetic redactor. Whether or not one subscribes to such a notion, clearly there is a prophetic narrative framework that functions as the backbone in the books of Kings.

The first prophet we meet is Ahijah the Shilonite (1 Kings 11:26-40), who finds Jeroboam, a bureaucrat working for Solomon, on the road. Shiloh, important in the Samuel materials, is a major cultic and political center during the pre-monarchic period. Jeroboam flees to Egypt when Solomon attempts to have him assassinated. The Jeroboam and Ahijah narrative precedes the wisdom tale of the demise of the united monarchy under Rehoboam.

The prophetic tenor of the Deuteronomistic History (DH), of which 1 and 2 Kings are a part, provides plot and core conflicts for what might otherwise be an annal of royal accomplishments and failures. The predominant theme in DH is that God does nothing without first revealing the event through a prophetic word. No leader by sheer force of might or tribal right can exercise power absent a divine sanction administered by a prophet/priest. Saul and David depend on Samuel for their divine imprimatur. Jeroboam has his prophet Ahijah. Similarly, Black pastors are often used as veritable furniture or background figures in U.S. politics today. Rehoboam had only human advisers before his unfortunate foray into power politics at Shechem (1 Kings 12:1-24).

The core conflict reflects African concerns—namely, the intersection of faith and identity enmeshed in tribal traditions. Recent books on ethnic identities in biblical literature indicate a broad interest in the topic. However, the texts transgress tribal boundaries as often as they conform to them.

Early Prophetic Stories (1 Kings 11–14)

Prophetic sanction and support do not seem to correlates highly with faithfulness. Jeroboam understood the political consequences of having Jerusalem as the one place for sacrifice. So he chose the politically reasonable strategy of building a new religious infrastructure within the boundaries of his own kingdom. This action put Jeroboam, an apostate, in direct opposition to the pro-Jerusalem editor of the books of Kings. Prophetic support proves both necessary and undependable. Support shifted for Jeroboam (1 Kings 13:1-34). Even as a desperate father, Jeroboam can find no support among the prophets when he sends his wife in disguise to Ahijah (1 Kings 14:1-18).

The Elijah and Elisha Cycles

Elijah has a remarkably brief call narrative (1 Kings 17:1-7) that does little to underline his credentials. The stories of Elijah describe the mighty acts that God does through him, which stand as his credentials, instead of the more formal call vision report that we see with the Major Prophets.

Elijah becomes an apt model for Black prophecy because desire serve as the backdrop for divine power through prophetic action. The first major story in the Elijah cycle involves the widow of Zarephath (1 Kings 17:8-24). The story indicates the need to trust a prophetic messenger amid scarcity.

African prophecy confronts the intersection of public policy and theology. Elijah confronts Ahab. The contest between the prophets of Baal and Elijah and his confederates exonerates the Yahwistic parties and denounces the Baalistic parties. When Elijah shrinks from life and longs for death, there are two caveats. First, the distance in time often obscures the sociopolitical backdrop the writer assumes we know, which in fact we may not know anymore. Second, many scholars argue that the essence of African spirituality privileges prophetic public theology. Material in Kings gives us the only description of transitions from one prophet to another. The story of the whirlwind that took Elijah (2 Kings 2:1-25) into heaven represents one of the most famous biblical texts. Within Jewish tradition, Elijah figures prominently in the Passover Haggadah. One can easily overlook the zealous Elisha, who twice requests the spirit of Elijah (2

Kings 2:9) and who did not get taken away in the whirlwind. Randall Bailey (1991) reminds African readers of the danger of overidentifying with the wrong character. Often in the history of African peoples, we forget those who carry on the ministries of those who get "taken up." The tradition of passing the mantle as a transfer of authority has emerged in contemporary culture; consider the role of Kente cloth or quilts (Tobin and Dobard 1999). A careful reader notes the role of water in the story amid the drought, the backdrop of much of Elijah's ministry. One also observes the play on the Exodus traditions (Exodus 14, Josh. 4:1—5:1), where the mantle splits the water, like the Sea of Reeds and the Jordan River were both split. Elisha's first act of prophetic power is the transformation of brackish water to potable water (2 Kings 2:19-22).

When the kings of Israel, Judah, and Edom appear to be in danger, they need a prophet. Jehoshapat seeks a prophet, and Elisha's first public theological encounter occurs. This initial act paves the way for a narrative collection of transformative prophetic performances (2 Kings 4:1-8:6). Their focus is on public theology and prophetic address that foment a Syrian revolution (2 Kings 8:7-15) and later one in Israel (2 Kings 9:1-37). This revolution leads to Joram's, Ahaziah's, and Jezebel's assassinations; ends the Omride dynasty, and builds the Jehu dynasty; in its place (2 Kings 10:1-36).

The Elisha cycle ends by interrupting the annals of Kings (2 Kings 13:14-21). Once again, the context is the Israelite Aramean controversy. By this time, Elisha is deathly ill. Nonetheless, disappointment with monarchs continues. The sick-unto-death Elisha still has more vitality than King Joash, whose failure of nerve points to the limited victory his people will achieve over the Arameans. Even the bones of the dead Elisha can bring a Moabite back to life (2 Kings 13:20-21).

The narratives of Hezekiah are part of the annals, and part of the prophetic backbone. These prophetic narratives (2 Kings 18:13—20:19) are remarkably similar to materials found in Isaiah (36–39). The background for these stories is Assyrian

power under Sennacherib and his campaign(s) into Israel (701 B.C.E.).

ANNALS

- General annals: 2 Kings 10–16
- Fall of Samaria: 2 Kings 17
- Hezekiah: 2 Kings 18–20
- Transition: 2 Kings 21
- Josianic Reform: 2 Kings 22–23
- Fall of Jerusalem: 2 Kings 24–25

The plot of the books of Kings continues the mythic construction of the Davidic house. Its prophetic backbone does not provide the only voice. The annals lift up the priests' voice as well. Priests serve as defenders of the faith in the Athaliah story as well as during Jehoash's reign (2 Kings 11–12). Just as prophets may be good or derelict, the narrator sets forth a conflict between good priests and derelict priests, namely the priests of Jehoiada (2 Kings 12:7).

While the annals may not meet today's readers as the most compelling genres in Kings, they nonetheless shape the core understanding of Israel's and Judah's history. The story of the Shalmaneser V's (727–721 B.C.E.), who captures Samaria, indicates that the Assyrian deportation and relocation practices ended racial and religious connections between the northern peoples, who would become known as the Samaritans, and the southern peoples, who would become known as the Judeans (see 2 Kings 17). The writer describes their common fate, deportation (2 Kings 17:19-20), and then builds on the consequences of the policy for the northern kingdom (2 Kings 17:21-41).

Stories about King Jehoash, along with the royal reformers Hezekiah and Josiah, provide the only successful temple refurbishing recorded in the annals. Hezekiah's reforms (2 Kings 18) build a bridge between annals and prophetic narrative, these reforms, preceding his visit to the prophet Isaiah (2 Kings 19). The subsequent story (2 Kings

20:1-11) parallels prophetic healing stories in the Elijah and Elisha cycles earlier in the Kings material.

The transition annals that recount the wickedness of Manasseh and Amon (2 Kings 21) provide the necessary backdrop for Josiah's activities (2 Kings 22–23). The story of his reforms demonstrates narrative skill and political understanding. The story involves a wide range of participants (the secretary of the house of the LORD, the high priest, and the prophetess Huldah) and their attending constituencies. Thus the writer depicts a reform with broad-based support from the king, the priests, and the prophets. Josiah's reform goes through this more elaborate process of buy-in before the public reforms that the writer of the Hezekiah narrative indicates were part of that failed attempt at reform. This marks a key reform connected to the discovery and reading of the document (2 Kings 23:2b). During temple restoration after the exile, the Torah will be read at the Water Gate (Nehemiah 8) as part of the inauguration of a new awakening of faith. Reading the book of the covenant was part of the reform; another element was a renewal of the liturgical place of Passover (2 Kings 23:21).

Probably the greatest mystery in Kings is Josiah's disappearance. His death receives little notice. A theology that indicates that Josiah should live a long and prosperous life fails to attend to his end. This gap is just the sort that African interpreters over the years have played on like a "riff" in a jazz or blues piece that invites the readers/speakers to improvise on the story.

The final annals of the books of Kings try to find what comfort they can in small things. The new empire, the Babylonians personified in King Nebuchadnezzar, stands as an overwhelming force for the post-Josianic community. Josiah's leadership is replaced with the likes of the coward Zedekiah, the puppet who rebelled against Babylon but only ineffectually. Jerusalem was conquered twice (597 and 587 B.C.E.). The temple was ransacked as an act of theological terrorism and also because temples in antiquity often were centers with vast resources.

Both wealth and meaning were concentrated in them. The Babylonian puppet Gedaliah was assassinated, which we surmise prompted a third attack and deportation (2 Kings 25:22-26). The only ray of hope is the "rightful king" Jehoachin's release from prison (2 Kings 25:27-30), which ends the books of Kings.

The books of Kings establish an idealized romance of the Davidic monarchy as model. The writers connect this monarchy to the temple's power as the nation's theological and political center. The prophetic backbone of the books problematizes actual monarchic practices. The annals corroborate the challenge of public theology and theocracy laid out in the Davidic model in practice. African communities have used these same texts to reflect on the challenges of public theology and the inheritance of African life and rhetoric.

References

Bailey, Randall C. 1991. "Beyond Identification: The Use of Africans in Old Testament Poetry and Narratives." In *Stony the Road We Trod: African American Biblical Interpretation*, ed. Cain Hope Felder. Minneapolis: Fortress Press, 165–84.

Brueggemann, Walter. 1968. "David and his Theologian." *Catholic Biblical Quarterly* 30: 156–81.

DuBois, W. E. B. 1961. *The Souls of Black Folk*. New York: Fawcett.

Endres, J. 1988. *Temple, Monarchy and Word of God*. Wilmington, Del.: Michael Glazier.

Gates, Henry Louis, Jr. 1989. *The Signifying Monkey: A Theory of African-American Literary Criticism*. New York: Oxford University Press.

Rost, Leonhard. 1982. *The Succession to the Throne of David*. Sheffield, Eng.: Almond, 1982

Tobin, J. and R. Dobard. 1999. *Hidden in Plain View: A Secret History of Quilts and the Underground Railroad*. New York: Doubleday.

ISAIAH

Makhosazana K. Nzimande

I saw the severed hand of a black activist in a bottle at a Port Elizabeth police station.
The police told me it was a baboon's hand. They said to me:
"Look here, this is the bottled hand of a communist."
But I know that Sicelo Mhlawuli . . . was buried with his hand missing.
—*A detainee of the apartheid government*

A POSTCOLONIAL *IMBOKODO* READING OF THE BOOK OF ISAIAH IN SOUTH AFRICA

As recounted above, the gruesome verbal cameos at the Truth and Reconciliation Commission (TRC) hearings were bitter reminders of our existential situation as black South Africans during apartheid. Ideological use of the Bible justified gross human rights violations causing our oppression. Then we were prime terrorist suspects of the apartheid government; feasts for police dogs; human depositories for shrapnel, bullets, and tear gas; and targets of home arrests, exile, and detention without trial.

The year 1994 ushered in a new political dispensation with Nelson Mandela as the first democratically instituted black president. Long-awaited freedom was finally realized and received with great exuberance by mainly the black sector of the South African population. Yet, the new dispensation is not as blissful as anticipated. The postapartheid South African era has many new challenges, including xenophobia, unabated poverty, socioeconomic instability, unemployment, HIV/AIDS, and other related social ills. Whereas in apartheid South Africa the yearning was for political freedom from the shackles of colonialism and apartheid, in postapartheid South Africa the rampant upsurge in globalization must be reckoned with. The capitalist South African economic system, like other two-thirds-world countries, needs redemption from economic, cultural, linguistic, and other related entanglements of globalization.

I engage the book of Isaiah through the methodological prism of a postcolonial *Imbokodo*[1] (black South African women's) hermeneutics. This methodology, like its apartheid counterpart Black Theology in South Africa, focuses on using the Bible as a weapon of struggle for redressing colonialism's negative historical effects and, most recently, globalization's impact. I begin with an overview and then a critical interrogation of the book of Isaiah concerning the spatial positioning of South African blacks, particularly black women's agency. My focus concerns three tenets of a postcolonial *imbokodo* hermeneutics: historical restitution, African identity politics, and the struggle for socioeconomic survival.

THE BOOK OF ISAIAH: AN OVERVIEW

Scholars generally divide Isaiah into three parts: First Isaiah (1–39), Deutero-Isaiah (40–55), and Trito-Isaiah (56–66). In its entirety, the book of Isaiah is fraught with exegetical complexities. The history, theology, and literary composition of the book remain under scrutiny among scholars, although there is unanimity on its final form.

> In sum, the book of Isaiah as a whole portrays the revelation of YHWH's Torah to the nations and Israel in analogy to the revelation of Torah to Israel and the nations, in the Mosaic tradition. . . . Whereas the Mosaic tradition portrays this revelation as a means to establishing Israel in its own land, the Isaiah tradition portrays the revelation . . . to [demonstrate] YHWH's world-wide sovereignty and to reestablish Israel in Zion. (Sweeney 1996: 65)

First Isaiah is controversially acknowledged as literature regarding the forty-year historical and political activities of the eighth-century prophet Isaiah. The possible contemporaries of the prophet are Hosea, Amos, Micah, Zephaniah, and possibly Nathan (2 Samuel 7; 12:1-15). First Isaiah depicts the prophet as close to royal circles and quite familiar with state political matters (6:1—8:23 and 36:1—39:8). Operating during the Assyrian empire era, the prophet Isaiah emphasized establishing

God's sovereignty in Zion and over the nations. The failure of royalty to rule with justice would lead to God's inevitable judgment. Despite varied approaches to resolve the thematic structure of First Isaiah, there is no consensus among scholars.

Deutero-Isaiah, the second part of the book, is regarded as distinct in origin from chapters 1–39 given language, content, themes, and historical context. In Second Isaiah, "the gentile king in chaps.40-55 is Cyrus of Persia (fl. 560–530 B.C.E. cf. 41: 2-3, 25; 44:24—45:13; 48:14), not the Assyrian king of Isaiah (10:5-19). The people are in Babylon, not in Isaiah's 8th century Jerusalem; the message is to leave Babylon, cross the desert, and return to Zion" (Clifford 1992: 490). Within this corpus, the new historical intervention of Yahweh is articulated. God's new act of restoring Israel to Zion is envisaged (40:1-11). Conventionally, Isaiah 40–55 is dated around 540 B.C.E based on the anticipated Persian defeat of Babylon and the release of the first deportees by Yahweh's agent of the return, Cyrus (48:20-21).

Scholars generally accept that the theological crux of Deutero-Isaiah is the dramatic shift from impending judgment to restoration and the reenactment of the new exodus-conquest (Childs 1979: 325–38; Clements 1982). Deutero-Isaiah's message refers to earlier traditions on creation, the new exodus-conquest (40:12-17; 41:17-20; 43:16-17; 51:9-10), Abraham (41:8; 51:2), and David (55:3-5) (Watts 2004). Whybray opines on the absence of future judgment on ancient Israel in Deutero-Isaiah. Central themes are reassurance, God's unlimited good will toward God's people, and God's determination to restore them promptly to joy and prosperity (Whybray 1983: 13). Notable rhetorical elements in Deutero-Isaiah are the servant songs (42:1-4; 49:1-6; 50:4-6; 52:13—53:12), liturgical poetry, psalmic laments, oracles of thanksgiving, hymns, trial speech, thanksgivings, and victory songs.

With Third Isaiah, no consensus among scholars on the prophet's social location or the historical date of composition exists. Scholarly proposals range from the pre-exilic era (for 56:9—57:13) to the late Hellenist period (for 65; 66:3-24) (Seitz 1992: 502). The prophet's work in Third Isaiah is similar to Deutero-Isaiah and as anonymous. Stylistically, their similarities signal that they have the same author or disciple/group of disciples who emulated Second Isaiah's poetic style (Smith 1995: 22–49). The prophet's addressees once again live in Judah.

In Third Isaiah, there is a remarkable theological continuity between the circumstances of ancient Israel in the Babylonian exile and of the returnees in Judah. Postexilic Israel practiced the same kind of sins that had precipitated the exile—namely, the resurgence of non-Yahwist rituals. The return to Judah was not as blissful as Second Isaiah had predicted. Therefore, God's impending judgment was once again announced on oppressors and religious deviants. Still, Yahweh's creative redemption is promised: realized liberation of ancient Israel and vengeance on their oppressors (47:4; 49:7, 26; 52:3, 9; 54:5, 8). There is an eschatological center notable in Isaiah 60–62 (Blenkinsopp 2003: 38–39, 60–66).

ISAIAH AND HISTORICAL RESTITUTION (ISA. 3:16-17)

The restitution of positive black historical contribution remains a pertinent challenge in South African postcolonial biblical interpretation, particularly since Enlightenment paradigms of modernity, influenced by scientific racism and the supremacy of reason and logic, shoved colonized African people to the periphery of world history. Colonial historiography concealed roles of Africans as political actors while accentuating Eurocentric histories. Africa was labeled an "ahistorical dark continent," a perpetual child constantly needing European supervision. Calculated to dominate, subjugate, and domesticate Africans, colonization and apartheid denied the African majority in South Africa

access to their own histories (Eze 1997: 103–40). Given that colonialism survives by subjugating "other" historical narratives, postcolonial biblical readers must listen to "our Other canons, written and unwritten . . . because imperialism proceeds by denying the validity of the narratives and values of its victims, while it imposes its own 'master narratives' on them" (Dube 2000: 50). History is one of these subjugated "canons."

The call for historical recovery is underscored in South African Black Theology, especially in the historical-materialist hermeneutics of Itumeleng Mosala:

> [F]or black theology . . . to be genuinely liberating in its use of the Bible it will have to identify . . . contemporary forms of black history and black culture that will better situate it [to] reappropriate past struggles of black people in a critical and hermeneutically fruitful way. . . . Liberating biblical hermeneutical appropriation, however, is a long [process that critically appreciates] the hermeneuticians . . . [and] . . . the historical and cultural struggles of the biblical communities before finally confronting the signified expression of those struggles in the texts. (Mosala 1989: 98)

In postapartheid South Africa, blacks are engaged in decolonization, where historical restitution is mandatory. They are still licking wounds inflicted by colonialism and apartheid. Decolonization entails rediscovering and reappropriating what imperialism had suppressed in the natives' past: a conversation with the West and Europe to hear and engage transformation, to honor native histories, formerly forgotten and marginalized (Said 1993: 261). Only creating a counter-memory to empirical, apartheid thought can salvage South African blacks from historical annihilation. The African Renaissance movement pioneered by President Thabo Mbeki underscores the importance of black historical restitution whereby black people must be made audible, historical actors. New black historical subjects must create a new historical consciousness interpreted where black historical restitution creates a new, positive, black historical collective memory.

Their largely patriarchal ethos mars current postapartheid historical restitution efforts. Black women are historically silenced, misrepresented, and sometimes negatively depicted. The prism of *Imbokodo* postcolonial hermeneutics seeks to redress this historical imbalance by addressing the muting, negative depiction of South African black women's agency, particularly investigating the dialectic among empire, race, gender, and class; women's historical roles as active participants; and their concurrent patriarchal oppression.

Ancient Israelite and Judean struggles under the Babylonian empire that Isaiah sought to address are analogous to black people's struggles in postapartheid South Africa. "The ideological intent of the empire [was] to talk Jews out of Jewish perceptions of reality into the Babylonian definitions of reality, to define life in terms of Babylonian values, Babylonian hopes, and Babylonian fears" (Brueggemann 1992: 92). To assist exiled Jews in discerning a new of reality, Isaiah appeals to old memories and affirmations, a new imagining of reality at home in Zion, away from their exilic context. Therefore, one can appropriate Isaiah as liberative in postapartheid efforts to recover black history and culture. The prophet's appeal to old memories and affirmations is useful. Positive historical memories can assist in removing colonially inscribed perceptions of reality amid imperial domination.

Yet Isaiah exhibits a condescending attitude toward women, which inhibits black women's appropriation of the book. The prophet's view of "the daughters of Zion" as "haughty" and "glancing wantonly with their eyes, mincing along as they go, tinkling with their feet," and thus "deserving of the Lord's affliction" (Isa. 3:16-17) clearly indicates the prevailing attitude toward gender and sex in prophetic literature (Amos 4:1-3; Jeremiah 2:23-25, 33). Such patriarchal prophetic voices defeat eschatological justice that prophetic literature seeks to

promote and must be viewed with suspicion (Darr 1994; Exum 1995: 248–71). The prophet's voice melds with the colonizer's voice, for black women are similarly stereotyped as being oversexed.

As black women who lived under apartheid brutality, we witnessed such negative depictions of "native people" as being sexually deviant. While historical, cultural struggles of Jews under Babylonian captivity reconnect postapartheid readers with their silenced and distorted histories, women's depictions remain largely flawed by misogynistic stereotypes. Given that Isaiah sacrifices gender struggles to national struggles, women readers must exercise great caution when appropriating this text for historical restitution. Black women in South Africa can identify with Jewish national struggles only while suspiciously viewing silencing of gender struggles and portrayals of women as sexually evil.

THE BOOK OF ISAIAH AND AFRICAN IDENTITY POLITICS

Identity is linked to ethnicity. Evidently, in colonial and postcolonial contexts, ethnicity is a biologically, culturally, ideologically, and racially constructed form of otherness, "a hybrid formation" that largely promotes white interests. Similarly, ethnic, cultural, racial, and class identities of black South Africans are still colonial, apartheid constructs perpetually reinscribed by neocolonial privileging of hegemonic White identity. Such a meta-identity is the standard against which subaltern identities are measured (Steyn 2001). Such ethnicity and identity politics are a dimension of colonizers' political, hegemonic power. Colonized subjects always meet imposed identity politics with fierce resistance (Mamdani 1996). The apartheid state created ethnic, cultural, political polarization of black South Africans. The political organization of colonized spaces enforced South African racialized identity construction. The apex of this politicized identity construction was the geographical partitioning of black and white races whereby black South Africans were forcibly confined into ethnically structured geographical spaces called *bantustans,* or homelands, while white races were allocated the best portions of land. Black resistance and struggle against white domination fostered a collective African political identity whereby the colonized sought to deconstruct white superiority mythology by undermining apartheid constructions of blackness.

The colonial arrest of black women's consciousness by introducing alien codes of behavior, culture, aesthetics, and so forth mediated through missionary ideology remains a major challenge in reconstructing postapartheid black women's identities. Using the Bible in creating, constructing, and distorting African identities makes identity politics a matter of postcolonial hermeneutical scrutiny. The postcolonial *Imbokodo* hermeneutics seeks to decolonize colonially imposed stereotypical images of blackness utilizing Black Consciousness to engender black women's conscientization.

The postcolonial African identity problem involves missionaries' repudiation of the African religious world as a "*tabula rasa* on which a wholly new religious psychology was somehow to be imprinted" (Bediako 1992: 225). Postcolonial African biblical readers should use the Bible to reclaim their theological and African religious past, their integrity, and their identity (Bediako 1992: 237; 1995: 17–38). African Christians should adopt an open, exploratory attitude to the African identity crisis rather than providing absolute solutions (Maluleke 2001: 26–41).

Black women must develop counterhegemonic identity constructions that demystify ethnicity, emphasize self-worth and self-love, and dispel self-loathing mentalities regarding their hybridized postapartheid South African identities. Black South Africans in general, and black women in particular, must exercise great vigilance not to embrace negative psychological images of them inscribed by colonizers when reading biblical texts. African women's self-perceptions must be psychologically unchained, and they must acknowledge their con-

testing embodied identities (Reddy 2000). South African black women must vigorously interrogate their own hybrid identities (Bhabha 1994). Where apartheid biblical interpretation sought to demean and distort African identity, postapartheid biblical interpretation should be skillfully used as a weapon to counter colonially inculcated negative self-images.

Geographical removal of Jews from Judah negatively influenced their national and religious identity. Exile gave them a new geographical and theological identity. The temptation to embrace Babylonian religions and cultures was great, thus unleashing Yahweh's wrath and impending judgment as manifested in Isaiah 40–55. Norman Gottwald notes that Jewish exiles experienced conflicting identities between a powerless Judahite and a powerful Babylonian state (1992: 46). Lived memories of Judah shielded them from imperial religious enticements and gave them a new identity. As God's witnesses, their redemption from Babylonian captivity was promised and their new exodus from Babylon was imminent only if they amended their ways before God (Isaiah 43).

Black people in South Africa are similarly caught up in ideological contradiction between imperially imposed identities and their own indigenous identities. They struggle to maintain their African identity, yet they have embraced the imposed Western identity. Like the Babylonian Jews in Isaiah, black South Africans are experiencing an exilic identity. This complicated type of exile is a cultural and identity exile at home. Hence, President Mbeki's exhortation "Africa! Define yourself!" Western cultural modes of existence have turned black South Africans into a hybrid people who unashamedly mimic the Western cultural ethos. They have sheepishly surrendered to colonial mimicry, relinquishing their African identity. The imperial seductions of Babylon have historically been too strong to resist.

The prophetic, poetic voice in Isaiah reminds black South Africans who have lost their sense of identity to similarly "withdraw their allegiance from the illegitimate and dysfunctional empire" (Brueggemann 1992: 112). But South African blacks need to be reconscientized of their postapartheid exilic existence for them to realize their state of exile. For Jews in Babylon, the acceptance of exile was "an act of polemical theological imagination that guards against cultural assimilation" (Brueggemann 1992: 110). For black South Africans, it would be an act of imagining a new postapartheid African identity. Given the disadvantaging gender ramifications inherent in the quest for restitution of African identity, it should not be achieved at the expense of the religio-cultural oppression of African women. As Mercy Amba Oduyoye cautions, African women should "develop a keen sensitivity to the inherent dangers of tying identity to culture" (2001: 13).

THE BOOK OF ISAIAH AND BLACK WOMEN'S STRUGGLE FOR SURVIVAL

On a global socioeconomic scale, the post–Cold War colonial legacy is that ownership of the world's economic resources rests primarily with a Northern, predominantly white minority while the majority of the world's population remains in dire economic impoverishment. The postcolonial African socioeconomic dilemma is that

when citizens of Europe own the land and mines of Africa, this is the most direct way of sucking the African continent. Under colonialism the ownership was complete and backed by military domination. Today, in many African countries the foreign ownership is still present, although the armies and flags of foreign powers have been removed. . . . In other words, in the absence of direct political control, foreign investment insures that the natural resources and the labor of Africa produce economic value which is lost to the continent. (Rodney 1981: 22–23)

The granting of political independence has done little to restore the productive forces of the formerly colonized African countries. Political enfranchisement does not promote socioeconomic independence. Imperialist countries still own African economic resources and use financial proceeds from these for their own economic development and well-being. Therefore, it is not surprising that the sociopolitical defeat of apartheid in South Africa has ironically not yet granted independence from the socioeconomic usurpation and dependence inflicted by Western imperialism.

Whereas, before 1994, African forerunners in the liberation struggle opted for a Marxist economic alternative, postapartheid South Africa encourages vigorous debates on foreign investment, trade, a free market economy, and sustainable development. The ironic slant of this socioeconomic venture is that South Africa, like many other independent former colonies, remains deeply entangled in the global economic forum. Remarkably, there has been a radical shift from advocating communal Marxist sharing of economic resources to endorsing a capitalist economic framework for those who, during the pursuit of independence, were opposed to capitalism for its economic exploitation. The postapartheid state reform linked the market, state, and global economy in a way that re-entrenched hegemonic capitalist globalization and the "bitter economic legacy of white development and black underdevelopment" (Magubane 2002: 89).

While there is tremendous economic growth within sectors of the emerging black middle-class elite, the majority of black South Africans are yet to personally benefit from the democratic, economic bliss. Although many positive developments have taken place since 1994, alarming rates of poverty, forced evictions, poor health care, and unequal access to educational opportunities inexplicably continue to plague South African black women (and men). In postapartheid South Africa, global effects of neocolonialism, continued imperialist exploitation, and manipulation of third world economies by Europe and America continue to plague blacks. The Euro-American economic hegemony coerces postcolonial states into generating wealth for former colonial masters, creating perpetual economic dependence (Young 2001: 41).

Globalization and the late stage of capitalism are major inhibiting factors to black economic development and independence in South Africa. By falsely presenting a globe divided into three homogenous worlds, globalization sustains economic oppression of formerly colonized countries. Yet the concentrated bulk of foreign investment in advanced industrialized economies limits capitalist mobility between so-called first and third worlds. Financial flows are heavily concentrated in transnational corporations in North America, Europe, and Japan who promote Western investment and commodities manufacturing in formerly colonized territories, exerting control over national governance of financial and economic markets in so-called third world countries. Imperial wealth produced in marginal geographical spaces like Africa, Asia, and Latin America materially benefits Western metropolitan centers (Hirst and Thompson 1996). Thus relations between the West and the rest of the world retain a colonialist ethos.

Unequal economic power relations established during the colonial era are reproduced through complex, capitalist-based economic relations. Western political hegemony is still gravely felt amid foreign policies that promote Western superiority and Western currencies over peripheral economies in former colonies. The huge debt crisis whereby economic surplus from peripheral countries is extracted and managed by core economies in Africa and elsewhere attests to globalization's adverse effects. Unequal neocolonial distribution of economic resources between the West and the rest of the world thrusts the so-called third world into a devastating state of poverty and material deprivation that continues unabated as Western core nation states use third world countries as financial machinery for the transportation of wealth (Hoogveldt 2001).

Problems of unemployment and underemployment have plagued South Africa since the dismantling of apartheid at alarming rates: above 25 percent. Before the advent of democracy, proponents of Black Consciousness and Black Theology leveled sharp criticism against the concentration of wealth in a few irresponsible people, from Coca-Cola and hamburger cultural backgrounds. Likewise, fierce theological attacks were directed toward racial capitalism of apartheid, pervasive class stratification, bourgeois intellectualism of South African blacks, and adverse effects of these on poor, exploited South African blacks. For example, utilizing a neo-Marxist ideological grid, Mosala levels a sharp critique against post–World War II internationalization of capital under late monopoly capitalism and impotent biblical sociological approaches that fail to transform oppressive and exploitative class and economic ideologies (Mosala 1989: 55–56).

Evidently, Europe and America have emerged as the "Babylonian empire" of our time. Within this economically suicidal postapartheid context, the prophet's anti-Babylonian political stance in Isaiah is deeply needed in leveling a sharp theological critique against the capitalist exploitation of globalization and the subsequent suffering it inflicts on South African blacks. Global "exilic voices" within South Africa and in related postcolonial contexts anticipate the humiliation of arrogant Babylon and the socioeconomic restoration of contemporary postcolonial Judean contexts. Those dispossessed of their wealth by Western greed—for example, the International Monetary Fund and the World Bank—and those who have suffered tremendous loss of life due to Euro-American military aggression and arrogance cry out for the fall of Babylon (Isaiah 47). Likewise, in rejecting a capitalist-ordered society that enriches a few while dehumanizing others, black South Africans envisage an era analogous to the prophet's prediction, with no more oppressors and land destruction (Isa. 16:4).

South African women largely sustain households as single parents because men are still locked up in the migratory labor system as diggers of gold and diamonds in the mines, builders of railway lines, and other heavy and exploitative jobs. The postapartheid economic condition is that black women continue to suffer from the socioeconomic racial capitalism of apartheid. Most South African women are poor: unemployed, illiterate, widowed, and confined in underdeveloped rural areas and former *bantustans*. Although the new democratic era has brought some changes to South African black women's lives, these have not necessarily changed the conditions of material impoverishment that most women experience. Poverty and malnutrition remain two of the greatest challenges threatening black women's existence. Moreover, the HIV/AIDS epidemic is devouring scores of women and men every year, leaving behind many orphans, widows, and disillusioned, child-headed families. Evidently, as the doubly imperialized, African women bear the brunt of global economic policy and are even more prone to exploitation by capital giants than are men. African women in the two-thirds world are the worst affected by the neocolonization of global economic policies (Dube 2000: 150–53).

The new spatial positioning of South African women's agency is a space of anticipation, an in-between space between the dusk of a politically oppressive regime and the dawn of social and economic justice. This is a space of waiting for deliverance of material goods, antiretroviral drugs, adequate health care, education, housing, and adequate shelter for all. This new spatial positioning demonstrates that "the return to Judah," the new political dispensation, is not as blissful as envisaged during the long struggle against apartheid. Politically, black South Africans have left Babylon, crossed over the Jordan, and returned to Zion. The political fruits of this dispensation manifest in positive signs of government delivery (albeit not yet to the satisfaction of most poor South Africans), the freedom of expression, the freedom of movement, and so forth. Yet this spatial positioning is a liminal "postexilic" space that has placed black South Africans in a perpetual socioeconomic limbo. The

struggle for economic survival continues whereby most black South African women anticipate the government's delivery of basic services to meet their basic daily needs.

Therefore, in postapartheid South Africa, black South Africans anticipate a praxiological transformation of the exploitative status quo where they find themselves economically shackled by the neocolonialism of globalization and the steady process of government service delivery. The prophetic voice of Third Isaiah encodes the postdemocratic experiences of black South Africans. Thus black South Africans identify with the postexilic exile of Jewish deportees in Third Isaiah (Gregory 2007). Evidently, "the return to Judah" is not as blissful as anticipated during the apartheid era.

As far as Isaiah is concerned, a black woman reader faces enormous problems in any effort to identify socioeconomic struggles of women in the text. Rather, the prophet focuses on injustice affecting males in high positions of power within an imperialist setting. The struggles of women in the text are conspicuous only by their absence, although the prophet is vociferous about the absence of communal justice in the exilic community. Therefore, the book of Isaiah's silence on women's struggles betrays black women's struggle for economic independence. Women can identify with only national struggles in the book. Yet Deutero-Isaiah's historic appeal to the exodus-conquest traditions connects us black South Africans to our historic victory over the gigantic apartheid monster while pointing us forward to promised restoration of our nation to happiness and prosperity (Isa. 40:1-11).

Under neocolonialism and globalization, black South Africans are the "Suffering Servants" who constantly seek to remove the Babylonian hegemonic yoke while others benefit tremendously from it. This is mostly manifested in increased class stratification of postapartheid South Africa and the concomitant class consciousness. The struggle for socioeconomic independence should take into cognizance the prevalence of class. The black masses should be allowed to critique class elitism and the

Makhosazana K. Nzimande

privilege of black elites without being perceived as compromising racial solidarity. South Africa is flawed with growing class divisions among the black elite, "the haves," and the majority of poor blacks, "the have-nots." Regarding problems of class and potential exploitation of the less privileged by black elites, in the United States, bell hooks asserts, "progressive black folks who have class privilege must intervene when our most conservative and liberal counterparts seek to deny the reality of black on black cruelty and exploitation" (hooks 2000: 99). The problem of the black elite and its collaboration by default in sustaining the imperialist capitalist agenda is prevalent among blacks in post-apartheid South Africa.

For example, the movement of black women into the corporate world has increased demand for domestic labor. Large scores of lower-class black women are employed as domestics in black households, just as they are used in white households. These class dynamics have adverse effects for poor women, who benefit from the income such labor provides while being reduced to positions of inferiority. Colonial domination equally affects black people, but class status is increasingly becoming a divisive factor among those formerly colonized, black women notwithstanding. Renita Weems comments on class prejudice existing in American, competitive postapartheid, and other postcolonial settings:

> Within a capitalistic society such as our own, disparate economic relationships among women can distort perspectives of reality. Among the "haves," it breeds a false sense of superiority. Among the "have-nots," it breeds an irrepressible sense of inferiority. Wherever human worth and dignity are measured by purchasing power, there is always a problem of class prejudice. (Weems 1988: 10)

Therefore, black South Africans identify with the "Oppressed Servant" of Deutero-Isaiah who imaginatively embodies staying faithful beside

Babylonian hegemony and the Judahites' impulse to adopt hegemonic thinking (Gottwald 1992: 49). Black South Africans eagerly await a "Cyrus of Persia" figure to rescue them from the stranglehold of globalization and neocolonialism (Isa. 48:14). Hopefully, in God's appointed time, Babylon will be toppled over and justice shall prevail! But while "Cyrus" rescues us from Babylon, the peculiar South African situation demands a concomitant rescue from dehumanizing black-on-black class exploitation, especially if it takes place between women.

Reading the book of Isaiah from a postcolonial *Imbokodo* perspective in South Africa today impels readers to consider the following tenets: historical restitution, African identity politics, and the struggle for socioeconomic survival. Black South Africans in postapartheid South Africa are, like the Jewish deportees in Babylon, in exile. Moreover, postapartheid liberation is not as blissful as anticipated. While the book of Isaiah can be appropriated for effecting historical restitution, black South African women must view the privileging of national struggles over gender struggles and the prophet's prevalent condescending attitude toward women with suspicion. The conflict between Babylonian-imposed state identity and Judahite identity mirrors the black South African identity crisis whereby they are caught between their own denigrated African identity and enticements of embracing imposed Babylonian definitions of identity in our time. As "Suffering Servants" groaning under the yoke of Western neoimperialism, globalization, and socioeconomic exploitation, black South African women eagerly await the new exodus-conquest whereby Babylon will be destroyed.

Note

1. Imbokodo is the Zulu word for "grinding stone." I use imbokodo in a postcolonial sense to symbolize the relentless sociopolitical, sociocritical, and sociocultural struggles of South African women against

colonial and apartheid injustices. The association of imbokodo with women's struggles in political circles takes its cues from the much-acclaimed South African women's freedom song used during the Defiance Campaign of 1956: "Wathint' abafazi, wathint' imbokodo, uzokufa!" translated as "You strike a woman, you strike a grinding stone, you will be crushed!" See Nzimande 2005.

References

Bediako, Kwame. 1992. *Theology and Identity: The Impact of Culture upon Christian Thought in the Second Century and Modern Africa*. Regnum Studies in Mission. Oxford: Regnum.

———. 1995. *Christianity in Africa: The Renewal of a Non-Western Religion*. Studies in World Christianity. Maryknoll, N.Y.: Orbis.

Bhabha, Homi K. 1994. *The Location of Culture*. London: Routledge.

Blenkinsopp, Joseph. 2003. *Isaiah 56–66: A New Translation with Introduction and Commentary*. AB 19B. New York: Doubleday.

Brueggemann, Walter. 1992. *Prophetic Imagination*. London: SCM.

Childs, Brevard S. 1979. *Introduction to the Old Testament as Scripture*. Philadelphia: Fortress Press, 325–38.

Clements, Ronald E. 1982. "The Unity of the Book of Isaiah." *Interpretation* 36:117–29.

Clifford, Richard J. 1992. "Second Isaiah." In *Anchor Bible Dictionary*, vol. 3, 472–88. New York: Doubleday.

Darr, Pfisterer K. 1994. *Isaiah's Vision and the Family of God*. Louisville, Ky.: Westminster John Knox.

Dube, Musa W. 2000. *Postcolonial Feminist Interpretation of the Bible*. St. Louis: Chalice.

Exum, J. C. 1995. "The Ethics of Violence against Women." In *The Bible and Ethics: The Second Sheffield Colloquium*, ed. J. Rogerson and M. Davies. Journal for the Study of the Old Testament: Supplement Series, 207. Sheffield: Sheffield Academic.

Eze, Emmanuel Chikwudi, ed. 1997. *Race and the Enlightenment*. Oxford: Blackwell.

Gottwald, Norman K. 1992. "Social Class and Ideology in Isaiah 40–55: An Eagletonian Reading." *Semeia* 92:43–57.

Gregory, Bradley. 2007. "The Postexilic Exile in Third Isaiah: Isaiah 61:1-3 in Light of Second Temple Hermeneutics," *Journal of Biblical Literature* 126 (3): 475–96.

Hirst, Paul, and Grahame Thompson. 1996. *Globalisation in Question: The International Economy and the Possibilities of Governance*. London: Polity.

Hoogveldt, Ankie. 2001. *Globalization and the Postcolonial World: The New Political Economy of Development*. Basingstoke: Palgrave.

hooks, bell. 1981. *Ain't I a Woman? Black Women and Feminism*. Boston: South End.

———. 2000. *Where We Stand: Class Matters*. New York: Routledge.

Magubane, Zine. 2002. "Globalization and the South African Transformation: The Impact on Social Policy." *Africa Today* 49 (4): 89–110.

Maluleke, Tinyiko. 2001. "Identity and Integrity in African Theology: A Critical Analysis." *Religion and Theology* 8 (1): 26–41.

Mamdani, Mamhood. 1996. *Citizen and Subject: Contemporary Africa and the Legacy of Colonialism*. Princeton Studies in Culture/Power/History. Princeton: Princeton University Press.

Mbeki, Thabo. 2002. *Africa: Define Yourself*. Tafelberg: Mafube.

Mosala, Itumeleng J. 1989. *Biblical Hermeneutics and Black Theology in South Africa*. Grand Rapids, Mich.: Eerdmans.

Nzimande, M. K. 2005. *Postcolonial Biblical Interpretation in Post-Apartheid South Africa: The Gebirah in the Hebrew Bible in the Light of Queen Jezebel and the Queen Mother of Lemuel*. Unpublished Ph.D. diss., Brite Divinity School, Texas Christian University.

Oduyoye, Mercy Amba. 2001. *Introducing African Women's Theology*. Introductions in Feminist Theology, vol. 6. Cleveland: Pilgrim.

Reddy, Thomas. 2000. *Hegemony and Resistance: Contesting Identities in South Africa*, Race and Representation Series. Burlington, Vt.: Ashgate.

Makhosazana K. Nzimande

Rodney, Walter. 1981. *How Europe Underdeveloped Africa*. Washington, D.C.: Howard University Press.

Said, E. 1993. *Culture and Imperialism*. London: Chatto and Windus.

Seitz, Christopher R. 1992. "Third Isaiah." *Anchor Bible Dictionary*, vol. 3, 501–7. New York: Doubleday.

Smith, P. A. 1995. *Rhetoric and Redaction in Trito-Isaiah: The Structure, Growth and Authorship of Isaiah 56–66*. Supplements to Vestus Testamentum 62. Leiden: Brill.

Steyn, Melissa E. 2001. *Whiteness Just Isn't What It Used to Be: White Identity in a Changing South Africa*. Albany: State University of New York Press.

Sweeney, Marvin A. 1996. "The Book of Isaiah as Prophetic Torah." In *New Visions of Isaiah*, ed. Roy F. Melugin and Marvin A. Sweeney, 50–67. Journal for the Study of the Old Testament: Supplement Series 214. Sheffield: JSOT.

Watts, Rikk E. 2004. "Echoes from the Past: Israel's Traditions and the Destiny of the Nations in Isaiah 40–55." *Journal for the Study of the Old Testament* 28 (4): 481–508.

Weems, Renita. 1988. *Just A Sister Away: A Womanist Vision of Women's Relationships in the Bible*. Philadelphia: Innisfree.

Whybray, R. N. 1983. *The Second Isaiah*. Sheffield: JSOT.

Young, Robert J. C. 2001. *Postcolonialism: An Historical Introduction*. Oxford: Blackwell.

JEREMIAH

Madipoane Masenya (ngwan'a Mphahlele)

Ngwan'a magana go botšwa o wetše dikomeng, a re dikoma ke tšešo.
—Northern Sotho proverb

AN AFRICAN/SOUTH AFRICAN READING OF JEREMIAH

To bring the Jeremiah text home to Africa, I use the experiences of African peoples in South Africa (hereinafter referred to as "African–South African peoples") to interrogate the book around two themes. First is a theme that emerges in the proverbial parents' warning quoted above, a rather literal translation of which might be: "A child who refused to listen [to advice] landed in 'initiation schools' and claimed that the schools were his extended family."

The tenor of the proverb quoted above is that "one who does not listen to advice usually lands in trouble." In the context of education, a parent may warn a disobedient or "know-it-all" child that if she or he persists in misbehaving, she or he will end up

dikomeng, "at the initiation schools." The Northern Sotho word *koma* (plural in the proverb, *dikoma*) refers to a place in African and South African indigenous contexts in which maturing boys and girls are initiated into manhood and womanhood. The common action phrase used in the context of initiation is "go *wela,*" literally, "go into the deep." The phrase signifies even to the outsider with no initiation experience that the *koma* experience is pretty rough. A disobedient child who thinks he is a "Jack of all trades," including the *koma,* is warned by the proverb that he will eventually land in trouble!

In the book of Jeremiah, Judah is addressed as a persistently disobedient child, disobedient despite the prophet's constant warnings. Judah ends up in *dikoma.* Who could be described as a disobedient child on the landscape of *apartheid* and present South Africa? During the period of *apartheid,* there were prophets who continually challenged the *apartheid* ideologues and all the racist Afrikaners and other racist whites about the injustices that they continually perpetrated against Black peoples. In some cases, atrocities were carried out in the name of God (consider, for example, the racist state theology propagated by some of them). I use the Northern Sotho proverb, informed by themes derived from the Jeremiah tradition, to engage the events and dynamics surrounding the downfall of the South African *apartheid* regime in the mid-1990s.

A second theme is "In Exile at Home." I am a native of Polokwane in South Africa. Due to South Africa's political history, I only "acquired" South African citizenship in 1994 when South Africa became independent. I therefore have a full grasp of what it means to be "in exile at home."[1] Hailing from a Pedi rural setting, I was steeped in African lore (for example, proverbs, folktales, and so on) from early childhood. Such an upbringing, coupled with my intentional decision to foreground "Africa" in my writings, for example in my *bosadi* approach, influences the way I read the book of Jeremiah.[2]

A word about the *bosadi* approach is in order. The *bosadi* or "womanhood" approach is an approach to the reading of biblical texts that was developed with a view to the articulation of the concerns of African–South African women:

> It can be argued that the major hermeneutical focus of the *bosadi* biblical hermeneutics is the unique experiences of an African–South African woman, with a view to her liberation. It is first and foremost an African woman's liberation hermeneutic. African women, facing such multiple life-denying forces as sexism in the broader South African society, which were inherited from the legacies of colonialism and apartheid, sexism in the African culture, post-apartheid racism, classism, HIV/AIDS, and xenophobia, are made the main hermeneutical focus . . . [T]he experiences of the marginalized, in this case African–South African women, and not the contexts which produced

the Bible, serve as a starting point of one's encounter with the biblical text. (Masenya 2005: 747)

THE BOOK OF JEREMIAH: AN INTRODUCTION

The book of Jeremiah claims to report events that occurred in Judah's last years. Thus Jeremiah's prophetic ministry started during the reign of King Josiah (626 B.C.E.) and continued through Jehoiakim's reign (609–598 B.C.E.) and the exile of Jehoiakim (598 B.C.E.) until the death of King Zedekiah (598–587 B.C.E.; compare 52:34).

On the geopolitical scene, the superpowers of the time—Assyria, Babylon, and Egypt—vied for power over smaller states like Judah. Assyria dominated the landscape and took Israel to exile into 722/21 B.C.E. (compare Shiloh's fate in Jer. 7:12-15, 26:6). Sooner rather than later, Babylon gained ascendancy as the new imperial power. The monarchy contributed greatly to Judah's moral and spiritual decline. Eighth-century prophets already critiqued the ruling classes' greed for power and wealth at the expense of poor people (Chaney 1993: 255–60). Therefore, Jeremiah's message against the wickedness of the powerful was not new. The impact of Babylonian imperialism on Judah would not only severely influence Judah's inhabitants but also become the core of Jeremiah's message. For Jeremiah, but perhaps contrary to the perceptions of most of his hearers, these were not mere political events. They formed an integral part of Judah's deviation from the covenant stipulations. As Walter Brueggemann says: "The reality of Babylonian power is not denied but is firmly subordinated to and incorporated into the intention of Yahweh. The Book of Jeremiah thus mediates the reality of imperial politics through the theological claims of the covenant" (1998: 3; see also Stulman 2005: 202). I am captivated by the book of Jeremiah's ability to expose human pride in institutional power and to warn the powerful to act responsibly when in such positions.

The book of Jeremiah is complicated by its lack of a unified chronological structure. It is difficult to assign with any definitiveness any original author and/or editors of the book named after Jeremiah. Scholars, including Carroll, argue that it is impossible to retrieve the (work of the) historical Jeremiah: "We should treat the character of Jeremiah as a work of fiction and recognize the impossibility of moving from the book to the real 'historical' Jeremiah, given our complete lack of knowledge independent of the book itself" (Carroll 1989: 12; see also 1999).

Despite this lack of a unified systematic whole, what becomes clear when one reads the book in its present form is that most of the events narrated in the book shed light on the contexts of a late pre-exilic setting and an early exilic one. There is a general consensus among scholars that the book's recipients were the Jewish communities in the postexilic period: the late exilic and early postexilic periods.[3] Collins succinctly captures this consensus by saying:

> The book is the outcome of a process of transmission which actually shaped the material being transmitted. Hence, although the resulting book provides unsatisfactory information about the life of Jeremiah, it easily makes up for this deficiency by the insight it gives us into the religious thoughts and concerns of the late exilic and early post-exilic community. (1993: 120)

Traditional approaches, such as historical-critical methods, no longer monopolize scholarship. Some more recent approaches to the book include feminist/womanist approaches;[4] intertextual approaches;[5] and ideological-critical approaches.[6] Some insights from these approaches resonate with those entailed in my *bosadi* approach (Masenya 1996, 2004, 2005). Just as womanist/feminist hermeneutical frameworks insist that there is no value-free interpretation of the Bible, so also in

the *bosadi* methodology the experiences of *basadi* (women) are deliberately made a hermeneutical lens in one's interaction with the biblical text. The *bosadi* approach also emphasizes—and this will be significant for the methodology employed in this essay—that the struggle for the affirmation of African women should be informed and inspired also by the corporeality of the African mentality. It should thus really be a *gender* struggle, a struggle by *both* women and men for the affirmation of all African–South African peoples. It is particularly with the latter focus in view that the *bosadi* concept will serve as the methodological tool for my interaction with the book of Jeremiah.

Considering this variety of approaches to the book, Brueggemann describes it as rich with potential for interpretation, with no one approach dominating: a situation in which one may "remain and play and listen and notice," since God is not flat or mute in the book (Brueggemann 1998: xiii).

As I venture to "remain, play, listen, and notice," even as I try to make sense of Jeremiah through an African lens, I turn to interrogate the Jeremiah text in light of the two themes named above.

A LESSON FROM DISOBEDIENCE?

THE DIKOMA ANALOGY: SOUTH AFRICA AND JUDAH

The Northern Sotho proverb I have quoted above refers to the presence of disobedient children in indigenous African societies. In the African (Northern Sotho/Pedi) context, this proverb is usually cited to warn a child who refuses to take advice from the elderly that his or her stubbornness will land him or her in trouble. The proverb gives no room for exceptions to the underlying mentality—one of optimistic wisdom?—that bad actions will necessarily land one in bad situations. This mentality is similar to one of the key presuppositions underlying Deuteronomistic theology as evident in the book of Jeremiah, according to which Judah's disobedience to covenant stipulations will *of necessity* lead to Judah's punishment.[7]

During the South African *apartheid* era, many prophets (that is, Black theologians, liberation theologians, and others) and certain institutions (the South African Council of Churches [SACC], the Institute for Contextual Theology, and others) dared to challenge the South African government over the atrocities committed against the Black majority. Their boldness and persistence in prophesying were probably motivated by their conviction that, eventually, their message would be vindicated. After all, as the proverb warns, disobedient children, however adamant and defensive they are in their disobedience—even if they use religious texts to buttress their disobedience—ultimately do not get away with their behavior. They usually end up in initiation schools![8] Just so, the Afrikaners, the oppressors of African peoples during the apartheid era, have had to learn a similar lesson. Obsessed with election theology and a related biblical hermeneutics (see Masenya 2004: 55-66; Snyman 2007: 53-83), most of them believed that they were closer to God than were all the other "heathen" (Babylonian?) peoples. It may be argued that in their arrogance, like the "know-it-all" proverbial child, they deceived themselves into believing that they were untouchable (in the terms of the proverb, they claimed the *dikoma* belonged to their families) and so oppressed the powerless in the name of God. They boldly preached the purity and election of the Afrikaner race (*volk*), supported by a controversial Dutch Reformed theology, a type of royal-temple ideology. In a nutshell, they, like the disobedient child, acted as if they could do what they liked, as nothing bad would ever befall them. After the catastrophic event of the fall of the Afrikaner "empire" in 1994 (compare to Judah's in 587/6 B.C.E.), we may now hope that the previous oppressors have learned the lesson taught to stubborn children: disobedience comes with a heavy price!

Part of the heavy price includes the redefinition of Blackness and/or Black folks. How should

Afrikaners grapple with the fact that their former political subjects are now their political bosses? What does it mean for a previously despised African to be in charge now of her or his previous masters? The notion of white superiority (and privilege) also now begs redefinition. Where do notions of Afrikaners' election fit in relation to affirmative action, for example? One can speculate with ease that the question "Where is God?" was crucial among Judean exiles during Jeremiah's time. The critical questions that bother many South African white folks today are: What happened to the tenets of white theology? Does God still care for white South Africans? How may African peoples today "reread" the catastrophe that befell ancient Judah? And we African–South Africans: Are we, like the Babylonians of old, all of a sudden no longer the heathens of apartheid South Africa? Could it be that we have been used as agents of God's wrath to punish apartheid's disobedient children? If so, how and what does it mean to experience a reversal of roles?

I find the exercise of involving a deity in the interpretation of these catastrophic moments in both contexts (South Africa and Judah) not only problematic but also scary. Why? In both contexts, not everybody believed God was involved in the unfolding events. For those who did, their interpretations of God's involvement were very different. Interpretation becomes even more problematic when we consider that even among the Judeans there was no uniform understanding of YHWH's workings. The conflict between Jeremiah and false prophets (Jeremiah 28) is one case in point. Because of his heavy message, many of his listeners did not view Jeremiah favorably. Nevertheless, we may assume that many among the powerless, whose voice we unfortunately do not hear in the book, would have been affirmed by Jeremiah's message that challenged injustices committed against them. Jeremiah received opposition from kings and prophets, some of whom designated him a false prophet (Mottu 1993: 315). I am not sure if Nebuchadnezzar viewed his capture of Judah more as the

Babylonian gods' intervention or simply as part of his imperialist expansionist agenda. I do not believe that he was convinced that his capturing Judah made him the servant of Judah's God (27:6).

In the South African situation, although there might be generalizations (particularly in certain Christian circles) that the events of 1994—the catastrophe of the Afrikaner empire and the rise of Black Power—might be viewed as having revealed the intervention of, and even vindication by, God and/or the ancestors, such will remain just that: generalizations. However, note that many Christians (and people of other faiths) did pray during those difficult times. As stated previously, some Christians used the same prophetic oracles to condemn apartheid's injustices. Similarly, those white South Africans who dared to speak against apartheid in the name of God might view the attainment of democracy as God's answer to their prayers.

I think for the new South African government, comparable in the analogy being developed here to the postexilic audience of Jeremiah's message, Judah's catastrophe teaches the following lessons. Leaders, particularly African leaders, must resist a deep-seated mentality that believes "once in power, always in power," a mentality that might have been inherited from the African traditional system of *dikgoshi* (traditional leaders). People gain power in many ways, including by default, by the popularity of certain individuals in their political parties, or for many other reasons. Once in power, all leaders need to serve the people by exercising justice for the powerless, averting all forms of greed, and being self-critical, challenging and uprooting corruption among themselves, and so forth.

The 587 B.C.E./1994 C.E. catastrophes in Judah and white South Africa, respectively, show that no human leader is indispensable. Thus human leaders need to remain humble and vigilant even as they serve fellow human beings who have equally been created in the image of the divine leader.

The main thrust of Jeremiah's message before the Judean exile was that continued disobedience would lead to a troubled end. Their *dikoma* would come in the form of "a foe from the North" (6:22; 20:1-6; 23:9ff, 27; 28). Earlier in his message (Jer. 3:11-14; 22-23; 7:1-15; 26:1-5), Jeremiah gave his hearers some hope that if they repented and turned to YHWH wholeheartedly, they would avoid impending judgment. With time, however, as the Judean peoples persisted in their idolatries, adulteries, and oppressions (7:1-15; 18:18-20; 22:13-17), Jeremiah warned that their salvation would come through their submission to the Babylonian yoke (27:12). As stubborn children, *bo-ngwan'a magana go botšwa,* the Judeans would meet a disastrous end!

Another important question remains, however: could we safely conclude that the "children" were *all* disobedient? Or was the prophet, inspired by the Israelite corporeal mentality (compared to the African one) in which the entire group suffers for an evil committed by an individual? This understanding makes sense, particularly if we consider that his message was directed mainly against the ruling classes (see Chaney 1993; Mottu 1993; Mosala 1993). Another Northern Sotho proverb comes to mind: y*a ja lebele, e fetetša tše dingwe* (translated, "once a goat eats a crop, it affects all the other [innocent] goats"). Its tenor is: if one person in a group commits an error, everyone is punished because of his or her mistake. Or is it, as one commentator stated, a matter of later redactors trying to vilify Jerusalem and those who remained in it?

INTERROGATING THE CORPOREAL MENTALITY WITHIN JUDAH'S PUNISHMENT

Reading as a justice-seeking *bosadi* Bible reader, I am bothered that although the prophet's message was mainly directed against male members of the ruling class and the religious establishment, the negative repercussions of their corrupt and failed leadership (see Domeris 1999) affect those who did not eat the proverbial crop, according to Jeremiah. How could womenfolk, given their exclusion from public religious life, fully access the prophet's message?

Even more unsettling is that women, already marginalized in that patriarchal society, are further marginalized by the prophet's problematic use of female sexual imagery to depict the type of punishment (*dikoma*) that would befall the whole nation (see Weems 1995; Diamond and O'Connor 1999). The core (judgment) message directed to the *whole* nation (symbolized by male leadership) is more often clothed in sexual imagery that vilifies women. The language sounds very rough to the ears of an African person whose tradition has always avoided speaking publicly about matters of sex and sexuality (see Masenya 2004), let alone when one hears such words as an "insult" or attack on human sexuality. In the Pedi culture, for example, if someone offends another person, the latter may deliberately swear at the offender by referring to his or her mother's genitals! Specific reference to a mother's genitals in such a conflict setting intends to make sure offenders *really* will be hurt. The troubling practice (as in Jeremiah) exposes and attacks *mostly* female sexuality. In Jeremiah's case, might we agree with Domeris that in his attempt to create an antisociety through the use of an antilanguage, Jeremiah "exaggerated" the situation to drive a specific point home (Domeris 1994, 1999)? If that was the case, why did the exaggeration have to occur through the use of problematic sexual female imagery (2:20; 3:6; 3:11; 4:30)?

Such misogynistic depictions of sexual female imagery, particularly in the oracles portrayed as coming from a deity, make it difficult for present-day Africana female readers to identify with such oracles, and with the deity portrayed therein. Commenting on Jeremiah's marriage metaphor (Jeremiah 2–3), Diamond and O'Connor rightly argue that Jeremiah's portrayal of the divine-human relationship, which shows the deity as long-suffering, undermines itself "by reinforcing cultural images of a punishing, unjust God, of punishing, unjust husbands, and of wicked independent women" (1999: 145).

Note that not all Judeans of Jeremiah's time (including Jeremiah himself) participated in the Babylonian exile. The text not only mentions a remnant designated the poorest of the land but also the existence of the "righteous" in the land (compare and contrast 5:1-6 and 12:1-4). In that way, Jeremiah deconstructs his own message regarding the wholesale condemnation of the Judahites (see Carroll 1999). One cannot safely conclude that all of Judah's children were disobedient (for not all tasted the exile) nor argue that all those who experienced the exile were disobedient. According to the book of Jeremiah, the majority of Judeans ended up in exile.

Again, Jeremiah believed the only relief and hope for the Judean future was to submit to the Babylonian yoke. We now ask: How may such a positive Jeremian notion of exile shape an Africana reading of the theme of exile in Jeremiah?

Exile and Life: Reconcilable?

"Choose exile and live!" (Jer. 38:17-18; 21:1-10: 27:1-7; 8) seems to be Jeremiah's call to his people. Jeremiah 21:8-9 captures the core of this call succinctly:

> And to this people you shall say: Thus says the Lord: See, I am setting before you the way of life, and the way of death. Those who stay in this city shall die by the sword, by famine and by pestilence; *but those who go out and surrender to the Chaldeans who are besieging you shall live* and shall have their lives as a prize of war. (21:8-9, italics mine; see also 27:8)

The opening contradictory phrase "choose exile and live" seems to capture Jeremiah's perception of a future hope for Judah. Such a painful theme reminds me of my encounter in one of the rooms in the Elminah Slave Castle in Ghana in 2000. In that upper room, I saw a board with a quotation from Ps. 132:14. The gist of its message was: "God is in this place"! Invoking a biblical text in that context invited me to grapple with the possibility of God's presence in the house of slavery. Is that what Jeremiah meant (21:1-10) when he encouraged Judeans to choose exile rather than their own homeland, implying that God could be actively present in exile? It is worth remembering that those Africans who were captured in the seventeenth century were in fact in exile in Ghana, their native land! One wonders how enslaved people could have understood Jeremiah's message that there is life in the house of slavery.

"IN EXILE AT HOME": AN AFRICA IN EXILE IN HER OWN TERRITORY

In earlier writings (Masenya 2003: 338–39; see also 2007), I have used the phrase "In Exile at Home" in my reimagination of the Vashti character in Esther to show the state of "exiled" African women in South Africa. I will use this phrase broadly in the present text to include the "exiled" state of Africana peoples to investigate what the above "contradictory" phrase on Jeremiah's message could mean in African (South African) contexts.

Historically, and today, Africana peoples have been the victims of a variety of ruthless systems—such as slavery, colonialism, and apartheid—ironically in their own territories. Although with slavery there was a forced removal of African peoples from the mother continent, in most cases, in the earlier stages, the slaves would first taste what it meant to be in exile at home (see the Elmina Castle incident described earlier).

Various Africana peoples have therefore tasted the experience of exile in their own territories! *Ke maho a go tšwa dipitšeng* ("they are the wooden spoons from the cooking pots"). They have had firsthand experiences of being in exile in their own homes! As victims of such evil systems, Africana peoples therefore know fairly well what it means to be in "exile at home," to be designated a "foreigner" in one's native land, where captors impose foreign cultural and political systems, languages, religions, and values on them. Exile, therefore, is a place of limited or no access to resources (depending on the generosity of the captors). The experience of

African and Judean exiles losing their lands to foreigners was painful. Land is the most invaluable religious and material asset for African peoples. *Lehumo le tšwa tšhemong*, "wealth comes from a field," says an African saying. The effects of land loss during colonial and apartheid South Africa are felt still by African–South African people today, an effect that has given birth to "socioeconomic exiles" amid political freedom! Such exiles cannot hope for a swift return if the South African government continues to implement slowly its land redistribution policy. In present-day South Africa, many African peoples experience what one would call "socio-economic" exile. Forty-two percent of the South African population earns R250-00 (about US $30) per month, even as the gap between rich and poor people continues to increase. The economy remains in the hands of the historical winners.

African women continue to be victimized by patriarchy in many respects (particularly in the home and the church). In our day, womenfolk feel the brunt of patriarchy through the impact of HIV/AIDS. If we add the observation that violence against women and children is at its peak in present-day South Africa, the reader will come to appreciate the reality that indeed one can be at home and yet in exile! These already "exiled" peoples, captured on their own territory, know well that exile cannot mean life. They will struggle to make sense of the message of Jeremiah.

For the Judeans of Jeremiah's time, the best option amid impending doom was to choose exile. Exile would be the only source of hope for Judah, its leaders, and its peoples. Jeremiah's message was strange because people were discouraged from putting their trust in their own heritage—their historically esteemed assets, such as the Jerusalem city, its temple, and the highly esteemed royal-temple ideology. Convinced that he indeed spoke on behalf of Yahweh, Jeremiah continued with his dreadful message notwithstanding the risk to his own life. The fact that one's home can actually turn into a place of pestilence, famine, hunger, and death (see 21:8-9) has been (and still is) tasted by many

Africana peoples. Though the message resonates, many Africans might dislike it, because to embrace the message means that imperialism, usually touted as a divine agent (for example, colonialism and apartheid in South Africa), always wins the day. In most cases, imperialism wins at the expense of many a powerless victim (see the proverbial goat described earlier). In that sense, Jeremiah's message might be viewed as a call for the powerless—the powerless nations, minority groupings, and "powerless majorities" (women in patriarchal contexts and Blacks in apartheid South Africa)—to show resignation among the powers that be. Africana women who continue to remain at the bottom of the societal ladder may not be encouraged to confront patriarchy!

The irony is that when Jeremiah himself was confronted with a choice between home and exile, he chose home (40:1-6). Did he dread the unknown and so refuse to abide by his earlier message? Was he afraid to face those whose judgment he had boldly predicted? I find no clue in the text to help answer these questions.

What is perhaps a vindication of Jeremiah's prophecies of doom (*dikoma*) is that it appears the exilic experience indeed benefited many exiles. The fact that very few exiles in Egypt or Babylon returned home when they were allowed to points in that direction (see Carroll 1981: 248; Boadt 1984: 384).

This positive portrayal of exile makes one suspect that those who benefited from the Babylonian exile had a larger share in the book's revision. Not only is the Babylonian exile glorified, but it also occupies more space in the book. Little, if any, space is given to those who went to exile in Egypt (Africa); the latter, like the Babylonian exiles, continued to thrive there. Similarly, those who remained in Judah are portrayed in a negative way, the poorest of the land (40:7). Should the latter be taken literally, also implying that the Judeans could not hope for any future from these? Should it be interpreted positively to imply that these, unlike "the cream of the land" who were "hurled" to exile, were more faithful to YHWH's covenant stipulations? A similar situation seems to prevail in postapartheid South Africa. There seems to be an underlying perception by the ruling party that South Africa's future (particularly in terms of political leadership) lies with those of their own (for example, the African National Congress) who experienced "political" exile during the apartheid era. For the powerful, those who remained in the land to experience the harsh reality of living in death's shadow, incarceration, and being "exiled at home" cannot be worthy candidates to rule the country. In the Judean situation, it was a Judean against a Babylonian; later on, it became a Jew against a Jew! In South Africa, it was a black person against a white person; now, it is a black person against a fellow black person! Doesn't this reveal just how self-serving and greedy *any* human being can be?

Even the political exiles of many Black South Africans during the apartheid era benefited the exiled then and even now. They benefited then because their flight out of their native land saved them from torture, denigration, and even death. Some of them benefited because they obtained educational opportunities for themselves and their children. As noted above, many of these are still benefiting because of the warped way in which political leadership is devised.

Depending on the experiences and ideology of a particular African–South African reader, then, the notion in the book of Jeremiah that exile and life are compatible may invoke very different reactions.

To enable readers to continue further dialogue with the book of Jeremiah, I end this interrogation with the words of the wise in Africa. I intentionally leave these words open-ended by not providing their tenors. Each reader needs to figure out for himself/herself what their tenors might be. As readers take time with these proverbs, if they offer new vistas on the materials in the book of Jeremiah they will have served their purpose.

Serokolwana se senyane se ikoketša ka go nkga.
("A small herb increases itself by releasing a strong odor.")

O se bone go akalala ga bonong, go wa fase ke ga bona. ("Do not envy the great heights at which an eagle flies; it will soon fall down.")

La go hlabela o le orele, ka moso le hlabela ba bangwe. ("When it [the sun with its rays] falls on you, avail yourself; tomorrow it will fall on others.")

Kgotlelela moepa-thuse, ga go lehumo le le tšwago kgauswi. ("Persevere, you digger of *thuse* [a "hard-to-find" fruit]; no wealth comes easy.")[9]

Notes

1. Masenya 2003: 338–39; Masenya 2007.
2. On the foregrounding of Africa, see Masenya 2005: 741–46; on the *bosadi* approach, Masenya 1996; 2004; 205: 741–51.
3. Bruggemann 1998; Collins 1993: 120; Stulman 2005; Diamond and O'Connor 1999; Wessels 2004: 479.
4. Bird 2000; Mbuwayesango 2001; Weems 1995, 2004; Mbuwayesango 2007.
5. Carroll 1999: 220–43; Diamond and O'Connor 1999: 87–145.
6. Mottu 1993: 313–28; Carroll 1999: 220–43.
7. See Jer. 7:1—8:3; 11:1-17; 13:1-11; 16:1-13, 26, 27; 17:5-8; 29:10-20; 32; 33:1-13; 42:7-22; 44; 45; and Carroll 1988: 24. Scholars basically agree about the influence of the Deuteronomistic editors on the book (see also Brueggemann 1998; Wessels 2004: 470-483; Weems 2004: 214; Scheffler 1994: 385).
8. Notice that the proverb speaks of initiation *schools,* in the plural, indicating that the severity of the punishment does not depend on the relationship of the disobedient child with one or another *mongkoma* (a leader in the *koma* exercise). As already noted, the initiation-school experience could never be an easy one.
9. Literally, "no wealth comes from nearby." There is no consensus on what *thuse* means. Some scholars regard it as the name of a very scarce root used for therapeutic purposes; others understand it to refer to a very small ant. With either option the main idea seems to be that a particular valuable object is hard to find; therefore if one *really* wants to find it, one needs to work *very* hard, as ordinarily no treasure comes easy.

References

Bailey, Randall C., ed. 2003. *Yet with a Steady Beat: Contemporary U.S. Afrocentric Biblical Interpretation.* Atlanta: Society of Biblical Literature.

Bird, Phyllis A. 2001. "A North American Feminist Response." In *Other Ways of Reading: African Women and the Bible*, ed. M. W. Dube, 199–206. Atlanta: SBL, Geneva: WCC.

Brueggemann, Walter. 1998. *A Commentary on Jeremiah: Exile and Homecoming.* Grand Rapids, Mich.: Eerdmans.

Boadt, Lawrence. 1984. *Reading the Old Testament: An Introduction.* New York: Paulist.

Carroll, Robert P. 1981. *From Covenant to Chaos: Uses of Prophecy in the Book of Jeremiah.* London: SCM.

———. 1989. *Jeremiah: Old Testament Guides.* Sheffield: Sheffield Academic.

———. 1999. "The Book of J: Intertexuality and Ideological Criticism." In *Troubling Jeremiah*, ed. A. R. Pete Diamond and Kathleen M. L. O'Connor, 220–43. Sheffield: Sheffield Academic.

Chaney, Marvin L. 1993. "Bitter Bounty: The Dynamics of Political Economy Critiqued by the Eighth-Century Prophets." In *The Bible and Liberation: Political and Social Hermeneutics*, ed. Norman K. Gottwald and Richard A. Horsley, 250–63. Maryknoll, N.Y.: Orbis.

Collins, T. 1993. *The Mantle of Jeremiah: The Redaction Criticism of the Prophetical Book.* Sheffield: JSOT.

Diamond, Pete, and O'Connor, K. M. 1999. "Unfaithful Passions: Coding Women Coding Men in Jeremiah 2–3(4:2)." In *Troubling Jeremiah*, eds. A. R. Pete

Diamond and Kathleen M. O'Connor, 123–45. Sheffield: Sheffield Academic.

Domeris, William R. 1994. "Jeremiah and the Religion of Canaan." *Old Testament Essays* 7 (1): 7–20.

———. 1999. "When Metaphor Becomes Myth: A Socio-Linguistic Reading of Jeremiah." In *Troubling Jeremiah*, ed. A. R. Pete Diamond and Kathleen M. O'Connor, 244–62. Sheffield: Sheffield Academic.

Masenya (ngwan'a Mphahlele), Madipoane. 1996. "Proverbs 31:10-31 in the South African Context: A Bosadi (Womanhood) Approach." Unpublished D.Litt. et Phil. Thesis, University of South Africa, Pretoria, South Africa.

———. 2003. "A Small Herb Increases Itself (Impact) by a Strong Odour: Reimagining Vashti in an African–South African Context." *Old Testament Essays* 16 (2): 332–42.

———. 2004. *How Worthy Is the Woman of Worth? Rereading Proverbs 31:10—31 in African–South Africa*. New York: Peter Lang.

———. 2005. "An African Methodology for South African Biblical Sciences: Revisiting the Bosadi (womanhood) approach." *Old Testament Essays* 18 (3): 741–51.

———. 2007. "Invisible Exiles? An African-South African Woman's Reconfiguration of Exile in Jeremiah 21:1-10." *Old Testament Essays* 20 (3): 756–71.

Mbuwayesango, Dora R. 1997. "Childlessness and Woman-to-Woman Relationships in Genesis and in African Patriarchal Society: Sarah and Hagar from a Zimbabwean Women's Perspective." *Semeia* 78: 27–36.

Mosala, Itumeleng T. 1993. "A Materialist Reading of Micah." In *The Bible and Liberation: Political and Social Hermeneutics*, ed. Norman K. Gottwald and Richard A. Horsley, 264–95. Maryknoll, N.Y.: Orbis.

Mottu, Henri. 1993. "Jeremiah vs. Hananiah: Ideology and Truth in Old Testament Prophecy." In *The Bible and Liberation: Political and Social Hermeneutics*, ed. Norman K. Gottwald and Richard A. Horsley, 250–63. Maryknoll, N.Y.: Orbis.

Patte, Daniel. 2004. *Global Bible Commentary*. Nashville: Abingdon.

Scheffler, Eben H. 1994. "The Holistic Historical Background against Which Jeremiah 7:1-11 Makes Sense." *Old Testament Essays* 7(3): 381–95.

Snyman, Gert F. 2007. "Collective Memory and Coloniality of Being as a Hermeneutical Framework: A Partialised Reading of Ezra-Nehemiah." *Old Testament Essays.* 20 (1): 53–83.

Stulman, Louis. 2005. *Jeremiah*. Nashville: Abingdon.

Weems, Renita J. 1995. *Battered Love: Marriage, Sex and Violence in the Hebrew Prophets*. Minneapolis: Fortress Press.

———. 2004. "Jeremiah." In *Global Bible* Commentary, ed. Daniel Patte, 212–25. Nashville: Abingdon.

Wessels, Wilhelm J. 2004. "Setting the Stage for the Future of the Kingship: An Ideological-Critical Reading of Jeremiah 21:1-10." *Old Testament Essays* 17 (3): 470–83.

EZEKIEL

Dexter E. Callender Jr.

OVERVIEW

Opinions on the date, composition, and setting of Ezekiel vary (Zimmerli 1979: 1–15). Ezekiel's activity contextually unfolds with the establishment of the neo-Babylonian Empire as the undisputed regional dominant power, controlling trade routes from Western Asia to Africa. The superscription of the book indicates that Ezekiel was among those deported with Jehoiachin when Jerusalem submitted to Babylon in March of 597 B.C.E. The many dates given throughout the book suggest a period of prophetic activity from 593 to at least 571. Ezekiel employs the discourse of the priestly theological tradition to make sense of the devastation wrought by Babylon against ancient Israel.

The principal divisions of the book are relatively clear. Chapters 1–24 contain oracles of judgment concerning Judah and Jerusalem. These are followed by a collection of oracles against foreign nations in 25–32. Chapters 33–39 proclaim restoration for ancient Israel and include further oracles against foreign nations. The final section (40–48) gives the plans for the new temple and new polity.

Perhaps *exile* is the overriding theme and context of the book, which explains and wrestles with the alienation of people from their ancestral environs. A second and related theme, *suffering and responsibility*, regards the prophet's interest in causal explanation. In this respect, the book gives attention to Israel's history as a history of rebelliousness and engages the issue of human and divine responsibility. A third important theme is the *presence (or absence) of God*, explored in the prophet's visions of the throne chariot. A fourth theme is *restoration*, articulated most systematically in chapters 40–48 and memorably depicted in chapter 37 in the vision of the valley of dry bones.

EXILE AND DIASPORA

The extent to which the biblical record comments on exile as an ultimate manifestation of God's wrath testifies to exile as a central concern for the guardians of the received tradition and provides some indication of how harsh the experience was for many of the survivors. The Babylonian exile encompassed both deportation from and destruction of ancestral setting. The dated oracles of the book hinge on the destruction of Jerusalem; oracles dated prior to Jerusalem's destruction are condemning, and those dated after bring comfort. Even the oracles against foreign nations involve the destruction and depopulation of Jerusalem. The shorter of these oracles explicitly presuppose Jerusalem's destruction (25:3, 8, 12, 15; 26:2), while the dates of the longer oracles (29–32) fall within one year of the city's destruction. Destruction is *the* issue of the book.

Ezekiel's text reflects an acute awareness of diasporic life and its implications for identity. The fact that the Babylonian government had resettled Jerusalem's elites as a community made possible continued cultural cohesion that provided the conditions for discursive reflection, as preserved in Ezekiel and subsequent exilic and postexilic writings. The same cannot be said for the deportees of the northern kingdom, who were dispersed and assimilated into new cultural environs and became effectively "lost." The book reveals significant interest in the fate of the northern tribes, evident in the oracles' expressing hope for reunification (11:15; 37:15-27) and in the copious references to "scattering" (for example, 11:16; 12:15; 20:23; 28:25; 34:5f). Fears of losing cultural identity no doubt intensified among the elites who comprised the exile community in Babylon when Jerusalem and its temple were destroyed.

Twenty-three centuries later and an ocean away, the intense suffering of sudden deracination

coupled with the harsh conditions of the Middle Passage and enslavement in the New World drove many to their deaths and countless others toward despair. The pain wrought by the loss of ancestral geography, the rupturing of family ties, and alienation from community found expression in the African American (Negro) spirituals: "Sometimes I feel like a motherless child / A long ways from home." Here, and in the second verse, "Sometimes I feel like I'm almost gone," the sufferer laments a loss articulated in both geographic and existential terms.

The conditions of Jerusalem's deported were different, given that they were largely people of means whose experience was not that of chattel slavery and who retained some control of their economic destiny (2 Kings 24:14-16; Coogan 1974). Still, their tradition of exile as emblematic of their experience resonated with surviving victims of the African slave trade, who engaged it in a variety of ways. Exile became a formative concept in Rastafari thought, in which "Babylon" is Jamaica and, more generally, Western oppression (Murrell and Williams 1998: 327; Breiner 1986: 32). Manifestations of the concept of exile are complex and compounding, seen for example in the socioeconomic dimensions alluded in Martin Luther King Jr.'s 1963 Lincoln Memorial address. Laying bare the irony of "emancipation" amid the bondage of segregation and discrimination, King observed that "the Negro lives on a lonely island of poverty . . . languishing in the corners of American society and finds himself an exile in his own land" (Carson 2001).

SUFFERING AND RESPONSIBILITY

The prophet's vocation report in the book's opening vision, where he receives a scroll containing lamentation, mourning, and woe (2:8-10), reveals Ezekiel's interest in the suffering endured by the community. This interest, of course, places him in the company of prophets who freely engage the catastrophic events of life—those considered true prophets according to the definition of Jer. 28:8.

Curiously enough, Ezekiel is commanded to eat the scroll, which, more surprisingly, we are told tastes "as sweet as honey" to the prophet (3:1-3; see also Jer. 15:16, 18). Ezekiel's oracles give verbal form to the suffering of exile and explore the exile in causal terms, considering human and divine responsibility. With respect to the people's fate, Ezekiel avoids rendering both Israel's complicity and God's involvement in simple terms.

HUMAN RESPONSIBILITY

Ezekiel explores the idea of human corporate responsibility for the exile by emphasizing "rebellion" against God throughout Israel's history. Israel's complete history of rebelliousness distinguishes the book of Ezekiel from other prophetic works and expresses in theological terms the terrifying reality of Jerusalem's destruction and the magnitude of ancient Israel's suffering. Chapter 16 describes Jerusalem's rebelliousness in terms of marital faithlessness throughout her covenantal relationship with YHWH. The oracle of chapter 20, based in the Exodus tradition, portrays corporate Israel as rebellious against God from the beginning. Israel's rebellious activity began immediately upon Yahweh's selection of Israel in Egypt (20:5-8), continued through the wilderness period (20:13, 21), and persists to the prophet's day (20:27-30). Chapter 23 combines marital with Exodus imagery to make the same point for both northern and southern kingdoms.

Throughout, Ezekiel places responsibility on various classes of leaders for such issues as mismanagement of foreign policy, inattention to social justice, and lapses in maintaining the orthodoxy of the national cult (Mein 2001: 260). Ezekiel indicts the elders, officials, princes, priests, and prophets (8:11-12; 11:1-4; 21:25-27; 22:26-31). In the oracle of 17:1-10, Ezekiel portrays Zedekiah, who sought alliance with Egypt, as a vine, "transplanted" in hopes of bearing fruit. The oracle continues by asking the vine, "will it prosper?" and states to the contrary, however, that the fate of the vine is to wither such that it needs not even be pulled from the ground to remove it (17:9-10). The confounding reality of the complicity of African rulers in the four centuries that culminated in the 1860s of the Atlantic/Americas slave trade poses similar opportunity for reflection. While the idea of divine punishment as explanation for oppression is clear in Rastafari thought, it is most frequently tied to the alleged curse of Ham tradition in Gen. 9:18-27 (Murrell and Williams 1998: 331).

Ezekiel includes statements that implicate God and question divine justice. In 9:4-6, God gives an order to slay all but "those who sigh and groan over all the abominations." The order, however, explicitly includes killing "small children" (9:6). Similarly, the comprehensive and indiscriminate scope of God's wrath appears again in the oracle of 21:1-7, where it is directed "against *all* flesh from south to north" and specifies the Deity's intention to cut off "both righteous and wicked" (21:3-4). Such language plainly reflects the indiscriminate killing that commonly attended war and, to some degree, what would have been the Babylonian attitude toward commoners upon entering the city. In tension with such statements, however, other passages (3:16-21; 14:12-23; 18; and 33:1-20) reflect on personal responsibility and uphold divine justice by linking individual destiny to acts of righteousness or wickedness. According to 18:4, "only the person who sins shall die." These oracles are less concerned with explaining exile than with promoting an ongoing moral imperative in the life of the individual (Mein 2001: 262). Ultimately, the book moves beyond causal explanation and preserves concern for the present existential condition of the individual.

THE PRESENCE OF GOD AND THRONE-CHARIOT VISIONS

The book opens with Ezekiel's report of a vision of the glory of God experienced among the exiles at the river Chebar (1:3). A storm wind "from the north" accompanies the vision suggesting geographic proximity to the exile community, although subsequent reports locate the appearance in Jerusalem. Ezekiel experiences God in exile as robustly as we might expect of one with ties to the Jerusalem priesthood. Like the vision of Isaiah (ch. 6), Ezekiel's vision describes YHWH in royal imagery and shows interest in the manifestation of YHWH's glory (*kabod*). God is enthroned above a firmament of sapphire and is only obliquely described. The wheels described in the vision suggest mobility, reflecting the imagery of a chariot. The vision associates the wheels with "living creatures," whose spirit is within the wheels, controlling their movement (1:20-21). The creatures are later identified with cherubim in chapter 10 and said to have human form (see Greenberg 1983: 44, 54-55).

The appearance of the throne chariot recurs in the vision of 8–11, where God's glory appears at the temple entrance (8:4), departs from the temple (10:15-19), and ultimately departs from the city (11:22-24). God's glory recurs again in the final vision of 40–48, where it returns to a restored Jerusalem and God subsequently promises to live with the Israelites forever (43:1-9). The recurring vision and its departure and return have been variously understood (Block 2000: 15–42; Strong 2000: 69–95; Tuell 2000: 97–110). Ezekiel's vision of the throne chariot and the glory of God in the midst of the exile presents the notion of the appearance of God *in and through* the gravest of circumstances.

The throne-chariot vision found expression in various ways in African American spirituals, typically reduced to the image of a "wheel in the middle of a wheel" (see 1:11). Of the many allusions to the wheel, several themes recur. "Faith" and "the grace of God" motivate the wheel, combining human and divine agency (Johnson 1940: 35). The wheel, associated with the word of God, is sometimes called the "Gospel wheel" (Courlander 1963: 51). The wheel-within-the-wheel is identified with "Jesus Christ," and the "big wheel" itself is identified with "God himself" (Perkins 1922: 243). As a symbol of the experience of the sacred apart from the visionary experience, the wheel is 'rollin'

in the heart of the believer" (Perkins 1922: 235). Further, Ezekiel's allusions to human elements emerge in references to the "spokes," identified as "humankind" or "human cries." The wheel invokes all-encompassing temporality or perhaps timelessness, being called the "wheel of time" (McLaughlin 1963: 72). It conjures the imagery of judgment in death—natural or eschatological—by association with the "chariot" of Elijah (Courlander 1963: 51). Still, in the spirituals, the focus on the wheel emphasizes salvation *in the present experience* of the believer. The believer's present experience of salvation provides certainty of a future dispensation of salvation in "Little Children, Then Won't You Be Glad," which includes an oblique reference to the vision of Ezekiel:

> Little children, then won't you be glad
> That you have been to heav'n
> And you're gwine to go again
>
> . . . Don't you hear what de chariot say?
> De fore wheels run by de grace of God.
> An' de hind wheels dey run by faith.
> (Allen 1995/1867: 87)

As James Cone observes of the spirituals: "For black slaves, Jesus *is* God . . . breaking into [humanity's] historical present and transforming it according to divine expectations. [Liberation] is already at hand in Jesus' own person and work, and it will be fully consummated in God's own ordained future" (Cone 1972: 57, emphasis added).

Another example within the African Diaspora that relates the throne chariot of Ezekiel to the context of suffering, both eschatologically and in the present world, appears in the teachings of Elijah Muhammad and the Nation of Islam. The "mother plane" concept presents Ezekiel's wheel as a military airship and a symbol of racial empowerment that will end suffering by vanquishing the oppressors of "the American so-called 'Negroes'" (Lieb 1998).

Restoration and the Valley of Dry Bones

The final vision of chapters 40–48 and oracles scattered throughout the book proclaim the restoration of Israel. Though cast in terms of a historical postexilic future, Ezekiel's vision of restoration is not simply a plan for a future physical Jerusalem. Rather, his vision is a heavenly exemplar that figured in the exilic life of the community (Tuell 2000).

Callahan observes in African American spirituals and African American preaching traditions a relative absence of allusions to the Bible's postexilic narratives (Callahan 2006: 80). The graphic portrayal of the restoration of Israel in the valley of dry bones in chapter 37 is a notable exception. God leads the prophet in ecstatic vision to an unnamed valley, full of bones. Upon surveying the bones, he notes "they were *very* dry" (37:2). The dryness of the bones emphasized in the text testifies to the utter absence of life. The prophet is instructed to "prophesy to these bones, and say to them: O dry bones, hear the word of the Lord" (v. 4). God tells Ezekiel to announce that the bones would be given breath and be reconstituted. Immediately following the prophetic performance, the bones are reconstituted, rattling and coming together individually ("bone to bone"; v. 7) before ultimately standing together as a vast corporate body—"an exceedingly great army" as rendered in the King James Version (v. 10). The group is the "whole house of Israel" (v. 11), a reunited greater Israel also proclaimed in the subsequent oracle of the two sticks (37:15-28). The spiritual "Dem Bones" recounts the various bones connecting but makes no reference to the corporate group, thus suggesting an emphasis on individual revival. In the refrain "Now hear the word of the Lord," as in Ezekiel's vision report, the bones find life in the context of the word of God.

Other allusions in the spirituals tradition to Ezekiel's vision express the notion of an individual restoration in the post–physical death future, as in "Dry Bones Gwine er Rise Ergin."

If you 'spect to git heav'n when you dies,
Dry bones gwine er rise ergin,
Better stop your tongue from tellin' lies . . .
(Perkins 1922: 242)

Here, one's present moral conduct has a bearing on the hope of a future post-death dispensation of salvation. Still, the following stanza voices the understanding of a *present* experiential restoration, where it is difficult not to sense allusion to the raised "army" of the KJV reading:

Got my breastplate, sword, and shiel',
Dry bones gwine er rise ergin,
Gwine boldly marchin' through de fiel'
(Perkins 1922: 242)

In a quite different exploration of the vision of the valley of dry bones, August Wilson presents the watery grave of the Middle Passage in place of the valley in the play *Joe Turner's Come and Gone*. The protagonist Herald Loomis reports an ecstatic vision in which bones rise up out of the water and start marching. They sink again and are washed onto shore; however, they are no longer bones but, in the words of Loomis, "They got flesh on them! Just like you and me!" (Wilson 1988: 53–54). The allusions in Wilson's portrayal of Loomis's vision embody symbolic death and rebirth and look forward to a return to Africa (Richards 2000: 747). The ecstatic experience figures prominently as well.

Similarly, the Middle Passage coalesces with the valley of dry bones in Henry Dumas's *Ark of Bones*. The Ark of Bones is "the house of generations," where "every African who lives in America has part of his [or her] soul," echoing Ezekiel's reference to "the whole house of Israel" (Dumas 1974: 15; Mitchell 1988: 302). Dumas suggests a present experiential restoration in *Ark*, apparent in allusions to the tradition of Ezekiel's wheel and the themes that echo in the spirituals. As in Ezekiel's initial vision of the throne chariot, a storm heralds the Ark's arrival. Prior to its appearance, the character Headeye "points out over the water and up in the sky," observing the "signs" that the Ark is coming (Dumas 1974: 7). The protagonist Fish-hound describes: "I see this big thing movin in the far off, movin slow, down river, naw, it was up river. Naw, it was just movin and standin still at the same time. . . . I looked up and what I took for clouds was sails. The wind was whippin up a sermon on them" (10). More directly, the story relates that the Ark is propelled by a loudly churning paddle wheel and that it rocks "like it's floatin on air" (12). Fire burns "near the edge of an opening which showed outward to the water" (14). Upon its arrival, Fish-hound invokes imagery akin to that of the wheel as chariot and transport: "I figured maybe we was dead or something and was gonna get the Glory Boat over the river and make it on into heaven" (10).

The Ark as the "house of generations" is consonant with the presence of humanity in the wheel of the spirituals, following Ezekiel's allusions to human form. Fish-hound's later description underscores the human experiential dimension: "The rain had reached us and I could hear that moanin like a church full of people pourin out their hearts to Jesus in heaven" (10). Dumas's sensibilities concerning restoration are evident in a private letter, in which he voices an abiding interest in the "Power of the word, The Word, if you will, the Word not only of the lyrics, but the Word of God as it is interpreted by either the group or the performer" (Dumas 1974: xii). Such sensibilities probably would have resonated with the prophet.

A BRIEF WORD ABOUT WOMEN AND EZEKIEL

Although I have based this commentary primarily on the historical use of Ezekiel in African American thought, the commentary would not be complete without mention of the graphic and, in places, misogynistic ways in which Ezekiel describes women and uses them in his metaphorical world. Especially in chapters 16 and 23, the prophet

depicts the fallen nation of ancient Israel as a loose woman, a whore who deserved whatever shameful and vile treatment she received from the lovers with whom she betrayed Yahweh. Renita Weems has argued that such graphic and, in places, horrific language is intended to arrest the attention and seize the imagination of a mainly male audience (Weems 1995: 13 passim). And it does. What is troubling is that it continues to do so in Africana settings with little effort to resist this depiction of these metaphorical women, often the vanguard of a way that Africana women are perceived, not only in dominant cultures but also in Africana ones. When one speaks of women in these negative sexual stereotypes, it invites invectives and verbal and physical abuse. More thought needs to be given to this problem in Africana biblical scholarly and pastoral work.

The book of Ezekiel emphasizes the self-revelation of YHWH through the tragic events of exile and destruction. This finds expression in the oft-repeated formula "and you/they will know that I am YHWH" (Zimmerli 1979: 52; Lapsley 2000: 121–24). God speaks through the prophet to portray human suffering, communal and personal responsibility, and the hope that is embedded in the nature of reality. Amid death lies the potential for life, realized through the engagement of the word of God, signified in a variety of ways.

References

Allen, William Francis, et al., eds. 1992. *Slave Songs of the United States*. Reprint of the original 1867 edition. Baltimore, MD: Genealogical Publishing Company.
Block, Daniel I. 2000. "Divine Abandonment: Ezekiel's Adaptation of an Ancient Near Eastern Motif." In *The Book of Ezekiel: Theological and Anthropological Perspectives*, ed. M. S. Odell and J. Strong, 15–42. Atlanta: Society of Biblical Literature.

Breiner, Laurence A. 1986. "The English Bible in Jamaican Rastafarianism." *Journal of Religious Thought* 42 (2): 30–43.

Callahan, Allen D. 2006. *The Talking Book: African Americans and the Bible.* New Haven, Ct.: Yale University Press.

Carson, Clayborn, ed. 2001. *A Call to Conscience: The Landmark Speeches of Dr. Martin Luther King Jr.* New York: Warner.

Cone, James. 1972. *The Spirituals and the Blues: An Interpretation.* New York: Seabury.

Coogan, Michael D. 1974. "Life in the Diaspora: Jews in Nippur in the Fifth Century B.C." *Biblical Archaeologist* 37 (1): 6–12.

Courlander, Harold. 1963. *Negro Folk Music, U.S.A.* New York: Columbia University Press.

Dumas, Henry. 1974. *Ark of Bones and Other Stories.* New York: Random House.

Greenberg, Moshe. 1983. *Ezekiel 1–20: A New Translation with Introduction and Commentary.* Garden City, N.Y.: Doubleday.

Johnson, J. Rosamond. 1940. *Album of Negro Spirituals.* New York: Edward B. Marks Music.

Joyce, Paul. 1989. *Divine Initiative and Human Response in Ezekiel.* Sheffield: JSOT.

Lapsley, Jacqueline. 2000. *Can These Bones Live? The Problem of the Moral Self in Ezekiel.* Berlin: de Gruyter.

Lieb, Michael. 1998. *Children of Ezekiel: Aliens, UFOs, the Crisis of Race, and the Advent of the End Time.* Durham, N.C.: Duke University Press.

McLaughlin, Wayman. 1963. "Symbolism and Mysticism in the Spirituals." *Phylon* 24 (1): 69–77.

Mein, Andrew. 2001. *Ezekiel and the Ethics of Exile.* New York: Oxford University Press.

Mitchell, Carolyn A. 1988. "Henry Dumas and Jean Toomer: One Voice." *Black American Literature Forum* 22 (2): 297–306.

Murrell, Nathaniel Samuel, and L. Williams. 1998. "The Black Biblical Hermeneutics of Rastafari." In *Chanting Down Babylon: The Rastafari Reader*, ed. Nathaniel Samuel Murrell, William David Spencer, and Adrian Anthony McFarlane, 326–48. Philadelphia: Temple University Press.

Perkins, A. E. 1922. "Negro Spirituals from the Far South." *Journal of American Folklore* 35 (137): 223–49.

Richards, Sandra L. 2000. "Dry Bones: Spiritual Apprehension in August Wilson's *Joe Turner's Come and Gone*." In *African Americans and the Bible*, ed. V. L. Wimbush and R. Rodman, 743–53. New York: Continuum.

Strong, John. 2000. "God's *Kabod*: The Presence of Yahweh in the Book of Ezekiel." In *The Book of Ezekiel: Theological and Anthropological Perspectives*, ed. M. S. Odell and J. Strong, 69–95. Atlanta: Society of Biblical Literature.

Tuell, Steven S. 2000. "Divine Presence and Absence in Ezekiel's Prophecy." In *The Book of Ezekiel: Theological and Anthropological Perspectives*, ed. M. S. Odell and J. Strong, 97–116. Atlanta: Society of Biblical Literature.

Weems, Renita. 1995. *Battered Love: Marriage, Sex, and Violence in the Hebrew Prophets.* Minneapolis: Fortress Press.

Wilson, August. 1988. *Joe Turner's Come and Gone: A Play in Two Acts.* New York: Penguin.

Zimmerli, Walther. 1979. *Ezekiel I: A Commentary on the Book of the Prophet Ezekiel, Chapters 1–24.* Philadelphia: Fortress Press.

HOSEA

Wallace Hartsfield

My reading of the book of Hosea is from four distinct yet interrelated positions: *under* the text, *behind* the text, *within* the text, and *above* the text. Under the text, I read as a Christian submitting to this literary witness as scripture. From behind the text, I read as a theologically trained historical critic who regards this document as a composite literary tradition. I approach and accept the literary constructed world of Hosea as an actual but disinterested reader (though hardly an uninterested one!). Finally, as a black male living in America, I read from over the text, imparting meaning as essentially response.

The book of Hosea is a prophecy that denounces the ancient Israelite cult for its idolatrous and syncretistic practices that presumably resulted in ultimate devastation of ancient Israel's and perhaps even Judah's exile. Poignant expres-

sions of desperation and hopeful rhetoric frame this prophetic reproach, and it seeks the redemption, restoration, and reunification of the former relational "utopia" that once existed between Yahweh and ancient Israel. Dissonance created by polar messages is literarily represented by a variety of images derived from natural phenomena, agrarian realities, and familial structures that illustrate intriguing and oftentimes disturbing depictions of the strained divine-human relationship between Yahweh and ancient Israel.

Three matters of significance that jut from the very fabric of the Hosean text include ancient Israel's struggle to maintain religious fidelity in the context of Canaanite culture; very human illustrations of divine pathos; and frequent usage of metaphor for God, the people of Israel/Judah, and the divine-human relationship. To interface with these textual issues, I raise three potential considerations as an impetus and interpretive framework for contemporary reflection on the book of Hosea. First is the issue of *faith and culture*—that is, the challenges of identity and assimilation associated with a minority religious expression practicing its faith amid a dominant culture. Second is the *movement from pathos to pathology*—that is, suffering that leads to extreme behaviors demonstrating desperation and violence. Third is the possible *misuse and disuse of metaphor*—that is, the development of responsible appropriations of the Hosean text for use in contemporary interpretation.

HOSEA: THE BOOK, PATRIARCHY, SHAME, AND BLACK LIFE

Hosea 1:1 introduces the book as Yahweh's revelation to Hosea during the reigns of Israelite and Judean monarchs during the latter half of the eighth century B.C.E. The initial disclosure is shocking as Yahweh instructs Hosea to marry a promiscuous woman. The woman apparently personifies the cosmic dissolution perpetrated in the land because of Israel's idolatrous conduct (1:2). Three children, whose names are given by Yahweh through Hosea, are born to this union. They epitomize Yahweh's disillusionment with the people of Israel (1:3-9). Subsequent to this disparaging attitude Yahweh expresses toward the people of Israel, the Hosean prophecy peculiarly depicts Yahweh anticipating the exaltation of, compassion for, and reestablishment of Israel as the people of God (1:10—2:1).

With a swift change in mood, Hosea/Yahweh, who are seamlessly blended together in parallel speech, plead with the children to convince their mother/Israel, who no longer is recognized as wife/consort, to cease her promiscuous behavior, which consists of acts of infidelity and perversion, or Hosea/Yahweh will disgrace, debase, detain, and ultimately destroy her and declare her children ille-

gitimate (2:2-13). Immediately following this act of divorce and threat of further humiliation, Yahweh bizarrely imagines seducing Israel via a rousing wilderness rendezvous (2:14-18). From this passionate reunion, Israel will truly know Yahweh as husband because Israel will eliminate the Baals and reestablish covenant, and the land will be filled with peace as Yahweh betroths Israel again for righteousness and justice (2:14-23).

The Hosean prophecy continues with another illustration wherein the prophet, obedient to Yahweh, purchases a promiscuous woman who already has a lover and then requires her to be sexually abstinent with all men, including him, for the duration she would be under his control (3:1-3). These conditions were to parallel Israel's extended period without monarchial leadership, the temple cult, or divine manifestation (3:4). Moreover, this abstinence would lead to ancient Israel's return, where they would seek Yahweh's presence and the Davidic monarchy would be restored (3:5).

Ancient Israel, an intensely patriarchal society, views Hosea's/Yahweh's behavior toward Gomer/Israel as normal, justified, even admirable. Male behavior, whether Hosea's or Yahweh's—stripping the wife (Gomer/Israel), exposing her nakedness, punitively caging her, and even disfiguring her for her unfaithfulness, in particular sexual infidelity—gets viewed as a man protecting his honor. In a society where a man being shamed was frowned upon and deemed unimaginable, a woman's promiscuity at the man's expense must be discouraged via dehumanizing methods.

Shaming of men by women is obvious; however, there exists another threat to male dominance from within unexpected patriarchal quarters: dominance or superiority of males over males. While patriarchy privileges all males over non-males, clearly there exists another degree of privileging among men of differing cultural, socioeconomic standings. Males were justified in dominating other males based on their value in a given society. Apparently, this occurred in ancient Israel and other ancient Near East patriarchal societies.

Beginning with Yahweh then the king, the priest, and so forth on to the male slave, a male hierarchy existed. That the Deity is imaged in terms of maleness, in the book of Hosea, has far-reaching implications for the honor/shame potential regarding Yahweh in ancient Israel. Regarding the *land,* Yahweh is considered a wilderness deity. Yahweh, unlike Canaanite gods, especially Baal, was an outsider unknown to the indigenous people. Both Yahweh and Israel try to make a name for themselves in the land. In Hosea, Yahweh's honor is at stake because of the faithlessness of Israel as the female consort, and because Canaanite deities, particularly Baal, occupy dominant positioning in Canaanite culture. Thus Hosea casts this struggle for honor on Yahweh to address the fact that faithless Israel (the woman) has jeopardized Yahweh's supposed or probably desired status as dominant deity.

Chapters 4–14 contain several condemnations of idolatrous practices, especially in Israel/Ephraim and Judah. Essentially, there are two extended sections within this prophetic corpus (4:1-11 and 11:12—14:9). Both units conclude with meager but compelling messages of hope (11:8-11 and 14:4-9). Just as in chapters 1–3, metaphorical depictions for God (for example, as maggots and rottenness, 5:12; a lion, 5:14 and 11:10; a bird catcher, 7:10-11; a farmer, 10:11; a parent, 11:1-4, 8-9; some sort of wild animal, 13:7-8; and a physician, 14:4); the people (for example, as dissipating dew, 6:4; a heated oven, 7:4-7; a silly dove, 7:11-12; a defective bow, 7:16; chaff in the wind, 13:3); and the divine-human relationship (for example, parent-child, 11:1-11; husband-wife, 1–2; and man-woman, 3) abound in these chapters and serve as the dominant rhetorical device for prophetic presentation throughout the remainder of the prophecy.

The first section unfolds around the accusation that the land's inhabitants have no knowledge of God (4:1—11:11). The verb "to know" with God as the object is a recurring motif throughout Hosea (see also 2:20; 4:6; 5:4; 6:3, 6; 8:2; and 11:3). While, at one level, knowledge of God is sexual in nature and connected with the before-mentioned husband-wife relational metaphor, in this section this knowledge refers to specific covenant violations: idolatry, swearing, lying, murder, stealing and adultery (4:1-3), perversion of the cult by priests and the prophets (4:4-19), corruption and instability in Israelite monarchial rule (5:1-7), and Israel and Judah's persistent use of violence and turning from God to traditional enemies for military support against external threats and each other (5:8—6:6). Verse 10:15 further develops each of these supporting indictments regarding the degradation of these roles and declares and describes the sociopolitical and economic consequences. This section closes with pathetic disillusionment coupled with God's expression of obligation as a frustrated parent addressing a wayward child, who cannot follow through with previously planned punitive actions consisting of disowning and ultimately destroying the child.

God's acts of deliverance and Israel's deceptive tendencies organize the second section (11:12—14:9). This section's preface summarizes Israel's general character of being flawed by deception (11:11—12:1). Examples used to support the prophetic indictment of Israel's deceptive nature focuses mainly on the ancestor Jacob, who attempted in the womb to supplant his brother Esau, struggled with God as a human with intentions of prevailing, and encountered God at Bethel, which ultimately became a questionable religious site for Hosea and other biblical proponents (12:2-6). Given that Jacob was seen as Israel's ancestor, the Hosean prophecy posits that, in Israel's life, contemporary instances of social injustice where the marginalized are exploited reflect the nation's inherently deceitful character (12:7-9). The remaining verses of this chapter contrast God's acts of deliverance and Israel's deeds of deception (12:10-14). Israel's history of deception is consequentially doomed because an angry God will attack, slaughter, and utterly destroy the nation for its deceit (13:1-16). In contrast, the final chapter presents a moving plea for repentance (14:3); a promise of healing and restoration (14:4-7); and, a proverbial maxim probably intended to add credence to the overall prophecy.

The challenge of religious identity and assimilation for black Christians in the United States has a history that predates their arrival on American shores as enslaved people. In Hosea, the issue of faith and culture is encountered in the struggle of Yahwism to survive as a religious tradition in the context of Canaanite culture.

FAITH AND CULTURE

The issue of faith and culture is first encountered in Judges, where Israelites are continually depicted as breaking relationship with Yahweh to partake in the perceived benefit of Canaanite culture. In Hosea, this reality is more pronounced, for Yahwism, the Israelites' religion, seemingly has been totally compromised because of Israel's infatuation with Canaanite culture. They reshape Yahweh into the figure of Baal.

The Black Church, essentially an unplanned offspring of African traditional religions and Christianity, has always struggled with its identity—that is, with what it means to be authentically black and Christian and live in the United States. In Hosea, the notion of true Yahwism seems more an ideal than reality. Apparently Israel, like U.S. black Christians, represented a multivaried spectrum of people, where syncretism probably was always present. That Hosea called them back to Yahwism probably reflected more wishful thinking than realistic possibility. That the Black Church has a unified history of religion also is a myth, for while African traditional religions have many commonalities, fragmentation has always existed. The encounter of European Christianity with African traditional religions makes it reasonable that the nonmonolithic Black Church has always been syncretistic.

Moreover, emphasizing prosperity in the Black Church context appears to reflect this issue also. That Israel turned to Baal because of this deity's association with fertility, especially as it pertains to crop growth, is absolutely essential for survival in an agrarian society. The same is true of blacks flocking to Christian churches with this emphasis. The fact is, prosperity is absolutely essential for survival and self-actualization in the United States.

Lastly, the challenge of identity and assimilation for Black Christianity is probably best seen in debates surrounding segregation versus integration. That we still use the descriptor "Black Church" instead of talking about the role of blacks in the Christian Church is evidence that this issue is still troubling and without resolve.

MOVEMENT FROM PATHOS TO PATHOLOGY

Again, imaging of divine maleness and issues of honor and shame, with Israel as female consort, problematizes who and what Yahweh does and can cause a malaise if readers try to apply this text to their lived realities. This image of God moving from pathos to pathology can be problematic in black communities as it potentially affirms acts of desperation and violence against women by suffering black men. In black communities, even though leadership is prominent among black women, patriarchy unfortunately still is assumed. Black men who have their honor, especially sexuality, threatened by women who have become intimate with men from other races often punitively confront these women. While often not spoken of in these terms, the man experiences hurt by the woman leaving. Unfortunately, black men's suffering has often led to pathological responses, including the beating, public humiliation, and even murder of women who could not otherwise be controlled.

Beyond the potential shame of being "dissed" by other women and by other black males, what may be even more damning in white America is when the black male falls at the very bottom of the sociocultural hierarchy. The black male feels the need to handle his business—that is, the black female—by asserting himself as a force to be reckoned with.

AMOS

Cleotha Robertson

THE BOOK OF AMOS is the third of the Minor Prophets in the Hebrew Bible, adopted by Protestant and Catholic canons. In the Septuagint, however, the book of Amos is placed second before the book of Joel. The Peshitta and the Vulgate follow the order of the Hebrew Bible (Harrison 1969: 833). According to Amos 1:1, his activity occurred during the eighth century B.C.E. along with Hosea and Micah. Other Neo-Assyrian Period prophetic contemporaries included Jonah and Isaiah. Amos lived in Tekoa, which was located five miles southeast of Bethlehem. Apart from what appears in the book of Amos, nothing is known about him (Harrison 1969: 883). Amos was a shepherd and fig cultivator (Amos 7:14). With Amos, the idea of the welfare and survival of the nation pertains to Torah covenantal fidelity for the first time since Moses (Deuteronomy 28) (Bullock 1986: 55). Amos

applied this principle to the northern kingdom and set the standard for succeeding prophets (Bullock 1986: 55).

AFRICAN AMERICAN AND AFRICAN CONTEXTS OF BIBLICAL REFLECTION

A discussion of the book of Amos within African American and African communities must begin with an examination of context and history of the application of the Bible in general. The appropriation of the Bible in both African American and African contexts raises concerns that both must be considered and addressed.

The use of the Bible by antebellum African Americans exhibits a dual complexity. There was an acceptance of the Bible and contextualization of it in the lives of adherents. Sanders notes how slave owners exposed enslaved persons to Christianity to make them more compliant servants. However, enslaved African Americans used Christianity to enhance their self-worth and foster dreams of freedom (Sanders 1998: 589). Mitchell chronicles some important abolitionist endeavors within the African American religious experience in the United States. One of the important aspects of the African American religious experience was the social activism of the early Black Church (Mitchell 2004: 131). Northern African American churches provided influence and rhetoric that helped combat chattel slavery evils. These abolitionist orators articulated necessary trends within African American religious communities that led to such commitments. The major weapon in this fight was African American religious experiences interpreted through biblical lenses.

Bible use in Africa encountered similar experiences of abuse. First, Westerners used the Bible to exploit Africa's wealth and to subjugate African continent peoples. Second, there is the concern of the contextualization of the gospel in Africa. The following anecdote is well known in South Africa and can also be heard in other parts of Africa: "When the white man came to our country he had the Bible and we had the land. The white man said to us, "let us pray." After the prayer, the white man had the land and we had the Bible" (West and Dube 2001: 30). This anecdote illustrates the dilemma concerning the role the Bible has played in Africa's colonization, exploitation, and national oppression. Most early Western missionaries found it difficult, if not virtually impossible, to distinguish between Christian faith and Western civilization (Tutu 1979: 486). In other words, in associating Christianity so closely with Western culture, missionaries often equated conversion to Christianity with acculturation into their own culture (Stinton 2004: 113).

In Africa, as elsewhere, the Bible must be contextualized and read through the lenses of cul-ture and experience or via contextual theological reflection (West and Dube 2001: 595). Contextual theological reflection is a particular commitment to the context of poor and marginalized people (West and Dube 2001: 595). Within this context, liberation and justice is the starting point for action and reflection (Carroll 2002: 67). This reading style, both in African American and African contexts, has created a "hermeneutic of suspicion," taking into account issues of power, economic fairness, justice, and collective relationships. "There is no innocent interpretation, no innocent interpreter, no innocent text" (Tracy 1987: 79).

CONTEXT OF AMOS

The book of Deuteronomy provides a worldview that connects both the internal life of the nation and its international context. According to curses and blessings articulated in Deuteronomy 28-32 and Leviticus 26, both the economic welfare of the nation and its international stability were contingent upon its obedience to the Torah. In light of this worldview, both the internal and international settings must be examined as one interprets Amos.

NATIONAL CONTEXT

Amos's ministry occurred during the reigns of Uzziah of Judah (792–740 b.c.e.) and Jeroboam of Israel (793–753 b.c.e.). These two kings experienced extended reigns (Anderson and Freedman 1989: 18). Uzziah reigned fifty-two years, and Jeroboam reigned forty-one years. Both reigns were exceptional for their times (Anderson and Freedman 1989: 18), especially Jeroboam's reign, given the turbulence during the existence of the northern kingdom (931–721 b.c.e.) (Thiele 1983: 116).

INTERNATIONAL CONTEXT

Jeroboam II's reign was enhanced by a lull in the confrontations with Aram (Jones 1984: 513–14). Amos is understood against this backdrop of respite from external military enemies and internecine

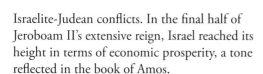

Israelite-Judean conflicts. In the final half of Jeroboam II's extensive reign, Israel reached its height in terms of economic prosperity, a tone reflected in the book of Amos.

OUTLINE OF AMOS

The book of Amos is a short book. It consists of nine chapters. According to the Masorah at the end of the Hebrew manuscript, there are 146 verses (Anderson and Freedman 1989: 23). By word count there are about 2,053 words (Anderson and Freedman 1989: 23). The book of Amos contains eight diverse ingredients—judgment oracles against the nations, exhortations, plagues, hymns, woes, oaths, visions, and eschatology (Anderson and Freedman 1989: 14–15).

STRUCTURE

Stuart outlines the book as follows: (1) introduction and superscription (1:1); (2) the first group of oracles (1:2—6:14); (3) visions and related narrative (7:1—8:3); and (4) the final group of oracles (8:4—9:15) (Stuart 1987: 287). This straightforward outline provides an overall perspective of the book's structure. After the superscription, section 2 begins with a group of oracles addressed to six surrounding foreign nations (1:2—2:3). The oracles crescendo to Yahweh denouncing both Judah and Israel (2:4-8), followed by a historical recital and threat against Israel by the deity (2:9-16). Verses 2:9-16 lead into a renewed condemnation against Israel (3:9—4:3). After condemnation of the cult in the North (4:4-5), there is a list of plagues (4:6-11). The final part of section 2 (5:1—6:14) consists of oracles of woe. In 5:1-27, there are exhortations to Israel and Judah.

In section 3, one finds a group of four visions and a confrontation between Amos and Amaziah in 7:1—8:3. In section 4, one finds a group of woes (8:4:14) that are followed by the fifth vision (9:1-6). Section 4 concludes with an epilogue (9:7-15).

THEMES

The major themes of the book are Yahweh's sovereignty; idolatry and immorality; visions from Yahweh; Amos and the Mosaic covenant; economic oppression; and injustice on both an international and a national scale (Stuart 1987: 288–94).

Yahweh is depicted as a sovereign deity over all nations and creation. This sovereignty, articulated by three different vantage points in the book of Amos, is expressed in oracles against foreign nations, hymns that laud the Deity, and covenant curses stipulated for covenant disobedience. The oracles are the first of three ways in which Amos exhibits Yahweh's sovereignty. The oracles against foreign nations (1:1—2:3) exhibit the belief that Israel's deity has both right and jurisdiction over the nations of the earth. The oracles in Amos 1:3—2:16 are the longest group of oracles against foreign nations in the Minor Prophets (Stuart 1987: 308). Amos depicts Yahweh as the deity who "roars" from Zion. The language of God "roaring" is parallel in Amos 1:2 to Yahweh giving "his voice." The parallel language of Yahweh "roaring" and "giving voice" occurs again in Amos 3:7-8. This language uses imagery of judgment and aggression by the Deity. In the second rhetorical question (3:4-6), one sees the full significance of this language as a symbol of attack and impending judgment.

The hymns of Amos are the second means by which Amos displays the sovereignty of Yahweh. The hymns (4:13, 5:8-9, and 9:5-6) provide a creedal theology concerning Yahweh's sovereignty as Creator and one who has jurisdiction over created order (Watts 1997: 10–27).

The third means by which Amos expresses Yahweh's sovereignty is by the use of covenant curses and blessings. The curses include starvation (4:6), drought (4:7), agricultural disaster (4:9), pestilence (4:10), war and its consequences (4:10), exile (5:27), and oppressive enemies (6:14). Amos depicts Yahweh as the protagonist against Israel for covenant infractions. Amos ends with promises of renewed divine favor (9:11-15). Yahweh will restore Israel's power over her enemies (9:11-12), provide agricultural bounty (9:13), return Israel from exile, and enable the repossession of the land (9:14-15). Implementation of curses and blessings listed in Deuteronomy 27 and 28 and Leviticus 26 in the context of oracles of Amos assumes a deity who is sovereign and controls the natural order (Stuart 1987: xxxi–xlii).

REFLECTION AND CONTEXTUALIZATION

Reflection and contextualization through the lens of the African and African American experience provides a unique vantage point for the interpretation of Amos. The nuances of Amos' oracles and the experiences of Africans and African Americans are interwoven. The language of Amos, enmeshed in cultural expressions of music, art and literature, is used to articulate themes in the history of Africans and African Americans.

Use of Hymns in the African and the African American Experience

The use of hymns is a phenomenon that is an important part of the religious history of people of African descent. Hymns contain the theology, pathos, and unspoken messages of African people, especially the spirituals. Spirituals such as "Steal Away," "Swing Low Sweet Chariot," and "Were You There" have a dual message that dealt with the immediate context of enslaved life and coded messages that were signals for other African slaves. The use of spirituals is understood against the larger historical backdrop of the role of music in West African culture, where appropriate music attends almost every activity in individuals' and the community's lives from birth to beyond the grave. The transatlantic slave trade may have been the genesis for many of these songs, from trading posts such as Elmina and Cape Coast of Ghana, as brokers in human cargo transported Africans to the Caribbean and the Americas as enslaved persons, held against their will.

Idolatry and Immorality

Amos' oracles denounced Israel's and Judah's idolatry (2:4, 8, 12). Jeroboam established a rival cult center in Northern Israel that violated Deut. 12:1-19. According to 1 Kings 12:25-33, Jeroboam established the center to provide unity for the Northern Kingdom of Israel (931–721 B.C.E.), which mimicked David's rationale in securing Jerusalem as both the central geographical headquarters and the unifying worship center of the United Kingdom. According to Amos, Jeroboam's worship centers exploited worship for personal aggrandizement and immoral behavior (2:6-8; 3:10; 4:1; 5:10); also, Amos maintained that the people lacked personal ethics (2:7) (Stuart 1987: 292).

God, Humanity, and Society in West Africa

In West African society, God is the cohesive factor of the society. In West Africa, the action or conduct of one individual can affect the other members for good or for evil. To prevent individuals for becoming rebellious and endangering the welfare of society, there are established codes of behavior for the individual and the community as a whole (Awolalu and Dopamu 1979: 212). Among the Yoruba, the word for immoral action is *eewo*—"things forbidden, things not done" (Awolalu and Dopamu 1979: 212). The Igbo call immoral actions *nso Ani*—"things forbidden by Ani, the earth goddess" (Awolalu and Dopamu 1979: 212). With the breaking of these codes of conduct, there are appropriate penalties imposed by the community and the belief that the Deity will punish the offending party (Awolalu and Dopamu 1979: 215).

Amos and Mosaic Covenant

The oracles of Amos use condemnation and curse language like one finds in Deuteronomy 27–28 and Leviticus 26. Amos reapplies Mosaic legislation into the context of covenant disobedience of the eighth century B.C.E. The curses and blessings cataloged in the Torah now find application in the context of apostasy of the northern kingdom. Amos uses ideas introduced in the Pentateuch in a new context. There is continuity and discontinuity with the material of Amos and the Torah.

ECONOMIC OPPRESSION

Throughout the book of Amos, economic oppression is condemned (2:6, 2:8, 3:15, 4:1, 5:11, 6:1-6; 8:5-6). The repeated references to economic oppression indicate the problem was frequent and widespread throughout all strata of the northern kingdom. Oppressing the poor occurred extensively, frequently, and casually. The list of infractions include economic oppression of the poor (2:6; 2:8; 5:12; 8:5-6); misuse of wealth (3:15; 4:1); and injustice. For example, Yahweh promises to destroy the rich because of their extravagance evidenced by winter and summer homes. In 4:1, Israel's women are excoriated and referred to as "cows of Bashan," because the poor suffer exorbitant taxes that fund these women's opulent lifestyles. In the marketplace, the poor are exploited by unjust business practices where merchants "buy the poor for silver" and the "needy for a pair of sandals." These practices are in direct violation of the Torah's call for equity, fairness, and provision for the poor, the widow, and the orphan (see, for example, Deut. 14:22-29; 16:9-12, 13-15; 24:17-18, 19-22; and 26:12-15) wherein justice and favoritism for the widow and the orphan were vital portions of community life not only for the nation of Israel but also for the entire ancient Near East culture (Bennett 2002: 24–30).

COSMOLOGY OF BOTSWANA

The cosmology of Botswana is informed by its interpretation of Gen. 1:1-10. In Botswana, interdependence is an important part of cosmology. The skies provide rain that waters the earth. People and animals depend on the land and the seas for their livelihood. These relationships in the created order exhibit a sense of interconnectedness and mutuality (Dibeela 2001: 384). The Setswana creation myth asserts that people were created with property. They came with corn, furniture, tools, and animals (Dibeela 2001: 397), according to their interpretation of Gen. 2:26-28. These beliefs lead them to affirmations of self-determination and self-sufficiency. As such, they view oppressing poor people as a violation of God's intentions in creation and as an injustice that must be addressed. So the prophet's assertion that "they trample on the heads of the poor as upon the dust of the ground, and deny justice to the oppressed" is an abomination to the Lord and a violation of the created order—that is, self-sufficiency of individuals and communities (Dibeela 2001: 398).

IMPORTANT PASSAGES IN THE AFRICAN AMERICAN EXPERIENCE

AMOS 7:17 AND THE THEME OF DIVINE INTERVENTION

Amos 7:7-9 provides the memorable vision where Amos sees Yahweh standing on the wall of Jerusalem with a plumb line in his hand. The vision symbolizes impending judgment of the nation and its destruction at the hands of the Assyrian Empire. The assurance of divine intervention and judgment for societal wrongs is a celebrated and essential theme in African American religious thought and practice. The African American religious community can confidently engage in the struggle against racism and all forms of oppression based on the conviction of Yahweh's involvement and assurances of justice and victory.

AMOS 7:14-15 AND TRUE POWER

A second important passage in African American religious thought is Amos 7:14-15. Amos states that he is not a prophet for hire but has been called to this office by Yahweh. In his immediate past profession, Amos was a cattle herder and fig cultivator (Watts 1997: 29–39). This passage is a favorite in the African American religious tradition for at least two reasons. First, the humility of the prophet is one that has captured the imagination of the African American religious psyche. Amos dissociates himself from the prophetic guild and the religious establishment. Amos's authority to prophesy and his legitimacy as a prophet derive from his call. Consequently, Amos is free from the manipulation and compromise that exist where power is exercised. Second, one sees in this retort Amos's disassociation from the religious establishment and the political leadership of King Jeroboam.

This passage connects with at least three important themes in people of African descent's experience. First, Amos experiences social disruption as a prophet from the South in Tekoa as he relocates to the North. DuBois notes problems that social dislocation created for African Americans in Philadelphia in his classic study *The Philadelphia Negro* (DuBois 1996: 235). Second, Amos's economic livelihood helps describe his identity. And finally, Amos maintains that he receives his calling as a prophet from a direct encounter with the Deity. Exclusion from established temporal, sacred, and secular power structures cannot deny one access from supernatural power. The presence of divine authority that does not cater to earthly standards of prestige but advocates and upholds a universal standard of fairness and equity is a theme that poignantly applies to African American religious history.

The role of the African American athlete touches on this theme of fairness. On one level, if given a fair chance, the African American athlete has come to symbolize the worth and value of people of color. Jack Johnson was the first African American heavyweight-boxing champion in history. Ward, in *Unforgivable Blackness: The Rise and Fall of Jack Johnson* (2004), calls Jack Johnson "the most celebrated and most reviled African American of his age." As a heavyweight champion in 1908, Johnson embodied the hopes and affirmation of

personhood-denied African Americans in the post-emancipation period. Jack Johnson's boxing prowess and his public repudiation of white social dating norms made him the most hated man in America.

Jack Johnson's life unfolds against the larger backdrop of the roles of African American athletes and their influence on society. The roles of such celebrated athletes as Jesse Owens, Muhammad Ali, Tiger Woods, Jackie Robinson, Arthur Ashe, Althea Gibson, Jackie Joyner-Kersee, Wilt Chamberlain, and Bill Russell have had and continue to have a profound effect on the psyche of America. For African Americans, the African American athlete is the affirmation of personhood in the face of indignity. Athletes provide a concretization of the aspirations of African Americans. Athletes achieve the economic status and social acceptability, though fleeting and elusive, that is denied many African Americans.

Amos 5:18-27 and True Worship

The third passage in Amos that is important in the experience of African Americans is 5:24. In Amos 5:18-27, one finds an oracle concerning those who wish for the Day of the Lord. In this oracle, the Deity makes a demand for justice. The combination of ritual performance without the appropriate acts of righteousness is an issue addressed previously in the history of Israel (Malachi; Psalm 50). In 5:24, the prophet requests the performance of righteousness along with the performance of ritual requirements of worship. In 5:22-24, the Deity rejects offerings and their concomitant worship music. In 5:25, the prophet uses the exodus theme as a point of reference to develop the importance for proper fulfillment of worship requirements. During the wilderness wanderings of the exodus, the nation of Israel did not bring sacrifices to Yahweh. This part of their religious experience highlights the importance of the appropriate behavior that must accompany worship that is acceptable to Yahweh.

The petition for the presence of justice in 5:24 is a favorite in the experience of African American

Christianity for several reasons. Southern white evangelical Christianity supported the proliferation of slavery and provided a religious, philosophical rationale for the slave trade and slavery (Sanders 1998: 589). Slave owners used the Bible to support slavery not only as a legal institution but also as a moral and religious institution. Africans and African Americans experienced the irrationality and inhumanity of this position. For the African American religious experience, slavery and the Bible were mutually exclusive. From the perspective of the African American religious community, no one who maintained that slavery was a viable institution could be Christian. The southern evangelical Christian rhetoric of piety was invalid and did not contain the values and actions consistent with the worship of Christ Jesus.

Second, people remember and revere this passage for its use in the March on Washington, August 28, 1963, in the speech by Dr. Martin Luther King Jr. This writer saw and read the actual copy of the speech when the writings and books of Dr. Martin Luther King Jr. were on display and auction at Sotheby's in New York City. Some of the more severe language with respect to the plight of African Americans and the experience of racisms was "softened" and "deleted" in the actual delivered speech. Gotthemeir, in *Ripples of Hope: Great American Civil Rights Speeches*, notes a change from the original intended speech at the conclusion of King's address (Gotthemeir 2003: 234).

The message of Amos has a rich heritage in African American and African religious communities. Oracles that address poverty, injustice, and equality resonate with the lives and experience of these respective religious communities. The presentation of Yahweh, a universal deity who has standards of justice that when violated incur wrath, are components of the native cosmologies of Africans and the beliefs of African Americans. Yahweh is the source of the music and myths of people of African descent. African and African American music celebrates and muses upon Yahweh's presence and

lordship, and places in Yahweh the substance of the hopes and prayers of people of color. The belief that the Lord is one who intervenes in the affairs of those unjustly treated leads to the struggle and engagement against the evils perpetrated against Africans and African Americans. Yahweh as the Lord of creation will not idly stand by in the face of injustice but will intervene with justice, judgment, and deliverance.

References

Anderson, Francis I., and David N. Freedman. 1989. *Amos*. Anchor Bible. New York. Doubleday.

Awolalu, J. Omosade, and P. Adelumo Dopamu. 1979. *West African Religion*. Ibadan, Nigeria: Onibonoje.

Bennett, Harold V. 2002. *Injustice Made Legal: Deuteronomic Law and the Plight of Widows, Strangers, and Orphans in Ancient Israel*. Grand Rapids, Mich.: Eerdmans.

Blassingame, John W. 1979. *The Slave Community: Plantation Life in the Antebellum South*. New York: Oxford University Press.

Bullock, C. Hassell. 1986. *An Introduction to the Old Testament Prophetic Books*. Chicago: Moody.

Carrol R., M. Daniel. 2002. *Amos—The Prophet and His Oracles*. Louisville: Westminster John Knox.

Dibeela, Moiseraele Prince. 2001. "Setswana Perspective on Genesis 1:1-10." In *The Bible in Africa: Transactions, Trajectories and Trends*. 384–99. Boston: Brill.

DuBois, W. E. B. 1996. *The Philadelphia Negro: A Social Study*. Philadelphia: University of Pennsylvania Press.

Gottheimer, Josh, ed. 2003. *Ripples of Hope: Great American Civil Rights Speeches*. New York: Basic Civitas.

Harrison, R. K. 1969. *Introduction to the Old Testament*. Grand Rapids, MI: Eerdmans.

Jones, Gwilym H. 1984. *1 and 2 Kings, Volume II*. The New Century Bible Commentary. Grand Rapids, Mich.: Eerdmans.

Mbiti, John S. 1999. *African Religions and Philosophy*. 2nd ed. Portsmouth, N.H.: Heinemann.

Mitchell, Henry. 2004. *Black Church Beginnings: The*

Long-Hidden Realities of the First Years. Grand Rapids, Mich.: Eerdmans.

Raboteau, Albert J. 2004. *Slave Religion: The Invisible Institution in the Antebellum South.* Oxford: Oxford University Press.

Sanders, Cheryl J. 2003. "African Americans, the Bible and Spiritual Formation." In *African Americans and the Bible: Sacred Texts and Social Structures*. Edited by Vincent L. Wimbush, 588–602. New York: Continuum.

Smith, Gary V. 1998. *Amos: A Commentary*. 2nd ed. Mentor Commentaries. Geanies House, Fearn, Ross-shire, IV20 1TW, Great Britain: Christian Focus Publications.

Southern, Eileen. 1983. *The Music of Black Americans: A History.* 2nd ed. New York: Norton.

Stinton, Diane. 2004. "Africa, East and West." In *An Introduction to Third World Theologies*, ed. John Parratt, 105–36. Cambridge, UK: Cambridge University Press.

Stuart, Douglas. 1987. *Hosea—Jonah*. Word Bible Commentary. Waco, Tex.: Word.

Theile, Edwin R. 1983. *The Mysterious Numbers of the Hebrew Kings*. Grand Rapids, Mich.: Zondervan.

Tracy, David. 1987. *Plurality and Ambiguity: Hermeneutics, Religion, Hope*. San Francisco: Harper and Row.

Tutu, Desmond M. 1979. "Black Theology/African Theology—Soul Mates or Antagonists?" In *Black Theology: A Documentary History, 1966–79,* ed. Gayraud S. Wilmore and James H. Cone, 483–91. Maryknoll, New York: Orbis.

Ward, Geoffrey C. 2004. *Unforgivable Blackness: The Rise and Fall of Jack Johnson*. New York: Knopf.

Watts, John D. W. 1997. *Vision and Prophecy in Amos*. Macon, Ga.: Mercer University Press.

West, Gerald O., and Musa W. Dube, eds. 2001. *The Bible in Africa: Transactions, Trajectories and Trends*. Boston: Brill.

Wilmore, Gayraud S., and James H. Cone, eds. 1979. *Black Theology: A Documentary History, 1966–1999*. Maryknoll, N.Y.: Orbis.

Wimbush, Vincent L. 2003. *African Americans and the Bible: Sacred Texts and Social Structures*. New York: Continuum.

OBADIAH

Elelwani B. Farisani

THE BOOK OF OBADIAH, the shortest book of the Old Testament prophets, contains only twenty-one verses. Nothing is known or said about the author in the text. The only thing revealed is his name, which means "servant of the Lord," a name he shares with eleven other persons in scripture, none of whom can be identified as the author. Scholars' debate varies widely on dating the book, from the ninth to the sixth century B.C.E. (see Faussett 1997; see also Finley 2003: 306). What is more important to us here, rather than authorship, is the book's message.

The book of Obadiah is presented mainly in two parts. The first part speaks of the doom of Edom for their pride and wrong against Jacob (vv. 1-16) (Baker 1985: 1455). The Edomites, descendants of Esau, had a grudge against Israel because Jacob cheated their ancestor out of his birthright

(see Gen. 25:21-34; 27:41). Perhaps that deception contributed immensely to the animosity Edomites had against ancient Israel. As Baker puts it, Edom took tremendous pride in her enormous wealth, gained from mining, trading, and theft, and in her strategic geographical location (Baker 1985: 1455). The book of Obadiah speaks of the danger of the sins of pride and arrogance, the feeling of superiority that often results from taking advantage of others.

The second part focuses on the deliverance and restoration of the house of Jacob (vv. 17-21) (Baker 1985: 1455). The turning point champions God's promise for deliverance and for cleansing Mount Zion. One of the results of restoration is the repossession of the land, the temple, the city, and the kingdom.

CONTEXTUALIZATION

The animosity between the Edomites and the Israelites is one of the oldest examples of discord in human relationships. The conflict began with a struggle between Jacob and Esau in the womb of their mother, Rebekah (Gen. 25:21-26). Their descendants inherited the animosity and continued fighting against each other. Ethnic tension described by Obadiah between the Israelites and the Edomites may have relevance in Africa today, especially in the context of recent xenophobic attacks on foreign nationals in South Africa.

Biblical texts have been abused to foment ethnic segregation and conflict in Africa. Maimela argues that, in Africa, ethnic diversity has been used by "politicians to destructive ends" (Maimela 1997: 118; see also Oddland 1997: 83; deJong 1999: 5). The destructive ends include "tribal or ethnic conflicts which have given rise to civil wars, conflict, refugees, and destruction of African society" (Maimela 1997: 118; see also Pierli et al. 1999: 36; Farisani 2004: 24–25). Maimela explains that dominant white culture in South Africa implemented apartheid, their political ideology, to exploit ethnic diversity for their own socioeconomic and political interests (Maimela 1997: 118).

What then should the role of the churches be in addressing ethnicity? Moving from the fact that many people affected by ethnic conflict are church members, the church has a role to play in encouraging coexistence and harmony among different ethnic groups. Thus she will have to insist that the problem is not ethnicity but the "polarising and destructive forms of ethnicity" (Nambala 1997: 33; see also Getui 1999: 10ff; Gichure 1999: 25ff; Farisani 2004).

For the church to address ethnic conflicts effectively in society, it will have to address ethnic conflicts within itself first (Nambala 1997: 33; see also deJong 1999: 6). Oddland argues that the church has to promote unity within diversity in this situation (Oddland 1997: 64; see also Shorter 1999: 64; Farisani 2004). Thus churches, bearing in mind

that ethnic categories within scriptures have been used to "manipulate and to rule," should encourage the use of scripture as "modes of resistance" to ethnic conflicts (Brett 1996: 8; Farisani 2004), toward inclusiveness and healing.

References

Baker, Walter L. 1985. *The Bible Knowledge Commentary: An Exposition of the Scriptures*. Wheaton, Ill.: Victor.

Brett, M. G. 1996. "Interpreting Ethnicity: Method, Hermeneutics, Ethics." In *Ethnicity and the Bible*, ed. M. G. Brett. Leiden: Brill.

deJong, Albert, ed. 1999. *Ethnicity: Blessing or Curse?* Nairobi: Paulines.

Farisani, Elelwani. 2004. "Ethnicity in Ezra-Nehemiah." *Theologia Viatorum* 28 (1): 24–55.

Faussett, A. R. 1997. "The Book of Obadiah." In *A Commentary, Critical and Explanatory, on the Old and New Testaments*, ed. Robert Jamieson, A. R. Robert, and David Brown. Oak Harbor, Wash.: Logos Research Systems.

Finley, Thomas J. 2003. *Joel, Amos, Obadiah: An Exegetical Commentary*. Dallas: Biblical Studies.

Getui, M. N. 1999. "At Variance but in Harmony." In *Ethnicity: Blessing or Curse?* ed. Albert deJong, 9–19. Nairobi: Paulines.

Gichure, P. 1999. "Ethnicity and Enculturation: Challenges and Promises." In *Ethnicity: Blessing or Curse?* ed. Albert deJong, 20–26. Nairobi: Paulines.

Maimela, Simon. 1997. "Cultural and Ethnic Diversity in Promotion of Democratic Change." In *Democracy and Development in Africa: The Role of the Churches*, ed. J. N. K. Mugambi. Nairobi: All Africa Conference of Churches.

Nambala, S. V. V. 1997. "Ethnicity and the Church in Africa." In *Church, Culture and Ethnicity in Present Ethiopia*, ed. Iteffa Gobena, 25–35. Addis Ababa: Mekane Yesus.

Oddland, O. 1997. "Revisiting the Cultural Anthropological Concepts of Culture and Ethnicity: An

Introduction to the Present Cultural Diversities in EECMY." In *Church, Culture and Ethnicity in Present Ethiopia*, ed. Iteffa Gobena. Addis Ababa: Mekane Yesus.

Pierli, F., et al. 1999. "Ethnicity and Human Development: The Missing Link." In *Ethnicity: Blessing or Curse?* ed. Albert deJong, 33–55. Nairobi: Paulines.

Shorter, A. 1999. "The Curse of Ethnocentrism and the African Church." In *Ethnicity: Blessing or Curse?* ed. Albert deJong, 27–32. Nairobi: Paulines.

JONAH

Valerie Bridgeman

INTRODUCTION

The book of Jonah begins, like most of the pro-phetic books, with the formulaic phrase, "the word of the Lord came. . . ." That beginning ends the similarities between the books, however, as Jonah begins to read like a short story, a cautionary tale whose meaning remains as open-ended as the question that ends the book—that is, the question about how YHWH ought to behave toward "that great city" Nineveh.

SO THE STORY GOES

The book sets forth a straightforward story. God calls. Jonah runs. A great storm endangers the lives of the sailors on the boat because of Jonah's life. Jonah is thrown overboard. A great fish is "appointed" to swallow Jonah before he can drown.

Jonah laments and worships in the womb of the sea. Jonah gets a second chance because "the word of YHWH" comes again, reiterating that Jonah should speak what he has been told. Jonah preaches an ambiguous word, "Nineveh will be overturned." Nineveh repents, much to Jonah's chagrin. Jonah and YHWH have a great argument. That is the story, in short: a great call, a great fleeing, a great storm, a great fear of YHWH in the sailors and the Ninevites, a great city, and a great theological dilemma.

Jonah seems to be a midrash on the classic ancient Israelite liturgical confession found first in Exod. 34:6-7 (compare to Jonah 4:2) and in variations throughout the Hebrew texts (see Num. 14:18; Neh. 9:17; Ps. 86:15; Ps. 103:8; Psalm 145; Psalm 8; Joel 2:13; and Nah. 1:3). Hans Wolff adds that it may be commentary on the prophet Jonah, son of Amittai, the prophet from Gath Hepher in 2 Kings 14:25, and an illustration of God's promise to renounce punishment on any nation that turns from wickedness in Jer. 18:7-8 (Wolff 1986: 81; see also White 1992: 213). Even though the book seems to tie the story to the life of the prophet mentioned in 2 Kings, we may not assume that the prophet is in fact the same as the one in 2 Kings. Nevertheless, it is important to know that the "other Jonah" of 2 Kings was also sent to prophesy to the enemy.

CLASSIFYING JONAH IN AFRICANA SETTINGS
When reading Jonah as a member of the Africana community, one must remember that it is not, primarily, a Christian text, though it has been retained in the Christian Bible. This fact may seem too obvious, and thus too ridiculous to mention—and I might agree, except that people often go too quickly to Christian constructs to understand texts in the Hebrew bible.

Jonah, rooted in the ancient, pre-Christian world, is a farce, a hyperbolized satire: a cautionary tale. Since many Africana communities have been taught to read the biblical text as "word of God," handed down directly from heaven, and as history, conversations around the text in these communities often have centered on whether the "great fish" was a whale, or real. But getting Africana communities to consider that the historicity or factuality of the Jonah text is neither of primary importance nor even the most interesting question to raise regarding Jonah's "whale of a tale" is a major task. The inculcating presence of conservative evangelicalism that requires unquestioned loyalty to the text as *the* "inerrant word of God," meaning accurate in facts and theology, foments rabid resistance when scholarship tries to point out the text's troubling questions.

Jonah has captured Africana imagination in literature and in sermonic content. In this essay, I examine Jonah in light of a typical African-American sermon on Jonah, the literary work of Zora Neale Hurston, and the memoir of Bishop Desmond Tutu as it relates to the Truth and Rec-onciliation Commission (TRC) of South Africa after the political dismantling of apartheid in that country.

JONAH AND POSTCOLONIAL THOUGHT

I examine the text, considering postcolonial criticism and the work of reconciliation as a lens for interrogating the Jonah text. Colonization requires colonizers to view the colonized as savages— "consequently, Christianizing, colonizing, civilizing, as well as enslaving became part of the mission to save" (Dube 2000: 10). In reading Durham's sermon and the critique of mission work embedded in Hurston's literature, one sees that Jonah has been used as a colonization tool because the text itself alludes to a "repentance" that calls for the denouncing of one's own cultural gods. Whether this usage may be "faithful" to the text is not the question. Rather, what are the implications of an imported faith into a culture vastly different from one's own?

According to Dube, the primary reason peoples are colonized is to advance one's religious notions, to rape the land and peoples of their resources, and to gain personal glory for being a conqueror (consider Columbus or any number of explorers) (Dube 2000: 13). When one adds an "us-them" paradigm that divides humanity into believers and unbelievers or good and evil, these three concepts often conflate to provide a sacred canopy for the violation of a cultural reality to exist.

MISSIONARY IMPULSES, RECONCILIATION, AND THE DANGER OF BLANKET AMNESTY

At least two concerns in the book of Jonah have an impact on Africana peoples: one, the evangelizing, missionary impulse and the ways in which people have presumed the text is a mandate for converting others; and two, the apparent call to reconcile one's most heinous enemies to one's own deity. For those persons on the inside and underside of empirical power, this rich story is troubling and difficult. Divine mercy and justice trump human notions and belief systems of the same (De la Torre 2007: 24).

The reconciliation De la Torre speaks of may best be exemplified by the TRC hearings that took place in South Africa, led by Bishop Desmond Tutu. These hearings sought to bring to light atrocities done in the name of a brutal apartheid system, and to help the country "move forward." No one could doubt that apartheid was just a governmental, military operation, any more than ancient Assyrians would be able to argue that they had nothing to do with the advancing conquering armies of their time. Assyrians benefited from the "fruits" of war and empire-building just as white South Africans benefited in the apartheid era of South Africa. Black South Africans were trodden down by apartheid. There were those who might have claimed not to have participated in the system and "who might have said they were opposed to apartheid but had nonetheless gone on enjoying the privileges and huge benefits that apartheid provided them—just because of an accident of birth, a biological irrelevance, the color of their skin" (Tutu 2000: 6).

Reconciliation cannot, however, mean "without accountability." What went missing in Jonah, according to De la Torre, was any attempt to change the culture so that, once the fasting and praying was done, Assyria would not be a dangerous neighbor. But the how of that task may be why the book ends so ambiguously. The answers are not in a dialogue with the Deity per se, but within the global human community, where humans are challenged to effect the change they desire—that is, to bear God's mercy in behavior toward neighbors, even dangerous ones. This challenge requires a balancing act that brings justice with mercy. As Tutu noted, the task of the TRC was to "balance the requirements of justice, accountability, stability, peace, and reconciliation" (2000: 23). But there is no such balancing act apparent in the Jonah text.

Jonah runs in the opposite direction from the word that comes to him, for good reason (1:3).

He cannot see how this word can be anything good for his own tribe. "Jonah disobeyed God out of his deeper loyalty to his own people" (De la Torre 2007: 77). The word, directed at an enemy of ancient Israel, Assyria, opens the door for that empire to survive only to ultimately destroy Jonah's nation-state. His nationalistic hopes are up against a theistic universalism. De la Torre notes that Jonah's story reveals a rebellious, marginal prophet who is angry with God about being merciful with the enemy and who is adamant regarding his oppressors' destruction. This God quickly dispenses mercy and redemption to the undeserving (De la Torre 2007: 24).

Seemingly, YHWH offered Nineveh a blanket amnesty, since there is no evidence that repentance meant repair the damage or change their bloodthirsty, land-grabbing, people-enslaving ways. The same question that confronted the TRC in South Africa confronted the Jonah writer: "Is it ever enough for perpetrators merely to apologize and be humiliated through public exposure? What about justice?" (Tutu 2000: 30). But, as Tutu observed, "blanket amnesty leads to amnesia. . . . The past, far from disappearing or lying down and being quiet, has an embarrassing and persistent way of returning and haunting us unless it has in fact been dealt with adequately" (2000: 28).

Reconciliation begins with utterance. The book of Jonah recounts a stark utterance by the prophet: "Forty more days and Nineveh will be overturned." And the "great city" or important city, as "great" may be translated, does overturn by repenting with hopes that YHWH also will repent. They repent under "great fear," under duress.

JONAH, HURSTON, AND A PARABLE OF REPENTANCE UNDER DURESS

To examine what happens when a people repent under duress, or when a people are forced to take on another people's god, becomes apparent in *Jonah's Gourd Vine*, by Zora Neale Hurston (1962/1990). Hurston introduces protagonist John Pearson as a man who leaves his elemental, earthy existence, where sexuality and sensuality are clear gifts of creation, to cross the river and find his "civilizing" wife, Lucy, who introduces him to Christianity and to guilt and words. He becomes the pastor of Zion Hope Church.

John represents Jonah's desire to escape from the Deity's grasp—John wants to escape from conventionality and not be confined by Christian expectations. Ciuba points out that Hurston's protagonist, John, like Jonah, resists delivering God's word—that is, becoming a preacher. "And just as Jonah's bitterness at the repentance of the Ninevites reveals how he has failed to internalize his own message about forgiveness, John calls for conversion but cannot achieve his own definitive change of heart" (Ciuba 2000: 127).

John's conversion is from his own spirituality, steeped in the rhythmic soul of African worship, especially the drum and the dance. John is forced to comply with an orthodoxy that is dissonant to his own encounter with God; at one point, he notes that he never felt guilty before crossing the river into Lucy's world. In addition, John's spirituality becomes specifically word-centered, and he is "compelled to learn language to express his new spirituality as his newly Christian God moves from the physical and natural world around him into the rarefied and hitherto inaccessible realm of words" (Wilson 2003: 65).

Like John, Jonah knows the power of utterance. Jonah resists it because to speak in God's name is to put God in motion. He knows the ancient creeds in which the people chanted, like a mantra or an incantation that YHWH is "slow to anger, having plenty of mercy" (4:2). Jonah fully expects that God will actively work against the judgment that he was commanded to speak. He expected, at least at the level of the text, for mercy to prevail in the face of injustices. In fact, "mercy no longer tempers justice but overrides it entirely" (White 1992: 228). And, for the sake of his own

people, running seemed the most appropriate thing for Jonah to do, given that years after the prophecy the Assyrians would ravage Israel and Judah and carry their elite citizens into captivity (see 2 Kings 17 and 18).

This story line also serves to stifle revolution and resistance. The question in 4:4, 9—"it is right for you to be angry"—serves to stifle any anger oppressed people would rightly have in the face of atrocities. As readers/hearers are confronted with this question, the assumed answer is "No, it is not right for me to be angry." The dissonance of such an answer, however, wars against impulses of survival. Jonah is sent on a mission that effectively aids and abets an enemy in the destruction of his own culture and peoples. He has every right to be angry. So we must ask the question, how does anger factor into justice making, evangelization, and reconciliation?

THE PROBLEM OF PREACHING JONAH

The concerns about evangelization, the missionary impulse, and reconciliation can be seen in two typical African American sermons found on blacksermons.com. In the sermon "A Preacher Who Went on Strike," L. R. Durham refers to the whale as a "strikebreaker." The sermon employs the metaphor of labor unions, and of a Deity who allows no "free agency" clause in the prophet's call. Durham equates preacher with prophet. The book of Jonah, then, becomes the quintessential call narrative—the call to go, the refusal, and then the relenting to God's will. Jonah puts into action what Jeremiah says he wishes he could do—not speak in God's name because every attempt is thwarted by the irresistibility of the call (Jer. 20:1-7). For Jonah, the irresistibility is connected with his desire to continue to live. He cannot run from God, no matter how hard he tries (compare Ps. 139:7-12).

Durham portrays everything and everyone in the story but Jonah—the wind, the whale, and the waiting Ninevites—as obedient. But in the end, the sermon is not about repenting citizens of Nineveh and the larger social implications of people and animals fasting. The sermon concerns individualistic Christians: "Don't you know that it is dangerous to strike against God's program? It's not just dangerous for preachers; it's dangerous for everybody who has been washed by the blood of the Lamb" (Durham 2007: 8).

Also on blacksermons.com, the anonymous author of a sermon titled "The Common Plight of the Goose and the Gander" posits that the lesson in Jonah for African Americans is this:

> It's time to soften our approach and give peace a chance . . . a real chance. It's time to let bygones be bygones. Its time to "put a little love in your heart" where you may have had a tendency toward hatred. Have we not all sinned and fallen short of the glory of God? [The preacher then names some possible outcomes such allowance might yield, from the end of ill feelings between individuals to the opportunity to cut the former enemies' hair. And, the preacher proclaims,] "stranger things have happened." (4)

CONCLUSION

Both sermons lean in the direction of personal piety and do not take seriously the conundrum in which Jonah found himself—that is, how can a people be in relationship with another people who want to destroy them? And, what do we do with Jonah's anger and our quest for justice? Audre Lorde reminds us that anger does not destroy; hate does (Lorde, 1984: 129). Anger provides energy so we may engage in analysis, protest, survival, and justice. This use moves us toward an effective use of power. Jonah's anger signals an opportunity for Africana communities to name pain, suffering, and oppression. That anger can help us discern our complicity or lack thereof. It also can galvanize us to speak with

impeccability, work for justice, and share our stories. We may then move toward reconciliation, recognizing the capacity for choice and the significance of God to do what human beings cannot.

References

Chen Nan Jou. 2004. "Jonah." In *Global Bible Commentary*, ed. Daniel Patte, 291–94. Nashville: Abingdon.

Ciuba, Gary. 2000. "The Worm Against the Word: The Hermeneutical Challenge in Hurston's Jonah's Gourd Vine—Critical Essay." *African American Review* 34 (1): 119–34.

"The Common Plight of the Goose and the Gander." Sermon no. 1151, 1–5. www.blacksermons.com (accessed September 19, 2007).

De la Torre, Miguel A. 2007. *Liberating Jonah: Forming an Ethics of Reconciliation*. Maryknoll, N.Y.: Orbis.

Dube, Musa W. 2000. *Postcolonial Feminist Interpretation of the Bible*. St. Louis: Chalice.

Durham, L. R. 2007. "A Preacher Who Went on Strike." 1–8, www.blacksermons.com (accessed September 19, 2007).

Howe Gaines, Janet. 2003. *Forgiveness in a Wounded World: Jonah's Dilemma*, ed. Dennis T. Olson. Studies in Biblical Literature. Atlanta: Society of Biblical Literature.

Hurston, Zora Neale. 1962/1990. *Jonah's Gourd Vine: A Novel*. Foreword by Rita Dove. New York: Harper & Row.

Lorde, Audre, "The Uses of Anger: Women Responding to Racism," 124–33, in *Sister Outsider: Essays and Speeches*. Berkeley: The Crossing Feminist Press Series, 1984, 2007.

Trible, Phyllis. 1998. "Divine Incongruities in the Book of Jonah." In *God in the Fray: A Tribute to Walter Brueggemann*, ed. Tod Linafelt and Timothy K. Beal, 198–208. Minneapolis: Fortress Press.

Tutu, Desmond. 2000. *No Future without Forgiveness*. New York: Image.

Valerie Bridgeman

White, Marsha C. 1992. "Jonah." In *The Women's Bible Commentary*, ed. Carol A. Newsom and Sharon H. Ringe, 212–14. Louisville, Ky.: Westminster John Knox.

Wilson, Anthony. 2003. "The Music of God, Man, and Beast: Spirituality and Modernity in *Jonah's Gourd Vine*." *Southern Literary Journal* 35 (2): 64–78.

Wolff, Hans Walter. 1986. *Obadiah and Jonah: A Commentary*. Minneapolis: Augsburg.

MICAH

Elelwani B. Farisani

THE BOOK OF MICAH is one of the books of the eighth-century B.C.E. prophets. Little is known about the author of this book (Richards 1996, 550). Although most scholars accept that Micah 1–3 was written by Micah the prophet, some believe Micah 4–5 was added during the exile, and Micah 6:1—7:6 concerns later anonymous prophecy from the period of king Manasseh. However, Hughes argues that the repeated expression "listen" (1:2; 3:1; 6:1) and the book pattern of alternating sections of judgment and salvation support the unity of the book and that the repeated phrases in no way undermine the single authorship of Micah (Hughes 2001, 349).

Scholars concur that the date of Micah's prophecy is in the reign of three kings of Judah—Jotham (750–731 B.C.E.), Ahaz (743–715), and Hezekiah (728–686) (Hughes 2001, 351; Henry 1996;

Martin 1985, 1475); however, there are slight differences among scholars over the specific date or period of reign of the kings (Hughes 2001, 351). Although Micah mentioned the destruction coming on the northern kingdom of Israel (Martins 1985: 1475), his main audience is the people of the southern kingdom of Judah (Martins 1985, 1475; Hughes: 2001, 351).

Generally divided into three main parts, the first part speaks about coming judgments (chaps. 1–3). The book shows that the prophet attacked the corruption eating deep into the fibers of Israelite society. Richards and Richards (1987) maintain that the "major thrust of Micah's message was against Israel's and Judah's social sin. Micah lashed out at greedy nobles who defrauded the poor in their land, and who were quick to evict widows" (Richards and Richards 1987, 477; Willington

1997, 479). Clearly the prophet spoke against the greed of wealthy and powerful people, the venality of priests and prophets, and the dishonesty of merchants. The prophet also spoke about the worship of other gods that had replaced or adulterated the worship of Israel's God.

The second part of Micah examined the prophetic promises of deliverance (chaps. 4–5). The third part mainly discusses exhortations and confessions of national sins, coupled with promises of restoration. Significantly, though the theme of judgment is prominent in each of Micah's three messages, the prophet also stressed restoration.[1] Micah wrote that the nation would ultimately be restored to prominence and prosperity.[2]

CONTEXTUALIZATION

The book of Micah is very relevant to Africa. Although Micah's prophecies signal the political and social circumstances of his time, the basic message from the book transcends time and has universal value and application. Micah's meticulous relevance for Africa intensifies as poverty, corruption, HIV/AIDS, and moral decay plague the African continent. Accordingly, there is a need for socioeconomic, political, and moral renewal in Africa.

The particular context of Micah's relevance concerns current socioeconomic conditions in Africa. Africa has for many years been devastated by institutionalized racism, colonialism, and the cold war legacy. Africa is also facing the AIDS epidemic, which is extremely high. Poverty continues to hit most women and children; war and genocide are the order of the day.

Accordingly, the African continent needs economic, political, and religious/moral renewal. We are fully aware that different concepts such as Africanism, Pan-Africanism (Nkrumah 1961; 1962; 1963a; 1963b; 1963c; 1964; 1965; Nasser 1955), cultural renewal (Diop 1956), African socialism

(Senghor 1964; 1958), decolonization (Fannon 1965), and African Renaissance (Mbeki: 1998 1999) have been used in a quest for the renewal of Africa. For the purposes of this discussion I will only briefly highlight the relevance of Pan-Africanism, African Renaissance, and moral renewal in Africa.

My analysis of both Pan-Africanism and the African Renaissance elsewhere (Farisani 2002) shows that despite the fact that the former emerged out of a context of colonialism and slave trade, while the latter has been more canvassed during the postcolonial era, they both share a common goal in that the major concern of both concepts is to address, transform, and renew the socioeconomic and political conditions in Africa. In other words, they both call for the renewal of Africa. This renewal involves reconstruction and transformation of our continent with the ultimate goal of making Africa a reborn or renewed continent, free from slavery, tribalism, racism, and economic and political exploitation.

Neither Pan-Africanism nor African Renaissance is a theological term. Rather, they are concepts coined by politicians to emphasize the need for Africans to stand together in addressing cultural and socioeconomic challenges facing Africa. The term *Pan-Africanism* was coined as a result of colonialism and slave trade in Africa. Its main aim was to mobilize Africans to be united against the oppression taking place in Africa. Several African political leaders believed that Africa had to be rid of colonialism and slave trade and that to achieve that end Africans had to stand together, united, in order to confront the socioeconomic conditions brought to Africa by these historical realities and to renew and reconstruct the African continent.

Similarly, African Renaissance is the realization that, in the wake of the damage caused by colonialism and apartheid in Africa, Africans themselves should take the lead in designing strategies and programs that will best address the current socioeconomic conditions of civil war, poverty, foreign debt, AIDS, refugees, and the abuse of women in Africa.

Accordingly, the African Renaissance is about the renewal, transformation, and reconstruction of the African continent, with a view to effectively addressing the above-mentioned conditions.

One main focus of both Pan-Africanism and African Renaissance is the moral renewal of the African continent. On several occasions, Nelson Mandela, South Africa's former president, called for moral renewal of Africa. John Mbiti, Kenyan scholar of religions, has famously asserted that Africans are notoriously religious, meaning that Africans center their lives around belief systems, rituals, and practices that make life meaningful and purposeful for them (Pityana 1999:138). Accordingly, scholars and politicians have correctly acknowledged that economic and political renewal without moral values will not bring social development.

> South Africa is also grappling with issues of how to bring about a stable and sustainable transition to political democracy. However, political democracy alone will not automatically create healthy economic conditions for development and growth in the country. History has shown that there are different routes to development. In Africa political liberation has not changed the plight of the poor. In fact, the continent is today poorer and more marginalised than before (Teffo 1999: 149).

Thus, politics and economics undoubtedly have a role to play; however, without a moral conscience, "society is soulless" (Teffo 1999: 168; Vil-Nkomo and Myburgh 1999: 269).

For that matter, Pityana has noted that African societies are riddled with the decay in moral values and the withering away of a sense of responsibility (Pityana 1999: 140). South Africa is rife with human rights violations that are national as well as personal. Pityana argues that South Africans must examine vicious, persistent, and gratuitous violence against people at all ages, including robbing elders of their money, raping young children, and stealing workers' wages. This violence, according to Pityana,

defies culture and tradition as well as morality (Pityana 1999: 147; see also Teffo 1999: 149).

However, Pityana believes the harshest moral indictment is reserved for those who fold our arms and do nothing (Pityana 1999: 147–48). Khoza argues that in Africa worries are not only about personal morality; they are, perhaps more importantly, about public morality. Problematically, institutionalized public immorality has resulted in obscene, unjust, corrupt consequences and leadership (Khoza 1999: 285).

Thus, if moral values are to have any value for modern Africa, they must be transformative. There is a sense that the development of an African ethical standard, drawing from the reservoirs of tradition that were suppressed under the weight of Western cultural hegemony, emerged as subversion in South Africa. Now that this standard is emerging from subversion, care must be taken that it does not become the new oppressive orthodoxy. Hopefully, African moral values will help situate this new search for African identity and spur efforts toward social renewal (Pityana 1999: 148; Teffo 1999: 149).

While politicians and cultural leaders have invented such renewal concepts as Pan-Africanism and African Renaissance, theologians are talking about such concepts as reconstruction theology (Mugambi 1995, 2003; Villa-Vicencio 1992; Karamaga 1997; Chipenda, Karamaga, Mugambi, and Omari 1991; Getui and Obeng 1999) and reconciliation theology (Bosch 1986: 159–171; Domeris 1987: 77–80; Bosman, Gous and Spangenberg 1991; Turner 1998: 8). All such different concepts tell us of a quest by theologians to design a new theological paradigm relevant to current socioeconomic, cultural, and religious changes in Africa. In their quest for a renewal theology, these theologians suggest different biblical paradigms (Mugambi 1995; Villa-Vicencio 1992).

The most important way to reflect on the eighth-century prophet Micah is to use him as a new paradigm in a quest for an African theology of renewal, transformation, reconciliation, and reconstruction. Micah conveys a strong message about the promise of deliverance and restoration. His message of hope, that his nation would ultimately be restored to prominence and prosperity, is very relevant in our context today as it stresses the very messages recently conveyed in our own history by advocates of both Pan-Africanism and African Renaissance.

Notes

1. Martins, 1985, 1475.
2. Martin, 1985, 1476; Henry, 1996.

References

Bosch, D. 1986. "Processes of Reconciliation and Demands of Obedience: Twelve Theses." Pages 159–71 in Tlhagale and Mosala 1986.

Bossman, H. L., I. P. G. Gous, and I. J. J. Spangenberg (eds.), 1991. *Plutocrats and Paupers: Wealth and Poverty in the Old Testament*. Pretoria: J. L. van Schaik.

Chipenda, J. B., A. Karamaga, J. N. K. Mugambi, and C. K. Omari. 1991. *The Church of Africa: Towards a Theology of Reconstruction*. Nairobi: All Africa Conference of Churches.

Diop, C. A. 1956. *The Cultural Contributions and Prospects of Africa*. Paris: Presence Africaine.

Domeris, W. R. 1987. "Biblical Perspectives on Reconciliation." *Journal of Theology for Southern Africa*, 60: 77–80.

Fanon, Frantz. 1965. *The Wretched of the Earth*. Trans. Constance Farrington. London: MacGibbon and Kee.

Farisani, E. B. 2002. *The Use of Ezra–Nehemiah in a Quest for a Theology of Renewal, Transformation, and Reconstruction*. Unpublished Ph.D. thesis, University of Natal.

Getui, M. N. and E. A. Obeng (eds.) 1999. *Theology of Reconstruction*. Nairobi: Acton.

Henry, Matthew. 1996. *Matthew Henry's Commentary on the Whole Bible: Complete and Unabridged in One Volume* Peabody: Hendrickson.

Hughes, Roberts B. 2001. *Micah*. Tyndale Concise Bible Commentary. Wheaton, Ill.: Tyndale House Publishers.

Karamaga, A. 1997. "A Theology of Reconstruction." Pages 190–91 in Mugambi 1997.

Khoza, R. J. 1999. "The Institutional Structures that Should Underpin the African Renaissance." Pages 279–88 in Makgoba 1999.

Makgoba, M. W. (ed.) 1999. *African Renaissance: The New Struggle*. Johannesburg and Cape Town: Mafube and Tafelberg.

Martins, John A. 1985. "Micah." *The Bible Knowledge Commentary: An Exposition of the Scriptures*. Ed. John F. Walvoord, and Roy B. Zuck. Wheaton, Ill.: Victors Books.

Mbeki, T. 1998. *Africa: The Time Has Come*. Cape Town: Tafelberg.

———. 1999. "Prologue." Pages xiii–xxi in Makgoba 1999.

Mugambi, J. N. K. 1995. *From Liberation to Reconstruction*. Nairobi: East Africa Educational Publishers.

———. 1997. *Christian Theology and Social Reconstruction*. Nairobi: Acton Publishers.

———. (ed.) 1997. *Democracy and Development in Africa: The Role of the Churches*. Nairobi: All Africa Conference of Churches.

Nasser, G. A. 1955. *Egypt's Liberation: The Philosophy of the Revolution*. Washington: Public Affairs Press.

Nkrumah, K. 1961. *I Speak of Freedom: A Statement of African Ideology*. London: Heinemann.

———. 1962. *Towards Colonial Freedom: Africa in the Struggle Against World Imperialism*. London: Heinemann.

———. 1963a. "Principles of African Studies." Address delivered at the time of the official opening of the Institute of African Studies, University of Ghana, Legon. *The Voice of Africa* 3 (2), 10.

———. 1963b. "United We Stand." Address to the Conference of Heads of State at Addis Ababa.

———. 1963c. *Africa Must Unite*. London: Heinemann.

———. 1964. *Consciencism: Philosophy and Ideology for De-Colonisation and Development with Particular Reference to the African Revolution*. London: Heinemann.

———. 1965. *Neo-Colonialism, The Last Stage of Imperialism.* Thomas Nelson and Sons: London and Edinburgh.

Pityana, N. B. 1999. "The Renewal of African Moral Values." Pages 137=48 in Makgoba 1999.

Richards, Larry, and Lawrence O. Richards. 1987. *The Teacher's Commentary.* Wheaton: Victor Books.

Richards, Lawrence O., 1996. *The Bible Readers Companion, Electronic Edition.* Wheaton: Victor Books.

Senghor, L. S. 1958. "A Community of Free and Equal Peoples with Mother Country." *Western World* 18,5.

———. 1964. *African Socialism.* Translated with an Introduction by Mercer Cook. London: Pall Mall Press.

Teffo, L. 1999. "Moral Renewal and African Experience(s)." Pages 149–69 in Makgoba 1999.

Tlhagale, B. and I. J. Mosala (eds.). 1986. *Hammering Swords into Ploughshares: Essays in Honour of Archbishop Mpilo Desmond Tutu.* Johannesburg: Skotaville.

Turner, E. A. 1998. *Reconciliation amidst a Socio-Economic Crisis: A Rhetorical Critical Reading of Nehemiah 5 against the Background of the Socio-Economic Situation in Judah during the Reign of the Achaemenids.* Ph.D. thesis. Stellenbosch University.

Villa-Vicencio, C. 1992. *A Theology of Reconstruction.* Cape Town: David Phillip.

Vil-Nkomo, S. and J. Myburgh. 1999. "The Political Economy of an African Renaissance: Understanding the Structural Conditions and Forms." Pages 266–78 in Makgoba 1999.

Willington, H. L. 1997. "Micah." *Willmington's Bible Handbook.* Wheaton: Tyndale House.

NAHUM

Valerie Bridgeman

THE BOOK OF NAHUM displays gloats by a prophet who delights in a blood-thirsty deity. The key theme of Nahum is vengeance. The primary weapons are humiliation and rape. "The absence of Nahum from the lectionary presents an implicit confession. Nahum is a book that makes the church uncomfortable, one that it seldom, if ever, opens" (García-Treto 1996: 619). This absence does not mean the book's sentiments are unknown in the African Diaspora, however. At core is the prophet's desire to see Assyria receive its "just due" violently.

A contemporary of the prophets Habakkuk, Zephaniah, Jeremiah, and Ezekiel, Nahum puts the character of God on the line, leading with the notion that "jealous" and "vengeful" is God. Hebrew text word order gives clues to the power of this jealousy and vengefulness. The Deity's wrath is continually sustained (1:1-2).

Nahum uses a variation of the ancient Israelite confession: YHWH is slow to anger (Exod. 34:6-7), uttered by the Deity. It would be an interesting study to compare the confession in its various settings in the Hebrew Bible, though partial in most places and changed. Seemingly, the confession may adapt to its surroundings. Also, in Num. 14:18, Moses repeats it back to the Deity to avert the people's destruction, in the psalms at 86:15, 103:8, and 145:8. Nehemiah includes a portion of the confession during the repentance and confession of those who returned to Jerusalem after the walls are rebuilt (Neh. 9:17). Moses repeats the confession to the Deity (Num. 14:18) in an effort to avert a catastrophic annihilation of ancient Israel. The prophets Joel and Jonah also use variations of the confession (Joel 2:13; Jon. 4:2).

Neither of these passages focuses on punishment; rather, they highlight the idea that the Deity "relents" of "evil." But for Nahum, the credo points to the power of Israel's deity, for whom neither Nineveh nor its allies is a match. Israel's God—one who kicks up storms with divine feet (1:3)—is a force to be reckoned with. For Nahum, the great confession is a prelude to the Deity's consuming, punitive, and devastating power. God will not let the guilty go unpunished. That is true justice, according to the prophet.

Nahum depicts Nineveh as a harlot who uses sorcery to seduce others (3:4). The Deity threatens her with a lifted skirt and filth flung on her (3:5-6). Careful readers should hear the threats as not only directed at Nineveh; lady Israel should know that the ranting warrior/husband god will do to her, whom he has legal license to punish, what he has done to lady Nineveh, a prostitute to whom he is not legally bound. Renita Weems helps us understand ways in which prophets use sexual language so that it "depended in the end on their ability to convince their audiences that viable connections could be drawn between the norms governing the sexual behavior of women and God's demands on Israel" (Weems 1995: 3). Consequently, sexual aggression allusions intend to invoke fear and repulsion. One does not know when an offense will occasion a beating or a rape, as Judith Sanderson reflects in her article on Nahum (Sanderson 1998: 232–36).

Nahum does at least indicate what constitutes the prophet's idea of fidelity. He tempers his words by saying YHWH is "good" or, as verse 7a notes, "Good is YHWH," again leading with the attribute. Africana people who are recipients of certain kinds of Christianity will recognize the liturgical exclamation "God is good [all the time] and all the time, God is good." This confession sometimes allows people to deny suffering, pain, and apparent unjust responses from the Deity.

Many Africana artists have tried to capture anger and rage mirroring what the prophet reports as the Deity's rage. Jamaican musician and Rastafarian prophet Bob Marley, born February 6, 1945, is one such artist. His song "One Love," often sung as an anthem for world peace, asks a key question not unlike the judgment Nahum portends: "There is one question I'd really love to ask. . . . Is there a place for the hopeless sinner who has hurt all mankind just to save his own?" In other words, should not those who hurt all humanity suffer for their deeds? Biographer Timothy White chronicles Marley's deepening dismay in the failure of nonviolent means to effect justice (White 1998).

Nahum declares that everyone will clap with joy over Nineveh's destruction, for who has ever escaped their relentless cruelty (3:19)? Justice—cruel, swift, and punishing—would come because God stands against Nineveh (2:13, 3:5). Nineveh's allies, including the African nations of Thebes, Ethiopia, Egypt, Put, and Libya, cannot successfully intervene (3:8). The mention of these nations attests to their might in the ancient world.

Sentiments found in Nahum's prophetic words are also clear in the writings of at least one African American in nineteenth-century United States history. David Walker, a free black and abolitionist, preceded Nat Turner's uprising.[1] Originally from the southern United States, Walker advocated slave revolts. In the *Appeal*, published September 1829, he wrote that "whites have always been an unjust, jealous, unmerciful, avaricious and blood-thirsty set of beings, always seeking after power and authority" (Walker 1995). As a result, he warned white America that "unless you speedily alter your course," white America would die at the hands of those they enslaved.[2] While Nahum did not explicitly call for an uprising from the people, his words clearly indicate that God will rise up against Assyria.

Nahum calls for violence. The book calls for swift and deadly justice. For Nahum, violence equals deadly justice. There is a distinct difference, however, between violence and liberating nonviolent justice—for example, nonviolent direct action as employed during the Civil Rights Movements in the United States or the "singing revolution" of South Africa. For a people under the boot of oppression and struggle, Nahum's blood lust–filled

Valerie Bridgeman

words must have sounded like good news (1:12-15). In the Africana Diaspora throughout the world, the call to end oppression with violence also is sometimes appealing. The question will remain, however; does not violence simply beget more violence?

Notes

1. During the early days of slavery in the United States, Nat Turner led a band of eight slaves in rebellion. The first killings were on August 22, 1831. Turner's rebellion was put down, but he claimed divine revelation for the bloodshed. From "The Southampton Slave Revolt," HistoryBuff.com, http://www.historybuff .com/library/refslave.html (accessed June 15, 2007).
2. See Africans in America, "David Walker's Appeal," PBS.org, http://www.pbs.org/wgbh/aia/ part4/4h2931t.html (accessed June 15, 2007). Taken from Walker 1995.

References

Achtemeier, Elizabeth. 1986. "Nahum." In *Interpretation, A Bible Commentary for Teaching and Preaching: Nahum-Malachi*, ed. James L. Mays, 5–30. Atlanta: John Knox.

da Silva, Valmor. 2004. "Nahum." In *Global Bible Commentary*, ed. Daniel Patte, 301–5. Nashville: Abingdon.

García-Treto, Francisco O. 1996. "Nahum." In *The New Interpreter's Bible: A Commentary in Twelve Volumes*, vol. 7. Nashville: Abingdon.

Sanderson, Judith E. 1998. "Nahum." In *The Women's Bible Commentary with Apocrypha*, 232–36. Louisville, Ky.: Westminster John Knox.

Walker, David. 1995. *David Walker's Appeal, in Four Articles: Together with a Preamble to the Coloured Citizens of the World, but in Particular, and Very Expressly, to Those of the United States of America*. Rev. ed. with an introduction by Sean Wilentz. New York: Hill and Wang.

Weems, Renita. 1995. *Battered Love: Marriage, Sex, and Violence in the Hebrew Prophets*. Overtures of Biblical Theology. Minneapolis: Augsburg Fortress.

White, Timothy. 1998. *Catch a Fire: The Life of Bob Marley*. New York: Owl Books.

HABAKKUK

Cheryl Kirk-Duggan

HABAKKUK ECHOES THEMES of Job and exudes an atmosphere of violence, vision, and victory: a matrix of injustice, theodicy, and triumph. The violence, framed as the passionate lament of a psalmist, parallels laments and woes of those today who are in Africa and the African Diaspora. The prophet's distress resonates with the pain and suffering of chattel slavery, genocide, systematic rape as a strategy of war, and other oppressions. These distresses force God's children, in hues from ebony to ivory, into exiles of terrorism, apartheid, and dislocation. Habakkuk's vision regarding trustworthiness offers testimony where the prophet's task is faithful dedication to God's justice amid worldly injustice. Habakkuk's voice echoes in the voices of other prophets ever since slave ships first left African shores bearing stolen human cargo.[1] Voices of the seventeenth, eighteenth, nineteenth, and twentieth centuries—from Harriet Tubman to Nelson Mandela—knew the anvil of oppression too well. We, too, receive the prophet Habakkuk's call to hold firm to God's justice, even when all human reality indicates the opposite. At these junctures, Habakkuk calls us to faithful endurance amid victory cloaked in troubling warrior language. Amid this faith, hymns emerged like "We've come this far by faith, leaning on the Lord," hymns that proclaim the ultimate victory of divine justice.

This article views Habakkuk through the lens of violence, vision, and victory, and frames the conversation by divine justice and liberation, using a womanist, interdisciplinary perspective that exposes matters of oppression (class, gender, race, age, ability). Itumeleng Mosala's PAP model—Polemical, referring to the argument; Appropriative, to the liberative message; and the Projective phase, referring to transformation hermeneutics—undergirds this exegesis.

VISUALIZATION: THEOLOGICAL, CONTEXTUAL OVERVIEW

Many African American congregants, when prompted by their pastor saying "God is Good!" respond "All the time!" Would Habakkuk assent to this mantra? Consider that Habakkuk begins protesting against God with lament and ends with an extraordinary vision of divine salvific presence. The lament complains bitterly and blames God for a hopeless situation (Brown 1996: 83–84). Habakkuk's warrior-storm God controls history and the world through violence. This poetic book involves debate between God and Habakkuk, five woes, and a liturgical, theophanic psalm. Amid rampant human and divine violence and domination minus justice, God acts on God's will. God claims that arrogance and wealth are temporary; that the righteous will wait faithfully for the downfall of oppressors (Sanderson 1992/1998: 237–39).

Achtemeier posits that the question is not God's justice or human doubt but God's will and purposes for God's world—that is, God's providence (1986: 31–32). Most scholars claim that Habakkuk, in traditional prophetic fervor, bemoans the injustice of an unjust world. Providence and justice are not mutually exclusive. There are three theological-literary moves in the book: violence amid a complaint and judgment speech; the vision of justice; and the closing victory hymn. The text implies that the turmoil of injustice took place during Jerusalem's final days (597–586 B.C.E.) prior to the Babylonian captivity, during Zedekiah's reign (Hiebert 1996: 623–26).

VIOLENCE AMID SUFFERING: COMPLAINTS — HABAKKUK 1:2-4, 12-13

Polemically, Habakkuk exposes injustice in which the victims, the poor, experience harshly limited freedom. Imperial injustice questions divine just rule. Habakkuk speaks for the victim, accusing God of inattentiveness and being inactive, prob-lematizing divine justice. Habakkuk complains a second time, highlighting God's immortality, and wrestles with the classic problem of theodicy: God's absolute righteousness amid tremendous world evil (Hiebert 1996: 630–32, 638–40). Complaint language includes terms of violence, trouble, pillage, wrong, contention, and strife. The first complaint is against native violence; the second against the Chaldeans (Ward 1985: 4, 12). Habakkuk laments that Judahites abandoned God's order for justice and righteousness during King Jehoiakim's reign (609–598 B.C.E.). They forgot covenantal, Deuteronomistic law, and Habakkuk faced unanswered prayer regarding a sick society. This weary prophet maintains his own faithfulness, conceding that Judah's punishment by Babylon is divine judgment against Judah's sin. The text implies that God's judgment and God's punishment are justified for they bring salvation (Achtemeier 1986: 34–40). The prophet laments the crisis situation, wondering how God can allow the wicked to oppress the righteous in a decadent society. YHWH responds that the Chaldeans, a new nation, will punish the evildoers. The dialogue/debate continues with 1:12-13, followed with YHWH responding again. The book's motif follows the call and response found in most African American music, often with a soloist or small group uttering a call and the larger group, orchestra, choir, or congregation responding.

Problematically, God remains silent amid unrelenting violence and evil. God's response is that, ultimately, evil and violence will fail and the righteous will live by their faithfulness, echoing the Exodus/Sinai liberation event (Smith 1984: 95–99). Habakkuk 1:2-4 exposes divine silence and inaction, where nonintervention sanctions violence justified by an eschatological promise that eventually it will all work out.

From an Appropriative stance, *Glory*, a film based on Colonel Robert Gould Shaw's letters, echoes Habakkuk 1:2-4, 12-13. The film chronicles the experimental development of the first Union army company of black soldiers (54th Massachusetts Volunteer Regiment) under all white officers, during the U.S. Civil War. Gould, from a privileged past, faces issues of class as he leads mostly illiterate former slaves and confronts racist prejudice in his officers, himself, and the enemy. This epic climaxes when the Union army attacks Fort Wagner and suffers huge black casualties; the black soldiers are immortalized for their bravery. They lived through the violence of slavery and then fought for the ultimate goal of freedom, which comes in limited fashion with the Emancipation Proclamation in 1863.

Alice Walker's *The Color Purple* demonstrates a Projective approach toward transformation. Walker's book, an epistolary novel and persecution text, explores relationships between God and Celie as Celie navigates a dysfunctional, abusive, black, southern family. The story reflects symptoms of the human predicament that involve scapegoating, victimization, and domination. Like Habakkuk, the violent story ends in victory. Celie's transformation as agape replaces Girardian mimetic rivalry with mimetic intimacy.[2] Celie recognizes her deep anger and grief after she realizes her harsh treatment by Mr. _____.[3] She comes to love herself, chooses noble authenticity, and embraces a God who loves and a sexuality that celebrates human communion (Kirk-Duggan 1994: 266–86).

VIGILANCE AND VISION AS DIVINE ANSWER (2:2-4)

Polemically, Hiebert posits that God tells Habakkuk to write or record the vision or revelation. Then Habakkuk, as herald or messenger, can run or carry the message and proclaim it to people. The vision, a witness to divine activity, will happen, even if delayed. Whether the focus is the credibility of God's vision or the faithfulness of the righteous, the issue is fidelity or steadfastness. Thus, Habakkuk is to be faithful to divine justice even when it appears delayed. In Rom. 1:17 and Gal. 3:11, Paul references Hab. 2:4 for Christians experiencing persecution regularly who lived after Jesus' preach-

ing and before the unfolding of God's rule on earth (Hiebert 1996: 640–42). The mystifying message about the runner and the text (2:2b) probably concerns a divine message for public broadcasting. God guarantees the message is sure and that, in God's time, the vision will occur (Brown 1996: 89–90). Habakkuk contends that one's faithfulness fulfills one's relationship with God. Faithfulness embodies intimacy, trust, and closeness to God, not cultic or ethical duties (Achtemeier 1986: 46). Habakkuk asks God why God employs the Chaldeans, who are more wicked than the Judahites they are used to punishing. God does not respond (Bellis 2000: 372). Next, the prophet calls attention to the proud and arrogant. Is the arrogant one an invader or someone closer to home as an Israelite oppressor—Greek, Assyrian, or Babylonian? Smith suggests the wicked one, *chayamah*, is Babylonian.

An Appropriative, liberative reading of a prophetic vision occurs in the spiritual "I Got Shoes, You Got Shoes, All God's Children Got Shoes." This spiritual creates a dialogue among diverse people, so that all those intended get the vision amid and across their sociocultural, ethnic, and religious differences.[4] Like the prophet, the spiritual's psalmist seeks to disseminate a message of hope through liturgy and teaching to produce holistic salvation and liberation, a call to see that liberation must emerge from the spirit, mind, *and* body. Oppressive encumbrances deaden sensibilities and mute the message of intimacy with God. When the enslaved psalmist and his or her audience did not have shoes, all could envision when their offspring would have shoes of leather, freedom, dignity, and justice (Kirk-Duggan 1997: 330–31; Kirk-Duggan 2006: 81).

Projectively, Mary McLeod Bethune (1875–1955), educator, administrator, politician, and diplomat, embodied her vision as she founded Bethune-Cookman College (1904). In her 1954 "Last Will and Testament," like the prophet, she declared her vision to help transform the lived experiences of her college and community. Retired and aware that her death was on the horizon, Bethune recognized that her life experiences could be inspirational. She formally bequeathed to her constituents love that builds, hope toward dignity, the challenge of developing confidence in one another, thirst for education, respect for power usage, faith, racial dignity, desire for harmonious living, and responsibility to young people (Bethune 1954).

VICTORY: DIVINE PRESENCE IN VIOLENCE (3:3-13)

The violence in chapters 1 and 3 stands in conceptual tension. Violence meted out by human hands results in self-destruction, with its self-glory producing hatred and humiliation. Violence begets more violence, evident in the millions who died in the twentieth century because of war or related government-sanctioned military violence. This does not even address recent militarism against terrorism, national systemic oppression of the poor and disenfranchised, or domestic violence in the twenty-first century. Intriguingly, God engages in violence, as nature and creation—with mythological language—wails and moans in travail. God uses violence to reconfigure and dismantle seats of power (Brown 1996: 93). Habakkuk gets to see the vision God promised. God conquers chaos, just as God did in creation. The divine cosmic battle ensues to save humanity (Achtemeier 1986: 56). Pinker states that a loud crowd, not Habakkuk, shouts questions to God regarding the focus of divine rage (Pinker 2003: 5)

Appropriatively, Alvin Ailey's dance suite "Revelations" embodies the chapter's victory, as it weaves cultural memory as body wisdom with fierce pageantry amid synthesized religious/folk song and masterful technique. The dance evokes holy liberation, liturgical rhetoric, archetypal protest, and psychic intensity in a systemized representation of dignity, order, and public possibility, celebrating and communicating a phenomenal black aesthetic (DeFrantz 2004: 3–4, 90–93, 239).

From a Projective, transformative perspective, in Toni Morrison's *Beloved*, Baby Suggs Holy, a former slave and a "woods preacher," embodies victory with her celebratory sermon in the Clearing.[5] The sermon is framed as a participatory aesthetic of *poiesis* (a creative calling-into-existence of that which did not exist before) and an improvisatory, poetic pedagogy as an aesthetic of a radically open (self) love. This survival formula engages relationality, which produces spiritual resources to help them face, defy, and overcome natural and human-created tragedy. The Clearing scene evinces Rudolf Otto's notion of holiness, the nonrational that cannot be held within reason, of *mysterium tremendum*—of wonder, awe, and mystery, a catalyst for one's physical body and spiritual restoration (Morrison 1987: 88–89, 177, 247; Milligan 1999).

VIEWING HABAKKUK AGAIN: CONCLUSIONS

Habakkuk's prophetic, poetic proclamation is protest and praise. Habakkuk exposes divine and human injustice and honors divine providence. For readers of faith not privy to biblical scholarship and for scholars, hope is the needle in a haystack of violence. Faith says God must have a reason for violence against innocence. Reason questions God's silence amid injustice. Faith and reason note that Habakkuk reflects the lives of oppressed peoples, that life is not fair, that God's ways are peculiar. Habakkuk cannot have a "happily ever after" ending when God uses divinely ordained violence to corral human violence; still, cultural artifacts testify to human resilience and divine presence. In sum, it is what it is: a warning of human vulnerability and divine incomprehensibility.

Notes

1. Early slave ships went to Europe, South America, and the Caribbean before being introduced into the American colonies, later known as the United States.

2. Mimesis pertains to imitation, the way most people learn. Mimetic rivalry occurs when two persons or groups desire the same object. Thee Smith coined the term *mimetic intimacy*, which concerns reconciliation where "an enemy functions intimately as an accomplice in the process of one's own transformation." Theophus H. (Thee) Smith, "King and the Quest to Cure Racism," in *Curing Violence* (Sonoma, Calif.: Polebridge, 1994), 236.

3. His name is left blank in this movie/book. When the two are reconciled as equals and friends at the end of the story, the audience finally learns his name is Albert.

4. One must hear the spirituals to grasp their message; reading their words alone will not suffice. Their message is complex, a series of doubles: double consciousness (context), double bind (story); double voicing (music), and double relatedness (faith and thought). See Kirk-Duggan, *Exorcizing Evil*. Only those invited into the community can fully understand the experience communicated in these songs.

5. Baby Suggs Holy, matriarch, storyteller, priestess, and tribal elder, makes a living with her heart: advising, healing, protecting, loving people into wholeness, and helping them to imagine their own grace, the only grace accessible to them; that community and survival emerge through their bodies amid shared emotional experiences. Love is the antithesis of injustice and the only response to evil.

References

Achtemeier, Elizabeth. 1986. "Nahum-Malachi." In *Interpretation: A Bible Commentary for Teaching and Preaching*. Atlanta: John Knox.

Bellis, Alice Ogden. 2000. "Habakkuk 2:4b: Intertextuality and Hermeneutics." In *Jews, Christians, and the Theology of the Hebrew Scriptures*, ed. Alice Ogden Bellis and Joel S. Kaminsky. Atlanta: Society of Biblical Literature.

Bethune, Mary McLeod. 1954. "Last Will and Testament." http://www.cookman.edu/about_BCU/history/lastwill_testament.html.

Brown, William P. 1996. *Obadiah through Malachi*. Louisville, Ky.: Westminster John Knox.

DeFrantz, Thomas F. 2004. *Dancing Revelations: Alvin Ailey's Embodiment of African American Culture*. New York: Oxford University Press.

Hiebert, Theodore. 1996. "The Book of Habakkuk." In *The New Interpreter's Bible: A Commentary in Twelve Volumes*. Vol. 7. Nashville: Abingdon.

Kirk-Duggan, Cheryl A. 1994. "Gender, Violence, and Transformation in Alice Walker's *The Color Purple*." In *Curing Violence*, ed. Theophus Smith and Mark Wallace, 266–86. Sonoma, Calif.: Polebridge.

———. 1997. *Exorcizing Evil: A Womanist Perspective on the Spirituals*. Maryknoll, N.Y.: Orbis.

———. 2006. *Violence and Theology*. Horizons in Theology. Nashville: Abingdon.

Milligan, Jeffrey Ayala. 1999. "Love, Jazz, and a Sense of the Holy: Conceptualizing the Teacher in Toni Morrison's *Beloved*." http://www.ed.uiuc.edu/eps/PES-Yearbook/1999/milligan_body.asp (accessed June 17, 2007).

Morrison, Toni. 1987. *Beloved*. New York: Knopf.

Pinker, Aron. 2003. "Problems and Solutions of Habakkuk 3:8." *Jewish Bible Quarterly* 31 (1): 3–8.

Sanderson, Judith E. 1992/1998. "Habakkuk." In *Women's Bible Commentary*, ed. Carol A. Newsom and Sharon H. Ringe. Louisville, Ky: Westminster John Knox.

Smith, Ralph L. 1984. *Micah-Malachi*. Word Biblical Commentary. Waco, Tex.: Word.

Ward, Williams Hayes. 1985. "Habakkuk." In *A Critical Exegetical Commentary on Micah, Zephaniah, Nahum, Habakkuk, Obadiah and Joel*, ed. John Merlin Powis Smith, Williams Hayes Ward, and Julius A. Bewer. Edinburgh: T. & T. Clark.

Zwick, Edward. 1989/1998. *Glory*. DVD. Sony Pictures Home Entertainment. ASIN: 080017.

ZEPHANIAH

Dora Rudo Mbuwayesango

ALTHOUGH I TEACH at a historically black seminary in the United States, my reading of the Bible is largely informed by my context of origin, Southern Africa. There are at least two aspects of this socio-historical context that inform my reading of the book of Zephaniah. The first aspect is the ambiguous role of the Bible in Southern Africa, where it has been used as both a book of oppression and a book of liberation. As a book of oppression, the Bible was used as justification by Europeans to colonize Africa. As a book of liberation, the Bible serves as a guide in the search for national identity and sustainability in an ethnically diverse, post-colonial Southern Africa. Both these themes run through the book of Zephaniah.

The words of YHWH in the book fall into three main parts that deal with three interrelated themes: announcement of the Day of YHWH—a day of judgment on Judah primarily for abandoning its God, YHWH (1:2-18); a call for repentance that includes the destruction of foreign nations (2:1—3:13); and an assurance of salvation for a remnant of the Judeans (3:14-20). The overall message is an exclusive one.

Although the book begins with a universal perspective, it presents a view of God that is dangerously exclusive and nationalistic. Zephaniah primarily concerns the chosen people of YHWH in the southern kingdom of Judah, who, according to the prophet, have been corrupted by foreign peoples with different morals and religious practices. The central thrust of the prophecies is that the wrath of YHWH will result in total destruction of the whole earth, followed by establishment of a new world order that guarantees safety, security, and prosperity, but only for the faithful people of

YHWH. The turning point from wrath to restoration for the people of YHWH begins by signaling a reconstitution of the people of Yahweh after judgment. Not only will the people of YHWH have a pure common language characterizing united service to their God, but the new beginning also will involve gathering those who scattered to regions beyond "the rivers of Cush" (3:10).

That the primary, if not the only, concern of the book of Zephaniah is the fate of the chosen people emerges clearly in the section against foreign nations (2:4-15). These foreign nations are in two categories. One category consists of Judah's immediate neighbors: Philistia (2:4-7), Moab, and Ammon (2:8-11). The other category consists of distant imperial powers, Cush (Ethiopia) and Assyria (2:12-15). The fate of all these nations is total destruction. The lack of interest for the well-being of foreign peoples is striking. The destruction of Judah's neighbors and of world empires that threaten the welfare of the chosen nation demonstrates the effect of the concept of divine election on those not elected. The destruction of these nations will result in a new world order that guarantees safety, security, and prosperity for the faithful people of YHWH, but for no one else.

Zephaniah's insistence that the new society he proclaims be exclusive and homogenous is dangerous. Such insistence leads to destruction without regard to the value of the lives of those who may not be seen as "chosen." The dangers of the exclusive perspective, which celebrates or wishes for the destruction of those who do not conform, whether within or without, are seen in such African countries as Rwanda and Sudan, where ethnic cleansing is rampant and the powerless are overrun and destroyed because they do not fit into the desired "norm" of a society. Thus it is important to consider the full implications of prophetic messages before we embrace them.

References

Chidester, David. *Savage Systems: Colonialism and Comparative Religion in Southern Africa*. Studies in Religion and Culture. Charlottesville, Va.: University Press of Virginia, 1996.

Dube, Musa W. *Postcolonial Feminist Interpretation of the Bible*. St. Louis, Mo.: Chalice, 2000.

Floyd, Michael. *Minor Prophets Part 2. The Forms of the Old Testament Literature*. Vol. 12. Grand Rapids, Mich.: Eerdmans, 2000.

Mofokeng, T. "Black Christians, the Bible and Liberation." *Journal of Black Theology* 2 (1988): 34–42.

Mosala, Itumeleng J. *Black Theology in South Africa*. Grand Rapids, Mich.: Eerdmans, 1989.

O'Brien, Julia M. *Nahum, Habakkuk, Zephaniah, Haggai, Zechariah, Malachi*. Nashville: Abingdon, 2004.

Sanneh, Lamin. *Translating the Message: The Missionary Impact on Culture*. Missiology Series, vol. 13. Maryknoll, N.Y.: Orbis, 1989.

Sugirtharajah, R. S. *The Bible and the Third World: Precolonial, Colonial and Postcolonial Encounters*. Cambridge: Cambridge University Press, 2001.

West, Gerald, and Musa W. Dube. *The Bible in Africa: Transactions, Trajectories and Trends*. Leiden: Brill, 2000.

HAGGAI

Kenneth N. Ngwa

Cyrus's edict in 539 b.c.e. that allowed the Judeans in Babylon to start returning home ushered in a sense of freedom from imperial powers as well as hope for restoring the nation. The temple, as a symbol of past religious prestige, now stood to remind the Judeans of the devastation they had endured (2:3). Also, the dominant political powers that threatened small nations still remained in place (2:20-22): a time for a new theology, a theology of reconstruction (Magumba 2002).

Haggai engaged in such a theology during the reign of Darius I (522–486 b.c.e.), urging his audience to work for holistic, community-oriented, postcolonial reconstruction.

NEW THEOLOGICAL LANGUAGE ABOUT THE HOMED AND THE HOMELESS (1:2-15)

The crisis of exile touched directly on the "house of God." Unlike Nathan, who argued that God did not want to be "housed" (2 Samuel 7), and unlike the exilic prophets (such as Ezekiel) who saw visions of God as a mobile deity (Ezekiel 1), Haggai challenged his audience with the image of a God in need of a house. In the reconstruction vision, Haggai saw YHWH in an unacceptable state of homelessness. The people lived in paneled houses, while the house of YHWH lay in ruins (1:4, 9; 2:3). In that community of the homed and the homeless, YHWH became the voice of the homeless, challenging both the religious and political leadership about the futility of an unbalanced reconstruction mentality that relegated the pressing, existential needs of some community members to some distant future. Consonant with the African religious concept of community well-being (Ray 2000), Haggai's vision was one whose sociopolitical and religious ethic was and is rooted in the belief that the community of God's people can never succeed unless all its members have been homed.

BUILDING A COMMUNITY FOR ALL

The image of God as a member of the postexilic community provides theological resources for addressing the needs of many Africans on the continent and those in Diaspora who have been either displaced by natural disasters or dehumanized by human conflict and exploitation, and who can quite adequately be described as the *Les Damnés de la Terre* (*The Wretched of the Earth*, Fanon 1961). First, we have a God that engages God's people in dialogue and persuasion ("Thus says the Lord . . . these people say . . ."; 1:2), not through political and religious commands. Second, God's act of judgment on the people for forgetting the poor, needy, and homeless (2:15-17) suggests that any community that ignores the plight of the homeless lives under divine judgment. Third, God's presence within the community reminds its members of the reality of life that goes beyond the physical and material to the spiritual (2:20-23). Healing and reconstruction must address this three-dimensional aspect of intellectual, socioeconomic, and spiritual needs of the victims of political and economic exploitation.

To read the book of Haggai is to be challenged not just about *what* one believes but also about *how* one believes. A community that addresses the needs of the poor is one that lives under divine blessing and healing and moves toward a better future (2:3-19). In the African context, it is such a community endeavor that will lead to the African Renaissance that has been advocated by a number of African leaders (Ngwa and Ngwa 2006).

References

Fanon, Frantz. 1961. *Les Damnés de la Terre*. Paris: Maspero.

Magumba, J. N. K. 2002. "From Liberation to Reconstruction." In *African Theology Today*, series 1, ed. Emmanuel Katangole, 189–206. Scranton, Pa.: Scranton University Press.

Ngwa, Wilfred, and Lydia Ngwa, eds. 2006. *From Dust to Snow: The African Dream?* Princeton, N.J.: African Ambassador Corp.

Ray, Benjamin C. 2000. *African Religions: Symbol, Ritual, and Community*. 2nd ed. Upper Saddle River, N.J.: Prentice Hall.

ZECHARIAH

Jerome Clayton Ross

THE BOOK named after Zechariah ben Berechiah is listed among the twelve Minor Prophets in the Hebrew Bible. Its superscription (1:1) and endorsement of reconstruction of the Jerusalem temple suggests its origins in conjunction with the book of Haggai (see Hag. 1:1-11). Though both parts (chs. 1–8 and 9–14) are located in the Persian period (Peterson 1984: 20, 109–110; 1995: 3–23), the latter is distinguished from the former by repeated references to future events (for example, "on that day"—12:3, 4, 6, 8 [twice], 9, 11; 13:1, 2, 4; 14:4, 6, 8, 9, 13, 20) and its label, *massa'*, which sections it into two parts (chs. 9–11 and 12–14) that are in sequence with Malachi (see 9:1; 12:1; Mal. 1:1).

The former chapters address Judah's restoration concerns as a Persian province during the early Persian period, serving as an alternative vision of reconstruction to Ezekiel's (see chaps. 40–48)

(Peterson 1984: 1–8, 117–19), while the latter chapters consider a later reconstruction during the Persian period. Thus two different prophets are responsible for the book (the namesake being accredited with chaps. 1–8 and an anonymous disciple with chaps. 9–14), addressing the circumstances in Judah during the Persian period.

THE PERSIAN PERIOD

The Babylonian exile (586–538 B.C.E.) precipitated Jewish colonialism—that is, the dispersion of the Judahite upper class to foreign lands in extensive settlements or colonies and subservience to larger empires' political dominion as well as remnants of the Judahites and Israelites who remained in Palestine (Gottwald 1985: 421f; Ahlström 1993: 799f). These complex double loyalties and jurisdictions that ran at cross-purposes fostered tensions as the exiles struggled to maintain their identity as Yahwists and to satisfy demands of particular overlords, under whose supervision they lived. In response to the Babylonian exile, proponents formulated early Judaism as a survival strategy that enabled southern Yahwists to maintain their identity. Constituting Davidic-Zionistic Yahwism minus a monarchy, the exile provided an international network linking dispersed Yahwists with Yahwists who remained within Palestine.

Judaism's early formation facilitated the emergence of a transcultural religious identity that fixed traditions, customs, and canons. First, the northern kingdom and southern kingdom Yahwistic traditions were collected, compiled, and reinterpreted in light of the exile. These traditions were transformed to address prevailing Judahite circumstances, specifically the exilic catastrophe. Believers interpreted the exile as fulfilling prophetic messages, which declared YHWH's imminent punishment for repeated disloyalty to the Yahwistic standards (Noth 1958: 296f; Soggin 1993: 266f) (see also Ezekiel 8–11; Jeremiah 23–24).

Explaining the cause for their exile depicting YHWH's departure from Judah for idolatry, Ezekiel argued that ideological contamination and constitutional violation caused the southern kingdom's downfall. The people compromised Yahwistic standards, prompting the Babylonians to destroy the land, deport inhabitants, and suggest the Judahite's best option for survival was to accept Babylonian colonization by establishing Yahwistic colonies (see Ezek. 8:3, 7, 14, 16; 43:1-2; 48:35 passim). Disciples collected and compiled prophetic messages. This process included sequencing and editing messages appropriated for use by later generations (Westermann 1967: 205–10). Compilation involved redacting messages so they reflected a continuum from unconditional judgment to conditional calls to repentance and later, during the end of the exile, developing oracles of salvation and

blessings as new circumstances arose. Collaborators/redactors wrote the Deuteronomistic History (DH) during this time, presenting an apologetic theodicy to defend YHWH's justness/justice and to explain the exile as resulting from violation of Torah and covenant, as expressed in their constitutional standards. More about the DH may be learned in the article elsewhere in this volume (pp. 112–14); here it is sufficient to note that the school of scribes and prophets responsible for its production wielded considerable theological and religious power.

Early Judaism as a survival strategy was concretized during the Persian period at the hands of the Persian administration. In 540 B.C.E., after attacking Babylonia, Cyrus recruited exiled Judahites who had assimilated into Babylonian society—possibly following the prophet Jeremiah's advice in Jeremiah 24–25, 27–29, and 37–38—for his mission in Judah. In 539 B.C.E., Cyrus emerged as king of Anshan and defeated the Babylonian army at Opis, ending Babylonian rule and officially beginning widespread Persian rule (Ahlström 1993: 814–16; Soggin 1993: 276; Purvis 1988: 165). Cyrus introduced a new policy for the subject peoples, which allowed them to return to their homelands, repair their temples, and keep their cultic traditions, specifically some of the *gôlah* party or exiled Judahites. This policy facilitated peaceful and compliant relations among subject peoples, diminishing unrest and revolt, spawning economic growth and development, and solidifying Cyrus's political and military positions. In his concern to secure his border against Egypt, Judah became a target area for reconstruction, since the Babylonian conquest had severely weakened it socioeconomically, destroying and depopulating major sites. Internally, Judah was disorganized, reflecting identity loss and land rights loss due to uncontrolled syncretism as men married foreign women (see Neh. 10:30; 13:23-24; Ezra 9–10; Mal. 2:10-16); unregulated market practices, such as selling on Shabbat (Neh. 10:31; 13:15-18); neglected jubilee practices, such as seventh-year land rest (Neh. 10:31); neglected caring for Levites and the sanctuary (Hag. 1:1-11; Mal. 2:4-9; Neh. 10:32-39; 13:10); sanctuary and offerings abuse/misuse (Mal. 1:1-14; 3:6-12; Neh. 13:4-5); and infidelity among priests (Mal. 2:13-17).

The Davidic monarchy's end caused these features, as it had provided economic and political structure, including royal officials and the temple. Rivalry among leaders who remained in the land (particularly priests) developed in the absence of a politically endorsed community ideology and the Judahite population's increased de-urbanization, which included land loss, weakened socioeconomics, and conflict between those who remained in the land and the exiles, conditions reflected in Ezra and Nehemiah. In response to structural deficiencies, Cyrus's policy to establish local autonomy for political stability and military security effected through repopulation of devastated areas; to endorse cults and ideologies of deportees from targeted areas; and to redevelop key sites (Peterson 1984: 19–23) became the agenda for several Persian-authorized, exilic descendants who returned to Judah.

Yahwists who remained in the land (that is, Judahites as well as Israelites and Samaritans) were the main hindrances to these agendas as they were reluctant to embrace the returning *gôlah* party. The nonexiled Yahwists perceived the *gôlah* party as a threat. Returnees represented both remnants of the Davidic regime and a new phase of subjugation under the Persians. Essentially, property rights—which included rights over women, as Washington observed (Washington 1994: 234–38)—and political control fueled differences between the two groups. The property struggle regarding women necessitated prohibiting exogamous marriages and promoting genealogical reckoning as "ideologies of descent." Conflict between the groups necessitated a delay in the temple's reconstruction as the Judean province's administrative center and overlord enforced the Persian "restoration" policy. Thus the book of Zechariah presupposes efforts in 538 B.C.E. by Sheshbazzar and in 520 B.C.E. by Zerubbabel.

HERMENEUTICAL LENS FOR READING ZECHARIAH

A hermeneutic properly labeled *contextualization under the auspices of minority sensitivity* is appropriate. I propose "minority sensitivity" as opposed to Afrocentricity and color consciousness, discarding the category of "race" as a superimposition upon biblical interpretation by those who are racists—blatant or recovering—and dismissing it as a postbiblical, Eurocentric, and North American–appropriated construct, foreign to biblical times. The prevalence and dominance of Egypt in ancient times have been well documented in biblical research, though such research has not been appropriately appreciated by those who garner ethnic or racial propensities (see Felder 1991; Bailey 2003; and Brown 2004).

My contextualization consists of three main steps. The first phase of contextualization is historical reconstruction. Reconstruction employs liberal arts education—social sciences, humanities, and natural sciences in concert—providing reconstructions that render appropriate historical contexts and realistic cultural circumstances, in which to read or listen to the Bible; and character sketches of real persons behind the texts.

The second phase envisions texts within some sociopolitical contexts. The Bible reflects internal diversity, so to decode biblical theology, biblical statements must be read as minorities' positions within a minority within diverse reconstructed contexts. Since minorities all mostly lived under circumstances that were not completely within their control, they had to confront and navigate political circumstances and cultures that were offensive toward survival—the normal desire to be free.

The third phase is minority sensitivity and employs principles for survival as the "Rosetta Stones" for understanding their history and statements. Those principles require the literature genre, for reading realistically, creating the concept and what the concept is (for example, who advocates some agenda within the Yahwistic leadership or international superpowers); and rhetorical strategies of the work to determine its agenda and intent—that is, targeting requirements for survival, using imagination that logically derives from critical research and data (Vaughn 2004: 368–85). Vaughn holds that a theologically useful Israelite history can be written by incorporating negative history (that is, the scientific endeavor sets boundaries on interpretation and provides corrective lenses for misinterpretation) and positive history (that is, understanding and experiencing texts as narrative) via imagination—the mental capacity to integrate disparate pieces of data into comprehensible "snapshots" (Vaughn 2004: 368–69, 376–81, 384).

Archaeology serves a threefold purpose: to detect discrepancies between biblical narratives and archaeological data; to determine consistency/inconsistency between descriptions in the Bible and archaeological data; and to provide reliable data for increasing our imaginary capacity to engage biblical narrative worlds (Vaughn 2004: 373, 381, 383). The goal is to "hear the text in context." Who spoke it? Who wrote it? To whom was it spoken? To whom was it written? For whom was it spoken? For whom was it written? When was it spoken? When was it written? Where was it spoken? Where was it written? What is it addressing? How is it presented? Why is it presented? These questions lead us to understand the Hebrew Bible as the ancient Yahwists' oral or written conversations probably occurring in their various, original sociopolitical situations: sociopolitical propaganda aligned with Persian-imperialistic aims who sought to reestablish the Judahite community in Judah centered around the Jerusalem temple cultus over against prevalent forms of Yahwism. This strategy for survival evolved as early Judaism—Davidic-Zionistic Yahwism minus a Yahwistic monarchy. The following discussions briefly summarize the salient points of the prophet.

ZECHARIAH 1–8

This part of the book consists of an introduction (1:1-6), a series of vision reports accompanied by oracular responses to explain different aspects of the visions (1:7—6:15), and a concluding section that contains prophetic speeches (7:1—8:23). The overtones of the discussions are theological; the undertones are sociopolitical since vision reports and oracles are predominant genres employed to address survival requirements (Peterson 1984: 110, 124) and reflect propaganda that advocated the Persian administration's agenda for Judah.

In Zechariah 1–8, YHWH was displeased with the ancestors, including prophets who were exiled (1:2, 4-5). This displeasure constituted grounds for exile and the basis for repentance (1:3-4) for those returned from and those who did not go into exile. Repentance signifies return to compliance with community standards expressed as the "words and statutes of YHWH" (1:6). The prophet's effort is directed toward Davidic-Zionistic Yahwism—that is, ideological standardization, particularly amid competing Yahwistic claims.

In the first section, Zechariah conveys various visions that reflect a spectrum of concerns and uses metaphors from several walks of life, such as military ("horse riders," 1:7-17), builders ("measuring lines"), and a courtroom scene that cleanses the high priest and rebukes Satan (3:1-10). The section includes metaphoric language of lamp stands, bowls, seven lamps, and olive trees, which represents YHWH's surveillance over the process of appointing leaders and laying the temple's foundation (4:1-13), and a flying scroll, signifying a worldwide curse (5:3-4) that connotes judgment of covenant violators as Judean society will be ordered again according to tenets of Davidic-Zionistic Yahwism (see 7:9-10; 8:16-17). Next, a vision occurs where Wickedness, represented by a woman, is removed from society by justice, symbolized by two women who remove Wickedness (probably to Babylon) so that Judah is ready for YHWH's presence. The final vision shows four horse-drawn chariots who pass between bronze mountains and survey the earth as sentries (6:1-3). The spirit of YHWH, however, blows only over the north, signifies YHWH's approval, and authorizes returnees to build the temple (6:8, 10, 12-15). The concluding oracles (chaps. 7-8) summarize themes the prophet presented in the previous sections.

ZECHARIAH 9–14

The second part of Zechariah (chaps. 9–14) addresses concerns similar to earlier chapters. This writer shows concerns about militarization, commercialization, ruralization, and collectivization (Peterson 1995: 19-20; Hoglund 1991: 54–71). These issues respectively betray efforts to fulfill specific requirements for survival: administrative structure, economic independence, land, assimilation, and population. References to Sûccôth as a prominent festival (14:16, 19), to future events (such as, "on that day"—12:3, 4, 6, 8 [twice], passim), and to the label *massa'*, in sequence with Malachi (see 9:1; 12:1; Mal. 1:1) (Peterson 1995: 24–25, 29), suggest a time closer and prior to the drafting of Ezra-Nehemiah (Ross 1997: 116–18).

Zechariah 9–14 has two parts marked off the label *massa'* (9:1; 12:1): chapters 9–11 and chapters 12–14, mainly of oracles of judgment and salvation. The first section generally focuses on administration (that is, the leadership) and counters a sense of vulnerability that ensued from the devastation of Judah. In 9:1-8, the writer announces judgment on foreign nations that had dominated Judah, while in 9:9-13 the writer expresses YHWH's preference for and elevation of Zion and Judah. Predictions of deliverance are interspersed within these two passages, which reflect YHWH's protection of Judah, specifically Zion (9:7-8, 14-17). Administrative restructuring happens by military mobilization (10:3-6), whereby the land is reclaimed (10:9, 10) and repopulated (10:8-10), and the constitutional

identity (ideology) of the people as YHWH's is re-embraced (10:5, 6, 9, 12).

In the second section (12–14), YHWH fights for and delivers Judah with plague and panic, thereby militarily and economically securing Jerusalem and the remnant therein. In 12:1-14, special attention is given to people and place. YHWH restores the "house of David" as "governors" (12:5, 6, 7, 8, 10, 12, 13) with the Levites as priests (12:13) in conjunction with securing Jerusalem and Judah (12:2, 3, 4, 6, 7, 9, 11, 12), a reversal of fortunes for the Davidides—that is, the third- or fourth-generation descendants of the Davidic regime. In 13:1-9, the prophetic book pictures administrative overhaul to include competing ideologies' eradication and their proponents' execution as "scattering" (13:7) and "refining" (13:9) that secures a remnant of the people (13:8).

SUMMARY

Throughout these discussions, the prophet (or prophets) employs several major themes: YHWH's universal sovereignty; the exile as punishment by YHWH for covenant (constitutional) violations; Persian Judean restoration mission as the second exodus; and Jerusalem as YHWH's designated preference for an administrative center and place for inhabitation or indwelling. Zechariah joins a host of exilic and postexilic prophets who promote Persian policies as the best option for surviving the exile, though not without opposition (see Isa. 56:1; 58:2, 5-9). Thus, the book of Zechariah (and others) reflects establishment views—those who won out or had clout to enforce their policies. However, in doing so, they did not eliminate diversity, and they unintentionally provided a context where Yahwistic pluralism survived—particularly underground movements that perpetuated the antihierarchical aspects of Yahwism, especially since religious power brokers could not coerce adherence in outlying areas (Peterson 1995: 22f; see also Zevit 2001: 254, 265, 621, 643, 688).

References

Ahlström, Gösta. 1993. *The History of Ancient Palestine from the Palaeolithic Period to Alexander's Conquest.* Journal for the Study of the Old Testament: Supplement Series 146, ed. Diana Edelman. Sheffield: JSOT.

Bailey, Randall C. 2003. *Yet with a Steady Beat: Contemporary U.S. Afrocentric Biblical Interpretation.* Semeia Studies. Atlanta: Society of Biblical Literature.

Barth, F., ed. 1969. *Ethnic Groups and Boundaries: The Social Organization of Culture Difference.* Boston: Little, Brown.

Brown, Michael. 2004. *Blackening of the Bible: The Aim of African American Biblical Scholarship.* Harrisburg, Pa.: Trinity.

Carter, Charles E. 1994. "The Province of Yehud in the Post-Exilic Period: Soundings in Site Distribution and Demography." In *Second Temple Studies 2: Temple and Community in the Persian Period*, ed. Tamara C. Eskenazi and Kent H. Richards. Journal for the Study of the Old Testament: Supplement Series 175. Sheffield: JSOT.

Coote, Robert B., and David Robert Ord. 1991. *In the Beginning: Creation and the Priestly History.* Minneapolis: Fortress Press.

De Roche, Michael. 1983. "Yahweh's *Rib* against Israel: A Reassessment of the So-Called "Prophetic Lawsuit" in the Preexilic Prophets." *Journal of Biblical Literature* 102:563–74.

Douglas, Mary. 1975. "Deciphering a Meal." In *Implicit Meanings*, 249–75. London: Routledge and Kegan Paul.

———. 1993. "The Forbidden Animals in Leviticus." *Journal for the Study of the Old Testament* 59:3–23.

———. 1999. *Leviticus as Literature.* Oxford: Oxford University Press.

———. 2005. *Purity and Danger: An Analysis of Concepts of Pollution and Taboo.* London: Routledge and Kegan Paul.

Eskenazi, Tamara C., and Eleanore P. Judd. 1994. "Marriage to a Stranger in Ezra 9–10." In *Second Temple Studies 2: Temple and Community in the Persian Period*, ed. Tamara C. Eskenazi and Kent H. Richards, 266–85. Journal for the Study of the Old Testament: Supplement Series 175. Sheffield: JSOT.

Felder, Cain Hope, ed. 1991. *Stony the Road We Trod: African American Biblical Interpretation.* Minneapolis: Augsburg Fortress.

Gammie, John G. 1989. *Holiness in Israel.* Overtures to Biblical Theology. Minneapolis: Fortress Press.

Glazier-McDonald, Beth. 1987. "Intermarriage, Divorce, and the *Bat-'El Nekar*: Insights into Mal. 2:10-16." *Journal of Biblical Literature* 106:603–11.

Gottwald, Norman K. 1985. *The Hebrew Bible: A Socio-Literary Introduction.* Philadelphia: Fortress Press.

Hoglund, Kenneth. 1991. "The Achaemenid Context." In *Second Temple Studies 1: Persian Period*, ed. Philip R. Davies, 54–71. Journal for the Study of the Old Testament: Supplement Series 117. Sheffield: JSOT.

Koch, Klaus. 1978. *The Prophets: Volume One. The Assyrian Period.* Tr. Margaret Kohl. Philadelphia: Fortress Press.

Levine, Lee I. 1996. "The Nature and Origin of the Palestinian Synagogue Reconsidered." *Journal of Biblical Literature* 115:425–48.

Milgrom, Jacob. 1991. *Leviticus 1–16.* AB Commentary 3. New York: Doubleday.

Noth, Martin. 1958. *The History of Israel.* 3rd ed. Tr. Peter R. Ackroyd. New York: Harper and Row.

Oden, R. A. 1987. "Religious Identity and the Sacred Prostitution Accusation." In *The Bible without Theology: The Theological Tradition and Alternatives to It*, 131–53. San Francisco: Harper and Row.

Peterson, David L. 1984. *Haggai and Zechariah 1–8: A Commentary.* Old Testament Library Series. Philadelphia: Westminster.

———. 1995. *Zechariah 9–14 and Malachi: A Commentary.* Old Testament Library Series. Louisville, Ky.: Westminster John Knox.

Purvis, James D. 1988. "Exile and Return." In *Ancient Israel: A Short History from Abraham to the Roman Destruction of the Temple*, ed. Hershel Shanks, 156–65. Washington, D.C.: Biblical Archaeology Society; Englewood Cliffs, N.J.: Prentice Hall.

Soggin, Alberto. 1993. *An Introduction to the History of Israel and Judah.* Tr. John Bowden. Valley Forge, Pa: Trinity International.

Ross, Jerome C. 1997. *The Composition of the Holiness Code (Lev. 17–26)*. PhD diss., University of Pittsburgh; Ann Arbor: University of Michigan.

Smith-Christopher, Daniel. 1994. "The Mixed Marriage Crisis in Ezra 9–10 and Nehemiah 13: A Study of the Sociology of Post-Exilic Judaean Community." In *Second Temple Studies 2: Temple and Community in the Persian Period*, ed. Tamara C. Eskenazi and Kent H. Richards, 243–65. Journal for the Study of the Old Testament: Supplement Series 175. Sheffield: JSOT.

Talmon, Shemaryahu. 1987. "The Emergence of Jewish Sectarianism in the Early Second Temple Period." In *Ancient Israelite Religion*, ed. Patrick D. Miller Jr., Paul D. Hanson, and S. Dean McBride. Philadelphia: Fortress Press.

Vaughn, Andrew G. 2004. "Can We Write a History of Israel Today?" In *The Future of Biblical Archaeology: Reassessing Methodologies and Assumptions*, ed. James K. Hoffmeier and Alan Millard, 368–85. Grand Rapids, Mich.: Eerdmans.

von Rad, Gerhard. 1962/1965. *The Message of the Prophets*. New York: Harper and Row.

Washington, Harold C. 1994. "The Strange Women of Proverbs 1–9 and Post-Exilic Judean Society." In *Second Temple Studies 2: Temple and Community in the Persian Period*, ed. Tamara C. Eskenazi and Kent H. Richards, 217–42. Journal for the Study of the Old Testament: Supplement Series 175. Sheffield: JSOT.

Westermann, Claus. 1967. *Basic Forms of Prophetic Speech*. Tr. Hugh Clayton White. Philadelphia: Westminster.

Zevit, Ziony. 2001. *The Religions of Ancient Israel: A Synthesis of Parallactic Approaches*. New York: Continuum, 254, 265, 621, 643, 688.

MALACHI

Stacy Davis

Growing up Pentecostal, I became accustomed to hearing the recitation of Mal. 3:8-10 right before it was time to pass the offering plate. It was the only Malachi passage I remember being used. The entire book, however, is a rhetorical critic's delight—a witty dialogue between God and God's disgruntled people, struggling to rebuild their lives after the exile of 586 b.c.e., written from a priestly perspective. God and the people argue about proper sacrifices (1:6-14), appropriate priestly behavior (2:1-9), divorce (2:10-16), and preparing for the last judgment (3:13—4:6), with God always having the last word about the importance of obedience and justice. True to my own upbringing, however, this article focuses on the rhetorical exchange about tithing and how the prosperity gospel's argument that faithful tithing to God guarantees wealth (Coleman 1995: 161) distorts the biblical text.

God calls the people robbers because they do not give their "tithes and offerings" (3:8 nrsv). In the Torah, the discipline of tithing helps the poor and ensures that the Levites, God's chosen servants, can fulfill their obligations without worrying about money (Num. 18:21-24; Deut. 14:22-29). According to Mal. 3:10-11 and Deut. 14:29, those who tithe will receive a blessing. In Malachi, the specific blessing is fertile farmland. In African American prosperity theology, the reward is guaranteed freedom from debt (Atlanta-based pastor Creflo Dollar), a hundredfold return on your financial investment if you tithe from your *gross* income (Jakes 2000: 57, 66, 73–74), and/or the assurance that God wants the giver to be rich and to flaunt her or his wealth (Kim 1996: 19). In West Africa, some Pentecostal ministers have berated followers who place only coins in the offering plate (Hackett 1995: 202).

Although African spiritual traditions have long believed that religion should help one to live the good life (Hackett 1995: 208; Nwankwo 2002: 61), the good life should not be defined solely by wealth. Such a definition excludes those who give their tithes faithfully yet remain in poverty. Christians who advocate for the prosperity gospel, those who claim a divine quid pro quo between tithing and wealth, reduce the "overflowing blessing" of Mal. 3:10 to monetary gain. The most literal reading of Mal. 3:12, however, does not promise great wealth—only that "all nations will count you happy, for you will be a land of delight, says the LORD of hosts." The biblical view of tithing offers not the guarantee of individual financial abundance but, rather, the promise that the basic need for food will be met (Mal. 3:11) and the hope of shared blessing, the hope that in giving to others we all will be satisfied (Deut. 14:26, 29).

References

Ayegboyin, Deji. 2006. "A Rethinking of Prosperity Teaching in the New Pentecostal Churches in Nigeria." *Black Theology* 4 (1): 70–86.

Coleman, Simon M. 1995. "America Loves Sweden: Prosperity theology and the cultures of capitalism." In *Religion and the Transformations of Capitalism: Comparative approaches*, ed. Richard H. Roberts, 161–79. London: Routledge.

Dollar, Creflo A. 2000. *No More Debt! God's Strategy for Debt Cancellation*. College Park, Ga.: Creflo Dollar Ministries.

Hackett, Rosalind I. J. 1995. "The Gospel of Prosperity in West Africa." In *Religion and the Transformations of Capitalism: Comparative approaches*, ed. Richard H. Roberts, 199–214. London: Routledge.

Kim, Sang-Bok Davis. 1996. "Bed of Roses or a Bed of Thorns." *Evangelical Review of Theology* 20, 1: 14–25.

Jakes, T. D. 2000. *The Great Investment: Balancing Faith, Family, and Finance to Build a Rich Spiritual Life*. New York: Berkeley.

Nwankwo, Lawrence Nchekwube. 2002. "'You have received the Spirit of power . . .' (2 Tim 1:7): Reviewing the Prosperity Message in the Light of a Theology of Empowerment." *Journal of the European Pentecostal Theological Association* 22:56–77.

AFRICA AND THE AFRICAN DIASPORA

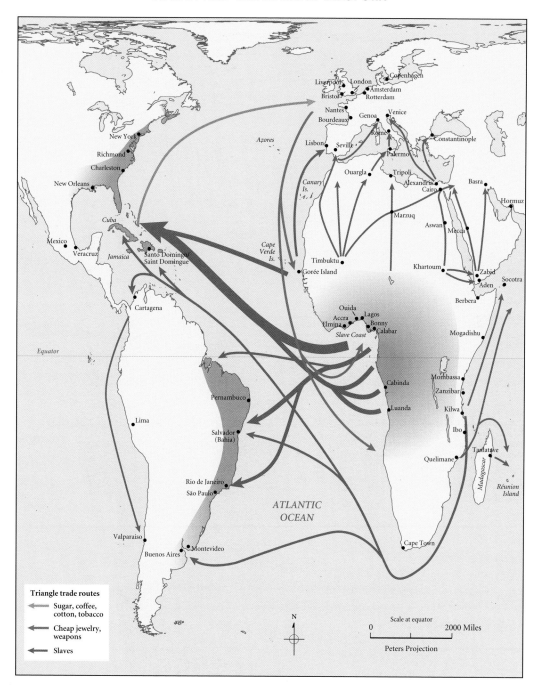

Fig. 1 The African Diaspora is in large part the result of the slave trade in which European and American powers forcibly transplanted Africans, overwhelmingly to the Americas, as slaves. As significant as the collective trauma experienced by those generations of Africans and their descendants is the resiliency that allowed them to preserve and pass on cultural traditions even as they adapted aspects of Euro-American Christian and other cultures and made them their own.

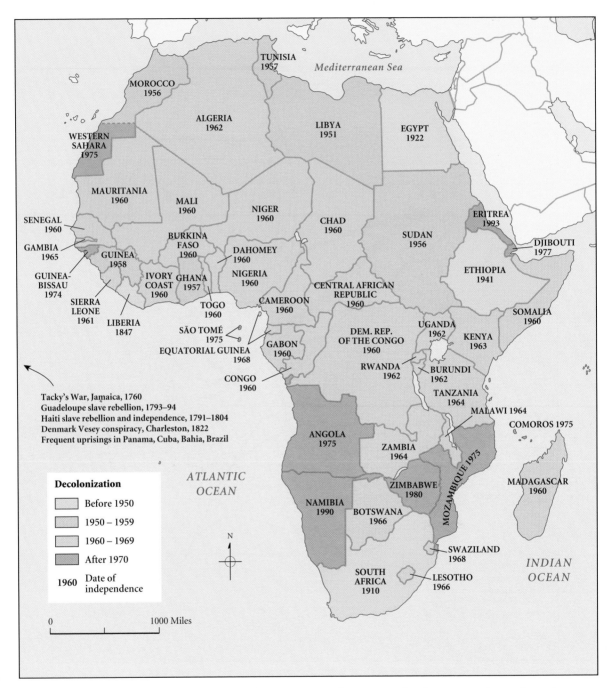

Fig. 2 The Africana world today consists of many nations that, except for the spectacular eighteenth-century wars of independence in Haiti and the rest of the Caribbean, have only in the last century won freedom from colonialism and only in recent decades from legal racism (in the United States) and apartheid (in South Africa). Many of these nations continue to struggle under the neocolonialism of neoliberal economic policies.

The Poetics of Daily Life and Made Things
A Gallery of Images from Ancient Israel and the Africana World
Hugh R. Page Jr.

WE UNDERSTAND THE LIFE AND FAITH of peoples past and present through made things. Such artifacts shed light on what might be termed the "poetics of daily life." Among the more important of these made things are visual images such as sculptures, figurines, paintings, and photographs. Through such artifacts, we are able to experience, however imperfectly, the daily lives of ordinary folk. We hear their concerns and questions echoed in the words they write and the things they craft by hand.

This is a case in a world in which Israel's scriptures took shape. The material cultures of ancient Israel, Lebanon, Syria, Palestine, Jordan, Iraq, and Egypt are well attested in the archeological record. These artifacts help flesh out the skeletal information provided in the First Testament itself. The same is true for the Africana cultures wherein many of Israel's sacred writings have been, and continue to be, read. The entries in this book offer insight into the ways the literature, music, folklore, and lived experience of peoples on the continent of Africa and those living in Diaspora throughout the world have encountered and been in conversation with those writings.

The images in this gallery come from two worlds: the ancient milieu in which the Hebrew Bible, the Apocrypha, and various pseudepigraphic writings were written and the Africana world within which those writings were read, prayed, interpreted, adapted, challenged, and—at times—intentionally overlooked. This assemblage is representative as opposed to comprehensive, suggestive rather than definitive. It speaks to the complex interrelationship of domains of cultural knowledge (for example, religion, politics, technology, and family) and the "texts," understood expansively, that embody them. It points to intersections between ancient Near Eastern material cultures, Israel's scriptures, and Africana life.

Attentiveness to such information, whether archaic or modern, is absolutely vital. In their study of ancient Israel's iconography, Keel and Uehlinger rightly urge that "anyone who systematically ignores the pictorial evidence that a culture has produced can hardly expect to recreate even a minimally adequate description of the culture itself" (1998: xi). The same is true for Africana life, the rhythms and seasons of which are captured in an assortment of artistic genres. These represent, in the words of Richard Powell, "the things that significant numbers of black people do" (2003: 15). Although Powell is speaking especially of "black diasporal culture" and the artistic modes that have emerged from it as "alternative to mainstream counterparts" (2003: 15), his description of the agents involved—is equally true of the whole of the Africana world. These agents are "the women, men, and children of African descent who because of the transatlantic slave trade, European colonialism, Western imperialism, and racism are globally dispersed, culturally hybrid, and narratively

engaged in multilingual, Pan-African polemics with each other and with the world-at-large" (16). The factors Powell names have suffused the entirety of the Africana world, not just the diaspora, with hybridity and engendered a kind of global "polemics." The effects are evident in visual representations as well as in literature.

Therefore, aged figurines, shrines, and sacred writings; reliefs, sculptures, and paintings; illuminated manuscripts; quilts and stylized personal items; Blues art and Psalm-derived intercessions inscribed on parchment and placed under "dressed" candles: such things are "poems" speaking to those with "a heart to understand, eyes to perceive, and ears to discern" (Deuteronomy 29:4) an unfolding mystery. They also constitute a poetics of made things and everyday existence—a Diasporan *mélange* at once Ancestral, biblical, Africana, and profoundly human. ◼

Fig. 3 "Build houses and live in them; plant gardens and eat what they produce" (Jer. 29:5). A man tends to a small plant beneath a palm tree in a relief from ancient Mari, Syria (early dynastic period, 3000–2685 B.C.E.). National Museum, Damascus. Photo: Erich Lessing/Art Resource, N.Y.

Figs. 4–6 Personal artifacts such as these portraits of ancient Israelites offer a vital connection with other cultures. From above left: Man's head, found in a sanctuary from ancient Ashdod, Israel; Israel Museum, Jerusalem. A woman wears a diadem of pearls and two rows of pearls around her neck, from the region of Hebron (ivory, Late Iron Age II; Reuben & Edith Hecht Collection, Haifa University). A woman wears an Egyptian hairstyle from ancient Gaza, 1550–1200 B.C.E (Late Bronze/Early Iron Age; Reuben & Edith Hecht Collection, Haifa University). All photos: Erich Lessing/Art Resource, N.Y.

Fig. 7 A woman's face carved in ivory. Phoenician, ninth–eighth century B.C.E. 11 x 8.85 cm; British Museum, London. Photo: Trustees of the British Museum/Art Resource, N.Y.

Fig. 8 Comb (wood, 336 mm), from a village of the Djuka maroons on the Tapanahoni River, Surinam, collected in the 1920s. Photo: Denis Finnin; American Museum of Natural History Library.

Fig. 9 A small domestic shrine, the model of a temple with two pillars with voluted capitals, probably dating from the beginning of the Israelite monarchy; from Megiddo. Clay; Israel Museum (IDAM), Jerusalem. Photo: Erich Lessing/Art Resource, N.Y.

Fig. 10 Not surprisingly, many of the artifacts from ancienet Israel bore apparent religious significance. These figurines represent women playing a tambourine and an aulos, instruments associated with worship. Clay; around 800 B.C.E. Israel Museum (IDAM), Jerusalem. Photo: Erich Lessing/Art Resource, N.Y.

Fig. 11 *Blue Repertory.* Africana, Christian, Jewish, Native American, and European religious traditions converge in African American *conjure.* In this cultural amalgamation, Scripture, the Psalms in particular, plays an important role. This painting evokes several of the streams feeding this tradition: a small green felt amulet bag known as a "hand," *toby,* or *mojo,* among whose contents may be handwritten passages of Scripture; a chaplet with gold cross and white beads, representing Christian influence; and a red seven-day candle that may be set as a light upon a written petition and/or used in a psalm-based ritual. Painting by Hugh R. Page Jr.

Fig. 12 The miniature replica of Michelangelo's sculpture of Moses on the left provides an interesting contrast to the "Moses, Giver of the Law" vigil light on the right (© 2004, Lucky Mojo Curio Company). The latter presumes that Moses is a celestial intercessor to whom votaries can appeal. It has been "dressed," that is, treated with special natural ingredients. A label on the back offers a biography of the great liberator as well as directions for securing his aid: write one's name nine times on a sheet of paper, place the paper under the lit candle, and offer a personal prayer. Sculpture and candle from the personal collection of Hugh and Jacquetta E. Page.

Fig. 13 *Faith Tonic.*
Passages from the First and
Second Testaments are proposed as Scriptural medicinals
for health and wholeness in
this painting, on display at
the House of Blues in New
Orleans (photograph by
Hugh R. Page Jr., January
2007).

Fig. 14 The furnishings of a Canaanite shrine with
steles, from ancient Hazor. Basalt. :Israel Museum (IDAM),
Jerusalem. Photo: Erich Lessing/Art Resource, N.Y.

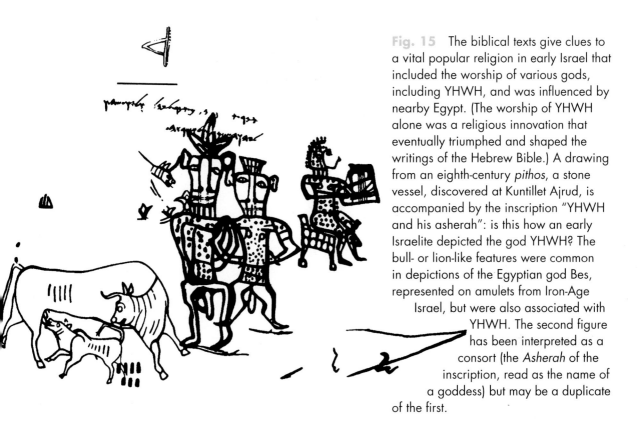

Fig. 15 The biblical texts give clues to a vital popular religion in early Israel that included the worship of various gods, including YHWH, and was influenced by nearby Egypt. (The worship of YHWH alone was a religious innovation that eventually triumphed and shaped the writings of the Hebrew Bible.) A drawing from an eighth-century *pithos*, a stone vessel, discovered at Kuntillet Ajrud, is accompanied by the inscription "YHWH and his asherah": is this how an early Israelite depicted the god YHWH? The bull- or lion-like features were common in depictions of the Egyptian god Bes, represented on amulets from Iron-Age Israel, but were also associated with YHWH. The second figure has been interpreted as a consort (the *Asherah* of the inscription, read as the name of a goddess) but may be a duplicate of the first.

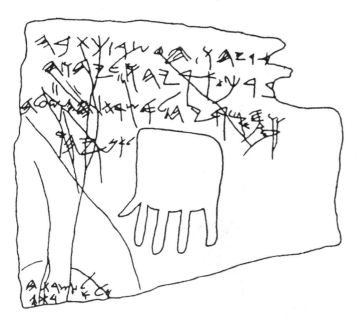

Fig. 16 Another inscription, scratched in a tomb at Khirbet el-Qom, depicts a hand reaching down (in blessing or protection?); the inscription reads, in part, "Uriyahu, the honorable, has written [this] . . . Blessed is/be Uriyahu by Yahweh / And . . . from his oppressors, by his *asherah*, he has saved him. . . ." The inscription has been taken as evidence that YHWH's *asherah* was a cult object, probably a tree, associated with divine blessing. See Othmar Keel and Christop Uehlinger, *Gods, Goddesses, and Images of God in Ancient Israel* (trans. Thomas H. Trapp; Minneapolis: Fortress, 1998), 210–48.

Fig. 17 The artifacts of empire confirm the power and influence of Egypt on Israel's horizon. The earliest impulses to monotheism came from the innovations of the Pharaoh Akhenaton, here depicted offering sacrifice to Aton, the sun god, with his family. Stone relief from Amarna, Egypt, ca. 1350 B.C.E.; 105 x 50 cm. Egyptian Museum, Cairo. Photo: Erich Lessing /Art Resource, N.Y.

Fig. 18 (left) Egypt was one of the earliest sources of writing and the profession of the scribe was one of prestige in any royal court. Here one of the ministers of King Amenhotep III is depicted honorifically as a scribe. New Kingdom, 18th Dynasty (1390-1352 B.C.E.) Egyptian Museum, Cairo. Photo: Werner Forman/Art Resource, N.Y.

Fig. 19 (left) Cleopatra of Egypt, clearly depicted with African features in a Ptolemaic relief from the first century B.C.E. In contrast, Hellenistic and Roman sculptures usually represented her in Hellenistic style and with European features. Private collection; photo: Werner Forman/Art Resource, N.Y.

Figs. 20 and 21 (left/right) African American artist Edmonia Lewis depicted *The Death of Cleopatra* (1876) and *Hagar* (1869) in classical style. Lewis identified with Hagar, an Egyptian woman cast into the wilderness after bearing Abraham's child; artists have often fixed on Hagar as a symbol of African-American slavery. (*Death of Cleopatra*: marble, 63 x 31-1/44 x 46"; gift of the Historical Society of Forest Park, Illinois; location: Smithsonian American Art Museum, Washington, D.C. *Hagar*: marble, 133.6 x 38.73 x 43.18 cm. Smithsonian American Art Museum, Washington, D.C. Prejudice regarding African features influenced the English translation of Song of Solomon 1:5 ("I am black but comely," KJV) until 1993, when the NRSV translated "I am black and beautiful." In the 1930s Earl R. Sweeting painted his portrait of the *Wife of King Solomon: An Egyptian Lady* (not shown) as a Black woman.

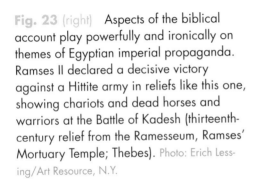

Fig. 22 (left)   At the core of the Hebrew Bible is the Exodus, YHWH's mighty deliverance of "a mixed multitude" of slaves from Egypt; likely from the dynasty of Ramses (depicted here in a monumental portrait from the Valley of the Kings). Photo: public domain.

Fig. 23 (right)   Aspects of the biblical account play powerfully and ironically on themes of Egyptian imperial propaganda. Ramses II declared a decisive victory against a Hittite army in reliefs like this one, showing chariots and dead horses and warriors at the Battle of Kadesh (thirteenth-century relief from the Ramesseum, Ramses' Mortuary Temple; Thebes). Photo: Erich Lessing/Art Resource, N.Y.

Fig. 24 Exodus recounts Moses' birth to a Hebrew slave woman, her hiding him along the banks of the Nile to protect him from the evil Pharaoh, the baby's discovery by the daughter of Pharaoh, and her taking the boy into the Pharaoh's palace to be raised within the Egyptian court—only to turn against Pharaoh and deliver the Hebrew slaves from bondage by the miraculous power of YHWH, who sends plagues that defile and destroy all that is sacred and powerful in Egypt. At various points this account parodies aspects of Egyptian royal mythology, according to which Horus, the god who protects the Pharaoh, was found along the banks of the Nile by the goddess Isis (pictured here nursing Horus in a painting from an Egyptian tomb). After the death of Osiris, Isis' consort, he becomes lord of the underworld and judge of the dead; Horus succeeds him—a mythical representation of the continuity of the Egyptian dynasty. In Exodus, the tenth plague strikes down all the first-born of Egypt—including the son and heir apparent of Pharaoh himself. Based on a drawing by E. A. Budge.

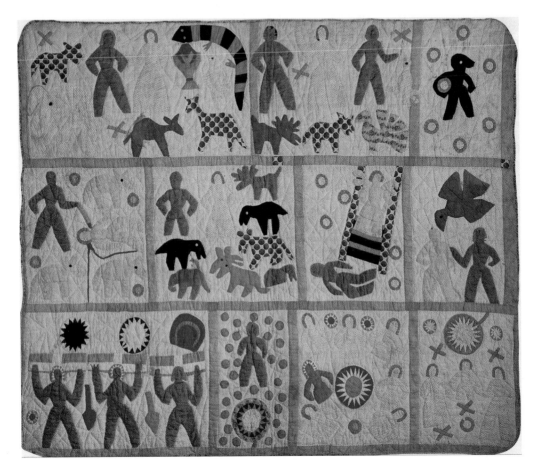

Fig. 25 African American art has long shown a fascination with biblical themes. Raised as a slave, Harriet Powers wove biblical stories into her quilts, now recognized as some of the best preserved examples of the Southern U.S. quilting tradition. Bible quilt, 1886. The fabric has faded considerably; the light tan background was originally deep pink, and the brown sashing between squares was green. Gift of Mr. and Mrs. H M. Heckman; National Museum of American History, Smithsonian Institution, Behring Center.

Fig. 26 African American artist Henry Ossawa Tanner made extensive travels in the Middle East; his experiences infused his paintings with an evocative realism. *Moonlight Hebron* (1907; 25 $\frac{11}{16}$ x 31$\frac{7}{8}$" oil on canvas). Gift of Mr. and Mrs. Thomas Whipple Dunbar; Milwaukee Art Museum; photo: John R. Glembin).

Fig. 27 Turner, *Daniel in the Lion's Den* (ca. 1916; oil, 41.25 x 50"; Los Angeles County Museum of Art). Subsequent African American artists incorporated into their art both more tension and more troubled identification with biblical characters who experienced dispossession and migration. The contrast between Henry Ossawa Tanner's rather impressionistic watercolor *The Destruction of Sodom and Gomorrah* (1928) and James Lesesne Wells's *The Destruction of Sodom* (1958), which evokes modern scenes of mob violence, is a case in point (both discussed in Romare Bearden and Harry Henderson, *A History of African-American Artists: From 1792 to the Present* (New York: Pantheon, 1993). Similarly, Wells's *Escape of the Spies from Canaan* (1932) depicted the biblical figures in a modern urban landscape and in modern dress: see www.negroartist.com/negro_artist/JAMES_LESESNE_WELLS/index.htm.

Fig. 28 African Christian art has often illustrated themes of deliverance in the Hebrew Bible; here, *The Three Hebrews in the Fiery Furnace*, from an illustrated parchment manuscript of The Canticles of the Prophets. Paintings of Old Testament subjects are rare in Ethiopian art. Painted leather binding on wood, 128 x 157 mm. The artist, known from a number of manuscripts, was one of the most inventive of his time and worked close to the Ethiopian court, ca. 1720–40.

Fig. 29 Jonah being swallowed by the whale, and his preservation afterward. Courtesy of Sam Fogg Ltd, London (Private Collection, www.samfogg.com).

References

Keel, Othmar, and Christoph Uehlinger. 1998. *Gods, Goddesses, and Images of God in Ancient Israel.* Translated by T. H. Trapp. Minneapolis: Fortress Press.

Powell, Richard J. 2003. *Black Art: A Cultural History.* 2nd ed, *Thames and Hudson World of Art.* London: Thames and Hudson.

THE AFRICANA BIBLE

READING ISRAEL'S SCRIPTURES

FROM AFRICA AND THE AFRICAN DIASPORA

THE
HEBREW BIBLE
Writings

The KETUVIM

A RATIONALE

Madipoane Masenya (ngwan'a Mphahlele) and Rodney S. Sadler Jr.

THE KETUVIM, OR WRITINGS—the third division and final section of the Hebrew Tanak (that is, Torah, Nevi'im, and Ketuvim)—represents a disparate collection of biblical texts. Notions of genre, diachronic nature, common theology or wisdom perspective, and areas of focal concern, among others, do not unify these books. Instead, the Ketuvim comprise a hodgepodge of different texts, a miscellany of biblical material. The lack of unity and coherence of all these, however, should in no way diminish the reader's appreciation for these texts. This division, presented here in the order of the Hebrew Bible, enjoys a variety of genres, such as Wisdom books (Proverbs, Job, Qoheleth [or Ecclesiastes]), Songs (Psalms and Lamentations), the Megilloth (or Scrolls, read on specific occasions in Judaism: Ruth, Song of Songs, Qoheleth [or Ecclesiastes], Lamentations, and Esther), and the histori-

cal books, such as much of Daniel, Ezra-Nehemiah, and 1 and 2 Chronicles. In many ways, the collection of Kethuvim is constituted by texts that touch on the range of feelings, experiences, and stories that unite the Africana community.

What unifies the treatment of this miscellany of biblical material, though, is the Africana lens through which the books are reread. The authors have deliberately used their varied Africana realities to engage these biblical books as depicted in the following brief survey.

WISDOM TEXTS COMPRISE:

Proverbs: A variety of Wisdom themes pertinent to Africana life—such as the need for healthy family relationships, the unsung Africana heroines (vis-à-vis the celebrated *Eshet Hayil* of Prov. 31:10-31), hard work, and other related themes—are dealt with from an African Diasporan perspective.

Job: Two responses to individual and collective (communal) suffering (loss of lives, diseases, poverty, social injustices) and some key concerns raised by the author of Job are presented from both an African and an African American perspective.

Qoheleth (Ecclesiastes): A disturbing book that is rich with a variety of ideas, including joy, meaninglessness (vanity), folly, madness, wisdom, toiling, and subtle absolutism. These issues are reread through an African Diasporan lens to foreground the untenable nature of life in the African Diaspora.

THE SCROLLS (MEGILLOTH) FOR FESTIVALS ARE:

Ruth: Pertinent issues forming part of Africana reality, such as marriage, sex, gender, and family, are radically recontextualized from the perspective of African American experiences with a resultant fresh and engaging reading of this scroll.

Esther: The African reality of the Ewe peoples of South Eastern Ghana serves as a hermeneutical lens through which the feast of the Purim, the pivot around which the book revolves, is read.

Song of Songs: A refreshing Afro-Caribbean hermeneutic is applied to this book of poetry. The reality of African Diasporan women is used effectively to bring the Beloved's Songs to life in these women's contexts.

The other Megilloth are Qoheleth, discussed above, and Lamentations, discussed below.

THE SONGS INCLUDE:

Psalter: This is a threefold, fresh division of the Psalter (vis-à-vis the traditional fivefold one), a division that is basically informed by the varied Africana experiences through which the various Psalms are "played with," bringing an enriching perspective to Psalter scholarship.

Lamentations: The African American reality of pain and suffering serves as a hermeneutical lens to engage the theology of suffering as it is portrayed in this book.

THE HISTORICAL BOOKS ARE:

Ezra-Nehemiah: The rhetoric of the antebellum period in Black America is actively, critically, and sarcastically brought to bear on a similar rhetoric in Ezra-Nehemiah.

1 and 2 Chronicles: The Chronicler's work, especially on the worshiping, praying, praising community, is engaged through a refreshing African American cultic lens.

Daniel: This apocalypse, with its emphasis on exile and exiles, enjoys a fuller Africana engagement as the African interpreter, who now lives as an exile, uses his Africana experiences to engage the book.

AN EDITORIAL NOTE

As is true with the other sections of the *Africana Bible*, the readings in this section explore a range of Africana ideas and issues through the unique lenses of the authors' interests and experiences. Like the disparate nature of the works in the Ketuvim, the authors of these essays mine the richness of the Africana experience and allow the distinctiveness of their own identities and experiences to shape their readings in ways unconventional in traditional biblical scholarship. As a result, readers who live in a world that often tries to distill the Africana people and their experience down to one essentialized notion of "blackness" will be inevitably confronted in this section with the breadth of what is Africana—from the richness of folk experiences from various traditions on the African continent, and the depth of suffering of Africans in the Americas and the Caribbean confronting slavery, to contemporary reflections from diasporan perspectives on such issues as marriage, rape, prosperity preaching, suffering, poverty, child-rearing, worship, exile, immigration, and a range of other concerns through the media of spirituals, the blues, jazz, hip-hop, poetry, proverbs, narrative, folktales, rituals, and protest discourse.

As the Ketuvim in the Tanak serve as a constant reminder of the diversity of thought, cultures, ide-ologies, and theologies that could be found among the "people of the book," this section—intentionally unassimilated in form, focus, or perspective—reflects the range of thought, cultures, ideologies, and theologies among others found in Africana communities in various global contexts. May you come, through the scope of the vision of the authors in this section, to both a new understanding of the various books in the Ketuvim and an expanded vision of the God who emerges from the essayists' perspectival readings of these biblical texts.

PSALMS

Nathaniel Samuel Murrell, David T. Shannon, and David T. Adamo

THIS ENTRY CONTAINS the work of three scholars, each of whom has treated the Psalter from a particular vantage point within the Africana experience. Nathaniel Samuel Murrell reflects on Psalms 1–50 from the point of view of the Black Diaspora in the Caribbean. The late David T. Shannon's contribution offers a reading of Psalms 51–100 with an eye toward the North American Diaspora. David T. Adamo places the African experience in the foreground of his reading of Psalms 101–150. This threefold subdivision of the Psalter is clearly at odds with the traditional fivefold breakdown that one finds in the Jewish canon. Its purpose is to highlight reading strategies in three distinct, and at times overlapping, Africana communities.

After Dr. Shannon's unexpected death in 2008, his work has been folded in with that of Dr. Murrell. Thus this essay itself reflects a reshaping of herme-neutical traditions in the face of unexpected crisis, a dynamic ubiquitous elsewhere in the Africana milieu. Though unusual, and in some ways transgressive, this essay shows how the privileging of contextual realities can influence the subdivision of and encounter with the Bible and its constituent books.

PLAYING WITH THE FIRST ONE HUNDRED PSALMS IN THE AFRICANA EXPERIENCE

Nathaniel Samuel Murrell

FOREGROUNDING A PHENOMENON
Africana peoples associated with Abrahamic religions have had an enduring relationship with the Psalms. The large collection of poems was

first called *Psaltērion* (Psalter) and *Psalmoi* (in the Septuagint) by Alexandrian-Africa Jews in Egypt who translated them from Hebrew to Greek circa 300–275 B.C.E. As the Psalter itself intimates, from antiquity African peoples shared in psalmody and may have contributed to the composing of the Psalter. A Benjaminite from Ethiopia seems the rightful composer of Psalm 7 (Felder 1999: 116), and Moses, an Egyptian Jew who wedded an Ethiopian, composed Psalm 90. Ethiopians and Egyptians participated with the Hebrews in the worship of Yahweh with Psalms in Africa and Jerusalem (Pss. 87:4-6; 68:28-35). Egyptians and Ethiopians, especially the *Beta Israel* (*Falasha*), maintain their ancient Hebraic and Christian faiths (Coptic, Ethiopian Orthodox, and others) to the present—with their attendant interest in the scriptures, including Psalms (Kaplan 1992: 110–11). The Psalter found it significant to show Jacob as having lived in the land of Ham (Egypt) for a while (Pss. 78:51; 105:23, 27; 106:22), and a psalmist refers to Egypt as *Mitzraim* and "the land of Ham" (Ps. 105:23, 27), probably because Egypt—mentioned hundreds of times in the Bible—was colonized by Joseph's extended family and later by descendants of the tribe of Ham (Felder 1999: 105, 116–17; Randall Bailey: 1991: 171, 174).

Early Christians, including those from northeast Africa, took great pride in their use of Old Testament scriptures and liberally cited a large number of Psalms in various aspects of their interpretation of the Christ phenomenon (see McCann 2005: 216–18). Cappadocian Fathers from North Africa (Gregory of Nazianzus, Gregory of Nyssa, and Basil), Cyril, Origin, and Clement of Alexandria (Egypt), and Tertullian of Carthage (now Libya/Tunisia) produced dozens of homilies on the Psalms each year for their mostly African parishioners; many of those homilies are extant (see *Encyclopedia of Early Christianity* (EEC), 1990: 432–33, 441, 467). To fulfill liturgical requirements "of scriptural precepts" for their clerical office, these divines recited entire psalms or groups of psalms with biblical canticles and antiphon chants used in their playful but theological orations (EEC 1990: 659–61). Many Africans from "Catholic Congo" and Angola would have been quite familiar with the Psalms before they were sold into slavery in the Americas; Christian missionaries exposed many other Africans to the sacred text (Adamo 2000). Melva Costen affirms that antebellum slaves were introduced "to psalm singing in religious and informal colonial gatherings. Religious instruction for slaves included instruction in Psalmody, which apparently appealed to the new 'converts.' When African Americans were granted freedom to organize their own religious meetings, the singing of Psalms was a requirement" (Costen 2004: 98). As Eileen Southern records, a Methodist minister, Samuel Davis of Virginia, wrote this to his friends in London in 1755 about the proclivity for psalmody in the lives of "his Africans" in American captivity:

> The books were all very acceptable, but none more so than the Psalms and Hymns, which enable them [the slaves] to gratify their peculiar taste for psalmody. Sundry of them have lodged all night in my kitchen, and sometimes when I have awakened about two or three o'clock in the morning, a torrent of sacred harmony has poured into my chamber and carried my mind away to heaven. . . . The Negroes have an ear for [Musick] and a kind of [extatic] Delight in Psalmody; and there are no Books they learn so soon or take so much pleasure in as those used in that heavenly Part of divine worship. (Southern 1983: 27–28; Small 1987: 83)

Notwithstanding Minister Davis's hyperbole, he speaks to the history and love affair Africana peoples have had with the Psalter historically. As Wilma Ann Bailey observes, by the time of the Civil War, African Americans, enslaved and free, "were in a broad sense familiar with the historiography of ancient Israel and . . . did incorporate some of those traditions into their own expressions of pain" (2008: 151), which they consoled with ancient Hebrew scriptures.

The Psalms comprise a series of songs, poetic narratives, sonnets, and prayers containing dirges, laments, solicitations, canticles of praise, and other forms of poetry used by Hebrew people as tools in conversation with Yahweh. A story from the Rabbinic tradition says the Ketuvim, or Writings, of which the Psalter is an essential part, are positioned in the Tanak after the Torah (Law) and the Nevi'im (Prophets) because in the Writings are the individuals' thoughts and search for God, rather than God's addresses to them. Many of the poems claim a composer; some are composites, and others seem to be edited from earlier versions. About 80 percent carry superscriptions of personal names and performers, but they are largely anonymous compositions that evolved over a period of about nine hundred years—between the time of Moses and early Judaism (Felder 1989: 65). Close to 50 percent of these Psalms claim to be written by, about, or for David, and others are attributed to Asaph (Pss. 50; 73–83). Many are ascribed to the sons of Korah (Pss. 42, 44–49; 50; 73–85; 87–88), Moses (90), Solomon (72), Herman (88), Ethan (89), Jeduthun (Pss. 39; 62; 77), and others. These names, however, add little to the meaning of the Psalms.

In spite of the Psalms' literary beauty and spiritual meaning, many questions dog their interpretation. Should they be read as one book, or five, or 150? Is their numbering sequence of any importance? What does the canonical shape of the Psalter say about its authorship, authority, and purpose as theological literature? Are their times and places of writing important for their meaning? How should we categorize and read the Psalms? The most popular Psalms express gratitude or thanks for divine favors or deliverance from distress, but just as many are laments arising from situations of oppression and transgression. Some Psalms concern the coronation of God (2; 21; 45; 72) and express confidence in God's sovereign power, protection, and provision. Others contain a motif of exodus and liberation while bemoaning bondage, distress, suffering, and the silence of God. A few Psalms repli-

cate wisdom genres (Pss. 1; 37; 73; 128), prophetic speech (Pss. 50; 81; 95), and battle hymns or the call to war (McCann 2005: 199–203). Psalms 19, 37, 40, 78, 81, 105, 112, and 119 seem to link wisdom with obedience to Hebrew law (Felder 1989: 65). Often one finds several of these features and emphases in one psalm. Those of us who read the Psalms with an eye for literary genre observe that all of them share common features: they use parallelism, repetition, and assonance, and they have liturgical content (if not formulas) for religious worship. McCann says that the "genre designation" of the poems, however, "may be misleading, since it is clear that the ancient authors and performers of the Psalms were not form critics in the contemporary sense" (2005: 199, 206).

Scholars commonly hold that the doxologies concluding four Psalms are strategically placed in the collection (Pss. 41:13; 72:19; 89:52; and 106:48) to indicate that the Psalter is arranged in five books of uneven length: Pss. 1–41, 42–72, 73–89, 90–106, and 107–150. Dianne Bergant (1997: 52), Toni Craven (1992: 17–18), and other scholars say it is possible that the fivefold division could have been accidental or that it could have been a rabbinic play on the Psalter designed to match the five-scroll Torah or a three-year liturgical cycle (see McCann 2005: 208; Anderson 1983: 22–23). In their canonical shape, the poetic songs show no chronological, historical, logical, or even theological flow. Each of the five books has some of every type of psalm. They also were written in no systematic order and arose impromptu from a variety of individuals' situations in life (*Sitz im Leben*) as they lived, encountered, and negotiated both life's traumas and life's pleasantries. As there is no one way to read these poems, one may choose to play with the Psalter: have the Hebrew poems speak to one; and in return, read them in light of their literary beauty, similarity to, and influence on our African life experiences and artistic and literary genre. The Psalms read and form us by forcing us, as Ellen Davis says, "to bring into conversation with God feelings and thoughts that most of us think we need to get rid of before God" can hear us (Davis 2001: 5; see also Witvliet 2007: 30).

For practical reasons, the fivefold division of the Psalter is not employed as a schema in my "play" with the Psalms in the Africana experience. Our beloved colleague, Dr. David T. Shannon, who passed away as this essay was being completed, recognized that the Africana use of the Psalms over the centuries has not been driven by mere academic questions of organizational structure, literary genre, or form and style of the poems. In his Black Church, folks have not been bothered by concerns over the fact that the Psalms were collected from such different time periods and locations as to make their authorship as uncertain as their historical context. His parishioners have learned that the Psalms were written and sung by people like them—vocalists, shepherds, farmers, musicians, washerwomen, paupers, clerics, soldiers, and kings—but they have seen in them divine agency and a source of spirituality, liberation, and rejuvenation. I hope that David, a master at playing with scripture (Shannon 1991), will be pleased that I continue here his insights into our people's playful but serious use of the Psalms under the following categories: (1) Oppression-Distress Lament; (2) Transgression-Reformation; (3) Ritual Rejuvenation.

PLAYING WITH OPPRESSION-DISTRESS LAMENTS

Personal and communal tragedies evoke lamentation among all peoples. They accent human suffering, give a voice to the voiceless, and plead the cause of justice and mercy. Oppression-distress laments, a large collection of poems in the Psalter (more than forty), reflect the pain of people in distress (for example, Pss. 11; 13; 28; 35; 44) as they lament personal and national disasters, utter pleas for deliverance, and make imprecatory solicitation for vengeance to "let God arise and scatter the enemy" (Ps. 68:1). Lament Psalms, as McCann observes, almost always begin with the interrogative *why?* (13:1), an entreaty (17:1), or a vocative,

"Lord" (3:1), "O, God" (6:1), or "My God!" (6:1; 22:1). They then proceed with a description of a distress, utter a plea for help (12:1), "often express confidence in God's ability to respond, and make a promise to God in return for aid" (McCann 2005: 199). The distress is often over human foibles (Psalm 51), oppression (Pss. 17; 22; 43; 54; 55), false accusation (Psalm 7), persecution (Pss. 38:12-20; 41:5-11), or illness and death (Pss. 3; 6; 38). In many of these poems, it is difficult to identify the precise reason for the complaint. Roland Murphy say this is "because the imagery is so extravagant; Psalm 22, for example, mentions 'bulls of Bashan,' 'dogs,' the sword, the lion, and wild oxen. But this can be an advantage for modern readers, who can interpret the vivid language of the psalmists in light of their own distress" (1993: 627). Although individuals seek protection and deliverance from God for great distress and evil enemies (Pss. 56:1-2; 57:1, 3; 59:1-3; 61:1-3), only occasionally is an enemy actually named (for example, Egypt or Tyre). In place of an identifiable source of distress, the cause of Hebrew pain is often euphemistic—for example, the enemy, the abyss, Sheol, the pit, the waves and billows, storms, war armor (sword), and ferocious animals.

Africana people express their lament over oppression and distress in many genres, including song, dance, sculpture, painting, drama, poetry, and narrative literature. Although their literary styles differ, one sees strong similarities between Hebrew and Africana laments. The spirituals "Deep River," "I Am Troubled in Mind," and "My Way Is Cloudy" represent a cadre of laments that retell a painful Africana story with serious playfulness around biblical liberation. These and other songs, says Vincent Wimbush, "as well as numerous sermons, addresses, and exhortations, reflect a hermeneutic characterized by a looseness, even playfulness, vis-à-vis the biblical text themselves" (1991: 88). Costen noted that the spirituals, emerging first during the antebellum slave period as the earliest authentic form of American folk song, "express the peculiar context, nature, experience, values, and longings of the specific folk who created them" (2004: 96). Most Africana laments are cast in the first person and possessive singular, but they are the voices of a voiceless people in distress; people claim in the laments, such as "Sometimes I Feel Like a Motherless Child . . . a long way from home," or "Come Here, Lord!" and "Cum by Yah Me Lord," to express in mournful and playful song their collective pain, oppression, or stress. Like Martin Luther King Jr.'s "I Have a Dream" speech, these songs are not individualistic; they are the dreams of and for the people.

These spirituals represent a community's cry for divine intervention in any number of ills: slavery and its masters' whips, brutality, and the sexual abuse of women, the long-dreaded nights of Jim Crow lynching, centuries of suffering impoverishment, disfranchisement, almost a hundred years of legal discrimination and its miseries, resurgence of racism, and other transgressions against African peoples. Wilma Bailey says of African American women's laments: "The language tends to be more generally expressed as 'Got hard trial' and 'Nobody Knows the Trouble I've Had.'" They do not "speak specifically of sexual abuse" or of being whipped while pregnant or having multiple miscarriages. Though dirges from these experiences were no doubt rampant, they were probably "reserved for the moaning and groaning songs that are often referred to in the literature" (Bailey 2008: 155). This moaning-groaning motif seems a page taken from the Hebrew Bible. A psalmist wrote: "I have become weary with my groaning" (Ps. 6:6). Another insisted: "Let me complain and let me moan, evening, morning, and noon" (Ps. 55:18). A third pleaded: "Let me remember, O Lord, let me moan" (Pss. 73:3; 77:4). Bailey says that the moans of the black woman were no light sighs; they echoed ineffable mental and physical trauma (2008:160).

The cause of the trauma is not named in the distress signal but, like Bob Marley and the Wailers chanting, "Come we go chant down Babylon one more time!" and the thousands of Civil Rights marchers singing, "You Got a Right . . . in freedom's land" as they marched on Selma, Alabama, they knew what their target was. African spirituals influenced the melancholic "rural blues" and gospel that succeeded them and "retained many elements of antebellum shouts, hollers, yells, work songs" and cries to "voice complaint, dissatisfaction, or helplessness [and] despair at injustice and social conditions" (Brown and Brown 1994: 598). They do this with a playful hermeneutic on scriptural idioms: "No! Woman Nuh Cry" (Marley and the Wailers, imitating Jesus, "Daughter! Weep not!"); "O, Brother, Don't Get Weary!"; "O, Rocks Don't Fall on Me!"; "My Good Lord, Show Me the Way"; and "My Lord Says He's Going to Rain Down Fire." James Evans says: "In the sacred music of African slaves, 'Go Down, Moses's chronicles the liberating act of God on behalf of the oppressed. 'Oh, Mary, Don't You Weep' celebrates God's defense of the oppressed against Pharaoh's army" (1992: 40–41). With them, Africans playfully typologized slavery and its legacy and the slave master as Pharaoh.

Most of the laments are cast in the singular but only occasionally represent the community as they do in the Africana tradition. A psalmist pleads: "Save me, O God, by your name, and judge me by your strength. . . . For strangers have risen up against me and oppressors seek after my soul" (Ps. 54:1-3). The chief musician cries: "Give ear unto my prayer, O God! . . . because of the voice of the enemy, because of oppression of the wicked: for they cast iniquity upon me" (Ps. 55:1-3). Another entreats God: "Be merciful to me, O God, for men hotly pursue me, all day long they press their attack" (Ps. 56:1 NIV). Such African American spirituals as "Don't Be Weary Traveler," "Didn't My Lord Deliver Daniel," and "Deep River" seem to play with the refrain: "Save me, O God; for the waters have come over my soul. I sink in deep mire. . . . I am weary of crying!" (Ps. 69:1-3); "Make haste, O God, to deliver me; make haste to help, O Lord!" (Psalm 70); "Deliver me, O my God, out of the hand of the wicked!" (Ps. 71:4); "Let my prayer come before you: incline your ear unto my cry; for my soul is full of troubles and my life draws nigh unto the grave" (Ps. 88:2-3). All of these want to alleviate personal pain and distress, to settle a score on injustice as the poet sees it.

An essential feature of the distress genre in the Psalms and the Africana experience is an imprecation (plea) that justice should not be silent and that vengeance should be speedy upon the enemy. The Psalter abounds with vengeful imprecatory prayers: "Destroy, O Lord, and divide their tongues: for I have seen violence and strife in the city. . . . Deceit and guile depart not from her streets" (Ps. 55:9, 11). Heman the Ezrahite asked: "Lord, why do you cast off my soul? Why do you hide your face from me?" (Ps. 88:14). When God appeared unresponsive, the psalmists pleaded: "Do not keep silence, O God: do not hold your peace, and do not be still." God, "Make their nobles like Oreb, and Zeeb." While you are at it, "O My God, turn them into a wheel; as the stubble before the wind. . . . Fill their faces with shame. . . . Make all my enemies bleed . . . that [they] may know that you are Jehovah" (Ps. 83:1, 9, 11, 13, 15-18). Many psalmists thought their God was *deus absconditus* (a silent or hidden God). The poets prayed: "O Lord God, to whom vengeance belongs; O God, to whom vengeance belongs show your self. Lift up yourself, thou judge of the earth: render a reward to the proud" (Ps. 94:1-2). A distressed and exasperated Hebrew entreated: "Listen to my prayer, O God, do not ignore my plea. . . . I am distraught at the voice of my enemy . . . for they bring down suffering upon me and revile me in their anger" (Ps. 55:1-3 NIV).

While God kept silence, the enemies of the Hebrews plotted secretly against them and gloried in their evil actions, saying, "no one shall see us" (Ps. 64:1-6). I wonder whether KKK lynch mobs followed this script as they waited in dark alleys for their innocent black victims, to noose them by the neck or slit their throat under cover, saying, "no one shall see us!" They expected law enforcement to look the other way, as recalled in the song "Look away! Look away! Dixie land!" Like the Jews, millions of Africana people raise the age-old question: Why do the innocent and righteous suffer but the wicked are not punished? Felder says: "The expressed anguish of the pious takes the form of laments that sharply pose the problem of theodicy." In Psalm 22:1, the problems of the pious are more explicit: "My God, my God, why hast thou forsaken me? Why art thou so far from helping me, from the words of my groaning?" (1989: 65, KJV). "How long, Lord? Will you be angry forever? Shall your jealousy burn like fire? Pour out your wrath upon the heathen" (Ps. 79:6). Bob Marley can wait no longer on God. He chants, "Stop that train I am leaving. . . It won't be long, whether I am right or wrong" ("Stop That Train"). "Man and people will fight you down" and make you "trudge through great tribulation" so "we are leaving Babylon. We are going to the Father's land" ("Exodus").

Lamenting the impact of colonialism and slavery with their legacy of oppression and poverty in Jamaica, Rastafarians playfully join the Hebrew refrain from the Babylonian captivity, singing, "By the rivers of Babylon, there we sat down, yea, we wept, when we remembered Zion. For there they carried us away captive, required of us a song . . . but how can we sing the Lord's song in a strange land?" (Ps. 137:1-4). Rastas, however, refuse to wait for help from the silent Judeo-Christian God who sanctioned the Jewish Babylonian captivity, "four hundred years" of African enslavement, and black oppression. They sing: "Buffalo Soldier in the heart of America, stolen from Africa . . . fighting on arrival," still "fighting for survival" (Marley and the Wailers). Rastas take charge of their own destiny by "Chanting Down Babylon" with "Confrontation and Rebel Music," through "Uprising and Exodus," coded in "Survival and Rastaman Vibration," because "A Hungry Mob is an Angry Mob!" (Marley and the Wailers). Rastas settle a question of theodicy in the Psalms by looking to a human deity they believe was predicted in Ps. 68:31, and they affirm their own divinity through a masoretic reading of Ps. 82:6-7: "You are godlike beings, and all of you sons [and daughters] of the Most High." Rastas see here not only a premise for former Ethiopian emperor Haile Selassie as their divine messiah but a means of affirming their spiritual worth in the economy of their redefined god. We humans are god-men; like Selassie the god-man, we share in the nature of the divine who fashioned us. As Ras Michael Henry admonishes: "Remember, we are all chosen of God. You are all Gods and children of the Most High" (Spencer 1999: 81).

Although the Psalter shows the Hebrew people questioning God's silence, the lament Psalms do not recall poets abandoning belief in God. In the same way, Africans in general do not have a long tradition of abandoning faith in God; whether God is recognized as Yahweh, Jehovah, Jesus, Onyonkopon, Olodumare, or Jah, the nonreligious and the religious alike direct their laments at the divine.

Speaking under the influence of the brutality of apartheid, South African church leader and theologian Allan Boesak echoed the lament of an African American bishop of the mid-1800s: "I began to question the existence of God, and to say: 'If he does exist, is he just? If so, why does he suffer one race to oppress and enslave another, to rob them by unrighteous enactments of rights, which they hold most dear and sacred?' . . . Again, said I: 'Is there no God?'" (Boesak 1983: 32). Boesak comments: "Here God is not conveniently declared to be 'dead,' because he obstructs our human plans and desires. No . . . Here is someone who knows that he cannot and does not want to live without God, but who at the same time has a strong feeling that God is no longer in his life, in his history, in his world with its pain and desolation" (1983: 32).

To Boesak, people who experience the oppression that he and other Africans endured at the hands of Afrikaners in South Africa ask: "Where is God? . . . Who is he? Belief in a provident God, who holds his people in his hand and shapes world history according to his will, seems a fortuitous relic of a more religious-minded age" (1983: 32). Boesak and other South Africans redefined the God of their oppressors, but their question of theodicy does not lead logically to atheism.

Laments may have lost their popularity in some Christian circles, or the "functioning canon,"

as Walter Brueggemann (1986: 107) and Witvliet (2007: 31) assert, but Africana people continue to lodge their laments in conversations, prayers, drama, music, art, sculpture, angry soliloquies, and other genres. The laments of pop culture artists (for example, reggae, hip-hop, gangster rap, jazz, R&B) are replete with coded as well as unmasked expressions of suffering, pain, and anger in art and song. In *Holler If You Hear Me*, Michael Dyson, an authority on "black folk culture," tells the riveting story of the popular hip-hop/rap artist Tupac Amaru Shakur (2 Pac) who, before his untimely and violent death, was obsessed with the idea of the provenance of God in his life in the ghetto. Tupac's laments are reflected in the lyrics of his hits that "drip with a sense of the divine." Dyson says: "In *So Many Tears*, [Tupac] asks God to intervene in his suffering, 'God can you feel me? / Take me away from all the pressure and all the pain.' In *Only God Can Judge Me*, Tupac seeks an answer for his existence and his friends' deaths, and in *I Wonder if Heaven Got a Ghetto,* Tupac ponders his destiny." Dyson adds, "In *Staring at the World Through My Rearview* Tupac sarcastically questions the divine presence when, like the biblical prophet Elijah to the prophets of Baal, he urges 'Go on baby scream to God, he can't hear you.'" Dyson concludes that Tupac's "*White Man's World* combines his request for divine favor and retribution in a fashion reminiscent of the Psalms: 'God bless me please / . . . Making all my enemies bleed'" (2001: 202–3). This imprecatory prayer is a popular lament in the Africana tradition.

PLAYING WITH THE TRANSGRESSION-REFORMATION GENRE

An important element of Israel's motif of transgression-lament is their pleas for absolution, for individuals, and occasionally for the nation. Israel's national laments over transgression and a plea for communal reform seem fewer in the Psalms (Psalms 58, 67, 74) than other laments in the Psalter, Lamentations, the Prophets, and the

Torah. The transgression motif in the Hebrew Bible is a serious concern of the Torah and the Prophets. Classical prophets (for example, Isa. 1:4; 43:27; Jer. 2: 5-8; 3:20-25) jealously chastised the nation for ignoring its covenant relation with Yahweh. Like the prophets, psalmists treat transgression as a violation of a law and an omission or neglect of duty in an assumed covenant with God. They deal with morality, justice, political oppression, and economic exploitation. As an active dishonorable human act requiring reform, transgression pervades the first one hundred Psalms (38, 51, 54, 59, 64, 69, and 77); many of these show admission and penitence for personal guilt and a plea for catharsis and restoration.

In the various tapestries of transgression in the Psalms, poets implicate many parties: themselves, other individuals, their nation, neighboring tribes or countries portrayed as a source of aggravation to the Hebrews, and international powers that dominated and oppressed the Israelites, often held as a vassal nation. In this sense, the Psalter's construal of Hebrew transgression could easily be a blueprint for the Africana ascription of this ill, which casts a very wide net; it envelops African peoples, their families and neighbors, oppressors, social structures, systems and institutions, ideologies, and governments' policies. As the psalmists have done, Africana people lament transgression against their God, individuals, and community. They have a tradition of showing contrition and remorse, individually and as communities of faith, for their transgressions, and seeking absolution.

Dyson laments U.S. and African American transgressions: "The resurgence of racism and xenophobia; the development of underground drug economies and gang violence in the inner city; the painful collapse of a liberal consensus on race; the increase in sexual violence among teens; a chilling rise in rates of black imprisonment; the expanding material misery of the working-poor and ghetto-poor" (Dyson 1996: 210). For these national transgressions, some of us are angered and want to embrace the lyrical confessions "I Shot the Sheriff"

and "Burning and Looting Tonight" because we have too "Many Rivers to Cross" (Cliff).

Often, artists in rap, hip-hop, reggae, R&B, jazz, and other art genres wrap their transgression-laments and pleas for reform in creative artistic expressions, some of which often go unnoticed. Michael Dyson writes: "In *Are You Still Down?* [rap artist] Tupac pleads for salvation: Please God come and save me / Had to work with what you gave me'. Then in *Picture Me Rolling*, Tupac wonders if God's forgiveness is forthcoming as he asks, 'Will God forgive me for all the dirt a nigger did to feed his kids?'" (Dyson 2001: 202–3). Ultimate salvation, black folks believe, may be in heaven, but justice is "to be sought also on earth" (Small 1987: 84). Marley chants: "Jah came to break oppression, rule equality, wipe away transgression, and set the captive free" ("Exodus"). The now-famous Jeremiah Wright wrote: "The coded messages of the spirituals in which 'heaven' was equated with 'goin' up' North or going back to Africa" were not pies in the sky. "'Joshua Fit de' Battle of Jericho,' 'Oh Mary, don't you weep, Oh Martha, don't you mourn. Pharaoh's army got drowned!' and 'If I had my way, I'd tear this building down' are neither other worldly nor compensatory"; they are for the here and now (Wright 1999: 97).

PLAYING WITH THE RITUAL REJUVENATION MOTIF

The Psalter provides a communicative speech genre unmatched in any large collection of canticles in the Tanak (Hebrew Bible). Since pre-exilic times, psalms were a source of religious inspiration for Hebrews, who later complemented their collections with the pseudepigraphal Psalms of Solomon and the Hodayot (Thanksgiving) Hymns of Qumran (*EEC* 1990: 441). Although John Witvliet says he finds "relatively tepid enthusiasm for the Psalms in worship throughout vast stretches of North American Christianity" (2007: xiii), perhaps few books in the Bible are used as often in Christian rituals as the Psalms. Many popular great hymns of the church are psalmody-benefactors, and most branches of the faith use the Psalter on a weekly basis to enrich liturgy, inspire religious devotion, and energize belief (Anderson 1983: 15–16). Glenn Hinson says this of worship in the Black Church: Scripture reading grounds the "soulful stirrings in the Word. Often drawn from the Psalms, it both establishes the fitness of praise and sets the service in a historical continuum that stretches back to biblical times" (Hinson 2000: 320). The Psalms ignite our passion because "they convey the whole range of human emotion, from despondent sorrow (Psalm 88) to ecstatic joy (Psalm 47 or 48), from ravaging guilt (Psalm 51) to profound gratitude (Psalm 136)."

One of the most enduring artistic features of the Psalms is their musical redolence. Much of the Psalter, certainly more than in any biblical book, calls for musical performance and worship. The original Hebrew Tehillim (hymns) and Greek Psalterion (instrument for musical accompaniment of the songs) indicate the nature, intent, and use of the unique collection of lyric poetry. Psalms 18–22 are likely written by musicians. Such title superscriptions as "To the Chief Musician," "To the Choir Director," and "To the Leader" show that many of the psalms were sung at cultural-ritual and political performances, including royal weddings (Psalm 45). Lucetta Mowry says that Psalms 2, 21, and 72 show that at the celebration of the king's coronation, "musicians sang odes" to "his just rule and victory over the nation's enemies." Priesthood choirs often sang familiar hymns of praise (Ps. 98:5-6), made petition (Psalms 44, 74, 79, 80, 83), and offered thanksgiving (Psalms 30, 66, 106–8) (Mowry 1993: 533–34). The title also "probably designates a collection of songs and also suggests organized liturgical music" (Good 1993: 535). Although the title "hymn" as a superscription occurs only in Psalm 145, a large number of Psalms are hymns (for example, 8, 19, 29, 33, 46–68, 76, 84, 92, 95–100). Others are either labeled songs (46, 48, 76, 87) or "carry musical or liturgical direction: 20, 26, 27, 66, 81, 107, 116, 134, and 135" (*Jerusalem Bible,* 1966: 779).

That the psalmists praise God for relief from transgression is typical: "When we were overwhelmed by sins, you forgave our transgressions" (Ps. 66:1). Saturated with the celebration of God's deliverance from transgression are Psalms 67–68, 73, 75, 85, 89, 91, and 95–101. So inspiring is this array of Hebrew songs that they make one want to shout with Mahalia Jackson, "Mama, I Want to sing!" because "All God's Chillen Got Wings" and can dance like David in the presence of the Lord. David was an over-ascribed psalmist (not all seventy-four Psalms given to him are his), but he was known to be a gifted musician on the lyre and harp (I Sam. 16:16-24) (like Dizzy Gillespie and Wynton Marsalis on the trumpet), and the Psalms ascribed to him are all said to have originally been set to music. Psalmists encourage people to "Sing unto the Lord a new song"; to praise God with the tambourine and dance, the Puerto Rican *tambore,* the Brazilian *samba,* the Trinidad and Tobago steel drums; and to worship God with reggae and stringed instruments (Pss. 149:1; 150:4). They say, "'Make a joyful noise unto God . . . make his praise glorious'" (Ps. 66:1, 2) (Hinson 2000: 46). This Hebrew genre of celebration and thanksgiving did not escape our gospel artists—Leontyne Price, Marion Williams, Aretha Franklin, J. Robert Bradley, James Cleveland, Albertina Walker, Roberta Martin, Clara Ward, and a host of others—who mirror the jubilation of the Psalms in gospel and other related musical genres.

PARTING WORDS

Africana people "play seriously" with Psalms as entreaty in danger or as a protective charm, healing therapy (Adamo 2000: 342), psychological comfort, a means of solace, and a font of spiritual strength and rejuvenation. Africana scholars say the canonical shape of the Psalms as Holy Scripture appealed to African people ipso facto, out of practical socioeconomic and spiritual concerns; our reading and play with the Psalms are pragmatic in nature, "contextual and existential in approach" (Ukpong 2002: 17; Adamo 2004: 151), and unabashedly soul- and self-gratifying. We love the poetic play of the Psalms because they satisfy our insatiable appetite for a good story, made palatable when wrapped in assonance and packaged in an ethical call for justice; they call for the humbling of our enemies, oppressors, the unjust, or evildoers but proffer justice, peace, and liberation to the downtrodden (for example, Psalms 2–7). When we read, sing, or dance Psalms, they "conscentize" us (bring us into play) with our contextual situation and, as Costen says, make us feel "lifted closer to God and to each other" (2004: 43–44) so that, in spite of our bleak situation, we can sing "I'm Going to Heaven Anyhow!" We play with the Psalms as tools to fight political, economic, health, social, and psycho-spiritual battles because they provide a "refuge in thunder," a place of shelter from the storms of life. They speak to suffering, sorrow, ecstasy, and vision in the human psyche and convey to the depths of the soul something ineffable yet profoundly human.

PSALM 101–150 IN AFRICAN CONTEXT

David Tuesday Adamo

INTRODUCTION

Between 1930 and 1980, the business of biblical interpretation in Africa was in the hands of missionaries who controlled Christianity in Africa. Few African scholars who interpreted the Bible followed verbatim the Eurocentric methods of those aforementioned biblical scholars. African biblical scholars began to recognize the importance of the role that culture plays in biblical interpretation and that this role must be understood in order to make Christianity and biblical interpretation authentically African. African biblical scholars— such as Samuel Abogunrin, professor of Old New Testament at the University of Ibadan, Nigeria; Justin Ukpong, professor of New Testament at the University of Uyo; David Tuesday Adamo, professor of Old Testament at Kogi State University,

Anyigba, Nigeria; G. Abe Adekunle, Ajasin University, Akungba, Nigeria; Gerald West, professor of Old Testament at University of Kwazulu-Nata, South Africa; Madipoane Masenya, professor of Old Testament at the University of South Africa, South Africa, and others—began serious studies with emphasis on Afrocentric biblical interpretation. Although we did not abandon Eurocentric interpretation, African worldview, culture, and religion began to dominate our hermeneutics. What follows below are examples of how Psalms 101–150 can be interpreted using an African cultural hermeneutic.[1]

The words of the Psalms are "words of the dead" and words that linger with power and authority after their speakers are gone (Brueggemann 1984: 12). Perhaps because we are speech creatures, the most enduring thing about us is our speeches to one another. So, I take these words as the "voice of the dead" that are most living, present, and powerful among us. These are words in songs that were spoken by the authors of the Psalms who have been buried a long time (Brueggemann 1984: 12).

The book of Psalms is traditionally divided into five books (1–41; 42–72; 73–89; 90–106; and 107–150). Each of these books ends with doxology. While the entire book of Psalms in the Masoretic Text (MT) contains 150 Psalms, the Septuagint (LXX) contains 151 Psalms. This part of the essay, on Psalms 101–150, does not follow the traditional division of the text, since it includes part of book 4 and book 5 according to that traditional division.

I will briefly discuss the Western interpretation of Psalms 101–150 and give greater attention to the Afrocentric interpretation thereof. This interpretation of Psalms in an African context may seem a little bit strange to the reader, yet it is a common practice in churches throughout the African Diaspora. What I mean is that this type of interpretation is practiced not only among the African Indigenous Churches but in other denominations in Africa and beyond. It is a reality also among African Diasporans all over the world (Yorke 1997: 145–64).

Eurocentric/Western Interpretation of Psalm 101-150

Although the traditional belief was that David was the author of the book of Psalms, including 101–150, this view has been abandoned by many scholars since the days of Herman Gunkel. Gunkel classified the Psalms into different types, including Hymns, Yahweh's Enthronement, Individual and Communal Complaint, Individual and Communal Thanksgiving, and Wisdom Psalms. Among the Psalms considered here (101–150), Psalms 103–105, 111, 113, 114, 117, and 135–150 are classified as Hymns (Collins 2004: 269);[2] none belong to Yahweh's Enthronement (Collins 2004: 269);[3] Psalms 102, 109, 120, 130, and 140–143 are Psalms of Individual Complaint; none are Psalms of Communal Complaint; Psalms 116, 118, and 138 are Psalms of Thanksgiving (Collins 2004: 269);[4] Psalms 101, 110, 132, and 144:1-11 are Royal Psalms;[5] and Psalms 112, 119, and 128 are Wisdom Psalms.[6]

Psalms 120–134 are called the Songs of Ascent, which is associated with pilgrimages to Jerusalem, although only Psalm 122 actually alludes to a journey with Zion (Collins 2004).

In the section containing Psalms 101–150, ten Psalms—called Halleluyah Psalms—stand out. The Hebrew word *halleluyah* contains three parts: first, the imperative of the verb for praise, *halle*; with its object, *lu*; and a short form of the name Yahweh *yah*. *Halleluyah*, therefore, literally means "praise the Lord." Eight of the *Halleluyah* Psalms repeat the word at the end (106, 133, 135, 146–150), but three only mention the word at the end (115, 116, 117). Psalms 113–118 are called Egyptian Hallel Psalms.

The section called Halleluyah Psalms is comprised of psalms in praise of Yahweh for his good deeds, perhaps to upset the terrible rebellious acts of the children of Israel in the wilderness. These acts of Israel's rebellion include tempting God in wilderness, opposing Moses and Aaron, the worshiping the golden calf, having little faith about the Promised Land, refusing to drive the people out of the land, and the consequences of engaging in idolatory and sexual misconduct (106) despite God's deliverance (Pss. 135:4, 19-20; 115:9). These psalms emphasize the election of Israel, which represents the nation's chosenness to minister to the entire world. Yahweh's strength and knowledge surpasses humanity's understanding (147:5). He knows the name of each star and the numbers in heaven (147:3-4).

According to this group of Psalms, a human being's simple act of kindness and demonstration of charity to the needy receives a very high commendation (112:5, 9). Everyone should bow to the Lord who is incomparable and lift the poor up from ashes (113:3, 5, 7). Those who inflicted pain on Yahweh's people must be punished (149:6, 9), for this, too, is part of Yahweh's justice.

Psalm 150 is the climax of the entire Psalter. This word *halleluyah* was repeated about ten times in Psalm 150. The psalmist encouraged children of God to raise their voices in praising the Lord by singing "Halleluyah."[7] Brueggemann classified the following: Psalms 145, 104, 119, 112, 111, 133, and 131 as Psalms of Orientation; Psalms 137, 109, 143, and 130 as Psalms of Disorientation; and Psalms 114, 113, 138, 124, 114, 146, 147, 148, 149, and 150 as Psalms of New Orientation (Brueggemann 1984).

Afrocentric Interpretation of Psalms 101–150

Reading Psalms for Therapeutic Purposes

With the advent of Christianity in Africa, the indigenous therapeutic method of biblical interpretation was considered not only barbaric and fetishist but also an abomination to Christianity. African Christians searched the Bible to find that source of power that the missionaries did not want to reveal to them. They found the power that they sought in the Bible, especially in the book of Psalms. Some Psalms may therefore be classified as therapeutic, protective, and success Psalms.

In some indigenous communities, reading of the Bible has also been combined with African indigenous methods of healing. Thus absolute faith in the word of God and in God himself is maintained, but with the combination of herbs, prayer, fasting, and use of the names of God in the healing process. Adherents to these practices believe that virtually all types of illnesses are curable with the combination of reading the Psalms and using African materials. Although these practices are mostly predominant among the pastors, prophets, evangelists, and apostles of African Indigenous Churches and their members in West Africa (particularly Nigeria), pastors of main missionary churches are also involved.[8]

Although other Psalms outside the section considered here have also been identified as therapeutic, I will discuss Psalms 109, 115, 119:176, and 126. For example, for stomach trouble (Adeboyejo 1988: 21), Psalm 115 is prescribed with other passages of the Bible (Psalms 19, 24, 53, and 54; Isaiah 47; Hebrews 11; and Luke 9:2-7; 10:9-16). It is to be read for three days with the following holy names: *bilasulika, labilasu, hubasabilahhuka* seven times, *Jehovah Araji* three times, *Salaja Eloi* three times, *Yod He Van He* seven times, and *Wasara* seven times. Pray for victory in different ways over it, and then drink two full spoons every morning and night.

One major problem responsible for family breakup and polygamy in Africa is barrenness and infant mortality. The biblical remedy for these are said to be Psalm 121 according to Prophet Samuel Akin Adewole (1991: 22). He recommends that a barren woman should pray and remind God that if she had not been borne by her mother she would have not existed and that it is God's wish and commandment for her to multiply. Such a woman should also ask God in prayer to bless her womb so that unbelievers should praise the Lord as soon as possible (Adamo 2001).

For safe delivery, Psalm 126 is recommended. Psalm 126 is a prayer to God to restore Israelite fortune. According to Ogunfuye, this chapter is good for infant mortality. As soon as a woman with the experience of infant mortality is aware that she

is pregnant, she should start reading this Psalm. It should be read to the water used for bathing, drinking, and washing every day. This same Psalm could also be written in the four parchments with the holy names *Sinni, Sinsuni,* and *Semanflaf* to be put into the four corners of the house (Ogunfuye n.d: 85). Psalms 102 and 109 can be used to cure epilepsy through the same process of reading.

Reading Psalms for Protection in African Contexts

The missionaries, with good intention to promote the kingdom of Christ, built not only maternity wards, dispensaries, and hospitals where Western medicine was dispensed. The truth, however, is that the hospitals, dispensaries, and maternity wards were not enough for the people. Those who were fortunate enough to have access to these hospitals and maternity wards could not afford the cost of conventional/Western medicine. The result was that not all Nigerians had access to the Western medicine. Others who believed they knew the source of the diseases and misfortune (enemies such as witches and wizards) sought protection from the traditionalists (who were not necessarily witches but native doctors) for what befell them. Hospitals and Western medicine could not deal effectively with the role of belief in that aspect of African understandings of pathology.

Psalms as Medicine for Protection

One way of mounting offensive and defensive battle against the evil ones and enemies in the Nigerian African indigenous tradition is the use of herbal and nonherbal medicine. The reading and writing of the word of God in conjunction with herbal and nonherbal medicine, and the citing and reciting of the holy names of God and angels to secure protection, has become a way of life in African Indigenous Churches.

Within Psalms 101–150, T. N. Adeboyejo prescribes for protection against enemies Psalms 101, 110, 114, and other Psalms (10, 14, 24, 28, 34, 50, and 91; Isa. 41:8-16; Isa. 47) with special instructions. Below are his exact words:

On Wednesday a white candle in each corner of your room three or two white candles, one yellow candle in the middle of the room, read these Ps. 10, 14, 110 and 114 each at the corner of the room in front of three candle at the middle, put bucket, pan or pot in which you have put palm front inside then, put calabash of water near it, read Ps. 28, 91 and Isaiah 41:8-16 into the water in the bucket, outside of your body over the water in the bucket, then pray for victory over all your enemies. Ask God to let them fall in spirit and physically let them be destroyed over the water in the calabash. After purification bathe with the water in the bucket and retain some for drinking, after that use incense of victory. Throw the water in the calabash outside or where you know that your enemies will step. (Adeboyejo 1988: 21)

The pregnant woman should bathe with the water and then fast.

Psalms 109 as well as other Psalms (9, 27, 51, and 91; and Gen. 11:1-9 and Matt. 15:29-38) are prescribed for protection against extravagance. Prophet Samuel Adewole prescribes the above passages with a coconut. A hole should be made on the coconut. Pour in lime juice from three to seven fruits, a spoonful of ocean water, and a small bottle of perfume.

Psalms 116, 121, 125, 102, 110, 114, 124, 126–127, 130, 137, and 119:137-44 are also prescribed for protection (for more details, see Adamo 2001).

Reading the Psalms for Success in Life

Among the Yorubas of Nigeria, success goes beyond mere riches or education. Success pertains to the totality of life's endeavors. It concerns getting a job or obtaining promotions in a current job. If one is jobless, there is no success. If one secures a job but has no appreciable promotion on the job, it means there is no success. Success includes accumulation of money and riches. It includes multiplication of wives and children. Traveling on water, land, and air without accident and achieving the purpose of traveling is success. Success in love relationships is important. Finding favor in the sight of God and people is success. All means are used to enhance success. Apart from hard work, medicine such as prayer, rituals, potent words, and faith in God are employed. All of these, according to African understanding, are medicine. Some Psalms were identified by the Christian converts and used with some indigenous materials. The Psalms that are identified as success Psalms are believed by the African Indigenous Churches to have the power to bring success if used with faith, with such rituals as prayer, fasting, and rehearsal of some specific symbols, and with a combination of other animate or inanimate materials.

Success in Examinations

For success in studies or examinations, Pss. 119:9-16 and 134 are identified. These Psalms should be read in conjunction with other Psalms (4, 8:1-9; 9; 23; 24; 27; 46; 51). Students should cut a candle stick into four segments. They should light them and make a circle with the candles. They should be in the middle of the candles while reading the Psalms.

According to Prophet Adewole, Ps. 119:9-16, Deut. 33:1-3, and Josh. 1:1-8 are for improved memory. Cook one local egg. After removing its shell, put it in a cup or glass of water and read the above passages over the water and the egg. Eat the egg, and drink the water. Or, one may read the word of God over honey or olive oil for drinking or licking (Adewole n.d: 33). According to Adewole, Ps. 119:9-16, Deut. 33:4, and Josh. 1:1-8 should be read on Thursday during fasting for memory, wisdom, and knowledge. At exactly 6 p.m. on Thursday, put the egg in a cup of water and read these passages on the water and egg with the holy names *Kosniel, Skrunniel,* and *Mupiel.* Pray for wisdom and knowledge and memory; then eat the egg and drink the water in the cup. At the end of the fast on Thursday, read Ps. 119:9-12 three times (Adewole 1991: 10).

Securing the Love of a Woman or Man

Psalm 133 is classified as a Psalm that will help one secure the love of a woman or a man. For example, if any man is looking for a girlfriend or a wife and has a history of failing at this; if a wife is losing the love of her husband; or if a husband is looking for the love of his wife, who is at the verge of divorcing, the individual should read this Psalm while following these important instruction:

> Draw some water with your mouth into a bottle. Put some water that will fill the bottle into a bowl. Wash your face and armpit seven times in the water in the bowl. Add the water in the bowl to the one in the bottle to fill it up. Then call the name of the woman/man and the name Eve/Adam 21 times. Read Psalms 133, Ruth 1:16-17 and Solomon and John 1:1-4 into the water at midnight and if the person is known give the water to her/him to drink. (Adeboyejo 1988: 27)

Chief Oguntuye recommends Psalm 133 for husband and wife, family, society, and church to avoid disharmony (Ogunfuye, no date: 88–89). Prophet Sam Adewole (Adewole 1991) also recommends Psalms 51 and 133 and Isaiah 60 for securing the love of a woman or a man using the following instruction:

> Sew blue cloth on four corners. Buy coconut. Write his or her name around the coconut with a biro three times. Make three signs of the cross around the name. Burn incense and sprinkle original perfume. Call these holy names: *Jehovah, Jehovah Emmanuel, and Jehovah Nissi* twenty-one times. Read Psalm 51, 133, and Isaiah 60.

In another booklet called *The Revelation of God for 1992*, Adewole identifies Psalms 13 and 51 to be read thirteen times and Psalm 133 to be read twenty-one times for love of a woman or man. According to the prophet, one should use early morning water or direct rain that falls especially on Wednesday or Sunday. After calling the names *Holy Mary* (twenty-one times) and *Jehovah Jire* (twenty-one times) on the water, one should drink it (Adewole 1991b: 21).

Psalms 110, 111, 114, 126, 132, and 140 are also recommended for various types of successes.

CONCLUSION

There is a temptation for Westerners to immediately condemn this Africana interpretation of Psalms as fetishistic. But a closer look at the faith that lies behind it should be taken. Such practice by biblical people should make us cautious to condemn. This Africana approach is also based on African tradition concerning the power in names, particularly in the enormous power in the names of God. This interpretation is also based on the African tradition based on the power in both the spoken and written words in Africana and biblical tradition. For example, it is said: "For the word of God is quick and powerful, and sharper than any two-edged sword"(Heb. 4:12). In Genesis 1, the world was created by the word of God. He sent his words, and the people were healed. The word of God will not go out without accomplishing the purpose for which it is sent (Isa. 55:11).

As stated before, this practice is not limited to the African Indigenous Churches but also involves other churches, including Catholic, Baptist, Anglican, and others in Nigeria and among the African Diasporas all over the world.[9] As a result of this Africana interpretation, the African Indigenous Churches are growing while most of the mainline missionary churches are declining. This has probably prompted these missionary mainline churches to begin to adopt this type of interpretation. This method of interpretation can also be seen as part of the African genius of applying African spirituality and experience instead of depending on the poverty of Western spiritual experience, which is indeed very strange to Africans even though we can imitate it perfectly.

Notes

1. This method was started by African Indigenous Churches. Full details of different aspects of African cultural hermeneutics can be found in my "The Historical Development of Old Testament Interpretation in Africa," *Old Testament Essays, New Series* 16, no. 1 (2003): 9–33.

2. Other passages that are also classified as hymns that are beyond the assigned range of texts are 8, 19, 29, 33, 65, 67, 68, 96, 98, and 100.

3. Only 93, 9, and 99, which are outside the assigned texts, are regarded as Enthronement Psalms.

4. Psalms 18, 30, 34, 40:1-11, 41, 66, and 92 are others outside the assigned texts.

5. Psalms 2, 18, 20, 21, 45, and 72 are outside the assigned texts.

6. Psalms 1, 14, 37, 73, and 91 are others.

7. It is important to mention that these Psalms do not fall into a single section within the traditional division of the book of Psalms. As the numbering of the rest of the Psalms differs, so also is the numbering of the Masoretic Text different from the Septuagint in the section that is assigned to me. Examples of this include the following: Psalms 11–13 in the MT are Psalms 10–112 in the LXX; 114–115 in the MT are 113 in the LXX; 116 in the MT is 114–115 in the LXX; 117–146 in the MT are 116–145 in the LXX; 147 in the MT is 146–147 in the LXX; 148–150 in the MT are 148–150 and 151 in the LXX.

8. A few of the African Indigenous Churches are Christ Apostolic Church (CAC), Cherubim and Seraphim Church (C&S), the Church of the Lord (Aladura), Celestial Church of Christ (CCC), and African Church. These churches have spread all over Africa and abroad. Some of the main missionary churches are affiliated with such denominations as the Anglican, Baptist, Four Square, and Seventh Day Adventist churches.

9. In 2002, I had the opportunity to visit some churches in the Northern Province of South Africa during my academic visit to the University of Pretoria. I worshiped with St. John Apostolic and the Zion Christian Churches at Mashabela in the Northern Province of South Africa, who practiced the same method of interpretation of the Psalter.

References

Adamo, David Tuesday. 2000. "The Use of Psalms in African Indigenous Churches in Nigeria." In *The Bible in Africa: Transactions, Trajectories, and Trends*, ed. Gerald West and Musa Dube, 337–49. Boston: Brill.

———. 2001. *Reading and Interpreting the Bible in African Indigenous Churches*. Eugene, Ore.: Wipf & Stock.

———. 2003. "The Historical Development of Old Testament Interpretation in Africa." *Old Testament Essays, New Series* 16 (1): 9–33.

———. 2004. "Psalms." In *Global Bible Commentary*, ed. Daniel Patte et al., 151–62. Nashville: Abingdon.

Adeboyejo, T. N. 1988. *St Michael Prayer Book*. Lagos: Neye Ade & Sons.

Adewole, Sam. 1991a. *Awake Celestials, Satan Is Nearer*. Lagos: Celestial Church of Christ.

———. 1991b. *The Revelation of God for 1992 and the Years Ahead*. Lagos: Sam Adewole.

Anderson, Bernard W. 1983. *Out of the Depths: The Psalms Speak for Us Today*. Philadelphia: Westminster.

Archaeological Study Bible: An Illustrated Walk through Biblical History and Culture. 2005. Grand Rapids, Mich.: Zondervan.

Asante, Molefi Kete, and Abu S. Abarry. 1996. *African Intellectual Heritage: A Book of Sources*. Philadelphia: Temple University Press.

Bailey, Randall C. 1991. "Beyond Identification: The Use of Africans in Old Testament Poetry and Narratives." In *Stony the Road We Trod: African American Biblical Interpretation*, ed. Cain Hope Felder, 165–84. Minneapolis: Fortress Press.

Bailey, Wilma Ann. 2008. "The Lament Traditions of Enslaved African American Women and the Lament Traditions of the Hebrew Bible." In *Lamentations in Ancient and Contemporary Cultural Contexts*, ed. Nancy C. Lee and Carleen Mandolfo, 151–62. Atlanta: Society of Biblical Literature.

Bergant, Dianne. 1997. *Israel's Wisdom Literature: A Liberation-Critical Reading.* Minneapolis: Fortress Press.

Boesak, Allan. 1983. "He made us all, but. . ." In *Apartheid Is a Heresy*, ed. John W. De Grouchy and Charles Villa-Vicencio, 1–9. Grand Rapids: Eerdmans.

Brown, Marian Talley, and William A. Brown. 1994. "Music: History and Development." In *Encyclopedia of Black America*, ed. W. Augustus Low and Virgil A. Cliff, 585–610. New York: Da Capo.

Brueggemann, Walter. 1984. *The Message of the Psalms: A Theological Commentary.* Minneapolis: Augsburg.

———. 1986. "The Costly Loss of Lament." *Journal for the Study of the Old Testament* 36:57–71.

Collins, John. 2004. *Introduction to the Hebrew Bible.* Minneapolis: Fortress Press.

Costen, Melva Wilson. 2004. *Spirit and in Truth: The Music of African American Worship.* Louisville, Ky.: Westminster John Knox.

Craven, Toni. 1992. *The Book of Psalms.* Collegeville, Minn.: Liturgical Press.

Davis, Ellen E. 2001. *Getting Involved with God: Rediscovering the Old Testament.* Cambridge, Mass.: Cowley.

Davis, Samuel. 1983. "Letter Dated 1755 to Friends in London." In *Readings in Black American Music*, ed. Eileen Southern, 27–28. New York: Norton.

Dyson, Michael Eric. 1996. *Between God and Gangster Rap: Bearing Witness to Black Culture.* New York: Oxford University Press.

———. 2001. *Holler If You Hear Me: Searching for Tupac Shakur.* New York: Basic Civitas.

Ellis, E. Earl. 1991. *The Old Testament in Early Christianity: Canon and Interpretation in the Light of Modern Research.* Grand Rapids, Mich.: Baker.

Encyclopedia of Early Christianity (EEC). 1990. Ed. Everett Ferguson et al. New York: Garland.

Evans, James H. 1992. *We Have Been Believers: An African American Systematic Theology.* Minneapolis: Fortress Press.

Felder, Cain Hope. 1989. *Troubling Biblical Waters: Race, Class, and Family.* Maryknoll, N.Y.: Orbis.

———. 1999. "The Presence of Blacks in Biblical Antiquity." In *Holy Bible, African American Jubilee Edition, KJV*, 109–25. New York: American Bible Society.

Good, Edwin M. 1993. "Music and the Bible." In *The Oxford Companion to the Bible*, ed. Bruce Metzger and Michael D. Coogan, 535–38. New York: Oxford University Press.

Hinson, Glenn. 2000. *Fire in My Bones: Transcendence and the Holy Spirit in African American Gospel.* Philadelphia: University of Pennsylvania Press.

Holy Bible, African American Jubilee Edition, King James Version. New York: American Bible Society.

Jerusalem Bible. 1966. Garden City, N.Y.: Doubleday.

Kaplan, Steven. 1992. *The Beta Israel (Falasha) in Ethiopia: From Earliest Times to the Twentieth Century.* New York: New York University Press.

McCann, J. Clinton, Jr. 2005. "The Book of Psalms." In *The New Interpreter's Bible: Old Testament Survey*, ed. Leander E. Keck, 197–221. Nashville: Abingdon.

Mowinckel, Sigmund. 1962. *The Psalms in Israel's Worship.* Trans. D. R. Ap-Thomas. 2 vols. Nashville: Abingdon.

Mowry, Lucetta. 1993. "Music and Musical Instruments." In *The Oxford Companion to the Bible*, ed. Bruce Metzger and Michael D. Coogan, 533–35. New York: Oxford University Press.

Murphy, Roland E. 1993. "Psalms, The Book of." In *The Oxford Companion to the Bible*, ed. Bruce M. Metzger and Michael D. Coogan, 626–29. New York: Oxford University Press

Ntintili, Prince Vuyani. 1999. "The Presence and Role of Africans in the Bible." In *Holy Bible, African American Jubilee Edition, KJV*, 97–107. New York: American Bible Society

Shannon, David T. 1991. "An Ante-Bellum Sermon": A Resource for an African American Hermeneutic." In *Stony the Road We Trod: African American Biblical Interpretation*, ed. Cain Hope Felder, 98–123. Minneapolis: Fortress Press.

Small, Christopher. 1987. *Music of the Common Tongue: Survival and Celebration in African American Music.* Hanover, N.H.: Wesleyan University Press.

Southern, Eileen. 1983. "Readings in Black American Music." In *The Music of Black Americans: A History.* 3rd ed. New York: Norton.

Spencer, William David. 1999. *Dread Jesus*. London: Society for Promoting Christian Knowledge (SPCK).

Ukpong, Justin S. 1995. "Rereading the Bible with African Eyes." *Journal of Theology for Southern Africa* 91:3–14.

———. 2002. "Intercultural Hermeneutics: An African Approach to Biblical Interpretation." In *The Bible in a World of Context: An Experiment in contextual Hermeneutics*, eds. Walter Dietrich and Ulrich Luz, 32–48. Grand Rapids: Eerdmans.

Wimbush, Vincent L. 1991. "The Bible and African Americans: An Outline of an Interpretive History." In *Stony the Road We Trod: African American Biblical Interpretation*, ed. Cain Hope Felder, 81–97. Minneapolis: Fortress Press.

Witvliet, John D. 2007. *The Biblical Psalms in Christian Worship: A Brief Introduction and Guide to Resources*. Grand Rapids, Mich.: Eerdmans.

Wright, Jeremiah A., Jr. 1999. "An Underground Theology." In *Black Faith and Public Talk: Critical Essays on James H. Cone's Black Theology and Black Power*, ed. Dwight N. Hopkins, 96–102. Maryknoll, N.Y.: Orbis.

Yorke, G. L. O. 1997. "The Bible and the Black Diaspora." In *The Bible in African Christianity: Essays in Biblical Theology*, ed. Hannah W. Kinoti and John M. Waliggo, 145–64. Nairobi: Acton.

JOB

Madipoane Masenya (ngwan'a Mphahlele) and Rodney S. Sadler Jr.

THE CHAPTER is an attempt by two scholars, one from the African continent (African South Africa) and one from the African Diaspora (African America), to bring some pertinent issues addressed by the book of Job to bear on the Africana reality in its variety. The authors and their communities seem to grapple with the Deity, who, while not always making sense, can still be the object of their trust!

Let the readers then give these narrators their ears.

JOB: AN AFRICAN READING

Madipoane Masenya (ngwan'a Mphahlele)

The book of Job is a fireball. It destroys the neat arrangement devised by some adherents of the religion of Israel to reject painful questions. It disturbs the harmony of biblical teaching about God's plan. . . . *It refuses to soften what everyone seeks to control, suffering and misfortune.*
—Duquoc and Floristan 1983: vii; italics added

Therefore I will not restrain my mouth;
I will speak in the anguish of my spirit;
I will complain in the bitterness of my soul.
—Job 7:11

Letlalo la motho ga le bapolelwe fase
"a person's skin cannot be crucified on the ground"
—African proverb

In the story that follows, the narrator, a contemporary Job, picks up on some of the issues raised by the character of Job in the Hebrew Bible in own her struggle to wrestle with God amid suffering. Her relationship with God, a relationship that started in her teen years, was nurtured both culturally and religiously by the belief that God is the sustainer of the moral order and the guarantor of retributive justice. Suffering has been her lot in recent times: the loss of good health by some family members, the loss of financial gains (because of robbery by people whom her family was trying to help), and topping it all, the loss of a human being! All of these she has suffered despite her commitment to God, with whom she also constantly interceded for her family. She finds her courage and determination to approach the Sacred Other with questions.

This contemporary Job is aware of the different, unsettling, and yet relevant wisdom perspective that the author of the book of Job presents. She has taught the book in her classes and used it in some of her counseling sessions as a clergy person. At the moment, overwhelmed by grief, the pain of loss, the perception of being an unjust sufferer, and a sense of betrayal and abandonment by the divine parent, she seems to be stared in the eye by the truth underlying the proverbial saying "Physician, heal yourself!" As part of her healing process, she will venture to speak to God about her suffering.

STRUGGLING THROUGH UNJUST SUFFERING: AN AFRICAN WOMAN WRESTLES WITH GOD

AN INDIVIDUAL'S STORY OR A COMMUNAL ONE?

Although my story is that of one grieving African–South African woman,[1] like the Hebrew Bible story of Job it can also be regarded as a collective[2] (see Dussel 1983: 61; see also Ntreh 2004: 141–58; Tamez 2004: 103–11). Just as the "individualized" narrative of the biblical Job was meant to address, among others, the socioeconomic inequities suf-

fered by the (righteous) Jews in the early postexilic Yehud, both from fellow Jews and from the Persian colonial masters (see Ceresko 2005: 68–70; see also MacKenzie 1983: 3–5), in its present South African setting, this story can be regarded as a collective. Why? It is likely a story of many grieving South African parents who wrestle with God amid (unjust) suffering, the latter not least because of the excruciating pain connected with the loss of a child. The argument in favor of collectivity is advanced because of the fatalities on South African roads in recent years. Statistics have shown that car crashes claim approximately fourteen thousand lives per annum! Also, because of the HIV/AIDS pandemic, which claims many young Black South African lives daily, my wrestling with God in the present story is most likely typical in the hearts and mouths of many affected parents (Masenya 2005). One common thread runs through most of these stories: parents' wrestling with God amid unjust suffering.

PROVERBIAL WISDOM

An African proverb says *Letlalo la motho ga le bapolelwe fase*, "a person's skin cannot be crucified on the ground." Why? A human being's (*motho*) final exit out of earth is always bound to inflict pain on the living—unless the moral order had been disturbed in one way or another. Also, in the African worldview, a causal link exists between the calamity and certain factors or forces, or a Force (Masenya 1989; 2005). Isn't that the same mentality that preoccupied the friends who were trying very hard, albeit irrelevantly, to comfort Job?

> Think now, who that was innocent ever perished? Or where were the upright cut off?
> As I have seen, those who plow iniquity and sow trouble reap the same. (Job 4:7-8)

The insistence by Job's friends that he brought all the misery on himself (see 8:1-8; 11:5-6;

20:5-8)—their refusal to adjust their status quo theology accordingly— brings to mind another proverb: *Sešo se baba mongwai wa sona*, "a sore itches to the one who has it!" Naturally, the sore's "outside" observer has no clue about the intensity of its "itchiness." The pertinent question is this: Why do outsiders to suffering approach those with sores as though they, the outsiders, have all the answers? Was Job to be intimidated by the problematic view of the majority? No! In an earlier article, in which I deliberately changed the biblical male character Job to a female character, Mmalehu, I argued: "Irrespective of her 'volatile' condition, she (Mmalehu), contrary to the status quo, refuses to regard the majority as the norm. If the theology of the healthy majority is faulty, she will not heed it" (Masenya 2001: 196).

My further engagement with the opening proverb breeds more questions: Why did my son die? How could *leitšibulo*[3] *la ka* depart from me so suddenly? So tragically? So unjustly? Tumisho, how on earth did you dare to leave me, your dad, your siblings, and your two-year-old Kamo so prematurely? Oh God, where were you when all these things happened? Tumisho, this same God with whom I now wrestle is the one whom your parents introduced to you at an early age as a caring, protecting father. Remember? I cannot but ask: Does God still have the capacity to be a keeper who would not let the feet of God's children be moved (Ps. 121:3)? Valid and good questions, but few or no answers![4] Says Job:

> "Even when I cry out, 'Violence!'
> I am not answered;
> I call aloud, but there is no justice." (Job 19:7)

Unlike Job, the man who, when pained by the loss of his children (Job 1:18-19), had the courage to curse his birthday (Job 3:1-10), I cannot. I dare not! Job not only curses his special day but he questions the usefulness of the female knees that eased his entry onto Mother Earth. Alas, even the breasts whose nurturing milk raised him come under his

scathing attack (Job 3:12)! Let me assure you, *Buti wa Marino*, that Job has no clue whatsoever about the duration of the labor pains that I suffered on that cold June day, night, and day—the longest I have ever experienced! Laboring to usher you to Planet Earth. God forbid that, even in my deep pain of losing the caring, resourceful young man that you were, I curse that day. Neither can I curse the day on which my mother bore me even as I continue to direct my anger and frustrations to the Sacred Other about your sudden departure. Despite the many yet-to-be answered "why" questions on this untold misery, I, your mother, whose knees received you, whose breasts you sucked, do not have the courage to curse the day that enabled me, for the first time in my life, to share in the blessing of cocreating with God, the divine mother.

Ruminating on the opening proverb leads to further questions and suspicions: Why did it happen to me? The question that runs through Job's encounter with his friends and God . . . is it not the work of a *thagelakgole*? *Thagelakgole* is a *muti* believed to have powers to enable a prescribed calamity to occur far from the victim's home.[5] Perhaps the ancestors are punishing her for being such an independent woman? A woman who chose to hold her own in the world; a woman whose thought patterns are still Eurocentric and patriarchal? Others may speculate about this with a measure of certainty. What exactly has she done to deserve God's punishment? Has she been tithing regularly? Did she really nurture her children according to God's standards? She might be reaping the consequences of her heretical, feminine/ist (demonic?) theologies!

Aren't all of the suspicions and questions raised in this text prompted by my/our incapacity to want to receive bad things from God as well as good things (see Job 2:10; see also Isa. 45:6-7; Amos 3:6; Lam. 3:38)? Can the optimistic worldview of the wise of Africa and of Israel win the day amid the present crisis? Amid the HIV/AIDS crisis? Definitely not! (See Masenya 2005.)

Yours, a tragic death. Senseless. Unjust. Your body? Made to bear the consequences of the apartheid racist legacies. When the white Afrikaner boy who (out of drunkenness? whatever?) overtook a car at a blind spot and hit your car so terribly, why did he run away from that gruesome scene? Leaving you to bleed profusely? If the bodies of your car's occupants were white, would your killer have run away from the scene of the crash? Oh God of justice, in and through all these injustices, where were you? As if the very incident of my son's death was not enough punishment, the how part only serves to add salt to my injury:

> For the arrows of the Almighty are in me;
> My spirit drinks their poison;
> The terrors of God are arrayed against me.
> (Job 5:4)

I stood in that hospital emergency unit, shocked, frustrated, and stunned. No words! Could I deny that he had died when confronted with his motionless, lifeless body? How were his parents expected to handle the taboo in African cultures that parents cannot bury their children?

Struggling through Job's story in the midst of pain enables me to reach at least the following conclusions:

- "Naked I came from my mother's womb, and naked shall I return there; the LORD gave, and the LORD has taken away" (Job 1:21). I thought I owned him. How wrong I was! Didn't he first and foremost belong to God? Isn't it typical of humans to believe that they own, among others, the material, physical, and political benefits? Were the perpetrators of the inequities in Yehud aware that the possessions they owned (?) unjustly could end at any time? As humans, we have a need to remain humble, responsible stewards of all that God has entrusted to us even as we need the capacity to let go when God recalls that which has been so dear to us—that is, our loved ones.

- The retributive philosophy that has dominated for so long (and continues to dominate) the religious landscape of both Africa and Israel needs to be applied with caution. It does not always work. It has not worked in the present story and in many related South African stories.

- The righteous will also go through the excruciating pain connected with the loss of a loved one, even if such loss comes unjustly. Even in such conditions, God is, God was, God will be: "Within the boundaries of a divine worldview, retribution is not necessary and the logic of causality does not necessarily apply to God's actions. People's world-views and religious beliefs depend on God, but God does not depend on their views, beliefs and actions" (Kamp 2004: 12).

- While we have the courage to yell at God and pour out our frustrations about the injustices suffered in our midst, we should also do the same toward the pillars of the evil structures that, in most cases, are directly or indirectly responsible for the inequities in our midst. Whether Job's complaints ever reached the ears of the perpetrators of the injustices of the time is unknown.

- So huge and sovereign is this Sacred Other, who has become and continues to be the object of our yelling, anger, criticisms, and frustrations, that God remains patient with all those who wrestle with God in the midst of unjust suffering. If these sufferers persist in their steadfastness with God, they, like the biblical Job, will eventually say: "I had heard of you by the hearing of the ear, but now my eyes sees you" (Job 42:5).

Ngwaga wo o sa nthatego, Selaganya! Let the year that does not like me, pass quickly!

We now listen to another voice from the African Diaspora.

JOB: AN AFRICAN AMERICAN PERSPECTIVE

Rodney S. Sadler Jr.

The story of Job is one of the most potent narratives in the whole of scripture. Job is a wealthy and powerful man who begins the narrative with respect for God, the love of his family, and the envy of his entire community (Job 1:1-5). His sudden fall, which occurs in the space of two brief introductory chapters, is emblematic of the tenuous nature of life itself, for fortunes can change without a moment's notice. Perhaps his story is most troubling because this good man's change of fortunes comes about because of the will of YHWH, the God in whom he has placed his trust. How frightening the first two chapters of Job are, for though they posit that God is in control of human lives, the reasons for the suffering that God apparently allows remain beyond our understanding.

Issues of theodicy, from the Greek *theo* ("God") and *dike* ("justice"), are thought to be the basis for the story of Job. Theodicy in essence asks the question "Is God just?" This question is unavoidable in a world where "bad things happen to good people," as it were. In fact, it is a necessary question to ask when the deuteronomistic equation of "do good and be blessed and do evil and be cursed" has proven a far too simplistic estimation of circumstances in this world. Perhaps this was the case in postexilic Judah when the reconstituted nation reminisced about its immutable covenant with YHWH, the impenetrable walls of Zion, and the promise of a perpetual king on David's throne, all of which came to a sudden end as its fortunes changed drastically in 586 B.C.E. So the Job narrative may well represent the queries of a people who perceive their world to be less predictable and their

God to be less just in the aftermath of the greatest tragedy in their collective history.

On a meta level, Job functions as the story of another people who have lost everything and learned to question everything about their God and their fortunes. Having been stolen from their lands and brought to a new land where they experienced unimaginable brutality, enslaved Africans' narratives are often inspired by and beholden to the Job story. The stories of James Albert Gronniosaw, Ottobah Cugoano, and Olaudah Equiano begin in similar fashion, recalling their days in an idyllic kingdom as children of privilege in African villages. Suddenly, each of their fortunes changes when they are stolen from their lands and thrust into hellish Job-like situations of loss, where their very lives are all but forfeit. Job's tale provides a vocabulary for the suffering of enslaved and recently freed Africans, couching the pain of families being sold away,[6] the anguish of a life in chains,[7] the horror of the loss of loved ones,[8] and even the hope of future redemption,[9] in the typology of this key biblical figure.

But like the account of Job, many narratives of formerly enslaved Africans emphasize the undeniable nature of Providence. For Job, Providence is what he comes to accept after his conversations with God (chs. 38–41), beginning with the following exclamation:

> Then the LORD answered Job out of the whirlwind: "Who is this that darkens counsel by words without knowledge? Gird up your loins like a man, I will question you, and you shall declare to me. (Job 38:1-3, NRSV)

In an extended monologue, God extols God's own ability to do things so far beyond human agency as to render Job's questions irrelevant. Unable to respond to the Deity, Job thus accepts his fortunes and bows to God's will (42:1-6). After accepting that he is not fit to question YHWH's will and repenting "in dust and ashes" (v. 6), Job is rewarded with "twice as much as he had before" (v. 10). Similarly, after questioning their lots in life and struggling to reconcile their fortunes with God's justice, the authors of many of the narratives of formerly enslaved Africans celebrate God's providence, noting that even amid their trials and travails, God's hand is apparent. Reflecting on the difficulties of his life, Olaudah Equiano notes:

> I believe there are few events in my life, which have not happened to many: it is true the incidents of it are numerous; and, did I consider myself an European, I might say my sufferings were great: but when I compare my lot with that of most of my countrymen, I regard myself as a *particular favourite of Heaven,* and acknowledge the mercies of Providence in every occurrence of my life.[10]

As with many of Equiano's fellow formerly enslaved Africana siblings, God's providence serves as a recurrent motif running throughout Equiano's narrative, ascribing theological significance to the pathos he endures and offering him the promise of a better life in this world and the next.

The appeal to Job was not limited only to extended narratives, for African American hymnody expresses the enduring power of the Job narrative to inspire hope in the otherwise hopeless. Brutalized, enslaved Caesar, after suffering the relentless abuse of his slaver, composed and sang this verse of hope to the chagrin of all who heard it: "We suffer here like father Job, But soon will go to wear the robe."[11] Emma Ray, reflecting on God's grace amid her own suffering, cites the following line from an unnamed song: "Is not Thy grace as mighty now, As when Elijah felt its power; When glory beamed from Moses's brow, Or Job endured the trying hour?"[12] Perhaps it is this character's appeal to others who suffer that leads Elizabeth Keckley to canonize him as "that divine comforter, Job."[13]

The lessons from each of these Africana witnesses to the significance of Job's tale are undeniable. Although the will of God is not clearly discernible, although bad things do happen to good people, although suffering is often all but unbearable, we still are to "keep on keeping on." The night of our suffering may be long, and the reasons for our suffering may be beyond our comprehension and our control, but we take heart in the Africana adage: *mayo ga se maboelele!* ("trouble don't last always!"). The goodness of the Lord comes just in the nick of time. As the song says: "He may not come when you want him, but He'll be there right on time, He's an on time God, Yes he is!"

As we conclude our reflections, the following African wisdom sayings come to mind:

> *Mayo ga se maboelele* (To go [to a place] does not imply to return to it [the same place]).
> *Modimo ga o lahle ngwana wa ona* (God will not throw away God's child).

Notes

1. African–South African women's individual experiences form one of the main foci of the *bosadi* biblical hermeneutics (see Masenya 1996; 2004; 2005).

2. Dussel, in "The People of El Salvador: The Communal Sufferings of Job," argues rightly in this regard: "To try to apply the message of Job, whether analogously or allegorically, to a whole people, can well appear a risky, if not an impossible undertaking. But remember the biblical figure or hermeneutical concept of the 'incorporating personality', used of the person of Israel, for example: a historical individual whose name is applied by analogy to the Hebrew *people*, to Jesus, to the early Christian community (the 'new Israel'), to the Church itself as a whole. In this sense, Job can equally be *a* person, or *a* people. There can be a collective Job, a Job-community. A suffering, persecuted, crucified Job-people" (Dussell 1983: 61).

3. The word *leitšibulo* is the Sotho word for a child (whether male or female) who opened the womb of a woman—that is, the firstborn child.

4. It is my belief that the God with whom I am wrestling is so huge that God is not bothered by any question that any human being can ask. Whether in

God's view such questions make sense or not, God has the capacity to answer (or not to answer) such questions accordingly and in God's own time, if we can even speak about time insofar as the Sacred Other is concerned,

5. In this context, it is usually believed to have been prescribed by concerned witches and wizards—in certain instances, in collaboration with or through the encouragement of a traditional healer or healers to make the calamity (death, disease, and so forth) occur far away from the victim-to-be's place of misfortune.

6. W. H. Robinson, *From Log Cabin to the Pulpit, or Fifty Years in Slavery* (Eau Claire, Wis.: James H. Tifft, 1913), 49–50.

7. Peter Wheeler, *Chains and Freedom: or, The Life and Adventures of Peter Wheeler, A Colored Man Yet Living . . .* (New York: E. S. Arnold, 1839), 21.

8. Bishop Isaac Lane, *Autobiography of Bishop Isaac Lane LL.D. with a Short History of the C.M.E. Church in America and of Methodism* (Nashville: Methodist Episcopal, 1916), 110.

9. Amanda Smith, *An Autobiography: The Story of the Lord's Dealings with Mrs. Amanda Smith . . .* (Chicago: Meyer and Brother, 1893), 144.

10. Olaudah Equiano, *The Interesting Narrative of the Life of Olaudah Equiano or Gustavus Vassa, The African*, vol. 1 (London: published by author, 1789), 2–3.

11. Rev. S. H. Platt, *The Martyrs, and the Fugitive; Or a Narrative of the Captivity, Sufferings, and Death of an African Family, and the Slavery and Escape of Their Son* (New York: Daniel Fanshaw, 1859), 82.

12. Emma J. Ray, *Twice Sold, Twice Ransomed: Autobiography of Mr. and Mrs. L. P. Ray* (Chicago: Free Methodist, 1926), 31.

13. Elizabeth Keckley, *Behind the Scenes, or, Thirty years a Slave, and Four Years in the White House* (New York: G. W. Carleton, 1868), 119.

References

Ceresko, A.R. 2005. *Introduction to Old Testament Wisdom: A Spirituality of Liberation*. Maryknoll, N.Y.: Orbis.

Duquoc, C. and Floristan, C. 1983. "Editorial." In *Job and the Silence of God*, ed. R. MacKenzie, vii-viii, Edinburgh: T. & T. Clark.

Dussel, E. 1983. "The People of El Salvador: The Communal Sufferings of Job." In *Job and the Silence of God*, ed. R. MacKenzie, 61–68. Edinburgh: T. & T. Clark.

Kamp, A. 2004. "With or without a Cause: Images of God and Man in Job 1–3." In *Job's God*, ed. E. Van Wonde, 9–17. London: SCM.

MacKenzie, R. 1983. *Job and the Silence of God*. Edinburgh: T. & T. Clark.

Masenya, M. J. 1989. In the School of Wisdom: An Interpretation of Some Old Testament Proverbs in a Northern Sotho Context, Unpublished MA dissertation, University of South Africa, Pretoria, South Africa.

Masenya (ngwan'a Mphahlele), M. 1996. Proverbs 31:10-31 in a South African Context: A Bosadi (Womanhood) Approach, Unpublished D. Litt. et Phil. Thesis, University of South Africa, Pretoria, South Africa.

Masenya (ngwan'a Mphahlele), M. 2001. "Between Unjust suffering and the 'Silent' God: Job and HIV/AIDS Sufferers in South Africa." *Missionalia* 29 (2): 186–99.

———. 2004. *How Worthy is the Woman of Worth? Rereading Proverbs 31:10-31 in African–South Africa*. New York: Peter Lang.

———. 2005. "The Bible, HIV/AIDS and African/South African Women: A Bosadi Approach." *Studia Historiae Ecclesiaticae XXXI (1)*, 187–201.

———. 2005. "The Optimism of the Wise in Israel and in Africa: Helpful in the time of AIDS?" *Old Testament Essays* 18 (2): 296–308.

Kamp, A. 2004. "With or without a Cause: Images of God and Man in Job 1–3." In *Job's God*, ed. E. Van Wonde, 9–17. London: SCM.

Ntreh, B. A. 2004. "Job." In *Global Bible Commentary*, ed. D. Patte et al., 141–58. Nashville: Abingdon.

Tamez, E. 2004. "From Father to the Needy to Brother of Jackals and Companions of Ostriches: A Meditation on Job." In *Job's God*, ed. E. van Wonde, 103–11. London: SCM.

PROVERBS

Naomi Franklin

THE BOOK OF PROVERBS is part of the corpus of wisdom literature found in the Hebrew Bible. It comes from the postexilic period, although it does contain material from the preexilic period, namely those pieces known as the "Solomonic collections" (chapters 10–21 and 25–29). The first nine chapters contain extensive discourses that center around one main figure: "Woman Wisdom." She describes herself elaborately as God's companion, there "with Him at the creation of the world." Proverbs 10:1—31:9 consists of six proverb collections containing sets of proverbs of a few verses each. The end of the book consists of a short poem in praise of the "capable wife." The main objective of the Wisdom discourses in Proverbs is to develop a strong sense of morality in the youth of the community, so as to ensure for them a stable life and future that includes by necessity a rightful place in the community. Wisdom has a dual benefit. It helps both the young person who is receiving instruction and the community of which the person is to become a productive member in the future.

The book of Proverbs contains evidence of definite Egyptian influence. Contemporary research has clearly established that Prov. 22:17—24:22 contains parallels to the Egyptian work known as the Instruction of Amenemope. The Egyptian material found in Proverbs was "adapted and modified in order to suit the new Hebrew framework" (Shupak 2005: 209). The content and objectives of Prov. 22:17—23:11 and Amenemope are similar. Shupak also points to the difficult nature of the Hebrew text and its incomprehensibility, without the illumination of the Egyptian Amenemope text (2005: 210). This speaks prominently to the

African presence and influence in the text of the Hebrew Bible.

According to Proverbs, there are two places where moral development is formed: the home and the larger community. Both are places where wisdom is to be taught and found. Within the confines of these two places, two types of wisdom discourses can be found. One, in the home, is parental/disciplinary discourse; the other, in the community, is the discourse of wisdom, which moves past the disciplinary nature of the discourse in the home to that of revelation and invitation. This is found in chapters 8 and 9 (Brown 1996: 43). Within Proverbs, one finds much advice about the use of wisdom, the virtuous woman as opposed to the loose woman, as well as guidance regarding wealth and poverty. The texts that deal with wealth and poverty exhibit, among other things, a concern for justice for the poor while decrying the oppressive and dishonest means that are often used to acquire wealth. There are also wise words advising against adultery and the proliferation of offspring by multiple partners (see 5:15-20). It also advises against laziness (see 6:6-11).

The proverb, as found in the book of Proverbs, is a "saying," at times in the form of comparisons (see, for example, 20:2 and 28:13) or popular sayings, some of which are well known and popular even now. One example that readily comes to mind is Proverbs 1:7a: "The fear of the Lord is the beginning of knowledge." Within the African Diaspora communities, certain sayings are passed down mostly by grandmothers and mothers to the next generation. Many Afro-Caribbean persons have learned sayings from their mothers and grandmothers, such as "Moon run till day catch him" (meaning that when you do something wrong, you can get away with it perhaps for a while, but in the end you will be caught) and "a still tongue keeps a wise head" (meaning that being silent rather than talking at the wrong moment can at times save one's life). Mercy Amba Oduyoye cites proverbs from Africa that are similar to those found in the book of Proverbs. One example is, "If there is something

to be gained from promiscuity, then the goat would be king" (Oduyoye 1995: 56). Her work provides many more examples that are insightful as to the wisdom of Africa.

Within Israelite society, wisdom was considered to be a very important element, woven into the tapestry of both the culture and the religion. As noted earlier, she held preeminence within the creation event. She was created before the world. As shown in 8:22-31, she is the foundation of everything. It is implied within the text, especially in verses 27–30a, that God used wisdom in all acts of creation. If, indeed, she was beside him, then it can be suggested that it was to Wisdom that God said, "Let us make humankind in our image, according to our likeness" (Gen. 1:26a). This adds to the understanding of creation, the reality that human beings were created with an innate capacity to acquire and use wisdom.

One of the most fascinating aspects of Wisdom's story is the seven pillars that she uses to build her house. It states in 9:1: "Wisdom has built her house; she has hewn her seven pillars." Careful examination of the Hebrew text reveals wisdom's seven pillars. They are seven feminine words that speak to the aspects of Wisdom, who is, herself, feminine. They are *torah*, instruction; *t'vunah*, understanding; *da'at*, knowledge; *armah*, shrewdness; *mezimah*, prudence/sound judgment; *tachbolet*, skill; and *melitzah*, a saying. In addition to Wisdom's seven pillars with which she builds her house, it is also of interest that most of the words connected with wisdom are feminine. An example of this is found in 3:21 in the word *tushiyah*, which is translated as "sound wisdom" or "common sense." It is also of note that words that indicate some negative aspects of knowledge and demeanor/behavior are also feminine, such as those indicating "pride" and "perverted speech."

Proverbs 14:1 presents a translational problem, and thus one of transmission of meaning as well. The Hebrew states: "The wisdom of women builds her house." This is what the actual translation should be, but this is not shown in the biblical translation into English. It is glossed over. The translation that is given verges on being interpretation (Meyers 2001: 306). Meyers sees this verse as being a term for the family household. She also sees it as an expression of female agency (2001: 306). What is found within this text is the understanding of the collective wisdom of the foremothers throughout the generations coming forward and influencing the female members of successive generations as they build households, nurture offspring, and pass on their wisdom to their daughters. Implicit in the text is the understanding of the transmission of wisdom as an aspect of oral pedagogy, which is a combination of tradition and practice.

One of the most popular sections found in the book of Proverbs is Prov. 31:10-31. It has often been preached on Women's Day in many African American churches. Although beautiful in its lyrical form in the Hebrew, the passage can also be considered problematic by many Africana women who read it and try in some way to identify with or live up to this woman who appears to be ideal.

The woman portrayed in this passage is a married, wealthy woman with servants, her own business, and a prominent husband. Many persons reading this section might question how this section, this paradigm, can in any way be relevant to Black women on the whole, due to the fact that many do not fit into the patterns. The possibility is miniscule at best. However, there are yet possibilities for identification within the text. Were there to be an adjustment in the translation of the adjective used to describe the woman, it would open up the possibility of identifying with this woman being described in the text. The adjective in the text used to describe the wife/woman can also be translated as "strength," "power," or "courageous." Thus, it can legitimately be translated as "a woman of strength" or "a woman of power" or "a woman who is courageous." With this retranslation of the text, by saying "whoever finds a strong woman, a 'courageous woman' or a 'powerful woman,'" one finds a paradigm within which an Africana woman

can place herself. Also, it is not necessary to translate the word that is translated to mean "wife" as such. The word in Hebrew is also validly translated as "woman." Thus, again with a valid retranslation of the text, a place can be found for the woman who is single with children and who faces life with strength and courage daily. Thus, this woman becomes real for Africana women.

There have been countless Afro-Caribbean and African American women throughout history—unsung heroines—who have risen to that level. Afro-Caribbean and African American mothers, grandmothers, and even great-grandmothers have for centuries risen to the challenges that arose for them and their families, meeting them valiantly, capably, and successfully. Within our histories are many untold stories of women who have tirelessly worked with the willing hands of verse 13; women who have awakened while it was still night and began to work, as noted in 31:15, just to ensure that their families would have a meal before they went to work. These are the women who stayed up late at night, just as noted in 31:18b, to make sure that their family's needs were met. They did not have financial wealth, but their wealth of spirit and courage in the face of overwhelming odds and their ability to stretch their money in order "to make do," speak to their valiant spirit and their enormous capabilities. These women abound in our present day and in our past. Within African Diaspora communities, it has long been the practice for those who have little to extend a helping hand to those who have less. There exists ample evidence, among the women of these communities, of the strength and dignity noted in 31:25. One need only look at the matriarchs throughout the African Diaspora for examples. What has been often woefully lacking is the praise due these women.

Child rearing is emphasized in Proverbs. The teaching found in 23:13 and 22:15 refers to *musar* ("instruction"). It must be made clear that discipline and instruction are meant to be used in a nonabusive way (Fox 1994: 241–43). In Proverbs, the term *instruction* (*musar*) exhibits a disciplinary nuance. This "instruction" is used in the context of child rearing. Careful examination and application of the text is necessary.

Proverbs stresses righteousness. In 14:34, it states: Righteousness exalts a nation, but sin is a reproach to any people. A clear understanding of righteousness is needed to apply this verse to the lives of people. In the biblical context, righteousness must be exercised in one's dealings both with God and one's fellow human beings. Examination of the corpus of biblical laws makes this clear. Sin within community, in whatever form it may take, is the undoing of a community and indeed becomes reproach. Sin against God inevitably leads to alienation from God and will lead to a breakdown in community. It functions in a reciprocal continuum. One leads to the other and feeds on the other. True righteousness in one area cannot help but lead to true righteousness in the other. This was fundamental for Martin Luther King Jr. when he quoted Amos 5:24. Righteousness bears fruit [see Amos 6:12], as do all actions. The prescriptions and guidelines given in Proverbs serve as a guide, a plumb line, if you will, for the community of faith. The task is to bring it to life in the lives of consecutive generations and create a sense of purpose within the continuum of a history that is lived and created daily.

There is much within the work that can be utilized in character formation and community building for members of the community of faith, whether advising children about education, friendships, business, or family life. It is all there and indeed applies even today. For members of the African Diaspora, that its source is to some extent from the continent of Africa makes it worth even more. That the mother is affirmed as teacher and largely the backbone of her household affirmingly, speaks to the reality of the African Diasporan familial condition. The strength, power, diligence, and commitment of African Diasporan women to their children, family, and community are confirmed and affirmed within the pages of Proverbs. The book

guides, affirms, and enlightens us on this journey called life.

References

Cannon, Katie Geneva. 2003. *Katie's Canon: Womanism and the Soul of the Black Community*. New York: Continuum.

Fox, Michael V. 1994. "The Pedagogy of Proverbs 2." *Journal of Biblical Literature* 113:241–43.

Fry Brown, Teresa L. 2000. *God Don't Like Ugly, African American Women Handing on Spiritual Values*. Nashville: Abingdon.

Greenspoon, Leonard. 2005. "Translating Biblical Words of Wisdom into the Modern World." In *Seeking Out the Wisdom of the Ancients: Essays Offered to Honor Michael V. Fox on the Occasion of His 65th Birthday*, ed. Ronald L. Troxel, Kelvin G. Friebel, and Dennis Margary. Winona Lake, Ind.: Eisenbrauns.

Meyers, Carol. 2001. "Wise Women Building Her House." In *Women in Scripture: A Dictionary of Named and Unnamed Women in the Hebrew Bible, the Apocryphal/Deuterocanonical Books, and the New Testament*, ed. Carol Meyers, Toni Craven, and Ross S. Kraemer. Grand Rapids, Mich.: Eerdmans.

Oduyoye, Mercy Amba. 2002. "Acting as Women." In *African Theology Today*, ed. Emmanuel Katongole. Scranton, Pa.: University of Scranton Press.

———. 2005. *Daughters of Anowa: African Women and Patriarchy*. Maryknoll, N.Y.: Orbis.

Redwine, F. E. 1998. "What Woman Is." In *Daughters of Thunder: Black Women Preachers and Their Sermons, 1850–1979*, ed. Bettye Collier-Thomas. San Francisco: Jossey-Bass.

Shupak, Nili. 2005. "The Instruction of Amenemope and Proverbs 22:17—24:22 from the Perspective of Contemporary Research. In *Seeking Out the Wisdom of the Ancients: Essays Offered to Honor Michael V. Fox on the Occasion of His 65th Birthday*, ed. Ronald L. Troxel, Kelvin G. Friebel, and Dennis Margary. Winona Lake, Ind.: Eisenbrauns.

Spearing Randolph, Florence. 1998. "Woman, the Builder of Her House" [a sermon delivered in New-

INTERPRETIVE ISSUES

MARRIAGE

The Afro-Asiatic cultures that produced, and the global cultures that have canonized, Ruth highly esteemed heterosexual conjugal partnerships, marriage, even though there is no specific term in Biblical Hebrew for marriage, nor any description of ritual practices associated with sanctioned unions. There are of course socially accepted conjugal unions in the text, but the smallest level of the Israelite kinship system is the maternal or paternal household, not a conjugal couple. Both matrilineality (Rebekah's mother's household in Genesis 24:15, David's sister's sons in 2 Samuel 2:18, the bride in the Song of Songs 8:2) and patrilineality (the dominant expression, as seen in Genesis 11:31; Numbers 1:5; 2 Chronicles 1:1, and so forth) are attested in the Hebrew Scriptures.

Marriage is a contentious category in the United States as some are asking who can and should marry, others are demanding the right to marry as a fundamental civil and human right, and still others are insisting on preserving a particular biblical paradigm. But marriage is a normative category in most of Africa and Asia. At the same time, the normative experience of black women in the Americas who do not marry shapes a reading of Ruth that may not be congruent with Africana readers in other contexts for whom marriage is normative. Asian and Africana readers frequently share a sense of cultural familiarity with the story of Ruth because of the focus on the mother-in-law/daughter-in-law relationship, the cultural and societal vulnerability of widows, and the necessity of producing live offspring, preferably male, to secure a woman's status and economic well-being and that of her family.

As an Africana reader, I am particularly interested in how issues of translation affect how scriptures are read, heard, understood, and interpreted in the broader African diaspora. In a working paper on African feminist postcolonial biblical interpretation, Musa Dube notes the rarity of women on committees responsible for major translations of the scriptures (such as UBS; this is also true for NRSV, JPS, and others) and the tendency for translators and their translations to advance the aims of empire. Construction of gender and gender roles, including marriage and motherhood, is one well-attested aim of empire. An Africana translation-sensitive reading of the book of Ruth calls into question the virtue and value of Ruth's marriage to Boaz even as it recognizes the import of marriage in the ancient and contemporary African and Asian contexts from which the scriptures emerged and in which they continue to be venerated.

The normative portrayal of marriage in Ruth is a particular problem for English readers because it masks sexual and domestic violence in a text that has been canonized as *scripture* for Jews and Christians. There are at least three indicators that Ruth was abducted into marriage: (1) the use of the verb *ns'*, "lift," with "woman," instead of the standard *lqch*, "take (as wife)," (2) the long-standing Israelite practice of abduction or rape-marriage, and (3) the preferential abduction of foreign women for rape-marriages.

The verb in Ruth 1:4, *vayis'u*, from *ns'*, "to lift" or "pick up," may be taken to indicate that Ruth and Orpah, both Moabite women, were abducted into marriage. I translate the first three words of Ruth 1:4, "They-abducted for-themselves Moabite-women. . . ." The verb *ns'* occurs 661 times in the MT. The primary meaning of *ns'*, according to *The Hebrew and Aramaic Lexicon of the Old Testament (HALOT)*, is "to carry" or "to lift." In virtually every translation of *ns'* in which the object is not a person, the verb is rendered with some form of "lift," "carry," "take," or something similar. Any thing or person may be the object of *ns'*: the hand (Deut. 32:20), prayer (Jer. 7:13), or sin may be lifted off of a person or community (Isa. 53:11), and so forth. In Ruth *ns'* is also used to indicate lifting grain in 2:18. Women are the object of *ns'* five times: Judges 21:23; Ruth 1:4; Ezra 10:44; 2 Chr. 13:21 and 24:3. Note that in Judges, the context is the abduction of sexually naïve girls from Shiloh into forced or rape-marriages for the purpose of progeny. The verb *chtph* in Judges 21:21, "to catch" (women), functions as a synonym. In Ezra, the women in question are specified as foreign. In 2 Chr. 13:21, Abijah's collection of women and the resulting offspring is cited as evidence of his *strength* in the previous verse, suggesting that these were abduction-marriages. (Jehoida's acquisition of women for his son Joash is not elaborated upon in 2 Chr. 24:3.)

The normative verb indicating marriage in the Hebrew Scriptures, *lqch*, "to take," with a woman as the object, indicates in every case in the Hebrew Scriptures socially sanctioned union (Gen. 4:19; Exod. 6:20; Jer. 16:2, and so on). Later in Rabbinic Hebrew, *niysuin*, from the stem *ns'*, indicates normative marriage; but this form does not occur in Biblical Hebrew. (Marcus Jastrow's *Dictionary of Targumim, Talmud Bavli, Yerushalmi and Misdrashic Literature* derives *niysuin* from *ns'* and connects it to the practice of relocating a wife to one's home, citing Mishnah, *Kethuvim* II:1, and Talmud, *b. Yebamoth* 37b.) Rape-marriage as a normative practice is introduced in Numbers 31, where sexually naïve girls are abducted as "booty," *shalal*. It is codified subsequently in Deuteronomy 20, 21, and 24. Among the modifications introduced are the shift of focus from any outsider girl whose people are designated as "enemies" (as in Num. 31:19) to "beautiful" women and girls among the enemy (Deut. 20:11). Deuteronomy 20:12-13 also calls for the abducted women and girls to be stripped, their heads shaved, and their nails cut.

In 2 Chronicles 28, Israelites are castigated by the prophet Oded for treating Judean captives like foreigners, including holding women and girls as booty (vv. 8-9); they were released and the naked among them were clothed (v. 15). The abduction of foreign women is not critiqued. Lastly, there is a suggestion that Moabite women are particularly vulnerable is Isaiah 16, in which they are described as "scattered nestlings" seeking protection in verses 2-4. The very name, "Moab," literally "from [my] father," evokes the alleged incestuous and therefore despicable nature of all Moabites according to the Israelite account of their origins in the Genesis 19 account of Lot and his daughters. As a result, Moabites, particularly Moabite women, are highly sexualized in the scriptures of Israel, as are many contemporary Africana women readers of those same scriptures.

Given the specific vocabulary deployed in the text and Ruth's identity as a Moabite woman—which she never escapes—Ruth is multiply marginalized, socially and sexually vulnerable. Ruth and Orpah's marriages, therefore, hide dirty not-so-little secrets, covered up by generations of male translators. Yet the experience of abduction-marriage and forcible pregnancy is not unimaginable to contemporary Africana readers. In some parts of Eastern and Central Africa, women are still abducted and raped into marriage.

The Associated Press (AP) ran a story on June 21, 2005, under an Addis Ababa, Ethiopia, dateline in which a twelve-year-old girl, kidnapped by men who wanted to force her into marriage, was rescued by three lions that chased off her abductors and guarded her until police and relatives located her. Sergeant Wondimu Wedajo of the local police reported that the men had held the girl for seven days, repeatedly beating her: "Often these young girls are raped and severely beaten to force them to accept the marriage."

The AP report noted that in Ethiopia, kidnapping has been part of marriage customs for quite some time and that the United Nations estimates that more than 70 percent of marriages in Ethiopia occurred by abduction, particularly in rural areas where the majority of the country's population lives. (The AP report did not delineate its sources.)

Interpreters appealing to biblical narratives to describe idealized marriage have in many cases legitimized violence in marriage. Religious authorities (Bible translators, pastors, seminary professors) have been negligent (and, I argue, criminally so) in failing to expose the ways in which the biblical narrative sanctions and contributes to the abuse of women in general and wives in particular. By

Wil Gafney

highlighting Ruth's embrace of Naomi and Naomi's god, interpreters of the book of Ruth have regularly overlooked the violence with which Ruth was initiated into marriage (and relationship with Naomi), as specified by the Biblical Hebrew vocabulary of that union. Biblical interpreters, like all readers, are shaped by their own constructed cultures, which they in turn lay onto the text even as they identify "biblical principles" for marriage. In so doing, lay and professional, clergy and academic interpreters of the Bible overlook the violence in which many women live, particularly in their marriages. Men in every part of the world rape their wives. According to Molly Egan and Jason Wood's 1999 Lehigh University report, *The Abolition of Marital Rape Exemption*, in the United States, spousal rape was criminalized by only seventeen out of fifty states in 1996. By 2007, all fifty states and the District of Columbia had criminalized spousal rape. (The state of New York relies on the ruling of an appeals court in 1984, *People vs. Liberta*, because an exemption for married men accused of raping their wives remains on the books.) Spousal rape affects all people in the United States and beyond, including those in the African dispersion.

SEX AND MARRIAGE

The book of Ruth also provides an opportunity to reflect on cultural and religious values about sex and marriage. In most parts of the African diaspora, normative sexual conduct is restricted to heterosexual intercourse after marriage. Of course, sexual activity in the diaspora is not limited to that context. Ruth's abduction into marriage and subsequent sexual initiation presents evidence of forced sexual contact that was culturally and religiously accepted. This presentation, however obscured it has become in contemporary Bibles, is problematic because it seems to sanctify forcible sex acts. The story of Ruth can be the starting point for a discussion on healthy and unhealthy heterosexual intimate practices.

Naomi's instruction to Ruth, to approach a drunken Boaz under the cover of darkness without being discovered, evokes sexual intimacy in the text and its interpretation. Naomi's instructions are telling: "When he lies down, memorize the place where he lies; then, go and uncover his thighs and lie down; and he will tell you what to do" (Ruth 3:4, my translation.) The word, *margeloth*, "at the feet" or "thighs," derives from the noun, *raglayim*, "feet," which includes the thighs and regularly has a genital or sexualized connotation (see Deut. 28:57; Judg. 5:27; 2 Kings 18:27; Isa. 7:20). When Naomi tells Ruth that Boaz will tell her what to do, what is left unsaid is that she should do whatever he says; it is certainly possible that he will demand sex. Her position relative to his suggests oral sex.

GENDER AND MARRIAGE

Gender in marriage is a particularly contentious issue in the Anglican Communion at the present moment, pitting some African voices against each other and pitting some African voices against voices in the United States and Canada. This struggle is not confined to the Anglican Communion; other communions, particularly in the United States, Canada and Europe, all of which include Africana voices, are vigorously debating these issues. Heterosexual conjugal unions are normative in the scriptures and in the African diaspora. The recognition of gay and lesbian couples as legitimate (socially, religiously, legally) conjugal partners is not the norm in spite of limited legal status for same-gender marriages and partnerships in a few places. This is true in the overwhelming majority of Jewish and Christian communities.

Ruth's commitment to Naomi in 1:16-17 is frequently taken out of its same-gender, non-sexual context and applied to heterosexual couples in Christian marriage ceremonies and homilies. My translation follows:

Do not beg me to leave you anymore, woman, or to turn back from following you, woman. For where you go, woman, I will go; where you rest, woman, I will rest;

your people, woman, will be my people;
and your God, woman, will be my God.
Where you die, woman, I will die
and there I will be buried.
May YHWH do this to me and more
if anything but death separates me from you,
    woman.

However, in the few Jewish communities that affirm same-gender unions, this text is regularly used in lesbian commitment ceremonies and marriages. In a related liturgical practice attested by Rabbi Marcia Falk in *The Book of Blessings*, the love poetry in the Song of Songs is used contemporarily by gay and lesbian couples in the same way that the poetry has been used traditionally by heterosexual married couples. The Sabbath "blessing of the beloved" is done with gender-specific language in the Song: if the one to be blessed is male, poetry with masculine grammatical markers from the Song is used, and if the one to be blessed is female, poetry with feminine grammatical markers from the Song is used.

The Christian practice of changing the gender context of this passage, as is done in the (heterosexual) marriage liturgy of the Episcopal Church (USA), is intriguing and unbalanced. There is among the proponents of normative heterosexual marriage a great reluctance to change the biblical text in any way—or at least any way that would make room for sexual minorities. Yet modifying words of commitment between two women to apply them to a woman and a man is deemed acceptable.

Ruth's embrace of Naomi is particularly striking remembering that they were from different ethnic communities, practiced different religions, and Naomi was there—and presumably did not object—when Ruth and Orpah were abducted into marriage.

FAMILY FIRST
The relationship between Ruth and Naomi is significant for multigenerational households and families identified by outsiders as "extended families." These

family members call themselves "families." Naomi's motivation is the well-being of her family. Her sons need wives. They get wives. When her sons die without progeny, the wives are expendable, and Naomi does her best to dispose of them. Orpah leaves; we do not know her fate. But we know her intent: to return to her people, the land of her ancestors and her gods.

As a postmenopausal widow bereft of her childless sons, Naomi had no family left. But she still had a home. Naomi returned to her people, the land of her ancestors. She never left her god, but her god had apparently abandoned her:

Women-folk, call me no longer Pleasant-
    Naomi,
you all must call me Bitter-Mara, for Shaddai,
    [Mother-God], has embittered me terribly.
I was full when I left, and empty when
    YHWH, [Father-God], brought me back;
why do you women call me Pleasant-Naomi
when YHWH, [Father-God], has so answered
    me,
and Shaddai, [Mother-God], has brought evil
    to me?" (My translation of Ruth 1:20-21)

Shaddai, the Breasted One who earlier sustained Naomi with Divine nurture, has rejected her from the Divine embrace. (See Genesis 49:25 where Shaddai, the Breasted One, blesses with blessings of *shadim*, breasts, and *rechem*, womb.) And, YHWH the Warrior-King has failed to protect her. Now, abandoned by Mother and Father God, Naomi tastes only bitterness.

BORDER AND BOUNDARY CROSSING
Africans and persons of African descent in the Diaspora are border-crossing people: internal African border crossing, involuntary Atlantic Ocean border crossing made possible by the violation of personal and communal boundaries, the complicated return voyages to Africa including the founding of Liberia and recent voluntary immigration to Europe and

North America. There are parallels to each of these moves in the story of Ruth.

Naomi and her family left Israel, Bethlehem, because of economic privation according to the narrative. Their flight across the border into Moab was intentional, but not voluntary. They cross borders and boundaries, abducting local (to them, foreign) women. Eventually, the men folk cross the border between life and death. When Naomi attempts to send her daughters-in-law away, neither wishes to leave her. Orpah's return to Moab is secondary to Naomi's rejection of her. Her trip home is not, initially, voluntary. Naomi crosses the border to return home, voluntarily, but not happily. Ruth crosses a border to gain access to Boaz's property. Ruth also crosses a boundary to give Boaz access to her body. Their descendant, David, would cross borders and boundaries and set new borders for his community. Their descendant, Jesus, would cross borders and boundaries and set new boundaries for his community.

CONCLUSION

Ruth was abducted into the messianic lineages of David and Jesus. But the text should not be read as an endorsement of abduction. It is in Ruth's power to choose where she will make her way in the world. She chooses her mother-in-law, chooses to stay with her, worship her, and support her. When Ruth gives birth, she is a surrogate for Naomi:

> "Blessed be YHWH, who has not left you, woman, without redeeming kin this day; and may that name be proclaimed in Israel! That one shall be to you, woman, a restorer of life and a provider when your hair grays, woman; for your daughter-in-law, she who loves you, woman, she has given birth—she who is more to you, woman, than seven sons." Then Naomi took the child and laid him in her bosom, and became his nurturer. The women of the neighborhood gave him a name, saying, "A son has been born to Naomi." (Ruth 4:14-17, my translation)

References

Akpera, Jacob. *Tiv levirate Custom and the Book of Ruth: A Comparative Method.* Ph.D. diss., Westminster Theological Seminary, Philadelphia, 1997.

Brenner, Athalya. *Feminist Companion to Ruth.* Sheffield: Sheffield Academic, 1993.

———. *Ruth and Esther: A Feminist Companion to the Bible.* Sheffield: Sheffield Academic, 1999.

Donaldson, Laura. "The Sign of Orpah: Reading Ruth through Native Eyes." In *Vernacular Hermeneutics,* ed. R. S. Sugirtharajah. Sheffield: Sheffield Academic, 1999.

Dube, Musa W. "Divining Ruth for International Relations." In *Other Ways of Reading: African Women and the Bible,* ed. Musa W. Dube. Atlanta: Society of Biblical Literature, 2001.

Dube, Musa W. "Towards Postcolonial Feminist Translations of the Bible." Unpublished Paper, 2006.

Gafney, Wilda C. M. "Mother Knows Best: Messianic Surrogacy and Sexploitation in Ruth." In *Mother Goose, Mother Jones, Mommy Dearest: Mother/Daughter, Mother/Son Relationships in the Bible,* eds. Cheryl A. Kirk-Duggan and Tina Pippin. *Semeia Studies* (forthcoming).

Falk, Marcia. *Book of Blessings.* Boston: Beacon, 1999.

Halpern, Baruch. *David's Secret Demons: Messiah, Murderer, Traitor, King.* Grand Rapids, Mich.: Eerdmans, 2001.

Mitchell, Anthony. "Lions to the Rescue! Big Cats Save Kidnapped Girl." Associated Press, June 21, 2005.

Nadar, Sarojini. "A South African Indian Womanist Reading of the Character of Ruth." In *Other Ways of Reading: African Women and the Bible,* ed. Musa W. Dube. Atlanta: Society of Biblical Literature, 2001.

Nayap-pot, Dalila. "Life in the Midst of Death: Naomi, Ruth and the Plight of Indigenous Women." In *Biblical Studies Alternatively: An Introductory Reader,* ed. Susanne Scholz. Upper Saddle River, N.J.: Prentice Hall, 2003.

SONG *of* SONGS

Nathaniel Samuel Murrell

A BLACK WOMAN'S SONG?

Perhaps no inspired writ so uniquely celebrates the beauty, credulity, and sexuality of a woman wooing her "Sugarman" in such unique and daring lyrics as does Song of Songs. This premier sensual canonical book shows the most intimate dialogue among biblical characters. Cast in magnificent Hebrew poetry and roughly thirty love songs, under a superscription assigned to Solomon, Song of Songs (hereafter "Songs") brazenly carves a space in the canon, even though its intrepid embrace of the erogenous audaciously arouses sexual passion with candor. The Latin Vulgate's title *Canticum Canticorum*, like the Septuagint's Greek *Aisma Aismaton*, captures the essence of the Hebrew superlative in the superscription "Song of Songs." The book of poems is the best of the biblical songs, the "Most Excellent

of Songs" (Weems 2006: 263); it surpasses David's song (1 Chron. 16:8-36), the canticles of Isaiah (Isa. 12:25), and other Hebrew songs.

PROSCRIBING SONGS

Although one of the most concise in the Hebrew Tanak (Bible), Songs has challenged as many secular and religious interpreters as any biblical book. Its frank exposé of a secular subject, its free use of natural imagery to showcase the power of the erotic, and the absence of consciousness of the divine made it easy for many to question whether it "soiled the hands," whether it qualified to be among canonized Hebrew writings. Readers ask: Is Songs a single or composite work, and when and where were the poems written? Does Songs dramatize a Tammuz fertility cult rite of Mesopotamia celebrating a marriage of the deity to humans? Should Songs be read as strictly poetic and fictitious or as historical? If Solomon is the object of the poet's passion, who would his paramour be? Is the "dark-skin" (*shehorah*) woman in the epic none other than an Egyptian queen, or another black African? Why are such seductive poems in the canon?

Martin Luther, a Protestant reformer often hostile to Judaism, wanted Songs expunged from the Bible because he thought it was too sexually explicit and had no spiritual value. Rabbis, however, justify Songs' place in the canon by allegorizing its lover as God who woos a beloved people Israel from unresponsiveness to their covenant obligations. Although at a later stage in rabbinic interpretation, God's lover in the Songs came to be linked with the Sabbath, the allegory finds correlatives in the Torah (Exod. 20:1-5; Deut. 24:1-4) and the Nevi'im (for example, Hosea 2-4; Nahum 2; Ezek. 16 and 23; Jer. 2, 3, 5, 7, 13, and 23), where Yahweh, Israel's beau, chastises her on grounds of infidelity. In that sense, Songs reminds Israel of the love God showers on them.

Neither the origin of Songs nor the gender of its writer is known for certain. In some poems (for example, 2:1-2; 6:11-12; 8:11-13), the speaker is not transparent and the book's tripartite colloquy may even be a fictitious cast of characters. The longest poem probably comes from the pen of the male lover (4:1-15), but a black woman is Songs' alpha voice; close to 75 percent of the poems come from her, and issues of sexual passion and sensitivity about her color are her primary concerns (1:1-6). Although the black woman is the most likely candidate for Songs' authorship, Solomon is declared its author for reasons in sundry: he was an acclaimed writer of a large number of songs and proverbs (1 Kings 4:32; 5:11-12); he was a man of much wisdom, fame, and fortune; he had an insatiable appetite for beautiful women and a luxuriant lifestyle (1 Kings 11:1-2); his wealth and power are featured frequently through the poems (Songs 1:5,

12; 6:8, 9); and he is named as cosigner of Songs (1:1, 5; 3:7, 9, 11) or its primary author. However, the translation of the opening verse, "I will sing the song of all songs to Solomon that he may smother me with kisses," in the *New English Bible with the Apocrypha*, points to the author. Most likely, Songs is written by and about a black woman proselyte from Egypt.[1] She said she is *shehorah* (1:5-6); *shahar* in the Tanak (Lev. 13:31, 37; Zech. 6:2, 6) means "black." She encountered color distinction and intimated that she was abused by nonblack sentinels at a time when her search for her swain made her vulnerable (3:3; 5:7).

SONGS IN BIBLICAL CONTEXT

Like the Psalter, Songs alludes to no datable historical event and offers vague clues of its *Sitz im Leben*. Linguists find vocabulary and syntactical structure in the poems pointing to postexilic Talmudic-Mishnaic Hebrew. The play on multiple references to "Daughters of Jerusalem" (3:5, 10, 11; 5:8; 8:4) and metaphoric images minted in subtropical fruits, spices, flora, animals, and trees of Lebanon give the poems the scent of Palestine or Israeli but no dating. Northeastern Africa (Egypt or Ethiopia) also cannot be ruled out completely (1:9). Unless the songs are strictly poetic and their characters imaginary, their vista suggests that they were written long after Solomon's reign (1:5 and 6:13), and most likely at a time when Africana women were having closer contact with fairer women from Palestine, Arabia, or Europe, during the Babylonian exile or shortly thereafter. The suggestion that Songs is a woman's bold response to the social-political reform under patriarchy in postexilic Israel is tenable. Politically intolerant Ezra and Nehemiah, concerned with their ravaged nation's new identity and the compromising of perceived race and ancestral purity, enforced strict ethnic and sexual codes of conduct in Second Temple Judaism (Weems 2006: 266; Melanchthon 2004: 181). They monitored marriage relations and forced Jewish husbands to abandon their Babylonian, Canaanite, and African-Egyptian wives, thus causing great social trauma and mayhem (Ezra 9:1—10:44; Neh. 13:23-29) among the Hebrew *goyim* (returnees). The Shullamite could have been among the women abandoned in Egypt in the name of ethnic purity.

Nothing in Songs precludes the passionate lover from being a noble African, Ethiopian, or Egyptian—perhaps Pharaoh's famous daughter, as Theodore of Mopsuestia (5th century c.e.) suggests. Scholars noted that Songs shows affinities to Egyptian love songs performed by professional singers for entertainment on festive occasions. The fact that Pharaoh's daughter is singled out for special affection and is mentioned at least four times in Solomon's biography (1 Kings 3:1; 7:8; 9:24; 11:1-2) is significant (Sasson 1989: 408–9). After Solomon's marriage to his African queen, in league with the pharaoh of Egypt, he brought her to Jerusalem (1 Kings 3:1) and, as she reports, took her into his private chamber and showered her with love (Songs 1:4). Later, she invites the daughters of Jerusalem and Zion to come and see him wearing his crown on his festive wedding day (3:11). The Shullamite's frequent address, "daughters of Jerusalem" and Zion (1:5; 2:7; 3:5; 5:8, 16), may be a mere poetic device, but it may also provide a hint as to her identity, as a person of foreign descent.

A Black Woman's Exploits

The black woman in Songs is one among many models of an ideal Africana woman. Although she fights vulnerability and the deferment of her dreams, she is an autonomous, assertive, resilient, and debonair woman who takes control of her destiny. Navigating her songs with exclamations, "cohortatives" (1:1; 4:16), imperatives (1:4; 3:5; 4:1; 2:7, 15; 3:5; 4:8, 16; 5:8; 8:4, 6, 14), and first-person soliloquy (1:2-4), she sounds the alarm that she is passionate and daring. Even like our "Black Queen" at the Super Bowl, when her Sugarman throws caution to the wind and removes her "pastie," she fears no wardrobe malfunction (see 5:3-4) because she is "a wall and [her] breasts are like towers" (8:10). Though many biblical texts make the woman's body a problem, in Songs it possesses no malaise (Weems 2006) and is not compartmentalized on lines of secular and sacred, "the rational and affective, the public and private" (Melanchthon 2004: 184). Her friends call her "the most beautiful of women" (1:8; 5:9; 6:1), full of youth (1:5), and a Shullamite (6:13). She affirms her African ethnicity with bravado—"I am black and beautiful, O daughters of Jerusalem, like the tents of Kedar, like the mountains of Solomon" (1:5). To ensure that her color is not a factor in her love equation, she wants a colorblind engagement: "Do not gaze on me because I am black, because the sun has blazed on me" (1:6).

Disregarding old fables and conventional propriety on dating, the woman waits on no Prince Charming to pop the question. She throws the first salvos of love: "Let him kiss me with a kiss in the mouth" (1:1). With *savoir-faire*, she showers uninhibited affection on her Sugarman like she treats no other (5:10f). She praises his kisses, youthful gazelle-like vigor, and voice, and she beckons closer so they can share love that is "better than wine" (1:1-4). She knows exactly what she wants and embarks on a relentless quest to get it, searching every street, theater, and pub for him (3:1-3). When she finds her Sugarman, she holds him fast and no thoughts of sexual harassment releases him from her grip (3:4). Like Toni Morrison's dying Pilate, she urges her Milkman: "Sing a little something for me" (S/Solomon, 340). She wants him to squeeze her in his arms (2:6) and "whisper sweet loving nothings" in her ears.

Although she is daring and adventurous, Black Beauty is no Sapphire woman who is out to swindle the one she woos. She is a morally upright and principled lover. Like most Africana women, she is committed totally to her only Sugarman, from whom she expects uncompromising monogamous love and affection (2:16; 6:3, 9; 7: 10; 8:14). Even though there are "sixty queens and eighty concubines and maidens without number" around Sugarman, he is hers alone. Sugarman is swept off his feet by her beauty and words (1:10, 13; 4:1; 6:4; 7:1, 6) and is left bereft of diction to describe her ineffable love. Like Milkman, he wants to sing: "Sugargirl don't leave me here / Cotton balls to choke me / Sugargirl don't leave me here / Buckra's arms to yoke me" (*S/Solomon*, 340).

Songs Speaks in a Creole World

Two popular hymns of the Caribbean church in which I grew up were influenced by the lyrics of the Songs: "He is the Rose of Sharon, He is the Lily of the Valley, the Bright and Morning Star" (compare to Songs 2:1), and "His love! His banner over me is love. He brought me into the banqueting house and his banner over me is love" (compare to Songs 2:4). Even worshipers who do not read such big words as *allegory* are sure these songs speak of Christ and the church rather than of human sexuality. When my church's youth group performed a dramatization of Songs, the erotic lines that placated our immature odes to human love were interpreted as a spiritual sexuality associated with Jesus, notwithstanding the anachronism of Songs predating Christ by over four hundred years. Canadian and U.S. missionary founders of our church would approve of no secular reading of the Songs. I learned later, however, from its exquisite passionate intent to ennoble human sexuality that Songs speaks not to Israel or Christ and the church! It is a black woman's search for her Sugarman who "done cut cross the sky" (see 3:1; 5:6) and left her dry lips longing for a real "kiss in the mouth" (1:1).

Songs offers a paradigmatic ode to love for the celebration of Africana sexuality and interracial intimacy. Weems says it best: "The Song of Songs advocates a balance in female and male relationships, urging mutuality not domination, interdependence not enmity, sexual fulfillment not mere procreation, uninhibited love not bigoted emotions" (1992: 160). Songs provides an answer to the question: Do black men have a moral obligation to marry black women? The exclamatory "No!" is unpopular among women who sing "Where have all the black men gone?" Out of grave concern for the acute shortage of eligible black male mates in non-incarcerated America, some black women issue a passionate call for a moral moratorium on black

men suiting white women. Theirs is a plea not to "betray the race" or resurrect "miscegenation"!

But Africana peoples have always found the biologistic idea of ethnic purity objectionable and churlish. We embrace all of our interracial forebears and, like current president Barack Obama, many of us are creole with richly mixed blood. *All the Women Are White, All the Blacks Are Men, but Some of Us Are Brave* mirrors the complicated reality of our saga (Hull and Smith 1982). Some men marry whites because, like the black woman in Songs, they sought and found true love. Others suit whites because they, like Morrison's Pecola Breedlove, who was "born black and ugly," pray for "the bluest eyes" and "beautiful children" to lift the race; because "high yellow children" are the closest "we folks" can come to beauty (Harris 2000: 163). Songs inverts any call for ethnic purity and unreservedly celebrates love in whatever race it is found. It bids us sing a song of Love to the one we love! Who can be born black and not sing? (Evans 1975).

Note

1. As Weems notes, many scholars have found similarities in mood and lyrical style between Songs and the love poetry and songs of ancient Egypt, which date back to the New Kingdom (circa 167–1085 B.C.E.). Some carry the features of the "Ramesside texts" and may have been composed for performance, festive and erotic entertainment, and even to console in times of grief (Weems 2006: 267). See also Fox 1985, 244–47.

References

Evans, Mari. 1975. *I Am a Black Woman*. New York: William Morrow, 1975.

Fox, Michael. 1985. *The Song of Songs and the Ancient Egyptian Love Songs*. Madison: University of Wisconsin, 1985.

Harris, Angela. 2000. "Race and Essentialism in Feminist Legal Theory." In *Reflections: An Anthology of*

African American Philosophy, ed. James A. Montmarquet and William H. Hardy, 157–66. Belmont, Calif.: Wadsworth.

Hull, Gloria T., Patricia Bell, and Barbara Smith, eds. 1982. *All the Women Are White, All the Blacks Are Men, but Some of Us Are Brave: Black Women's Studies*. Old Westbury, N.Y.: Feminist, 1982.

Lyke, Larry L. 2007. *I Will Espouse You Forever: The Song of Songs and the Theology of Love in the Hebrew Bible*. Nashville: Abingdon, 2007.

Meek, T. J. 1922. "Canticles and the Tammuz Cult." *American Journal of Semitic Languages and Literature* 39 (1): 1–14.

Melanchthon, Monica Jyotsna. 2004. "Song of Songs." In *Global Bible Commentary*, ed. Daniel Patte et al., 180–85. Nashville: Abingdon.

Mills, Charles. 2000. "Do Black Men Have a Moral Duty to Marry Black Women?" In *Reflections: An Anthology of African American Philosophy*, ed. James A. Montmarquet and William H. Hardy, 167–82. Belmont, Calif.: Wadsworth.

Sasson, Victor. 1989. "King Solomon and the Dark Lady in the Song of Songs." *Vetus Testamentum* 39 (4): 407–14.

Weems, Renita J. 1992. "Song of Songs." In *The Women's Bible Commentary*, ed. Carol A. Newsom and Sharon H. Ringe, 156–60. Louisville, Ky.: Westminster John Knox.

———. 2006. "Song of Songs." In *The New Interpreter's Bible: Old Testament Survey*, 262–69. Nashville: Abingdon.

ECCLESIASTES

Jamal-Dominique Hopkins

ECCLESIASTES IS ONE of the most difficult books of the Bible to interpret. Possibly penned by multiple writers,[1] the nature and tone of the book are, at times, unsettling; ideas of joy, meaninglessness (vanity), folly, madness, wisdom, toiling, and subtle absolutism are juxtaposed throughout the entire work. Moreover, the overall content of Ecclesiastes projects a sense of fatalistic determinism despite a prolepsis of hope. The presence of these elements speaks to the uncertainties and variable nature of life, especially in light of the divine. As regards the African Diaspora, the untenable nature of life mainly has been understood via social ethics. From the colonization of African countries to the enslavement and development of African people in the Caribbean and the Americas, Ecclesiastes resounds decisively.

Ecclesiastes (Qoheleth in the Hebrew manuscripts) falls into the division of biblical literature known as the Writings section (Ketuvim) of the Hebrew Bible. Part of the biblical Jewish wisdom literary tradition (to which Job and Proverbs also belong), Ecclesiastes explores the aspects of life relevant to philosophy, relationships, and politics. In narrative style, the acknowledged teacher-leader (preacher) of the community is introduced as the son of David, the current king in Jerusalem: "The words of the Teacher, the son of David, king in Jerusalem. Vanity of vanities, says the Teacher, vanity of vanities! All is vanity" (Eccles. 1:1-2).[2]

This description, as well as the overall instructive content of Ecclesiastes, evokes the image of Solomon (especially borrowing from the context of 1 Kings 3–11), David's biological son and immediate successor to Israel's throne (1:1, 12). Despite this descriptive image, the name Solomon does not appear in Ecclesiastes, hinting at a late compositional date. Moreover, linguistic evidence (the appearance of Aramaisms and Persian loan words) exists to support the claim that the work comes from the fifth to third centuries B.C.E. In spite of these concerns and problems concerning the literary structure of the document, the content is filled with a rich cadre of instructive wisdom with particular regard to human experience. Similar to the book's historical audience, these teachings provide useful insight for communities within the African Diaspora.

The main protagonist of this work also is the bearer of the book's Hebrew name, Qoheleth. The name *Qoheleth*, translated as either "teacher" or "preacher" in English, discloses learned lessons from experiential circumstances. One may ask what kindles this illumination of wisdom, this public revealing of personal knowledge? Wisdom emanates from tragic situations, experienced turmoil, the trials (or struggles) of life, and, at times, the folly and madness of wantonness. It is along these lines that we are able to see the larger themes dealt with throughout the book. These themes include (1) the meaninglessness (vanity) of life in contradistinction to toiling and (2) the acknowledgment of divine control and divine order (that is, "the fear of God" described in 5:7; 7:18; 8:12-13; 12:13) in the larger context of human toil and pleasure. It is here that a parallel theme of hope for a better future also is intimated. The duality of life with particular regard to madness, folly, vanity, and toiling sets the backdrop for these larger themes. As suggested in 1:3, 9, 14; 2:11, 17-20, 22; 3:16; 4:1, 3, 7, 15; 5:13, 18; 6:1, 12; 8:9, 15, 17; 9:3, 6, 9, 11, 13; and 10:5, the acknowledgment of the divine also is to infer that all circumstances fall under the matrix of preexisting authority (there is nothing new "under the sun").

From a social-cultural perspective, this article examines the variable nature of life within Ecclesiastes (especially as this relates to communities of the African Diaspora) based on its juxtaposing themes surrounding human life. Ecclesiastes in conversa-

tion with the African Diaspora must take seriously the historical contours and the development of this people group. This study pays particular attention to the way Ecclesiastes shapes an understanding of wisdom, which emanates out of an opposition to societal madness, while at the same time projecting a proleptic intimation of hope.

ECCLESIASTES AND AFRICANA COMMUNITIES: DRAWING THE CONNECTIONS

Ecclesiastes opens with the acknowledged teacher-leader (v. 1) posing a philosophical question (in v. 3), which reflects a larger fundamental human reality. To his audience, Qoheleth utters, "What do people gain from all the toil at which they toil under the sun?" This question, along with the overall tone of the book, challenges the ambition and agenda of humanity in general and, in particular, reveals a kind of objective reality for the preacher himself as well as provides an understanding of the divine. According to the preacher, such a realization is thus understood by the document's recipients too. Human toil without this knowledge results in what Qoheleth concludes as meaningless: "Vanity of vanities! . . . All is vanity" (1:2; also noted in 1:14; 2:15, 17, 19, 21, 23, 26; 3:19; 4:4, 7-8, 16; 5:7, 10; 6:2, 4, 9, 11; 7:6; 8:10, 14; 9:2; 11:8, 10; and 12:8), and "a chasing after a wind" (noted in 1:14, 17; 2:11, 17, 26; 4:4, 6, 16; and 6:9).

Akin to Ecclesiastes, acknowledgment of the divine similarly has been understood within the context of the African Diaspora. Traditionally in the Black community, the spiritual and the socio-civil (that is, the sacred and the profane) aspects of life are held in delicate balance. Hence, many aspects of life are viewed through the lenses of certain hermeneutical sensibilities. Qoheleth denotes the variable nature of human life as madness and folly (1:17; 2:3, 10-13; 7:25; 10:1, 6). In North

Jamal-Dominique Hopkins

America, this variable nature is best observed via the influence of the Black sacred rhetorical tradition (which borrows from Black Christian preaching) and is preserved in Black literature, Black art, Black comedy, and Black music.

In Black literature, the variable nature and the duality between the spiritual and socio-civil aspects of life are best reflected in James Weldon Johnson's *God's Trombones: Seven Negro Sermons in Verse*, Zora Neale Hurston's *Their Eyes Were Watching God* and *Jonah's Gourd Vine*, James Baldwin's *Go Tell It on the Mountain* and *The Fire Next Time*, and Toni Morrison's *Song of Solomon*. In Johnson's *God's Trombones*, the "old-time Negro preacher" waxes eloquently a proleptic message of divine and social hope in the face of calamity. This message, delivered in a syncopated and poetic fashion, is described in the sermons "The Prodigal Son," "Noah Built the Ark," and "The Judgment Day." The tension between wisdom and folly, between madness and joy, similarly comes through the writings of Baldwin. In his *The Fire Next Time*, Baldwin's critique of American's behavioral rectitude is measured via his Black Pentecostal Christian background. As he noted in his address to the World Council of Churches in 1968, Baldwin's moral critique stands as one who is deeply shaped, informed, and engaged with the Black Christian experience yet, at the same time, standing outside of it: "I address you as one of those people who have always been on the outside, even though one tried to work in it."

Reflecting on the variable nature of life and the balanced tension of duality between the sacred and profane brings to mind an ancient African proverb that states, "to stumble is not to fall, but to move forward faster." Whether brought about by self or imposed without warrant (by the wicked that oppress, denoted in 3:17; 7:15, 17; 8:10-14; 9:2; 10:13), the preacher in Ecclesiastes acts out of a sense of humility and instructive responsibility. Despite Qoheleth's seemingly many foolish inclinations, which likely contributed to his humility and wisdom (seen throughout 2:1-11, but especially from 1:17; 2:1, 3, 8, 10, 20; and 7:15, 23-25), the instructive wisdom given is replete in acumen and is lucidly candid.

CONSCIOUS RECKONINGS

In classic Hebraic tradition, Qoheleth serves as a type of rabbi (a learned scholar and teacher) and is grounded in a kind of communal consciousness (for example, aware of the social concerns that plague his communal group and, hence, consciously addressing these concerns): "If you see in a province the oppression of the poor and the violation of justice and right, do not be amazed at the matter; for the high official is watched by a higher, and there are yet higher ones over them" (Eccles. 5:8).

Similar to this tradition, certain groups and leaders within the African Diaspora also project a communal consciousness, which is brought about by unwarranted societal madness. Like Qoheleth, this consciousness brings about a courage that emanates from wisdom that also projects a sense of proleptic hope.[3] Black Nationalists, arising out of the American Civil Rights movement of the mid-twentieth century and borrowing from the influences of Toussaint L'Ouverture, Harriet Tubman, Marcus Garvey, and others, demonstrated a similar awareness and collective consciousness. Wisdom, emanating from a sense of collective consciousness, was the tool that undergirded Black militants in their plight against the madness of societal injustice. Akin to those from the nonviolent movement, Black militants possessed the wisdom to understand their resistance as a prolepsis of hope toward social and cultural egalitarianism. This also was the notion articulated by W. E. B. DuBois (as a kind of Qoheleth) with regard to his commitment to social and civil uplift for Black Americans. His notion of the "talented tenth" (that is, the most gifted Negros who had been trained and educated with the highest standards possible) was envisaged as leading the Black "race" to a socio-civil egalitarian status in America. DuBois, a noted African American scholar and activist, fought for civil and human rights in America and abroad. He was known as the father of the National Association for the Advancement of Colored People (the NAACP, which also was the direct legatee of DuBois's earlier Niagara movement) and the Pan-African movement, which helped to liberate and begin the decolonization process of African countries.

Struggle, and the wisdom that subsequently results, has not been uncommon for people of the African Diaspora. In North America, in particular, the madness surrounding the veracity of slavery also seeded wisdom that (to borrow from the thinking of DuBois as taken from his *The Souls of Black Folks*) produced a sense of two-ness (a double consciousness) that the American Negro feels. Double consciousness thus leads to a curious state: being despised as Black and yet celebrated as an American. Because of the larger American psyche and social consciousness, or its lack thereof, being Black and living a Black reality (despised) and yet having to view oneself and to function as Black through the eyes and reality of Whiteness has led to what Paul Laurence Dunbar has described in *We Wear the Mask*:

We wear the mask that grins and lies,
It hides our cheeks and shades our eyes,
This debt we pay to human guile;
With torn and bleeding hearts we smile,
And mouth with myriad subtleties.

Why should the world be otherwise,
In counting all our tears and sighs?
Nay, let them only see us, while
We wear the mask.

We smile, but, O great Christ, our cries
To thee from tortured souls arise.
We sing, but oh the clay is vile
Beneath our feet, and long the mile;
But let the world dream otherwise.
We wear the mask! (Dunbar 1895: 896)

Double consciousness was the attitudinal reality for many enslaved Africans. While the slave asserted a passive, docile, and obsequious role, resistance fueled the mind. The passive-resistant slave pretended to acquiesce to the enslaver's every demand, yet this obsequious attitude wielded certain power to overtake the enslaver in many aspects. The result of triumphant struggle against societal madness, in concert with humility toward the divine, yielded variant forms of liberation (educationally, socially, economically, and politically).

Unlike Qoheleth, the Black Nationalist and the enslaved, collective consciousness is faintly evident in the hip-hop movement. Although directly indebted to the historic traditions of Black music, culture, and politics, and without casting hip-hop as largely monolithic in its expression (widely divergent forms of articulation are conveyed via music, fashion, literature, and demeanor), this movement is largely riddled with extreme nihilism and narcissist mores (madness and folly). Hip-hop projects a descriptive reality of urban lethargy and inner-city decadent life. Similar to Qoheleth's realization of earthly vanity (2:1-24), and in light of Solomon (who is alluded to as the Qoheleth), wherein he partakes in the folly of foreign idol worship and polygamous non-Jewish relations, many rapper-preachers within hip-hop defiantly engage in the folly and madness of a life of ineffectuality (vanity). The rapper-preacher attempts to cast descriptive commentary with regard to urban existence. This portrayal, however, is self-circumvented by the movement's own subjugation to the commoditization (that is, financial excessiveness), commercialization, and the praxis engagement of degenerative reality. This resembles what Stanley Crouch and Wynton Marsalis allude to concerning the sacred and profane in Black music; many elements of hip-hop propound the glorification of the ludicrous and the profane (Vanity of vanities! . . . All is vanity). Like Solomon in 1 Kings 10, this resembles the exploitation of wisdom, the self-abrogated act of a compromised collective consciousness. In the case of hip-hop, the teacher-preacher indirectly speaks to the philosophical question poised by the Qoheleth in verse 3 (similarly restated in 2:22; 3:9; 5:16): "What do people gain from all the toil at which they toil under the sun?"

WISDOM FROM THE DUALITY OF LIFE

Beginning at 3:1, Qoheleth presents an overview concerning the duality of life. Here, the seasons of life (3:1-8) correspond with the cycle of the created order in 1:4-7. In like fashion, Qoheleth contends that, in light of fate, there is no eternal advantage to being wise or wealthy; these are but temporal aspects subject to the divine. So, too, it is with other aspects of socio-civil life. Qoheleth contends that oppression, too, is but vanity (4:1-4, 13-16). The oppressed here, like DuBois's description on double consciousness, appear to have a greater sense of consciousness in that they are able to engage multiple realities, multiple reckonings, multiple strivings, and multiple (broader) perspectives (4:13-16; also highlighted in 8:10-14). Ecclesiastes is similar to what is brought out in the New Testament, where Paul declares that the master, too, is subject to a greater authority and thus must acquiesce (Eph. 6:9; Col. 4:1); this disposition was lacking in the American enslaver. Whereas the institution of slavery in the New Testament largely ascribed certain patterns of class-oriented governance, slavocracy in America demeaned Black people with acts of barbarism, which have continued for nearly half a millennium. Acts of barbarism also have been evident under African colonization and apartheid. Other aspects of human relations dealt with here, particularly in regards to fate, include the individual (4:7-8), couples (in 4:9-12), and the wisdom of youth juxtaposed to the elderly (4:13-16).

The duality of life in relation to wisdom and folly is further examined in 7:1-14. Whereas the duality of life in 3:1-8 corresponds to the various cycles of created order, here duality is scrutinized (to borrow from the thought of Cornel West) to determine whether one embraces nonmarket values of caring, sharing, nurturing, and connecting over against titillation and short-term stimulation (West

2001: xvi). Wisdom exclaims that it is better to take moral positions over against the folly and madness of human desire, wherein one may be overtaken (10:1—11:6).

Ecclesiastes is a book of shared experiential wisdom. The wisdom that emanates from life is varied. As much as it is important to learn from personal trials, struggles, and triumphs, Ecclesiastes bears witness that wisdom can be garnered from the learned lessons of others. In this, Qoheleth speaks to the varied situations of humanity in general and to the African Diaspora in particular. The proverb "If a person does not know their history they are bound to repeat it" is a common adage in Black communities. Nowhere better than throughout the African Diaspora is it understood that the generations today stand on the shoulders of pioneering foremothers and forefathers; this has been evident in the fate rise of America's first Black president, Barack Obama. In this sense, *there is nothing new under the sun.*

Notes

1. In light of this, this study will take a more thematic examination of Ecclesiastes.
2. All biblical passages are taken from the New Revised Standard Version unless otherwise indicated.
3. Due to the breadth of communities within the African Diaspora and the space constraints here, this study will focus its attention primarily on the Africana communities within the North American context.

References

Adeyemo, Tokunboh. 2006. *Africa Bible Commentary: A One-Volume Commentary Written by 70 African Scholars.* Grand Rapids, Mich.: Zondervan.

Baldwin, James. 1953. *Go Tell It on the Mountain* Reprint, New York: Bantam Dell, 1985.

———. 1963. *The Fire Next Time*. Reprint, New York: Vantage International, 1993.

———. 1985. "White Racism or World Community?" In *The Price of the Ticket: Collected Nonfiction 1948–1985*, 435–42. New York: St. Martin's.

Conyers, James L., Jr., ed. 2001. *African American Jazz and Rap: Social and Philosophical Examinations of Black Expressive Behavior*. Jefferson, N.C.: McFarland.

DuBois, W. E. B. 1903. *The Souls of Black Folks*. Reprint, New York: Barnes and Noble Classics, 2005.

Dunbar, Paul Laurence. 1895. "We Wear the Mask." Reprinted in *The Norton Anthology of African American Literature*, ed. Henry Louis Gates, 896. New York: Norton, 1997.

Gates, Henry Louis, and Nellie Y. McKay, ed. 1997. *The Norton Anthology of African American Literature*. New York: Norton.

Hurston, Zora Neale. 1934. *Jonah's Gourd Vine*. New York: Harper Perennial, 2008.

———. 1937. *Their Eyes Were Watching God*. New York: Harper Perennial, 2006.

Johnson, James Weldon. 1927. *God's Trombones: Seven Negro Sermons in Verse*. Reprint, New York: Penguin, 1990.

Lincoln, C. Eric. 1999. *Race, Religion, and the Continuing American Dilemma*. Rev. ed., New York: Hill & Wang.

Morrison, Toni. 2004. *The Song of Solomon*. New York: Vintage.

Towner, W. Sibley. 1997. "Ecclesiastes." In *The New Interpreter's Bible Commentary*, vol. 5, 265–360. Nashville: Abingdon.

West, Cornel. *Race Matters*. 2001. 2nd ed. New York: Vintage.

LAMENTATIONS

Wilma Ann Bailey

THE BIBLICAL BOOK of Lamentations contains five poems that describe the suffering (including starvation, rape, and murder), confusion, bewilderment, and anger experienced by those who remained in Jerusalem after the Babylonian conquest (587/586 B.C.E.) The book aids the grieving process by giving permission for the various emotions associated with suffering to be expressed.[1]

The theology of the poems understands God to be behind the suffering of God's people (1:15; 2:1-8; 3:43-45). That theology, which was normative for ancient Israel, had taught God's people that suffering was the outcome of sin. Therefore, their suffering was to be interpreted as deserved, and the appropriate response was self-examination and turning back to God (3:40). However, the poems also indicate, in subtle ways, that the Jerusalemites were not comfortable with that theology. The

absence of a naming or listing of sins suggests that they were not convinced that their sins—whatever they might have been—merited the unleashing of such utter devastation on their community. Moreover, the affirmation that "the steadfast love of the Lord never ceases" (3:22 NRSV) gave the community hope. This is the theology to which they clung. God had not abandoned them and never would. Hence, the poems contain both conventional theological understandings and challenges to that theology.

African American traditional theology either rejected the idea that God was responsible for human suffering or the idea was suppressed in the materials that have come down to us (spirituals, autobiographies, and conversion stories). They did believe, with the ancient Israelites, that God would ease their sufferings and release them from pain.

The fifth chapter of Lamentations reveals a very clear class division in Jerusalem. Most of the complaints there indicate that, much to the dismay of the elite in Jerusalem, the war had reversed the social structures. Those who had been privileged were now forced to endure the dangers, indignities, and hard work previously reserved for the poor. Those who had been at ease now labored in the hot sun all day, grinding grain and being subjected to rape and abuse, while those who were previously servants ruled over them (5:8, 10, 13). The victims in this chapter clearly describe their own miserable situation but not an awareness that their current condition is the lot of the poor every day.

Although the poems in the book of Lamentations were passed down to us solely as words, undoubtedly other elements accompanied them, including tunes, ululations, silence, dance, and perhaps drama. Internal evidence—such as first-person voices, physicality (stretching out hands, weeping), groaning/moaning, sitting in silence, and "crying out"—suggests this.

The African American tradition includes a practice of moaning/groaning songs (wordless or sparsely worded tunes sung slowly in a drawn-out manner) as a response to suffering. The function of these tunes is to express grief in a way that does not leave one vulnerable to further abuse or misunderstanding because the reasons for the sadness are not articulated. This tradition may shed light on the practice and function of moaning in ancient Israel in that it may not have been inarticulate ejaculations but sung responses to pain.

Note

1. This essay relies upon the fuller discussion in Bailey (forthcoming).

References

Bailey, Wilma Ann. Forthcoming. "Lamentations." In *Ecclesiastes, Song of Solomon and Lamentations*, with Douglas Miller and Christina Bucher. Believer's Church Bible Commentary series.

ESTHER

Dorothy Bea Akoto (née Abutiate)

THE MULTIPLICITY of Euro-American male voices, which offers no place to African voices in Bible commentaries, makes the *Africana Bible* project very appropriate. The book of Esther, a royal/court intrigue/novella, a Sophia/Wisdom tale (White 1992: 125; Niditch 1995: 195) memorializing the Jewish Purim feast, addresses existential issues of identity, survival, and cultural preservation by a Diaspora minority against a majority. It also addresses gender and power issues as well as the interrelationship of divine intervention by a "hidden God" and human agency. This commentary on Esther addresses issues that affect and have lasting relevance for African peoples, albeit with only local/communal, regional, and ethnic-specific interpretative differences. The use of the term *African* may be very broadly understood in reference to the complexity of African cultures. However, in this article,

its use is peculiar to southeastern Ghana Ewe peoples of sub-Saharan Africa.

Traditional commentaries on Esther address historicity, theology, structure, and other critical issues of provenance, but this article attempts to find themes in Esther that resonate with those relevant for the Africana cultural contexts. Taking Esther as the traditional cornerstone for the Jewish feast of Purim, which marks a period of "relief"/"rest" (9:16, 18) and the victory of Jews over Persians (9:20-23) (see Berg 1979: 40, 123; Clines 2000: 354, 358), this article construes two annual festivals of migration/deliverance (Glidzi and Hogbetsotso) among the Ewe peoples of southeastern Ghana as Purim. It is argued that in Esther, as in African royal settings, patriarchy is entrenched through court/royal disputes in which queens are used to achieve male agenda. Such an argument demands that we read the book of Esther through a gender-sensitive lens.

CONTEXT OF ESTHER

Esther belongs to the Ketuvim/Writings (hagiographa) and has no authorial superscription. Apart from an implicit reference to deliverance from "another quarter" (4:14), divine activity and human agency in the Persian Diaspora (see Ezra 6–7), Esther does not mention the word *God*. Nor does Esther mention major Jewish cultic practices in the Torah or covenant except Queen Esther's request for a three-day fast, likely related to prayer (4:16-17). Furthermore, descriptions of the expansive Persian Empire, magnificent Susan palace (1:1), elaborate postal system (3:13; 8:10), and custom of impalement (2:23; 5:14; 7:10) (Clines 1988: 353) make a Jewish authorship disputable. Although a Persian Jewish authorship with limited access to Judean traditions is a possibility, a Persian/Achaemenid (538–332 B.C.E.) setting for Esther is suggested by extrabiblical sources (see Wong Wai Ching 2004: 136; Moore 1999: 352).

Clines (1988: 353), referring to Herodotus, suggests that reference to Ahasuerus in the past tense (Esther 1:1) places Esther in the reign of Xerxes I (486–465 B.C.E.). However, White (1992: 124–55), arguing that Amestris, not Vashti, was Xerxes' queen, prefers a later dating, in the early fourth century B.C.E. Furthermore, the amicable coexistence of Jews and Persians in earlier chapters of Esther (see also Daniel 1–6; Ezra/Nehemiah) favors a Persian origin. By contrast is the extreme hostility between Jews and Gentiles under the Seleucids (see 1 and 2 Maccabees) in the Hellenistic period (198–143 B.C.E.). In spite of arguments concerning the authorship and dating of Esther, this article construes Esther as depicting times of peaceful coexistence and tensions, which often mark tribal/regional conflicts between the powerless minority and the powerful majority African peoples, and the part played by divine intervention and human agency.

Since the Reformation, Christians and Jews have debated whether Esther is historical/theological or fictional/allegorical. In this light, Moore offers a "combination theory" (1999: 351), showing Esther as a combination of both characteristics. Thus Esther's literary form comprises three stories, which include a royal harem tale (Esther 2:7-18); a tale about Vashti (Esth. 1:10-22); and two independent stories, one about Mordecai (2:5-10, 19-23; 3:4b-6; 4:1-3, 9-17; 5:9-14; 6:2-13; 7:9; 8:1b-15; 9:20–10:3) and the other about Esther, whose Jewish name is Hadassah (2:7-18; 4:4–5:8; 7:1–8:8; 9:12-14) (White 1992: 125; Moore 1999: 351). Moore (1999: 350) and Niditch (1995: 195) see Esther as a composite secular "Jewish romance," like the stories of Joseph (Genesis 37–50) and Daniel (Daniel 1–6). Similar stories of intrigue and wisdom abound in African royal settings, which possess characteristics of both history and fiction.

STRUCTURE/CONTENT OF ESTHER

Esther relates the stories of King Ahasuerus, his courtiers, their wives, and Esther, Mordecai, and the Jews. The two feasts, which open the story, end in the divorce of Queen Vashti (1:19) and the remarriage of Ahasuerus to Esther (2:17). Two of the king's eunuchs are executed (7:9b) when their plot to assassinate the king (2:21ff) is discovered. Also, Haman's open hatred for Mordecai and the Jews (8:3ff) is revealed and his treachery and plan to have the Jews massacred in an evil pogrom is discovered and foiled (3:2ff; 8:9ff; 9:16). He is impaled while Mordecai is honored for his faithfulness. This culminates in the massacre of seventy-five thousand Persians and the salvation of all twenty-seven thousand Jews (8:9ff; 9:16). This salvation/deliverance of the Jews, which establishes the Purim memorial feast in Esther, could be related to African cultural and broader global contexts, where issues of hatred calling for survival are prevalent. Here, those in authority are not always the most intelligent, and queens are often used to fulfill male agendas (for example, courtiers inform queens of plots and the queens in turn inform kings), so evil plots are foiled and justice is served.

COMMENTARY ON ESTHER

The vanity of the Persian court is portrayed by the festivities, which culminate in the divorce of Queen Vashti, who refuses to satisfy the male egocentric agenda (1:4-8, 9-10ff; see also Dan. 5:1-4—King Belshazzar's feast in Babylon). Here, King Ahasuerus is portrayed as a puppet, manipulated by his subjects and wives (1:14-22; 2:2-4; 3:8-11; 7:3; 8:3; 9:13), while Esther and Mordecai are very intelligent. Additionally, Vashti mirrors an independent African woman of substance and dignity, in control of her affairs, who defies societal norms. Although she is banished and divorced as a deterrent to other Persian and Median women (1:16ff), her action shows women's power at work in the empire and court. This scene, while ridiculing patriarchy and revealing the insecurity of the courtiers (1:21), also mirrors the causes and effects of extreme tensions between different genders/classes/ethnic groups in African contexts and in the Diaspora.

Despite Esther's intelligence, Susan Niditch describes her beauty, docility, and obedience in concealing her Jewish identity to win the love of a heathen king from a harem of very beautiful virgins (2:2) as "structured empathy" (1995: 200). Esther's action here raises moral questions as to why Esther, a Jewess, shows no regard for dress code, *kosha* diet, or Jewish culture (2:5-15). In the African context, wife inheritance and promiscuity have their part in the court, but situations for survival often force young women into unhealthy marriages and polygamy.

Esther's beauty, position, and wisdom (4:17ff) put her in charge of the affairs in the kingdom (2:21-23) and lead to the deliverance of herself and her people from destruction (3:1-6, 7ff). This contrasts with the autocracy and rashness of Ahasuerus (3:23), which destroy his people. Although this hardly depicts the real struggles for survival of exiled people, it mirrors the reality of bitter ethnic, tribal, or regional conflicts in royal intrigues and the vital part played by gender and power. The beauty and tactfulness of African queens/women are powerful in devising means for good to win over evil.

The Purim (9:1-19, 20-32), which is related to an ancient Persian New Year feast adopted by Diaspora Jews, is probably a later appendage to Esther to justify the Jewish celebration (Clines 2000: 354). Nothing is peculiar about this feast except in relation to *pur*, meaning "lot," with the Hebrew masculine plural nominal ending *im*. It probably refers to Haman's lots to determine the day for assassinating the Jews (White 1992: 125; Moore 2000: 352). In line with the foregoing, this article sees two migration festivals, Glidzi and Hogbetsotso, among the Ewe peoples in Ghana as a type of Purim.

THE RELEVANCE OF ESTHER IN THE AFRICANA CONTEXT

Esther raises issues pertinent to the realities and impact of colonialism on African cultures, in which extreme anger and bitter local, ethnic, regional, tribal, communal, and other jealousies (see Esther 3–7) are fanned by political or imperialistic tendencies. In this context, arranged marriages, divorce and remarriage, royal/court intrigues, kinship, and family/ethnic ties exist. Additionally, extreme patriarchal/male domination, sexism, gender, classicism, and social status (or *kyriarchical*) relationships, in which "elite educated propertied men hold power over wo/men and other men" (Schüssler-Fiorenza 2006: 211) exist. Wars, counter wars, and victories and defeats also exist. In such existential issues, divine intervention (by the Supreme Being) and human agency collaborate to effect deliverance, as happens in Esther, where the Jews trust their "hidden" God and act in their predicaments.

In the African context, royal legislations are supported by the ruling king's ethnic group, who protect his interests but are opposed by rival parties, who constantly attempt to foil his plans, depose, and even assassinate him. Here, African queens/women tend to be the "ears" of the court. They hear, counsel (see Haman's wife in 6:13b), and reveal plots against kings, foil the plots through wisdom, and bring the perpetrators to justice as Esther does (2:22-23; 7; 8).

GLIDZI AND HOGBETSOTSO FESTIVALS AS PURIM AMONG THE EWE PEOPLES OF SOUTHEASTERN GHANA, WEST AFRICA

African peoples celebrate various annual feasts to mark victories and deliverances from despotic kings and oppressive rulers. The Adaklus and Anlos, of southeastern Ghana, celebrate the Glidzi (which literally means "over the fence wall") and the Hogbetsotso (meaning "departure from the source"), respectively. Both festivals commemorate the deliverance/migration of these ethnic groups from the despot King Agorkorli and his subjects. As minorities in a foreign land, the Adaklus and Anlos develop strategies to outwit their oppressors. Their women devise a wise plan of throwing all the water from their laundry or dishwashing basins against a sidewall of their city. As the wall saturates with water, the people break it down and clamber over. The entire group departs secretly overnight, walking backward (that is, facing Agorkorli's city) so that the direction in which they are going cannot be noticed. As their enemies attempt to pursue them, the thick forests consume the group and arrows kill some of the enemies, some of whom defect to the camp of their subjects while others flee for their lives. Annually, these peoples reenact their enslave-

ment/deliverance, which they see as divine intervention, with festival/durbar, abundant food, drink, and frenzied rejoicing. The whole community rests on that day (as Jews do at Purim), eating, drinking together, showing solidarity with one another, and making peace through forgiveness. They also affirm faith in the Supreme Being for wisdom and for their victory over their oppressors, as the Jews do in Esther.

The circumstances surrounding the Glidzi and the Hogbetsotso portray how hostilities between majorities and minorities degenerate into bitter conflicts, resulting in destruction of life and property. Gender and power issues also play their part. The women's wisdom and the shrewdness of the Adaklus and Anlos in outwitting Agorkorli and his subjects find expression in Esther. She flatters and teases her hosts, Haman and King Ahasuerus, with her beauty at the banquets before coming to the real issue of the day. Although good wins out in Esther and in African contexts most of the time, ethical/moral issues are raised as to who determines what is good and evil and what makes the destruction of or deliverance from one people over others justifiable?

The establishment of Purim in Esther can be related to the Adaklu Glidzi and the Anlo Hogbetsotso migration festivals. The canonized Esther presents the outcomes and results of vagaries, of rash and foolish decisions. Ethnic feuds, extreme hatred, pride and minority/majority power conflicts, resulting in massive destructions of life and property, as mirrored by Esther, are prevalent in African contexts. African queens/mothers play vital roles of mobilization, organization, and strategizing, as does Esther. The political/imperial concerns, court intrigues, feminist/gender, class/status, race, and patriarchal issues in Esther are relevant to Diaspora Jews, but they also are to African Ghanaian Ewe peoples on the continent, in the Diaspora, and for other peoples globally. God may seem "hidden" in all these situations, but God is actively involved with the cosmic order.

Dorothy Bea Akoto (née Abutiate)

References

Alt, A., O. Eißfeldt, and P. Kahle, eds. *Biblia Hebraica Stuttgartensia.* 1997. Stuttgart, Ger.: Deutsche Bibelgesellschaft.

Berg, Sandra B. 1979. *The Book of Esther: Motifs, Themes, and Structure.* Society of Biblical Literature Dissertation Series 44. Missoula, Mont.: Scholars.

Clines, David J. A. 1984. *The Esther Scroll: The Story of the Story.* Journal for the Study of the Old Testament Supplementary Series 30. Sheffield: JSOT.

———. 1988. "Esther." In *Revised Edition Harper Collins Bible Commentary,* ed. James L. Mayes, Joseph Blenkinsopp, Beverly R. Gaventa, et al., 353–59. San Francisco: HarperSanFrancisco.

The Jewish Publication Society Hebrew-English Tanakh: The Traditional Hebrew Text and the New JPS Translation. 1999/2000. Philadelphia: Jewish Publication Society.

Levenson, Jon D. 1997. *Esther: A Commentary. Old Testament Library.* Louisville, Ky.: Westminster John Knox.

Moore, Carey A. 1999. "Esther, Book of (and Additions)." In *Dictionary of Biblical Interpretation,* A-J. ed. John Hayes, 349–53. Nashville: Abingdon.

Niditch, Susan. 1985. "Legends of Wise Heroes and Heroines." In *The Hebrew Bible and Its Modern Interpreters,* ed. Douglas A. Knight and Gene M. Tucker, 445–56. Chico, Calif.: Scholars.

———. 1995. "Short Stories: The Book of Esther and the Theme of Woman as a Civilizing Force." In *Old Testament Interpretation: Past, Present, and Future Essays in Honor of Gene M. Tucker,* ed. James L. Mays, David L. Petersen, and Ken H. Richards, 195–209. Nashville: Abingdon.

Schüssler-Fiorenza, Elisabeth. 2006. *Wisdom Ways: Introducing Feminist Biblical Interpretation.* Maryknoll, N.Y.: Orbis.

Semenye, Lois. 2006. "Esther." In *Africa Bible Commentary,* ed. Tokunboh Adeyomo, Solomon Adria, Issiaka Coulibaly, et al., 559–68. Nairobi, Kenya: WordAlive/Zondervan.

Suter, David W. 1985. "Esther." In *The HarperCollins Bible Dictionary,* ed. Paul J. Achtemeier, Roger S. Boraas, Michael Fishbane, et al., 308–10. Reprint, San Francisco: HarperSanFrancisco, 1996.

White, Sidney A. 1992. "Esther." In *The Women's Bible Commentary,* ed. Carol A. Newsom and Sharon H. Ringe. Louisville: Westminster/John Knox, 124–29.

Wong Wai Ching, Angela. 2004. "Esther." In *Global Bible Commentary,* ed. Patte, Daniel, J. Severino Croatto, Nicole W. Duran, et al. Nashville: Abingdon, 135–40.

DANIEL

Andrew M. Mbuvi

EXILES/IMMIGRANTS/REFUGEES

The book of Daniel is usually divided into two
major sections: chapters 1–6, the narrative of
Daniel and the Jewish young men; and chapters
7–12, visions and dreams about the kingdoms of
the world and God's dealings with them. Chapters
1:1—2:4a and 8–12 are written in Hebrew, while
chapters 2:4b—7:28 are written in Aramaic (the
official language of the Babylonians). Aramaic subsequently became the dominant language among
Jews in first-century Palestine during the time of
Jesus. Because the story is about life in the Diaspora, I intend to read it in tandem with my own
experience as a postcolonial African who lives in the
Diaspora while also incorporating the experiences
of other Africans in Diaspora.

Although the historical dating of the book
remains contested among modern scholars—sixth
century B.C.E. (Longman 1999: 1) or second century B.C.E. (Goldingay 1989: xxxvii) provenance—
the setting of the story is in the period of the
Babylonian exile following the destruction of Jerusalem in 587 B.C.E. It was at a time when Babylon
was a world power, sacked Jerusalem, and exiled the
Judeans to Babylon (2 Kings 24–25).

READING DANIEL IN BABYLON:
AN "IMMIGRANT/REFUGEE/EXILE/SLAVE/
COLONIZED" READS DANIEL

I come to the book of Daniel as a different kind of
"exile." While not forcibly brought to America by a

conquering army, I find myself in a situation where, as an immigrant (or, as we are officially known, "resident aliens"), I still check to ensure that I am not green (and that I have no antennae on my head!) in America. I also struggle to maintain my Kenyan identity while taking advantage of the "king's bounty" that America has to offer me as a professor in an American learning institution.

Even though my learning has been so "Babylonian" that my style of writing has been shaped by the Euro-American education that I have received, I have struggled to find my own voice in my attempt to express myself as an African immigrant scholar.

Not unlike Daniel's and his companions' positions in the biblical narrative, my story begins with a forfeiture of a position of privilege. In parallel fashion to the story in Daniel, the beginning meant something of a social dislocation and a loss of privilege. For the four Jewish young men, it meant having to start from scratch about learning a new culture, language, and economic and social systems—the conquerors' systems. It entailed a downward spiral from royal status in Judah to mere students with little ability to choose even what they ate or learned.

For me, loss of privilege meant going from being a professor in a liberal arts college in Kenya to being a graduate student in America. One evening, as I cleaned the blackboard as part of my janitorial duties at a seminary in Grand Rapids, Michigan, it occurred to me how the blackboard had become a metaphor for my experience. I had moved from *using* the blackboard as a sign of authority and status, and for dissemination of information as a teacher, to *cleaning* the blackboard as a means of raising funds for my living expenses while earning a minimum wage as a graduate student and a janitor.

In the setting of the book of Daniel, Babylon (and subsequently Medo/Persia) was the superpower of the day, parallel to the role played by contemporary America. Daniel and his three companions struggled to keep their Jewish religious heritage while also being faithful to their new home in

exile. For example, their abstinence from the royal food was a symbolic refusal to assimilate (Goldingay 1989: 19). The primary reason of conflict with the Babylonians is the insistence by the four to remain faithful to their religious heritage even after they had imbibed some of the educational and social trappings of Babylon.[1]

There is a juxtaposition of one's faithfulness to the newly adopted home and to the home of origin that tends to create tension. This is a position that any émigré embodies in relation to his/her country of origin, whether the relocation was forced or not. The sense of loyalty to one's country of origin continues to encumber the émigré, leading sometimes to conflict of interest. In the case of Daniel and his friends, who are racially designated as the *Jews*— "yehudai" (3:8)—by their Babylonian accusers, it was not just political ambivalence but a religious one too.[2] Having been referred to earlier as simply the *young men* (1:17) or Daniel's *friends* (2:13), they are suddenly racially designated. The story is in Babylon, but the Jewish young men stand out for their difference and distinct identity.

NAMING AS POWER TO CONTROL

An incident I remember well happened on my first day in grade school. Having been named after my maternal grandfather, whose baptismal name is Andrew, I remained oblivious to this designation since I was usually called by my Ki-Kamba name at home, Mūtūa. With dire repercussions, I failed to recognize this as my name when during the roll call the teacher kept calling the name in the roll without my response. To this authority figure in school, it did not matter what they called me at home—"from now on, you will be called Andrew in school" she seemed to emphatically imply. I did not have a choice in the matter, even though both were my given names from birth.

An ominous part of the story of Daniel and his Hebrew colleagues (for enslaved Africans in the Americas) has historically been the incident of name changes (1:7) from their Hebrew names (Daniel, "God is my judge"; Hananiah, "God has been gracious"; Mishael, "Who is what God is"; and Azariah, "God has helped") to their Babylonian ones (Beltheshazzar, "*Bel* [Babylonian deity] protect his life"; Shadrach; Meshach; and Abednego (*abed-nabu*?), "slave of *Nabu*" [Babylonian deity]).[3] As Goldingay notes: "Giving of (new) names as a sign of (new) ownership and thus (new) destiny . . . was common court practice" (1989: 17). This one section of Daniel haunted the enslaved Africans and their progeny who experienced a similar reality when their names were changed to that of their masters' choosing. They essentially lost any identity that was connected to those names and their African heritage. This moment is vividly captured in *Roots*, the 1970s television miniseries on American slavery, written by Alex Haley, when Fiddler renames Kunta Kinte:

FIDDLER: "You Toby, I Fiddler!"
KUNTA: grabs Fiddler's wrist and shouts, "Kunta! Kunta Kinte!"

Kunta's initial resistance in his emphatic response is in vain, and he eventually succumbs to the control not only of the slave owner but of the expansive land that consumes his every effort at escape.

Naming and power were well understood by the enslaved Africans in America, and the mirroring of this image in the story of Daniel might have caused them to embrace the image of the four Jewish young men. They recognized the sense of powerlessness that accompanied the (re)naming and exile of a people. For this reason, they were able then to ask the question in the Negro spiritual "Didn't My Lord Deliver Daniel?":

Refrain:
Didn't my Lord deliver Daniel,
Deliver Daniel, deliver Daniel,
Didn't my Lord deliver Daniel,
An' why not every man?

Stanza:
He delivered Daniel f'om de lion's den,
Jonah f'om de belly of de wale,
An' de Hebrew chillen f'om de fiery furnace,
An' why not every man?
(Johnson and Johnson 1925: 20)

However, it is interesting that the book of Daniel does not seem to have provided as large a redemptive framework for the enslaved Africans in America as the exodus motif (see the book of Exodus) did. Among the enslaved Africans in America, the story of Daniel seems to have been mainly recounted in light of God's redemptive work that gave hope to the slaves for their own eventual liberation from slavery.[4] Perhaps the difference for them lies in the treatment of the Jewish young men to the King's bounty versus the slaves' own inhumane treatment at the hand of their white slave masters removing any parallels of identification.

Even though the characters in Daniel and the enslaved Africans were both in exile after being forcibly taken from their home to a foreign land, the parallels seemed to end there for the enslaved Africans whose lives were horrendous. And so, for the enslaved Africans, when the stories were heard, their emphases were not so much on the parallels with the Jewish young men (as was the case with identification with Israel in the Exodus motif) as on God's ability to redeem.

A parallel scenario for postcolonial Africans involves the legacy of European names that Africans acquired at baptism. To be recognized as a Christian, a person was given a new name (usually a biblical or European name) at baptism that at once alienated the convert from his or her kinfolk and aligned him or her with the colonizer. It is against this legacy that, in the 1970s, the then Zairean (now Democratic Republic of Congo) president Mobutu Sese Seko was reacting when he ordered every Zairoi to drop his or her European name in favor of (re)adopting African names.

DREAMS, VISIONS, AND THEIR INTERPRETATIONS (DANIEL 2, 7–11)

For Africans, arguably the greatest attraction to Daniel (the liberation element notwithstanding!) may be the interpretation of dreams and visions. Daniel is granted a special divine ability to understand and interpret dreams and visions (1:17; 2:19ff), which came in handy on several occasions, saving both his life and that of other Jews in Babylon (2; 4; 5). The elaborate visions and dreams (see Daniel 7–11) outline predictions of Babylon's future, also signifying Daniel's God's control of the cosmic order.

Dreams were (and still are) a central part of the spiritual psyche that permeates African religiosity, which filters into the African Christian experience (Adeyemo 2006: 993).[5] This cultural continuity in African Christianity is especially prevalent in the so-called independent churches where African spiritualities are intricately enmeshed into and closely intertwined with the Christian faith to form a vibrant but uniquely African Christian expression (Mbiti 1969: 307).

In the historical order of the traditional African spiritual leaders—prophets, priests, seers, oracles, shamans, medicine men and women, and so forth—most pioneers of African Independent Churches, such as Isaiah Shembe of the Zionist Church in South Africa, Simon Kimbangu of the Kimbanguist Church in Congo, and prophet William Wadé Harris of Liberia, trace their Christian calling to spiritual encounters in a dream or a vision.

A seer in my grandfather's community had predicted, via dreams and visions, the coming of the white man (missionaries) into our homeland. When I later asked my grandfather, a Christian and itinerant preacher for over eighty years, whether he believed that God had communicated this message to the seer long before any Christian missionaries arrived, he seemed to consent to that possibility. Difficult as it was for my grandfather to assent,

his recognition of the possibility of God's revelation outside of the Bible or a Christian messenger resonates with Daniel's story and rebuffs the prejudiced European missionary teachings that identified everything religiously African with demons, evil, and the devil. Instead, my grandfather recognized that God could communicate with a people through seers even when those seers did not recognize the Christian deity. This is the message of Daniel 7–12, that indeed *ēla šamai*—"the God of heaven" (that is, YHWH, god of the Jews)—is the god who controls not just the fortunes of the Jewish nation but also the destinies of all the world's nations.

In this sense, one cannot see God working only in one particular part of the world and not in another, even when the nations and peoples of the world do not recognize that God is the one controlling the cosmic events. Such a perspective is reinforced by the dream that was revealed to the Babylonian king Nebuchadnezzar by "the God of heaven" (2:28) and to Belshazzar in the handwriting on the wall (chap. 5), even though neither recognized YHWH as his God.

AFRICAN REFUGEES AND NEBUCHADNEZZAR'S STORY (DANIEL 4)

Nebuchadnezzar's divine punishment in Daniel 4 reads more like the story of the modern refugee. In many respects, the life of the refugee is characterized by the inhumane and animal-like conditions to which people are subjected in their flight from danger. It is these elements of utter dehumanization and desperation (4:23-26) that would have many refugees perceive their conditions as divine punishment. For many innocent refugees, there is no clear reason as to *why* it is happening to them. At least Nebuchadnezzar had been informed *why* he was being reduced to inhuman conditions, and later he was even granted a chance to repent (Dan. 4:27). In this regard, when Nebuchadnezzar's proclamation after restoration is put in the mouth of the refugee, it turns out as a statement not of trust in God but of despair: "All the peoples of the earth are regarded as nothing. He does as he pleases with the powers of heaven and the peoples of the earth. No one can hold back his hand or say to him: 'What have you done?'" (4:35 NIV). Regrettably, such a perspective would only perpetuate the traditional African image of a detached God (*deus absconditus*), resulting in a sense of hopelessness.[6]

XENOPHOBIA AND THE LION'S DEN (DANIEL 6)

For a foreigner, one's speech accent, dressing, and other "cultural quirks" mark him or her as an outsider. It matters not how long one has been living in the adopted home country. The so-called natives will always identify one as an outsider with the seemingly innocuous question, "So where are you *originally* from?" "To assimilate or not to" is the ever-present challenge for the exile/refugee/immigrant. Yet, this is not entirely up to the individual. It also depends on acceptance by the "natives." Perhaps the most devastating example of this xenophobia in recent history remains that of Auschwitz and the Jewish holocaust. However, more recent examples of genocide in Africa—Rwanda and Darfur—also are not devoid of xenophobic propaganda.

Daniel and companions learn of the Babylonian natives' xenophobia in the incidents of "the fiery furnace" (Daniel 3) and of "the lion's den" (Daniel 6). The natives are the ones who zealously report to the authorities about the foreign Jews who were being unpatriotic (3:8; 6:12-14). Notice how their identity is highlighted in their accusations; the three young men become *the Jews* (3:8), while Daniel is referred to derogatorily as the "Judean exile" (6:14), even though he was a high-ranking Babylonian official at that point. A modern equivalent of this xenophobia is in such countries as South Africa, whose economic growth at the end of apart-

heid has attracted a growing number of foreigners, causing restlessness in the native South African population and resulting in a lot of killings of foreigners who are supposedly taking jobs that belong to South Africans.

Many Arabs in the United States today, for example, continue to find themselves in the "lion's den" simply for, among others, their profiles, religion, and heritage, which link them to the events of 9/11. It is Daniel's commitment to his Jewish heritage and religious convictions (note how "praying facing Jerusalem" [Dan. 6:11] bears resemblance to Muslims who pray facing Mecca!) that lands him in the lion's den following the complaints of the "natives" to the authorities about his prayer habits, much in the same way that the three Jewish young men were thrown into a fiery furnace for their refusal to worship an idol, an abomination in their faith.[7]

DANIEL'S PRAYERS AND AFRICAN PRAYER LIFE

Prayer in Africa is a central spiritual aspect of religious expression. Prayer is invoked ubiquitously in African communities. Interpretation of dreams, related as an answer to prayer (2:20ff), makes sense to African spirituality, in which solutions to every last problem, from the most sublime to the most mundane, are besought via prayer.

When the prayer in Daniel is addressed to the "God of our ancestors" (2:23), most readers readily identify this reference to Daniel's Jewish ancestors, including such patriarchs and matriarchs as Abraham and Sarah, Isaac and Rebekah, and Jacob and Rachel. African readers, however, see reference to more than just Jewish ancestry in this passage. Since God is God of all nations, according to Daniel, then God is the same God of our (African) ancestors and thus Africans have a rightful heritage to claim our place as God's children too. In this respect, the African has no need to echo Nebuchadnezzar's words—

"Truly, *your* God is the God of gods, the Lord over kings, a revealer of mysteries, for you have been able to reveal this secret" (2:47)—since the African can instead say, "Truly, [*our*] God is the God of gods, the Lord over kings, a revealer of mysteries, for *he has* been able to reveal this secret."

RESURRECTION IN DANIEL 12: HOPE AND DEATH IN THE AFRICAN CONTINENT

The message of resurrection in Daniel 12 strikes very close to the heart of reality in Africa today. The continent has been so ravaged by diseases (malaria, typhoid, and the now ubiquitous HIV/AIDS), droughts and famines, wars and counter wars, and coups and counter coups that death is a reality that is ever too close to home. Such devastation of human life has led some to call it the "bleeding continent," the "cursed continent," or the even racially tainted "dark continent." Hope for any sense of a better life seems to have disappeared for many people. Yet, a glimmer of hope prevails—resurrection hope! That Africa is home to the fastest-growing church in the world speaks of a spiritual conviction of justice in the afterlife.

While the concept of the afterlife is not new to African religiosity, a sense of a final resurrection accompanied by divine justice, as espoused in Dan. 12:1-2, has been fully embraced by the African Christians. Subsequently, Daniel's overall message of faith and hope in a God who is in control even when human reason seems to indicate otherwise means that even death is not the end of the story.

Notes

1. Although the Jewish young men avoided the king's bounty as a symbol of resistance to assimilate (Dan. 1:8-16), it is paradoxical that by becoming more sophisticated in the ways of the Babylonians than any of the Babylonians (Dan. 1:19) and by defying the king's order to worship his idol, they end up being made Babylonian government officials, which they do not resist.

2. For Daniel, the term *Jew* has both religious and political identity inextricably entwined, unlike most modern national identities that are largely devoid of religious characteristics.

3. These may reflect a deliberate corruption of Babylonian names by the Jewish author of Daniel to "heighten the gross paganism of foreign theophoric names that replaced the Israelite theophoric names" (Goldingay 1989: 5).

4. My cursory and very limited survey of some Negro spirituals seems to suggest that their favorite stories were largely those of the three Jewish young men in the fiery furnace and of Daniel in the lion's den.

5. See further discussion in Adeyemo 2006.

6. The concept of God in Africa is one of a deity who is removed from the daily affairs of people and only intervenes (or should only be sought) in times of severe community emergencies, such as droughts, floods, and so forth.

7. Indeed, one must acknowledge that this fear of the foreigner is not limited to Babylonians and that other parts of the Jewish scripture contain evidence of Jewish xenophobia—for example, in "*herem*" commands that have to do with total destruction of a conquered people lest they corrupt the Israelites (see, for example, 1 Sam. 15:3; Jer. 5:21).

References

Adeyemo, Tokunboh, ed. 2006. *Africa Bible Commentary*. Nairobi and Grand Rapids, Mich.: World Alive/Zondervan.

Callahan, Allen Dwight. 2006. *The Talking Book: African Americans and the Bible*. New Haven: Yale University Press.

Goldingay, John E. 1989. *Word Biblical Commentary: Daniel*. Vol. 30. Dallas: Word.

Johnson, J. W., and R. Johnson. 1925. *The Books of American Negro Spirituals*. New York: Viking.

Laubenstein, Paul F. 1932. "An Apocalyptic Reincarnation." *Journal of Biblical Literature* 51 (3): 238–52.

Longman III, Tremper. 1999. *NIV Application Commentary: Daniel*. Grand Rapids, Mich.: Zondervan.

Mbiti, John. 1969. *African Religions and Philosophy*. New York: Praeger.

Towner, Sibley. 1984. *Interpretation: A Bible Commentary for Preaching and Teaching: Daniel*. Atlanta: John Knox.

EZRA *and*

NEHEMIAH

Herbert Marbury

THE BOOKS OF EZRA AND NEHEMIAH were originally a single literary work. Written sometime in the early Hellenistic period (after 332 B.C.E.), they recount the idealized story of a reconstituted but small Jerusalem community threatened with obliteration by imperial rule (Ezra 9:7-10), interethnic strife (Ezra 9–10; Nehemiah 13), and the abusive excesses of an elite class (Nehemiah 5). Both Ezra and Nehemiah respond to the Jerusalem community's suffering by enacting internal reforms that strengthen the community's cultural identity. Ezra and Nehemiah's reforms become legendary. By the end of the story, the two emerge as cultural heroes who restore order and hope and give identity to a people in disarray.

EZRA AND NEHEMIAH AS LEADERS

While the narrator presents both Ezra and Nehemiah as clearly heroic figures, the actual social positions that the two reformers occupy reveal a bit more ambiguity and complicate the story. As impe-

rial officials, Ezra and Nehemiah have the crown's trust (Ezra 7:11-26; Neh. 1:11—2:8). The Persian ruler commissions Ezra's work in Jerusalem and underwrites the cost of his mission. Similarly, the king dispatches Nehemiah with imperial imprimatur to function as governor over the province. Meanwhile, the narrator informs the reader that both reformers hold deep loyalties to the Jerusalem collective. Ezra immigrates to Jerusalem to offer his expertise in Mosaic law (Ezra 7:1-6). Nehemiah's concern for the sorry condition of the infrastructure in Jerusalem prompts him to leave the Persian court and to initiate the rebuilding of the wall (Neh.1:1-6).

In these conflicting roles, both reformers deploy strategies of accommodation and resistance. On one hand, the reformers call for mass divorces that separate their community from those whom they termed "the peoples of the land" (Ezra 9:1-4; 10; Neh. 13). The divorces wreak horror upon the community and rend families asunder. However, these same divorces simultaneously create new spaces of cultural flourishing for what is now a small, homogeneous Jerusalem collective. Ezra's reforms appeal to the law of Moses (Nehemiah 8) and call the people toward a cultural unity that resists imperial domination. On the other hand, Ezra's reforms and Nehemiah's fortification of the infrastructure give the province the political stability that the Persian officials desire. Consequently, the two officials succeed in appeasing the crown while saving their people.

THE MULTIVALENT RHETORIC OF REFORM

The reforms are presented as separatist rhetoric (Ezra 9–10; Nehemiah 10, 13). The rhetoric's stark language is both poignant and provocative and its content is morally disturbing, leaving the reader with unsettling questions. Were Ezra and Nehemiah too intent on pleasing the Persian crown at the expense of the people? Were they complicit in Persian repression? Did their reforms succeed only in creating interethnic conflict by pitting disempowered members of the Jerusalem community against even more disempowered "peoples of the land"? Or were their reforms, although problematic, the only reasonable means to ensure the survival of their community? These books' final chapters continue to raise important issues for marginalized communities in their own struggles against repression.

A hermeneutical turn to rhetoric of the antebellum period in the United States provides a rich analogue to the rhetoric in Ezra and Nehemiah. African Americans held in chattel slavery understood the political value of multivalent rhetoric. Take, for example, the song "Swing Low, Sweet Chariot," sung on antebellum plantations throughout the South. The lyrics read:

Swing low, sweet chariot,
Coming for to carry me home;
Swing low, sweet chariot,
Coming for to carry me home.
I looked over Jordan,
And what did I see,

Coming for to carry me home,
A band of angels coming after me,
Coming for to carry me home.

If you get there before I do,
Coming for to carry me home,
Tell all my friends I'm coming too,
Coming for to carry me home.[1]

Clearly such rhetoric accommodated the repression of slavery. It allowed the slaveholding class to participate in the myth of slaves' contentment with their social condition. The white slaveholding class heard African Americans singing this song on Sunday mornings in brush arbors and during the workday in the fields. For them, the song alluded to the story of the prophet Elijah in 2 Kings. It dramatized Elijah's reward for his faithfulness to Yahweh. The slaveholding class understood the elder prophet's ascension in Elisha's presence as a sign of God's satisfaction with his service. For them, the song articulated their slaves' future hope that after a lifelong tenure of acceptable service, God would allow them, also, to participate in Elijah's heavenly reward.

The same rhetoric simultaneously facilitated resistance amid repression, however. African Americans held in chattel slavery constructed a far different meaning from that of their slaveholding counterparts. They heard the lyrics and knew that the "sweet chariot" was a metaphor for the Underground Railroad. "Raising" that song in church or in the field meant that the "train" was stopping in the vicinity that week or that evening. To "swing low" meant to stop by and pick up new passengers. "Home" was not some spiritual afterlife, but rather life after slavery—that is, life anywhere north of the Mason-Dixon Line.

The second stanza recalled the Jordan River, the last natural boundary that the Israelites would encounter on their forty-year journey to freedom from Egyptian bondage. For African Americans, this marker was the Ohio River, the watery boundary that extended the Mason-Dixon Line, separating slave and free states. To "look over" the Jordan was to envision all of those who had already escaped to freedom and beckoned their sisters and brothers to join them.

The third stanza is almost self-evident. It acknowledged the rigors and the risks of the route from slavery to freedom. Not all could join the band of escapees. Some were in no condition to make the long, hazardous journey. Some were afraid. Some stayed behind to facilitate the journey for others. The last line, however, articulated a universal hope that all would "get there" someday.

Within a matrix of overwhelming repressive power, the rhetoric of the spiritual and its ability to "play" in and among the interpretive gaps and disjunctions between the social worlds of slave and slaveholder became a powerful subversive tool against repression. Such rhetoric is political; it takes sides. It simultaneously subverts and directs power. Black preachers and others who employed the song for political purposes carefully crafted a multivocal rhetoric in which both slave and slave master could participate, albeit with very different interests and understandings.

Since the rhetoric was appropriately constructed to attend to each group's social and political interests, each group could participate in their own symbolic world of meaning. The slaveholder certainly would not have been aware that the rhetoric signaled the arrival of the Underground Railroad and the slaves' intent for freedom here instead of in the hereafter. Those slaves who had not read 2 Kings or heard the story of Elijah preached might not have been aware that there was another signification for the rhetoric in the planter class's romanticized notions of slave piety. Only those individuals, who traveled between both worlds, such as slave preachers, would have understood the rhetoric's double signification and why the song needed such a multivalent character to be effective.

The separatist rhetoric of Ezra 9–10 and Nehemiah 10–13 is similarly multivalent. Like the spiritual "Swing Low, Sweet Chariot," the rhetoric of Ezra and Nehemiah also emerges from a context of repression. Judah suffered under Persian dominion

that was no less brutal than that of the Assyrians and Babylonians before them or that of the Greeks and Romans who succeeded them.

MULTIVALENCE AND PERSIAN POLICY

Persian policy targeted temples and their priesthoods for their utility to the empire. Because Darius I the Great, the Persian emperor (522–486 B.C.E.), authorized and funded the construction of the Jerusalem temple, the priesthood there was especially beholden to Persian authority. Since ancient temples possessed vast wealth, the harsh yoke of Persian rule levied high taxes against their huge repositories. Larger temples in Babylon and Egypt struggled under the brunt of these demands, but smaller temples, like the one in Jerusalem, were threatened with the loss of their very existence. Moreover, Persian authorities employed temples and their religious ideologies as a more cost-effective method of pacifying local populations than military force.[2]

Under such repressive power, the rhetoric that culminates both the books of Ezra and Nehemiah takes on new meaning. Such rhetoric, produced in a context of imperial dominion, employs positions of both resistance and accommodation to subvert imperial control. Just as the spirituals of our forebears held meaning for both slave and slavemaster, the separatist rhetoric in Ezra and Nehemiah allowed both the Persian officials and the Jerusalem community to participate in the same rhetorical discourse but toward vastly different political ends. For the Persians, expelling the "peoples of the land" consolidated power in the hands of the loyal collective whom they had freed from Babylon and for whom they had constructed a temple. At a time when tension with Egypt and Greece ran high, the Persians needed loyalty and stability in this Western border province. A more religiously unified province that would support the temple with its finances (Ezra 8:24-35; Neh.10: 28-32; 13:10-14) also centralized the collection of taxes.

IMPLICATIONS FOR JERUSALEM

For the Jerusalem community, the rhetoric of these chapters, imbued with the familiar symbols of their collective ancestral memory, conveyed a far different meaning. At each turn, the rhetoric recalls their ancestral story (Ezra 9:7-11; Neh. 9:7-31) and calls members to recommit themselves to resisting the loss of cultural identity and returning to practices that affirm cultural survival. Expelling so-called "foreigners"[3] became a communal and public affirmation of cultural unity in the face of forces that threatened the community's obliteration. The mass divorces prevented the transference of wealth and land to so-called "outsiders" and preserved wealth in the hands of the collective. The pledge to support the temple (Neh. 10:32-39) and to obey Ezra's law (Nehemiah 8–9) bound them with a *religio-cultural* ideology that began to shape what would become a new *ethnic* identity.

This separatist rhetoric, like its antebellum analogue, the spiritual, functioned in an ambiguous space. Both rhetorics assumed postures of accommodation to appease repressive powers as well as postures of resistance to inspire a marginalized community. However, the deployment of multivalent symbolism was not limited merely by the reformers' rhetoric. In the politico-cultural landscape of the province, Ezra and Nehemiah themselves become ambiguous figures with subversive intent. We find a useful hermeneutical frame for reading this aspect of the activities of Ezra and Nehemiah in the work and rhetoric of the much-maligned and similarly ambiguous Booker T. Washington.

WASHINGTON AND DUBOIS: INTERPRETIVE PARADIGMS

During his lifetime, Booker T. Washington dominated the nineteenth-century U.S. political landscape as its most prominent African American. His staunch public advocacy of industrial education and commercial endeavor for African Americans gained the support of conservative and liberal whites alike. History, however, has diminished his legacy, owing in large part to the African American community's preference of W. E. B. DuBois's competing philosophy to that of Washington. DuBois emphasized the need for liberal arts education and civil and political attainment *before* the pursuit of industrial education and commercial endeavors.

While both men spent their lives working for African American advancement, their differing proximities to white brutality may have influenced their distinct political philosophies. DuBois, born after the end of slavery, grew up in the North and was educated at Fisk and Harvard. Washington, however, was born into slavery and was educated in the South. Similar to Ezra and Nehemiah's proximity to the Persian crown, Washington's context gave him firsthand exposure to the brutality of American slavery and the violence that southern whites could inflict on blacks with impunity. Unlike DuBois, Washington had also lived through Reconstruction and the heartbreaking Compromise of 1877 that followed. He had seen black civil and political advances dismantled with the stroke of a white man's pen and had known the political, social, economic, and psychic devastation wrought upon black communities throughout the South. Such a context, totalized by southern white power and black vulnerability, led Washington to defer publicly on social and civic advancement for African Americans until blacks first achieved a mastery of commerce and industry. Washington believed that such achievement could not be written away as had been the case with gains under Reconstruction. Harnessing these twin forces, commerce and industry, Washington believed African Americans could build an economic base with which to sustain advances in the civic and social arena.[4]

Like Washington, both Ezra and Nehemiah emerged from positions at the center of imperial administration. They also had seen repressive power at close proximity. Perhaps this explains why they both enlisted the support of the Persian crown for their missions. Perhaps their proximity to the crown also prevented them from criticizing Persian rule. Instead, Ezra spoke of imperial dominion as divinely ordained (Ezra 9:8-9; Neh. 9:35-37). Ezra recast Persian dominion as God's punishment and encouraged the community to rebuild Jerusalem under Persian authority as a way of participating in God's "steadfast love." At the same time, Nehemiah, savvy in matters of imperial diplomacy, entertained both imperial officials and members of his own community at his table (Neh. 5:14-17).

In his famous 1895 Atlanta Cotton Exposition speech, Washington admonished African Americans, saying, "To those of my race who depend on bettering their condition in a foreign land or who underestimate the importance of cultivating friendly relations with the Southern white man, who is their next-door neighbor, I would say: 'Cast down your bucket where you are—cast it down in making friends in every manly way of the people of all races by whom we are surrounded. Cast it down in agriculture, in mechanics, in commerce, in domestic service, and in the professions.'"[5] His response to a social world dominated by pervasive white power was to advance a program and a rhetoric that achieved the economic and immediate educational ends of black southerners without raising the white community's suspicions or inciting their violent reprisals. Similar to Ezra and Nehemiah, he sought to advance the cultural life of his community without arousing the repressive political forces that threatened its obliteration. In the same speech, Washington seemingly concedes any pursuit of civil rights in lieu of economic attainment, saying, "In all things that are purely social, we can be as separate as the five fingers, yet one as the hand in all things essential to mutual progress."[6]

Yet neither of these descriptions adequately captures Washington's attitude toward the races. He did not expect African Americans to allow whites to violate their basic human dignity. In spring 1884, he declared before the National Education Association in Madison, Wisconsin: "Now, in regard to what I have said about the relations of the two races, there should be no unmanly cowering or stooping to satisfy unreasonable whims of Southern white men, but it is charity and wisdom to keep in mind the two hundred years' schooling in prejudice

against the Negro which the ex-slaveholders are called upon to conquer."[7] In the same speech, he repeated his long-held belief that whites would have no choice but to endow blacks with rights properly due to full citizens if African Americans surpassed them in the commercial sphere. In a similar way, Ezra and Nehemiah at times explicitly resisted imperial repression. Ezra criticized Persian rule as slavery (Neh. 9:36-37), while Nehemiah repeatedly confronted imperial officials who attempted to prevent the community from repairing Jerusalem (Neh. 2:19-20; 4:1-23; 6:1-14).

The biblical reformers and the nineteenth-century educator alike were ultimately pragmatists. Washington was no more wedded to the ideology of accommodation than Ezra and Nehemiah were wedded to separatism for its own sake. Washington, like Ezra and Nehemiah, succeeded in deploying both rhetorical modes of accommodation and resistance to subvert repressive power. Publicly, his accommodating speech afforded him funds from wealthy, liberal, white philanthropists and segregationist alike. Indeed, he would come to be known as the most powerful African American in the country. Privately, however, his activities would underscore the ambiguity that constituted his persona. Contrary to his benefactors' expectations, Washington financed some of the earliest antisegregation litigation.[8] At the same time, while his Tuskeegee Institute, tucked away in Alabama, trained African Americans in agriculture, commerce, and the trades, it also boasted one of the most progressive liberal arts curriculums in the South, where classical training in Latin, Greek, and philosophy was at the heart of the curriculum.

Deploying similar rhetorical modes of accommodation and resistance, Ezra and Nehemiah succeeded as well. With the confidence of the crown, Ezra (Ezra 7:11-25) called this reconstituted and culturally homogenized community to reinterpret Mosaic law for a new generation (Neh. 8:1-12). Nehemiah brought important infrastructural improvements that fortified the city of Jerusalem for both the Persian Empire and his Jerusalem community (Neh. 2; 5:15-19).

In the end, the work and rhetoric of both Washington and the biblical reformers achieved their ends, but not without doing irreparable violence. For nineteenth-century African Americans, Washington's program meant ceding civil liberties and, in some cases, human dignity and accepting painful second-class citizenship. For the Jerusalem collective, one can only describe as unspeakable the horror of the mass divorces and violence done by scapegoating women and children.

Ultimately, Washington's work and speech and the rhetoric and work of the biblical reformers have much to teach contemporary marginalized communities engaged in their own struggles for freedom. Both affirm struggles for human dignity against repression. And both warn that compromises in struggles for freedom may beget the repression of those struggles.

Notes

1. Traditional spiritual. Published in *Songs of Zion*, ed. J. Jefferson Cleveland and Verogla Nix (Nashville: Abingdon Press, 1984), No. 104.

2. See John M. Lundquist, "What is a Temple? A Preliminary Typology," in *The Quest for the Kingdom of God: Studies in Honor of George E. Mendenhall*, ed. H. B. Huffmon, F. A. Spina, and A. R. W. Green (Winona Lake, In.: Eisenbrauns, 1983). For specific examples of temple and state engagement, see M. A. Dandamaev, "Neo-Babylonian Society and Economy," in *The Cambridge Ancient History: The Assyrian and Babylonian Empires and Other States of the Near East, from the Eighth to the Sixth Centuries B.C.*, ed. John Boardman, I. E. S. Edwards, et al, (New York: Cambridge University Press, 1991), 269–70. See M.A. Dandamaev, *Slavery in Babylonia from Nabopolassar to Alexander the Great* (626–331 B.C.) (DeKalb: Northern Illinois University Press, 1984), 107–8. See also Christopher Tulpin, "Darius's Suez Canal and Persian Imperialism," *Achaemenid History* 6 (1991): 260–61, and M. A. Dandamaev, "Achaemenid Babylonia," in *Ancient Mesopotamia: A Collection of Studies by Soviet Scholars*, ed. I. M. Diakonoff (Moscow: Nauka Publishing House, 1969), 310–11. John H. Kautsky's schema on aristocratic empires and Gehard Lenski's study of agrarian societies both offer helpful theoretical frames for an understanding of temple and court relationships. See John H. Kautsky, *The Politics of Aristocratic Empires* (New Brunswick, N.J.: Transaction Publishers, 1997), 250–51, and Gerhard Lenski, *Power and Privilege: A Theory of Social Stratification* (Chapel Hill: University of North Carolina Press, 1984), 255–66.

3. The term *foreigners* is the writer's designation for "the people of the land." The term however, can be misleading since it assumes some cultural difference between the community that Ezra and Nehemiah are constructing and others living in Yehud. The differences are not cultural or ethnic but are constructed as Ezra and Nehemiah erect the boundaries of this new community.

4. See John Hope Franklin, *From Slavery to Freedom: A History of Negro Americans* (New York: Alfred Knopf, 1980), 274. For W. E. B. Dubois's critique of Washington's program see chapter 3 in his book *The Souls of Black Folk* (Chicago: McClurg, 1903).

5. Booker T. Washington, *Up From Slavery: An Autobiography* (New York: Doubleday, 1919), 219–20.

6. Ibid., 240.

7. Louis. R. Harlan, ed., *The Booker T. Washington Papers: Volume 2 1860–1889* (Champaign, Ill., 1972), 259.

8. Louis R. Harlan, "The Secret Life of Booker T. Washington," *Journal of Southern History* 37:3 (1971), 393–416.

References

Clines, David J. A. *Ezra, Nehemiah, Esther.* New Century Bible Commentary. Grand Rapids: Eerdmans, 1984.

Klein, Ralph. "Ezra-Nehemiah." *ABD* 2:731–42.

Washington, Booker T. 1884. Speech before the National Education Association, Madison, Wisc.

———. 1895. "Atlanta Compromise." Address before the Cotton States and International Exposition in Atlanta. Available online at http://historymatters.gmu.edu/d/39.

Williamson, H. G. M. *Ezra, Nehemiah.* Word Biblical Commentary 16. Waco: Word, 1985.

Throntveit, Mark. "I and II Chronicles" in *The HarperCollins Bible Commentary* (San Francisco: HarperSanFrancisco; 2000).

1–2 CHRONICLES

Renita J. Weems

As an American and as a woman of African ancestry, stories of people struggling to preserve their cultural identity, reclaim their historical memories, and find language to name their own identity strike a deep chord within. As someone whose ancestors were brought to these shores in chains from Africa some four hundred years ago, stripped of language, culture, religion, and kin, I have both witnessed and know what it is personally to take an active part in my own people's struggle to reclaim their historical memories and carve out an identity that strikes a balance between one's African roots and American memories. But I am also a citizen of the largest empire in the West, and though I work hard to resist the Christian meta-narrative of the West and its complicity with the imperialistic ambitions of the West, I don't fool myself into thinking that I have not benefited from America's superpower status. I am a First World woman with Third World commitments. But despite those commitments I watched the television in horror in 2003 as the country I live in invaded, raided, and decimated a smaller, comparatively defenseless country by the name of Iraq, some of whose population is predominantly Muslim. I stared in disbelief as my country stormed in and deposed that country's leader, destroyed its monuments, looted its national treasures, and imposed martial law on its citizens. That experience, coupled with my own memories as an African American woman, have reinforced in my mind the chaos that erupts when a people's cultural memories are virtually erased.[1]

People with a cultural memory see themselves as part of a collective story. Cultural memory includes things like narratives, values, martyrs, leaders, and heroes woven into an account that helps people see themselves belonging to something larger than themselves.[2] Reading 1 and 2 Chronicles, one begins to appreciate the effort the writer put into creating a narrative that instilled a sense of mission, national pride, and divine purpose in a people that had once been displaced from their homeland and robbed of their cultural memories. Convincing the exiles to return to their homeland was one thing. Persuading them to remain loyal to the god of their ancestors and to make the sacrifices necessary to create their own memories and rebuild their monuments was another. The Chronicler surveyed the archives of Israel's past kings and prophets and wars and found in the story of its martyrs, leaders, and heroes inspiration and fulfillment in the restoration of YHWH's rebuilt temple. The Chronicler was eager to inspire the inhabitants of Judah to hope again and to throw themselves behind a national effort to rebuild and to restore order to their homeland.

As we have seen from stories of war-torn areas such as the DR Congo, Sudan, Rwanda, Liberia, and from stories of natural disaster as nearby as New Orleans, it is not easy to go back home once one has been displaced from one's homeland. There is a lot of anguish involved. And if one decides to go back home, it is not always possible to simply pick up where one left off. The returnees were forced not only to adjust to their new reality but also to rediscover God's purpose for them under new circumstances. Instead of asking why the disaster happened to them like his theological counterpart the Deuteronomistic Historian years before, the Chronicler retells the story of Israel's past in order to answer the questions "Are We Still the God's People?" and "What do God's promises to David and Solomon mean to us, today?"[3]

THE COMPOSITION OF CHRONICLES

The books of 1 and 2 Chronicles were most likely originally one book. We have the translators of the Septuagint to thank for dividing the books into two under the title *Paralipomenon*, meaning "Things Omitted." The latter probably refers to the fact that Chronicles includes supplemental material not found in the other historical books, namely Samuel and Kings (Hezekiah's reforms: 2 Chron. 29-31; Manasseh's repentance: 2 Chron. 33).

The fourth-century translator of the Latin Vulgate suggested that the name *Chronicon or* "A Chronicle of All of Sacred History" more aptly described the book and thus gave it the name "Chronicles" since the material in the book purports to span a period stretching all the way from Adam to Cyrus the Great (538 B.C.E.). In the Hebrew Bible, Chronicles belongs to the third division of the Hebrew canon, the *Ketuvim* (The Writings), following Ezra–Nehemiah. While Chronicles is the last book in the Hebrew Bible, it is considered one of the historical books in English Bibles and appears after 1–2 Kings and before Ezra–Nehemiah.

First Chronicles retells the story of King David from a priestly point of view, playing up the association with the Ark of the Covenant, the Jerusalem cult, and detailed preparations for the building of the Jerusalem temple. Judah was David's and the kings' ancestral home, which explains why Judah and its institutions are the Chronicler's focus and why there's hardly any mention of the northern kingdom and its tradition. Second Chronicles continues the priestly saga left off in First Chronicles of the building of the Temple, picking up with Solomon and his exclusive contribution as a cult-observing, worshiping king. The rest of the book is devoted to recapitulating the books of Kings in chronicling the reigns of the Davidic kings who were Solomon's successors ending with Cyrus's decree (538 B.C.E.) and the restoration the exiles to their homeland (2 Chron. 36).

Edited in its final form during fifth-century Persian domination, 1 and 2 Chronicles, indeed the Bible itself, is protest literature or what some call Diaspora literature. Definitions of such literature are obviously fluid. But one thing is clear: the Chronicler is written to explain how a people who found themselves as part of a catastrophic event managed to survive whole, find freedom, and rebuild their lives. They were not content to let their oppressors have the last word or define their history.

Perhaps the best modern example of protest or survival literature would be African American slave narratives. By their very existence, the narratives demonstrated that African Americans were people with mastery of language and the ability to write their own history. The narratives told of the horrors of family separation, the sexual abuse of black slave women, and the inhuman workload blacks endured. They told of free blacks being kidnapped and sold into slavery. They described the frequency and brutality of flogging and the severe living conditions of slave life. They also told exciting tales of escape, heroism, betrayal, and tragedy. The narratives captivated nineteenth-century readers, portraying the fugitives as sympathetic, fascinating characters. Slave narratives were proof that slaves were human, just as books like 1 and 2 Chronicles were testaments that despite the destruction of the Temple and the bondage of exile, the hopes and dreams of a national revival of Israel could never be extinguished. After all, Israel's destiny was tied to God and not to human powers. The message of the Chronicler was unmistakable: Yahweh, the Lord of history, is in control, ordering the destinies of all empires and their inhabitants. This, perhaps, explains why Chronicles is the last book of the Hebrew Bible.

For the Chronicler the golden age of Israel's past came during King David's rule and the Davidic monarchy was a stable part of worship in Jerusalem. Reflections on this period inspired life at that moment. They were a model for Judah's reconstruction and restoration in the postexilic period. The Chronicler is interested in drawing on the best of Israel's history to remind the community that apathy has not always been a part of their past; there was a period when Israel served Yahweh with all its heart.

It comes as no surprise then that select portions of 1 and 2 Chronicles, with their emphasis on Israel worshiping, praising, and praying its way through one hardship after another, have found deep resonance within the Africana community over the years. For example, David called for the Levites to appoint from among themselves singers who would be accompanied by mechanical instruments in "lifting up the voice with joy" (1 Chron. 15:16). Of the 24,000 who were "set forward for the work of the house of the Lord. . . . four thousand praised the Lord with instruments" (made by David? 1 Chron. 23:4-5). First Chronicles 25:7 reflects 288 skilled singers employed for the praising of God. Lively music and singing have long been an important part of African worship and celebrations. Worship engages the whole person: the spirit, the intellect, and the body. If one were to walk into the average African or African American church today, one is likely to find worship with enthusiastic singing, clapping, dancing, and even spirit-possession.[4] Second Chronicles 20 is the story of African American church audiences love to narrate about not waiting until one's troubles are over to thank and praise God. Aware that his tiny kingdom was no match for the vast army marching toward it, Jehoshaphat called the inhabitants to join him in fasting and prayer (20:3-4). After reassurances from Jehazial the prophet and from God, he leads his people to the battlefield with sounds of praise and prayer. The passage serves to remind oppressed people that (1) no matter how intimidating the mighty may seem, nothing and no one can be compared to the Almighty's power and (2) that with fervent prayer and praise to God, circumstances can change.

Regarding prayer, the center of the Chronicler's theology for the returnees is obtained in Solomon's dedicatory prayer in 2 Chronicles 7:14. God's response to Solomon is crucial for this theology. God will forgive and restore those under judgment when they "humble themselves, pray, seek [God's] face, and turn from their wicked ways." Most of the major themes of the Chronicler are found in this story of King Jehoshaphat. It includes (1) the importance of holding firm to faith and relying totally upon God, (2) God sending words of warning and assurance through prophets and through priestly leadership in worship, (3) and God's promise of blessing upon a faithful worshiping community and the assurance of answered prayer (2 Chron. 7:14). In the story of Jehoshaphat's prayer, these elements combine to reassure the Chronicler's Second Temple audience. Their efforts to rebuild were constantly undermined by interference from the inhabitants who were direct descendants of the contingency that challenged King Jehoshaphat (see Neh. 2:19; 4:1-3; 7-9; 6:1-4; 13). With much prayer, though, comes much power, says the Chronicler.

Another prayer has gained lots of attention in recent years. Few people had ever heard of the obscure, sentence-long prayer lodged deep in 1 Chronicles. However, American evangelist Bruce Wilkinson changed all that by his book on 1 Chron. 4:10 that sold over eight million copies globally. The main words are purported to have been first spoken by Jabez: "And Jabez called on the God of Israel, saying, 'Oh, that you would bless me indeed, and enlarge my territory, that your hand would be with me, and that you would keep me from evil, that I may not cause pain!'"

The success of Wilkinson's "The Prayer of Jabez" is based partly on his interpretation of the ancient prayer as a plea for personal blessing and for more opportunities to do God's work. The fact that God honors Jabez's prayer and blesses him with great riches proves, say some, that if people in pure heart ask God for a blessing—and do so using the exact words that Jabez prayed—then God would give them wondrous gifts. But isn't it true that each of us can pick out individual passages seeming to suggest that God will give us whatever we wish as long as it is asked for from a pure heart? Who among us has not known Christians with deep prayer lives yet with no material blessing? Are we to believe that it was because they failed to pray with Jabez's conviction? While I do not want to discount these passages summarily,

there is something plastic and misleading about this sort of theology. The expectation that with the right prayer, miraculous blessings can be obtained resides in the heart of prosperity gospel preaching. The latter has spread throughout Christianity. It threatens to drown out the voices of prophets who speak on God's behalf against injustices and systemic evil in the world. Prayers like Jabez's, may help inspire individuals here and there in their quest for success, but it does nothing for the masses of people lingering in poverty because of systemic oppression.

This is a particularly fascinating period to study for those of us who are of African descent because of the insight it gives into Diasporan religion and what we can learn about how Judah's understanding of race, ethnicity, and nationality evolved as its people came into closer contact with people from different parts of the world. Writings like that of the Chronicler deserve closer study because we discover how the Chronicler tried to rouse interest in Levitical cultic practices by showing that the kings' and the people's failure to worship God properly had led to the nation's downfall and the monarchy's collapse.

In the United States, there has been a long tradition of calling for the separation of church from state, yet a powerful inclination to mix religion and politics if it helps the cause of particular people. Throughout our history, great political and social movements—from abolition, women's suffrage, civil rights, today's struggles over abortion and same-sex marriages, to our nation's military campaigns to spread freedom and democracy around the world—have drawn upon religious institutions for moral authority, inspirational leadership, and organizational muscle. It is dangerous however, when a nation equates its policies with God's will. History would be far different if we did not tend to hear God most clearly when we think God is telling us exactly what we want to hear.[5]

Renita J. Weems

Notes

1. Suzy Salamy, "Erasing Memory: The Cultural Destruction of Iraq," provides visuals of Iraqi art destroyed and looted in the invasion and discusses the logic that says, in effect, "We had to destroy the city in order to save it." See http://www.mediarights.org/film/erasing_memory_the_cultural_destruction_of_iraq.

2. Rodriguez, Jeannett, and Ted Fortier, *Cultural Memory: Resistance, Faith and Identity* (Austin: University of Texas, 2007), 17.

3. Mark Throntveit, "I Chronicles," in *HarperCollins Bible Commentary*, James L. Mays, ed. (San Francisco: *HarperSanFrancisco*, 2000): 325.

4. C. Eric Lincoln and Lawrence Mamiya. *The Black Church in the African American Experience* (Durham: Duke Univeristy Press, 1990), xi.

5. Madeline Albright, *The Mighty and the Almighty: Reflections on America, God, and World Affairs.* New York: HarperPerennial, 2006: 24

References

Allen, Leslie C. 1999. "I and II Chronicles: A Commentary" in *The New Interpreter's Commentary*, volume 3. Nashville: Abingdon.

Klein, Ralph. 2004. "Africa and Africans in the Book of Chronicles." *Currents in Theology and Missions.*

Laffey, Alice. 1998. "1 and 2 Chronicles." In *The Women's Commentary*, eds. Carol Newsom and Sharon H. Ringe, 117–22. Louisville: Westminster John Knox.

Lincoln, C. Eric, and Lawrence H. Mamiya. 1990. *The Black Church in the African American Experience.* Durham: Duke University Press.

Oded Lipschitz, and Manfred Oeming. 2006. *Judah and the Judeans in the Persian Period: In the Persian Period.* Winona Lake, Ind.: Eisenbrauns.

Throntveit, Mark. 2000. "I and II Chronicles." In *The HarperCollins Bible Commentary* (San Francisco: HarperSanFrancisco.

THE AFRICANA BIBLE

READING ISRAEL'S SCRIPTURES

FROM AFRICA AND THE AFRICAN DIASPORA

THE DEUTEROCANONICAL AND PSEUDEPIGRAPHIC WRITINGS

INTRODUCTION *to the*

DEUTEROCANONICAL *and*

PSEUDEPIGRAPHIC WRITINGS

Stacy Davis and
Nathaniel Samuel Murrell

THE FOLLOWING eighteen articles introduce texts that are not included in the Hebrew Tanak and the Protestant Bible. Many of the texts appeared in the earliest Greek and other translations of the Hebrew scriptures and either became a part of the Roman Catholic and Eastern Orthodox or Coptic (Egyptian) canon or Ethiopic canon (or both) or were preserved also in African languages (Syriac, Coptic, and Ethiopic). Good precedent exists for Africans' use of these books/chapters. Diaspora Jews in Alexandria, Egypt, included fourteen of the writings in the first Greek version (Septuagint) of the Hebrew Bible (circa 250 B.C.E.), and early Christians, especially in North Africa, are known to have used some of them. Of course, influential Jews at the Synod of Jamnia (circa 90–100 C.E.) excluded these writings from their canon for various reasons: they appeared too late in the biblical period, after the

Hebrew canon was formed; many were written in Aramaic and Greek, then Coptic and Syriac, under pseudonyms; some rabbis did not believe they "soiled the hands" of the users, or were sacred or inspired; although they were not read as widely as books in the Hebrew Bible, they were used by early Christians who were in tension with the Jews over the death of Jesus and the new "Christian cult"; and rabbis thought their authentic Jewish heritage was in jeopardy of being eroded by cultural syncretism, political disfavor, and Christian apocalyptic visions (Douglass 1974: 54).

Christian scholar Jerome (354–420) held that Tobit, Judith, Wisdom of Solomon, Sirach (or Ecclesiasticus), Baruch, Letter of Jeremiah, Suzanna, Additions to Esther, Additions to Daniel, Prayer of Azariah, Song of the Three Young Men, Bel and the Dragon, and 1 and 2 Maccabees may be read for personal edification but not for confirming church doctrine. He then sought to exclude them from the biblical canon as apocryphal (hidden, secret, and uninspired) but was urged by North African scholar-cleric Saint Augustine of Hippo (354–430), leaders at Carthage (now Libya and Tunisia), and Pope Damasus I (304–386), to whom he was private secretary, to include them in what became the standard Latin Vulgate. The Catholic, Eastern Orthodox, and other North African churches kept the books as a part of the biblical canon without question—until European Protestants seriously challenged the books' canonical status in 1519—and preserved many of them in superior uncial manuscripts: Sinaiticus, Alexandrinus, Vaticanus, and codex Ephraimi Rescriptus (Dentan 1964: 546).

When Andreas Bodenstein of Carlstadt published *de Canonics Scripturis Libellus* at Wittenberg in 1520, he labeled the books apocryphal and excluded them from his Protestant translation, probably also since some of the books recognized purgatory (Washington 2000: 327). The Council of Trent, however, decreed twelve of these books canon worthy in 1546 and placed them after the Song of Songs. In 1566, Sixtus of Sienna named all fifteen books deuterocanonical writings, and the Synod of Jerusalem reaffirmed their place in the canon in 1672 (Dentan 1964: 546; http://www.copticnet/EncyclopediaCoptica/).

Although the content of these writings varies considerably and effects perceptions of their value and integrity for African peoples, they are composed mostly in literary forms similar to those of the Hebrew canon: historical narratives (Judith and the Maccabees); delightful short stories with folktales of death, demons, and angels (Tobit and Bell and the Dragon); practical ideas of wisdom as morality (Ecclesiasticus and Wisdom of Solomon); apocalyptic visions (2 Esdras); and devotional poetry. Some books contain little that might be classified as spurious and theologically untenable. Judith captures Israel's stress under Babylonian invasion. The books of 1 and 2 Maccabees are

historical surveys of accounts and responses to real Greek suppression of the Jewish people in Palestine and their fight to preserve their culture. Tobit encourages "adherence to God's laws," "the Golden Rule," "tender consideration for women," and "racial brotherhood" (Washington 2000: 327). Wisdom of Solomon, among the finest examples of Hebrew Wisdom literature, and Ecclesiasticus, a guidebook for the good life, are two marvelous collections of poems and proverbs and arguably the most important of the deuterocanonical books (Douglass 1974: 53).

As Margaret Washington says, African Americans' use of the scriptures extends way beyond the boundaries of the Hebrew Bible to include "forbidden books." Perhaps, writes Washington, the "fifteen esoteric, profoundly, lyrical guides for living were withdrawn from common use when teaching enslaved people, just as were certain portions of the Old Testament. That Charleston rebels had Bibles with the Apocrypha was revealed at the trial of Mingo, where an enslaved man William testified: 'At Mingo's house I took up the Bible and read two chapters from the prophet Tobit'" (Washington 2000: 326; see also Kennedy and Parker 1970).

Also included here are articles on the most popular of the pseudepigraphic writings in Coptic/Ethiopic Africa: The Prayer of Manasseh, 3 and 4 Maccabees, Sibylline Oracles, Psalm 151, 1 Enoch, Adam and Eve, 2 Esdras, and Jubilees. Not considered here are Letters of Aristeas, Testaments of the Twelve Patriarchs, Psalms of Solomon, 2 Baruch, Testament of Job, Testament of Moses, Lives of the Prophets, Ascension of Isaiah, and Apocalypse of Elijah. These are pseudonymous writings that are attributed to such biblical figures as Abraham, Adam, Noah, Enoch, and Moses but were never a part of the official Jewish or Christian canon. They were written by Jewish sages, mainly in the Diaspora (between 200 B.C.E. and 200 C.E.), attempting to preserve Hebrew faith and culture under recovery from centuries of invasions, destruction, and cultural "pollution." They address similar concerns expressed in the deuterocanon, show tensions between loyalty to Jewish religion and Greco-Roman culture, and "provide an important link between the Old and New Testament periods, when Jewish thought was profoundly influenced by Greek ideas" (Harris and Platzner 2003: 347–48, 369). Along with the second canon, these writings provide a rich source of information on the nature of postbiblical religion of Jewish communities in the African Diaspora (Egypt, Syria, Ethiopia, and so forth) and Palestine (Bandstra 2004: 501–3). For example, 1 Enoch, a frequently used pseudepigrapha, references the Enoch of Genesis and appears in the apocalyptic New Testament book of Jude (Bandstra 2004: 504–5) as a text worthy of citation. Others are cited in the NT pseudepigrapha.

Including those books in this work both acknowledges the denominational diversity of Africana Christians and allows the texts to be claimed by all readers for the insights they offer and the questions they may pose. Like a number of biblical books, these writings by and to diasporic Jews attempted to strengthen their Jewish faith while they were away from the land of Israel and the temple they called home. Their historical context mirrors the experience of contemporary Africana peoples, many of whom live outside of Africa as a result of historical circumstances. The stories told by the original authors will be retold for a new Diaspora audience, utilizing Africana traditions, ranging from folklore to spirituals, as well as history

and theology. Whether the reader is familiar with these texts or is being introduced to them through this work, the deuterocanonical, or second canon, books offer first-order comfort and challenge for peoples of Africana descent.

References

Bandstra, Barry L. 2004. *Reading the Old Testament: An Introduction to the Hebrew Bible*. 3rd ed. Belmont, Calif.: Thomson/Wadsworth.

Dentan, Robert C. 1964. *The Apocrypha: Bridge of the Testament*. New York: Seabury.

Douglass, J. D., ed. 1974. *The New International Dictionary of the Christian Church*. Grand Rapids, Mich.: Zondervan.

Harris, Stephen L., and Robert L. Platzner. 2003. *The Old Testament: An Introduction to the Hebrew Bible*. New York: McGraw-Hill.

Kennedy, Lionel, and Thomas Parker. 1822. *The Trial Record of Denmark Vessey*. Introduction by John Oliver Killens. Reprinted as *An Official Report of the Trial of Sundry Negroes*. Boston: Beacon, 1970.

Washington, Margaret. 2000. "The Meaning of Scripture in Gullah Concepts of Liberation and Group Identity." In *African Americans and The Bible: Sacred Texts and Social Texture*, ed. Vincent L. Wimbush, 321–41. New York: Continuum.

1–2 ESDRAS

C. L. Nash

AFRICAN AMERICAN WOMEN, TRUTH AND STRENGTH

People of African descent have long been told that slavery, mercifully, introduced Africans (and, later, African Americans) to Christianity. However, this assertion is not completely true. Proof of this is found in 1 and 2 Esdras, two apocryphal books that have roots connecting them directly to two African countries—Ethiopia and Egypt. Much of the content in the two books is repeated in Ezra, Nehemiah, and 2 Chronicles. The book of 1 Esdras, estimated to be written in the first century, is canonical for Coptic Christians. (The word *Coptic* describes the Afro-Asiatic language of the Copts. Coptic Orthodox Christianity is said to have been established by the Apostle Mark in Egypt during the first century.) The book of 2 Esdras, developed between the second and third centuries c.e., was written in Greek, presumably by the Christian Church. In addition, 2 Esdras is absent from the Western Christian canon but is canonical for Ethiopian Christians. Many Western Christians will recall the New Testament story of the Ethiopian eunuch who was baptized by the Apostle Philip (Acts 8:27). The Ethiopian Church still credits its beginnings to the evangelism of Philip. Equally important is the significance of 1 and 2 Esdras as books of vision and insight.

While those in the African Diaspora, in general, may be helped by 1 and 2 Esdras, African American women in particular may be helped by chapter 4 of 1 Esdras. Of interest is the story in Chapter 4 that depicts the king's three bodyguards competing to prove the meaning of true strength. It is the third bodyguard, Zerubbabel, who wins the contest by combining knowledge of womanhood and truth to highlight strength. He speaks with high regard, making such statements as woman "gives birth to kings and causes men to leave their families behind for her" (4:26-27). Yet, Zerubbabel portends two images of women—the concubine or mistress, and the dutiful wife. Attaching images or even labels to women is nothing new. For example, since most Black women during antebellum America were enslaved, many in society expected them to play the role of plantation "mistress." This usually occurred through either coercion or force. Historically, Black women were rarely perceived as the "dutiful wife," as there were no legal systems to protect this social designation for the enslaved. Among other things, marriage was seen as a sign of civilization and social stability. In this way, Zerubbabel helps by highlighting the strength and social contributions of wives and mothers.

Contemporary literary critics suggest that the fictional writings of Black women in nineteenth-century America demonstrate a dialectic tension between marriage and freedom. This could be attributed to many factors. For example, enslaved Black women were rarely afforded protection or status through marriage. While Zerubbabel's admiration of women is undoubtedly high, his two images of womanhood are rather narrow. Contemporary Black women might ask, "Are we only mothers or mistresses?" Perhaps this serves as a reminder that even the best intention to define women can be insufficient: no one can define us better than we can.

References

Ackroyd, P. R., et al. *The Cambridge Bible Commentary New English Bible: 1 & 2 Books of Esdras*. Cambridge: Cambridge University Press, 1979.

Braxton, JoAnne M. *Black Women Writing Autobiography*. Philadelphia: Temple University Press, 1989.

"Coptic." *The Free Dictionary* Web site. http://www.thefreedictionary.com/Coptic (accessed February 10, 2009).

Duff, Archibald. *The First and Second Books of Esdras*. 1903; reprint, Whitefish, Mont.: Kessinger, 2004.

"Early Jewish Writings: 2 Esdras." http://www.earlyjewishwritings.com/2esdras.html (accessed February 10, 2009).

Tate, Claudia. "Allegories of Black Female Desire; or, Rereading Nineteenth-century Sentimental Narratives of Black Female Authority." In *Changing Our Own Words*, ed. Cheryl A. Wall. New Brunswick, N.J.: Rutgers University Press, 1989.

TOBIT

Stacy Davis

PART OF THE Roman Catholic First Testament, Tobit tells the story of its title character, a long-suffering but righteous Israelite who receives the angel Raphael's assistance in order to recover from blindness, retrieve treasure, and obtain a wife for his son Tobias. Chapters 3–8 narrate the marriage of Sarah and Tobias and thus explain Raphael's designation as the patron saint of singles. The angel's intervention lends the folktale some "romance," but such patriarchal romance is not life-affirming for African American women.

Having lost seven husbands on seven successive wedding nights to an envious demon, a humiliated and still-virgin Sarah prays for death. Instead, God sends Raphael to arrange the nuptials between Sarah and her nearest male relative, Tobias, "for Tobias was entitled to have her before all others who had desired to marry her" (3:17 NRSV). Pekka

Pitkanen notes: "Family life in Israel has in one way or another served as a model of family life for those later generations who stand in the Judeo-Christian tradition" (2006: 104). Tobit's idealized view is no exception (Soll 1998: 166). Sarah belongs to Tobias, "for she was set apart for [him] before the world was made" (6:18 NRSV); her father acknowledges this reality, Raphael captures the demon, and all live as they should in fairy tales, happily ever after.

From a womanist perspective, the story is problematic. As Cheryl Townsend Gilkes writes: "African American women, by choice and by circumstance, violate nearly every dimension of American gender norms" (2001: 188). Such norms "have been shaped by the ideology of a White patriarchal, racist culture" (Douglas 1997:241), in which African American women supposedly lacked the moral rectitude of European women (Douglas 1997: 238–39). Since emancipation, some African American women have attempted to show their moral worth through the politics of respectability, or living by the same moral standards as European women; the consequences, however, have included an internalization of patriarchy and middle-class values that have marginalized working-class and lesbian women, to name only two groups (see Gaines 1996 and Collins 2004).

The combination of Christianity and patriarchy is even worse. Marriage is established as the ideal for women, as opposed to sexual relationships without legal or ecclesiastical sanction or the single life; in a sermon on Proverbs 31, Juanita Bynum argues that "you ain't a real woman until you've birthed out a man" through faithfully supporting a husband and "always [keeping] him on top" (Bynum 2003). Defining true womanhood through a woman's attachment to a man is problematic, regardless of whether an ancient text or a contemporary African American woman makes the claim. Toinette Eugene insists: "Womanist movements or meetings do not resurrect the myths or the archetypes that exemplify and exercise pure and unbridled power and control over the lives of others" (1997: 133). Womanist communities should challenge patriarchy wherever it appears, including biblically sanctioned patriarchy. Slavery is in the Bible as well, but no one calls for a return to the plantation.

References

Bynum, Juanita. 2003. "Let's Keep It Real and Get It Right." CD included in Thomas Weeks, *Teach Me How to Love You: Communication and Intimacy in Relationships: The Beginnings* . . . Denver: Legacy.

Collins, Patricia Hill. 2004. *Black Sexual Politics: African Americans, Gender, and the New Racism*. New York: Routledge.

Davis, Angela Y. 1998. *Blues Legacies and Black Feminism: Gertrude "Ma" Rainey, Bessie Smith, and Billie Holiday*. New York: Pantheon.

Douglas, Kelly Brown. 1997. "Daring to Speak: Womanist Theology and Black Sexuality." In *Embracing the Spirit: Womanist Perspectives on Hope, Salvation, and Transformation*, ed. Emilie M. Townes, 234–46. Maryknoll, N.Y.: Orbis.

Eugene, Toinette M. 1997. "The Shaman Says . . . Womanist Reflection on Pastoral Care of African American Men." In *The Care of Men*, ed. Christie Cozad Neuger and James Newton Poling, 122–37. Nashville: Abingdon.

Gaines, Kevin K. 1996. *Uplifting the Race: Black Leadership, Politics, and Culture in the Twentieth Century*. Chapel Hill: University of North Carolina Press.

Gilkes, Cheryl Townsend. 2001. *"If It Wasn't for the Women . . .": Black Women's Experience and Womanist Culture in Church and Community*. Maryknoll, N.Y.: Orbis.

Jones, Charisse, and Kumea Shorter-Gooden. 2004. *Shifting: The Double Lives of Black Women in America*. New York: Perennial.

Morrison, Toni. 1991. *Beloved*. New York: Signet.

Pitkanen, Pekka. 2006. "Family Life and Ethnicity in Early Israel and in Tobit." In *Studies in the Book of Tobit: A Multidisciplinary Approach*, ed. Mark Bredin, 104–17. London: T. & T. Clark.

Soll, Will. 1998. "The Family as Scriptural and Social Construct in Tobit." In *The Function of Scripture in Early Jewish and Christian Tradition*, eds. Craig A. Evans and James A. Sanders, 166–75. Sheffield, England: Sheffield Academic Press.

Walker, Alice. 1983. *In Search of Our Mothers' Gardens: Womanist Prose*. New York: Harcourt Brace Jovanovich.

Weeks, Thomas. 2003. *Teach Me How to Love You: Communication and Intimacy in Relationships: The Beginnings* . . . Denver: Legacy.

JUDITH

Naomi Franklin

IN EVERY AGE there arises a deliverer who delivers his or her people from the hands of an oppressor. The Israelites had Moses and, later, Judith. Africana history has Harriet Tubman, Nat Turner, Denmark Vesey, and Toussaint L'Overture, to name a few. Alongside the act of deliverance, we find the use of violence. Judith is such a story.

Judith's story presents us with a complex description. She exists and acts in what might be deemed polar opposites. On the one hand, she is very pious. She fasts and prays daily, living on a rooftop "close to God." On the other hand, she is aware of the events of her community and rises to act as the Moses of her time when danger arises. She utilizes the most extreme form of violence to rid her people of the enemy. She beheads their leader. She uses manipulation, deceit, and seduc-

tion to achieve her goals. Through prayer, she gains God's acquiescence to her actions.

Judith as deliverer is successful. However, her use of the very extreme act of violence is disconcerting. God's acquiescence can also be troubling. There are those in the community of faith who find the presence of violence in the biblical text troubling. On the other hand, as Kirk-Duggan notes, there are those who would see justification in the use of violence to protect those who are in danger (2006: ix). Theologians speak of a just war, and the story of Judith definitely fits.

There is much within the story to which Africana persons can relate. Within the society in which she lives, Judith is profoundly "other" by virtue of her lifestyle (Levine 1995: 215). She is beautiful, wealthy, and yet an ascetic. For Africana people, the notion of being "other" is readily understood. Judith does not allow her beauty to be seen. She uses it only temporarily to seduce the enemy. Likewise, for so long, the beauty of Africana people has not been seen. Judith lives apart from her community yet is brought back into it by the necessity of the events that are taking place and temporarily is made a part of it. Likewise, Africana people often find themselves living the existential duality of being apart from the overall community and yet being a part of it when it is deemed useful, especially in times of war when they are needed for military duty.

While the act of beheading her enemy is in itself a difficult thing to identify with, it can be seen as a metaphor. The head is the site of the brain, the power of thought and action. Beheading can thus be seen as disempowering the power source of oppression and, in so doing, gaining agency. It is the attainment of freedom, which is a movement toward the sacred (Kirk-Duggan 2003: 124). The text of Judith bequeaths to the community of faith the gift of agency through disengaging from the cycle of oppression.

References

Bal, Mieke. 1995. "Head Hunting: 'Judith' on the Cutting Edge of Knowledge." In *A Feminist Companion to Esther, Judith and Susanna*, ed. Athalya Brenner. Sheffield, Eng.: Sheffield Academic.

Cannon, Katie G. 1988. *Black Womanist Ethics*. Atlanta: Scholars.

———. 2003. *Katie's Canon: Womanism and the Soul of the Black Community*. New York: Continuum.

Dube, Musa. 2002. "Rereading the Bible: Biblical Hermeneutics and Social Justice." In *African Theology Today*, ed. Emmanuel Katongole. Scranton, Pa.: University of Scranton Press.

Fry Brown, Teresa L. 2000. *God Don't Like Ugly*. Nashville: Abingdon.

Gottwald, Norman K. 2003. "African American Biblical Hermeneutics: Major Themes and Wider Implications." In *Yet with A Steady Beat: Contemporary U.S. Afrocentric Biblical Interpretation*, ed. Randall C. Bailey. Semeia Studies, no. 42. Atlanta: Society of Biblical Literature.

Kirk-Duggan, Cheryl A. 2003. "Let My People Go! Threads of Exodus in African American Narratives." In *Yet with A Steady Beat: Contemporary U.S. Afrocentric Biblical Interpretation*, ed. Randall C. Bailey. Semeia Studies, no. 42. Atlanta: Society of Biblical Literature.

———. 2006. *Violence and Theology*. Nashville: Abingdon.

Levine, Amy-Jill. 1995. "Sacrifice and Salvation: Otherness and Domestication in the Book of Judith." In *A Feminist Companion to Esther, Judith and Susanna*, ed. Athalya Brenner. Sheffield, Eng.: Sheffield Academic.

Pippin, Tina. 2003. "On the Blurring of Boundaries." In *Yet with A Steady Beat: Contemporary U.S. Afrocentric Biblical Interpretation*, ed. Randall C. Bailey. Semeia Studies, no. 42. Atlanta: Society of Biblical Literature.

Stocker, Margarita. 1998. *Judith: Sexual Warrior, Women and Power in Western Culture*. New Haven: Yale University Press.

Tragle, Henry Irving. 1971. *The Southampton Slave Revolt of 1831* [A Compilation of Source Material]. Amherst: University of Massachusetts Press.

Williams, Demetrius K. 2003. "The Bible and Models of Liberation in the African American Experience." In *Yet with A Steady Beat: Contemporary U.S. Afrocentric Biblical Interpretation*, ed. Randall C. Bailey. Semeia Studies, no. 42. Atlanta: Society of Biblical Literature.

The GREEK ADDITIONS *to* ESTHER

Randall C. Bailey

THE HEBREW TEXT of the book of Esther was problematic in its inclusion in the canon, since there was no reference to God in the text. The Greek text, however, contains several references to God, such as in 2:19, where Esther is said to fear God and keep the laws, and in 6:1, where God is the one who keeps the king awake, which leads to the honoring of Mordecai. It appears from this that disagreement arose in the ancient community as to whether the book should show God as an active agent in the struggle (Gottwald 1985).

Although the Hebrew text of Esther contains overt references to sexuality and uses several innuendos suggesting sexual enticement and seduction (Duran 2003; Bailey 2009), these elements are either deleted or rephrased in the Greek text. Generally, the Black religious traditions have ignored these elements found in the Hebrew text, with the exception of such clergy as the late Vernon Johns, the predecessor of Martin Luther King Jr. as pastor of Dexter Baptist Church, who depicted Esther's going to see the king in chapter 5 as a seduction scene. In contrast to this interpretation, Juanita Bynum's song "One Night with the King" speaks of an innocent romantic meeting between the two of them. This reading is more in line with the Greek text's presentation, where the king refers to Esther affectionately as "my wife" (7:8).

Besides these editorial changes to wording of the Hebrew text by the translators of the Greek text, certain manuscripts of the Greek text contain additional passages, such as the prayers and dreams of Mordecai and the prayer of Esther, which seem to change the tone of the whole work. In these prayers are references to the nature of God as "all knowing" as well as appeals to the Exodus event and the covenant with Abraham. These prayers tend to follow the genre of individual laments in the Psalms. Most interesting are the professions of innocence by Mordecai that he would have kissed the soles of Haman's feet (C: 13:13) and that Esther was not pleased with being married to the king (C: 14:15) and the king's desires for peace in the kingdom (B: 13:2).

The nationalistic tone of these prayers asking God to intervene on behalf of the nation is of the same tenor as David Walker's *Appeal to the Coloured Citizens of the World*, which states:

> Though our cruel oppressors, and murderers, may (if possible) treat us more cruel, as Pharaoh did the Children of Israel, yet the God of the Ethiopians, has been pleased to hear our moans in consequence of oppression, and the day of our redemption from abject wretchedness draweth near. . . . (Walker 1819: xiv)

In this way, the Greek text has more appeal to the U.S. Black religious tradition than the Hebrew text. While usually using the Protestant canon text of Esther, which follows the Hebrew text, the preaching of the book and the oral tradition associated with it are more in line with the wording and changes found in the Greek text, where Esther is chaste, Mordecai is upstanding, the king is sympathetic, and only Haman is the "bad boy."

References

Bailey, Randall C. 2009. "That's Why They Didn't Call the Book Hadassah: The Interse(ct)/(x)ionality of Race/Ethnicity, Gender, Class, and Sexuality in the Book of Esther." In *They Were All Together in One Place: Toward Minority Biblical Criticism*, ed. R. C. Bailey, T. B. Liew, and F. F. Segovia, 227–50. Semeia Studies, 57. Atlanta: Society of Biblical Literature.

Bynum, Juanita. 2006. "One Night with the King." Lyrics available at http://www.onlylyrics.com/hits.php?grid=11&id=1002515 (accessed September 19, 2008).

Duran, Nicole. 2003. "Who Wants to Marry a Persian King? Gender, Games, and Wars in the Book of Esther." In *Pregnant Passion: Gender, Sex, and Violence in the Bible*, ed. C. A. Kirk-Duggan, 7–84. Semeia Studies. Atlanta: Society of Biblical Literature.

Gottwald, Norman K. 1985. *The Hebrew Bible: A Socio-Literary Introduction*. Philadelphia: Fortress Press.

Walker, David. 1819. *David Walker's Appeal*, ed. C. M. Wiltse. Reprint, New York: Hill and Wang, 1965.

WISDOM *of* SOLOMON

Nathaniel Samuel Murrell

WHY NOT WISDOM?

Among people for whom the Bible is an essential
religious document, relatively few pay attention to
the second canon. Among the few who do, little is
known about how many read Wisdom, a book that
exists under different names and in many versions
(Vetus Latina, Syriac Peshitta, the Arabic Bible,
and the English Bible). A few early Christian writers, some of them from North Africa, referenced
the book occasionally. Among these are Irenaeus
(circa 140–206 C.E.), Clement of Alexandria,
Egypt (circa 175–232 C.E.), Origen (circa 185–257
C.E.), Jerome (circa 345–420 C.E.), and Augustine
of Hippo (354–430 C.E.). They saw in Wisdom a
great spiritual resource but were uncertain of its
canonical veracity; probably because it appeared
fairly late in both Greek and Hebrew.

There is little in Wisdom, however, to justify
its absence from the canonical books; its teachings
show no departure from biblical wisdom traditions
and contain none of the fanciful myths of other
books in the second canon. Of course, the author
of Wisdom is uncertain. Scholars who find in its
ideas, themes, and concerns similarities to the writings of Philo (circa 20 B.C.E. to 50 C.E.) speculate
on a common authorship. Wisdom's knowledge of
Israel's history and Greek and Stoic philosophical
ideas, however, suggest the author may have been
an educated, Greek-speaking Jew living in Alexandria, Egypt, between 300 B.C.E. and 50 C.E. (Morgan 1988: 1082; Reese 1988: 860).

WISDOM AND AFRICANA TRADITIONS?

Like early North African Christians, Africana peoples can rediscover Wisdom as a spiritual and theological resource since its most important religious themes resonate with the African experience: the wisdom tradition and the fourfold paradigm of righteousness, justice, resistance, and liberation. In Afro-Caribbean wisdom tradition, Orunmila, the African spirit in Santeria, is master of all wisdom and mysteries to whom Olodumare (God) has entrusted the world and a repository of the knowledge of all destiny. Orunmila manifested and assisted Olodumare in creation. This personified wisdom, which exists also in Elegba/Eshu, the trickster deity of wisdom, opportunity, and misfortune in Vodou, represents Olorun's (God) might, teaches his secret wisdom to the faithful, and mediates between heaven and earth as well as good and evil. Eshu resolves conflicts through Ifa divination bestowed by Olodumare, the true source of all wisdom.

Biblical wisdom and African wisdom have the same theology and objectives. God, the source of all wisdom and wise ruler of the universe, guides the morally upright and the just but also controls the final destiny of all (3:1–5:23). Wisdom is personified with great attributes and magnificent divine female beauty. She is sought after by the prudent and embraced as a guide to life; whoever possesses her is assured of immortality and is drawn closer to God (6:17-20). Through wisdom comes knowledge, good instruction, wealth, and mediation between God and humankind (9:1-18). Biblical wisdom is the source of wise counsel (8:8-9; 9:9, 11), was at the creation with God, protects from trouble righteous ones who serve *sophia* (10:6, 9-10), and rewards those who seek after her but punishes those who do not (11:15-26). Wisdom expresses itself as a resourceful woman in African society. A popular Ghanian proverb says, "The wisdom of an old woman is worth a thousand young men," so "A woman must not be killed. She is bought with elephant's tusk" (Mbiti 1991: 63–65). The woman is praised for being as virtuous and wise and as invaluable to society as *sophia* is in biblical wisdom. After hearing a case in court, an Ashanti tribunal says it "consulted the wise old woman"; it embraced a symbol of wisdom as final authority in judicial deliberations (Tufuo and Donkor 1989: 59–60).

WISDOM AND LIBERATION

The author of Wisdom makes Hebrew wisdom a path to liberation and the religious life by showing a moral connection between righteousness, justice, wisdom, and liberation through the Hebrew exodus. In this regard, the third section of Wisdom 11–19, as a theological survey of God's direction of the course of Israel's history, reproduces exodus narratives of the ancient Israelites' liberation stories. In all of those, wisdom is shown as a deliverer in present trials and a guide for the people's future (Morgan 1988: 1084). Little evidence exists that Africans in American captivity read Wisdom's version of the exodus event—perhaps because, as Margaret Washington feels, these "esoteric, profound, lyrical guides for living" were "withdrawn from common use when teaching enslaved people, just as were certain portions of the Old Testament" (2000: 326). Our forebears could have appropriated the exodus event through Wisdom, as a source and tool of liberation from slavery and oppression, as well as they did from the canonical text. Now, "as daughters of Sophia we prophesy, as sons of Sophia we dream [new] dreams, and in our vision we call for all people to share in the dance of liberation" ("Voices of Sophia").

References

Cheon, Samuel. 1997. *The Exodus Story in the Wisdom of Solomon: A Study in Biblical Interpretation*. Journal for the Study of the Old Testament: Supplement Series 23. Sheffield, Eng.: Sheffield Academic.

Kolarcik, Michael. 2005. "The Book of Wisdom." In *The New Interpreter's Bible, Old Testament Survey*, 494–502. Nashville: Abingdon.

Mbiti, John S. 1991. "Flowers in the Garden: The Role of Women in African Religion." In *African Traditional Religions in Contemporary Society*, ed. Jacob K. Olupona, 59–71. St. Paul, Minn.: Paragon.

Morgan. G. W. 1988. "Wisdom of Solomon." In *International Standard Bible Encyclopedia*, vol 4 (Q–Z), ed. G. W. Bromiley, 1082–84. Grand Rapids, Mich.: Eerdmans.

Reese, James M. 1988. "Wisdom of Solomon." In *HarperCollins Bible Commentary*, ed. James L. Mays, 749–63. San Francisco: HarperSanFrancisco.

Tufuo, J. W., and C. E. Donkor. 1989. *Ashantis of Ghana, People with a Soul*. McCarthy Hill, Accra, Ghana: Anowuo Educational Publication.

Washington, Margaret. 2000. "The Meaning of Scripture in Gullah Concepts of Liberation and Group Identity." In *African Americans and the Bible: Sacred Texts and Social Texture*, ed. Vincent L. Wimbush, 321–41. New York: Continuum.

BARUCH

Robert Wafawanaka

OVERVIEW

The book of Baruch, an apocryphal work of five chapters, is traditionally attributed to Baruch the son of Neriah, Jeremiah's secretary (Jeremiah 32; 36; 43; 45). However, commentators are not agreed about the exact authorship of this book. The mixed genres of prose and poetry, the shift in language and style, as well as the varied content of the book also contribute to the dispute in authorship. The date of the writing of this book is also disputed among scholars. In fact dates range from Babylonian times in the sixth century B.C.E. to Roman times in the first century C.E. While Baruch exists in Greek, there are also translations in other languages such as Latin, Syriac, Coptic, Ethiopic, Armenian, and Arabic. Three other books of Baruch can also be found in the pseudepigrapha (2, 3, and 4 Baruch).

THEMES AND DIVISIONS

The book of Baruch deals with the themes of sin, punishment, confession, and consolation. Consequently, it also engages the perennial question of theodicy. Borrowing much from the Hebrew Bible, especially Deuteronomistic theology, the writer argues that Israel's sin was the cause of its exile to Babylon. It is admission and confession of this sin that the nation does in order to be renewed.

In the first division of the book, the historical narrative introduction (1:1-14), Baruch reads his book to the exiled nation of Israel to demonstrate the nature of its sin leading to Babylonian exile. Due to this guilt, he calls upon the nation to pray and confess its sins in order to mitigate divine anger.

The second division of Baruch (1:15—3:8) contains the nation's prayer of confession and repentance. This section, heavy with Deuteronomistic theology of sin and punishment, absolves God from Israel's catastrophe. Such absolution of God and placement of responsibility on human agency is in line with Jones' concept of "humanocentric theism" (Jones 1973:178-202). Israel acknowledges its sin as the reason for its exile and punishment. This theological explanation is also intelligible from the African philosophy of causality. When catastrophic events happen, the primary question often asked is not "how" but "why" (Mbiti 1990:199-210; 1991:165-173). The writer's claim of national sin and responsibility appeals to African experience and makes this book relevant to the African context. Due to the belief that a wrong has been committed, Africans usually perform propitiatory rituals and ceremonies to rectify any offenses to the spirits or the Supreme Being (Mbiti 1991:78).

The idea of captivity and exilic existence is also pertinent to Africans. The experience of African slavery through no fault of their own is however contrary to Israel's exile as a result of self-confessed sin and disobedience. A new dimension is added by those Africans who experienced either self-imposed exile or left their homelands in search of better fortunes. Whatever way Africans found themselves in the Diaspora, like the ancient Israelites, they too can relate to the experience of colonial oppression, cultural dislocation, and identity crisis. In spite of Israel's admission of Torah disobedience as the major cause of its exile, the nation's demise may also be understood as the historical reality of its existence in an area dominated by ancient superpowers.

A definite shift in language and style is evident in the third section (3:9—4:4). Here the writer uses poetry to communicate God's providential gift of wisdom to Israel. This wisdom poem buttresses the theme of national suffering. Israel is in exile because it has forsaken God, who is equated with wisdom.

The final section (4:5—5:9) is a poetic composition with a message of consolation, comfort, encouragement, and restoration for a nation that has suffered the vicissitudes of exile. In an inclusio that forms a reversal of fortunes with the opening sections of the book, Israel will be consoled and restored back to Jerusalem while the nation of Babylon is threatened with punishment and destruction.

CONCLUSION

The book of Baruch describes the changing fortunes of Israel. Sin leads to national demise but repentance ushers in the hope of renewal and restoration. The question of theodicy is transformed into the problem of human culpability. Yet this neat formula is problematic as we try to appropriate this scripture in our modern and Christian context. On the one hand we see a God who punishes and restores one nation. Yet on the other hand we remain with the same God who threatens to punish but not restore another people. If God is the God of all humanity, the book of Baruch cautions us not to view ourselves as the sole recipients of divine favor. All of God's people should be equal recipients of divine punishment and salvation.

References

Jones, William R. 1973. *Is God a White Racist? A Preamble to Black Theology.* Garden City, NY: Anchor / Doubleday.

Kobia, Samuel. 2003. *The Courage to Hope: The Roots for a New Vision and the Calling of the Church in Africa.* Geneva: World Council of Churches.

Lartey, Emmanuel, Daisy Nwachuku, and Kasonga Wa Kasonga, eds. 1994. *The Church and Healing: Echoes from Africa.* African Pastoral Studies Vol. 2. Frankfurt am Main: Peter Lang.

Mbiti, John S. 1990. *African Religions and Philosophy.* 2nd edition. London: Heineman.

_____. 1991. *Introduction to African Religion.* 2nd edition, revised and enlarged. Oxford: Heinemann.

Moore, Carey A. 1977. *Daniel, Esther, and Jeremiah: The Additions.* AB 44. Garden City, N.Y.: Doubleday.

Saldarini, Anthony J. 2001. "The Book of Baruch: Introduction, Commentary, and Reflections." In *The New Interpreter's Bible.* Vol. 6., ed. Leander E. Keck. 927–82. Nashville: Abingdon.

Stone, Michael E. 1984. *Jewish Writings of the Second Temple Period: Apocrypha, Pseudepigrapha, Qumran Sectarian Writings, Philo, Josephus.* Philadelphia: Fortress Press.

Whitehouse, O. C. 1913. "1 Baruch." In *The Apocrypha and Pseudepigrapha of the Old Testament.* Vol. 1., ed. R. H. Charles. Oxford: Clarendon.

World Council of Churches. 2004. *For A New Africa with Hope and Dignity.* Geneva: WCC.

LETTER *of* JEREMIAH

Vivian L. Johnson

THE LETTER OF JEREMIAH dates to sometime during the sixth to second centuries B.C.E. This document, whose primary text exists in Greek, could, as survival literature, address any number of communities whose lives were dictated by empires during these centuries. As the prophet Jeremiah comforts his community with a definitive duration of their punishment in exile (Jer. 29:10), so too does the author of the Letter of Jeremiah; the exiles must serve a maximum sentence of seven generations for their transgressions against God (v. 2) before restoration. So addressed to a community in Babylonian captivity and exile, the Letter conveys the import of exclusive worship to God.

Although couched as a letter in the mode of Jer. 29:1-23, from which it derives its authority, the document reads like a sermon on the futility of worshiping Babylonian gods. The author explicates the absurdity of reverence paid to feckless idols, who are unworthy of worship because humans create and care for them (vv. 8-9, 13, 18, 24, 45), parasites cause them to decay (vv. 12, 20, 72), and they promote immorality among the priests who maintain them (vv. 10-11). The author's vituperative stance against Babylonian idolatry intends to keep his audience focused on the one true God (v. 6), who needs no physical representation (Exod. 20:3-5; Deut. 5:7-9). This God alone has the power to command the celestial realm (vv. 60-63), save the helpless (vv. 36-38, 54), and deliver the exiles (vv. 2-3). Unapologetically hailing his deity as supreme, the writer does not permit any nuanced understandings of the relationship between image and deity. In our modern world, which tends to value religious diversity, his highly polemical stance may indeed disturb us. His marked criticism, however, emanates from a desire for a colonized people to survive. He confronts the threat of assimilating into an imperial context with invectives aimed to counter the allure of Babylonian religion.

In a spirit and tone similar to the Letter of Jeremiah, the religious leaders of my Pentecostal church thwarted the attraction of other religions by presenting them as idolatrous. Buddhism and Hinduism, with their rich heritage of iconic imagery, were condemned as religions of idolatry. Among Christian traditions, Catholicism, unfortunately, bore the brunt of most attacks launched by my clergy. They assailed Catholicism because of its vivid representations of God, elaborate liturgies, and belief in saints. The leaders of my congregation equated many Catholic rituals with idolatry, or they considered Catholic rituals as superfluous distractions from proper divine devotion. Worship of God, they taught, did not require statues, incense, or high liturgy. Rather, true reverence for God required a clear heart and releasing one's life to God's perpetual care.

The clergy of my church concerned themselves with not only the threat of our conversion to other religions but also the threat of our assimilation into contemporary culture. Activities associated with American popular culture—such as wearing contemporary clothing, listening to popular music, dancing, and consumerism—were all deemed as idolatrous. The admiration of and concentration on the accoutrements of modern culture, in their view, inhibited complete worship of God.

Keeping focused on God, they instilled and required constant attention. Reading scripture daily and singing spirituals—such as "Where He Leads Me I Will Follow," "Power, Power Lord," "Come by Here My Lord," "We're Down Here Lord Waiting on You," and "Sweet Hour of Prayer"—all reinforced the necessity of exalting God as the sole source for positive change in our lives. The clergy of my upbringing, like the author of the Letter of Jeremiah, saw the hope of the survival of our community in absolute devotion to the one true God.

References

Doering, Lutz. 2005. "Jeremiah and the 'Diaspora Letters' in Ancient Judaism: Epistolary Communication with the Golah as Medium for Dealing with the Present." In *Reading the Present in the Qumran Library: The Perception of the Contemporary by Means of Scriptural Interpretations*, ed. Kristin De Troyer and Armin Lange, 43–72. Symposium Series. Atlanta: Society of Biblical Literature.

Harrington, Daniel. 1999. *Invitation to the Apocrypha*. Grand Rapids, Mich.: Eerdmans.

Moore, Carey A. 1977. *Daniel, Esther and Jeremiah: The Additions*. Anchor Bible. Garden City, N.Y.: Doubleday.

Weems, Renita. 2004. "Jeremiah." In *The Global Bible Commentary* ed. Daniel Patte, J. Severino Croatto, et al., 212–25. Nashville: Abingdon.

SUSANNA

Stacy Davis

PART OF THE Roman Catholic canon, Susanna is one of the additions to the book of Daniel, possibly written before the end of the second century B.C.E. This addition, like the others, adds detail to Daniel's story and, in this case, gives Daniel "a great reputation among the people" (Susanna 64). Daniel saves Susanna from execution for the false charge of adultery, leveled against her by lecherous judges with whom she refuses to be intimate. "A very beautiful woman" (Susanna 2), Susanna is also God-fearing and refuses to dishonor her marriage (Susanna 20–23). On first reading, it is easy to dismiss Susanna as a passive figure. The text gives descriptions of her beauty, grace, and righteousness, but Susanna herself hardly speaks. From a womanist perspective, however, Susanna is a model for oppressed Africana women, who are often forced to be silent but who know when a timely word can lead to their redemption.

The scholar bell hooks argues that enslaved black women could count on no one, particularly not on whites, for protection from sexual abuse; this lack of support continued after emancipation (hooks 1981: 36, 58). She concludes that "neither passive acceptance nor stoic endurance lead to change. Change occurs only when there is action, movement, revolution" (hooks 1981: 193). When the male assembly sentences Susanna to death for adultery, based on the false witness of her would-be rapists, the silent Susanna finally speaks, proclaiming to God her innocence (Susanna 42–43). "The Lord heard her cry" (Susanna 44) and sent Daniel to her rescue. Although it makes sense for a Hellenistic Jewish text, steeped in the prevailing patri-

312

archy of the day, to use a man as a redeemer figure, if Africana women had written the story, a woman would have been another woman's savior.

Womanist theologian Diana Hayes argues that Africana women's literature can serve "as a source for discovering, uncovering and recovering the spiritual values and voices of Black women" (1995: 33). In *Kindred*, Dana consciously chooses to save herself, being alternately passive or proactive as the situation warrants (Butler 1988: 50–51, 93, 101, 164, 176, 200–201, 260). When, in *The Color Purple*, Celie finally accepts her sister-in-law's and then her sister's advice to "fight them for yourself" (Walker 1982: 22, 131), she begins to envision the possibility of freedom, first Sofia's (96) and then her own (207, 213). *Beloved* uses women saviors throughout, from a poor Caucasian woman who delivers Sethe's youngest child (Morrison 1987: 101–3) to Baby Suggs's preaching (107–8) to Sethe's own escape from slavery (198, 243) to Denver's decision to rescue herself and Sethe (298–99, 309).

Hayes concludes that the biblical character Hagar is a worthy model for Africana women; Hagar "talked directly to God" (1995: 56).

Susanna, too, is a worthy model. Unlike Hagar, she did not speak with angels, but like Hagar in Genesis, Susanna's words move God to act on her behalf. Susanna has a womanist's faith, "a blinding faith that reveals a God who batters down the gates of prisons where the righteous are held captive and sets them free, but only with their own participation in bringing about that freedom" (Hayes 1995: 53).

References

Butler, Octavia E. 1988. *Kindred*. Boston: Beacon.

Hayes, Diana. 1995. *Hagar's Daughters: Womanist Ways of Being in the World*. New York: Paulist.

hooks, bell. 1981. *Ain't I a Woman: Black Women and Feminism*. Boston: South End.

Jones, Edward P. 2006. *All Aunt Hagar's Children*. New York: Amistad.

Martin, Valerie. 2003. *Property*. New York: Doubleday.

Morrison, Toni. 1987. *Beloved*. New York: Signet.

Walker, Alice. 1982. *The Color Purple*. New York: Pocket.

BEL *and the* DRAGON

Adam Oliver Stokes

BEL AND THE DRAGON, written in the second century B.C.E., is a Greek addition to the Book of Daniel. In its present form, the text represents the merger of two narratives. In the first story, Daniel refutes King Cyrus's claim that the idol Bel is a "living God" (*zōn theos,* Bel 6) by revealing a secret entrance whereby the priests of Bel enter and eat the food that is offered to the idol. In the second story, Daniel kills a giant serpent (Greek: *drakōn*) by tricking the serpent into drinking a special concoction. Daniel's actions incur the wrath of the Babylonians, who forcefully compel the king to throw Daniel in the lion's den. Yet even here God is with him and sends the prophet Habakkuk to rescue Daniel. The king sees such deliverance as proof that the God of the Jews is the true God.

Bel and the Dragon finds many parallels with the "trickster" narratives in black American folklore where the hero uses his or her wisdom to defeat a more powerful enemy. In the "Uncle Remus" stories, Brer Rabbit prevents himself from becoming Brer Lion's meal by leading the lion to a well. When Brer Lion looks down the well, he sees another lion (his own reflection on the water) and, thinking that he has found a larger meal, jumps in and drowns himself. Another example of such a trickster tale is found in the story "John Outwits Mr. Berkeley."[1] John, a figure who appears in various black folktales, repeatedly outmaneuvers his wealthier and stronger opponent, Mr. Berkeley.

On a deeper level, the theme emphasized in Bel and the Dragon of standing up for truth in the face of persecution resonates strongly with the experience of blacks in America. Just as the prophet Daniel uncompromisingly proclaimed the truth of one God, so the prophets and prophetesses of black history have uncompromisingly proclaimed the truth of the equality of all races in the eyes of the one God. Related to this is the role of the Gentile king in affirming the truth of one God. The king's support of Daniel is mentioned several times in the story, most notably in the statement made by the Babylonians that "the king has become a Jew" (*Ioudaios gegonen ho basileus*, Bel 28). Just as this story shows that not all of the heroes in Jewish history were Jews, so it is important for black Americans to remember that not all of the heroes of black history have been black. Other individuals, such as Viola Luizzo and James Reeb, also spoke out in support of the truth in spite of the opposition they faced from many of their peers and at the cost of their very lives. The story of Bel and the Dragon reminds us that we are never alone when we stand up for what is right.

Note

1. See "John Outwits Mr. Berkeley" in Abrahams 1985.

References

Abrahams, R. D., ed. 1985. *African American Folktales: Stories from Black Traditions in the New World*. New York: Pantheon.

Goodspeed, E. J., trans. 1989. *The Apocrypha*. New York: Vintage.

Hamilton, V. 1985. *The People Could Fly: American Black Folktales*. New York: Knopf.

Harris, Joel Chandler. 1983. *The Complete Tales of Uncle Remus*. Boston: Houghton Mifflin.

PRAYER *of* MANASSEH

Hugh R. Page Jr.

MANASSEH HAS NOT found a place alongside biblical kings such as David and Solomon in the popular imagination of contemporary African American readers. First Testament sources cast him as an enigmatic figure. In 2 Kings 20:21—21:18; 23:26; and 24:3 he is the ultimate antihero, a man whose legacy of evil was passed on to subsequent generations. In 2 Chron. 33:1—33:20, 23, he is recast as a penitent leader who mends his errant ways. The apocryphal Prayer of Manasseh fleshes out the brief account by the Chronicler so as to more fully portray him as a monarch who is contrite in his later years. Unlike biblical monarchs whose skill and political prowess are forthrightly celebrated, Manasseh is at best a fatally flawed and ambiguous figure—a leader whose legacy was saved from the metaphorical ash heap long after his death. How and why might this have happened? What light might realities in the Africana world shed on the process by which Manasseh was recast as a man of prayer?

Prowess has long been celebrated in Africana music, art, and literature in the North American Black Diaspora. The exploits of figures like David, the angels, Noah, Mary, Martha, Jacob, Jesus, John, Moses, Ezekiel, Isaac, Aaron, Joseph, and Joshua are recalled in the spirituals.[1] Folk poetry celebrates the power and independence of the maroon.[2] Twentieth-century blues songs—such as "Hoochie Coochie Man," "Mannish Boy," and "Aunt Caroline Dyer Blues"—call to mind the otherworldly power that accrues to those born under special circumstances or who have mastered the secret skills of the conjurer.

Hoochie Coochie Man[3]

On a seven hours
On the seventh day
On the seventh month
The seven doctors said
He was born for good luck
And that you'll see
I got seven hundred dollars
Don't you mess with me

Mannish Boy[4]

Sittin' on the outside
Just me and my mate
I made the moon
Come up two hours late
Well, isn't that a man?

Aunt Caroline Dyer Blues[5]

I'm going to Newport News
just to see Aunt Caroline Dye
[What you gon' ask her, boy?]
She's a fortune-telling woman, oh Lord,
and she don't tell no lie

Public officials, politicians, sports icons, entertainers, and clergy are often hailed for their prowess and contributions to civic life. They have, as it were, their own *axé*.[6] Peter Paris has noted that among Black Christians in North America, the latter group (clergy) is often accorded status akin to that of royalty (Paris 1995: 61) and that this is a modern reflex of a more widespread and long-standing African practice. One could argue that celebrity, in general, often confers noble status within the African American community. The deference and preferential treatment those in the public eye typically receive accords well with this observation. Nonetheless, one wonders what it is about athletic, military, leadership, and other

forms of prowess that makes those possessing them so deserving of special note? Why do specially gifted Africana women and men receive such special regard? Perhaps they are seen to represent the potentialities of our community on the whole. It may be that Condoleezza Rice, LeBron James, Venus Williams, Desmond Tutu, Vashti McKenzie, Nelson Mandela, and others are icons of what we are capable of becoming. Whatever the case, celebrities appear to assume larger-than-life status, at times seeming to embody our collective understanding of fully actualized personhood. It may be that such individuals, whether encountered in life or lore, are in effect the fictive royalty within whom inhere our hopes and dreams.

Prowess, strength, foresight, resoluteness, and independence are among those virtues in the ideal leader's repertoire frequently recounted in African American song and story. On the other hand, frailty, character flaws, indiscretion, and failure to conform to generally accepted norms of behavior have proven to be more problematic. As prevalent as the fallen and resurrected hero or heroine appears to be in the American imagination,[7] Africana conceptions in the North American Diaspora appear to be much more ambiguous. African American responses run the gamut from complete forgiveness and reacceptance to mild rebuke or abject scorn. One can see this most recently in the treatment of such figures as Martin Luther King Jr. (concerning plagiarism detected in his doctoral dissertation), track standout Marion Jones (regarding her use of performance-enhancing drugs), and Jesse Jackson Sr. (in reference to his comments about Barack Obama), to name just a few. Each has been lionized for unparalleled accomplishments and vilified for perceived shortcomings.

Perhaps the experience of Diaspora, whether one has in mind the dispersion of Jews in the postexilic and Second Temple periods or that of Africana peoples in Europe and the Americas from the sixteenth century to the present, leads to a more nuanced understanding of those in positions of authority. It may also foster greater tolerance for and understanding of those whose distinguishing characteristics and accomplishments had been considered nonnormative in an era when political realities were different. It may generate an ability to appreciate more fully persons who do not fit neatly into preexisting social categories (such as "good king" or "bad king"). It may even allow those living in Diaspora to rethink, reconceptualize, and reformulate ideas about personhood.

In the second or first century B.C.E. environment in which the Prayer of Manasseh was likely composed,[8] reclamation of this king may have represented the re-embrace of leaders within the community who had at one time been classified as marginal, unacceptable, or outside of the mainstream. An Africana reading of this text (and further reflection on the figure of Manasseh) today may contribute to a rethinking of the role of the "great man" and "great woman" in our collective history, and perhaps even a reassessment of our attitudes about public figures in general. Such rethinking may involve either a reconceptualization of prowess as a distinguishing trait for such figures or a reformulation of what that term connotes.

Notes

1. See, for example, the selection of lyrics in Herder and Herder (2001).
2. The lyrics to the poem "Wild Negro Bill" illustrate this well (Randall 1971: 7).
3. This rendition is that recorded by Gates and McKay (1997: 36).
4. This version is recounted by Touré (2003: 212).
5. These lyrics are found in Yronwode's online article about Caroline Dye (1995–2003).
6. This is the Yoruba term for spiritual power. On its importance in African societies and in Brazilian Candomblé, see Harding (2000: 77–79, 222 n. 1).

7. A provocative perspective on how those seeking to maximize media exposure through the use of this image is presented by Lant (1983: 17–18).
8. This is the approximate date range proposed by Charlesworth (1985: 627).

References

Charlesworth, James H. 1985. "Prayer of Manasseh: A New Translation and Introduction." In *The Old Testament Pseudepigrapha*, ed. J. H. Charlesworth. New York: Doubleday.

Gates, Henry Louis, Jr., and Nellie Y. McKay, eds. 1997. *The Norton Anthology of African American Literature*. New York: Norton.

Harding, Rachel E. 2000. *A Refuge in Thunder: Candomblé and Alternative Spaces of Blackness*. Bloomington: Indiana University Press.

Herder, Nicole Beaulieu, and Ronald Herder, eds. 2001. *Best-Loved Negro Spirituals: Complete Lyrics to 178 Songs of Faith*. Mineola, N.Y.: Dover.

Lant, Jeffrey. 1983. *The Unabashed Self-Promoter's Guide: What Every Man, Woman, Child, and Organization in America Needs to Know about Getting Ahead by Exploiting the Media*. Rev. 2nd ed. Cambridge, Mass.: JLA.

Paris, Peter. 1995. *The Spirituality of African Peoples*. Minneapolis: Fortress Press.

Randall, Dudley, ed. 1971. *The Black Poets*. New York: Bantam.

Touré, Ali Farka. 2003. "And It's Deep, Too." In *Martin Scorsese Presents the Blues: A Musical Journey*, ed. P. Guralnick, R. Santelli, H. Geroge-Martin, and C. J. Farley. New York: Amistad.

Yronwode, Catherine. 1995–2003. "Aunt Caroline Dye: African-American Root Doctor, Spiritualist, and Fortune Teller." http://www.luckymojo.com/aunt carolinedye.html (accessed February 10, 2009).

1–3 MACCABEES

Willa M. Johnson

The books of 1 and 2 Maccabees explore one of Judaism's most powerful historical periods. Both works are in the Apocrypha, but 3 Maccabees belongs to the Pseudepigrapha.

The books of 1 and 2 Maccabees present the challenges faced by Jewish communities following the death of Alexander circa 323 B.C.E. For several years thereafter, the Seleucus and Ptolemy families struggled for control over his empire. Finally, Antiochus III, a Seleucid, overthrew Ptolemy V. By about 168 B.C.E., Antiochus IV Epiphanes had emerged as king. Antiochus IV quashed a rebellion of Jews and enacted an oppressive program against them. Possession of the Torah scroll became criminal, as did circumcision and Sabbath worship. The Greek god Zeus was incorporated into the Jerusalem temple, and non-Jews were invited to worship in the temple. Torah laws regarding sacrifice were ignored.

Contemporaneously, the priest Mattathias Maccabaeus led a small group of Jewish rebels to challenge Antiochus IV. Most did not comply with the revolt, expressing a view similar to the Prophet Jeremiah regarding appropriate behavior during national difficulty (Cohen 1987; Cohn-Sherbok 2003:85). Support for the resistance developed after a pious, nonviolent group, the Hasideans—who had fled to the desert in protest—were slaughtered unjustly by the Seleucids. Thereafter, the rebellion strengthened. When Mattathias died, his son Judas Maccabaeus assumed the mantle of leadership with the help of the Hasmoneans, his clan. By December 15, 164 B.C.E., Judas Maccabeus had purified the temple, and Jewish people enjoyed independence briefly. Hanukkah commemorates this occasion (Cohn-Sherbok 2003: 84–88).

Thematically, 1 and 2 Maccabees deal with

Willa M. Johnson

revolution, martyrdom, and victory. They feature embedded letters that follow the formulae of Greek epistles. The function of the letters is similar to those in the book of Ezra. It was argued that the purpose of these insertions is to either "enliven" the text or to attest to the historical nature of the works (Nisula 2005: 202). The book of 3 Maccabees details the Diaspora's impending extermination at the hand of an arrogant king. The work dates to between 20 B.C.E. and 41 C.E., when Alexandrian Jews struggled to assert their rights for citizenship but were denigrated and subjugated (Cohn-Sherbok 2003: 102–4). The text features oppression, the weight of persecution, and God's liberation. Unlike other pseudepigraphic works, 3 Maccabees diverges from reliance on graphic apocalyptic imagery to establish its theses. It is written in powerful, very melodic prose. Stylistically, it shares more in common with the Letter of Aristeas than it does with the other books of Maccabees (Hadas 1949: 202).

The writings in 1, 2, and 3 Maccabees reiterate to Africans and the African Diaspora the horror of bondage, the grace of God's liberating presence, and the victory achievable through intervention in God's name. Portions of 3 Maccabees are so poignant that they might deceive the reader into assuming that the subject of the text is modern Africans during the Middle Passage rather than Jews in late antiquity. These texts are neither defeatist nor do they express victimization. The books of 1, 2, and 3 Maccabees reiterate victory and liberation. Thus, as Hanukkah memorializes the victory won, so too should we celebrate the victories of our past and regenerate renewed hope for succeeding generations.

African Americans face disproportionately high rates of high school dropouts, even though that rate has been reduced recently; childhood poverty (39.9 percent compared to 11.1 percent of white children); and male incarceration in state or federal prison (28 percent compared to 16.6 percent of Hispanic and only 1.1 percent of white men). Of all persons infected with HIV/AIDS, 43 percent are African American and 56 percent are women.

While the overall rate of infant mortality is decreasing in the United States, African American children are more than twice as likely to die in infancy than are white children (data from http://www.census.gov, cited on http://www.radford.edu). The outlook for African Americans may be perceived as overwhelmingly bleak or as the opportunity of a lifetime. In the same fashion that Mattathias Maccabeus undertook Antiochus IV Epiphanes, with new leadership we, too, can take on the battle of these destructive forces and ensure that, rather than being swept under the tide, we can overturn it.

References

Charlesworth, James H., ed. 1983. *The Old Testament Pseudepigrapha*. Vol. 2. Garden City, N.Y.: Doubleday.

Cohen, Shaye J. D. 1987. *From Maccabees to the Mishnah*. Louisville, Ky.: Westminster John Knox.

Cohn-Sherbok, Dan. 2003. *Judaism: History, Belief and Practice*. London and New York: Routledge.

Cousland, J. R. C. 2003. "Reversal, Recidivism, and Reward in 3 Maccabees: Structure and Purpose." *Journal for the Study of Judaism* 34 (1): 39–51.

Davies, Philip R. 2000. "If the Lord's Anointed Had Lived." *Biblical Interpretation* 8 (1/2): 151–60.

Doran, Robert. 1983. "2 Maccabees 6:2 and the Samaritan Question." *Harvard Theological Review* 76 (4): 481–85.

Edrei, Arye, and Doron Mendels. 2007. "A Split Jewish Diaspora and Its Dramatic Consequences." *Journal for the Study of the Pseudepigrapha* 16 (2): 92–137.

Hadas, Moses. 1949. "Aristeas and III Maccabees." *Harvard Theological Review* 42 (3): 175–84.

Nickelsburg, George W. E. 2005. *Jewish Literature between the Bible and the Mishnah: A Historical and Literary Introduction*. Minneapolis: Fortress Press.

Nisula, Timo. 2005. "Time Has Passed since You Sent Your Letter: Letter Phraseology in 1 and 2 Maccabees." *Journal for the Study of the Pseudepigrapha* 14 (3): 201–22.

Scurlock, Joann. 2000. "167 B.C.E.: Hellenism or Reform?" *Journal for the Study of Judaism* 31 (2): 125–61.

Shepkaru, Shmuel. 1999. "From after Death to Afterlife: Martyrdom and Its Recompense." *AJS Review* 24 (1): 1–44.

Weitzman, Steve. 1999. "Forced Circumcision and the Shifting Role of Gentiles in Hasmonean Ideology." *Harvard Theological Review* 92 (1): 37–59.

Williams, David S. 2001. "A Literary Encircling Pattern in 1 Maccabees 1." *Journal of Biblical Literature* 120 (1): 140–42.

4 MACCABEES

Emerson B. Powery

THE BOOK OF 4 MACCABEES is a "marginal" text. It has never been incorporated into any formal "canonical" collection, but it was regularly included among important manuscripts of the Greek Bible. Yet this story from the late first century C.E. has influenced circles of piety and resistance movements throughout the ages. This highly dramatic account about Maccabean martyrs under the regime of Antiochus Epiphanes (see 2 Maccabees 6–7) retells the incredible, tortuous deaths suffered by nine Jews faithful to the law. It is an anti-imperial story from within the empire. The author accepts a Hellenistic cultural paradigm for his thesis ("reason is sovereign over the emotions") and argues the case in the Hellenistic language (Greek), even though he portrays one of the book's leading protagonists—the mother of seven sons—speaking in the indigenous tongue, "Hebrew" (16:15-23).

Furthermore, the author of 4 Maccabees borrows the book's theological direction from its Hellenistic milieu. Whereas 2 Maccabees emphasizes the resurrection of the body (for example, 7:14), 4 Maccabees highlights the immortality of the soul (16:13; 17:12; 18:23), clearly influenced by cultural features originating outside the tradition.

The author uses the "master's tools." It was not uncommon for displaced persons to do so. But the content portrays the empire (especially its "tyrant,"[1] Antiochus Epiphanes) and its "way of life" critically. The author's goal is clear: to keep the Torah and value the ancestral traditions, customs, and way of living. This choice supports the overarching, philosophical thesis that "reason is sovereign over the emotions" (1:1).

This is also a story about dying for worthy causes. The author invents an inscription for the tombstones of the deceased: "Here lie buried an aged priest (Eleazar) and an aged woman and seven sons, because of the violence of the tyrant who wished to destroy the way of life of the Hebrews. They vindicated their nation, looking to God and enduring torture even to death" (17:9-10).

Coretta Scott King related that Martin Luther King Jr. knew he would not be blessed with a long life (King 1993). She wrote that he often told his children: "If a man had nothing that was worth dying for, then he was not fit to live." Mrs. King assuredly pronounced that her husband "faced the possibility of death without bitterness or hatred" (301). So is the case with this portrayal of the Maccabean martyrs. Indeed, the absence of clear references in 4 Maccabees to the revolutionary activity of Maccabean warriors may imply an alternative, competing position of nonviolent resistance as the proper response in the face of imperialistic oppression. It is this active perseverance (or obedience to Torah *only*), even by a female character who outmaneuvers Antiochus (see 15:28-30; 16:14), that has "paralyzed" the tyranny (11:24-25; see also 1:11).

Such a story, however, raises theological tensions with its message of redemptive suffering, whether the suffering was accomplished on behalf of the law (6:27-30; 17:21-22), religion or piety (*eusebias*; 9:24, 29), the nation (1:11; 6:29; 18:4), or the land (17:21).

Human history has seen unimaginable suffering. The Afro-Diasporic world has received more than its fair share in these tragic episodes of history. And, any ideology—political, theological, or otherwise—of "redemptive suffering" must be called into question. Any form of forced dehumanization *for the sake of* the "humanization" of others must be labeled mindless, human torture with no value. Contemporary martyrdom has no ideology worthy of adherence. To be fair to the author of 4 Maccabees, this story was an imaginative attempt to display the weak, the colonized, and the powerless as outdueling their powerful colonizer by using the only weapons at their disposal: their minds *and* their bodies.

Ancestors who have suffered from the colonial efforts of others should be remembered, but not as martyrs who have died for *worthy* causes but as those who have died because of senseless gain (for example, land acquisition, economic exploitation, race ideologies). Afro-Diasporic scholars have begun the difficult task of thinking through the implications of African conceptions of "ancestors" for biblical interpretation. This book may be a useful tool in this endeavor (see, for example, 4 Macc. 3:8; 5:29; 9:24; 16:20).

Note

1. In the deuterocanonical literature, the word *tyrant* is used forty-six out of forty-nine times in 4 Maccabees!

References

Aguilar, Mario I. 2002. "Time, Communion, and Ancestry in African Biblical Interpretation: A Contextual Note on 1 Maccabees 2:49-70." *Biblical Theology Bulletin* 32 (3): 129–44.

DeSilva, David A. 2007. "Using the Master's Tools to Shore up Another's House: A Postcolonial Analysis of 4 Maccabees." *Journal of Biblical Literature* 126 (1): 99–127.

King, Coretta Scott. 1993. *My Life with Martin Luther King, Jr.* Rev. ed. New York: Puffin.

Moore, Stephen D., and Janice Capel Anderson. 1998. "Taking It like a Man: Masculinity in 4 Maccabees." *Journal of Biblical Literature* 117:249–73.

Young, Robin Darling. 1998. "4 Maccabees." In *Women's Bible Commentary*, ed. Carol A. Newsom and Sharon H. Ringe, 330–34. Louisville, Ky.: Westminster John Knox.

SIRACH

Naomi Franklin

SIRACH, also known as Ecclesiasticus, is centered in the Wisdom literature tradition containing similarities to the books of Proverbs and Ecclesiastes. It was written by Jesus son of Sirach and translated into Greek by his grandson; thus the date of authorship spans 320–130 B.C.E. Sirach was born in Jerusalem but wrote the book in Hebrew in Alexandria, Egypt (McKechnie 2000: 1–26).

For Africana people, Sirach is problematic, for it contains misogynistic advice and negative advice about slaves. However, alongside that negative information, one finds constructive advice about living. His teachings are contradictory. In one chapter, he speaks of the "wickedness" and "anger of women" (25:13, 15), yet in the very next one he speaks about the happiness of the man who finds a good wife (26:1). His greatest appreciation seems to be for a silent wife, seeing her as a gift from the Lord (26:14). This reflects the influence on Sirach of Hellenism, with its narrow view of the place of women in society and its negative view of women (Camp 2005: 377). For Africana women in particular and the community in general, these teachings must be eschewed. Likewise, readers will find the negative advice about slaves and their treatment disconcerting, given our long and tortuous experience of slavery.

While Sirach is part of the corpus of Wisdom literature, there is much within it that cannot be considered wisdom in the modern context. His advice regarding women and children and how to live in society must be sifted in order to find that which can be useful in a modern context. For the community of faith, in terms of faithful living, Sirach offers helpful teaching. His statement that "the fear of the Lord is like a garden of blessing, and covers a person better than any glory" (40:27) is one that resonates in the lives of the Africana religious experience, for this very notion of being covered and sustained by the Lord is the religious ethos that has sustained the community throughout its journey.

The reader of Sirach faces many challenges. To gain from the experience, one must fancy oneself a gleaner, sifting through the material to find what is usable. Looking past the negativity about women and slaves, one finds advice that is indeed helpful in the quest for health and wholeness. There is much to be learned that is of intrinsic worth for communal survival and growth, and much to eye with great caution. His advice concerning the abuse of alcohol (31:25-30), the abuse of food (37:29-31), self-control (37:27-31), and wise conduct (32:18-33) is extremely valuable for those interested in building strong, healthy, and productive members of the community.

Sirach's misogyny must be understood as being in keeping with the cultural influence of his time and must thus be negated. Africana women have been and still are largely the backbone of the community, and therefore extreme caution must be exercised in using the wisdom of Sirach. Selectivity and care in the use of this text will make it indeed a useful pedagogical tool in community formation.

References

Camp, Claudia V. 2005. "Becoming Canon: Women, Texts and Scribes in Proverbs and Sirach." In *Essays Offered to Honor Michael V. Fox on the Occasion of His 65th Birthday*, ed. Ronald L. Troxel, Kelvin G. Friebel, and Dennis Margary. Winona Lake, Ind.: Eisenbrauns.

Cannon, Katie Geneva. 2003. *Katie's Canon: Womanism and the Soul of the Black Community*. New York: Continuum.

Fry Brown, Teresa L. 2000. *God Don't Like Ugly: African American Women Handing on Spiritual Values*. Nashville: Abingdon.

McKechnie, Paul. 2000. "The Career of Joshua Ben Sira." *Journal of Theological Studies* 51 (1): 3–26.

Mitchem, Stephanie Y. 2004. *African American Women Tapping Power and Spiritual Wellness*. Cleveland, Ohio: Pilgrim.

Oduyoye, Mercy Amba. 2003. "Biblical Interpretation and the Social Location of the Interpreter: African Women's Reading of the Bible." In *Biblical Studies Alternatively: An Introductory Reader*, ed. Susanne Scholz. Upper Saddle River, N.J.: Prentice Hall.

———. 2005. *Daughters of Anowa: African Women and Patriarchy*. Maryknoll, N.Y.: Orbis.

Redwine, F. E. 1998. "What Woman Is." In *Daughters of Thunder: Black Women Preachers and Their Sermons, 1850–1979,* ed. Bettye Collier-Thomas. San Francisco: Jossey-Bass.

Sawyer, Deborah. 1996. *Women and Religion in the First Christian Centuries*. London and New York: Routledge.

Trenchard, Warren. 1982. *Ben Sira's View of Women: A Literary Analysis*. Brown Judaic Series 38. Chico, Calif.: Scholars.

Wimbush, Vincent L. 2003. "Reading Texts through Worlds, Worlds through Texts." In *Biblical Studies Alternatively: An Introductory Reader*, ed. Susanne Scholz. Upper Saddle River, N.J.: Prentice Hall.

PSALM 151

Stacy Davis

PSALM 151 does not appear in my Protestant Bible. During the fight against apartheid, a United Methodist periodical wrote its own Psalm 151, perhaps without realizing that a canonical Psalm 151 exists. The psalm retells David's selection as Israel's second king and has two main versions, a longer Hebrew original (Pigue 1988: 30–32) and a shorter Greek translation. The Greek version, which includes David's miraculous slaying of Goliath, will be utilized here. Psalm 151 appears in the Ethiopic and Coptic (Egyptian) Christian canon, and its story of the triumph of the underdog resonates particularly with the Coptic Christian history of persecution and survival against all odds, an experience that should be familiar to all peoples of Africana descent.

From a rhetorical-critical perspective, Psalm 151 is written as a first-person account of David's

rise to power because of God's favor. The opening verse establishes the unlikelihood of David's selection: "I was small among my brothers, and the youngest in my father's house; I tended my father's sheep" (151:1 NRSV). The unassuming shepherd boy, however, receives Samuel's anointing because although his "brothers were handsome and tall . . . the Lord was not pleased with them" (151:5 NRSV). Although Psalm 150 and other psalms are sung during the receiving of Holy Communion, Coptic liturgy generally includes no readings from the First Testament; the exceptions are during "the Holy Days of Jonah, Lent, and the Holy Week," when the prophets are read during weekday services (http://www.coptic.net). Therefore, the scriptures that are the focus of this commentary do not have a comparable place in Coptic experience.

Nevertheless, the image of the unlikely survivor

326

is a part of Coptic history if not Coptic liturgy. In the Greek translation, Ps. 151:7 describes the shepherd David's killing of the warrior Goliath without mentioning the stones and slingshot made famous in 1 Sam. 17:40, 48-50. In Coptic tradition, both stones and shepherds find a place. In a fifth-century confrontation between Cyril of Alexandria's supporters and Roman officials, the Coptic monk Ammonius struck the Roman prefect Orestes with a rock and received the death penalty for his actions (Kamil 2002: 181). Additionally, one of the legends surrounding the fourth-century Coptic St. Shenuda, whose name the current Coptic pope bears, is that he was a shepherd as a child (Kamil 2002: 185).

Throughout their history, Coptic Christians have faced persecution in their homeland, and many have left Egypt recently for their own safety. Just like all African peoples, Coptic Christians labor to maintain their history and traditions as best they can. Like David, they choose to praise God for their selection and their survival. The writings of the Coptic-American poet Matthew Shenoda, particularly his poem "The Calendar We Live," testify to this reality.

References

"David and Goliath." Public Domain. Arranged by M. Kibble. *Take 6.* Produced by Mark Kibble, Claude V. McKnight III, and Mervyn E. Warren. 1988. Reprise Records.

Kamil, Jill. 2002. *Christianity in the Land of the Pharaohs: The Coptic Orthodox Church.* London: Routledge.

Pigue, Stanley Calvin. 1988. The Syriac Apocryphal Psalms: Text, Texture, and Commentary. Ph.D. diss., Southern Baptist Theological Seminary.

"Psalm 151: A Tutu-ian cry from South Africa's apartheid hell." 1988. *Christian Social Action* (May 1): 32.

Shenoda, Matthew. 2005. *Somewhere Else.* Minneapolis: Coffee House.

1 ENOCH

Hugh R. Page Jr.

VISIONARY EXPERIENCES, and traditions, both oral and written, that preserve the memory of such experiences, have been an important part of the Africana religious experience from antiquity to the present (see Holmes 2004: 34-38). For example, within some sectors of the Black Church, dreams, extrasensory experiences, and special revelations have traditionally been embraced as normative and divinely inspired, particularly when they support established theological orthodoxies. Moreover, the role of imagination and performance in African American homiletics has been well documented. The pulpit is, in fact, one of the most recognizable places where inspiration plays a role in allowing the preacher to converse with, fill in the gaps, exegete, and expand what one finds in the Bible (Andrews 2007: 218-220).

Within the milieu of African Indigenous Reli-

gions and what might be termed Diasporan Religious Amalgams in the Americas, such phenomena are not at all unusual.[1] In each of these settings, such encounters have at times been closely tied to grassroots freedom movements. The slave revolts involving both Denmark Vesey and Nathaniel Turner had, as their stimulus, numinous experiences of this kind (Raboteau 2001: 57-58). Freedom fighters like Harriet Tubman, abolitionists like Sojourner Truth, and civic leaders in the vein of George Washington Carver, Malcolm X, Howard Thurman, and Martin Luther King Jr. purportedly had such experiences (compare to the collection of short vignettes in Noll 1991).[2] Moreover, record of these encounters has often been preserved in works canonical (for example, autobiographies, biographies, and so forth) and—in at least one well-known instance (the *Holy Koran of the Moorish*

Science Temple of America)—through the mediation of a modern prophet of Allah.[3]

The book of 1 Enoch can be said to emerge from the "sanctified imagination," to use a designation popular among some of today's African American preachers, of a visionary or community wrestling with social dislocation and disenfranchisement. Although likely assuming its final form at some point in Syria-Palestine in the first century B.C.E., it is a text that bears some of the distinguishing traits of cultural artifacts produced in the Black Diaspora. Among the more important of these markers are evidence of "bricolage" (on which see Wimbush 2000: 13), agglutino-synthesis (see Page 2003: 118), and hybridity (see Ojaide 1998: 325). How it ultimately arrived in Ethiopia and why it was embraced there are mysteries yet to be resolved (Himmelfarb 1999: 333).

It is a heterogeneous anthology that brings together and creatively juxtaposes apocalyptic visions, eschatological predictions, parables, admonitions for prudent behavior, astronomical musings, and other midrashic materials. Its major subdivisions—1–36; 37–71; 72–82; 83–90; 91–105; 106–107; and 108, according to Himmelfarb (1999: 332)—appear to be demarcated by formal subdivisions or thematic disjunctions. The conflation of these genres makes the book difficult to classify because of the disparate pieces of which it is constituted. In this regard, it is a reflection of those who created, edited, and preserved its contents. One can see in it the continuing effects of social dislocation. Perusing it brings the sense that the very act of reading (or hearing) the book is intended to conjure a reality in which celestial verities that have an impact on the waking world can be clearly seen and touched.

The book of 1 Enoch has exercised considerable influence on Ethiopian Orthodox theology and political thought (Isaac 1983: 8-10). Although among Africana Protestant and Catholic Christians the book lies outside of the biblical canon, within the larger body of popular and esoteric works utilized by certain African American traditional healers (for example, Hohman 1971: 59), the person of Enoch and Enochian traditions are referenced nonetheless. The enigmatic nature of both have no doubt led to the view among select Africana reading communities that Enoch and other figures (for example, the Angels, Elijah, and Moses) are mediators of liberating truths. To the extent that social marginalization and limited access to structural power continue to be manifest within the Black Diaspora, 1 Enoch and works akin to it will likely continue as sites of imaginary, artistic, and theological engagement.

Notes

1. Among those systems of belief that fuse or form an amalgam of African and other religious elements, I would include Rastafarianism, Santeria, Shango, and Vaudou (on these and other related Diasporan belief systems see Koslow 1999: 158–62).

2. Malcolm X's revelatory encounter in prison is briefly recounted in his autobiography (1990: 186–89).

3. See, for example, the online version of this text (Ali 1927) available at http://www.hermetic.com/bey/7koran.html#Prologue (accessed August 12, 2008).

References

Ali, Drew. 2008. *The Holy Koran of the Moorish Science Temple of America Divinely Prepared by the Noble Prophet Drew Ali* (online version of original) 1927 [cited 12 August 2008]. Available from www.hermetic.com/bey/7koran.html#Prologue.

Andrews, Dale P. 2007. "Black Preaching Praxis." In *Black Church Studies: An Introduction*, ed. S. Floyd-Thomas, J. Floyd-Thomas, C. B. Duncan, S. G. Ray Jr. and N. L. Westfield. Nashville: Abingdon.

Himmelfarb, Martha. 1999. Enoch, First Book of. In *Dictionary of Biblical Interpretation*, ed. J. H. Hayes. Nashville: Abingdon.

Hohman, John George. 1971. *Pow-Wows or Long Lost Friend: A Collection of Mysterious and Invaluable Arts and Remedies*. Reprint of the 3rd (?) 1856 ed. Pomeroy, Wash.: Health Research.

Holmes, Barbara A. 2004. *Joy Unspeakable: Contemplative Practices of the Black Church*. Minneapolis: Fortress Press.

Isaac, Ephraim. 1983. "1 (Ethiopic Apocalypse of) Enoch: A New Translation and Introduction." In *The Old Testament Pseudepigrapha, Volume 1: Apocalyptic Literature and Testaments*, ed. J. H. Charlesworth. New York: Doubleday.

Koslow, Philip, ed. 1999. *African American Desk Reference*. New York: John Wiley and Sons.

Malcolm X. 1990. *The Autobiography of Malcolm X*. 27th reprint of the 1964 ed. New York: Ballantine.

Noll, Joyce Elaine. 1991. *Company of Prophets: African American Psychics, Healers and Visionaries*. St. Paul, Minn.: Llewellyn.

Ojaide, Tanure. 1998. Literature in Africa and the Caribbean. In *Africana Studies: A Survey of Africa and the African Diaspora*, ed. M. Azevedo. Durham, N.C.: Carolina Academic.

Page, Hugh R., Jr. 2003. "A Case Study in Eighteenth-Century Afrodiasporan Biblical Hermeneutics and Historiography: The Masonic Charges of Prince Hall." In *Yet With A Steady Beat: Contemporary U.S. Afrocentric Biblical Interpretation*, ed. R. C. Bailey. Atlanta: Society of Biblical Literature.

Raboteau, A. J. 2001. *Canaan Land: A Religious History of African Americans*. New York: Oxford.

Wimbush, Vincent. 2000. "Introduction: Reading Darkness, Reading Scriptures." In *African Americans and the Bible: Sacred Texts and Social Textures*, ed. V. L. Wimbush. New York: Continuum.

The SIBYLLINE ORACLES

Willa M. Johnson

The Sibylline Oracles are eclectic Jewish-Christian texts. For pseudepigraphic writings generally, it is difficult to discern whether texts emerge from and belong to either community or both (Harlow 2001). The matter is too complex for thorough examination here, but it bears mentioning that some Oracles seem to take a decidedly anti-Jewish tone after first expressing praiseworthy commentary on Judaism (book 3). This complexity mitigates against arguing that the texts are entirely Jewish or Christian.

In the fourteen books comprising the Sibylline Oracles, the elderly Sibyl makes pronouncements purportedly in ten (or more) diverse cultural milieus, including Persian, Egyptian, Jewish, and Cumaean contexts. Some argue that the primary goal of the Oracles is "political propaganda" (Charlesworth 1983: 320). For example, Oracle

portions are attributed to Nero's supposed reentry into the world as either the antichrist or Satan. However, these claims suffer inadequate support (van Henten 2000). Oracular references to the Babylonian exile, paired with both anti-Jewish claims and Christian apocalyptic eschatological views, reflect the notion that the Oracles were used to express dominant religious and political perspectives. Based on when the Sibylline Oracles were probably written, between 200 B.C.E. and 500 C.E., it is likely that the two agendas—the religious and the political—dovetailed, especially with respect to Christian views about Jewish people.

Thematically, the Sibylline Oracles focus on creation, messianism, the destruction induced by lawlessness, and resurrection. The Oracles are premised on biblical texts that are reconstituted to incorporate notions about the world. Even when the Sibyl's warnings seem to take a decidedly Christian angle, intricate knowledge of Jewish legal traditions is evident. Many of the writings express unwavering hope in God, who will deliver the pious and punish the sinful, all in spectacular fashion. Therein, these themes captivated the eschatological and often apocalyptic (or perhaps gnostic) emphasis of the work (Attridge 2000: 173–78). The Oracles are linked to ideas discussed by Greek philosophers. Some of the Sibylline Oracles became the fodder for serious debate by many church fathers (O'Brien 1997).

The Sibylline Oracles offer an undeniable glimpse into the world of apocalyptic eschatology. This type of literature is tied to communities experiencing ostensibly inescapable distress. Thus the Oracles help us understand spiritual movements of Africans all over the world, including deliverance from American slavery and South African apartheid. Perhaps more important, the premise for how the Oracles were created—rewriting the Bible's story to lead oppressed peoples to deliverance—remains a tool for postmodern people who are pinned in by unspeakable circumstances. They give us the mechanism to gather the wherewithal to overcome. They teach also by the crude anti-Jewish remarks in the text that we need not oppress the Other to be delivered from oppression. Whether addressing the HIV/AIDS crisis in Africa and in the United States, staring down the humiliation of black women in rap music and music videos, or delivering African American males from their one-in-three lifetime chance of incarceration, the Sibyl, not unlike the vaunted African woman, extends to us a unique opportunity to recast our situations and to act boldly.

References

Attridge, Harold W. 2000. "Valentinian and Sethian Apocalyptic Traditions." *Journal for Early Christian Studies* 8 (2): 173–211.

Charlesworth, James H., ed. 1983. *The Old Testament Pseudepigrapha*. Vol. 1. Garden City, N.Y.: Doubleday.

Cohen, Shaye J. D. 1981. "Sosates the Jewish Homer." *Harvard Theological Review* 74 (4): 391–96.

Felder, Stephen. 2002. "What Is the Fifth Sibylline Oracle?" *Journal for the Study of Judaism* 33 (4): 364–85.

Harlow, Daniel C. 2001. "The Christianization of Early Jewish Pseudepigrapha: The Case of 3 Baruch." *Journal for the Study of Judaism* 32 (4): 416–44.

Nickelsburg, George W. E. 2005. *Jewish Literature between the Bible and the Mishnah: A Historical and Literary Introduction*. Minneapolis: Fortress Press.

O'Brien, D. P. 1997. "The Cumean Sibyl as the Revelation-Bearer in the Shepherd of Hermas." *Journal of Early Christian Studies* 5 (4): 473–96.

van Henten, Jan Willem. 2000. "Nero Redivivus Demolished: The Coherence of the Nero Traditions in the Sibylline Oracles." *Journal for the Study of the Pseudepigrapha* 21:3–17.

LIFE *of* ADAM *and* EVE

Dexter E. Callender Jr.

THE TRADITION popularly known as the Life of Adam and Eve (LAE) is an expansion and midrashic exposition of details and thematic elements that appear in Genesis 2–5. Taking literary form between 100 and 600 C.E., the tradition is preserved in several versions: Greek, Latin, Armenian, Georgian, Slavonic, and Coptic (fragmentary). Discerning the precise relationships between the versions has been a tenuous affair. Common narrative elements include the couple's performance of penitence, in which Eve is again deceived by Satan; Adam's recounting of the transgression in paradise; Cain's act of fratricide; Satan's expulsion from heaven; and Adam's sickness, death, and burial.

One thematic element of the biblical narrative emphasized in LAE is guilt. Adam's guilt is minimized, and Eve accepts full responsibility for the transgression. Even in offering penitence, Eve

once again falls prey to Satan and is reproved by Adam. However, potential tension between the sexes is mitigated by Eve's unquestionable devotion to Adam. African Diasporan traditions drawing on biblical imagery exploit similar dynamics. Rastafari tradition invokes Adam and Eve to underscore woman as both pleasure and danger to man (Chevannes 1998). Eve, however, often finds more sympathetic treatment within the African Diasporan community—no surprise, given the dominance of the matrifocal ideal.

Compassionate engagement of Eve is evident in the sculpture of folk artist William Edmondson, in which the maternal protagonist wears a fig leaf and presents an upheld breast—a West African gesture declaring matriarchal authority (Callahan 2006: 27). Adam, the fruit, and the serpent are conspicuously absent. In Zora Neale Hurston's story

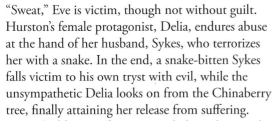

Dexter E. Callender Jr.

"Sweat," Eve is victim, though not without guilt. Hurston's female protagonist, Delia, endures abuse at the hand of her husband, Sykes, who terrorizes her with a snake. In the end, a snake-bitten Sykes falls victim to his own tryst with evil, while the unsympathetic Delia looks on from the Chinaberry tree, finally attaining her release from suffering.

Relief from suffering is similarly underscored in LAE. Adam, on his deathbed and in excruciating pain directly attributable to the transgression, sends Eve and Seth to the earthly paradise to seek the medicinal oil of mercy (in the Greek version, Seth offers to retrieve fruit from paradise for relief). The motif of a botanical cure to counter the effects of sin reminds one of the "balm in Gilead" of the African American spiritual. Although the spiritual's lyric is directly rooted in the prophet Jeremiah's brief allusion (Jer. 8:22), LAE reveals the true breadth of the theme.

References

Callahan, Allen D. 2006. *The Talking Book: African Americans and the Bible.* New Haven: Yale University Press.

Chevannes, Barry. 1998. "New Approach to Rastafari." In *Rastafari and Other African-Caribbean Worldviews*, ed. Barry Chevannes, 20–42. New Brunswick, N.J.: Rutgers University Press.

Hurston, Zora Neale. 1995. *Zora Neale Hurston: Novels and Stories.* New York: Library of America.

Jonge, Marinus de, and J. Tromp. 1997. *The Life of Adam and Eve and Related Literature.* Sheffield, Eng.: Sheffield Academic.

JUBILEES

Jamal-Dominique Hopkins

THE BOOK OF JUBILEES is a late Second Temple Jewish pseudepigraphic work that resembles and expands on the biblical Torah. Preserved among the Dead Sea Scrolls at Khirbet Qumran, this work, which is extant in multiple fragmented manuscript copies, functioned as an authoritative text to the people of Qumran (see Hopkins 2008: 239–52, Campbell 2005: 43–68, Ulrich 2000: 117–20, and VanderKam 1992: 1.638 for this discussion). A fuller account of Jubilees is preserved in Ethiopic (VanderKam 1989 and 2001). The book of Jubilees, which is part of the literary canon of the Ethiopian Orthodox Church, provides a descriptive account of God telling Moses to instruct Israel to adhere to the covenant and godly righteousness; this is largely demonstrated through the patriarchs' obedience to God. Moses is presented by God with the description of Israel's ancestors (Adam, Enoch,

Noah, Abraham, Isaac, and Jacob) as early priestlike figures. Although not called "priest" explicitly, they perform priestly duties (see Jub. 6:18-19). Because of their righteous attitude and obedience to God, the patriarchs are highly revered in Jubilees.

The author of Jubilees presents the patriarchs as archetypes who convey God's will for Israel. Akin to the community who preserved this work, African American communities likewise celebrate their ancestral past. Celebrated in particular are those who have stood for liberation, righteousness, and freedom in the face of racial opposition; figures like Harriet Tubman, Sojourner Truth, Frederick Douglass, Marcus Garvey, Richard Allen, Nat Turner, Toussaint L'Overture, Adam Clayton Powell Jr., and countless others are recognized as part of a celebrated ancestral legacy of leadership within the African Diaspora. These figures are celebrated during both Black History Month and the cultural holiday Kwanzaa. The status of Jubilees in the Ethiopian Orthodox canon likely speaks to how this group also celebrated and emulated its ancestral legacy.

The ancestral legacy celebrated in the African American cultic observance of Kwanzaa is somewhat similar to the way Jubilees was read by the people of Qumran. Maulana Karenga, the chief architect of Kwanzaa, describes several aspects of this observance as promoting the remembrance and celebration of the ancestors (Karenga 1998: 15–84). Several symbols reflect the remembrance and celebration of the past: the Mishumaa Saba, or the Seven Candles, representing the principles practiced by the ancestors (Nguzo Saba); the Kikombe cha Umoja, or the Unity Cup; and the ancestral "roll call."

A function of the Kikombe cha Umoja is to pour a libation. Karenga notes five basic reasons for pouring libation to the ancestors: (1) to remember and honor those who worked, walked, and paved the way (here the name of the ancestors are called out in a kind of "roll call" fashion); (2) to reaffirm our link and life through them; (3) to raise models before the community to imitate; (4) to express a recommitment to their legacy, thus preserving and expanding what they have done; and (5) to cultivate and sustain a cultural practice that sets a model for how the children remember, honor, and link with their ancestors.

As with the preservation of the book of Jubilees, remembering and reflecting on the ancestral past has been vital to communities of the African Diaspora. The preservation of the book of Jubilees in the Ethiopian Christian canon likely finds similar meaning in parallel with the observance of the Martin Luther King Jr. holiday, black history month and the celebration of Kwanzaa. These observances continue to provide spirit to the lives and legacies of people on whom the African Diaspora stands.

References

Campbell, Jonathan. 2005. "'Rewritten Bible' and 'Parabiblical Texts:' A Terminological and Ideological Critique." In *New Directions in Qumran Studies: Proceedings of the Bristol Colloquium on the Dead Sea Scrolls, 8–10 September 2003*, ed. Jonathan G. Campbell, William Lyons, and Lloyd K. Pietersen, 43–68. Library of Second Temple Studies 52. London: T. & T. Clark.

Hempel, Charlotte. 2000. "The Place of the *Book of Jubilees* at Qumran and Beyond." In *The Dead Sea Scrolls in Their Historical Context*, ed. Timothy H. Lim, 187–96. Edinburgh: T. & T. Clark.

Hopkins, Jamal-Dominique. 2008. "Hebrew Patriarchs in the Book of *Jubilees*: A Descriptive Analysis as an Interpretative Methodology." In *With Wisdom as a Robe: Qumran and Other Jewish Studies in Honour of Ida Frohlich*, ed. Karoly Daniel Dobos and Miklos Koszeghy, 239–52. Sheffield, Eng.: Sheffield Phoenix.

Karenga, Maulana. 1998. *Kwanzaa: A Celebration of Family, Community and Culture*. Los Angeles: University of Sankore Press.

Ulrich, Eugene. 2000. "Canon." In *Encyclopedia of the Dead Sea Scrolls*, vol. 1, ed. Lawrence H. Schiffman and James C. VanderKam, 117–20. Oxford: Oxford University Press.

VanderKam, James. 1992. "The Jubilees Fragments from Qumran Cave 4." In *The Madrid Qumran Congress: Proceedings of the International Congress On the Dead Sea Scrolls, Madrid, 18–21 March 1991*, vol. 2, ed. Julio T. Barrera and Luis V. Montaner, 1.635–43. Studies on the Texts of the Desert of Judah 11. Leiden: Brill.

———. 1989. *The Book of Jubilees*. Corpus scriptorum christianorum orientalium 511. Scriptores Aethiopici 88. Loranii: Peeters.

———. 2001. *The Book of Jubilees*. Sheffield, Eng.: Sheffield Academic.

NOTES FROM A STATION STOP:
AN EDITORIAL POSTSCRIPT

I PEN THIS postscript in Montpelier, Vermont, a fortuitous set of circumstances having brought me to this historic capitol in a state, several of whose cities and towns were purportedly home to stations on the Underground Railroad (Siebert and Hart 1898: 130–31). Gazing at its gold-domed state house and quaint shops, nestled between seemingly impenetrable mountains, I can only imagine the feelings the passengers on that freedom train must have harbored long ago. Clandestinely traversing the Green Mountains *via* early nineteenth-century transport must have been harrowing. Realizing that they had arrived in a state that had at one time declared itself an independent republic (1777–1791)[1] must have left them feeling, at best, guardedly optimistic. Dare they "settle in" and make a go of it here? Could they trust local residents not to yield to fugitive slave laws and return them to bondage? What sort of life might they be able to create in this beautiful, yet rugged, locale? Was this simply a temporary way station—an oasis on the way to Canada? Should they "press on" another 130 or so miles until they crossed the Jordan/St. Lawrence and arrived in Canaan/Montreal?

As I wander the streets immersing myself in the local culture of this unusually vibrant town, I appreciate how much has changed in more than two and one half centuries: how different my experience must be from that of my Africana forebears who came here in the early to mid-1800s on a different kind of journey. The leader of the free world is now African American. Vermont was a "Blue State" in the last presidential election. Cars with "Obama–Biden" bumper stickers abound.[2] I am here voluntarily, rather than through forced exodus. I am a citizen whose basic rights are protected by federal and state laws. I have a choice in lodging. I arrived by light of day, rather than under the cloak of darkness. For the most part, local merchants have greeted me with warmth. By and large, I am no different than any other tourist.

Yet, from time to time I am conscious of palpable feelings of "otherness." On some occasions I appear to be almost unnoticeable to passersby; on others, the continuous "gaze" of the random onlooker makes me feel hyper-visible. It could be that I am an obvious anomaly in a state with an overall population that is roughly 96.8 percent White and only 0.8 percent Black.[3] Perhaps it is because in a city of 7,760 any newcomer stands out, particularly if that woman or man is a person of color; or that at 52, I am twelve years older than the typical Montpelier resident.[4] Whatever the case, whether in clergy collar, business attire, or the urban bohemian garb de rigueur for so many, I seem to attract attention. Blending in is difficult to say the least. I have the occasional thought of perhaps retiring here. Yet, as was the case with those Africans who sought liberty here and farther north long ago, I am conscious of how race and the experience of Diaspora have been written onto my psyche and my physical body. I wonder how such may have been etched, subtly or overtly, into the collective consciousness of Vermonters. I realize that nearby cities like Jerusalem, Goshen, and Jericho reflect colonial American inscriptions of the Bible onto the state's landscape. I wonder what subtle messages about personhood, derived from that same source, have been comparably inscribed, and to what extent they are in conversation with the ideals espoused in the state's *Constitution* and the tradition of political autonomy that continues to find expression in local Green initiatives and secessionist rhetoric.[5] I wonder why there are so few African Americans in the state, and particularly in its capitol, given its remarkable history. I wonder why questions akin to these seem to arise whether I am at home or on the road. I also wonder if such musings about the Bible, personal safety, and local ethos have been and remain a hallmark of life in Diaspora?[6]

Nonetheless, I recognize that by *conjuring*—and refusing to relinquish—memories of the Underground Railroad, Montpelier has become, at least for me, holy ground; and my trip here has taken on a special quality. Consequently, this postscript has been transformed into a contemplative reflection on both *The Africana Bible* and the milieu from which it has come. As for my role in preparing these closing words, it has evolved. I am, for the moment, far more than simply a general editor writing a concluding essay from a hotel situated along the Winooski River. I walk in the footsteps, and hold close the memory, of those passengers for whom that secret railway was the route to freedom. I write realizing that *The Africana Bible* is, in fact, part of the cultural fabric they helped to weave.

Narratives of crisis, social dissolution, pilgrimage, exile, displacement, and restoration have been the primary texts through which many of ancient Israel's Scriptures have been parsed and alongside of which they have been read in various Africana settings. Every experience—actual, imagined, or hoped for—is a prism for interpretation, a canon for appropriation. The entries you have read in this volume demonstrate the complex relationship between these ancient writings and Africana life. As a whole, they depart considerably from some of the standard fare in commentaries, many of which provide hermeneutical monologue.[7] They are readings of texts held by communities, ancient and modern, to be authoritative. They present, as well, disparate visions of Africana life itself. Continental African and African Diasporan perspectives are represented. The voices of women and men are documented. There is great variety in terms of methodological approach, genre, and ideology among authors. Articles proceed from the assumption that Africana biblical hermeneutics is not so much a field to be controlled, as it is a cosmos into which scholars, musicians, artists, and others are enfolded. They seek to provide glimpses into that universe; to support those who live comfortably within it; and even to engage those who have grave reservations about the role that the Bible and cognate literatures have played and continue to exercise in the development of Western ideals as well as in the shaping of Africana societies, institutions, ethics, and conceptions of wholeness. They tell a story. They describe a long, and at times troubled, relationship between a heterogeneous community and a body of traditions. They call attention to enduring and emerging tropes derived from personal experience, the annals of the past, literature, music, the visual and plastic arts, and current events by means of which Africana life is formed, sustained, queried, and at times thoroughly refashioned.

Contributors to this volume have written from a variety of social locations.[8] Among them are faculty and administrators at colleges, universities, and seminaries; clergy; independent scholars; and doctoral students. Their readings highlight, rather than mute, the settings in which they live and work. Their distinctive insights bring biblical, apocryphal, and pseudepigraphic literatures, as well as the particularities of contemporary Africana life, into sharper focus. Together, they establish a set of broad parameters within which future Africana encounters with Israel's Scriptures can take place, while at the same time inviting an ever widening and increasingly diverse circle of fellow travelers to collaborate in the process. They make all too clear that Africana hermeneutics of the First Testament and other aspects of culture can be described as: an academic discipline; a body of interpretive work about and/or generated by Africana peoples around the world; and a way of life.

Thus, my personal musings from Montpelier are culturally and biblically inspired notes from a sacred journey: reflections that inform my understanding—as scholar and child of the American Diaspora. They speak of the lasting impact that the Bible, eighteenth-century abolitionist activities, and African migration from the southern U.S. to Canada have had on northern Vermont and elsewhere. Regarding my recent penchant for seeking and visiting significant "stops" on the Underground Railroad, such have become for me what labyrinth walking and pilgrimages to *Santiago de Compostela*, Walsingham (England), and Cape Coast Castle (Ghana) are for no small number of people today: a modern spiritual exercise; a bridge to ancient memories, hopes, dreams, joys, sorrows, rituals, and ancestors whose names are long forgotten. While there is a National Underground Railroad Freedom Center in Cincinnati, Ohio,[9] I am aware of no religious organization, Africana or other, which has officially declared retracing any of its routes a sacramental exercise.[10] Underground Railroad sites, and even the veracity of some related lore, are contested.[11] The original trek along what William Still has so aptly termed "the mysterious road" (Still 2007: vii) was, for many, scripturally grounded and divinely inspired.[12] It remains so for me today. It is a personal reminder that meaningful spiritualities and useful methodologies for interpreting canonical texts are often best derived from autobiographical musings as well as the ebb, flow, and surprises of the "here and now."

As for this *Africana Bible*, I view it as the first fruit of a discursive approach to ancient Israel's scriptures: one that explores deeply, generously, and rigorously their role as cultural matrix. My hope is that it will be seen as a point of reference for future biblical interventions, both scholarly and creative. Perhaps most of all, I pray that it is treated as a collectively articulated first word about Israel's scriptures and Africana life, rather than the last.

Hugh R. Page Jr.

Notes

1. Cf., the timeline maintained by the Vermont Division for Historic Preservation—www.historicvermont.org/sites/html/timeline.html (downloaded July 7, 2009).

2. Obama and Biden actually received 67.8 percent of the votes cast in Vermont—http://elections.nytimes .com/2008/results/states/vermont.html (downloaded July 8, 2009).

3. These are 2007 data, updated as of May 5, 2009—http://quickfacts.census.gov/qfd/states/50000.html (downloaded 08 July 2009).

4. The Montpelier, VT population figure comes from the U.S. census population estimate for 2008—http://www .census.gov/popest/cities/SUB-EST2008-4 .html (downloaded 08 July 2009). Demographic data (from 2000) available through the City of Montpelier's webpage – www.montpelier-vt.org/pdf/2000CensusMontProfile.pdf (downloaded June 8, 2009)—indicate a total of 8,035 residents, of which 52 are Black/African American (0.6 percent). These same data also indicate that the median age of its residents is 40.5 years.

5. Examples of the latter include the Second Vermont Republic movement and the newspaper *Vermont Commons*.

6. Barely a week after my return home from Vermont, Harvard professor Henry Louis Gates was arrested in Cambridge, for attempting to enter his own home—an episode that places in stark focus the tenuous nature of security and wellbeing among Africana peoples in the American Diaspora (Bello and Johnson 2009).

7. The genre needs to be the subject of more vigorous critical study among Bible scholars.

8. The autobiographical statements provide important insights into how authors self-identify and position themselves as biblical interlocutors.

9. The webpage is www.freedomcenter.org/underground-railroad/# (downloaded on July 8, 2009).

10. Neither the *Encyclopedia of African and African-American Religions* (Glazier 2001) or the Schomburg Center's *African American Desk Reference* (Koslow 1999) note the existence of any modern day religious practices centering on the Underground Railroad as pilgrimage route.

11. See Zirblis' thorough examination of persons, sites, and artifacts in Vermont (Zirblis 1996).

12. See, for example, Still's description of the concluding episode of Henry Box Brown's escape (2007: 53).

References

Bello, Marisol, and Kevin Johnson. 2009. Racial Profiling Debate Not Over. *USA Today*, http://www.usatoday.com /news/nation/2009-07-22-racial_N.htm.

Glazier, Stephen D. 2001. *Encyclopedia of African and African-American Religions, Routledge Encyclopedias of Religion and Society*. New York: Routledge.

Koslow, Philip, ed. 1999. *African American Desk Reference*. New York: Wiley.

Siebert, Wilbur Henry, and Albert Bushnell Hart. 1898. *The Underground Railroad from Slavery to Freedom*. New York: Macmillan.

Still, William. 2007. *The Underground Railroad: Authentic Narratives and First-Hand Accounts*. Abridgement of the original 1872 edition edited by I. F. Finseth. Mineola, N.Y.: Dover.

Zirblis, Raymond P. 1996. *Friends of Freedom: The Vermont Underground Railroad Survey Report*. Montpelier: State of Vermont.

INDEX OF AUTHORS

Index of Authors

Index of Authors

Index of Authors

INDEX OF SCRIPTURE

Names of biblical books are followed by pages listed in italics where primary discussions of those books may be found; occurrences outside those pages are indexed.

HEBREW BIBLE

GENESIS	*70–79*	5:1-32	65
		8:21-22	65
1	233	9:18-27	159
1:1—2:4a	65	9:24-27	42
1:1-10	176	9:25	65
1:1-2	50	9:29ff	49
1:5	66	10	65
1:18, 21, 24	82	11:1-9	65, 232
1:26-27	64	11:10-30	65
1:26a	245	11:28	48
1:27	50	11:31	250
2:4b-25	65	12:1—25:11	65
2–5	333	12	86
2:7-24	64	12:1-3	65
2:23	64, 65	12:1	66, 118
2:26-28	176	14:19-20	65
3:14-19	64, 65	15:12-21	65
3:22-24	66	16	50, 86
4:19	251	16:17-20	118